REAL ESTATE HOME INSPECTION

4th Edition

Mastering the Profession

Russell W. Burgess

Dearborn™

Real Estate Education

Vice President: Roy Lipner
Publisher: Evan Butterfield
Development Editor: David Cirillo
Senior Managing Editor: Ronald J. Liszkowski
Typesetting: Janet Schroeder
Design Manager: Lucy Jenkins

Published by Dearborn™ Real Estate Education, a division of Dearborn Financial Publishing, Inc.®
155 N. Wacker Drive
Chicago, IL 60606-1719
(312) 836-4400
http://www.dearbornRE.com

01 02 03 10 9 8 7 6 5 4 3 2 1

Library of Congress Cataloging-in-Publication Data

Burgess, Russell W.
    Real estate home inspection : mastering the profession / Russell W. Burgess.—4th ed.
      p. cm.
  Includes index.
    ISBN 0-7931-4532-5
    1. Dwellings—Inspection. 2. Building inspection. 3. Real estate business. I. Title.

TH4817.5 .B8697 2001
643'.12—dc21   2001031841

C ontents

5 ROOFING 115

6 PLUMBING 167

About the Author

Russell W. Burgess is the author of *Real Estate Home Inspection: Mastering the Profession,* 4th edition. Mr. Burgess has a degree in mechanical engineering, is a licensed real estate broker, a licensed real estate inspector, a certified applicator with the Structural Pest Control Board in Texas, a designated representative with the Texas Natural Resource Conservation Commission, and a Certified Code Inspector with the Southern Building Code Congress International and has been for many years. In addition, in 1977 he was one of the founders of the Texas Association of Real Estate Inspectors (TAREI), he was the first education chairman for TAREI and, in 1981, he was elected president of the association and was responsible for the legislation passed in Texas to require inspectors to be registered and bonded. This led to the licensing and required education of inspectors in 1986. These past experiences provide him with extensive knowledge relating to real estate agents, brokers, homebuyers, and homesellers in dealing with home inspections. He owns and operates a large real estate inspection business that was established in 1969.

In 1984, Mr. Burgess established a real estate inspection school, which is a leader in the field of instructing aspiring inspectors. The school's inspection courses are approved by the Texas Education Agency and the Texas Real Estate Commission, and are recognized by the U.S. Department of Education. *Real Estate Home Inspection: Mastering the Profession* is derived from these inspection courses and is adapted for the real estate professional. Mr. Burgess sold the school in 1995 but remains a consultant to the industry.

Acknowledgments

The author wishes to thank those who participated in the preparation of the fourth edition of *Real Estate Home Inspection: Mastering the Profession.* In particular, thanks go to the following individuals, who provided vital professional guidance and expertise during development of this edition:

Anthony J. Brueneman
The Home Inspection Institute, Cincinnati, Ohio

Patrick L. Casey, 1997 President
American Society of Home Inspectors, Inc.®

Nanci Hawes
Nanci Hawes Real Estate School, Dallas, Texas

Thomas G. Lauhon
Midwest Inspectors Institute, Lansing, Kansas

Dr. Dennis N. McIlroy
Lifetime Learning, Inc., Springfield, Missouri

Everett H. Rawlings, President
The Inspection Experts, Inc., Boca Raton, Florida

Burton B. Silver
Ideal Home Inspections, Inc., Pompano Beach, Florida

The author would also like to thank Dan Friedman, American Home Inspection Service, and Robert Tanenbaum, Tanenbaum Construction, Inc., for their reviews of past editions of the text.

Reprinted in the appendixes of this edition are the Standards of Practice and Code of Ethics from both The American Society of Home Inspectors, Inc.®, and The National Association of Home Inspectors, Inc. Appreciation goes to both organizations for graciously granting permission to reproduce these documents, as well as for their useful comments and assistance during development of this edition.

The author would like to recognize and thank the following businesses for their contributions of figures and information to this book:

Alopex Products Industries, Inc.
American Lumber Standards Committee
American Plywood Association
American Society of Home Inspectors, Inc.®
American Wood Preservers Bureau
A. O. Smith Water Products Company
Burgess Inspection Group, Inc.
Caloric Corporation
Carrier Corporation
Cedar Shingle and Shake Association
Delta Faucets
Dryvit
Environmental Protection Agency
General Electric Corporation
Geothermal Heat Pump Consortium, Inc.
Jacuzzi Whirlpool Bath Company
Jenn-Air Company
KitchenAid
Kohler
Lennox Industries
Magic Chef
Mueller Company
National Association of Home Inspectors, Inc.
National Roofing Contractors Association
National Wood Windows & Door Association
NBCCII
NEC
Norweco
NuTone
Raypak

SBCCII*
SBCCII – International Residential Code for
    One & Two Family Dwellings
Sears, Roebuck & Company
State Industries, Inc.
Texas Natural Resource Conservation
    Commission
Texas Structural Pest Control
The Trane Company, Unitary Products Group,
    an American-Standard Company
Thermador

U.S. Consumer Product Safety Commission
U.S. Weather Bureau
Vent-A-Hood Company
Watts Regulator Company
Weathermatic Sprinkler Division of Telsco
    Industries
York

Finally, very special thanks must go to Colleen Halpin for her invaluable assistance in preparing the manuscript for this edition.

Introduction

Real Estate Home Inspection: Mastering the Profession, 4th edition, is written for anyone desiring knowledge of the inspection business. Many people confuse real estate appraisals with real estate inspections. A real estate appraisal systematically analyzes the factors that bear on the value of real estate. The real estate inspection process evaluates and reports on the physical condition of the structural and mechanical components of the property.

This book covers the inspection process from start to finish. It includes a quiz at the end of each chapter, a checklist for each chapter, and a glossary. The book may be used as an inspector's guide in the field. Courses in inspections are also helpful to homeowners, real estate agents, appraisers, etc. The real estate industry has a growing need for well-trained real estate inspectors. According to the American Society of Home Inspectors, Inc. (ASHI), and the National Association of Home Inspectors, Inc. (NAHI), ten years ago real estate inspectors inspected approximately 10 percent to 15 percent of the homes sold. Today, they inspect more than 50 percent, and that percentage is expected to increase another 30 percent to 40 percent over the next five years. Real estate inspectors are hired primarily by home buyers. Sellers also may hire inspectors to comply with the disclosure laws, thus eliminating surprises and avoiding legal liability. Many banks, mortgage companies, and other lending institutions require that home inspection and repairs be made before funding the loan. Since the third edition of the book, several states now require that sellers reveal all known defects in their homes. Other states are expected to follow suit. In states without disclosure laws, courts have ruled against sellers who knowingly concealed defects.

The real estate inspection profession is one of the fastest growing businesses in the United States. There are many reasons for the demand for real estate inspectors. Who employs a real estate inspector? Homebuyers have the desire to know the condition of the property they are purchasing. Because of the high cost of homes today and large mortgage payments, it is difficult for the buyer to make major repairs. Sellers, in many cases, have their properties inspected prior to listing their homes to determine the condition. If necessary repairs are needed, it may make a major difference in the sale of the property. Every day, more and more mortgage lenders become interested in the inspection process because they must be aware of a property's condition and repair amounts in the event the mortgage company must foreclose on or seize the home for nonpayment of loan. Insurance companies are interested in the inspection process because of possible liability under insurance policies they issue. Some insurance companies employ inspectors to perform inspections on properties they insure. However, the type of inspection these inspectors conduct is not a complete inspection because insurance companies are interested only in areas covered in their policies.

Real estate inspection is a technical and complex field that demands a professional approach. Education is the key to developing essential skills for the real estate inspector.

Many states have strict laws to protect homebuyers against known defects when purchasing a home. Many states require that the seller provide the real estate agents and buyer with a disclosure statement revealing all known defects. Many states have passed licensing and/or registration laws for inspectors. Texas was the first to recognize the need for real estate inspection training when it passed legislation in 1985 requiring 90 hours of certified schooling and state examinations for licensing. States with laws requiring that inspectors be either registered or licensed with the state require education and examination to get a license.

Inspectors in Texas have been regulated for several years, first with a registration law passed in 1981 and then with a licensing law passed in 1985. A new, revised licensing bill, passed in 1991, requires that an inspector serve an apprenticeship for 15 months before becoming a licensed inspector. A licensed inspector must obtain continuing education courses to renew his or her license.

Real estate inspection is the art of identifying problem areas through observation; therefore, an inspector must be familiar with soils, foundations, construction, plumbing, roofing, HVAC and electrical systems, appliances, swimming pools, and spas. The inspector should be familiar with building codes that apply to the areas where the inspector operates. Although the inspection process is not considered as a code inspection, the inspector should be able to identify a health or safety problem as well as a structural or mechanical problem.

The person who desires to become an inspector should be at least age 18 (there is no upper age limit) and be bondable. The person seeking a career change in the inspection profession should be mechanically inclined or familiar with construction.

The inspection profession is an exciting career as well as a profitable one. Many persons have entered the inspection industry as a second career. An inspector should consider becoming a member of a recognized national society or association, such as ASHI or NAHI. There also are many reputable state and local associations. Like any business, it is important to check out any association or society before joining. Check with groups such as the Real Estate Commission, the National Association of REALTORS®, and the Better Business Bureau, Inc. If the organization offers certification, make certain the courses involved are approved by, for example, one of the model building code bodies or the education agency for the state where the organization is located. It is important for real estate agents as well as the general public to be careful that inspectors who display certifications be certified by a recognized, reputable organization. Few states have restrictions and regulations on real estate inspectors, and the inspection industry is relatively new to many areas. The effect of counterfeit organizations selling certifications can be disastrous for the real estate profession. When an inspector is asked for documentation, qualifications and type of school(s) he or she has attended, these should be approved by a state licensing agency.

The inspection business is a viable profession, with people ready to claim that they are certified inspectors. The only certified inspector is a code inspector who has a certification number on a certificate from the model code body that certified the inspector. The associations, societies, and approved schools give designations to their graduates after they have completed a course and passed examinations. An inspector does not have to belong to any society or association to be a competent inspector. However, he or she should have an education in the various areas of the inspection process.

Real estate agents in today's market must be educated. Know whether your state has any laws connected with the home inspection process. This is not a field to be taken lightly. Let us be professional by looking for professional inspectors to perform real estate inspections.

1 Establishing a Business

The inspection business is a high liability business. Legal bills can be catastrophic, so it requires that you, the inspector, be knowledgeable and thorough when performing an inspection. It is important that you be aware of the legal risks and liabilities all inspectors face in the inspection industry. In today's litigious society, any inspector can be sued, even if he or she performed the inspection correctly.

That is precisely why you should have a good attorney for sound legal advice when making your plans of operation. When picking your attorney, it is good if that attorney has some understanding of the real estate inspection business and has previous trial experience. Have your attorney draw up a contract for each inspection for both you and your customer to sign. The contract should state what you are going to do and not do so the customer understands the inspection procedure.

It is also helpful to have a Standards of Practice printed to show potential customers. You can make one up, or if you're in an area where there are regulations, there probably is a Standards of Practice that you are required to use. If not, the ASHI Standards or NAHI Standards could be used (with permission). Make this a part of your contract.

We said earlier that you can be sued even if you performed the inspection 100 percent correctly; even if you called out everything as defective. Most lawsuits of this nature are inspections that were performed without the purchaser present at the inspection. In many cases, the purchaser never received a copy of the report for some reason. Then there are people who are so disgruntled with agents or sellers that when they sue them, their attorney will include you.

It is important that you carry general liability insurance and errors and omission insurance (E&O), whether you are a single inspector company or a multi-inspector company. Understand your E&O Insurance before you purchase it.

Many important steps must be considered before starting a residential/commercial inspection business. We will try to address all areas of starting a business in the following sections.

■ GENERAL GUIDELINES ON OWNING YOUR OWN BUSINESS

Have you thought of the pros and cons of owning your own business? Consider the following:

Pros
- Being your own boss
- Development of your own ideas and thoughts
- Having the authority to make your own business decisions
- Personal satisfaction
- The chance to generate a comfortable living
- Job security
- Helping people make good decisions
- Flexible hours

Cons
- Financial risk
- Income may be unstable, unlike a salary
- No medical insurance
- You pay all Social Security taxes
- You bear the brunt of problems
- Long and hard hours to start out
- Limited free time until business is established

■ TYPES OF BUSINESSES

How should you operate your inspection business? There are three basic types of business: the sole proprietorship, the partnership, and the corporation. It is advisable to consult a lawyer to help you decide what is best for you.

Sole Proprietorship

Generally, *sole proprietorships* are a single-person business, including many self-employed individuals and home-based businesses. Most individuals will initially start their business as a sole proprietorship because it is the easiest method and requires the least amount of paperwork. An individual working alone will most likely be working out of a home office or have a small office elsewhere. This is one of the most exciting, independent, and economical ways to start a business because of the low overhead.

Advantages
- It is simple and does not require any legal action to start.
- You don't have to wait for legal papers to begin, although you will need a business license, and you may have to register to do business in your state.
- You will enjoy receiving all the profits from your business.
- You will have freedom to use the money as you wish.

Disadvantages
- You bear unlimited liability for yourself (your company).

Partnership

A *partnership* is formed when two or more people pool their money, abilities, and skills and partners proportionally share profits and risk. You can choose to have a general partnership or a limited partnership, and shares can be based on capital contributions, amount of time devoted to the business, or other mutual agreements.

A partnership does not pay federal income taxes; rather, income or loss flows through to the partners, who are taxed on their individual shares of partnership taxable income. The partnership is a tax-reporting entity that must file an annual partnership return.

Corporation

A *corporation* is considered by federal and state law to be an artificial legal entity that exists separately from the people who own, manage, control, and operate it.

With a corporation there is a great deal of paperwork. Establishing a corporation usually requires an attorney and legal fees. Also, as separate legal entities, corporations are subject to federal and state income taxes. This is effectively double taxation: once at the corporate level and again when those already taxed earnings are distributed as dividends. An S corporation eliminates the problem of double taxation.

The courts have historically upheld the principle that a corporation is separate from its shareholders, officers and directors. Shareholders risk their capital investment, but their personal assets are generally considered beyond the reach of business-related creditors and lawsuits. However, although shareholders' assets are usually shielded from lawsuits, employees, officers, or directors put their assets at risk when they sign a loan individually or guarantee anything personally.

Corporate ownership offers a number of other advantages, including increased availability of capital and easy transfer of ownership. Avoiding dissolution of the business is one of the strongest arguments for incorporating. It is one way of ensuring that the business will go on, even if one or more of the principals were to leave for any reason.

The downside of incorporating is that corporations are the most difficult and costly form to establish. They are usually at a tax disadvantage, and they often face some legal restrictions. It is important to have a knowledgeable attorney because it is necessary to have corporate meetings and maintain records of those meetings with your incorporation documents. Your attorney should guide you on the rules and regulations to make it more difficult for someone to pierce the corporate veil. If the corporate veil is pierced, you no longer have the protection of being incorporated.

■ UNDERSTANDING REAL ESTATE INSPECTION

A real estate inspection is an observation of the condition and operation of the major structural and mechanical components of a structure. The purpose of the inspection is to determine if the components are performing their intended function or need repair or replacement. A real estate inspector is not a code inspector; therefore, the components inspected are not subject to code approval, quality certification, or estimation of life expectancy.

Inspectors can do only a visual inspection. They cannot or should not dismantle any equipment for the purpose of inspection, even if licensed in the field to which the component belongs, such as HVAC or electrical. However, inspectors should remove inspection plates or covers to perform inspections of equipment. Inspectors should perform all inspections in a manner consistent with inspection industry standards. While exercising due care in the performance of these inspections, inspectors should not make representations or guarantees with respect to latent or unobserved defects that may exist or surface in the future. The inspection is good only for the time and day of the inspection. There are no warranties or insurance policies.

There are possibilities of additional business opportunities other than residential inspections for resale purposes. Some of the growing areas that will yield additional compensation are insurance inspections, construction monitoring, HUD and FHA inspections, subcontracting to municipal authorities for code inspection (if properly certified), expert witness testimony, etc.

■ AWARENESS OF SAFETY TECHNIQUES

Be aware of safety techniques, both before and during an inspection. These include, but certainly are not limited to, setting ladders on grass rather than on driveways, checking to see if overhead service is touching the house before laying the ladder against the roof, determining that the roof is dry prior to climbing (especially wood roofs), etc. Additionally, there are several important "tools" that you should consider using daily in the inspection process. These are listed at the end of this chapter.

■ DETERMINATION OF REGISTRATION/LICENSING REQUIREMENTS

You must determine licensing requirements, if any, for your state. First, are inspectors required to be registered or licensed by the state? Are there educational requirements that the individual must satisfy? Even if special education is not required, it is highly recommended that a person interested in entering the inspection business, regardless of background, should take educational courses pertaining to real estate inspections. It is important that the person understand the reasons for and the techniques of real estate inspections.

■ INITIAL START-UP COSTS

Determine the initial start-up costs of the business. Normally, a person can get started with an amount of capital ranging from a minimal amount up to $20,000, depending on initial expenses. It is advisable that inspectors have money set aside or some other form of supplemental income while getting started. Next, the entrepreneur must decide where to set up an office, the size of the office, and what office equipment is needed (telephones, desks, etc.).

■ NAME YOUR BUSINESS

After deciding how your business is going to be structured (sole proprietorship, partnership or corporation), you must pick a name for your business. If you have decided to be a sole proprietorship or partnership and the name is decided on, it must be filed at the courthouse as an assumed name. If you decide to incorporate, the name decided on for the corporation will be registered with the corporate documents. The assumed name must be filed in each county in which you plan to do business. This procedure protects the name from infringement by others and also protects others from their names being infringed on. You should check the law in your state when you file.

■ BANK ACCOUNTS/BUSINESS EXPENSES

Regarding bank accounts and business expenses, the inspector should consult with a certified accountant to determine the best way to organize his or her accounts to ensure proper recording of revenues and expenses. When opening the bank account, arrangements should be made with the bank to process and deposit credit card payments from the client. It is important to establish a line of credit with the bank to secure a good credit rating in the event operating capital is required.

The inspection business is a high liability business because preowned homes can have defects that are detected after the inspection. There are also latent defects that are not apparent until wallpaper, sheetrock, or paneling is removed. For this reason, it is important that an inspector consider having a preinspection contract that clearly spells out the scope of the inspection: how the inspector is going to perform the inspection, that there are no warranties or guarantees, etc. Unfortunately, there are many buyers who think they should not have any problems after they move in. For this reason, it is important for an inspector to have insurance. An inspector should carry general liability insurance and E&O insurance. Many real estate firms will not put your company on their list of inspection companies if you do not have these types of insurance.

■ HIRING INSPECTORS

Many inspectors expand their inspection businesses and hire other inspectors as employees. This increases their liability; therefore, it is important to train the inspectors you hire. It is helpful if you belong to a reputable inspectors' society or association because such organizations have educational programs along with inspection standards and codes of ethics that will help you be more professional. The inspection business is a challenging business because it doesn't make any difference how long you have been in the business— you are always learning.

Whether to offer salary or commission to the inspector employees is another option to consider. If additional inspectors are hired to perform inspections, the employer decides whether to pay salary or commission. If the decision is a salary, it will be a set amount to pay, whether or not any inspections are performed. Inspectors who are paid a commission receive payment for only inspections they perform. (Most inspectors prefer to work on a commission basis.) The commission plan is usually better for the company from the standpoint that if the inspector is not working, he or she is not getting paid.

The employer should have a written contract with the inspectors that is drawn up by a knowledgeable attorney. The contract should cover all pertinent information relating to the agreements between both parties. This contract should be renewed each calendar year. Items included in a contract should cover the following:

- **Compensation during training.** This should be a specific dollar amount for a specific time frame.
- **Salary/Compensation.** The method of compensation after training should be one of the following types: (a) salary—dollar amount with any benefits, or (b) commission—percentage with any benefits;
- **Claims.** The employer should cover a method for handling claims in the employee contract. For example, the employee will be responsible for 50 percent or 75 percent of the claim and the company is responsible for the balance. Usually, inspectors split the claims the same as the percentage that the employee receives.
- **Marketing.** If the employee is expected to do marketing for the company as part of his or her job, this must be stated in the contract. Additionally, the marketing materials should be readily available for distribution. (Some employers choose to hire a marketing person instead of requiring inspectors to perform this task.)
- **Educational courses.** The contract should state your requirements on education. If continuing education is required in your area, are you, the employer, going to pay for this education or pay a part of the cost?
- **Association dues and licensing fees.** Specify in the contract if these fees will be paid for by the company, by the employee, or split between the two.
- **Company policies.** It is advantageous to have a company Policy Manual that explains what is expected of an employee with regard to tardiness, dress code, peformance, vacation time, sick time, etc. By signing the contract, employees imply that they have read the company policies and agree to abide by them.
- **Business cards.** Business cards should be furnished by the company at no cost to the employee.
- **Recovery fund.** A recovery fund is a fund that is set up to help pay for insurance and attorneys' fees. The recovery fund comes from the inspection fee. It usually takes a dollar figure off the top of the gross inspection fee before any commissions are paid. For instance, if the inspection fee is $150 and you take $10 off the top for this special fund, the inspector (if on commission) is then paid his or her percentage based on $140.
- **Errors and omissions insurance (if available) and general liability insurance.** This is a business decision that each employer has to make. The premiums are usually paid out of the recovery fund.
- **Workers' compensation.** Indicate if you have it or not.

- **Uniforms.** If you are going to require uniforms for your inspectors, the contract should indicate this and who is going to pay for them (employer, employee, or split cost). Additionally, who is going to pay the maintenance, cleaning, and repair on the uniforms should be stated.
- **Payroll taxes.** Who pays? If the company is operating as an employer hiring inspectors as employees, the company would withhold and pay the payroll taxes. If the company contracts with the inspectors as independent contractors, then they must pay their own payroll taxes.

■ GENERATING BUSINESS FOR YOUR NEW COMPANY

There are many different ways to generate new inspections for your company. The most important are advertising and referrals.

Advertising

Advertising is important, but an inspector must determine where to advertise and how to get the best return on advertising. Telephone yellow pages can be very helpful, and advertising material such as scratch pads, brochures, Rolodex cards, etc., that have your name and phone number are good, inexpensive advertising materials.

Target the areas that give the most business, and keep expanding the business areas. It always helps to get acquainted with the real estate agents. Doing office presentations for real estate agents is a good way to increase one's business. When doing office presentations, take donuts or rolls for the agents. The following is a sample agenda for real estate office presentations:

Presentation for Real Estate Office Meetings

Thank the agents for inviting you to their meeting.

1. Introduce your company
   A. How long you have been in business
   B. Number of inspectors you employ (unless you are a sole proprietorship)
   C. Inspection area you cover
   D. How the name of your company was established

   E. Schools and education (to show why you are qualified to perform their inspections)
2. Purpose of presentation
   A. To assist real estate agents (when taking a listing) to identify a possible problem
   B. If agents identify a possible problem, how they should manage it with their clients
   C. The real estate agent's role at an inspection regarding the listing or selling of property during the inspection
   D. How the real estate agent should approach cosmetic items
   E. Explain latent defects: what they are, etc.
   F. The inspector's responsibility to purchasers and agents
3. Items to cover on a presentation
   A. Foundations (walking across room to see if it is sloping, etc.)
   B. Roof (when approaching a house, notice shingles, composition or tar and gravel)
   C. Shower pans—what are some focuses of a leaky pan (detergents, etc.)
   D. Electrical—copper and aluminum, double wiring, CO/ALR plugs
   E. Heating and air-conditioning—heat exchangers, air-conditioning check only above 60°F, etc.

Referrals

Real estate agents are a very good source for referrals. If they think you do quality inspections and work well with their clients, chances are they will refer you to others. The clients will refer you as well. Always give the client at least two business cards—one for the client to keep and one for a friend.

Remember that when you are inspecting a home for a client, the seller of the home also may be in the market for a home inspection. If sellers are present, give them your business card and tell them you will be glad to help them out when they're ready.

■ CLIENT/INSPECTOR RELATIONSHIP

Communicate with your client.

Have a set procedure for making your appointments. Many times a real estate agent makes the appointment for the inspection. When agents make appointments, ask for potential purchasers' addresses and phone numbers so you can call them (especially if out-of-town clients). There are three reasons for such calls: First, to introduce yourself; second, to ask if they have any special concerns about a property; and third, to find out if they can be with you for the inspection. Try to keep the real estate agents' involvement to a minimum. When you call potential purchasers, it gives you the opportunity to verbally explain the inspection process and its limitations. If you have a contract, review your contract with them, then fax it to them to sign if they cannot be with you for an inspection.

When clients cannot be with you, after you have completed the inspection, phone them and verbally describe the observations documented in the report.

Sometimes clients may want to discuss repair options and priorities. Make sure you have a toll-free phone number where they can contact you for clarification or more information.

The best inspection is useless to your clients if they don't understand your observations or can't read your handwriting. Good communication is a vital part of a service business.

Return phone calls promptly. Your clients most likely have deadlines and need answers quickly. Be accommodating to their needs. This is the biggest purchase of their lives.

A good, thorough inspection report is vital if you have to defend yourself in court and be successful. Along with good communication skills, it can keep you *out of court.*

■ SUGGESTED TOOLS AND OFFICE SUPPLIES

The following list represents the minimum tools and equipment recommended to perform most residential real estate inspections. This is followed by a short list of basic equipment and forms any start-up office should have.

Tools and Equipment

- Adjustable wrench—12″
- Amprobe (for amperage and voltage)
- Binoculars
- Briefcase
- Camera (Digital)
- Circuit analyzer
- Circuit tester (pocket check; Woodbow Model P-125 or equivalent is recommended)
- Coveralls (for crawling under house)
- Dustmask or facemask respirator
- Fireplace key
- Flashlight (2)
- Ground fault circuit interrupter (GFCI) circuit tester
- Gloves
- Hard hat
- Jumpsuit
- Knee pads
- Ladder (OSHA-approved)
- Leak-check (gas fittings)
- Moisture meter
- Nut drivers—¼″ and 5⁄16″.
- Plastic cup (microwave check)
- Pliers
- Cordless screwdrivers (blade and Phillips)
- Stapler
- Thermometer (AC—2)
- Oven thermometer (a mercury thermometer is recommended)
- Tiff 8800 (gas and carbon monoxide test)
- Towel
- Water meter key

Office Equipment and Forms

- Computer/typewriter
- Printer
- Facsimile machine
- Toll-free phone number
- Inspection report forms (either preprinted or report software)
- Routing slips (client information, address, day, etc.)
- Invoice forms and receipts for clients
- Web page and e-mail

2 The Inspection Report

■ INSPECTION PROCEDURES

This textbook is a resource for inspectors across the country. It is not possible to address all of the regional variations of the inspection process. Inspection procedures may not be the same nationwide. In many cases there may be more than one way of observing a specific system or element, but for the purposes of this book, we will give general inspection guidelines with the understanding that there may be deviations according to the area in which you will be performing inspections.

■ TYPES OF REPORTS

Different types of inspection reports may be used to record conditions and may include a checklist, narrative, or computer-generated report. Whatever form is used, the inspection report is the final, most lasting contact with the customer. It is considered a legal document and contract between the two parties. The information in the report is used by many purchasers to determine whether to purchase real property. It is the best advertising you have—be proud of it.

■ INSPECTION AGREEMENT

Many inspectors have a contract that details what will be inspected and how the inspection will be performed. The customer reads and signs the agreement before the inspector begins the inspection. (See Figures 2.1 and 2.2.)

The inspection report must include the inspector's and company's names. In some states, the inspector must be licensed to perform real estate inspections and must display the license number on the report.

Conditions

There are several conditions of the inspection of which all parties must be aware. The inspection is a visual inspection. (See Fig. 2.3—Scope of Inspection.) The inspector does not dismantle any appliance (other than removing inspection covers). The inspector inspects only items he or she views. If a defect is hidden under or behind furnishings or inside walls or is buried, it is impossible for the inspector to locate the defect.

The inspector does not inspect for compliance with building codes for two reasons. First, this is the jurisdiction of the municipality where the property is located. The municipality is responsible for ensuring that buildings are constructed according to standards for health and safety. Second, building codes constantly change, and codes in force when the house was built may not be current. It is impossible for an inspector to know all codes for all municipalities. The property may not meet the present code but may have been acceptable under the codes in effect when the structure was built. The method allowing the old codes is referred to as *grandfathering*. Although the home inspector is not a code official, it is a good idea for any inspector to become familiar with the minimum housing code or ordinance in the area in which he or she lives. This is because the minimum code is a statement of minimum health and safety issues in the community.

The inspector must not comment on design adequacy, capacity, or efficiency of any item in the house. Inspections are for items present at the time of the inspection. An inspector is not a troubleshooter or a design engineer. The purpose of an inspection is to determine whether items are performing their intended function.

Inspectors are generalists and must not portray themselves as specialists in any field or trade, even though most inspectors are plumbers, electricians, HVAC contractors, etc. However, it is important that an inspector, regardless of his or her background, have training in all phases of the inspection process.

The inspector should make a written disclaimer on the inspection report regarding any items or functions of items not inspected. For example, on a real estate inspection most inspectors do not inspect sewer lines or check environmental conditions. Many states require special training and licenses for a person to perform environmental inspections such as testing for radon, lead paint, asbestos, and indoor air quality. Special licensing may also be required for termite inspection, septic inspections, and water wells. Therefore, these types of inspections are optional, with an additional charge for increased costs and time to the inspector.

It is not a good idea for inspectors to include cost estimates (although a good percentage of them do) unless they bid to perform repairs on defects noted on the inspection report. In some areas, it is a conflict of interest if an inspector performs the inspection and repairs on the same property.

Disclaimer

The inspector always must attach a disclaimer to the inspection report. The disclaimer allows the customer to know what areas the inspection covers and what areas are not covered. The different areas of inspection may be broken down into groups, such as structural and mechanical. Structural would cover foundation, roof, roof flashings, superstructure (joists, rafters, purlins, roof vents, decking, insulation, etc.), chimney, drainage, etc. Mechanical would cover HVAC, electrical system, plumbing, water heater, dishwasher, kitchen exhaust, range, oven, and any other built-in appliance. Other mechanical equipment may include swimming pools, spas, saunas, etc. (See Figure 2.4.)

The disclaimer should also cover those things the inspector does not inspect:

- Compliance with building codes
- Soil
- Design adequacy
- Capacity
- Efficiency
- Size
- Value
- Flood-plain location
- Pollution
- Habitability
- Air or water quality
- Hazardous materials (such as lead paint, asbestos, UFFI insulation, radon gas, etc.)
- Engineering analysis

Environmental inspections are disclaimed on the standard inspection because of the special training, licensing, and extra cost and time involved in performing these inspections. Environmental inspections would include asbestos, UFFI, radon, lead paint, lead in water, etc. The disclaimer also covers method of payment and provides signature lines for both the customer and the inspector.

The disclaimer may be printed in your inspection report or as a separate sheet, but it is recommended that the disclaimer be reviewed by an attorney in the area of intended use.

The inspector discusses the inspection report results and reviews the report item by item with the customer to be certain he or she understands all items listed and their condition. The inspector answers questions to the best of his or her ability.

At least two copies of the inspection report should be made: one for the customer and the other for the inspector's files. The inspector always retains a file copy of the inspection form and copies of all correspondence regarding any inspection the inspector performs. The inspection report (Figures 2.1 and 2.2) can be either a pre-printed checklist or a computer-generated form.

■ **FIGURE 2.1** Inspection Report

Nº 1690

BURGESS
Inspection Group, Inc.

INSPECTION REPORT

SEE BACK OF FOURTH PAGE FOR IMPORTANT LIMITATIONS, DISCLAIMERS AND INFORMATION.

INSPECTOR _____ LICENSE NO. _____

THIS REPORT IS OUR INVOICE. INSPECTION FEE $ _____

NAME OF BUYER _____ DATE _____

ADDRESS OF PROPERTY _____ TIME _____

CITY _____ ❑ PAID ❑ BILL DIRECT DATE PAID _____

REALTOR _____ ASSOCIATE _____ PHONE _____

❑ VACANT   ❑ SINGLE STORY   WEATHER CONDITIONS _____
❑ OCCUPIED   ❑ TWO STORY   ❑ ADDENDUM ATTACHED TO THIS REPORT
❑ TOWNHOUSE/CONDO ❑ OUTSIDE TEMP. ___ ❑ TERMITE INSPECTION ATTACHED # _____

The left column headers (vertical): NOT INSPECTED | NEEDS IMMEDIATE REPAIR OR REPLACEMENT | PERFORMING INTENDED FUNCTION

STRUCTURAL FOUNDATION
(FOUNDATIONS ARE NOT TOTALLY OBSERVABLE)

NOTE: FOUNDATION ON CLAY SOIL REQUIRES ADEQUATE AND EVEN MOISTURE AROUND THE PERIMETER OF THE FOUNDATION THE ENTIRE YEAR TO PREVENT MOVEMENT. TREES AND SHRUBS CAN CAUSE FOUNDATION DAMAGE WHEN GROWING TOO CLOSE. WATER SHOULD NOT BE PERMITTED TO POND OR ERODE UNDER OR ALONG SIDE ANY PART OF THE FOUNDATION. DEPENDING ON THE DESIGN AND METHOD OF ORIGINAL CONSTRUCTION OF A PIER AND BEAM FOUNDATION. THE FLOOR SYSTEM MAY NEED LEVELING PERIODICALLY. ❑ **SLAB** ❑ **PIER & BEAM** ❑ **BASEMENT**

			OBSERVATIONS:
			VENTILATION
			CEILINGS & WALLS
			FLOORS
			DOORS
			INTERIOR STEPS, STAIRWAYS, BALCONIES, RAILINGS

DRAINAGE   WATER DRAINAGE (FOUNDATION AREA-SURFACE OR SUBSURFACE DRAINS ARE NOT TESTED)

			OBSERVATION:

EXTERIOR

			SIDING: ❑ STONE ❑ FRAME ❑ BRICK ❑ SHAKES ❑ CONCRETE BLOCK ❑ STUCCO
			PORCHES & DECKS
			WINDOW & DOOR TRIM
			SOFFITS-FASCIA
			GUTTERS-DOWNSPOUTS

GARAGE

			DOORS ❑ METAL ❑ WOOD
			GARAGE DOOR OPENER ❑ AUTO REVERSE

FIREPLACE

			FIREPLACE-LIGHTER
			FIRE BOX/FIRE BRICK ❑ METAL ❑ BRICK
			LINTEL-DAMPER-FLUE
			CHIMNEY ❑ CHIMNEY CAP

PAGE 1 OF 4

■ **FIGURE 2.1** Inspection Report *(Continued)*

N.I.	N.I.R./R	P.I.F.	

ROOF

NOTE: WEATHER CONDITIONS, WIND, HAIL AND EXTREME TEMPERATURES AFFECT ALL ROOFING FROM DAY TO DAY, SO, CONTINUAL OBSERVATION IS RECOMMENDED. ❏ **ASPHALT SHINGLES** ❏ **WOOD SHINGLE** ❏ **SLATE/TILE** ❏ **BUILT-UP** ❏ **METAL**

			OBSERVATIONS
			FLASHING
			ROOF VENTS-RAIN CAPS

ATTIC (ATTICS ARE NOT TOTALLY OBSERVABLE)

			TRUSS ROOF SYSTEM ❏ YES ❏ NO RAFTERS-PURLINS-COLLAR TIES ❏ YES ❏ NO
			DECKING
			INSULATION TYPE: ❏ BLOWN ❏ BATT ❏ ROCKWOOL ❏ CELLULOSE ❏ FIBERGLASS AVERAGE AMOUNT:
			VENTILATION ❏ RIDGE VENT ❏ TURBINE ❏ POWER VENT ❏ SOFFIT VENTS ❏ GABLE LOUVERS & SCREENS

WINDOWS

NOTE: ONLY A REPRESENTATIVE NUMBER OF ACCESSIBLE WINDOWS WERE CHECKED FOR OPERATION AT THIS INSPECTION. AS THERMALPANE WINDOWS LOSE THEIR VACUUM, MOISTURE MAY APPEAR, AND THEN DISAPPEAR, DEPENDING ON INSIDE AND OUTSIDE TEMPERATURE, BAROMETRIC PRESSURE, AND THE HUMIDITY LEVEL: THEREFORE WINDOWS ARE LISTED AS OBSERVED AT TIME OF INSPECTION ONLY, AND NO WARRANTY IS IMPLIED. ❏ **WOOD** ❏ **METAL** ❏ **SINGLE GLAZED** ❏ **THERMAL**

			WINDOWS
			SCREENS
			WATER PENETRATION

MECHANICAL APPLIANCES *NOTE:* THE FOLLOWING IS NOT INCLUDED IN THIS INSPECTION: CLOCKS, TIMERS AND AUTOMATIC COOKING OR CLEANING MODES OR INTERCOM COMMUNICATION MODES. MICROWAVES ARE NOT CHECKED FOR RADIATION LEAKAGE.

			COOK TOP/RANGE ❏ GAS ❏ ELECTRIC
			OVEN ❏ ELECTRIC ❏ GAS ❏ SELF CLEAN ❏ CONTINUOUS CLEAN ❏ MANUAL CLEAN
			#1 SETTING _____ ° TEMP _____ ° #2 SETTING _____ ° TEMP _____ °
			TIMER
			MICROWAVE
			KITCHEN EXHAUST ❏ VENTED ❏ NON-VENTED
			DISPOSAL
			DISHWASHER
			COMPACTOR
			INTERCOM

MISC.: ─────────────────────────────────────

■ **FIGURE 2.1** Inspection Report *(Continued)*

N.I.	N.I.R./R.	P.I.F.	

COOLING   *NOTE:* AIR CONDITIONING UNITS ARE NOT CHECKED WHEN OUTSIDE TEMP. IS BELOW 60°. WE RECOMMEND THE A.C. UNIT BE COMPLETELY SERVICED BEFORE EACH COOLING SEASON AND THE CONDENSATE DRAIN FLUSHED WITH A CHLORINE BLEACH EVERY 2 MONTHS DURING THE COOLING SEASON TO PREVENT CLOGGING.

TYPE OF SYSTEM   ❐ GAS   ❐ ELECTRIC   ❐ CENTRAL   ❐ ZONED

AIR OUT (SUPPLY) _____ AIR IN (RETURN) _____ TEMP. DIFFERENTIAL _____

			COMPRESSOR
			CONDENSER - COIL & FAN
			CONDENSATE DRAIN
			AUXILIARY CONDENSATE DRAIN **(ATTIC SYSTEM ONLY)**
			SUCTION LINE **(INSULATED)**
			CEILING FANS
			ATTIC FAN (WHOLE HOUSE)

HEATING   *NOTE:* ONLY THE EMERGENCY HEAT MODE IS CHECKED ON HEAT PUMPS WHEN TEMPERATURE IS ABOVE 80°. WE RECOMMEND THE HEATING SYSTEM BE COMPLETELY SERVICED BEFORE EACH HEATING SEASON. FILTERS SHOULD BE CHANGED AS NEEDED (AT L EAST EVERY 2 MONTHS). CHECKING HUMIDIFIERS, ELECTRIC AIR FILTERS AND PROPER AIR FLOW BALANCE IS NOT INCLUDED IN THIS INSPECTION.

❐ CENTRAL   ❐ ZONED   ❐ GAS   ❐ ELECTRIC   ❐ FLR/WALL   ❐ RADIANT   ❐ HEAT PUMP

UNITS (#   )   FILTER SIZE _____   LOCATION _____

			BURNER/ELEMENT
			DUCT-WORK ❐ METAL ❐ FLEX

INSIDE PLMBG.   *NOTE:* PIPES AND PLUMBING IN WALLS, IN OR UNDER CONCRETE SLABS OR CONCEALED BY PERSONAL EFFECTS AND THEIR QUALITY, CONDITION OR PURIFICATION OF WATER IS NOT INCLUDED IN THIS INSPECTION.

PLUMBING TYPE: ❐ COPPER   ❐ PVC   ❐ GALVANIZED   ❐ CAST IRON   NO. OF BATHROOMS (   )

			KITCHEN FAUCET & DRAIN
			LAVATORIES (#)
			TUBS (#)
			SHOWERS (#)
			COMMODES (#)
			WATER HEATER ❐ GAS ❐ ELECTRIC SIZE: UNITS (#)
			TEMPERATURE & PRESSURE VALVE OPERATION
			UTILITY ROOM FAUCET & DRAIN

MISC.: _____

_____

■ **FIGURE 2.1** Inspection Report *(Continued)*

Nº 1690

N.I.	N.I.R./R.	P.I.F.

OUTSIDE PLMBG.

NOTE: PIPES, PLUMBING EQUIPMENT AND RESERVOIRS CONCEALED IN ENCLOSURES OR UNDER THE GROUND WERE NOT CHECKED FOR LEAKS OR DEFECTS - ALSO - THE SERVICEABILITY OR CONDITION OF THE SEPTIC OR SEWER SYSTEM IS NOT INCLUDED IN THIS INSPECTIONS. SPRINKLER SYSTEMS WERE ONLY CHECKED IN THE MANUAL OPERATION MODE. POOL PLUMBING SYSTEMS ARE NOT LEAK CHECKED.

			METER-MAIN SHUT-OFF WATER METER CHECK ❏ VISUAL 5-MINUTE CHECK
			OUTSIDE FAUCETS (#)
			SPRINKLER SYSTEM ❏ BACKFLOW PREVENTER ❏ ANTISIPHON VALVE ❏ STATIONS (#)
			GAS LINE CHECK ❏ VISUAL 5-MINUTE CHECK

NOTE: LIGHTS AND EQUIPMENT ACTIVATED BY PHOTO CELL SWITCHES WERE NOT CHECKED. ALSO, LANDSCAPE AND EXTERIOR GROUNDS LIGHTING IS NOT INCLUDED IN THIS INSPECTION. - ANTIQUATED WIRING SHOULD BE UPDATED; IT CREATES A POSSIBLE HAZARD.
TYPE OF WIRING IN PANEL: ❏ COPPER   ❏ ALUMINUM   ❏ CIRCUIT BREAKERS   ❏ FUSES
NOTE: ONLY A REPRESENTATIVE NUMBER OF ACCESSIBLE OUTLETS ARE CHECKED. *SECURITY SYSTEMS ARE NOT INCLUDED IN THIS INSPECTION.

ELECTRICAL

			SERVICE ENTRANCE
			SERVICE PANEL - LOCATION _____ SUB SERVICE PANEL - LOCATION _____
			FIXTURES-SWITCHES AND OUTLETS
			❏ GFCI ❏ GARAGE ❏ KITCHEN ❏ BATHROOMS ❏ EXTERNAL ❏ POOL/SPA
			DOOR BELL/CHIME
			SMOKE DETECTORS (#) **(MANUAL TEST ONLY)**
			BATHROOM VENTS, FANS & HEATERS

POOL/SPA

NOTE: POOLS & SPAS ARE CHECKED FOR EQUIPMENT ONLY, NOT LEAKAGE. POOL TIMER FUNCTION NOT CHECKED. WE DO NOT BACKWASH SWIMMING POOLS.

			❏ GUNITE ❏ FIBERGLASS ❏ VINYL
			HEATER ❏ GAS ❏ ELECTRIC
			POOL SWEEP ❏ CONNECTED ❏ NOT CONNECTED
			❏ DIVING BOARD ❏ LADDER ❏ SLIDE

MISC.: _____

_____

_____

_____

_____

_____

■ **FIGURE 2.2** Property Inspection Report

Your Company Name Here
Your Company Address Here Including City, State, Zip Code
Your Phone, Fax Numbers Here

Property Inspection Report

The following report will be accompanied by details or remarks to support items in need of repair. Additional pages may be attached that are important to your understanding of the condition of the property. Please read them very carefully. This report may not be complete without the attachments. If an item is present in the property and has been inspected, a mark will be made in the "I" column. If an item is not present in the property a mark will be made in the "N/I" column. If an item is present in the property, but is not inspected, a mark will be placed in the "N/I" column. If the inspector determines that an item is in need of repair, the inspector will mark the "R" column. A mark in the "C" column indicates that comments are included that describe the condition of an item. Comments may be provided by the inspector whether an item is deemed in need of repair or not. Such comments are considered important and should be read.

I = Inspected   N/I = Not Inspected   R = Not Functioning or In Need of Repair   C = Comments

I	N/I	R	C	Inspection Item

I. STRUCTURAL SYSTEMS

☐ ☐ ☐ ☐   **A. Foundations**
Type: _____
Functioning as intended? ☐ Yes ☐ No
Crawl space accessible? ☐ Yes ☐ No   ☐ N/A
Method used to inspect crawl space: _____
Comments:

☐ ☐ ☐ ☐   **B. Grading & Drainage**
Comments:

☐ ☐ ☐ ☐   **C. Roof Covering**
Type: _____
Rooftop accessible?   ☐ Yes ☐ No
If not accessible, how was rooftop observed? _____
Comments:

☐ ☐ ☐ ☐   **D. Roof Structure and Attic**
Attic accessible?   ☐ Yes ☐ No
If not accessible, how was attic observed? _____
Approximate Insulation: _____
Comments:

☐ ☐ ☐ ☐   **E. Interior and Exterior Walls**
Comments:

☐ ☐ ☐ ☐   **F. Ceilings and Floors**
Comments:

☐ ☐ ☐ ☐   **G. Doors (Interior and Exterior)**
Comments:

■ **FIGURE 2.2** Property Inspection Report *(Continued)*

I	N/I	R	C	Inspection Item

☐ ☐ ☐ ☐   H. **Windows**
Comments:

☐ ☐ ☐ ☐   I. **Fireplace/Chimney**
Comments:

☐ ☐ ☐ ☐   J. **Porches and Decks**
Comments:

☐ ☐ ☐ ☐   K. **Carports (attached)**
Comments:

II. ELECTRICAL SYSTEMS

☐ ☐ ☐ ☐   A. **Service Equipment**
Visible wiring type: *service:* _____
    feeders: _____
Appropriate connections? ☐ Yes ☐ No
Comments:

☐ ☐ ☐ ☐   B. **Branch Circuits**
Visible wiring type: _____
Comments:

III. MECHANICAL SYSTEMS

☐ ☐ ☐ ☐   A. **Heating Equipment**
List type and energy source for each unit: _____
_____
Comments:

☐ ☐ ☐ ☐   B. **Cooling Equipment**
List type, energy source, supply temperature, return temperature, and temperature differential for each unit: _____
_____
_____
Comments:

    C. **Plumbing Systems**

☐ ☐ ☐ ☐   1. **Water Supply System and Fixtures**
Supply piping type: _____
Comments:

☐ ☐ ☐ ☐   2. **Drain, Wastes, Vents**
Drain/Waste/Vent piping type: _____
Comments:

☐ ☐ ☐ ☐   3. **Water Heating Equipment**
Comments:

■ **FIGURE 2.2** Property Inspection Report *(Continued)*

I	N/I	R	C	Inspection Item

D. Appliances

☐ ☐ ☐ ☐   1. **Dishwasher**
Comments:

☐ ☐ ☐ ☐   2. **Food Waste Disposer**
Comments:

☐ ☐ ☐ ☐   3. **Range Hood**
Comments:

☐ ☐ ☐ ☐   4. **Ranges/Ovens/Cooktops**
Comments:

☐ ☐ ☐ ☐   5. **Microwave Cooking Equipment**
Comments:

☐ ☐ ☐ ☐   6. **Trash Compactor**
Comments:

☐ ☐ ☐ ☐   7. **Other Kitchen Appliances**
Type: _____
Comments:

☐ ☐ ☐ ☐   8. **Bathroom Exhaust Fans and/or Heaters**
Comments:

☐ ☐ ☐ ☐   9. **Whole House Vacuum Systems**
Comments:

☐ ☐ ☐ ☐   10. **Garage Door Operators**
Comments:

☐ ☐ ☐ ☐   11. **Door Bell and Chimes**
Comments:

☐ ☐ ☐ ☐   12. **Hydro Therapy Equipment**
Comments:

☐ ☐ ☐ ☐   13. _____
Comments:

☐ ☐ ☐ ☐   14. _____
Comments:

☐ ☐ ☐ ☐   15. _____
Comments:

Page 3 of _____

■ **FIGURE 2.2** Property Inspection Report *(Continued)*

I	N/I	R	C	Inspection Item

IV. OPTIONAL SYSTEMS

☐ ☐ ☐ ☐   A. **Lawn Sprinklers**
Comments:

☐ ☐ ☐ ☐   B. **Swimming Pools and Equipment**
Comments:

☐ ☐ ☐ ☐   C. **Outbuildings**
Comments:

☐ ☐ ☐ ☐   D. **Outdoor Cooking Equipment**
Comments:

☐ ☐ ☐ ☐   E. **Gas Lines**
Comments:

☐ ☐ ☐ ☐   F. **Water Wells**
Comments:

☐ ☐ ☐ ☐   G. **Septic Systems**
Comments:

☐ ☐ ☐ ☐   H. **Security Systems**
Comments:

☐ ☐ ☐ ☐   I. **Fire Protection Equipment**
Comments:

☐ ☐ ☐ ☐   J. _____
Comments:

■ **FIGURE 2.3** Scope of Inspection

<u>**SCOPE OF INSPECTION**</u>

The inspection scope is furnished to you as part of the inspection report so that you may better understand the nature of the inspection performed on the areas and components contained in the report. We urge you to read the inspection scope and to refer to the scope of any item you might have a question about. In addition to any limitations listed in the following outlines or contained in the report, we do not inspect for building codes, design adequacy, capacity, efficiency sizing, value, flood plain location, pollution, or potability of water, nor do we inspect for insurability.

<u>**Definitions:**</u>

Performing intended functions: Carrying out the design purpose or intended operation of an item, part, system. component.

Needs Repair or Replacement: Not performing its intended function, needs repair, or shows evidence of prior damage, or a safety hazard.

Not Inspected: The structure was not equipped with the item, part, system, member, or that item, part, system **or** member was not inspected.

Foundation and related structural items:

This foundation and related structural components contained in this section were visually examined. Areas or components located in areas not affording complete visual access with out dismantling, uncovering, or the removal of storage or furnishings are expressly excluded from this report. Walls, ceilings. and flooring are examined for deficiencies related to structural performance and water penetration only. Cosmetic damage to walls, ceilings, doors, or flooring is not specifically identified nor addressed in this report. The condition of paints, stains, other surface coatings, or the condition of cabinets is not determined nor addressed in this report. Doors and windows are examined for proper operation, glazing, and evidence of physical damage. Thermal windows are examined for the presence of moisture or other signs of seal failure. Early stages of seal failure may not be detectable at the time of this inspection. Cleanliness, or weather conditions may affect the inspectors ability to detect seal failure therefore, only obvious seal damage is reported. Door and window screens are inspected for presence and condition. **The inspector does not** take soil samples, sightings, measurements, not use equipment in the performance of the foundation inspection. No warranty or guarantee is issued or implied as to the future performance of this foundation and the opinion rendered is based on the conditions existing at the time of this inspection

Chimney and fireplace:

The inspector will inspect the visible components and structure of the chimney and fireplace, the visible parts of the fire box and flue however, **does not** inspect for adequacy of the draft or performance of a chimney smoke test. The damper operation, the presence of non combustible hearth extension, the condition of the lintel, and material surrounding the fireplace, attic penetration of the chimney flue, where accessible, for fire stopping, gas log lighter valves for function and gas leaks, the operation of circular fans when present, and observe the coping or crown, caps or spark arrestor from a ground level at a minimum.

Porches and decks:

The inspector will inspect porches, decks, steps, balconies and carports for structural performance as to visible footings, joists, decking, railings and attachments points, where applicable. **The inspector does not** inspect detached structures or waterfront structures and equipment.

Roof, Roof Structure and Attic:

The inspection of the roof covering, flashing, plumbing vent caps, the roof structure, and components located in the attic space is limited to those areas and items that are accessible and visual without dismantling, uncovering, or, removal of storage to inspect. Underlayment, fasteners and all areas not affording proper head clearance are expressly excluded from this inspection. **The inspector does not** walk on roofs when it is determined that damage to the roof surface may result, or when considered unsafe

■ **FIGURE 2.3** Scope of Inspection *(Continued)*

as determined by the inspector. **The inspector does not** enter attic spaces with less than 5ft of head clearance. **The inspector does not** inspect for insurability.

Appliances:
All appliances are operated in the manual mode only. Self cleaning functions are not inspected. Appliances are inspected for proper operation, visible areas of damage, missing or defective parts, leaks, installation as to secure mounting and proper routing of hose connections, and for vibration or excessive noise during the operation of the appliance. **The inspector does not** determine the compacting ability of compactors, the grinding abilities of food disposal units, nor the vacuum capabilities of central vacuum systems.

Water Heaters:
The inspection of the water heater/s, and heater components are visual in nature and are limited to those items listed in this report. **The inspector does not:** Dismantle any equipment, controls, or gauges to inspect components; operate any valves, when in the inspectors reasonable opinion, damage to property or injury may result; determine proper sizing as to hot water needs; inspect any part, or component that is not completely visual and located in a accessible area; move stored items or furnishings to gain access to the water heater; determine the remaining useful life of the unit or any component; or remove insulation blanket to gain access to water heater components.

Cooling Systems:
The inspection of the cooling system is limited to those items listed in this report. **The inspector does not:** Operate a cooling system when the outside temperature is below 60 degrees Fahrenheit; determine the proper operation of condensate systems; inspect gas-fired refrigeration systems; inspect for the pressure of the system coolant or determine the presence of leaks; determine the efficiency of a system; inspect any equipment which is not in an accessible area or dismantle any equipment, controls or gauges; determine the electrical current draw of the system; program digital-type thermostats or controls; operate any set back features on thermostat or controls; inspect interior components of an evaporative cooler when the unit has been drained or shut down.

Heat Systems:
The inspection of the heat system is visual in nature and is limited to the items listed in this report. **The inspector does not:** Activate or operate heating systems which have been shut down or which do not respond to normal control devices; determine fully the performance of heat exchangers; [This would require dismantling of the system], inspect any equipment unless the equipment is located in an accessible area; dismantle any equipment, controls or gauges; inspect accessories such as humidifiers, air purifiers, motorized dampers, heat reclaimers, electronic air filters or wood burning stoves; inspect solar heating systems; determine the efficiency or adequacy of a system; activate heating or heat pump systems if the ambient temperatures or other circumstances are, in the reasonable opinion of the inspector, not conducive to safe operation without damage to the equipment;; program digital-type thermostat or controls; operate radiant heaters, steam heat or unvented gas-fired heating appliances.

Plumbing System:
The inspection of the plumbing system is a visual inspection in nature and is limited to the items listed in this report. **The inspector does not:** Operate any main, branch or shut-off valves; inspect any system which has been shut down or otherwise secured; inspect any component which are not visible and accessible,; inspect any exterior plumbing components such as water mains, private water wells, private sewer systems, sprinkler systems or swimming pools {unless agreed to by both parties and inspected as a separate inspection apart from the listed items contained in these report}; inspect fire sprinkler systems; inspect or operate drain pumps or waste ejector pumps; inspect the quality or volume of well water; determine the potability of any water supply; inspect water conditioning equipment, such as softeners or filter systems; inspect solar water heating systems; determine the effectiveness anti-siphon devices on appropriate fixtures or systems; operate free standing appliances; inspect private water supply systems,

■ **FIGURE 2.3** Scope of Inspection *(Continued)*

swimming pools or tanks; observe the system for proper sizing, design or use of proper materials; or inspect the gas supply system for leaks. This inspection can not fully determine, in most cases, if a shower pan is damaged and leaking in that most damage is not visual and , in some cased, prolonged use of water is necessary for leaks to become apparent. Because of the limited nature of the inspection and therefore mention possibilities, we do not offer nor imply any warranties regarding the absence of shower pan leaks, damage, nor the continual functional use of the shower pan.

Electrical Systems:
The electrical systems inspection is a visual inspection and is limited to the items listed in this report. **The inspector does not:** Move any objects, furniture or appliances to gain access to any electrical component; remove switch cover plates, except where aluminum wiring is observed in the main or sub panels; inspect any electrical equipment which is not in an accessible area; dismantle any electrical device or control; inspect ancillary systems, such as burglar and smoke or fire systems, antenna, electrical de-icing tapes, sprinkler wiring, intercom systems, any system controlled by timers or photo cells, landscape lighting, cable TV wiring, telephone wiring, load or voltage regulators; or trace wiring origins or wiring destinations.

Swimming Pool and Hot Tub:
The inspection is limited to a visual examination of the items listed in this report. **The inspector does not:** Dismantle or otherwise open any components or lines; uncover or excavate any lines or otherwise concealed components of the system, or determine the presence of sub-surface leaks: fill the pool or hot tub with water; determine the presence of sub-surface water tables; or inspect any ancillary equipment such as computer controls, covers, chlorinators or other chemical dispensers, or water ionization devices or conditioners.

Inspection of additional special structures or equipment (as requested):
> Guest House
> Cabana
> Workshop
> Solar System
> Whirlpool Bath
> Swimming Pool and Equipment
> Sprinkler System
> Spa/Hot Tub and Equipment
> Other_____

REPORT: The Company agrees to provide appropriate reports according to the specific service rendered. The report will indicate which items were inspected, which items are in need of service/repair, or, are not performing the function for which they are intended. Items not included in the report shall not be considered good or bad from any lack of notation. No verbal statements by inspector shall expand the scope of this agreement or the inspection report, nor will such statements be relied upon when solicited from the inspector by the Client at the time of inspection or any other time. The other inspections or tests will be on separate reports with qualified details of the specific subject - and in accordance with applicable professional and technical standards. The reports will be the property of the Burgess Inspection Group, Inc. and the Client and may not be used by any other person without their written consent. The parties hereby authorize distribution of copies of this report to:_____.

INSPECTION REQUIREMENTS AND LIMITATIONS: The building, its components and equipment, are to be ready and accessible for inspection on the date and time stated above. All utilities and pilot lights must be on and all equipment operational so the total inspection can be completed on that date. The inspector is not obligated to change light bulbs, light pilots, move furniture, obstructions or floor coverings, or remove panels to inspect any part of the building or its equipment. Pool/spa must be

■ **FIGURE 2.3** Scope of Inspection *(Continued)*

full, clean and operational. Deviations of these requirements that delay the inspection is just cause for an additional charge.

THE FOLLOWING SPECIFIC LIMITATIONS APPLY: Design problems are not within the scope of inspection. The Inspector will not determine the operational capacity, quality or suitability for a particular use of items inspected. No engineering, scientific or specialized technician test will be made by the inspector. No test samples will be taken from the roof or any other part of the structure unless specifically requested. The company will have no liability for latent defects which cannot be observed by a normal inspection nor can be determined by normal equipment operation; and it is specifically agreed and understood that: Mechanical devices and structural components may be functional one moment and later fail or malfunction; therefore, the Company's liability is specifically limited to those situations where it can be conclusively shown that the mechanical device or structural component inspected was inoperable or in the immediate need of repair or not performing the function for which it was intended at the time of inspection. The Client recognizes that there is **NO REPRESENTATION OF WARRANTY OR GUARANTEE** on the future life of items inspected. The inspector does not take responsibility for reporting non-compliance with any building, electrical, mechanical or plumbing codes established by municipal ordinances or any existing structure.

The intent of the inspector statements and any or all statements on the inspection report is not to be construed as being an endorsement or a condemnation of any appliance, system, structural component, or the building in its entirety. Nor, is it the intent to make any statement of property value.

The inspection report may not include minor settlement and minor crack in concrete, veneer and walls that would be within the normal tolerance or standard and does not impair the structural function of the building. The inspection report may not include cosmetic defects; minor cracks, scrapes, dents, scratches, soiled or faded surfaces of the structure or equipment. Also, soiled, faded, torn or dirty floor, wall or window coverings. The Inspection Report is not to be construed as a total list of defects, existing or potential.

SPECIAL DISCLOSURE: It is not uncommon to observe cracks or for cracks to occur in concrete slabs or the exterior and interior walls. Cracks may be caused by the curing of building materials, temperature variations, and soil movement such as: settlement, uneven moisture content in the soil, shock waves, vibrations, etc. While cracks may not necessarily effect the structural integrity of a building, cracks should be monitored so that appropriate maintenance can be performed if movement continues at an abnormal rate. Proper foundation maintenance is the key to the prevention of initial cracks or cracks enlarging. This includes, but not limited to, proper watering, foundation drainage and removal of vegetation growth near the foundation.

SPECIAL NOTE: The Client is hereby advised that other adverse problems may occur at slab cracks and other voids in the slab. Radon gas, termites and other living organisms, can enter a building through cracks and voids and may be a health hazard. Cracks and voids can be sealed effectively to prevent radon gas or other undesirable organisms from entering.

The inspector encourage the Client to obtain a second opinion from a qualified specialist (structural engineer, licensed electrician, licensed plumber, certified factory trained service person, etc.) when there is a condition that they question or are concerned about. The Client has a right to have more than one inspection, or more than one inspector.

The inspector recommends that all repairs are completed by, or under the direction of, a qualified specialist that is certified, licensed and bonded. Also, that the Client obtain a copy of the work order and the paid receipt of all completed work that was performed on the property within the last 6 months.

The Inspector thank you for giving us the opportunity to help you get a total view of your new investment through this report, the eyes of an experienced, qualified inspector. If you have any questions concerning this report, please feel free to call.

■ FIGURE 2.4

IMPORTANT AGREEMENTS AND LIMITATIONS

Scope: This is a visual inspection only. We inspect only what we see. We do not disassemble anything. We do not inspect for any environmental issues such as lead paint, asbestos, etc. We do not inspect for building codes, soil analysis, adequacy of design, capacity, efficiency size, value, flood plain location, pollution or habitability. Please remember that older houses do not meet the same standards as newer houses, even though items in both might be performing the function for which they are intended. We do not hold ourselves to be specialists for any particular item; nor are we engineers. We are a general real estate inspection company. This inspection report covers only the items listed in the report which are reasonably observable , and are based only on the present condition of those items.

For example, we do not move furniture, rugs, paintings, or other furnishings. There is no responsibility expressed or implied for latent defects, or for defects not reasonably observable at the time of the inspection, or for defects that would require the removal of major or permanent coverings for observation. No representation is made concerning any condition other than the operability of any item. No representation is made as to the future performance of any item. There are no warranties, either expressed or implied. If you would like a warranty or guarantee you must obtain it from a warranty company. *When an item is noted as not functioning or in need of repair, replacement or further evaluation by a specialist, the Purchaser agrees to contact a qualified specialist to make further evaluations of the item before you purchase the home.*

Dispute Resolution: In the event a dispute arises regarding this inspection, the purchaser agrees to notify (inspector). so as to give a reasonable opportunity to reinspect the property. **Purchaser further agrees that the (inspector) can either conduct the reinspection itself or can employ others (at its expense) to reinspect the property, or both.**

Defense Costs: In the event the purchaser files suit against (inspector) or its inspector, the purchaser agrees to pay all the company's legal fees, costs of expert witnesses, court costs, costs of depositions and all other such expenses incurred by (inspector) if the purchaser fails to prevail in the lawsuit.

Exclusivity: The report is prepared exclusively for the Client(s) named and is not transferable to anyone in any form. Client(s) gives permission for (inspector) to discuss report findings with real estate agents, specialists or repair persons for the sake of clarification.

By my signature below or the acceptance of this report, I acknowledge that I have read this agreement and limitations and the attached report, and that I understand the terms and conditions and I agree to be bound by these.

THIS REPORT IS OUR INVOICE

Inspection Fee $_____   Report #_____

Inspector/License No.:_____

Buyer:_____   Date:_____

■ SAMPLE PHRASES FOR INSPECTION REPORTS

Appliances

Range (Gas)
Pilots need adjusting
Electronic pilots do not operate
Pilot does not operate
Air-gas mixture needs adjusting
Strong gas odor; needs to be checked
Improper clearance to combustibles

Range (Electric)
Elements have hot spots
Element does not operate
When all burners are on high setting, breakers trip
Element does not reach proper heat
Control knob broken

Oven (Gas)
Oven does not have pilot light
Oven door hinges broken
Glass in door broken
Oven temperature checks hot; approximately 50°F
Door gasket damaged
Numbers worn off control knobs
Continuous-clean oven finish is damaged
Electronic pilot does not operate
Standing pilot does not operate
Oven timer does not operate

Oven (Electric)
Oven door hinges broken
Door glass broken
Door does not seal properly
Door gaskets damaged and/or missing
Thermostat checks hot; approximately 50°F
Self-clean mode does not operate
Oven timer does not operate
Handles are loose
Timer operates only top oven
Broiler element does not operate
Bake element does not operate
Oven needs to be anchored in cabinet
Numbers worn off control knob
Oven light does not operate
Thermostat needs to be properly anchored in oven
Elements have hot spots
Rotisserie does not operate
Self-clean window shield does not operate

Door lock does not operate
Self-clean mode operates with timer broken
Continuous-clean oven surface is damaged
Is no longer a continuous-clean oven

Dishwasher
Door gasket damaged
Door interior damaged or rusted
Tub liner damaged and/or rusted
Soap dispenser does not operate
Shows evidence of leaking
Top spray bar does not operate
Dishwasher needs to be anchored in cabinet
Timer does not operate properly
Door lock needs repair (does not lock properly or does not turn off when lock is in open position)
Door hinges broken
Heater does not operate
Dishwasher has excessive noise and/or vibration
Front panels damaged
Bottom and/or top rack damaged and/or needs rollers
Knobs or push-buttons missing

Disposal
Has excessive vibration (hammers missing and/or frozen)
Disposal leaks under sink
Disposal case has corrosion
Rubber splash shield damaged or missing
Disposal needs to be grounded
Check for proper installation—sewer drain below disposal drain
Disposal jammed; could not break loose

Kitchen Exhaust

Ductless
Needs two filters—one grease filter, one charcoal filter
Fan does not operate and/or fan has excessive noise and vibration

Ducted
Vents to attic
Fan and/or blower does not operate
Grease filter missing or damaged
Vent pipe needs to be sealed at joints and/or connections
Not vented out of kitchen

Jenn-Air
Motor overload trips; not vented properly
Not vented outside
Grease filter not properly installed
Vent not connected in cabinet

Compactor

Key missing
Ram does not operate
Door does not lock properly
Excessive noise and vibration
Door damaged

Microwave

Microwave needs a grounded outlet
Door glass cracked and/or broken
Door hinges and latches loose or broken
Oven shows evidence of arcing, wear, damaged door
    seals and gaskets, sealing on exterior and interior
    surfaces
Door does not close properly
Interlock does not operate
Oven appears to have been dropped and/or damaged
Stirrer and/or plastic stirrer cover damaged

Intercom

Radio inoperable
Static in radio and speakers
Speakers inoperable
Knobs missing on speakers and/or radio

Gas Grill

Handle broken (missing on cover)
Control knob missing
Burners rusted or damaged
Grill post rusted out
Grates rusted out or missing
Charcoal has been used in gas grill
No gas cutoff valve

Gas Light

Glass broken and/or missing
Mantels need replacing
Mantel holder broken
No gas cutoff valve

Refrigerator

Door gaskets damaged
Plastic liner broken or damaged
Door hinges need repair
Temperature checks: Refrigerator _____°F
    Freezer _____°F

Plumbing

Water meter

5 min. minimum leak check
Evidence of movement in meter; needs to be checked
Meter damaged; could not check
Meter full of water; could not check
Meter disconnected or meter locked; could not check

Gas line

5 min. minimum check
Meter has excessive movement approximately 1 cu. ft.
    in 5 min.

Kitchen sink

Swing spout needs repair (leaks)
Faucets leak around stems
Connections leaking under sink
No P-trap; using radiator hose for trap
Vegetable spray disconnected
Vegetable spray does not operate
Vegetable spray has low pressure
Vegetable spray leaking
Hot water dispenser leaking and/or inoperable
Drainstop inoperable
Water leak under sink has damaged the cabinet and
    under house
Faucets have low water pressure
Finish on kitchen sink damaged (chipped)
Faucets loose on sink
Hot and cold water reversed

Lavatories

Faucets leak
Leak at connection under sink
Drainstop inoperable
Loose at wall
Sink cracked
Top of lavatory needs to be sealed to countertop
Faucets loose on sink
Stops broken in faucets; need repair
Water hammer
P-traps
Hot and cold water reversed

Bathtubs

Tile loose and/or missing
Tub needs grout between tub, tile and corners
Shower diverter valve does not operate properly
Drainstop inoperable or missing

Soap dish missing
Hot and cold water faucets reversed
Faucets have no stops; need repair
Water hammer
Faucets leak

Shower

Plumbing loose in wall
Tile needs grout; tile broken; tile missing
Water hammer
Faucets leak
Shower head needs seals
Shower leaking; carpet/baseboard/drywall in adjoining
  area has water damage
Wood damage under house in subfloor, joist and/or
  beam
Enclosure door glass broken
Enclosure needs to be sealed (leaks)
Standing water test

Whirlpool Tub

Shows evidence of leaking
Pump has no pressure
Pump should be on a timer
GFCI is present and functional

Commodes

Loose at floor
Bowl or tank is cracked
Tank lid broken or missing
Seal leaking between tank and bowl
Flush mechanism inoperable
Leaking under house; wood damage
Bowl refill tube missing

Outside Faucets

Handles missing or damaged
No water
Faucets leaking in wall
Water cut-off handles broken and/or rusted off
Faucets need seals and washers
Antisiphon device missing
Pressure test

Sprinkler System

Controls inoperable
Missing and/or broken heads
No water to X station
Valve stuck on X station; shut off water at cutoff
Underground water leak

Heads need adjusting
Recommend estimate from pool company
Could not locate backflow prevention device

Utility Room

Faucets leak
Sheetrock has water damage
Subfloor has water damage
220V outlet is dead
Dryer vented in attic or under house

Water Heater (Gas)

Leaking at cold water cutoff
Leaking at cold and hot water connections at top of
  heater
Water lines installed properly; hot to hot, cold to cold
Leaking at drain valve
Leaking under tank
Case dented—water has some rust; should be checked
  for tank damage
Vent is blocked—no draft at draft diverter
Has two draft diverters (can have only one)
Class "B" vent pipe through ceiling, attic, and roof
Vent pipe improperly installed, disconnected
Thermostat inoperable
Strong gas odor
Copper gas line cannot pass through wall, floor, or
  ceiling
Vent pipe has to be double wall pipe through ceiling,
  attic, and roof
T & P valve exhaust line has been reduced
Water has bad odor; possible that anode rod needs
  replacing
Burner needs replacing
Wood damage in floor
No gas cutoff valve
Water heater not elevated where required

Water Heater (Electric)

Heat element inoperable
Damaged thermostat
Water leaks around heat elements
Wires to controls and element burned or disconnected;
  same general information above for gas heaters
  applies to electric
Water heater not elevated where required
T & P valve exhaust line has been reduced

Fireplace

Bricks in back of firebox need pointing up with fire clay
Back of facebrick needs to be sealed to lintel

Gas starter needs repair
Not a woodburning fireplace
Metal fireplace—metal firebox is damaged
Chimney needs brick pointed up with mortar
Mortar cap needs replacing at top of chimney, if visible
Damper is inoperable
No damper; has loose brick in firebox
Has loose brick in flue
Loose brick at top of chimney

Heating

Furnace (Gas)
Burners rusty and dirty; recommend service by heating company to check for heat exchanger malfunction
Needs to be checked by heating company for heat exchanger malfunction
Spillage noted; recommend service by heating company to check for heat exchanger malfunction
Evidence of rollout; recommend service by heating company to check for heat exchanger malfunction
Burner(s) need alignment; recommend service by heating company to check for heat exchanger malfunction
Lack of combustion air; needs opening to crawlspace or attic
Vent connector not sealed at flue; gas odor noted
Combustion air opening needs insulation pulled back
Gas lines show corrosion
Flexible gas line penetrates through wall, floor, ceiling, and/or cabinet of unit
Flexible gas line kinked
Copper gas line penetrates through wall, floor, and/or ceiling
Irregular flame noted at burner; recommend service by heating company to check for heat exchanger malfunction
Pilot flame is dirty (misaligned); recommend service by heating company
Blower has excessive vibration and noise
Belt worn, loose
Recommend furnace be cleaned and heat exchanger rechecked by heating company
No gas cutoff valve
No cutoff switch

Furnace (Electric)
Heat elements are inoperable
Wires burned or loose
Fuses blown
No cutoff switch

Furnaces (Both Electric and Gas)
Thermostat needs to be leveled and tightened to wall
Ducts disconnected and damaged in attic and/or under house
Ducts lying on ground; ducts beginning to rust under house
Return ducts not insulated
No provision for filters on return side of furnace
Electronic filter service light inoperable

Humidifier
Cannot check with air-conditioning operating
Humidifier not connected
Needs cleaning and service

Air-Conditioning
Compressor has excessive noise and vibration; needs to be checked
Condenser coil needs cleaning
Evidence of refrigerant leak at condensing unit
Condensing unit needs to be releveled
Condensate drain line disconnected and/or broken
No auxiliary drain on attic unit
Drain not in a conspicuous location
Insulation missing on suction line
Temperature too cold to check, below 60°F
Not cooling properly
Suction line is damaged
Suction line needs to be insulated (at cooling coil)
Compressor cycling
Evaporator coil needs cleaning, if visible
Condensate drain stopped up; needs service
Evaporator case rusted out; needs repair

Electric
Type of wire: aluminum or copper
Aluminum wire on 220V circuits
Copper wire on 110V branch circuits
Panel has double-wired breakers and/or fuses
Wrong size wire on breakers or fuses
Hot rheostat
Discolored wall outlet
Broken light diffuser
Missing fixtures
Wires lying on ground under house
Bare wires protruding from ceiling or wall
Knock outs missing
Neutral not bonded
Service entrance not grounded
Loose wall outlets

No weatherproof covers on outside outlets
GFCI (ground fault circuit interrupter) inoperable
No GFCI on pool light
Panel door and cover missing
Panel loose in wall
Weatherhead loose
Wires too low between house and garage
Bulbs missing from outside fixtures
Three-prong outlets have open grounds
Outlets connected in reverse polarity
Open wire splices in attic and under house
Electrical service drop too low
Pool motor needs external grounds
Doorbell does not operate
Bathroom heaters and/or fan does not operate
Attic fan does not operate; louvers covered with
   insulation; belt missing

Foundations

Pier-and-Beam

Piers missing, tipped
Piers need to be shimmed to support girder or beam
Floor joist, girder, or beam sagging
Floor joist, girder beam, or sill plate has wood damage
Subfloor has wood damage
Perimeter beam wall is cracked; shows evidence of
   movement
Floors not level
Stress cracks in sheetrock; shows evidence of movement
   throughout
Brick separation on exterior
Step cracking at foundation or corners
Structure appears out of square

Slab

Brick separation on exterior; some stress cracks in
   sheetrock; does not show evidence of major
   movement at this time; ground around foundation
   needs to be sloped away from foundation and kept
   moist
Brick separation on exterior; some stress cracks in
   sheetrock; striker plates have been adjusted; doors do
   not fit; bricks pulling from around windows; floors
   are not level; recommend a foundation company
Cable ports need to be sealed with mortar
Dirt too high on brick drainage; needs to be corrected
Shows evidence of water penetration; needs drainage
   corrected
Foundation shows evidence of minor movement—
   nothing major at this time—as evidenced by

settlement cracks in sheetrock, margins on doors,
   some brick separation on exterior; ground around
   foundation needs to be kept moist

Water Drainage

Dirt slopes to foundation
Drainage needs to be corrected

Roof

Composition Shingle

Roof is old, brittle; shows evidence of curled, cracked
   shingles and valleys; recommend estimate from
   roofing company
Broken and damaged shingles, valley, and ridge;
   recommend estimate from roofing company
Roof shows evidence of leaking; recommend estimate
   from roofing company
Shows evidence of sagging (applies to all roofs);
   recommend estimate from roofing company

Wood Shingle

Has broken, missing, loose, and curled shingles;
   recommend estimate from roofing company
Split and missing ridgerow; recommend estimate from
   roofing company
Roof is old; shingles show evidence of deterioration;
   recommend estimate from roofing company

Wood Shake

Has curled and worn shakes and has exposed felt paper;
   recommend estimate from roofing company
Has split and missing shingles; recommend estimate
   from roofing company

Built-Up

Has low areas, allowing water to pond; evidence of
   blisters; exposed felt or split seams; shows evidence
   of leaking; recommend estimate from roofing
   company
Flashing needs resealing
Flashings rusted out; need repair
Scuppers damaged/blocked/inadequate

Vents

Water heater vent rusted out; needs replacing
Furnace vent rain cap missing
Sewer vents need to be sealed on roof
Flashings need to be sealed; rain skirt needs to be sealed

Garage Door

Has some wood damage in bottom panel
Fingerjoints pulling apart
Panels have water damage
Loose and/or missing hardware
Hinges are loose
Track is damaged
Broken glass
Excessive sagging in door

Door Opener

Checked manual operation only; remote control not
   checked
Automatic reverse does not operate (safety)

Swimming Pool

Leaks at pumps and filter area
Heater full of leaves and debris; needs to be cleaned
   before lighting is checked
Pool has loose, cracked, and missing tile

Pressure gauge on filter broken
Pool sweep does not operate
Plaster chipped and/or worn through
Algae in pool needs to be cleaned
No water to slide
Pool fill line broken
Decking is cracked; Kool-crete sealing off
Skimmer opening cracked
Needs to be sealed between decking and coping
Water too dirty to check
No GFCI on pool light

Miscellaneous

Wood damage around exterior in fascia, soffit
Thermopane windows have lost their seals
Windows broken
Wood damage
Windows need caulking to brick
Paint; excessive chipping and/or peeling

3
Soils and Foundations

Soil conditions must be investigated to determine the suitability of construction materials. Field exploration provides soil samples from various strata. The bearing capacity and settlement characteristics of the foundation and the stability of slopes and earth pressures on supporting structures are determined from soil samples. Subsurface strata and groundwater conditions indicate potential problems in excavating and/or removing groundwater during construction. Residential construction precautions are necessary in some geographic areas because of sinkholes, caves, and mine tunnels.

Soil characteristics vary widely from one geographic region to another. Soil on steep slopes is generally less productive than soil on gentle slopes. Soil developed from sandstone is more sandy and less fertile than soil formed from shale. Soil properties are quite different when developed under tropical climates compared with temperate or arctic conditions. Scientists have recognized soil variations and have established classification systems of characteristics for identifying sandy, clay, loam, and other soils. Soil variations dictate the residential foundations viable in different geographic locations. Most foundation problems are diagnosed from analysis of soil composition.

■ SOILS

Soil is produced by material deposits and geologic forces. Soil characteristics are determined by physical and mineral composition of the parent material, climate under which the soil material has existed since accumulation, plant and animal life on and in the soil, topography, and length of time forces have acted on the material. All determining factors influence soil characteristics, and the significance of each factor varies from one geographic location to another. In one area a certain

factor may dominate soil formation, whereas in another area the same factor may be less important. The interrelationship of these factors is complex, and the effects of a single factor cannot be isolated and completely evaluated. (See Figure 3.1.)

Properties

Information relating to soil properties is collected during a soil survey. Evaluation of soil properties is based on field and laboratory tests of samples from the survey area and on laboratory tests of samples of similar soils in nearby areas.

During a soil survey, shallow borings are made and examined to identify and classify soils. Samples are tested in a laboratory to determine grain-size distribution, plasticity, compaction characteristics, and mechanical properties. General soil property information can be found for a specific geographic area by consulting the local county soil conservation service.

Survey

A soil survey is an inventory and evaluation of the soils to determine the suitabilities and limitations of land use. Residential construction should not be started without reliable information on the soil-bearing values of the site. Investigation of underlying materials is essential for foundation design. The location and approximate depth of rock, abnormal soil conditions and groundwater level must be considered before residential construction begins.

Soil-bearing values for structures subject to earthquake forces in combination with other vertical loads are increased by approximately 33 percent when the foundation is supported on natural, dense, relatively incompressible bearing strata, such as hardpan rock and

■ **FIGURE 3.1**

Soil characteristics are determined by composition, climate, plant and animal life, topography, and time forces.

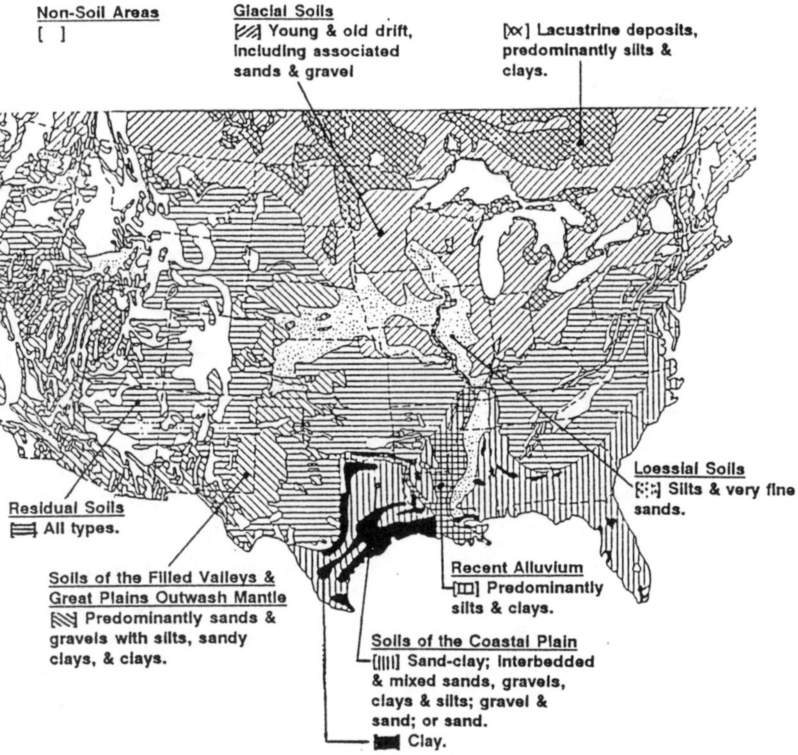

cemented or compacted sand and gravel. For tall, flexible structures, sites having firm soil or rock at shallow depth are preferred over sites having weaker soils, even if the sites with weaker soils are a greater distance from a fault. Short, stiff structures are most susceptible to damage when the site is near an active fault.

Ideal sites are relatively rare in seismic areas. Weak soil sites in seismic areas must be made suitable for construction by improving the sites. There is no standard test that will permit prediction of the response of the foundation soil to earthquake shocks. However, information can be obtained in the field and laboratory to assist in the evaluation of the probable behavior of certain soils.

In preparing a soil survey, soil scientists, conservationists, and engineers collect extensive field information on erosion, droughts, flooding, and other factors that affect various soil use and management. Field experience and collected information on soil properties and performance are used as a basis for predicting soil behavior.

Planners using soil survey information can evaluate the effect of specific land use on productivity and on the environment. Planners use the soil survey to create and

maintain a land-use pattern in harmony with the natural soil. Contractors use the soil survey to locate sources of sand, gravel, roadfill, and topsoil. Soil surveys also identify areas where bedrock, water, or firm soil layers are located.

Soil scientists conduct a soil survey by observing the length and shape of slopes, size of streams and pattern of drainage, native plants or crops, rocks, and soil profile. A soil profile is the sequence of natural layers in the soil from the surface to the parent material that has not been changed by leaching or by plant roots.

Soil characteristics are determined from test results, records, field experience, and state and local specialists.

Classifications

Soils are classified as gravel, sand, silt, and clay based on texture size. Most soil consists of loam. Loam is a mixture of two or more soil ingredients. A soil classification depends on the ingredient that has the most influence on the soil's behavior. A silty clay loam is primarily a silt, but contains clay. An organic silt is composed primarily of silt, but contains organic material.

■ **FIGURE 3.2**

Loam is classified by its clay, silt, and sand content.

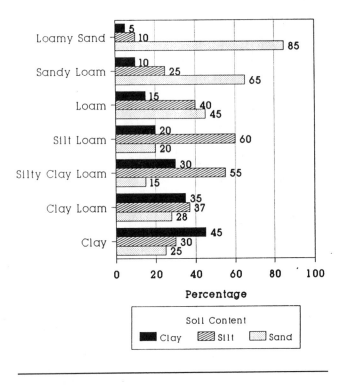

Mineral Soils
Mechanical Analyses

Most organic soils are weaker and more compressible than soils without organic material. (See Figure 3.2.)

Coarse-Grained Soils

Gravel and sand are coarse-grained soils. If individual particles can be seen by the naked eye, the soil is considered coarse-grained. Compacted coarse-grained soils are dense with few voids. Soil compressibility is the reduction of voids under a load and is the major cause of foundation settlement. Gravel and sand-based soils do not compress unless the grains are rearranged by erosion caused by poor drainage or vibration.

Soil shearing is a function that affects foundation performance. The weight of a structure may create stress forces that cause the soil to slide away from the foundation footing. The resistance in coarse-grained soils is due to internal friction. When the foundation footing has a sufficient bearing surface and proper soil compaction, the shearing strength of coarse-grained soils is very high.

Fine-Grained Soils

Fine-grained soils are silts and clays. Silts are finer than sands, but coarser than clays. Clays consist of microscopic flake-shaped crystalline minerals. Silts and clays are cohesive in nature and tend to compress, deform, and creep under a load. Generally, silts are more stable than clays. Clays tend to cause major problems in foundation stability because clays expand with moisture.

Three clays that cause foundation problems are kaolinite, montmorillonite, and illite. Montmorillonite clay is flakelike and is held together by a weak oxygen-bond linkage. Montmorillonite clay can swell 10 to 15 times its size and exert a force of 3 to 16 tons per square foot. The expanding clay can move a typical house that weighs 300 to 400 pounds per square foot.

A soil engineer rates the potential change of volume in a soil by the plasticity index (PI). The PI is the range of moisture content in which the soil remains plastic. The higher the PI rating, the greater the shrink-swell potential. The foundation design should be based on a report generated from a soil test. Color does not affect the expansiveness of clay; clay can be black, gray, orange, etc. Silts or sands obtain bearing strength by friction, and clays obtain bearing strength by cohesion.

Expansive Soils

Expansive clay soils react to climatic conditions like a sponge. Clay soils expand as they absorb water and then contract when they dry out. This causes differential movement on the building foundations. The highly expansive clay soils and changing weather conditions can cause homeowners costly repairs. Differential movement does not stop as buildings get older. Older structures with a history of minimal movement have been known to develop foundation problems in a very short time due to changing conditions at the outside perimeter of the foundations. As long as the foundation movement is not enough to damage the house or foundation, most people do not consider the movement to be a foundation repair problem.

A primary reason for foundation problems is the expansive nature of the clay soil that is supporting the building foundation. The clay expands or contracts as its moisture content changes with the weather. Depending on the area, the amount of shrinkage ranges upward of 60 percent of the total wet volume. This shrinkage accounts for the large cracks that form in the soil after a long dry period. The more expansive the clay, the larger the crack.

If a person wants to stop the seasonal foundation damage, the first thing to do is follow a controlled

■ **FIGURE 3.3**

Placement of soaker hoses and/or sprinkler heads at foundations.

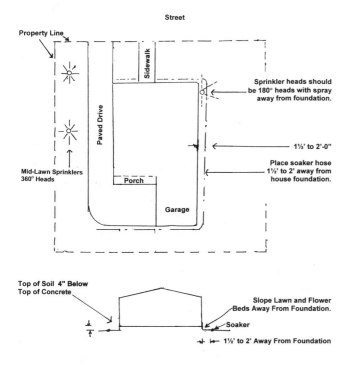

watering program to maintain constant moisture content of the soil under the foundation. Quite often foundation movement can be stopped. There are different ways of setting up a controlled watering program. The most expensive system would be to install an automatic lawn sprinkler system. The least expensive system is to place soaker hoses around the foundation placed 18″ to 24″ inches from the foundation. (See Figure 3.3.) The soaker hoses should be the bubbler type, and there should be enough hoses that, connected together, they will wrap the foundation so the foundation will be watered evenly. If a sprinkler system is installed, all heads by the foundation should be installed at least 18″ from the foundation with 180-degree heads spraying out from the foundation and no heads spraying water against the house or foundation. Water spraying against the foundation will undermine the soil under the footings causing the foundation to settle the same as if there were no moisture at all. Whether you have expansive soil or stable soil, the sprinkler pattern should never spray against the structure or foundation because this can cause soil erosion and foundation problems.

To keep a foundation stable during hot dry weather requires large amounts of water. If there are trees and shrubs close to the foundation it will require more water, because some large trees and shrubs will absorb as much as 200 gallons of water per day from the soil.

If a controlled watering program is desired, watering should be deep and done early in the morning. When the weather conditions are hot and dry, you may have to do this at least two to three times a week. If the soil starts pulling away from the foundation, it is an indication that the soil is not getting enough water. Without good drainage and water to keep the soil expanded around the foundation for support, the watering cycle needs to be increased. The reason for installing the sprinkler heads or soaker hoses 18″ to 24″ from the foundation is to allow the foundation and the soil under and around it to set up a capillary attraction, which pulls the moisture toward the foundation and keeps the soil expanded around and under the foundation.

Most people do not understand expansive soils, especially people who are moving from an area of stable soil to an area with expansive soil. An inspector who is performing a home inspection for those unfamiliar with expansive soils should always explain how to care for this type of foundation properly. When purchasers are moving to an expansive soil area from a stable soil area, where they try to keep moisture *away* from the foundation, it is not uncommon for them to have foundation problems or at least foundation movement because of their lack of knowledge about how to care for the foundation.

Water that stands or runs alongside a foundation may cause uneven settlement of the foundation. If the soil grading is such that the water does not drain away from the foundation but, instead, runs alongside it, and if water is allowed to stand or pond alongside the foundation, the water will flow below the foundation and dissolve the clay that supports it, causing the foundation to settle.

The homeowner can reduce the amount of differential settlement by following a few recommendations:

- During extended dry periods, water the soil evenly around the entire foundation to prevent the soil from pulling away from the foundation. If the soil appears to be pulling away from the foundation, it may be necessary to water daily and always evenly around the entire foundation. It is important not to let the water hit the foundation or run into the gap between the foundation and the soil. It is also important to water 18″ to 24″ from the foundation, allowing capillary attraction to pull the moisture to the foundation. Many homeowners install automatic sprinkler systems that eliminate the problem of moving hoses, forgetting to water, etc. In hot, dry weather, the foundation usually requires added moisture three to four times per week.

- Trees and shrubs that are too close to the foundation will absorb excessive amounts of water from the soil. Quite often a large tree will absorb more water than has been added with the watering system. Large trees' root systems extend out to at least the drip line of the tree, and one wants to remember that the feeder roots of trees and shrubs will go to moisture. Some homeowners will choose to root prune a large tree rather than lose it. A tree professional should do this. Root pruning is done by digging a trench away from the foundation, cutting the tree roots, and installing some type of barrier to prevent the roots from growing back under the foundation.
- Install gutters and downspouts to control water runoff and soil erosion, extending downspouts away from the foundation.
- There should be no low areas or high areas that block or hold water flow. Soil should slope gradually away from the foundation, 1½″ to 2″ in 4′ to ensure proper drainage.
- Sometimes the topography of the lot and the elevation of the house will not allow normal runoff of surface water. When this situation exists, it may be necessary to employ a structural engineer to design surface drains to remove the excess water. This can be expensive, but it is very important. If the foundation is going to be protected from failure, it must have good drainage.

It is important that an inspector be familiar with the areas that he or she inspects because of the local soil conditions. A prudent inspector needs to be knowledgeable about the various requirements of the local and national codes for good construction practice. While a real estate inspector does not inspect to codes and is not a code inspector, having code knowledge will help.

There are factors other than the type of soil that influence the construction of a foundation. The topography is very important, as is whether the property is situated near a lake, creek, or river; the depth of the frost line for the area; the depth of the water table or underground springs (although underground springs may not be active year-round)—all help determine the recommended depth and type of footing required.

Sometimes it is difficult because of landscaping to visualize the topography of the property as it was before the structure was built, but in most cases the inspector is able to determine if (1) the property is located in an area of hills, (2) the property is cut out of a hillside, or (3) the property is constructed on the side of a hill where it could be subject to erosion and/or mud slides. Other adverse conditions that the inspector should be aware of are whether the area is subject to earthquakes, wind loads, or snow loads. Also, is the property located in an area where there are no codes, such as out in the country or in a small village?

■ FOUNDATIONS

The foundation distributes the structure's load to the ground. Foundation walls are usually poured concrete, concrete block, or wood. The foundations used in different areas of the United States depend on climate, soil characteristics, building load, and the water table. The foundation footing should extend, at a minimum, 12″ below the finished grade or below the frostline. Finish grade should be a minimum of 8″ from the top of the foundation (6″ below wood siding, 4″ below brick). An inappropriate foundation may sink or settle.

The foundation must be checked in a residential inspection. Foundation settlement can cause internal stresses that weaken a structure. Differential settlement produces unsightly cracks in floors, exterior walls, and ceilings; it will cause unlevel floors, roof leaks, and inoperable doors and windows and will affect plumbing. All cracks should be reported. A structure that is perfectly square without settlement or significant cracking has an acceptable foundation.

Most structures experience some settlement. While most foundation problems can be corrected, repair work is usually expensive, and extreme problems may necessitate demolishing the entire structure. The inspector must recognize and report foundation problems to the client. A residential inspector must have a thorough knowledge of foundations to determine acceptable standards.

Basements

Foundation footing for basement construction must be a minimum of 12″ below the frost line to prevent damage from expansion and contraction of the soil during freeze and thaw cycles. The size and depth of the footings are determined by the size and weight of the structure they have to support and the soil type. When the basement is dug out, the opening should be larger than the actual foundation by approximately 2′ to 3′ all around. This allows room to waterproof the wall and to

■ **FIGURE 3.4**

Bracing foundation walls against lateral earth pressure.

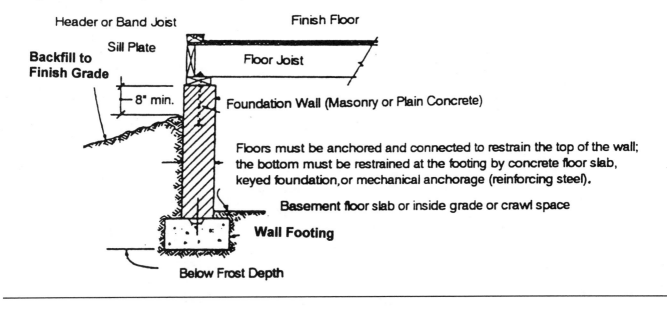

install drain tile around the footings to carry excess moisture away from walls.

Concrete Foundations

Poured concrete walls should be steel reinforced. In some foundation systems the footing when poured will have a V-shaped groove in the top of the footing with rebar from the footing exposed to tie the wall steel and provide a continuous concrete and steel reinforcement from the foundations through the wall corners and along the top tie beam. The concrete wall should be 8″ thick, and it should be poured in a single pour. After the concrete has cured for several days, the outside of the wall should be covered with a good waterproofing material.

The drain tile at the footing and the footing itself should be covered with gravel. The gravel should be washed and should be approximately ¾″ maximum size.

Basement walls should not be backfilled until after the house has been closed in. Care should be taken when backfilling not to damage walls, in particular any wall adjacent to or housing mechanical equipment. (See Figure 3.4.)

Concrete blocks, also referred to as con*crete masonry units* (CMU), are used as basement walls as well as retaining and crawlspace walls. Regardless of the end use, a concrete block wall must have a supportable footing. The requirements for a concrete block wall gen-erally are the same as for a poured concrete wall (width, depth, height, size, and reinforcement). (See Figure 3.5.)

A horizontal crack in a basement wall, even if it is only a hairline crack, can be the most significant crack observed and the most costly to repair. Occasionally, this type of crack occurs when the wall is backfilled in the construction process. If this is the case, the crack may not be significant structurally. Often, however, this type of crack occurs because of moisture-laden soil or hydrostatic pressure. If this is not corrected, the wall may fail, and the cost to repair is very high. (See Figure 3.6.)

Wood Foundations

A properly designed and installed wood foundation provides more value and benefit to the consumer than any other foundation available today if the property is located in an area with stable soils and free of wood destroying insects such as termites, carpenter ants, etc. It creates a lower level that is just as warm, dry and comfortable as the upper levels of the home. Wood foundations are very simple to finish, provide excellent energy efficiency and have tremendous design flexibility. Home inspectors face the challenge of separating the good foundations from the not-so-good foundations. There are a few key items the inspector should be looking for when inspecting a wood foundation. The total depth of backfill is what determines whether foundation wall studs should be 2 × 6s, 2 × 8s or 2 × 10s. The spacing of the

■ **FIGURE 3.5**

Foundation walls using a spread footing: A, crawlspace; B, basement.

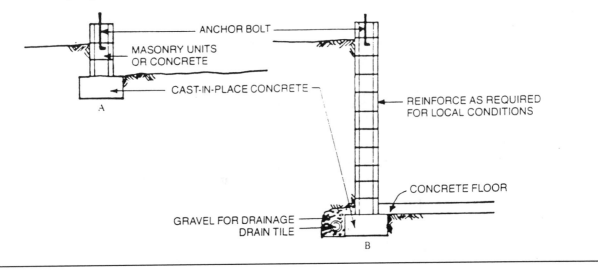

studs also varies with different backfill depths. If the wall studs show evidence of deflection from top to bottom, it is an indication of inadequate stud spacing and/or sizing for the existing backfill depth or settlement of the structure. A very important detail with wood foundations is proper connection of the foundation wall to the

■ **FIGURE 3.6**

Vertical steel beams 4 feet on-center can strengthen a cracked block. The beam must attach securely to the joists and slab. Where there is no slab, footings must be poured. Hiring an engineer should be recommended when this condition exists.

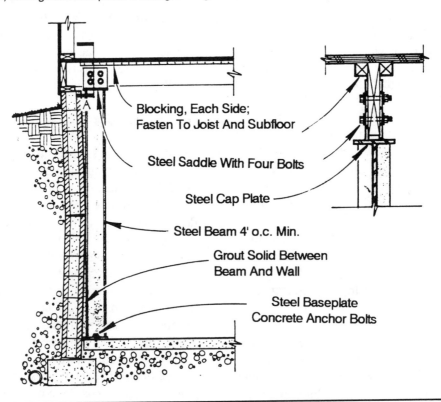

floor system of the structure above. Every floor joist must be fastened to the foundation top plate with a metal framing anchor. Where the floor joists run parallel to the foundation wall, there must be solid blocking installed between the floor joist and the foundation wall, and that blocking must be connected to the foundation wall with framing anchors. Without proper blocking and connections, the lateral pressure can push the top of the foundation wall inward. This is usually visible when sighting down the foundation wall from the exterior.

Another critical detail is the connection of the stud to the top plate. Some codes do not allow a specific nailing schedule to be used; however, the best way to make this connection is to place a metal joist hanger at the top of the stud. Studs pushing inward and pulling away from the top plate are indications of inadequate fastening.

Walkout basements create a design that is different from full-fill basements. The pressure of the full-fill basement on one side of the house is not offset by equal pressure from the walkout side. This unequal pressure can cause the foundation to lean toward the walkout side.

Walkout basements must be designed with the use of interior shear walls, which are interior partition walls with plywood sheathing properly fastened to one side. These intersect with the full-fill basement wall to prevent the foundation from being pushed toward the walkout side.

Wood foundations should not be backfilled until the basement floor and first floor have been constructed or the walls have been braced. For crawlspace construction, backfill or bracing will be installed on the interior of the walls' crawlspace before backfilling the exterior.

Wood foundations enclosing habitable or usable spaces located below grade must be adequately drained. A porous layer of gravel, crushed stone, or courses a minimum of 4" thick should be placed under the basement floor. Provisions must be made for automatic draining of this layer and the gravel or crushed stone wall footings. A moisture barrier must cover the porous layer below the floor. This moisture barrier should be 6-mil-thick polyethylene.

Wood foundations should be damp-proofed. The plywood panel joints should be sealed full length with a caulking compound capable of producing a moisture-proof seal under the conditions of temperature and moisture content prevailing in the area where it is applied and used. A 6-mil-thick polyethylene film should be applied over the below-grade portion of exterior foundation walls prior to backfilling. The space between the excavation and the foundation wall is backfilled with the same material used for footings. (See Figure 3.7.)

Concrete

Concrete is a mixture of Portland cement, aggregate and water. Portland cement consists of lime plus silica, alumina, and iron oxide. The proportional mix determines the strength and general properties of concrete. Sand, gravel, or crushed rock aggregate serve as filler material for concrete, and the cement acts as an adhesive to bond the filler material. Water added to cement causes hydration, which is the chemical reaction between water and cement in a concrete mixture. Other additives give concrete special properties.

Concrete is green (not cured) after the first few days of pouring. Curing is the hardening of concrete over a period of time. To cure properly, concrete must be kept damp and protected from freezing temperatures. Concrete reaches 70 percent of its ultimate strength in seven days. Under normal conditions, concrete cures in 28 days to approximately 90 percent strength and continues to cure with age. (See Figure 3.8.)

Steel Reinforcement

Concrete by itself is hard and brittle. Reinforcing concrete with steel allows slight deflection without breakage. Wire mesh and reinforcing bar (rebar) are reinforcements used in concrete.

Mesh is a welded wire fabric used to reinforce concrete. Wire mesh is supported on chairs or on half bricks placed at intervals around the area to be poured. Chairs hold wire mesh at the proper height in the concrete area. The mesh is available in wide rolls. Wire mesh must not bend or be displaced. (See Figure 3.9.)

Reinforcing bar (rebar) is steel bar used to reinforce concrete slabs, foundations, footing, and piers. The size of rebar is indicated by a number that indicates $\frac{1}{8}"$ increments in diameter; for example, $1 = \frac{1}{8}"$, $2 = \frac{1}{4}"$, $3 = \frac{3}{8}"$ and $4 = \frac{1}{2}"$. Reinforcing bars are placed either along the slab perimeter or, in a matt or pile cap foundation, at the rebar instersection area to be poured with concrete. In the latter, the bars are spaced approximately 16" apart and wired together at each intersection to form a grid. Chairs hold the rebar at the proper height in the concrete area.

Post-tension reinforcement is a method of pre-stressing concrete in which the tendons (reinforcing elements) are tensioned after the concrete has set. Post-

■ **FIGURE 3.7**

Typical details for wood foundation basement walls.

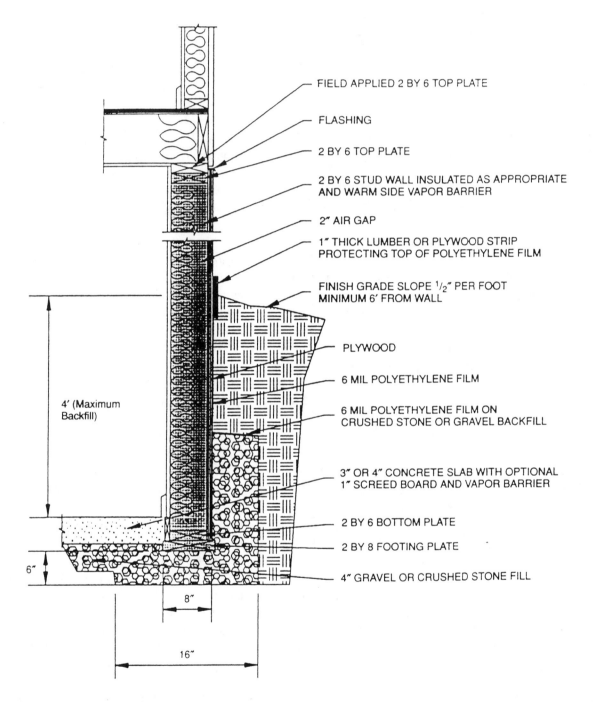

FIELD APPLIED 2 BY 6 TOP PLATE

FLASHING

2 BY 6 TOP PLATE

2 BY 6 STUD WALL INSULATED AS APPROPRIATE AND WARM SIDE VAPOR BARRIER

2" AIR GAP

1" THICK LUMBER OR PLYWOOD STRIP PROTECTING TOP OF POLYETHYLENE FILM

FINISH GRADE SLOPE 1/2" PER FOOT MINIMUM 6' FROM WALL

PLYWOOD

6 MIL POLYETHYLENE FILM

6 MIL POLYETHYLENE FILM ON CRUSHED STONE OR GRAVEL BACKFILL

3" OR 4" CONCRETE SLAB WITH OPTIONAL 1" SCREED BOARD AND VAPOR BARRIER

2 BY 6 BOTTOM PLATE

2 BY 8 FOOTING PLATE

4" GRAVEL OR CRUSHED STONE FILL

4' (Maximum Backfill)

6"

8"

16"

For SI: 1 inch = 25.4 mm, 1 foot = 304.8 mm.

■ FIGURE 3.8

Concrete slab showing plumbing risers and brick ledge.

Brick Ledge

tension reinforcement is used extensively in areas that have expansive clay. Before the concrete is poured, steel cables are laid on chairs, which hold reinforcement cable at the proper height in the concrete area. Cable spacing is approximately 4′ on center. After the concrete has set, a jack stretches the cable, and collar and spring-actuated steel wedges hold tension on the stretched cable. The cable is cut inside the cavity and the opening is sealed.

■ FIGURE 3.9

Mesh is a welded wire fabric, supported on chairs or halfbricks, used to reinforce concrete.

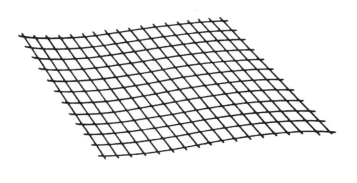

Because tension is applied after the concrete has set, the foundation is said to be *post*-tensioned. A post-tension slab holds together under compression. When properly designed and installed, it has excellent tensile strength. (See Figure 3.10.)

Block

Concrete blocks are often used as retaining walls. Because of the weight factor associated with concrete block structures, the perimeter footings require the same reinforcing as concrete walls. Concrete blocks must have vertical and horizontal steel reinforcement wall ties. (See Figure 3.11.) The vertical reinforcement is rebar located in the core holes of the block. The rebar is tied to the footing steel, and the core is then filled with concrete. (See Figure 3.12.)

Support

Foundational support must consider bearing pressure, bearing capacity, and structural loads. *Bearing pressure* is the force exerted by the foundation on the earth. *Bearing capacity* is the ability of the ground material to safely support a load. *Structural loads* are transmitted to the earth by footings, piles, and piers.

the inverted-T footing is equal to foundation thickness. (See Figure 3.13.)

In mild climates, the footing is often poured as one piece. In cold climates, the base of the footing is poured first and the foundation wall is poured second. The inverted-T footing will not perform well in areas with expansive clay because this footing provides more surface area for the clay to move the foundation when a moisture change occurs. In areas of expansive clay, a trench is often dug and the foundation wall and footing are poured as a single unit. The soil under the footing must provide a firm bearing.

■ FIGURE 3.10

Plastic chairs are used to position post-tension cable, rebar, and wire mesh above vapor barrier to ensure that reinforcement is properly encased when concrete is poured.

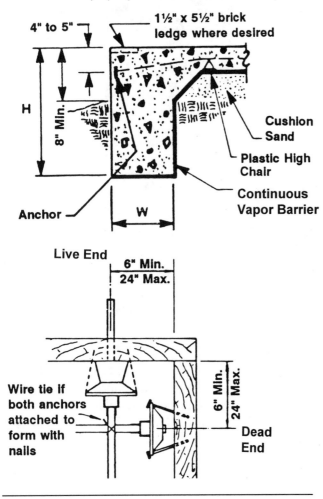

■ FIGURE 3.11

Some concrete block and brick structures require steel reinforcement wall ties.

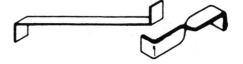

Metal Bar Anchors

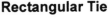

Z Tie

Rectangular Tie

Truss Tie

Ladder Tie

WALL TIES

Dovetail
Anchor
Slot

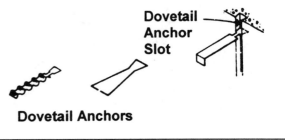

Dovetail Anchors

Footing

A footing usually rests on solid earth (or bedrock) where the foundation and/or piers are placed. The footing is the portion of the foundation that transfers the structural load to the ground. The footing spreads the bearing pressure over an area sufficient to spread the weight of the structure and minimize settlement. Most structures in stable soils are built on concrete footings. The major factors determining the size and shape of the footing are the weight of the structure and the bearing capacity and stability of the soil. In stable soil areas, the footing is constructed in the shape of an inverted T. The width of the inverted-T footing is generally twice the thickness of the foundation wall. The minimum depth of

■ **FIGURE 3.12**

Reinforced grouted masonry wall.

Partially Grouted Hollow Unit

Fully Grouted Hollow Unit

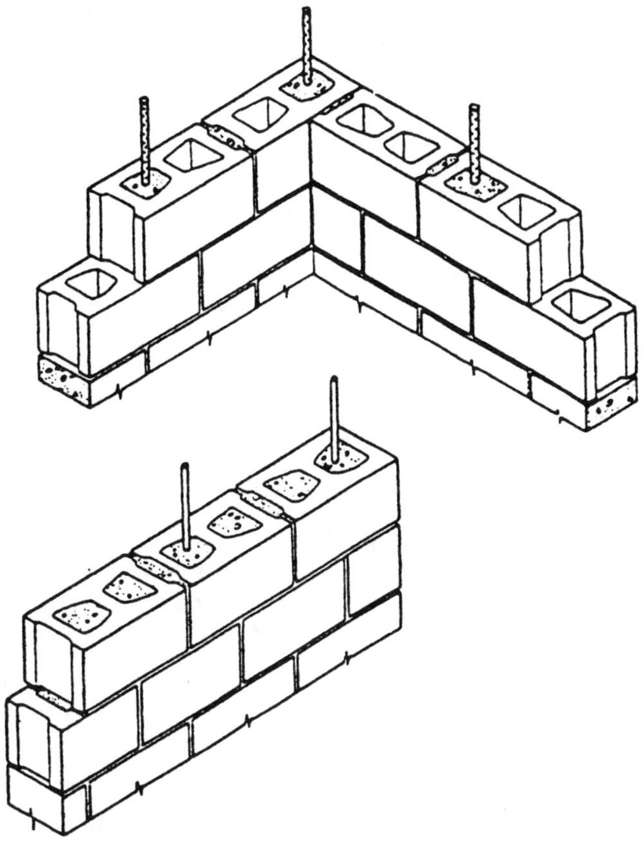

When a structure is built on sloped ground, a step footing alleviates the need for deep excavation and high foundation walls. A step footing is a footing with steps that follow the contour and grade of the land. It is often poured as one piece. In areas subject to earthquakes or where expansive and unstable soil is present, reinforcing bars are placed in the footing.

When constructing a basement, a footing is poured around the outside perimeter. The foundation wall sits on the footing. The sill plate, a board laid on the foundation wall on which the framing rests, is secured to the top of the foundation walls with anchor bolts or percussion nails. The framing is secured to the sill plate.

When constructing a structure with a crawlspace, footing and foundation walls are poured as one piece. In warm climates where soil conditions permit, foundation walls are used as the footing.

Piles

Piles are vertical foundation members of timber, concrete, steel, or a combination of these materials. Bearing pressure is distributed to the soil by friction piles or to bedrock by bearing piles. (See Figure 3.14.)

Friction piles rely on pressure and friction from surrounding soil to support the load. Bearing piles transmit loads to firm, bearing soil. Piles are often used in town houses, apartments and condominiums when soil conditions are unstable.

Piers

Piers are vertical foundation members that transfer the building load to the ground. In stable soil, the pier may be supported by a spread footing resting on the ground. A spread footing is a rectangular base placed beneath the foundation to distribute the building load over a larger area. A spread footing is not adequate in areas with expansive clay because the footing moves as the moisture level changes in the soil. To be functional, the pier must be drilled to a depth with constant moisture level where the clay stays damp and its volume will not change. Piers are often used to pass through soil with low bearing capacity to reach a satisfactory foundation material. Piers are often "belled out" or expanded at the

■ **FIGURE 3.13**

Inverted-T footing is used in stable soil areas.

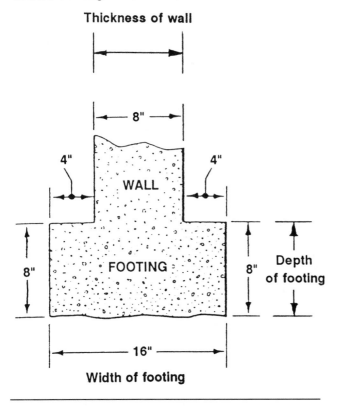

Thickness of wall

Width of footing

■ **FIGURE 3.14**

Town houses and apartments use bearing or friction piles for support in unstable soils.

PILE FOUNDATIONS

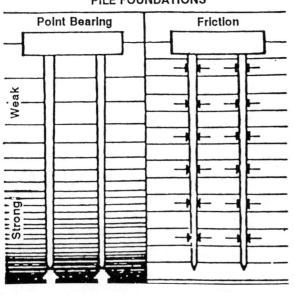

base to increase bearing surface. Piers resting on rock do not need to expand at the base.

Most residential construction with a crawlspace uses a combination consisting of piers for the interior and a beam wall with piers for the perimeter. Structures with crawlspaces often have piers that support the entire house. A pier is a post made from wood, concrete, or brick. Cedar and bois d'arc or pine or spruce specially treated for moisture resistance are common woods used for piers in residential construction. The bark of cedar is hairy, while bois d'arc bark is bumpy and hard. Bois d'arc will not rot and is resistant to termites, while untreated cedar, redwood, and pine will rot and are susceptible to termites.

Pier-and-Beam

Pier and beam foundations have crawlspaces. It is very important that the inspector observe the crawlspace for evidence of the following: excessive dampness, moisture penetration or efflorescence on masonry surfaces, plumbing leaks and lack of proper ventilation (causing wood decay and conditions that are conducive to wood-destroying insects that can cause damage to sill plates, joists, beams, and subflooring.) (See Figure 3.15.) There should be a minimum of 18″ of headroom in the crawlspace. It is important that the crawlspace be inspected. However, the inspector should not enter a crawlspace when entering could cause damage to the property or could endanger the inspector. Some hazards are moisture, standing water, wires lying on the ground, etc.

Pier-and-beam construction uses foundation walls and piers that support girders. (See Figure 3.16.) The girder is a structural member supporting floor joists in a pier-and-beam foundation and is made of solid wood, laminated wood or two or more planks secured together. A girder is required when the distance between the foundation walls is too great a span for the floor joists. The girder is supported by piers that transfer the load to the ground. Normally, girder pockets (beam pockets) are formed or cut into the foundation walls. (See Figure 3.17.) When the girder pocket is too low and spacers are used to raise the girder, steel shims should be used.

Approximately 4″ of the girder is placed in the girder pocket. One end of the floor joist sits on the sill plate and the other end rests on the girder. Floor joists are secured where they overlap the girder. In lieu of a girder pocket, an alternate method of construction places the girder on top of the foundation wall. Metal joist hangers secure floor joists to the girder. (See Figures 3.18 and 3.19.)

■ FIGURE 3.15

Crawlspace moisture problems often go undetected. Electrical wires should be anchored to floor joists. Sewer lines should not be on the ground, and lumber should not be on the ground attracting termites.

The beam wall or grade beam is supported by concrete piers. Vent openings in the beam wall or in the header space above the foundation wall will minimize the accumulation of moist air. (See Figure 3.20.)

Underpinning is a skirting material usually placed around the outside perimeter of the structure. Skirting material may be metal, brick, concrete block, plywood, or siding material. (See Figure 3.21.)

■ FIGURE 3.16

In pier-and-beam construction, girders supported by piers provide stability to floor joists at intervals between foundation walls.

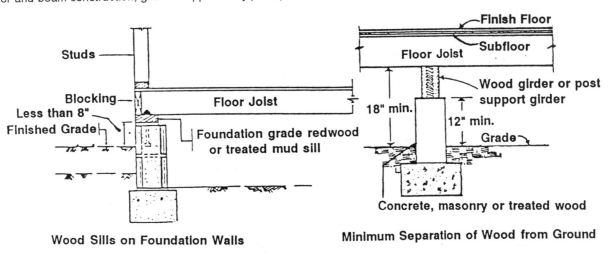

Wood Sills on Foundation Walls

Minimum Separation of Wood from Ground

■ **FIGURE 3.17**

A built-up wood girder is made of planks nailed together. Joints in the planks must be staggered and supported by piers. Girder ends are placed in pockets in the foundation wall.

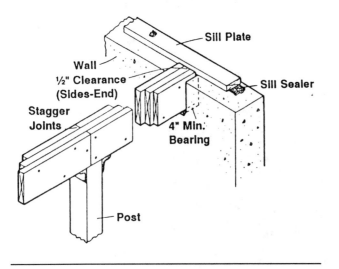

■ **FIGURE 3.18**

Joist hanger alternative.

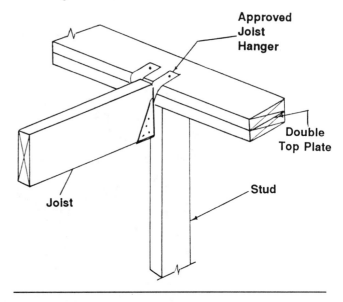

Slab-on-Grade

Slab-on-grade foundation is used when the structure is built directly on the ground. In warm climates, a trench dug into the soil is used as a form for concrete. A perimeter beam is the edge around the foundation that adds stiffness and stability to the slab. In a monolithic slab, the concrete foundation wall and floor slab are poured as one piece. In a floating slab, the concrete foundation wall and floor slab are poured separately. (See Figures 3.22 and 3.23.)

Monolithic Slab

A monolithic slab-on-grade foundation requires a wide base and steel reinforcement. A commonly used variation consists of a flared thickening of the slab edge.

■ **FIGURE 3.19**

A metal joist hanger is nailed to the girder and floor joist.

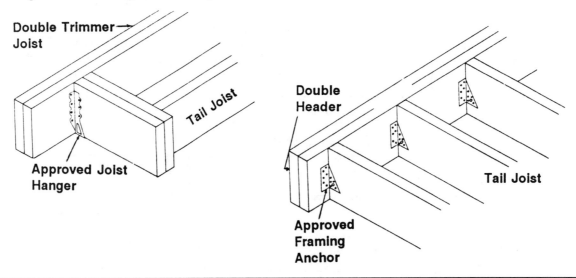

■ **FIGURE 3.20**

Crawlspace ventilation.

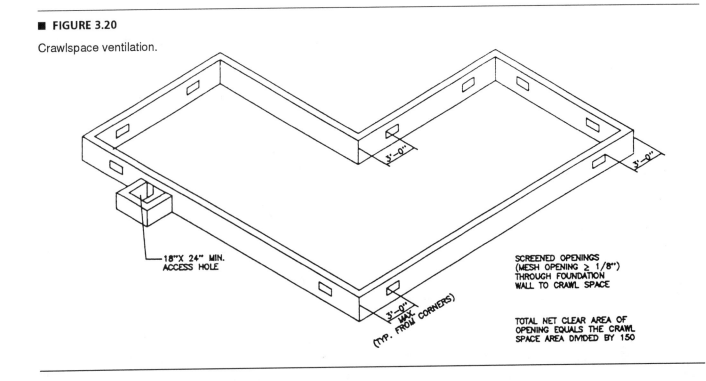

18"X 24" MIN. ACCESS HOLE

3'-0"

3'-0"

3'-0" MAX. (TYP. FROM CORNERS)

SCREENED OPENINGS (MESH OPENING ≥ 1/8") THROUGH FOUNDATION WALL TO CRAWL SPACE

TOTAL NET CLEAR AREA OF OPENING EQUALS THE CRAWL SPACE AREA DIVIDED BY 150

Because the slab floor will not support interior load-bearing walls, interior footing is trenched in before the slab is poured. This interior footing provides additional stiffness to the slab and supports the load-bearing walls. In cold climates, edge insulation reduces heat loss.

Often, ducts for the heating and air-conditioning system are set in place before the slab is poured. The weakest slab foundation is with an H-shaped floor plan, while the strongest slab foundation is a rectangular or square floor plan.

■ **FIGURE 3.21**

The crawlspace of a pier-and-beam house is covered by underpinning around the perimeter.

UNDERPINNING

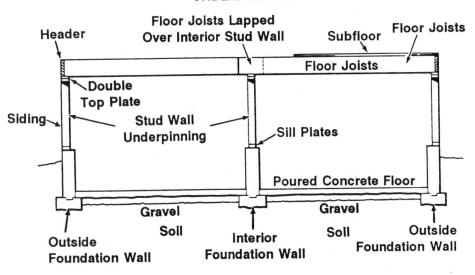

Header

Floor Joists Lapped Over Interior Stud Wall

Subfloor

Floor Joists

Floor Joists

Double Top Plate

Siding

Stud Wall Underpinning

Sill Plates

Poured Concrete Floor

Outside Foundation Wall

Gravel

Soil

Interior Foundation Wall

Gravel

Soil

Outside Foundation Wall

■ **FIGURE 3.22**

Monolithic slab is one solid piece consisting of the floor slab, foundation walls, and footing. Most slab-on-grade foundations are poured monolithically.

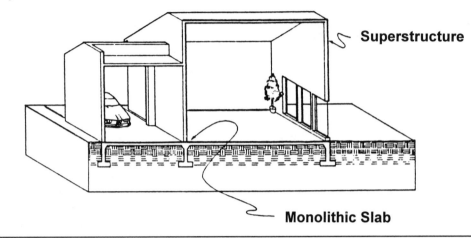

Superstructure

Monolithic Slab

Floating Slab

A floating slab is a reinforced slab placed between walls or footing. The footing poured for a floating slab is allowed to set and the forms are removed. The slab floor is poured inside the footing and is separated from it by an expansion joint. This process of pouring the slab separately allows the slab to rise or fall without causing cracks at the footing edges.

Screeded Slab

A screeded slab is a wooden floor built on a concrete slab. The space under the flooring is often a return air space for a heating and air-conditioning system. A screeded slab has no crawlspace and no vent openings. Wood damage or plumbing leaks are difficult to detect in a screeded slab.

■ FOUNDATION INSPECTION TECHNIQUES

A structure is only as good as its foundation. Basically, the foundation is built on either soil or rock, and it

■ **FIGURE 3.23**

Floating slab is poured as two separate pieces with an expansion joint. Floating slabs are commonly used in garages for pier-and-beam structures.

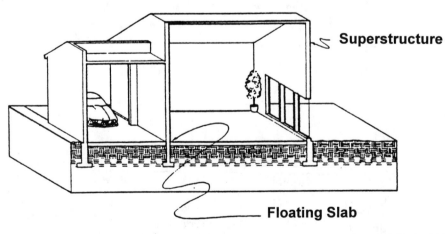

Superstructure

Floating Slab

must be solid to support the structure above. All building codes require that foundations be to a depth sufficient to ensure stability. Building codes may require that pilings or poured concrete piers be used with the concrete footings, depending on the soil conditions. For example, a soil that is a weak soil, such as silts that are finer than sand, will not compact to support a foundation.

Many older buildings were built without the benefit of any building codes. This applies to many rural areas, and it could apply to recently constructed buildings. There really weren't any national building codes prior to establishment of the FHA (Federal Housing Administration) in the early 1930s; however, many of the larger cities developed some building codes that they enforced. All regions of the country now have access to the national codes, although they are not uniformly enforced. Even today, many small villages and counties throughout the United States do not enforce any codes.

Basement foundations have been popular for centuries. However, they were not always called *basements,* but instead were called *cellars.* Cellars had two purposes: first, to get below the frostline for a more stable foundation; second, to store fruits and vegetables after the growing season.

In older buildings it was common practice to construct a foundation by laying stones one upon another. These may or may not have been laid in mortar and may or may not have been built on footings. When a stone foundation is encountered and the building is still standing, the foundation has stood the test of time. The most common problems are that water can penetrate, extensive settling can occur, pests can enter, floors will probably be uneven, and cost to repair may be prohibitive. The inspector should report any deficiencies observed.

Modern foundations are typically constructed of poured-in-place, steel-reinforced concrete. These may be in the form of monolithic slabs where frost penetration is not a factor and soil conditions permit. The monolithic slab has a thickened edge, usually 16" to 20" thick. The plans usually specify the number and size of rebar (steel bars) required, which run continuously around the perimeter of the structure.

All foundations must extend below the frost line as defined by the local building official. Any defects noted, even minor cracks, should be included in the inspection report. The inspector should report signs of settlement, serious cracking, or separations and distortions and recommend they be analyzed by a structural engineer. Foundation defects can lead to major repair costs and represent high claim concerns to inspectors.

Inspectors should become knowledgeable about detecting and analyzing settlement cracks and problems in accordance with the part of the United States that they are in. All buildings settle to some extent, usually within the first few years. This type of movement is normal and should be reported as such. Many cracks of less than ¼" fall in this category. Some cracks ¼" and even larger may be of little concern, depending on the age of the structure (if it is 20 years old or older) and if the crack is filled with dust, dirt, or paint and shows no evidence of being due to fresh movement. It should be reported, with a statement that the movement appears to have stabilized. (Be aware, though, that many structural engineers consider cracks as small as 2 millimeters (about the thickness of a nickel) to be significant.) An inspector cannot call for a structural engineer or expert to analyze every defect noted, or the customer will question the need for an inspector. Of course, if the inspector has any doubt as to a foundation's stability, a structural engineer should be consulted.

The inspection analysis is based on the opinion of the inspector, which is based on knowledge, experience, and judgment. When judging structural cracks, consider the location, size and freshness as well as the type of crack; for example, if the crack takes the form of a V, which indicates differential settlement or rotation of the footing, or if there are signs that one side of the foundation crack has remained stable and the other side shows signs of movement. The inspector must try to determine if these signs are significant. An inspector who is not sure of a structure's integrity should then recommend bringing in an engineer for evaluation.

Step cracks that follow the mortar joints in a concrete block foundation or a basement wall usually are not of any significance if they are hairline and uniform and not part of the corners, tie beam, or foundation itself. However, if they are wider at the top of the wall, heaving or settlement of the soil is indicated. Heaving may occur due to frost penetration or expansive clays. If the crack is wider at the bottom, some type of settlement is occurring. Foundations also should be inspected from the outside as well as the inside, if possible.

Spalling Concrete

Inspectors should be aware that in some areas, especially along the ocean (condominium balconies, concrete floors and floor joists, beams, and pilings in detached houses), there may be a problem with concrete spalling due to rusting reinforcing steel. Inspectors

■ **FIGURE 3.24**

Frostline depth must be considered when footing and foundation walls are constructed.

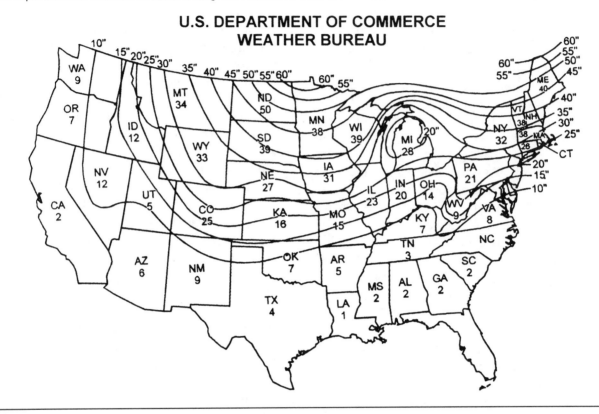

Climate

Climate is a major factor in determining the appropriate foundation. In northern regions, the foundation and footing must be protected against frost damage. When moisture in the soil freezes during cold weather, the soil expands and rises. The soil settles when the moisture thaws. To prevent damage caused by the expansion of frozen soil, the footing and foundation walls must extend below the frostline. This depth varies by locale. (See Figure 3.24.)

Because the footing must be placed deep in cold climates, most structures are built with basements. The foundation walls in structures with basements are usually 7' or 8' high. The footing supports structural members of the building and provides adequate headroom in the basement. A basement provides a minimum amount of heat loss in relation to the overall living area during winter and offers additional living and storage space.

Some structures in cold climates are built with a footing below the frostline and a slab floor at grade level.

Crawlspaces are often used in more moderate climates where the footing is less deep. A crawlspace is only 1½' to 4' high. The footing is laid deep enough to prevent frost damage. In the South and West, there is normally no need for a deep footing to protect against frost damage.

Frostline

A frostline chart provides information concerning how far below the surface soil may freeze. If soil freezes, the moisture within that soil will expand. The bottom of grade beams should sit in and rest on soil that will never freeze. The inspector should be familiar with the local code requirements for the areas in which they are doing inspections because most areas have their own codes that may be adopted from the national codes or modified to fit their needs. For example, in North Texas, 6″ is the average depth to which the soil freezes; however, North Texas building officials require a 10″ minimum depth.

Movement

The expansion or contraction of soils produces pressure on the foundation sufficient to move an entire structure. Uniform movement is usually harmless to structures. Nonuniform movement produces bending and twisting within the structure and results in noticeable defects. (See Figure 3.25.)

Nonuniform or unequal foundation movement is normally the result of changes in moisture content of soil caused by excess or nonuniform watering of flowers, shrubs or lawns adjacent to the foundation; poor drainage away from the foundation; or leaking plumbing lines.

Excessive water or lack of water causes volume changes and movement in soils at the base of the foundation. Soil movement, settlement, or upheaval is transmitted to the foundation.

Clay soil expansion exerts pressure on a foundation similar to the pressure produced by a hydraulic jack. When soil loses moisture, the subsoil shrinks and the foundation settles due to weight of the structure.

Foundation movement is generally evidenced by interior or exterior wall cracks, ceiling cracks, sticking doors or windows, pulled roof trusses, and broken windows. These structural indications are realized in pier-and-beam as well as slab foundations.

Drying Edge Effect

Drying edge effect is the removal of moisture from the soil along the foundation perimeter. Drying edge effect is a problem during hot summer days or during drought and causes downwarping of the foundation. Downwarping is the tendency for the perimeter of the foundation to settle.

As the soil dries, it pulls away from the foundation and cracks are formed. These cracks and openings increase the rate of evaporation under the footing. If there are fall rains, the soil does expand, but the soil and slab do not completely return to their original positions. The drying cracks also admit water that erodes soil away from under the footing. After several wet and dry cycles, the perimeter permanently settles and foundation repair is required. Most slab foundation problems involve downwarping. Wet and dry cycles also affect beam walls in pier-and-beam construction.

Transpiration

Transpiration is the removal of soil moisture by vegetation. Trees absorb moisture from surrounding soil under the foundation and cause downwarping of structures. River-bottom trees (e.g., weeping willow, pecan, cottonwood and mulberry trees) consume more water than other trees and should not be planted near a foundation. These trees have shallow root systems that spread under foundations and cause transpiration.

Trees with a deeper root system can cause foundation problems when located too close to the house. Tree branches that spread over the roof indicate that roots will be under the house. Even when not directly under the foundation, tree roots draw moisture from the soil through capillary attraction, the movement of water in a channel above a horizontal plane of the supply of free water. Capillary attraction in clay and silt soils is usually very high. A tree should not be placed closer to a residential structure than 1½ times its mature height. This distance is often not practical because of yard size.

A residential inspector should consider the effects of trees on a structure. A tree growing too close to a structure may indicate foundation and/or plumbing problems. The inspector should inform the homeowner about the importance of replacing the water removed from the soil by trees.

A tree can be root pruned to cut down water consumption. A trench is dug around the tree along its drip line to a depth of approximately 4' to cut surface roots. A barrier of corrugated fiberglass, concrete or lime is placed in the trench to prevent roots from growing toward the structure. Part of the tree will die when roots are cut.

Leaves emit moisture into the atmosphere. By pruning branches and leaves, less moisture is emitted and the need for water is diminished. If the leaf mass of a tree is decreased by 10 percent, the growth rate decreases by 30 percent. Bushes also consume large amounts of water and should be pruned and maintained just as trees.

Drainage

Soil is an important factor in drainage evaluation. Soil functions as a storage medium for water. Water moves through soil in the following ways: infiltration, the downward movement of water into soil; percolation, the soil's ability to absorb water; and drainage, the proper removal of excess water from root systems and foundations. Water flow has a direct effect on the struc-

■ **FIGURE 3.25**

SLAB FOUNDATION

CUPPING

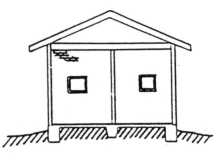

PROBLEM:

1— Cracks in exterior masonry.
2— Horizontal and vertical separation of windows from adjacent masonry or siding; general distortion of door and window frames and sticking of doors and windows.
3— Cracks and spalling at corners of foundation slab.
4— Horizontal cracks at joint between foundation slab and masonry.
5— Interior partitions separate from ceiling and, occasionally, from floor.

SOLUTION:

a. Drill mud jack holes through interior slab.
b. Pump soil cement grout to raise.

DOWNWARPING

PROBLEM:

1— Cracks in exterior masonry.
2— Horizontal and vertical separation of windows and doors from adjacent masonry or siding; general distortion of door and window frames and sticking of doors and windows.
3— Break in slab, noticeable in interior of house in some cases.
4— Noticeable tilt of exterior walls in some cases.
5— Cracking of interior gypsum board ceilings and partitions, particularly at door and window corners (Not shown).

SOLUTION:

a. Drill and pour deep concrete piers.
b. Drill mud jack holes through perimeter beam.
c. Mechanically raise in conjunction with mud jacking.
d. Pour concrete column.

Unequal foundation movement results in cupping when moist clay expands and downwarping when expansive clay dries and shrinks around slab-on-grade foundations.

■ **FIGURE 3.26**

The arrows show how the flow of surface water is directed by swales to flow away from the house.

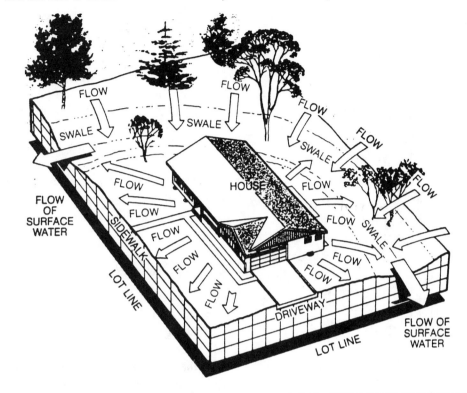

tural integrity of systems, durability of materials, schedule and construction cost, and maintenance cost. Residential inspectors should be aware of the principles and consequences of poor drainage and the influence of drainage systems on the function of property inspected.

Drainage systems remove subsurface and surface water from property. Subsurface drainage systems are used when slopes and soils of natural landscapes interfere with site structures and uses. Positive results of subsurface drainage include reduction in a high water table, reduction of construction cost, and elimination of structural/construction problems. The drainage systems used to remove water are drain inlets, catch basins, and perforated pipes and French drains.

Severe surface drainage problems cause water penetration into a structure. Correcting drainage problems is critical in areas of expansive clay. Because approximately 80 percent of foundation problems are caused by poor drainage, the excavator should slope the lot and cut in swales so water drains away from a structure with a slab-on-grade foundation. A swale is a small valley that channels surface water off the property. (See Figure 3.26.)

The outside perimeter of the foundation must be kept at a uniform moisture level. The ground should be graded to a gentle slope away from the foundation. Ideally, the slope should be 1 percent to 5 percent, which equals 1″ to 5″ in 8½′. In cases where the slope is steep, soil tends to wash away from the foundation. The steeper the degree of slope, the greater the run-off and possibility for erosion. The lesser the degree of slope, the greater the structure stability, which is directly related to soil type.

Regardless of the type of foundation, drainage is one of the most important concerns next to proper footings and foundation. Without proper drainage, subsurface water can build up tremendous pressure underground. No waterproofing system is designed to work without proper drainage. A waterproofing manufacturer will not warrant its product if drainage is missing or inadequate or if the structure is built on a site where proper drainage is impossible.

In many geographic locations, the minimum drainage for any structure is a perimeter footing drain. Depending on soil conditions, some buildings will

A retainer wall prevents erosion and corrects a steep slope. Retainer walls often require support from the back to resist overturning or sliding.

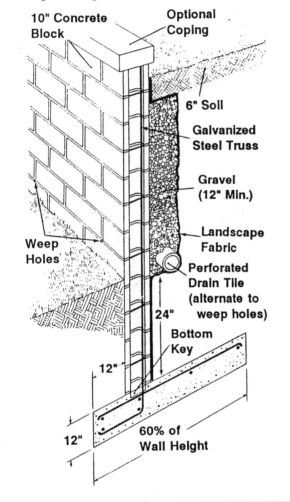

Unequal moisture caused by poor drainage results in foundation movements. Poor drainage also causes water to flow into a crawlspace, piers to move, and wood to rot. Water under a structure causes serious problems.

Plumbing Leaks

A plumbing leak under a slab-on-grade foundation can cause moisture retention and swell clay, causing uplift. Plumbing leaks can occur in either sewer lines or water supply lines. A leak in the water supply reduces water pressure and washes the ground from under the slab, causing settlement.

A plumbing leak under a crawlspace causes piers to rise or settle. Air-conditioning condensate flowing from the evaporator may cause movement.

■ MAINTENANCE

Expansive clay soil requires water to prevent settlement. An inspector should report whether the ground is cracking or pulling away from the foundation. As clay soil dries, shrinkage occurs and the slab could cantilever over the void and cause foundation failure. Because nature cannot be relied on to provide the proper amount of rain, a moisture maintenance program must be implemented to maintain foundation stability.

Watering

The homeowner must be informed of the importance and techniques of watering. Residential inspectors should ascertain whether the soil is an expansive clay before recommending a watering program. Watering a silty soil will lubricate the shear plane and could cause a foundation to settle, while watering a coarse-grained soil could cause erosion under the slab, particularly if there is poor drainage.

Many structures are built on shallow-depth wood or concrete piers (no beam wall). A "pier" structure should not be watered because it will cause foundation movement. The water washes under the perimeter piers and the structure settles. Because the piers under the center of the structure are sitting in dry ground they will not settle.

The ideal watering method is to slowly add water to maintain soil moisture. Permeability is the ability of a soil to absorb moisture. Sand is very permeable, but clay is not. Clay absorbs water slowly; it will absorb only approximately $\frac{1}{16}''$ of water per hour because the small pores in clay restrict water flow.

require an underground drain system and/or a sump pit with an ejector pump.

Retainer walls often are used to maintain the correct slope in lots with a steep grade. Correct slope should be maintained around the residential structure. Curbs for flower beds around a foundation usually trap water. Curbs should be sunk a *minimum* depth below the surface and should have drainage outlets to prevent pooling. (See Figure 3.27.)

Gutters and downspouts divert water from the foundation. Gutter extensions should direct the water away from the structure and property. Plugged gutters will cause overflows, which will create wet spots next to the foundation. Downspouts must be spaced equally to handle water.

A sprinkler system is an excellent means of watering soil around a foundation. Sprinkler systems are programmable and automatically cycle each zone "on" and "off" at desired times. Soaker hoses may be used in lieu of a sprinkler system. Position the soaker hoses about 18″ to 24″ away from the foundation with the holes facing the ground.

Soil shrinking away from the foundation is an immediate signal that the soil needs water. Soil must be watered uniformly. Excess watering in one area will result in unequal moisture levels and unequal soil movement.

In cases where the soil is extremely dry and has pulled away from the foundation, time will be required to replenish appropriate moisture. The soil must be watered each day until the gap between the soil and foundation closes. This may take several days or weeks, depending on the type of soil. Water maintenance is a continual job. Where concrete such as a patio or sidewalk lies adjacent to a foundation, the foundation will not require watering because the ground will stay moist from watering the ground adjacent to the patio or sidewalk.

There should not be an opening between the foundation and patio. Water could flow through the opening and cause foundation problems. Openings should be sealed. However, it is necessary to water around the outside edge of the patio to minimize soil movement. Four different climates exist around the four sides of a structure. The west and south sides tend to dry more than others. Most foundation problems occur at the southwest corner. The northeast side is usually in the shade and moisture will not evaporate as fast.

Fill Dirt

Soil around the foundation will compact and, eventually, low spots will form and water will pool. A clay-based soil should be added around the foundation to correct the problem. Clay-based soils will shed rainwater and divert it from the foundation.

At least 4″ of concrete should be showing below both brick and frame siding of structures on slab foundations. Dirt above the brick line allows water to penetrate into the structure, causing damage. Carefully pull the carpet back from the tackstrip and check for stains or rotting. A strong mildew odor is a sign of water penetration in the structure.

Add dirt to correct a drainage problem, or dig a swale to direct the water away from the house. The swale should be sloped ½″ per foot for 6′. Where landscaping will not correct the problem, area drains can be used. In cases where the house and lot are situated so drainage is impossible, sump pumps are used. The residential inspector should make the homeowner aware of existing swales in routing rainwater from the house. Fill dirt never should be added to swales in an attempt to level a yard.

■ REPAIRS

Upheaval of a slab foundation presents the most difficult foundation problem. If the upward movement is extreme, the theoretical cure is to break out the slab, excavate the base to the proper grade and repour the slab section. A more practical solution is to raise the lowest slab areas to the approximate grade of the heaved section. This operation is critical because the grade of the entire structure is being altered; care must be exercised not to aggravate the heaved area.

Mud-jacking is a process whereby a cement grout is pumped beneath a slab to produce a lifting force that can literally float the slab to a desired position. The cement grout is pumped through small holes drilled through the concrete. This process has the additional feature of chemically treating the soil to minimize future differential movement produced by soil moisture variations.

Pier-and-beam foundation movement is due to settlement or upheaval. Settlement is generally alleviated by mechanically raising the beam, removing existing piers, sustaining the beam position and installing new supporting piers. In heaved areas, the practical approach is to minimize the grade differential by raising the lowest areas. If the movement is substantial, lowering the high area is necessary. This is performed by undercutting the affected areas, installing new support pads or piers, removing existing piers, lowering the perimeter beam and resupporting the foundation with new columns. (See Figure 3.28.)

The interior of the structure is leveled by using shims on existing piers. The shimming process will not guarantee against future recurrence of interior settlement because the problem has not been resolved. However, the shimming process is relatively inexpensive and, as the rate of settlement decreases with time, the bearing soil beneath the pier will eventually compact.

Research on foundation problems has indicated that seasonal moisture content varies to a depth of 7′ to 8′. A foundation support must be a minimum of 8′ below the foundation (or to rock) to provide maximum protection against recurrences of foundation failures.

FIGURE 3.28 ■

Pier-and-beam foundation settlement causes cupping and upheaval causes downwarping.

PIER and BEAM FOUNDATION

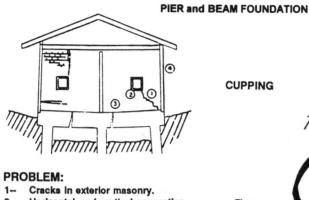

CUPPING

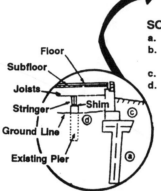

PROBLEM:

1– Cracks in exterior masonry.
2– Horizontal and vertical separation of windows and doors from adjacent masonry or siding; general distortion of door and window frames and sticking of doors and windows.
3– Breaks in perimeter beam, noticeable in interior of house in some cases.
4– Noticeable tilt of exterior walls in some cases.
5– Cracking of interior gypsum board ceilings and partitions, particularly at door and window corners (Not shown).

SOLUTION:

a. Drill and pour deep concrete piers.
b. Break existing piers and lower to grade.
c. Pour concrete column.
d. Raise or lower interior floors by shimming or notching existing piers.

DOWNWARPING

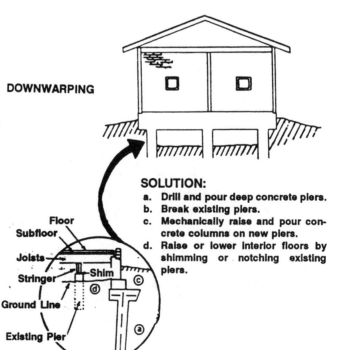

PROBLEM:

1– Cracks in exterior masonry.
2– Horizontal and vertical separation of windows and doors from adjacent masonry or siding; general distortion of door and window frames and sticking of doors and windows.
3– Breaks in perimeter beam, noticeable in interior of house in some cases.
4– Noticeable tilt of exterior walls in some cases.
5– Cracking of interior gypsum board ceilings and partitions, particularly at door and window corners (Not shown).

SOLUTION:

a. Drill and pour deep concrete piers.
b. Break existing piers.
c. Mechanically raise and pour concrete columns on new piers.
d. Raise or lower interior floors by shimming or notching existing piers.

■ REVIEW QUESTIONS*

1. There are four soil classifications.

   A. True
   B. False

2. Clay and sand are considered fine-grain soils.

   A. True
   B. False

3. Clay receives its bearing strength by cohesion.

   A. True
   B. False

4. Differential settlement may cause

   A. cracks in the foundation and/or walls.
   B. roof leaks.
   C. plumbing leaks.
   D. All of the above

5. The real estate inspector must recognize and report possible foundation problems.

   A. True
   B. False

6. Four basic footing types are commonly used in residential construction.

   A. True
   B. False

7. The footing used is determined by

   A. climate.
   B. soil type.
   C. building load.
   D. All of the above
   E. None of the above

8. The sill plate secures to the top of the foundation wall.

   A. True
   B. False

9. Foundations with a crawlspace do not require venting.

   A. True
   B. False

10. When the footing and floor are poured simultaneously, this is called a

    A. floating slab.
    B. monolithic slab.
    C. screeded slab.
    D. None of the above

11. Poor drainage causes what percentage of foundation problems?

    A. 0 percent
    B. 20 percent
    C. 50 percent
    D. 80 percent

12. Transpiration is the removal of moisture from the soil.

    A. True
    B. False

13. It is the responsibility of the inspector to detect visible evidence of wood damage.

    A. True
    B. False

14. That portion of the foundation that transfers the structural load to the ground is the

    A. truss.
    B. footing.
    C. sill.
    D. floor joist.

15. Drain tile at the base of a foundation should be covered with

    A. clay.
    B. sand.
    C. concrete.
    D. gravel.

Answers to all of the chapter review questions are located in Appendix C at the back of this book.

16. Ground water that would otherwise cause the basement to be moist can be collected in a _____ if drain tiles are installed around the foundation.

17. Ground water collected in the sump can be removed by a _____ Sump _____ pump.

18. To prevent settlement of expansive clay soil, a requirement is

    A. drain tile.
    B. water.
    C. transpiration.
    D. a vapor barrier.

19. When moisture in soil freezes, the soil

    A. contracts.
    B. expands.

20. Movement of a foundation in an expansive soil may be caused by

    A. poor drainage.
    B. a plumbing leak.
    C. nonuniform watering.
    D. All of the above

21. A tree growing too close to a house is a clue to check the foundation closely in that area.

    A. True
    B. False

22. A moisture maintenance program for silty soil may cause foundation failure.

    A. True
    B. False

■ INSPECTION CHECKLIST
Soils and Foundations

PRELIMINARY

Soil

Yes No

☐	☐	Sand
☐	☐	Silt
☐	☐	Clay
☐	☐	Gravel
☐	☐	Loam, sand
☐	☐	Loam, clay
☐	☐	Expansive clay

FOUNDATION

Type of foundation

Yes No

☐	☐	***Slab-on-grade***
☐	☐	Is at least 4″ of slab foundation above soil line?
☐	☐	Is soil sloped away from foundation?
☐	☐	Does the post-tension foundation have the cable ports sealed?
☐	☐	Are HVAC ducts in the slab?
☐	☐	Is slab cracked?
☐	☐	Are the floors level?
☐	☐	Any evidence of water penetration?
☐	☐	Any evidence of foundation repair?
☐	☐	***Screeded slab***
☐	☐	Does screeded slab foundation have weep holes for ventilation?
☐	☐	Is space between the floor and slab used for return air for HVAC?
☐	☐	Is the heating system an upflow furnace?
☐	☐	Any evidence of plumbing leaks when removing the filter and observing the return opening?
☐	☐	Does the house appear to have been treated for termites?
☐	☐	Is at least 4″ of slab foundation above soil line?
☐	☐	Is the soil sloped away from the foundation?
☐	☐	Any evidence of water penetration?
☐	☐	Any evidence of foundation repair?
☐	☐	Is the slab cracked?
☐	☐	Do floors appear level?
☐	☐	***Pier-and-beam***
☐	☐	Is the crawlspace properly ventilated?

Yes No

☐	☐	Does the crawlspace have adequate headroom?
☐	☐	Do all girders and joists have proper support?
☐	☐	Any evidence of wood damage in the crawlspace?
☐	☐	Any debris on the ground in the crawlspace?
☐	☐	Do any mildew problems (musty odor) exist?
☐	☐	Are the furnace ducts (supply or return) located in the crawlspace?
☐	☐	Do the ducts have proper support and not touch the ground?
☐	☐	Are the electrical wires properly terminated and secured to the joist?
☐	☐	Does the crawlspace have ponding or standing water?
☐	☐	Is the floor level and solid to walk on?
☐	☐	Does the soil slope away from the foundation?
☐	☐	Does the dryer or kitchen exhaust vent under the house?
☐	☐	Does water heater temperature and pressure (T&P) valve exhaust under house?
☐	☐	***Basement***
☐	☐	Are basement walls poured concrete or concrete and concrete block?
☐	☐	Do basement walls show evidence of water penetration?
☐	☐	Is soil sloping away from foundation?
☐	☐	Do window wells drain properly?
☐	☐	Is basement equipped with a sump pump?
☐	☐	Are all girders and joists properly supported?

WATER MAINTENANCE

Yes No

☐	☐	Is soil pulling away from foundation?
☐	☐	Are there weepholes in brick and are they open?
☐	☐	Is ridge line out of level?
☐	☐	Are trees too close to foundation?
☐	☐	Are there brick separations (particularly around window and door openings)?
☐	☐	Are wide mortar joints following a cracking pattern?
☐	☐	Are brick separations caulked?
☐	☐	Is brick pulling away from windows or doors?

Yes No

- ☐ ☐ Is trim sound around windows and doors?
- ☐ ☐ Are windows broken?
- ☐ ☐ Are gaps between window and lintel sealed?
- ☐ ☐ Is trim sound around frieze board?
- ☐ ☐ Is frieze board open at corners?
- ☐ ☐ Is caulking at corners excessive?
- ☐ ☐ Is trim open at corners?
- ☐ ☐ Is metal or plastic used at corners?
- ☐ ☐ Are post-tension cable ports exposed?
- ☐ ☐ Are there major cracks in perimeter beam of foundation?
- ☐ ☐ Is concrete in beam wall of pier-and-beam foundation crumbling?
- ☐ ☐ Are vents missing in pier-and-beam foundations?
- ☐ ☐ Is skirting (underpinning) tipped out on pier houses?
- ☐ ☐ Is there evidence of previous foundation repair?
- ☐ ☐ Are there signs of mud-jacking?
- ☐ ☐ Have brick cracks been pointed-up (brick sealed with mortar)?
- ☐ ☐ Has the foundation been repaired?
- ☐ ☐ Is there evidence of foundation movement?
- ☐ ☐ Is slab foundation on addition pulling away from original foundation?
- ☐ ☐ Are concrete steps dropping or pulling away from house?
- ☐ ☐ Is brick chimney pulling away from house?
- ☐ ☐ Is there brick separation at fireplace?

DRAINAGE

Yes No

- ☐ ☐ Is ground sloped toward house?
- ☐ ☐ Will backfilling solve this problem?
- ☐ ☐ Will cutting a swale solve this problem?
- ☐ ☐ Should a foundation or landscape company be consulted?
- ☐ ☐ Has sand been used for backfill?
- ☐ ☐ Is ground slope away from house too steep (no more than 45° angle)?
- ☐ ☐ Has soil washed away?
- ☐ ☐ Are retaining walls needed?
- ☐ ☐ Is ground uniformly sloped around the house?
- ☐ ☐ Have swales been filled?
- ☐ ☐ Can water shed off property?
- ☐ ■ Are area drains used?

Yes No

- ☐ ☐ Is there evidence of water pooling or moss around the house?
- ☐ ☐ Do drainspouts carry water away from foundation?
- ☐ ☐ Do flowerbed curbs trap water next to house?
- ☐ ☐ Do concrete patio or pool decks slope toward house?
- ☐ ☐ Are there gaps between house and patio (or pool deck)?
- ☐ ☐ Is dirt line high (within 4″ of brickline)?
- ☐ ☐ Check interior area for water penetration: Is wall, floor or baseboard stained?
- ☐ ☐ Is there a mildew odor?
- ☐ ☐ Carefully pull up carpet from affected wall. Is tackstrip stained or rotted?
- ☐ ☐ Are rooms below grade? Check for signs of water penetration under carpet.

GARAGE

Yes No

- ☐ ☐ Are bricks pulling away at garage door frame?
- ☐ ☐ Are there cracks in garage floor?
- ☐ ☐ Are sheetrock corner tape joints pulled and wrinkled?
- ☐ ☐ Is interior sheetrock cracked?

CRAWLSPACE

Yes No

- ☐ ☐ Is there evidence of water under the house?
- ☐ ☐ Are cinder blocks or bricks used for piers?
- ☐ ☐ Are concrete piers tipping? Check that pier was not poured at a slant.
- ☐ ☐ Do piers support girders?
- ☐ ☐ Are shims missing?
- ☐ ☐ Has girder been notched to fit pier?
- ☐ ☐ Do girders twist and turn?
- ☐ ☐ Are piers sinking?
- ☐ ☐ Are there sags in girder?
- ☐ ☐ Are there girder sags at the beam wall?
- ☐ ☐ Are there sags in the floor joists?
- ☐ ☐ Is wood other than bois d'arc used for piers?
- ☐ ☐ Is there wood damage caused by termites or rot?
- ☐ ☐ Is there a mildew odor under house?
- ☐ ☐ Is there evidence of mildew on floor joists or girders?

Yes No

☐ ☐ Is there evidence of wood damage at sillplate and floor joist around perimeter (particularly in areas of poor drainage or planter boxes)?

☐ ☐ Is there evidence of wood damage under bathroom, kitchen or laundry room?

☐ ☐ Is there evidence of wood damage in areas of poor ventilation?

☐ ☐ Is there evidence of wood damage where girders rest in beam pockets?

☐ ☐ Is there evidence of wood damage where girders sit directly on the ground?

Note: In homes where parts of the crawlspace are inaccessible, identify this on the inspection report. State what you could not inspect and why.

INTERIOR

Yes No

☐ ☐ Is sheetrock cracked or puckered (particularly above windows and doors)?

☐ ☐ Are sheetrock cracks patterned throughout the house?

☐ ☐ Are sheetrock corner tape joints pulled and wrinkled?

☐ ☐ Is there evidence of recent taping and bedding and fresh paint?

☐ ☐ Are there cracks inside closets?

☐ ☐ Are corner tape joints pulled and wrinkled inside closets?

☐ ☐ Is there evidence of patching?

☐ ☐ Do all doors align and close?

☐ ☐ Has striker plate been moved?

☐ ☐ Are door headers level?

Yes No

☐ ☐ Is there evidence that door casing has been changed?

☐ ☐ Have wedges been placed at top of door and painted over?

☐ ☐ Is floor tile cracked?

☐ ☐ Is there evidence that flooring has been shimmed, plywood or carpet padding used on slab foundations?

☐ ☐ Do floors slope and drop along outside perimeter? If slope cannot be felt by walking along perimeter, check with a 4' level.

☐ ☐ Do floors give along the perimeter of a screeded slab?

☐ ☐ Do floors on a slab foundation have step cracks?

☐ ☐ Do floors heave up?

☐ ☐ Do floors cup?

☐ ☐ Are there gaps at top of interior walls (ceiling)?

☐ ☐ Are there gaps at bottom of interior walls (flooring)?

☐ ☐ Is brick fireplace pulling away from sheetrock?

☐ ☐ Are cabinets pulling away from ceiling or wall?

☐ ☐ Are countertops pulling away from wall?

☐ ☐ Are trim boards pulling away from floor or ceiling?

Note: Carefully inspect a home with fabric-covered walls or wallpaper. Check for cracks through the fabric above doors and windows.

☐ ☐ Attic

☐ ☐ On stick-built houses, are rafters pulling away from ridge?

■ REPORTING GUIDELINES

Inspection reporting guidelines for structural system (soils and foundations) incorporating the above checklist:

- Report the type of foundation (for example, slab-on-grade, pier-and-beam, or basement).

- Report the condition of the foundation, related structural components, and/or slab surfaces.

- Report the crawlspace areas' general condition: the foundation components, ductwork, electrical, plumbing, wood rot, mildew, moisture. If not entering the crawlspace, report why and what method was used, if any, to observe the crawlspace condition.

- Report general indications of foundation movement that are present and visible, such as sheetrock cracks, brick cracks, out-of-square door frames, or floor slopes.

- Report as in need of repair any post-tensioned cable ends that are not sealed.

- Report as in need of repair a crawlspace that does not appear to be adequately ventilated.

- Report as in need of repair basement walls with cracks and/or showing evidence of water penetration.

- Report as in need of repair conditions or symptoms that may indicate the possibility of water penetration that is present and visible, such as improper grading around foundation walls.

- Report as in need of repair conditions that are present and visible, such as erosion or water ponding, that may be adversely affecting foundation performance.

- Render a written opinion as to the performance of the foundation. After evaluating the entire foundation, the inspector must decide whether the extent of foundation movement exceeds acceptable limits for your area. If numerous problems exist, recommend that a structural engineer or foundation company conduct an additional evaluation of the property.

4 Wood and Construction

A familiarity with basic construction details enables the residential inspector to evaluate the quality of a finished residential structure. The structural system has the function of supporting, enclosing and protecting residential internal spaces. The portions of the structure that provide support must resist forces of gravity, rain, earthquake, wind, and snow. The portions of the structure that provide enclosure must resist effects of heat and cold, solar radiation, noise, and biological or chemical agents. Some components of the structure furnish both support and enclosure.

The supporting members, both vertical and horizontal, are subjected to environmental and man-made forces. Floors transfer loads of equipment, occupants, goods, and their own structural weight to the vertical support elements. Floors also resist the horizontal forces of earthquakes and wind. Vertical support elements transfer forces and loads to the ground, as well as the weight of walls and equipment, the weight of snow, and the forces of wind.

Stresses are found in horizontal support elements (e.g., beams, joists, girders, slabs, the chords in a truss). Vertical support elements include posts, piers, columns, walls and the web members of a truss. All materials have specific strength characteristics to resist stresses. Structural members may be weakened by plumbing and electrical systems if holes are drilled or notched improperly.

■ WOOD

Both hardwoods and softwoods are used in construction. The terms *hardwoods* and *softwoods* have no direct relation to the actual physical hardness or softness or the strength of wood. Hardwood and softwood classifications refer to specific species of trees.

Hardwood comes from deciduous trees that lose leaves each year at the end of the growing season. Hardwood trees include oak, maple, ash, walnut, and cherry. Softwood comes from evergreen trees that retain needlelike or scalelike leaves at the end of the growing season. Softwood trees include pine, fir, and cedar.

Lumber

Trees yield structural lumber, plywood, or particle board that is identified by grade marks or certificates of inspection. All structural lumber used in residential construction is required to be graded by an approved agency under recognized grading rules. Lumber must be stamped showing species, grade, and other prescribed information. Lumber grades are determined by number, character, and location of imperfections that affect strength, durability, and use. Common imperfections are knots, checks, pitch pockets, shakes, and stains. The best lumber grades are free or practically free of imperfections. The lower lumber grades contain more imperfections and should not be used for structural construction. All softwood species are covered by grading rules. (See Figure 4.1.)

The National Grading Rule defines dimension lumber as surfaced softwood from 2″ through 4″ designed for use as framing members (e.g., joists, planks, rafters, studs, and small timbers). Lumber designation is reported in thickness and width. The finished size of surfaced lumber is smaller than the size designation; for example, 2″ × 4″ lumber is not actually 2″ × 4″, but rather 1⅝″ × 3½″ because of surfacing operations.

Unseasoned lumber is surfaced to larger dimensions than dry lumber to compensate for shrinkage due to moisture loss. Maximum allowable moisture content of

■ **FIGURE 4.1**

Grade stamps indicate species, grade and prescribed information on untreated lumber.

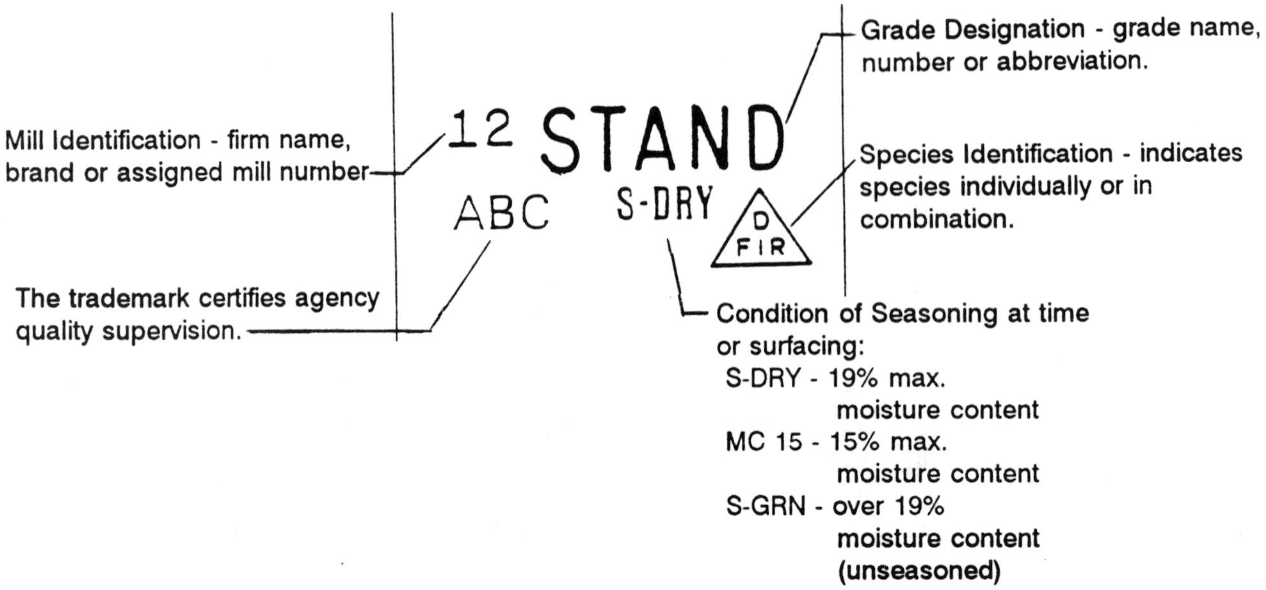

seasoned lumber is 19 percent. As the moisture content drops below 19 percent, there is shrinkage.

Green lumber is seasoned by air-drying or by kiln-drying before being used for wood structures in a house.

The moisture content of lumber used in a house will change, causing (1) warping, loosening of knots, checks, collapse, and honeycomb or (2) stains, mold, and decay. Chemical stain may occur in softwoods.

Decay and dry rot develop when moist conditions exist. Moisture penetrates wood pores, allowing fungus strands to grow in wood cells, and causes cell walls to dissolve. Affected wood will fail when subjected to a load. Rot is spread by microscopic spores in the air and ground. Rot cannot attack dry wood or pressure-treated wood. With moisture penetration and temperatures exceeding 40°F, failure-causing decay will occur in between six months and two years.

Plywood

Plywood is available in many grades and surface finishes. It is used in various applications, from sub-flooring and roof decking to siding and built-in cabinets. An inspector must be familiar with registered grade trademarkings. (See Figure 4.2.)

Grade Designations

The American Plywood Association (APA) identifies structural panel grades by the veneer grade used on the face and back of the panel (e.g., A-B, C-D) or by intended use (e.g., APA Rated Sheathing, APA Rated Sturd-I-Floor). Veneer grades determine veneer appearance in terms of natural unrepaired growth characteristics and the allowable number and size of repairs that are made during manufacture. High-quality veneer grades are "N" and "A." Panels with "B" grade or better veneer faces are always sanded smooth to meet requirements for cabinets, shelving and furniture. Minimum-quality veneer grades ("C" grades) are permitted in exterior plywood. "D" veneer grades are intended for interior use or applications protected from permanent exposure to weather. APA Rated Sheathing panels are not sanded. APA Rated Sturd-I-Floor, APA C-D Plugged, and APA C-C require only touch sanding to produce uniform panel thickness. (See Figure 4.3.)

Durability Classifications

APA-trademarked panels are produced in four exposure durability classifications: Exterior, Exposure 1, Exposure 2, and Interior. Exterior panels are fully waterproof and are designed for applications subject to permanent exposure to the weather. Exposure 1 panels

■ **FIGURE 4.2**

Plywood is identified by grade and designated use.

Typical APA Registered Trademarks

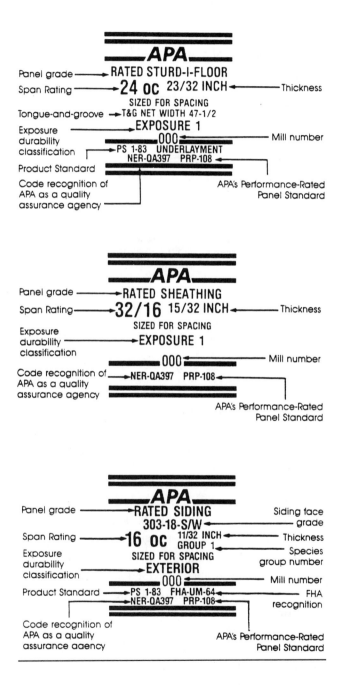

Roof sheathing should bear an exterior grade trademark. An inspector should observe the grade trademark when inspecting the underside of the roof.

Span Ratings

APA Rated Sheathing, APA Rated Sturd-I-Floor, and APA Rated Siding carry span ratings. Span ratings indicate maximum center-to-center spacing for supports over which the panels should be placed in construction applications. The span rating in APA Rated Sheathing trademarks appears as two numbers separated by a slash, such as 32/16 or 48/24. The first number is the maximum recommended support spacing when the panel is used for roof sheathing (decking) when long dimension or strength axis of the panel crosses three or more supports. The second number is the maximum recommended spacing of supports when the panel is used for subflooring with the long dimension or strength axis of the panel crossing three or more supports. For example, a panel marked 32/16 is used for roof decking over supports 32″ on center or for subflooring over supports 16″ on center.

Potential Wood Damage

Residential inspectors must be able to detect visible evidence of wood damage in the crawlspace or basement where sill plates, girders, floor joists, and subflooring are visible. The two primary causes of wood damage in homes are wood rot and wood-destroying insects. Wood rot is the end product of wood-destroying fungi, which are the major cause of damage to wood structural members. Wood damage due to attack by these fungi is as critical as that from wood-destroying insects such as termites and beetles. Conditions that favor termites such as subterranean termites and dampwood termites, and beetles, such as deathwatch (furniture) beetles, also are conducive to the growth of fungi; therefore, the potential destruction is compounded. (See Figure 4.4.)

Residential inspectors must understand why wood is susceptible to fungus attack and how to prevent it. Wood comes from hardwood and softwood trees, as mentioned earlier. Hardwood trees are slower growing than softwood trees, which usually have a shorter life span than hardwood trees. Hardwood trees have closely packed cell layers that produce hard-textured woods.

The cambium layer, just under the bark, is the area of actively growing cells in the woody parts of the tree. The cambium, or sapwood, may be only a few cells thick. The phloem is conductive tissue that moves sugars produced

are fully waterproof and are designed for applications where high moisture conditions are encountered. Exposure 2 panels are designed for interior use with intermediate glue intended to provide protection from moisture due to delays in construction. Interior panels are intended for interior use only.

■ **FIGURE 4.3**

Veneer Grades

N	Smooth surface "natural finish" veneer. Select, all heartwood or all sapwood. Free of open defects, allows not more than 6 repairs, wood only, per 4 x 8 panel, made parallel to grain and well matched for grain and color.
A	Smooth, paintable. Not more than 18 neatly made repairs, boat, sled, or router type, and parallel to grain, permitted. May be used for natural finish in less demanding applications. Synthetic repairs permitted.
B	Solid surface. Shims, circular repair plugs and tight knots to 1 inch across grain permitted. Some minor splits permitted. Synthetic repairs permitted.
C Plugged	Improved C veneer with splits limited to 1/8-inch width and knotholes and borer holes limited to 1/4 x 1/2 inch. Admits some broken grain. Synthetic repairs permitted.
C	Tight knots to 1-1/2 inch. Knotholes to 1 inch across grain and some to 1-1/2 inch if total width of knots and knotholes is within specified limits. Synthetic or wood repairs. Discoloration and sanding defects that do not impair strength permitted. Limited splits allowed. Stitching permitted.
D	Knots and knotholes to 2-1/2 inch width across grain and 1/2 inch larger within specified limits. Limited splits are permitted. Stitching permitted. Limited to Exposure 1 or interior panels.

■ **FIGURE 4.4**

Wood-decaying fungus begins with spores that germinate.

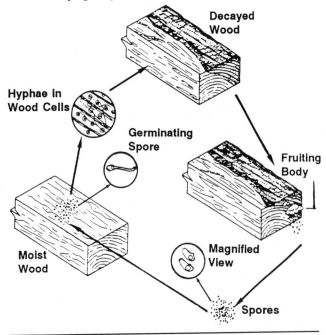

by the tree's foliage down into the roots for use or storage. The xylem moves water and nutrients up from the roots to the foliage. The movement of fluids allows nutrients to be moved to various areas of the tree as needed. It may also be a defense against enemies such as the bark beetle. As the beetle penetrates into the cambium layer to lay its eggs, a healthy tree will push fluids out of the opening and may be able to repel the attacker.

The green of trees and plants is caused by chlorophyll, the essential chemical for the process of photosynthesis, in which carbon dioxide and water are converted to sugars and oxygen and provide nutrition and energy to trees and plants. Oxygen is given off into the atmosphere as a waste product. Chlorophyll separates green plants from fungi.

As a tree grows, cell layers are pushed to the interior. Cells pushed into the interior are no longer living and growing, but they provide strength to the tree. The inner heartwood of dead cells is filled with resins, oils, and turpentine that provide resistance to attack by fungus and insects.

Trees grow most during the warmest months of the year. During the fall, cell production slows and cells move closer together. Latewood is the slow growth period of a tree and is responsible for creating annual rings. Latewood provides physical resistance to insect and fungus attack. Some trees, such as juniper, bald cypress, red cedar, redwood, mulberry, and black walnut, provide natural resistance to insect and fungus attack.

All wood contains water. Trees that have been dead for years and appear to be bone dry still contain water, as the cells strive to maintain equilibrium with outside humidity. The more humidity in the outside air, the more moisture in a tree's interior. A living tree may be composed of 90 percent water by weight, primarily within the cells, although cell walls could contain 30 percent water by weight. These maximum moisture levels are saturation points. When a tree is cut down and milled for lumber, the moisture content begins to drop immediately because the water source (from the roots) has been cut off. Depending on the outside latent humidity, the moisture content may drop to as low as 8 percent. Kiln-drying is the process of heating wood in a kiln to reduce moisture content and kill fungi. The kiln is not a permanent control. Lumber absorbs moisture again after it is used in a structure. Fungi must have moisture to grow in wood and usually cannot survive and grow in wood with less than 20 percent moisture content.

Building materials such as Masonite, particleboard, plasterboard, and plywood are useless if exposed to water, which breaks down adhesives in these building materials. Excessive moisture conditions, such as condensation in improperly ventilated bathrooms, may allow the growth of fungus and/or mold on walls, floors, tile, and grout. Moisture causes paint to blister, peel, and stain plaster. Moisture also causes bonding materials that hold wall and floor coverings to loosen and/or separate.

Wolmanized wood is chemically pressure-treated lumber that resists wood rot and termite damage. Lumber is placed in a chemical vat that forces chemicals into the heart of the lumber. Pressure-treated lumber is often used for sill plate construction to minimize the danger of termite infestation.

A residential inspector should not comment specifically about termite infestation. Most states require that a licensed pest control inspector comment about termites or living organisms. However, it is important that the residential inspector recognize wood damage and mention damage in the client report.

Destructive Fungi

Fungi are plants without chlorophyll. Fungi, usually seen as mushrooms, help to decompose wood that has died. Fungi are lower plant forms that produce spores that are distributed by wind and water. Spores are present where wood is cut, processed or used. Fungi feed on cellulose, decompose wood to organic matter, and return wood to the soil as nutrition for other plant life.

Stain fungi and decay fungi are two major fungi that occur on wood. Stain fungi are visible as discoloration of wood, and are most often seen as bluish stains. Stain fungi in the active stage feed on wood at a very slow rate and do not cause damage, although the presence of stain fungi as an active growth indicates that conditions are right for other fungi that may cause damage. Decay fungi include white rot and brown rot, which are major destroyers of wood. Pocket rot is another decay fungus that occurs in standing timber and will not survive after the tree is cut and wood is milled. Pocket rot appears as small pockets or pits of white mycelia and is usually not a problem to the lumber.

Wood rot is caused by fungi that feed on wood. They infect wood and will develop into a fungus under certain environmental conditions. All fungi require oxygen, favorable temperatures, and adequate moisture. Fungi and termites are often found together because they require similar environmental conditions. Moisture is the key to fungus development. Decay fungi cannot seriously damage wood that has a moisture content below 20 percent. Kiln-dried lumber is dried to approximately 14 percent moisture content to prevent wood rot because lumber will gain some moisture in shipping, storage, and construction.

Direct contact with water or high humidity conditions will cause wood to absorb water, resulting in wood rot. High-humidity conditions occur under a house with a crawlspace. Although other forms of fungi exist, decay fungi cause most damage in the crawlspace area. Fungi eat wood cell walls, which results in decomposition. Decay fungi include brown rot, white rot, soft rot, and dry rot.

Brown Rot

Brown rot is decay fungi that feed on the cellulose of softwoods. Under ideal conditions for growth, decay could begin in sound timber in as little as three months. The residential inspector must be concerned about brown rot because all structural framing, such as mudsills, sill plates, floor joists, subfloors, wall studs and roof members, is constructed from softwoods. These structural areas are most likely hidden from view, and moisture buildup caused by a water leak, poor drainage, and/or inadequate ventilation could escape detection for a substantial time and cause serious problems.

The two species of brown rot that affect the integrity of wood structures are teardrop fungus and *Poria inerassata* fungus. Teardrop fungus has water droplets that form sporophores on its fruiting body. This fungus species is a problem in cooler parts of the United States. *Poria inerassata,* the most common wood-destroying fungus in the United States, is a serious problem only with softwoods. Most organisms require food, water, oxygen, and proper temperatures to survive and multiply. Temperature extremes place fungi into a dormant state as spores. The ideal temperature for rapid growth of *Poria inerassata* fungi is 72° to 74°F, which is also a very comfortable temperature for humans. At lower temperatures, the growth rate of *Poria* will slow. *Poria* will resume growth as the temperature rises. *Poria* will not grow well above 80°F, and at approximately 115°F, the fungus will die.

Wood with moisture content below 20 percent will not support the growth of fungus. *Poria* fungus requires visible standing water to begin growth. Even if the cells of the lumber have absorbed all of the moisture possible, fungus growth cannot start until water droplets are formed outside the cells. Saturated lumber will not support fungus growth because there is insufficient oxygen. The speed at which *Poria* fungus will destroy lumber depends on temperature, moisture content, and lumber type.

Wood rot causes wood to break into small cubes with cracks running perpendicular to the grain. Wood rot is caused by recurring changes in moisture content from wet to dry. The wood becomes crumbly and strength decreases rapidly. Eventually, wood rot causes wood to become a brittle substance that can be crushed into a powder.

White Rot

White rot is a decay fungus that is common in crawlspaces that are consistently wet. White rot is a less common problem than brown rot. White rot attacks hardwoods, works very slowly, and feeds on cellulose and lignin (which binds wood cells together). White rot causes wood to have a spongelike consistency.

Soft Rot

Soft rot fungi attack wood from the surface inward and cause cavities to form. Soft rot is generally found in situations where wood is too wet to be attacked by other decay fungi.

Dry Rot

Dry rot is a water-conducting type of brown rot fungus. Dry rot has specialized rhizomorph structures that conduct water. Rhizomorphs are dirty white, become brown or black with age, and may range from ¼″ to 1″ in diameter. Dry rot fungus attacks wood that is resistant to attack by other decay fungi. This fungus can destroy large areas of wood in one to two years.

Conditions that allow water to contact wood cause rot. Poor drainage causes water penetration into a house and will cause wood rot to sill plates, floor joists, and girders. Poor flashing along windows and doors also results in water penetration and causes wood rot.

Whenever a dirt line lies above the sill plate, there is a possibility of water penetration and subsequent wood damage. Girders or floor joists resting on or in the ground allow water to come into contact with wood. Plumbing leaks in crawlspaces, screeded slabs, and basements can cause wood rot to flooring, floor joists, and girders. Plumbing areas that are particularly susceptible include areas under commodes, showers, laundry rooms, and kitchens. Concentrations of moist, humid air in crawlspaces or basements cause wood rot. Vent openings should be strategically located in beam walls of crawlspace construction, and air should flow in and out of a crawlspace to prevent humidity buildup because poor ventilation combined with poor drainage results in high humidity.

Residential inspectors should observe the perimeter of a house before examining a crawlspace. (See Figure 4.5.) Note areas with poor drainage, areas where the dirt level is high, or areas where there are exterior windows and doors. The residential inspector should be alert to musty odors, which are associated with high humidity and decay. Other wood rot signals include a brownish or whitish coating on the floor joists or sweating floor joists. Musty odor or wood damage should be noted on the report to the potential homebuyer.

Wood rot is often obvious, but other times it is difficult to detect. While inspecting under a house, inspectors should randomly stab the sill plates with an ordinary screwdriver. If wood damage is found, inspectors should also check the ends of floor joists. Wood that can be penetrated more than ¼″ to ½″ indicates probable wood rot damage.

Wood rot will spread from one piece of wood to another. Residential inspectors should check pocket

■ FIGURE 4.5

A combination of wood rot and termite damage.

girders for wood damage. Where the sill plate has rotted away, the floor joists and flooring may drop slightly around the edges. Where the ends of floor joists or girders have rotted away, the floor may drop or feel springy. If floor joists drop, the sole plate and frame wall could also drop.

Before going under the house, the inspector should check the bathroom, kitchen, and laundry areas, making sure to flush each of the commodes several times and run water in all bathtubs and showers and in the kitchen.

Treatments

Some wood species have a high resistance to decay and termites. Other wood species need a preservative treatment to resist decay and termites. Wood preservatives are divided into four major classes: (1) waterborne salt preservatives, (2) oilborne preservatives, (3) creosote and solutions containing creosote, and (4) borate.

Waterborne Salt Preservatives

Waterborne salt preservatives are most often used to pressure-treat lumber and plywood for residential construction and leave the wood clean, odorless, and easy to paint. Waterborne salt preservatives are durable and are recommended for wood members that are in ground contact and support building structures. All waterborne salt preservatives are relatively odorless and are paintable, provided the wood has the same moisture content required for untreated wood.

Oilborne Preservatives

Oilborne preservatives are used to treat lumber that will not come in contact with saltwater. Pentachlorophenol (Penta) is a preservative that is highly toxic to both fungi and insects, insoluble in water, and permanent. Penta varies in color from dark brown to colorless and is the most widely used oilborne preservative used to treat lumber.

■ **FIGURE 4.6**

Pressure-treated wood bears the AWPB certified agency trademark.

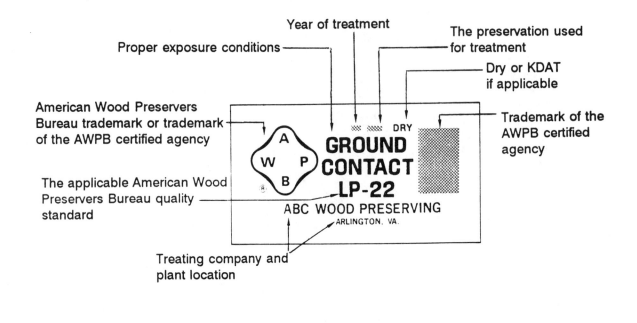

Creosote

Creosote is the most widely used of all preservatives. Creosote and solutions containing creosote are used where protection against wood-destroying organisms is of first importance, where painting is not required, and where an odor is acceptable.

Creosote/coal-tar mixtures are the most widely accepted preservatives for marine or saltwater installations and are ideally suited for treating pilings for shore dwellings, etc. Creosote/petroleum mixtures are used where economy is of first importance, but they should not be used for marine installations.

Two wood preservative treatments are (1) the pressure process and (2) the nonpressure process. The pressure process forces the preservative into wood under pressure. The nonpressure process applies preservative to the wood surface by painting, dipping, or spraying.

Borate

There are various borate treatments for preserving wood. Borate is largely used by the pest control industry as a treatment for wood that is in place. Additionally, many manufacturing plants are beginning to utilize borate preservatives in the assembly of roof trusses and other structural components.

Pressure-Treated Wood

Pressure treatments, in which preservative chemicals are applied under pressure to obtain maximum penetration, provide the best protection against decay and termite attack. The pressure preservation process provides the most dependable means of ensuring uniform penetration and distribution of preservative.

Protection is required for structures that are subjected to decay and termites, such as

- sills on concrete or masonry walls;
- sills or sleepers on concrete or masonry slabs in direct ground contact;
- ends of wood girders contacting concrete or masonry walls; and
- wood embedded in grade or areas that are subject to decay and termites.

The American Wood Preservers Bureau (AWPB) quality stamp provides visual assurance that a product has been pressure treated according to the appropriate standard. (See Figure 4.6.) A typical stamp provides

- year and month of treatment;
- preservative used;
- governing standard;

■ **FIGURE 4.7**

A 3'–4'–5' right triangle method is used to construct 90° batter boards.

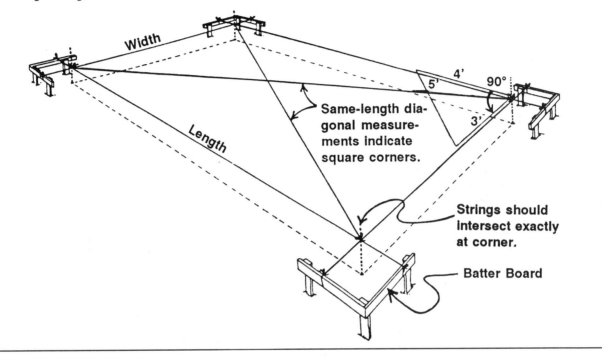

- TSO (treating service only)—the treating plant is not responsible for grade;
- moisture content;
- name and location of treating plant;
- chemical retention;
- chemical description of the preservative; and
- local quality control agency.

Non-Pressure-Treated Wood

Wood treated with a nonpressure process should not be used in contact with the ground or under severe conditions of decay or termite attack. The wood is not sufficiently impregnated with preservative to provide adequate protection.

■ FOUNDATIONS

Batter Boards

After the location and dimensions of the foundation have been established, corner stakes are driven into the ground. The topsoil, grass, shrubs, and other organic material are removed from the building foundation area. A set of batter boards, which are level ledger boards nailed to stakes that are driven into the ground, is erected 3' and 6' behind each corner stake. A line is stretched from each batter board across the tops of the corner stakes to the opposite batter board. These lines are reference points for preparing the ground for the foundation.

The top edge of the batter board is the desired elevation of the foundation and floor line. Sand is used to fill in uneven areas and raise the grade so the floor line reaches proper height. The floor line must be a minimum of 8″ above the dirt line outside the building to keep water and insects away from the residential structure.

Batter boards must have square corners. One method for ensuring that the corners are square is measuring diagonally from corner stake to corner stake. The corners are square if the two diagonal measurements are equal. Another squaring method is the 3'—4'—5' right triangle method. By measuring 3' in one direction and 4' in a perpendicular direction from the corner stake, the diagonal measurement should be 5', implying a 90° angle. (See Figure 4.7.)

Underground Plumbing

Plumbing must be installed according to strict building codes that dictate materials to be used and

■ **FIGURE 4.8**

A vapor barrier is used in residential construction to prevent moisture penetration through a porous concrete slab.

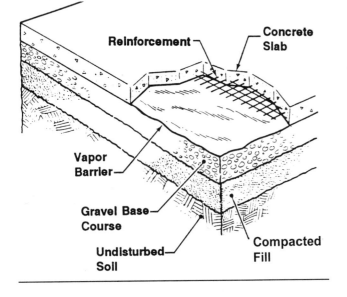

method of installation. Sanitary sewer pipe is manufactured from cast iron, PVC (polyvinylchloride), or other approved materials. Water supply piping is copper, although wrought supply copper (soft copper tubing) and plastic piping have been used more frequently because they preclude piping joints under the foundation slab.

Gas pipes are installed in walls and run overhead in the attic, where there is adequate ventilation. Underground plumbing is installed after forms have been set at proper elevations for the foundation. A plumbing contractor installs sewer pipe with an appropriate slope, which should be ¼″ per foot fall, toward the sewer for proper drainage.

Vapor Barrier

A vapor barrier consists of polyethylene sheet material placed below the concrete slab. The vapor barrier is laid over the ground; then either rebar or post-tension cables are installed, and concrete is poured. (See Figure 4.8.) A vapor barrier should be used under basement floors and behind walls. Basement walls should not use polyethylene materials as a vapor barrier. An approved vapor barrier sealant must be used to keep the moisture from penetrating through walls.

Concrete is a durable, dry, and porous material that induces capillary attraction. Capillary attraction is the movement of a liquid upward through a cellular

structure of fibrous strands or through a structure of other solids. Water penetrates concrete or masonry walls and slabs by capillary attraction. Capillary attraction is evidenced by the presence of a whitish powder (called *efflorescence*) at the base of an inner basement wall or at ground level on pier-and-beam construction.

On a concrete slab, moisture may cause floor tile to loosen and carpets to mildew. (Please note that floor tiles may become loose for other reasons than moisture. If floor tiles are found that are lifting, or "tenting," this can also be caused by poor slab preparation, installation over painted surfaces, faulty mortar mix, etc. Be careful of your diagnosis as to the cause of this. Causes should be stated, if known.) Moisture that reaches sill plates and studs and other wood structures by capillary attraction will cause rot. Plastic or asphalt sheet coating should be placed under concrete slabs or behind basement walls to stop capillary attraction and form a vapor barrier.

■ MASONRY

Masonry today refers to building with stone, brick, concrete block, clay tile, and other units that are held together by mortar. Masonry characteristics vary in strength, durability, and safety of the masonry units; the mortar; and the method of laying, bonding, joining, anchoring, tying, spanning, and reinforcing masonry units into a whole as part of the residential structure.

Stone

Throughout history, stone has been used as structural material (e.g., as building material, finish material, and flooring and roofing material). Stone is classified as sedimentary, igneous, or metamorphic. Sedimentary stone is composed of sands, clays, and organic materials deposited by water into beds where, under pressure or chemical action, the particles became stone. Igneous stone results from the application of heat until materials melt and then resolidify. Metamorphic stone results from a combination of pressure, heat, and moisture. Today, stone is used primarily for surface finishing.

Clay

The abundance of clay and the ease of forming it into desired shapes account for the appearance of fired clay objects such as brick, structural clay tile, terra-cotta, roof tile, and drain tile. Brick that has been fired is used for fireplaces, chimneys, siding on structures, decking, walls, and walkways. Structural clay tile is used for floors, decking, bathtubs, showers, and walls. Terra cotta means "baked earth," and is a hard-baked, glazed or unglazed, ceramic material used architecturally as a decorative surface for facings and tiles. Roofing tile is made in several different configurations. Roof tile is brittle and may be broken by walking on it or by heavy objects falling on it. Roof tile is heavy and weighs approximately 8 to 19 pounds (lb.) per square foot (sq. ft.), which requires additional bracing for the roof structure. Drain tiles have many uses, such as drains from gutters, French drains, foundation drains, etc.

Brick

Brick is rectangular block formed of clay and hardened by heat. Brick is graded by absorbency and compressive strength. Brick that is fired at higher temperatures has fused particles and closed pores, which produces an impervious surface. Soft brick is fired at lower temperatures and is absorbent and susceptible to weathering and erosion. The compressive strength of a brick wall depends on the type of brick and mortar used.

Adobe Brick

Adobe brick, a sun-dried brick that has been used for centuries, requires protection from moisture. Adobe brick must be laid on a waterproof foundation and be covered by a roof overhang. Adobe brick is extremely soft and also has a high absorption rate and a low compressive strength. It is important for adobe brick to have a protective coat of sealer applied, owing to its susceptibility to weathering and erosion.

Concrete Brick and Concrete Block

Masonry units of Portland cement and aggregate are classified as concrete brick and concrete block. Concrete bricks are available in the same sizes as clay bricks, but have lower compressive strength. Concrete blocks are hollow cell units available in various sizes and are load bearing or non-load bearing. Load-bearing blocks have lower compressive strength than clay brick, but have greater insulating qualities. Concrete blocks are available in standard weight and lightweight. Standard-weight block is produced from Portland cement and sand and gravel aggregate, and each block weighs approximately 40 lb. Lightweight block is produced from Portland cement and an aggregate of cinders, slag, shale, or pumice and weighs approximately 30 lb. per block.

Mortar

Mortar is used for bonding masonry units and is composed of cement, small aggregate, and water. The properties of mortar differ greatly, depending on the cement and aggregate used, the ratio of cement to aggregate, and the ratio of amount of water to solids.

Three cements used in mortar are Portland cement, natural cement, and various limes. Portland cement provides higher strength than natural cement or lime cements. Natural cement's properties show wide variations and predictability. When the ratio of Portland cement to lime increases, strength increases. Lime increases plasticity and volume stability (shrinkage/expansion). Lime from shells is soft and produces mortar of lower strength and durability than lime from limestone.

Mortar joint finishes are troweled and tooled joints. In troweled joints, excess mortar is cut off with a trowel and no additional finish is used. In tooled joints, a special tool is used to compress and shape mortar joints. Tooled joints provide maximum protection against water penetration. The tooling operation forces mortar tight against the masonry on each side of the joint.

A dependable troweled joint should shed water. The flush joint produces an uncompacted joint with a small hairline crack where the mortar is pulled away from the brick by the cutting action of the trowel. The struck joint and the raked joint produce a shelf on which water may collect.

Masonry anchors, ties, and joint reinforcement are used in masonry construction to hold brick and block in place. Bonding with metal ties is recommended for exterior walls. Metal ties allow slight differential movement between the facing and backing to relieve stresses and prevent cracking.

■ STRUCTURAL COMPONENTS

Structural components must provide support and resist natural forces such as gravity, wind, rain, snow and earthquakes. Components providing enclosure and protection must resist heat, cold, water, noise, solar radiation, chemical agents, and disease-producing conditions. Some structural components furnish both support and enclosure while other components provide only support or enclosure. (See Figure 4.9.)

Structural support is subject to both vertical and horizontal forces. Floors provide a means of transferring loads to vertical support elements. Horizontal supports

■ **FIGURE 4.9**

Housing Construction Terminology

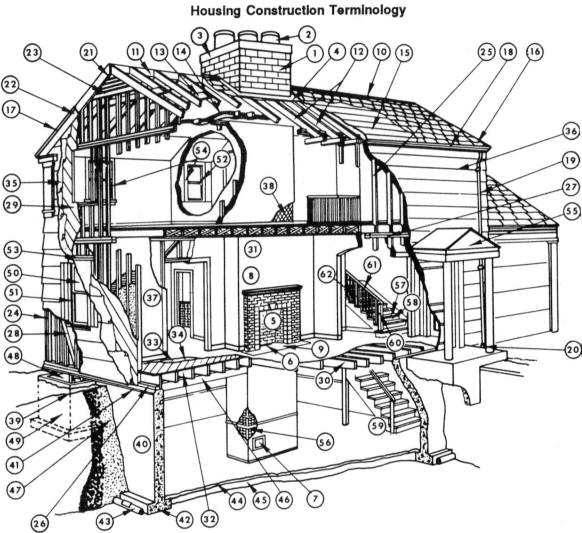

1. **Chimney**—A vertical masonry shaft of reinforced concrete or other approved, noncombustible, heat-resisting material enclosing one or more flues. It removes the products of combustion from solid, liquid, or gaseous fuel.

2. **Flue Liner**—The flue is the hole in the chimney. The liner, usually of terra-cotta, protects the brick from harmful smoke gases.

3. **Chimney Cap**—This top is generally of concrete. It protects the brick from weather.

4. **Chimney Flashing**—Sheet-metal flashing provides a tight joint between chimney and roof.

5. **Firebrick**—An ordinary brick cannot withstand the heat of direct fire, so special firebrick is used to line the fireplace.

6. **Ash Dump**—A trap door to let the ashes drop to a pit below, from where they may be easily removed.

7. **Cleanout Door**—The door to the ash pit or the bottom of a chimney through which the chimney can be cleaned.

8. **Chimney Breast**—The inside face or front of a fireplace chimney.

9. **Hearth**—The floor of a fireplace that extends into the room for safety purposes.

10. **Ridge**—The top intersection of two opposite adjoining roof surfaces.

11. **Ridge Board**—The board that follows along under the ridge.

12. **Roof Rafters**—The structural members that support the roof.

13. **Collar Beam**—Really not a beam at all. A tie that keeps the roof from spreading. Connects similar rafters on opposite side of roof.

14. **Roof Insulation**—An insulating material (usually rock wool or fiberglass) in a blanket form placed between the roof rafters for the purpose of keeping a house warm in the winter, cool in the summer.

■ **FIGURE 4.9** (Continued)

15. **Roof Sheathing**—The boards that provide the base for the finished roof.

16. **Roofing**—The wood, asphalt or asbestos shingles—or tile, slate or metal—that form the outer protection against the weather.

17. **Cornice**—A decorative element made up of molded members usually placed at or near the top of an exterior or interior wall.

18. **Gutter**—The trough that gathers rainwater from a roof.

19. **Downspout**—The pipe that leads the water down from the gutter.

20. **Storm Sewer Tile**—The underground pipe that receives the water from the downspouts and carries it to the sewer.

21. **Gable**—The triangular end of a building with a sloping roof.

22. **Barrage Board**—The fascia or board at the gable just under the edge of the roof.

23. **Louvers**—A series of slanted slots arranged to keep out rain, yet allow ventilation.

24. **Corner Post**—The vertical member at the corner of the frame, made up to receive inner and outer covering materials.

25. **Studs**—The vertical wood members of the house, usually 2″ × 4″ generally spaced every 16″.

26. **Sill**—The board that is laid first on the foundation and on which the frame rests.

27. **Plate**—The board laid across the top ends of the studs to hold them even and rigid.

28. **Corner Bracing**—Diagonal strips to keep the frame square and plumb.

29. **Sheathing**—The first layer of outer wall covering nailed to the studs.

30. **Joist**—The structural members or beams that hold up the floor or ceiling, usually 2″ × 10″ or 2″ × 12″ spaced 16″ apart.

31. **Bridging**—Cross bridging or solid. Members at the middle or third points of joist spans to brace one to the next and to prevent their twisting.

32. **Subflooring**—The rough boards that are laid over the joist; usually laid diagonally.

33. **Flooring Paper**—A felt paper laid on the rough floor to stop air infiltration and, to some extent, noise.

34. **Finish Flooring**—Usually hardwood, of tongued and grooved strips.

35. **Building Paper**—Paper placed outside the sheathing, not as a vapor barrier, but to prevent water and air from leaking in. Building paper is also used as a tarred felt under shingles or siding to keep out moisture or wind.

36. **Beveled Siding**—Sometimes called clapboards, with a thick butt and a thin upper edge lapped to shed water.

37. **Wall Insulation**—A blanket of wool or reflective foil placed inside the walls.

38. **Metal Lath**—A mesh made from sheet metal onto which plaster is applied.

39. **Finished Grade Line**—The top of the ground at the foundation.

40. **Foundation Wall**—The wall of poured concrete (shown) or concrete blocks that rests on the footing and supports the remainder of the house.

41. **Termite Shield**—A metal baffle to prevent termites from entering the frame.

42. **Footing**—The concrete pad that carries the entire weight of the house upon the earth.

43. **Footing Drain Tile**—A pipe with cracks at the joints to allow underground water to drain in and away before it gets into the basement.

44. **Basement Floor Slab**—The 4″ or 5″ layer of concrete that forms the basement floor.

45. **Gravel Fill**—Placed under the slab to allow drainage and to guard against a damp floor.

46. **Girder**—A main beam upon which floor joists rest. Usually of steel, but also of wood.

47. **Backfill**—Earth, once dug out, that has been replaced and tamped down around the foundation.

48. **Areaway**—An open space to allow light and air to a window. Also called a *light well.*

49. **Area Wall**—The wall of metal or concrete that forms the open area.

50. **Window**—An opening in a building for admitting light and air. It usually has a pane or panes of glass and is set in a frame or sash that is generally movable for opening and shutting.

51. **Window Frame**—The lining of the window opening.

52. **Window Sash**—The inner frame, usually movable, that holds the glass.

53. **Lintel**—The structural beam over a window or door opening.

54. **Window Casing**—The decorative strips surrounding a window opening on the inside.

55. **Entrance Canopy**—A roof extending over the entrance door.

56. **Furring**—Creating an airspace with thin strips of wood or metal before adding boards or plaster.

57. **Stair Tread**—The horizontal strip where we put our foot when we climb up or down the stairs.

58. **Stair Riser**—The vertical board connecting one tread to the next.

59. **Stair Stringer**—The sloping board that supports the ends of the steps.

60. **Newel**—The post that terminates the railing.

61. **Stair Rail**—The bar used for a handhold when we use the stairs.

62. **Balusters**—Vertical rods or spindles supporting a rail.

■ **FIGURE 4.10**

Blocking and nailing patterns for plywood subfloor panels. Deformed-shank nails are strongly recommended.

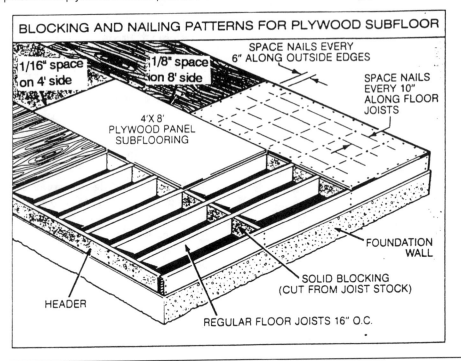

Floors

Floor framing in a wood frame house consists of piers (posts), girders (beams or stringers), sill plates, joists and subfloor. When assembled properly on a foundation, floors produce a level, anchored platform for the remaining structural components. Piers and center girders (wood or steel) that support the inside ends of the joists are sometimes replaced with a wood frame or masonry wall when the basement is subdivided. A house constructed with a crawlspace will normally have piers to support the girders. Crawlspace ventilation is important in areas with high humidity because poor air circulation in a crawlspace and poor lot drainage will cause wood damage.

A wood frame structure may be constructed on a concrete slab with lumber on the concrete slab. The subfloor is nailed to the lumber. This flooring construction method is referred to as a *screeded slab*.

The design of wood floor systems should equalize expansion and contraction of wood framing from the outside wall to center girders. As girders and joists approach moisture equilibrium, there are only small differences in the amount of shrinkage. A well-designed floor system will minimize cracks in walls and sticking doors, as well as other structural problems. (See Figure 4.10.)

Concrete Slab

A wood frame house constructed on a concrete slab must have a level foundation when the slab is poured. The sill plate is anchored to the concrete slab with anchor bolts or concrete nails. The remaining structural components are anchored to the platform.

Floor Framing

The sill plate rests on the vertical concrete wall or perimeter of the slab floor. Either way the sill is anchored to the concrete foundation in an effort to tie the substructure to the superstructure of the house. The foundation bolts are set into the concrete slab or wall during the pour. Then the sill plate is drilled for the bolts to pass through and secured with washers and nuts that will anchor the superstructure during high winds and, possibly, hold the house in place on the foundation during earthquakes. (See Figure 4.11.)

■ **FIGURE 4.11**

Combined slab and foundation.

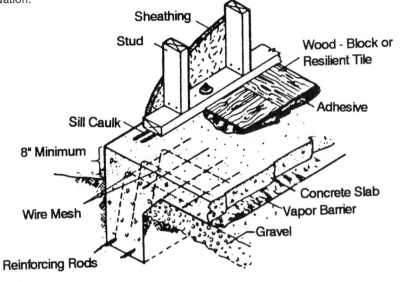

On top of the sill plates, in pier and girder construction, are the floor joists, end joists, and rim joists. (See Figure 4.12.) The joists in residential construction are placed either 16″ or 24″ on center. Then the subflooring is fastened on top of joists. In platform type construction, the stud walls are then built on top of the subflooring. In balloon framing, the vertical wall framing members extend from the sill plate fastened to the side of each floor joist upward to the ceiling of the top floor. Then fireblocking at each floor level is installed between each of the balloon studs.

Subfloor

The concrete slab acts as the subfloor on slab-on-grade construction. Pier-and-girder construction or a residential structure with a basement requires a subfloor that covers the joists. The subfloor can consist of either boards or plywood. Plywood is available in 4′ × 8′ sheets or larger and varies in thickness from ½ to 1⅛″.

Floor load requirements and joist spacing either 16″ or 24″ on center will determine the proper thickness of boards or plywood used for the subfloor. Plywood subflooring is stronger because sheets can be installed with the plywood glued and nailed or screwed to the joists. Plywood sheets should be installed with the face grain at right angles to joists and staggered so joints are not all on the same joists. When underlayment is used, whether for carpet or tile, underlayment joints also should be staggered. Plywood also can serve as combined plywood subfloor and underlayment.

Board subflooring may be applied either diagonally or at right angles to joists. When board subflooring is placed at right angles to joists, the finish floor must be laid at right angles to the subfloor. Diagonal subflooring permits finish flooring to be laid either parallel or at right angles to joists. End joints of the boards should be made directly over the joists.

Wall Construction

Homes built according to today's building codes are better and tighter. As a result, moisture problems can occur if moisture forms inside the walls. Moisture problems can occur in both cold and warm climates, when humid air comes in contact with a cold surface. Condensation on a window is easy to detect. However, when moisture forms inside a wall cavity, it can go unnoticed until structural damage appears. Moisture trapped inside the wall can cause mold, mildew, wood rot, and odors in a short period of time. Uneven drying of wood studs can lead to walls bowing and cracking in the sheetrock.

It is important that builders be familiar with the area where they are constructing new homes and understand the vapor drive in that area. In warm, humid climates, moisture vapor moves from outside to the cooler, drier air-conditioned inside. In cold climates, moisture in the warm inside air moves toward the cooler, drier con-

■ **FIGURE 4.12**

Pier and girder construction.

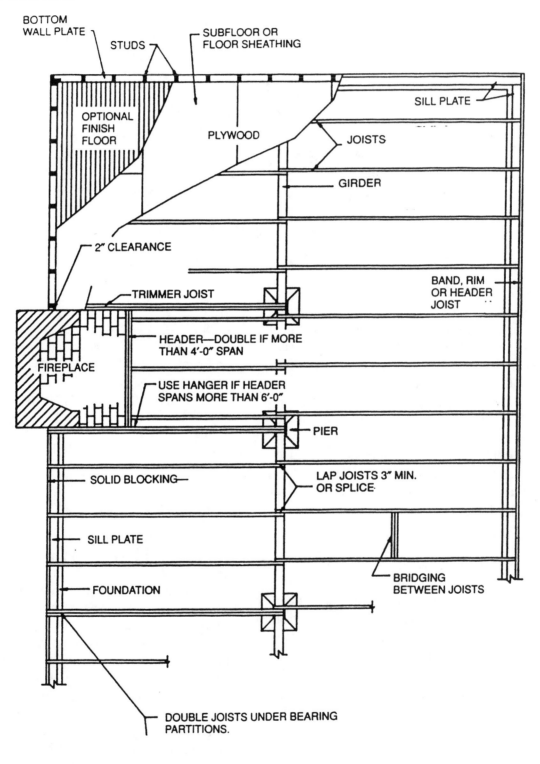

ditions outside. In warm climates, as water vapor travels through the wall, it comes in contact with cooler surfaces as it gets closer to the wall. Condensation most often occurs in walls with poor warm side vapor retarders and sheathing material with low R-values. To keep wall cavities dry, the ultimate goal is to keep the inside wall temperature above the dew point, the temperature at which moisture in the air condenses. When the temperature inside the wall reaches the dew point, drops of water will form and eventually soak the wood, cavity insulation, drywall, and/or inside wall covering. When materials in the wall remain wet, mold and mildew can form, causing odors and even health problems. Also, the wood studs and wood sheathing can rot and attract insect and structural damage. When constructing a moisture-resistant cavity wall, there are some important facts to remember:

- Moisture vapor condenses on cold surfaces.
- During cold weather, the inside surface of noninsulating sheathing will be colder than the inside surface of insulating sheathing.
- The thicker the wall cavity, the greater the condensation potential owing to the colder temperature toward the cold side.
- Moisture vapor can move through a wall assembly by diffusion and air transport.

Air transport is more important than diffusion in cold climates. Field studies show that walls sheathed with insulating sheathing are drier than walls sheathed with noninsulating sheathings.

Rigid foam insulation provides good thermal resistance. It can effectively raise temperatures in cavities above the condensation level and prevent thermal short-circuiting through the framing members.

In warm climates, when warm, moist outdoor air seeps into the wall cavity and comes in contact with the cool surfaces of the air-conditioned interior, water vapor condenses into liquid. To limit the chance of moisture condensation, it is important to reduce the amount of moisture that permeates the wall from the outside and allow any moisture that does enter the wall to dry. Rigid foam sheathing is moisture resistant, so water will not soak through the sheathing into the wall cavity. Wood-based sheathings can absorb moisture that soaks through exterior finishes. Wood-based sheathings must be installed with gaps between boards that allow air and moisture vapor intrusion into the wall. Such sheathings are often protected from moisture with house wraps or felt building paper. House wraps and felts are designed to let water vapor pass through, which means they do not

keep damaging water vapor out of warm-climate walls. The best sheathing for warm climates is rigid foam with plastic film facers that reduce water vapor and liquid water intrusion into the wall. Also, interior finishes such as latex paint or permeable wallpaper that let water vapor escape to the inside are best for warm-climate use.

Walls serve as structural support and separation of spaces. These two functions may be combined in one surface, as in bearing walls, or differentiated, with the structural function handled by beams and columns, while the walls become a nonbearing separating surface. Bearing walls support a vertical load. Nonbearing walls support no vertical load. Bearing and nonbearing walls frequently use the same construction techniques.

Separation between interior and exterior space of the residential structure provides a barrier against weather and controls airflow, water vapor, moisture and heat. Walls also provide privacy (sight and sound) and fire resistance.

Walls transmit vertical loads from other elements of the residential structure. They provide accommodation for heating, air-conditioning, plumbing, and electrical systems and are usually the principal location for openings for light and ventilation and a means for supporting doors, windows, or other amenities. Wall finish is determined by the construction used to meet the structural and/or separating requirements.

Wall Framing

Wall framing includes vertical studs and horizontal members, sole plates, top plates, and window and door headers of exterior and interior walls that support ceilings, upper floors, and roof. Wall framing serves as a nailing base for wall coverings.

Wall-framing members used in conventional construction are usually nominal 2″ × 4″ studs spaced 16″ or 24″ on center. Top plates and sole plates are nominal 2″ × 4″. Wall-framing lumber should be free from warps. All framing lumber for walls must be dry (15 percent moisture content is desirable; however, 19 percent is the maximum allowable moisture content). The common ceiling height of a residential structure is 8′. It is common practice to rough frame walls to a height of 8′ 1½″. In platform construction, when dimension material is 1½″ thick, precut studs would be 7′9″ long. This height allows for use of 4′ × 8′ sheets of drywall.

Wall framings commonly used in construction are platform and balloon. Wall framing in platform construction is erected above the subfloor. A combination of platform construction for first-floor sidewalls and full-

■ **FIGURE 4.13**

Typical wall, floor, and roof framing.

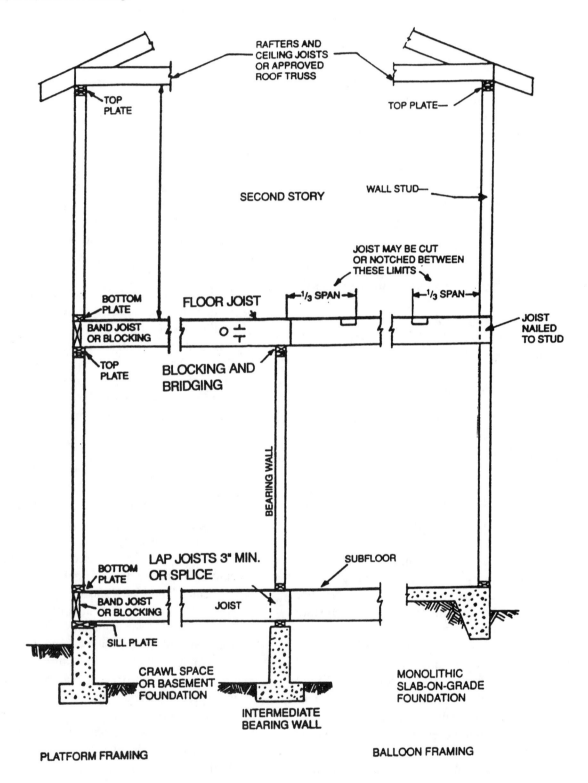

■ **FIGURE 4.14**

A typical exterior wall, showing corners, door and window openings, and a let-in diagonal brace.

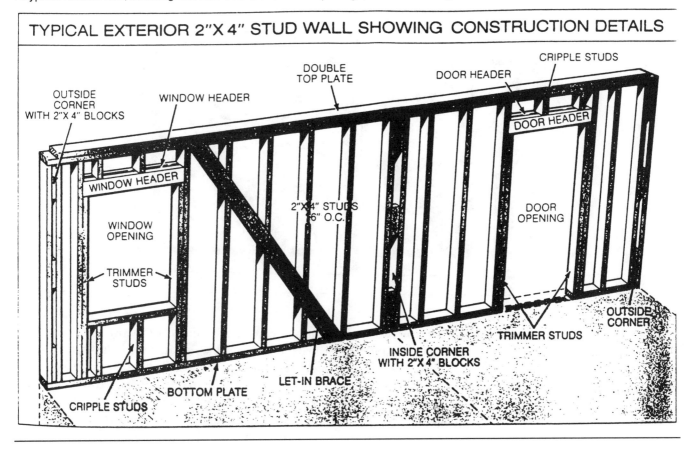

TYPICAL EXTERIOR 2"X 4" STUD WALL SHOWING CONSTRUCTION DETAILS

length studs for end walls extending to end rafters at gable ends is sometimes used in single-story dwellings. (See Figure 4.13.)

A horizontal assembly method of framing is used on the subfloor for tilt-up of wall sections. This system involves laying out precut studs, door and window headers, cripple studs, and windowsills. Sole plates and top plates are nailed to all vertical studs and adjoining studs to headers and sills. (See Figure 4.14.) The entire section is then erected, plumbed, and braced. Another method of assembly includes fastening the studs only at the top plate. When the wall is erected, studs are toe-nailed to sole plates that are nailed to the subfloor. Corner studs and headers are nailed together to form a single unit. Sheathing may be installed before the wall is erected in place. When all exterior walls have been erected, plumbed and braced, the nailing is completed. Sole plates are nailed to floor joists and headers or stringers. Corner braces are nailed to studs and plates; door and window headers are fastened to adjoining studs, and corner studs are nailed together.

Interior walls are fastened to intersecting exterior walls. Intersection must also provide nailing surfaces for drywall finish. After walls are erected, a second top plate laps the first at corners and wall intersections. Top plates can be partly fastened in place when the wall is in a horizontal position. Temporary bracing is left in place until ceiling and roof framing are completed and sheathing is applied. (See Figure 4.15.)

The finished ceiling height of a room is 8' to 10'. There are exceptions in rooms with cathedral or vaulted ceilings or in basement or attic rooms.

Balloon wall studs extend from the first-floor sill to the second-floor top plate or end rafter. Platform framed walls are constructed for each floor. Balloon frame construction requires that wall studs and floor joists rest on and be fastened to the anchored sill. The ends of second-floor joists bear on a 1" × 4" ribbon that has been let into the studs. Joists are nailed to studs at these connections. End joists parallel to the exterior on both first and second floors are nailed to each stud. (See Figure 4.16.)

■ **FIGURE 4.15**

The topmost plates of the double top plate overlap the plates below them at all inside corners.

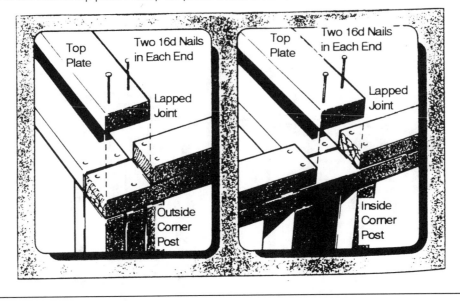

Firestops are required in balloon framing to prevent the spread of fire through open wall passages. Firestop blocking must be of the same material used for studs, and blocking must be nailed between studs.

Framing for end walls in platform- and balloon-framing construction varies. The method used for

■ **FIGURE 4.16**

Balloon-framing wall studs extend from the sill plate of the first floor to the top plate or end rafter of the second floor.

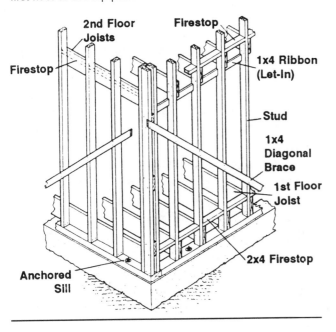

platform construction in two-story dwellings with finished rooms above the first floor includes materials and procedures similar to those of the first floor. The edge floor joist for the second story is toenailed to the top wall plate, subfloor, sole plate, and wall studs. The method used for balloon construction requires that the studs extend from the sole plate through the first and second floor. The edge joist must be nailed to each stud, and firestops must be used.

Large-volume tract builders use assembled walls delivered to the construction site. Walls are laid in proper location and then tilted into place. Custom builders assemble walls by laying studs on the subfloor and tilting them up in sections. Wall sections are then plumbed and braced.

In platform framing, both structural and space separation must be completed before construction of the second floor. A floor system of joists is erected, then covered with a subfloor of 1″ × 6″ or 1″ × 8″ boards or plywood. The subfloor extends over the joists to the extremities of the residential structure. Exterior walls and space separations are assembled on the subfloor and tilted into the proper locations. Procedures used to frame the first floor are repeated to complete the second floor.

Three advantages of using platform framing are as follows:

1. Walls and room partitions are assembled away from the building site.

2. Building walls and partitions in sections is done with minimum time and effort, as each floor provides a safe level work area to construct wall assemblies.

3. Platform framing does not require additional fire-stopping because each stud space is blocked off by wall and partition framing, so danger of fire is minimal.

Headers Headers or lintels span the tops of window and door spaces for support. The header ends rest on cripple studs or trimmer studs that are nailed to the adjoining studs. Header size must increase as the span increases. Headers must support vertical loads, and if not strong enough, they will sag and damage window or door areas. (See Figure 4.17.)

Flashing Flashing is used in locations where two different surfaces or two different materials join. Flashing is used where water may penetrate into a building. Flashing is used at more points than previously were considered necessary because of damaging effects of water entering the building through open junctions due to construction movement or shrinkage.

■ FIGURE 4.17

Headers should conform to the rough opening size of windows and doors.

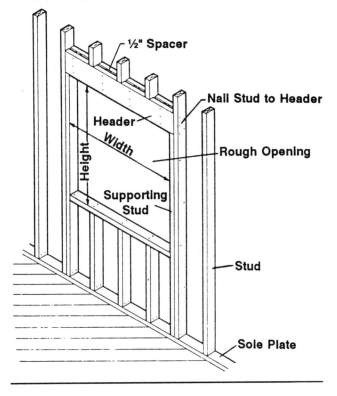

■ FIGURE 4.18

Flashing is used around door and window openings.

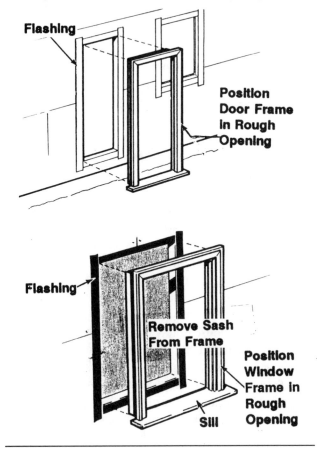

Single flashing is often inadequate, and a second counterflashing or cap flashing must be used. Flashing will not always be exposed; many times, it is concealed under siding or roof areas. Flashing material must be corrosion resistant and properly installed to make junction points leakproof. Flashing must withstand foundation movement, wind, and rain. (See Figure 4.18.)

Flashing used in residential construction is made from polyethylene, plastic, asphalt-felt, aluminum, copper, galvanized metal, and stainless steel. Copper and stainless steel are popular flashing materials used for gutters and downspouts.

Normally aluminum is not used as an exterior flashing material because of the chemical reaction between aluminum and the alkali in cement. Aluminum may be used if coated with asphaltum or another protective coating. Fasteners used in installing flashings must be corrosion resistant (i.e., copper, aluminum or galvanized nails, screws, clips). Flashing is used at the following locations in residential construction:

- Chimney and roof junctions
- Wall and roof intersections
- Roof valleys and roof penetrations (e.g., sewer vents, vents)
- Chimneys or masonry construction to frame or stucco walls
- Exterior windows, doors, and vent openings
- Masonry, wood, or metal copings and sills
- Wood trim projections and built-in gutters

Metal Framing

Metal framed buildings have been constructed for years but were mostly commercial buildings. Now metal framing is becoming more popular in residential properties in various parts of the country. Steel construction is becoming popular in areas where there are an abundance of wood-destroying insects (termites) and fungus (wood rot), as this eliminates any food source for them. When metal construction spread to homes, it was just the metal studs and this type of construction that moved further north to cooler climates.

The whole house is now framed with steel floor and ceiling joists, studs, and rafters that are made from cold-formed steel into various sizes and thickness channels. Steel framing gets its strength when the joists are standing on edge. The purpose of the gussets, bridging, and straps is to tie the structural members together to maintain proper alignment. *Racking* is rotation and twisting caused by wind or axial loading. The steel framing has a zinc coating (galvanized) to protect it from corrosion.

The floor system uses steel channels that require bridging to prevent racking. Racking of the floor joist is very serious, as it would allow the building's floor system to shift and even collapse. Bridging should be used in the center of the spans and below load-bearing walls that rest on the girder. It is required every 12′ of span. The floor system must be anchored to the foundation with bolts. (See Figure 4.19.)

In metal floor systems, a metal joist system must have bridging and web stiffeners, and all connections must be made using proper angle plate or gusset and screws. The subfloor is installed on the floor system with the sill plate, which is fastened to the joists with self-drilling corrosion protected screws along with the metal channel that supports the studs. (See Figure 4.20.)

Screws for all steel-to-steel connections shall be installed with a minimum edge distance and center-to-center spacing of ½″. Areas such as roof trusses might be spot welded and/or use metal straps to prevent high winds from lifting the roof system off the house. The

exterior wall and load-bearing studs must be a heavier gauge cold form steel than non-load-bearing studs. The metal channel that supports the metal studs is called *track*. There is a track that rests on the sillplate and another track at the top of the wall. The studs set in the tracks with self-drilling and taping corrosion-protected screws. (See Figure 4.21.) When constructing a second story, it is important that all the load-bearing steel studs be located directly in line with joists, trusses, and rafters with a maximum tolerance of ¾″ between their centerlines. The interior load-bearing walls shall be supported on foundations or be located directly above load bearing walls with a maximum tolerance of ¾″ between the centerline of the studs. Holes in wall studs and other structural members shall not be larger than 1½″ in width or 4″ in length. Holes are only permitted along the centerline of the web of the framing member. Holes shall not be less than 24 inches center to center and be a minimum of 10″ from edge of hole to end of member.

Steel studs, like the steel joists, must have lateral bracing (bridging) internally or externally to align the studs during construction and to maintain the structural integrity of the completed wall assembly. Bridging provides resistance to both rotation and axis bending caused by wind and axial loading. The bridging must be continuous, connected at each stud location, and connected at each wall end to a rigid part of the main structure. (See Figure 4.22.)

The sheathing must be connected to the top and bottom tracks of the wall assembly to enhance the restraint provided to the stud and stabilize the overall wall assembly. Steel roof framing shall be located directly in line with the load-bearing studs below with a maximum tolerance of ¾″ between the centerline of the stud and roof joist and rafter.

Ceiling joists bracing the bottom flanges of steel joists will be laterally braced with ½″ inch thick gypsum board minimum. Ceiling joists shall have a minimum load bearing length of 1½″ and shall be connected to the rafters, called *heel-joint connections*. (See Figure 4.23.)

Blocking or bridging shall be installed between joists in line with strap bracing at a maximum spacing of 12′ measured perpendicular to the joists. The third point bracing should be used for straps installed at closer spacing than third-point bracing, or when sheathing is applied to the top of the ceiling joist. Splices in ceiling joists are only permitted at interior load-bearing walls. Spliced ceiling joists must be connected with the same number and size of screws on each side of the splice as required for the heel-joint connection. (See Figure 4.24.)

■ **FIGURE 4.19**

Steel floor construction.

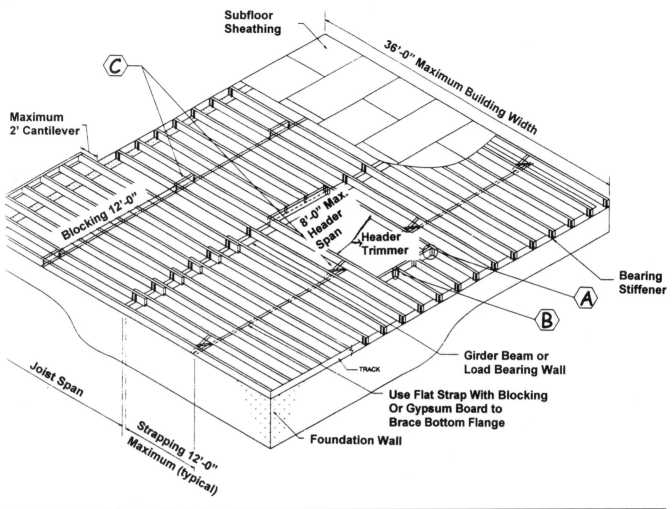

Rafters and other structural members cannot be spliced. Openings in the roof and ceiling framing shall be framed with headers and trimmers between ceiling joists or rafters. Header joists span cannot exceed 4 feet. Header and trimmer joists can be fabricated from joist and track sections, which will be the same size and thickness as the adjacent ceiling joist or rafter.

Rafter bottom flanges of steel rafters must be continuously braced with track section or 1½″ steel strapping at a maximum spacing of 8′, as measured parallel to the rafter. The track section or straps shall be fastened to the bottom flange of each rafter and shall be fastened to blocking and bridging installed between rafters in line with the continuous bracing. The decking and roof covering will be installed on the top flange of the rafter. (See Figure 4.25.)

Thermal Conductivity. Thermal conductivity or thermal bridging is a problem with metal frame houses in cold climates. Outside air temperature is transferred through the metal studs to the inside, causing condensation when the cooler air is mixed with the inside warm air, which causes condensation to form inside the wall. When condensation forms in the wall, it will often appear on the drywall as streaking. Streaks on the wall reflect the location of the metal framing in the wall. The streaks may be vertical or horizontal. Moisture and mold can form inside the wall cavity as well. Metal conducts heat and cold much faster than wood, and drops the R-value of the wall significantly. The thermal bridging problem is aggravated by using hardboard such as OSB (oriented strand board) for sheathing. One procedure is to install extruded polystyrene foam over the studs on

■ **FIGURE 4.20**

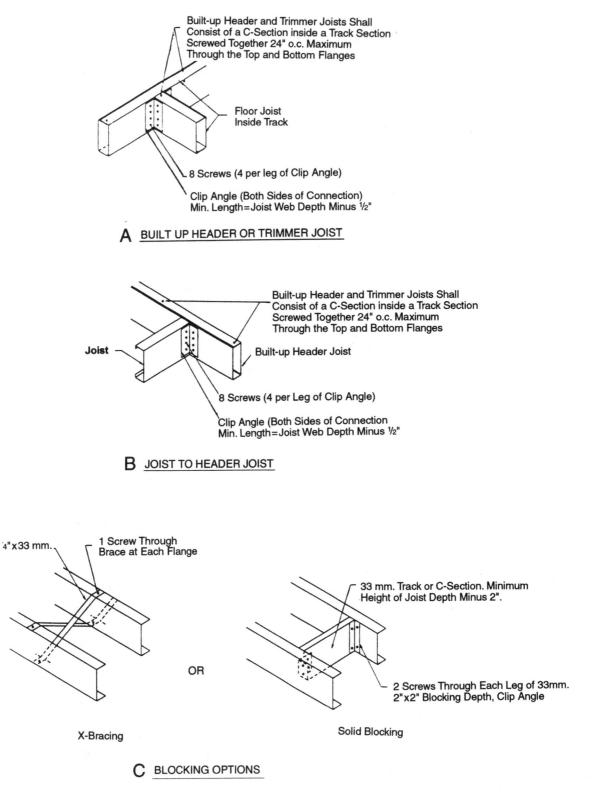

Built-up Header and Trimmer Joists Shall
Consist of a C-Section inside a Track Section
Screwed Together 24" o.c. Maximum
Through the Top and Bottom Flanges

Floor Joist
Inside Track

8 Screws (4 per leg of Clip Angle)

Clip Angle (Both Sides of Connection)
Min. Length=Joist Web Depth Minus ½"

A BUILT UP HEADER OR TRIMMER JOIST

Built-up Header and Trimmer Joists Shall
Consist of a C-Section inside a Track Section
Screwed Together 24" o.c. Maximum
Through the Top and Bottom Flanges

Joist

Built-up Header Joist

8 Screws (4 per Leg of Clip Angle)

Clip Angle (Both Sides of Connection
Min. Length=Joist Web Depth Minus ½"

B JOIST TO HEADER JOIST

¼"x33 mm.

1 Screw Through
Brace at Each Flange

33 mm. Track or C-Section. Minimum
Height of Joist Depth Minus 2".

OR

2 Screws Through Each Leg of 33mm.
2"x2" Blocking Depth, Clip Angle

X-Bracing

Solid Blocking

C BLOCKING OPTIONS

■ **FIGURE 4.21**

Wall-to-Wood Sill Connection

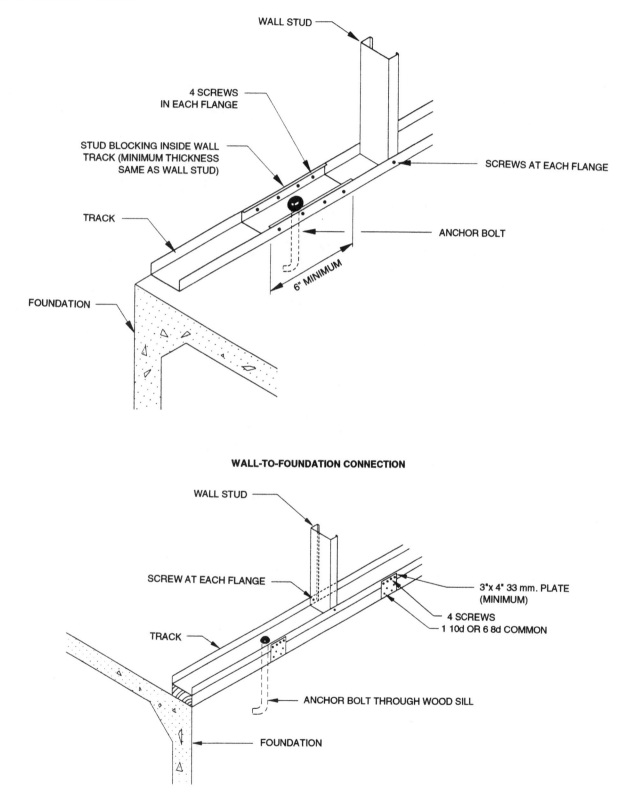

■ **FIGURE 4.22**

Steel wall construction.

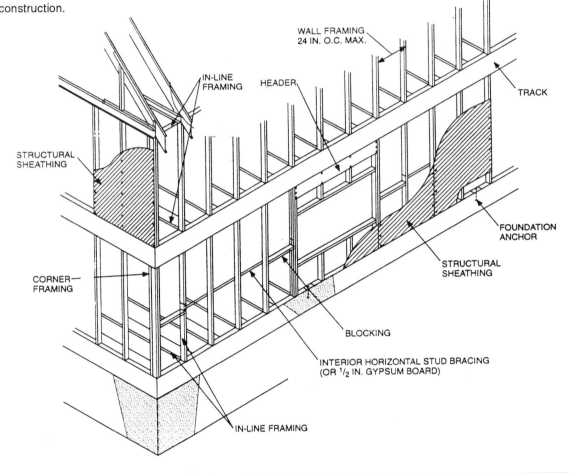

■ **FIGURE 4.23**

Heel-joint connection.

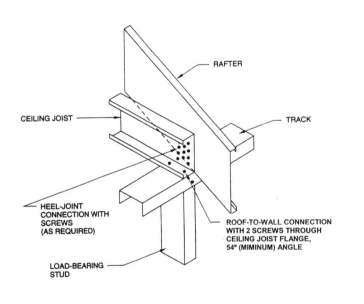

■ **FIGURE 4.24**

Spliced ceiling joists.

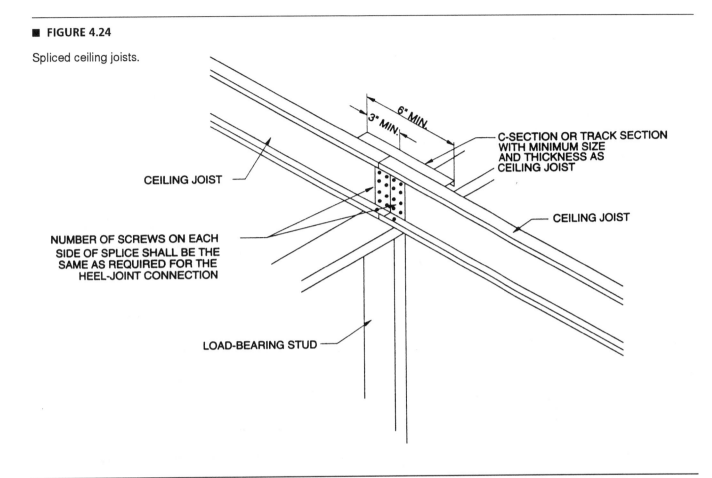

the cold side to reduce the condensation problem. This layer of foam acts as a thermal break. Even with the foam covering the studs, the fasteners still conduct cold to the studs and cause condensation. Research is being conducted on proper remediation and installation techniques to correct this problem. Any areas within the metal framework susceptible to air infiltration should be caulked or sealed with foam. If the condensation is not stopped, it can lead to rusting and possible failure of the metal studs, which could cause major structural problems.

Finishes

Interior

Interior finish materials include gypsum board, plywood, paneling, fiberboard, and wood paneling in various thicknesses. Gypsum board, dry wall, and plywood are fastened directly to wall framing. Furring strips are used on a masonry wall and the gypsum board or paneling is adhered to the furring strips.

In older construction, prior to the 1950s, plaster walls were common. Plaster walls consist of a wire mesh fastened to the studs, then a rough coat of mortar troweled onto the mesh, followed by a finish coat smoothed on the wall with paint or paper covering it.

Exterior

Exterior walls must be covered with weather-resistant siding. Exterior wall coverings include wood or wood-base materials and masonry, veneers, and metal or plastic siding. Wood siding is available in different patterns and finishes. Prefinished siding is also available.

Materials used for siding on structures should be identified in the inspection report, and if defects are observed, they should be reported. Cracks, separations, and deteriorating wood or siding should be reported and repair recommended.

Wood Siding   Wood has been used for siding for decades because of its abundance and its relatively low cost. However, wood is not as plentiful as it once was; therefore, it is not as reasonably priced. Owing to the growing shortage of lumber today, there have been many changes in the lumber industry to eliminate waste.

■ **FIGURE 4.25**

Steel roof construction.

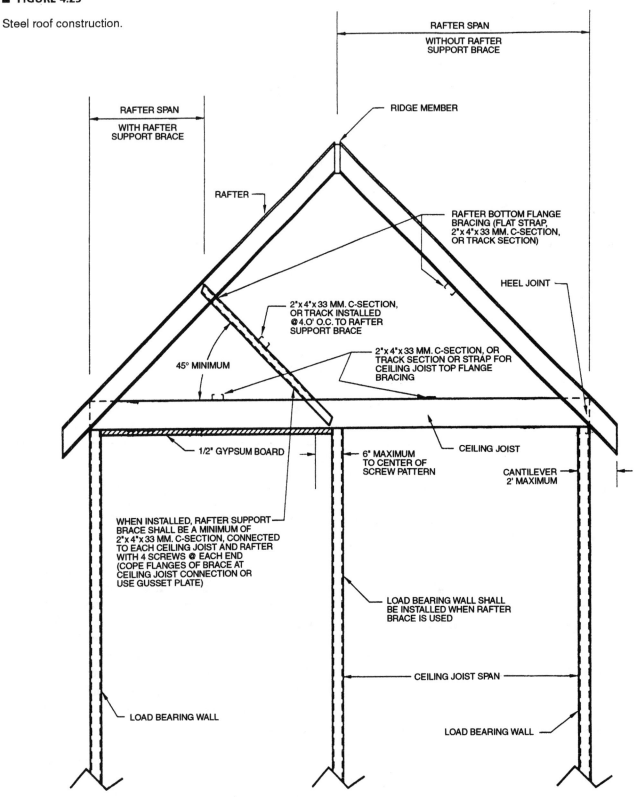

■ **FIGURE 4.26**

Wood-frame wall construction.

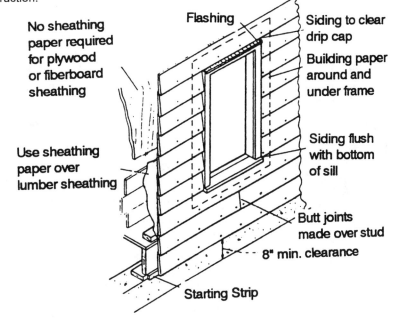

Many parts of a tree that once were thrown away now are converted into particleboard, hardboard, plywood, or shingles.

Wood is available in many varieties and is generally more reasonably priced than masonry siding, which has led to its widespread use. Wood siding in any form, if properly maintained, will last the lifetime of the structure. It is important that wood siding never come in contact with the soil because it will act as a wick to draw up moisture from the soil, which will cause damage from decay and termites or other wood-destroying organisms. It is a building practice to have a minimum of 8″ clearance from soil. (See Figure 4.26.)

Some woods, such as cedar and redwood, have a natural resistance to decay and rot. Others may be pressure-treated to resist decay and insects. Wood that has been pressure-treated will require some maintenance because of its exposure to the elements. Wood that has had no pressure treatment will require regular maintenance in the form of paint, stain, varnish, or some type of wood sealer.

Hardboard is a popular siding material made of wood fibers that are combined under pressure and heat. It may be treated with fire- and moisture-retardant chemicals. These products are especially vulnerable to decay and rot; therefore, it is necessary to keep hardboard

siding painted and sealed. Plywood siding has a tendency to delaminate. This is most obvious on the exterior face, where peeling may be evident. When this condition is present, the siding may have to be replaced. Generally, the structural integrity of the plywood is not affected, but the plywood is cosmetically damaged.

There are other types of siding materials that are popular, such as aluminum, vinyl, brick, exterior insulation and finishing systems (EIFS) and stucco.

Aluminum Siding Aluminum siding has been used on homes since the early 1950s, many times replacing wood siding. It can have either a smooth finish or a textured wood grain finish. Aluminum is vulnerable to dents and can be damaged by hail or falling branches. Aluminum siding has a baked enamel finish that, under normal conditions and minimum maintenance, will not require painting for 15 to 20 years.

Vinyl Siding Vinyl siding, like aluminum siding, is often used to cover some other type of siding or to cover the soffits, fascias, etc., on brick veneer homes. Vinyl products have their color all the way through the material and should never need repainting. Vinyl siding is flexible in warm to hot weather, but it is very brittle in cold weather and can crack or break if struck.

■ **FIGURE 4.27**

Exterior plaster-wood frame.

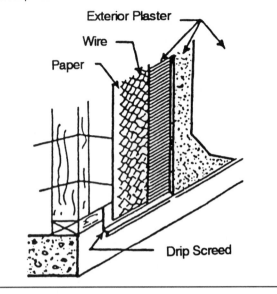

Asbestos Cement Siding Asbestos cement siding has not been used since the 1970s, but for approximately 30 years it was very popular. Although brittle and easily broken, asbestos siding was durable and many homes still have it. When remodeling, this product must be removed according to the Environmental Protection Agency (EPA) standards. The cost is significant, and the inspector should report this to the client. Only qualified contractors must do removal and disposal.

Stucco. Stucco can be applied directly to any masonry or concrete surface (as long as it is a clean surface) and is used over a metal lath in frame construction. Stucco is a Portland cement plaster that is durable and able to withstand repeated freeze/thaw cycles. (See Figure 4.27.) Stucco applied over a metal lath tends to crack and telegraph the joints in plywood sheathing, due to the expansion and contraction of the plywood. These cracks should be sealed to prevent moisture penetration from causing damage to the studs and interior walls. The inspector should report even hairline cracks to the client, and they should be repaired.

EIFS. Exterior insulation finish system, EIFS, is a wall finishing system that has the appearance of stucco. While it has the appearance of stucco, EIFS is actually a multilayered system. The multilayers act like layers of clothing on a cold day that insulate and keep the elements out. The outer layer is an acrylic finish coat that acts as a water barrier, shedding moisture and protecting the inner layers. Behind this layer is a base coat with a fiberglass mesh embedded in it. This layer adds impact strength to the finish. The innermost layer is expanded polystyrene, one to four inches thick, which is the layer that adds the insulating factor and allows aesthetic joints and features to the siding. EIFS is a nonstructural component of the wall. (See Figure 4.28.) There have been problems in the past with EIFS, which were mainly the result of installing the materials over wood framing instead of over masonry by inexperienced installers. The damage, in most cases, was from moisture seeping in behind the siding. Failures developed at roof rakes and chimneys; around windows, doors, and floor lines; where siding came in contact with the soil; etc.

Each EIFS manufacturer has developed detailed installation standards. Failure to follow the manufacturer's instructions and details will allow water to get into the wall. The cladding material then acts as a barrier, and the water cannot flow out but has to evaporate and get out as water vapor. During this extended time, the wood absorbs moisture, causing wood rot. Dryvit and

■ **FIGURE 4.28**

All EIFS walls are similar in construction.

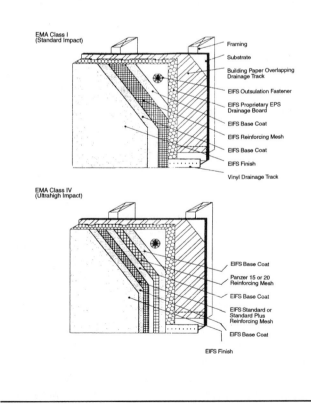

■ **FIGURE 4.29**

Termination at foundation.

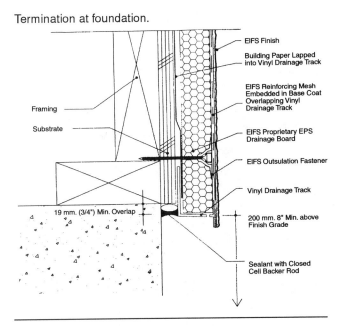

■ **FIGURE 4.30**

Outsulation expansion joint—dissimilar substrates.

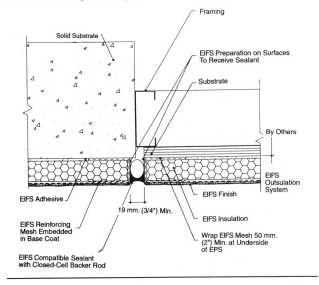

other manufacturers in the industry have developed a drainable system to prevent water from being trapped in the wall cavity. (See Figure 4.29.)

Home inspectors must be able to identify EIFS. Identifying the different hard coat stucco, polymer-based EIFS and polymer-modified EIFS is as important as understanding the potential for moisture damage related to the various types.

The inspector should be familiar with some, if not all, details of EIFS installation. The important part of inspecting EIFS is terminations. EIFS should be terminated at a minimum of 8″ above finished grade by backwrapping with reinforcing mesh and base coated onto the foundation. All terminations require backwrapping, which is where the reinforced base coat is continued from the face of the insulation board across the edge and onto the back side of the insulation board, a minimum of 2½″.

Expansion joints are required when the system terminates against a dissimilar material such as plywood or concrete block. The system should be held back ¾″ to allow for an expansion joint and caulking at project completion. Expansion joints are required at floor lines, at areas where there is a change in substrate, and at areas with significant structural movement. (See Figure 4.30.) Penetrations and terminations at penetrations such as light fixtures, hose bibs, dryer vents, and wall receptacles require backwrapping with reinforcing mesh and base coat. The insulation board should be held back from

the opening a minimum of ⅜″ to ½″ for proper sealant application. Sealants used at terminations at expansion joints, windows, and other openings must be properly caulked. Use only high quality sealants approved by the manufacturer.

Windows and doors can be a significant area of water intrusion. If a gap is observed between the sill and jamb, it should be caulked. Drip flashing should be installed continuously at the heads of openings, such as multiple, ganged windows to prevent water entry.

Flashings where roof and vertical wall meet—A diverter flashing is installed as the first piece of flashing at the end of the roof where it intersects the wall. All diverter joints must be soldered. Step flashing should extend up at least 6″. The purpose of the step flashing and diverter is to shed the water off the roof and keep it away from the vertical wall. (See Figure. 4.31.)

Crickets and chimney enclosure—Crickets are designed to deter the accumulation of snow and ice and deflect water around a chimney. Wood-enclosed chimney chases can be finished with a full EIFS with Expanded Polystrene Insulation (EPS). Flashing should continue about 6″ above the cricket. Flashing at the enclosure top must also be installed. (See Figure 4.32.)

There should be a minimum of 2″ between the EIFS and the roof.

Flashings should be used to properly direct water away from the structure. Door, window, and deck attachments are the most typical areas where flashing is used. Although flashing has been required for years, many

■ **FIGURE 4.31**

Flashing where roof and vertical wall meet.

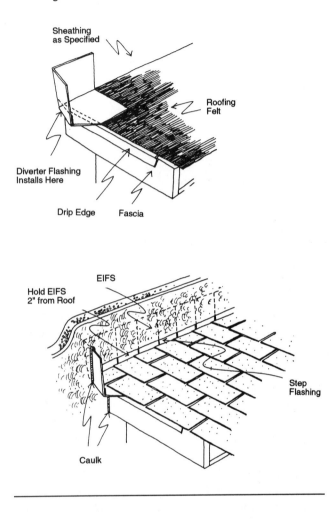

■ **FIGURE 4.32**

Flashing at chimney and cricket.

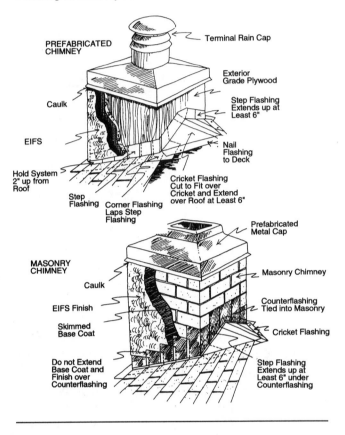

builders mistakenly felt that flashings on stucco type exteriors were not necessary. Therefore, inspectors should check for proper flashings. Flashing points, where a gutter meets a sidewall, are one of the most common areas for excessive moisture intrusion.

Foam should not terminate below grade. The foam substrate should be backwrapped and sealed to the foundation approximately 8″ above grade. This serves two purposes: (1) It prevents wicking of the foam and (2) it eliminates a termite trail into the structure. (The foam creates a great environment for termites that is impossible to treat.) Penetrations should be properly sealed, and no foam should be exposed. Look for all penetrations; not only the obvious ones. In addition to pipe penetrations, look for fasteners, lights, or any object that passes through the EIFS wall cladding material.

When installing a sprinkler system, sprinkler heads should be a minimum of 24″ from the foundation with no spray hitting the EIFS siding. Landscaping should be done by persons knowledgeable about EIFS siding and where to plant shrubs. All shrubs should also be 24″ from the foundation, and ivies and vines should not be allowed to grow on the walls. Areas that are cracked or damaged should be repaired. The finish coat and base coat material should be removed. If the insulation board is not damaged, the base coat, mush, and finish coat can be repaired. All repairs must be done with manufacturer's approved materials and should be made by people who are licensed and certified to do repairs on EIFS siding.

When inspecting EIFS siding the inspector should inspect the following:

- Step and kickout flashing should be in place where roof and vertical wall meet.
- Flashing at chimneys, crickets, dormers, etc., should be in place.

■ **FIGURE 4.33**

Masony veneer must have a brick ledge.

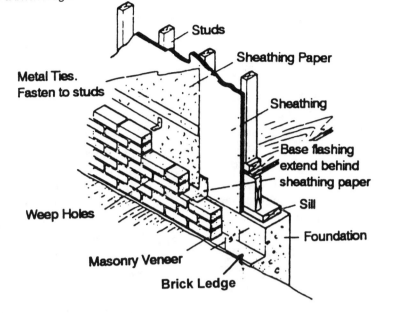

- Framing/substrate shall be flat with no planar irregularities greater than ½″ within a 4′ radius.
- Flashings should be in place around windows and doors.
- Check for damaged or deteriorated caulked seals between the EIFS cladding and windows and doors. Cracked or split sealant should be replaced immediately so water does not have a chance to penetrate the break.
- Seal light fixtures, outlets, hose bibs, shutters, downspouts, and other attachments to the home. There should not be gaps around these items where they attach to the wall.
- Defective gutters and downspouts that can let water into the structure should be replaced. Also, gutters should be kept clean so water flow is not obstructed.
- Make sure that ladders leaned against an EIFS wall have soft foam guard pads placed at the ends. Unprotected ladders can dent, puncture, or scar EIFS.
- Remove soil and mud splashes as soon as possible from EIFS. Freshly applied finish can become stained by repeated exposure to mud splash-ups, especially in areas with clay soil. Soil can be removed from EIFS with household cleaners.
- Mold, mildew, and algae should be cleaned with a commercial cleaner.
- Soil should be at least 8″ below an EIFS wall.

- Sealants used to repair EIFS walls should be approved by the manufacturer.

Masonry Veneer   When masonry veneer is used as an outside finish over wood frame walls, the foundation must include a supporting offset referred to as a *brick ledge*. (See Figure 4.33.) This results in a space of about 1″ between the masonry and the sheathing. Masonry veneer may be supported by wood foundations as well as by concrete or concrete block foundations. Base flashing is used at the brick course below the bottom of the sheathing and framing, and should be lapped with sheathing paper. Weep holes, which are required on 33″ centers to provide drainage, are also located at this course and are formed by eliminating the mortar in certain vertical joints. Corrosion-resistant metal ties are used to bond the brick veneer to the framework.

A common misconception is that 4″ brick veneer will stop all moisture penetration. It is important that you, as an inspector, know that brick is porous, absorptive material and that water can penetrate a brick veneer wall wherever there is a lack of material: settling cracks, between brick and mortar, bond cracks, and open mortar joints.

Water that penetrates a brick veneer wall is coming through the brick, mortar and through small cracks in the mortar. It doesn't matter how the moisture enters in the wall cavity, but it is important to have simple installation practices to prevent water problems. It is important that steps be taken to allow any moisture to drain from the wall. Water that penetrates the brickwork will travel down the back face of the bricks, be collected by through-wall flashing, and drain through exterior weep holes. It is important to keep mortar droppings out of the airspace and keep the area clear around the weep holes. The purpose of weep holes is to allow water that has been collected by the flashings and penetration to exit the wall system. Most codes require through-wall flashings; through wall flashing is required at the base of the wall, as well as at window and door lintels. Flashing is also required when brick veneer is installed above a roof.

Flashings are not always visible when inspecting the brick veneer, but weep holes are. If there are no weep holes or they have been plugged, the inspector should note it on the inspection report. Because the average homeowner or buyer does not know the importance of the weep holes, they may plug the weep holes so insects can't penetrate the house. However, it is important that the weep holes be left open for drainage.

Brick and stone should be laid in a full bed of mortar, with care taken to avoid dropping mortar into the space between the veneer and sheathing. The outside joints should be tooled to a smooth finish to get maximum resistance to water penetration. Masonry laid during cold weather should be protected from freezing until after the mortar has set up.

Masonry veneer should not support any vertical load other than the dead load of the veneer above. Veneer above openings (windows, doors, etc.) should be supported on lintels of noncombustible material; angle irons usually are used for the lintels.

When inspecting a structure constructed with a masonry veneer finish over wood, there are several areas to be observed. The inspector should move around the exterior, checking the corners of the frieze boards for open or mismatching corners, an indication of foundation movement. The inspector should sight along the length of the wall. Does it appear to be plumb? If not plumb, is the wall leaning out at the top or bowing in the center? This may indicate that (1) a foundation problem exists; (2) no wall ties were used when the wall was built; or (3) the house may have been rebuilt from the inside, possibly because of a fire. The inspector should pay strict attention when inspecting the interior, attic, crawlspace or basement for any signs of damage and report his or her findings.

The inspector should check that there are weep holes every 33″ on center, that masonry is sealed to window and door casings, and for any other wall penetrations.

The soil should be a minimum of 4″ below the brick line and slope away from the foundation approximately 6″ in 10′ for good drainage.

It is important that an inspector note all findings in writing.

Roofs

The roof serves as an enclosing surface between the interior and exterior of a structure. Structural loads result from equipment (i.e., solar collectors, mechanical equipment, signs) and external forces (i.e., wind, rain, snow, sun). The external surface of a dwelling may be required to have a fire resistance rating to prevent the spread of fire from one dwelling to another. The nature of the roof is a significant feature of the building's appearance. The roof provides a barrier against elements and controls the flow of moisture, heat, cold, and light. Thermal expansion and contraction can be a problem for connections and durability of roofing materials because solar radiation is a major factor. In areas subject to high winds or hurricanes, anchoring of the roof construction to the wall is critical to prevent uplift. The roof must also handle structural stress and movement due to expansive soils or seismic movement. A conventional roof is assembled on site, whereas a truss roof is prefabricated at a manufacturing facility and delivered to the site.

Roofs are classified on the relationship of the roof surface to the ceiling surface. Common roof-to-ceiling relationships are illustrated in Figure 4.34.

Roof configurations are sloping, flat, or arched. (See Figure 4.35.)

Common roof styles include the following:

- Shed roof—contains one sloping plane with no ridges, valleys, or gables.
- Mansard roof—contains two sloping planes with a different pitch on four sides.
- Gable roof—contains two sloping planes of the same pitch on each side of the ridge with a gable on each end. Normally, the gable has an attic vent.
- Gambrel roof—contains two sloping planes with a different pitch on each side of the ridge. The lower plane has a steeper slope than the upper plane. A gable is at each end.
- Hip roof—contains sloping planes with the same pitch on four sides. A hip roof has no gables.

■ **FIGURE 4.34**

Roofs are classified by the relationship of the roof surface to the ceiling surface.

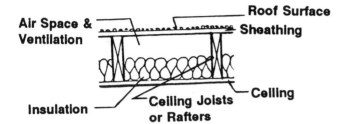

1. Roof surface and ceiling are opposite faces with air space between them.

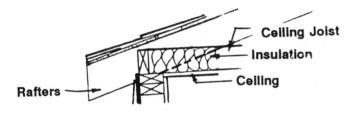

2. Structural elements support the roof and ceiling surfaces.

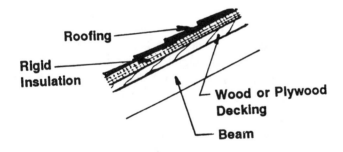

3. Structural elements are located under a deck, the underside of which is exposed as the ceiling.

- Flat roof—has little or no slope and is often referred to as a *dead level roof*. A flat roof may be within a parapet wall (extended wall) or end at the outer wall edge.
- Butterfly shed roof—contains two sloping shed-type roofs. The low side in the center causes a double pitch roof with a valley in the roof center.

Framing

In a conventional joist and rafter system, the spacing of the roof framing components affects the supporting wall structure but is not determined by the wall structure.

■ **FIGURE 4.35**

Common roof styles include flat, gable, shed, hip, gambrel, double pitch, and mansard.

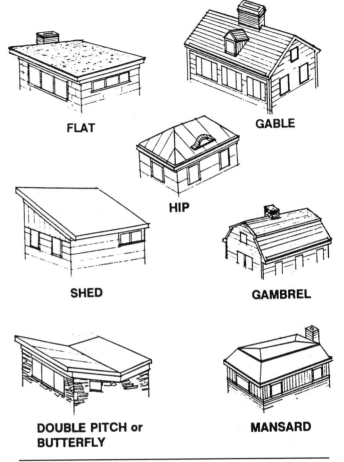

Beams, joists, rafters, and trusses are framing components generally used as light framing or more widely spaced at the same intervals as the columns or piers providing support. Ceiling joists and roof rafters are spaced 12″, 16″, or 24″ on centers. Joists span roughly one-half the width of the residential structure from the exterior wall to a center load-bearing wall, beam, or girder. Rafters are supported on exterior walls and bear against a ridge board at the high point of the roof. Rafters exert a thrusting force that tends to spread the outside walls. This thrust is resisted by the ceiling joists acting as ties from wall to wall and by the collar beams (ties). The sizes of joists and rafters depend on span, lumber species, spacing between joists and roof loads. Span can be reduced by installing purlins and braces between rafters and joists at load-bearing partitions. (See Figure 4.36.)

Joists and rafters can restrict flexibility of room planning because of the need for interior bearing walls.

■ **FIGURE 4.36**

Purlin and purlin braces.

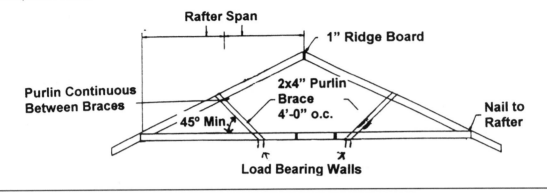

However, joists and rafters provide overhead space for installation of insulation and mechanical equipment and for expansion. Joist and rafter systems include the following (also see Figure 4.37):

- Ridge board—board at the top intersection that aligns and receives the rafters.
- Roof rafter—structural member that rests between the toprests on the top plate of the ridge board. Roof rafters support roof weight.
- Collar beam—lightweight structural member attached to rafters and used to brace opposite roof slopes. A collar beam or collar tie keeps the roof from spreading.

■ **FIGURE 4.37**

Joist and rafter systems consist of a ridgeboard, rafters, and a collar.

- Purlin—structural member laid horizontally to support roof rafters. Purlin braces connect to horizontal members and extend to ceiling joists at a load-bearing wall.
- Rafter anchors—various metal rafter anchors are used in roof construction. These devices help tie the rafter to the supporting wall. They are nailed to the rafter and to the top plates. (See Figure 4.38.)

Truss

Trusses require stress-rated members and must be built from engineered designs. Trusses are composed of framing members arranged in a series of triangles to form a roof. Individual framing members are connected by either wood or metal gusset plates, metal connectors, or gang nail plates. (See Figure 4.39.)

Truss systems consist of a lower chord and an upper chord, diagonals ("web members"), and gusset plates. Upper chords are the equivalent of collar beams and support rafter chords in the form of the letter W. All integral parts are assembled and held in place by gusset plates, bolt connections, or nails.

The truss supports greater roof loads and spans widths than do other framing systems. This span allows interior walls to be non-load-bearing and provides flexibility in placing and/or moving walls. Truss members are considerably smaller than their counterparts in a joist and rafter system and resist bending forces. Bending stresses are relatively small because of the structural action within a truss. Individual truss members resist compression and tension forces. (See Figure 4.40.)

In light framing, trusses are spaced 24″ to 48″ on center. Truss roof systems may be designed for flat or sloped roofs to receive membrane or shingle roofing

■ **FIGURE 4.38**

Metal roof anchors are devices that help tie the rafter to the supporting wall.

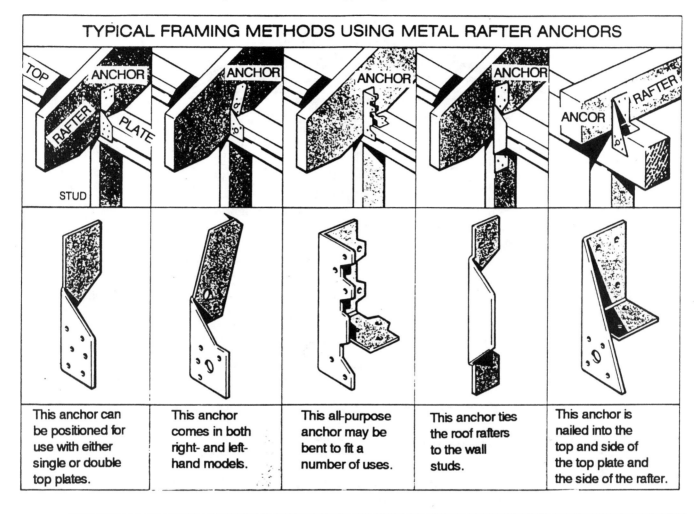

TYPICAL FRAMING METHODS USING METAL RAFTER ANCHORS

| This anchor can be positioned for use with either single or double top plates. | This anchor comes in both right- and left-hand models. | This all-purpose anchor may be bent to fit a number of uses. | This anchor ties the roof rafters to the wall studs. | This anchor is nailed into the top and side of the top plate and the side of the rafter. |

■ **FIGURE 4.39**

A truss is constructed of top chords, bottom chords, and web members tied together with gusset plates.

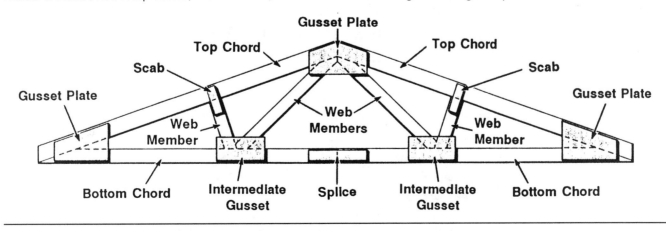

■ **FIGURE 4.40**

Roof trusses may span from exterior wall to exterior wall and do not require support from interior walls.

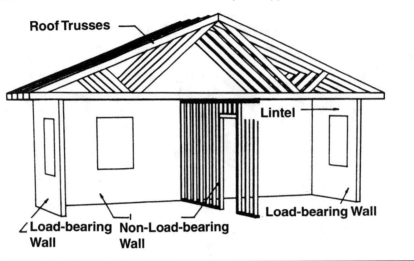

finishes. Truss roof systems commonly used in residential construction include the following (also see Figure 4.41.):

- King-post truss—consists of upper chord, lower chord, and center vertical post. Spans for this truss are

■ **FIGURE 4.41**

Roof trusses commonly used in residential construction are the king-post truss, W-type truss, and scissors truss.

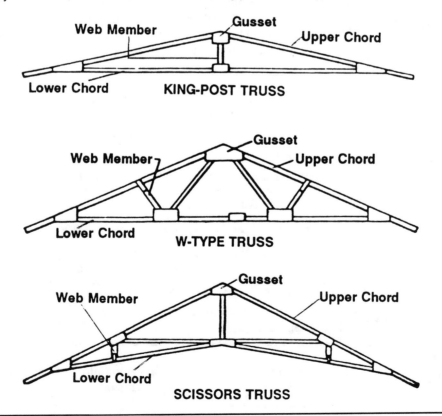

less than those for the W-truss when the same size materials are used. The king-post truss is normally used on low-sloping roof systems.

- W-type truss—most popular and extensively used light truss. Allows longer spans than the king-post truss.
- Scissors truss—used when a sloping ceiling is desired or if more clearance is desired under the center of the building.

Spacing for joist and rafter systems is 12″, 16″, and 24″ on center. Truss roof systems are on the same centers as joists and rafters and on some applications can extend to 48″ on center. Typical spacing for a truss roof system is 24″ on center, whereas typical spacing for a 2″ × 4″ stud wall is 16″ or 24″ on center. These dimensions are based on a 4′ × 8′ sheet of building material. Standardized construction materials and processes are used to reduce waste and building costs.

Gusset plates anchor the truss together. If the webs are removed, the truss and roof are no longer stable and will sag. Trusses should not be cut or drilled.

Most truss roofs are low sloping roofs because the web members will not allow for any storage space in the attic. The steeper pitched roofs are hardly ever truss. Usually they are stick built to allow for possible installation of the central heat and for storage space.

Insulation

All residential structures should be insulated. Insulation should be installed during construction; however, many older structures may require additional insulation. Insulation thickness determines the R-value. R-value indicates the resistance to heat loss. For example, loose or blown fiberglass insulation has an R-value of R-3 per inch or R-3.3 per inch in blankets or batts. Ten inches of insulation would have an R-value of R-30 (R-3 per inch × 10″ = R-30). Walls, floors, and roofs have a thermal insulation value that is enhanced by insulation material. (See Figure 4.42.)

Insulation is recommended in the northern states owing to the cold temperatures and in the southern states owing to the hot temperatures. The same R-value of insulation is required for protection against either hot or cold temperatures.

Calculation of heat loss or heat gain must consider thermal resistance (RT) of the construction assembly and air temperature differential. Other critical factors that must be considered are:

- building orientation, which affects solar heat gain and wind exposure, air movement, and infiltration;
- latent heat sources and heat gain from occupants, equipment, and lighting;
- surface color, reflectivity, and heat from building materials; and
- amount of insulation.

Insulating materials are categorized as follows:

- Batt or blanket—glass, mineral wool, or wood fibers, enclosed by paper and/or aluminum foil with or without a vapor barrier. Used to fill air spaces in walls, floors, attics, or roofs. (See Figure 4.43.)
- Board or sheet—glass, mineral fibers, foamed plastics, sheet plastics, wood, or cork with or without a vapor barrier. Used as wall sheathing for cavity fill, rigid roof insulation, and perimeter slab insulation. (See Figure 4.44.)
- Loose fill—vermiculite, perlite, glass, or mineral wool, and shredded wood. Used to fill wall cavities and flat areas above ceilings. (See Figure 4.45.)
- Reflective—aluminum foil combined in layers with air spaces. Used for roofs, walls, and floors above vented or unheated spaces. (See Figure 4.46.)
- Foam—concrete and plastics. Used for roof decks and irregular spaces. (See Figure 4.47.)

Sheathing

Roof sheathing is covering over rafters or trusses and usually consists of lumber or plywood. Wood roof planking or fiber board roof decking might be used on flat or low-pitched roofs. Diagonal wood sheathing used on flat or low-pitched roofs provides resistance against high winds. Sheathing should be thick enough to span between supports and provide a solid base for roofing material. It is standard practice to use 1″ × 4″ furring strips spaced on 4″ centers when wood shakes or shingles are used in damp climates, to provide ventilation for roofing material. The shingles or shakes are nailed to the furring strip. Plywood roof sheathing should be laid with the face grain perpendicular to rafters. Plywood roof sheathing should have an exterior glue line. End joints must be constructed over rafter centers and staggered. Edge joints should be supported by blocking between the joists or rafters or with the use of plyclips or H-clips between rafters.

Windows and Doors

Windows and doors are usually purchased as package units. Packaged windows are in frames complete with glass, exterior casing, and hardware. Wood

■ **FIGURE 4.42**

Residential structures use construction materials with varying thermal resistivity (R-value).

Material	Material	Resistivity
Thermal Resistivities of Construction Materials		
Wood	Plywood	1.25
	Hardwood	0.91
	Softwood	1.25
Concrete	Mortar -	0.20
	Stucco	0.20
	W/Lt. Wt. Aggregate	0.59
	Sand, Gravel Aggregate	0.11
	Masonry Common Brick	0.20
	Concrete Block	1.11
	Concrete Block w/ Lt. Wt. Aggregate	2.00
	Plaster	0.20
	Gypsum or Plaster Board (5/8 inches)	0.39
	Gypsum or Plaster Board (1/2 inches)	0.32
	Glass (Single Pane)	0.88
Finish	Carpet	2.08
Flooring	Cork (1/8 inches)	0.05
	Vinyl	0.05
Roofing	Asphalt Shingle	0.44
	Wood Shingle	0.87
	Slate	0.05
	Built-Up Roof	0.33
Air Space	Between Non-Reflective Surfaces	1.34
	Between Non-Reflective and Reflective Surfaces	4.64
Insulating Materials	Batt. (Mineral Wool)	3.12
	Loosefill (Mineral Wool)	3.70
	Perlite	2.78
	Boards (Glass Fiber)	4.17
	Expanded Polystyrene	4.00
	Mineral Fiberboard	2.94

doors may be prehung in a door frame with hinges installed or doors and frames may be purchased separately. Metal doors and windows and their frames are purchased as a complete packaged unit. Door casings usually have to be assembled. Rough openings for doors and windows must be sized correctly when framing is installed to allow for proper installation. Exterior doors and windows must have flashing (weather stripping, caulking, vinyl inserts) to seal casings to studs, headers, and sills to prevent water penetration and air infiltration. Doors and windows must have a seal to prevent air infiltration and water penetration. Felt paper is often used for flashing material in areas that are protected by siding and interior wall finish. The tops of exterior windows and doors should use a corrosion-resistant flashing to cover the drip cap.

Windows

Windows slide horizontally or vertically. Window frames are made from steel, aluminum or wood. Window quality depends on construction, security, and insulating factors. Window styles used in residential construction include the following (See Figure 4.48):

- Single hung window—sash window with movable bottom sash (not shown).

■ **FIGURE 4.43**

Batt or blanket glass or mineral wool is used to fill airspaces.

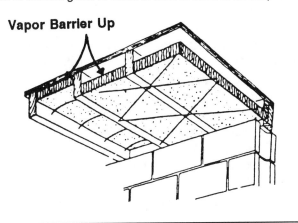

■ **FIGURE 4.45**

Ventilation spacer is used to provide air flow over insulation.

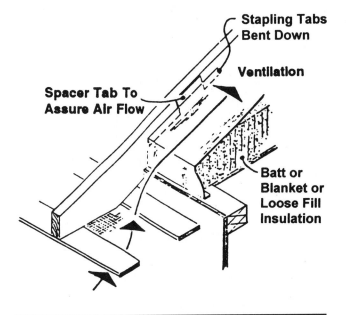

- Double hung window—sash window with two vertically sliding sashes. Both single and double hung window sashes are held in place by sash frame friction controlled by springs and/or weights.
- Glider window—sash window that opens by moving horizontally (not shown).
- Casement window—window having hinged sash that operates similarly to a door.
- Jalousie window—window formed by horizontal slats of glass that open and close horizontally by a handle driving a gear assembly.
- Fixed window—framed window that will not open and close.
- Awning window—window with sash hinged horizontally; opens from bottom to top.

- Ribbon window—window used in basement walls and bathrooms.
- Bow window—a single window that bows outward from the exterior wall.
- Bay window—a combination of three or more windows that extend outward from the exterior wall. These windows have special framing requirements.

Double Pane or Thermopane Windows

Double pane or Thermopane windows are windows that are hermetically sealed with a vacuum between two

■ **FIGURE 4.44**

Foam sheathing is used as wall sheathing.

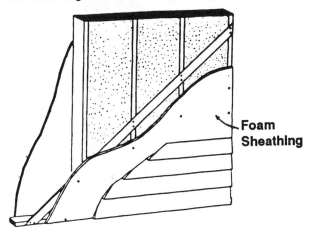

■ **FIGURE 4.46**

Reflective aluminum foil combined in layers with air space.

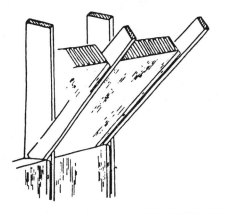

■ **FIGURE 4.47**

Foam concrete and plastics.

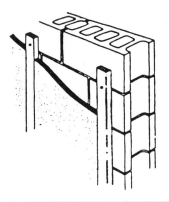

pieces of glass. This increases the R-value of the window unit. Doors can be made of wood or metal. If the seal is broken, a window will acquire moisture between the pieces of glass and in time will discolor.

When inspecting double pane or Thermopane windows, observers may see "rainbows" by daylight reflection. A similar effect can be seen at the point of tangency of the airspace surfaces in a collapsed insulating glass unit. This is a different phenomenon. On occasion, moisture-stained glass with "iridescence" is confused with interference fringes. Interference fringes are an optical phenomenon characterized by light, rainbow-like color patterns on double-glazed windows. Such fringes will appear, disappear, and reappear as lighting or viewing angle changes. However, actual fringes can

■ **FIGURE 4.48**

Windows used in residential construction include bay, bow, fixed, casement, awning, ribbon, double hung, and jalousie.

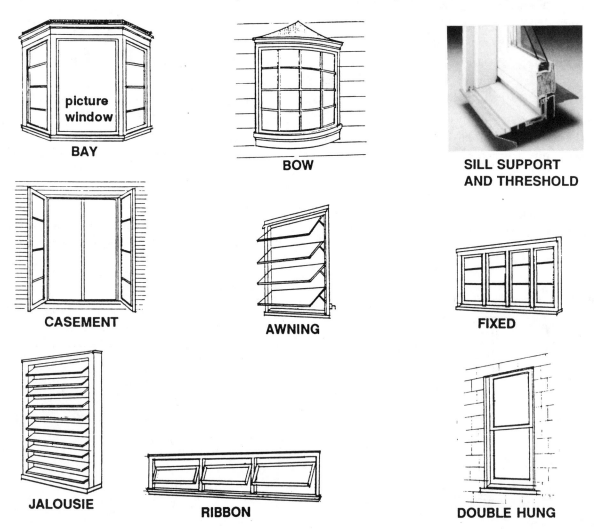

■ **FIGURE 4.49**

Basic door styles used in residential structures are flush doors, doors with glass inserts, and doors with louvered inserts.

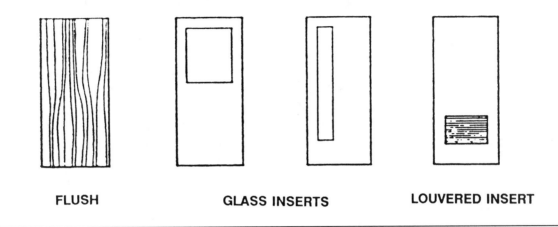

FLUSH   **GLASS INSERTS**   **LOUVERED INSERT**

be early identified by depressing the affected area. If the color pattern noted originally is indeed due to interference fringes, it will move or disappear, whereas stain that is permanently fixed will not disappear from view at the same viewing angle.

Interference fringes are sometimes referred to as *Brewster's fringes, Newton rings, Jamen fringes,* or *optical interference.* Interference fringes are caused by the reflection from two glass panels of almost identical thickness placed close together in parallel planes, as in insulated glass units. Actually, when two pieces of glass vary from each other in thickness up to only .0002″ (two ten thousandths of an inch), and are placed in matching, superimposed locations, there is a possibility of such fringes appearing under certain viewing conditions.

Some of these conditions are as follows:

- There must be at least two panels of glass in parallel planes.
- The panels must be of identical thickness within .0002″.
- There must be a reflection of light—this phenomenon does not occur with light transmission for all practical purposes.
- Viewing must be from a fairly acute angle.
- The background (behind the glass) should be dark.
- The reflecting light source must be diffused and monochromatic—such as fluorescent lights or high, overcast, single-color sky.

Doors

Door styles must be compatible with the house design. There are five basic door styles. (See Figure 4.49.)

1. Paneled door—Paneled doors may be used on both the interior and the exterior. Most interior paneled doors consist of solid wood or plywood with raised or flat panels. Exterior doors frequently have one or more panels of glass.
2. Solid core flush door—Solid core flush doors are flat on both sides, although some flush doors are flush on one side and paneled on the other. Flush doors are commonly veneered with a core of wood, glued together with staggered joints. The wood strips are glued to the sides, top, and bottom to create a smooth surface that can be cut and planed. The front and back faces are covered with a veneer on both the interior and the exterior surfaces. Solid core doors or fire-rated doors are used to separate a garage from living space.
3. Hollow core doors—Hollow core doors are flush doors with a core that consists of a grid of crossed wooden or cardboard slats. The door edges are solid wood and made to accommodate locks and hinges. The door faces are 3-ply plywood produced from various hardwoods. Hollow core doors are lighter than solid core doors and are used as interior doors. A hollow core door should never be used for exterior installation.
4. Louvered door—Louvered doors are interior doors used on closets or where air circulation is

required. Louvers are small slats of wood installed horizontally and angled in the door frame to allow air flow.

5. Sliding glass patio doors—Sliding glass doors have a metal frame with provisions for one door to be stationary and the other door to rest on a metal glide in the threshold. The sliding door moves on the glide by means of rollers that are adjustable for ease of movement. Sliding patio doors should have a sliding screen door that operates the same as the glass door. Most sliding doors can be removed from the frame by lifting the door up and pushing the bottom of the door outward. Sliding glass patio doors should be safety glass.

Interior door thickness is 1⅜″, and exterior door thickness is 1¾″. Wooden doors are manufactured from mahogany, birch, ash or oak. Metal doors are manufactured and used as exterior doors.

Fireplaces

Fireplaces are constructed of solid masonry, stone, brick, reinforced concrete, factory-built metal, or a combination of masonry with a metal insert. A normal fireplace uses only about 10 percent of the energy in the fuel to provide heat to occupants. High-efficiency circulating fireplaces can heat small homes. A circulating fireplace contains a metal insert that circulates heat by fan or by convection.

Fireplaces with gas logs must have a damper block on the damper to prevent the damper from closing. This device eliminates any risks of operating gas logs with a closed damper and dumping flue gases into the dwelling. When gas logs are present in a fireplace, the inspector should observe the damper block and report if it is not present.

Improperly built fireplaces are dangerous if they do not draw properly. They will smoke and may be a serious fire and safety hazard. Careful attention must be given to fireplace construction.

Fireplace fires are caused by thin walls, combustible materials, wood mantels, unsafe hearths, and broken or missing dampers. Hazardous conditions also occur when the firebox and flue are not properly installed and sealed. Fireplaces currently built include the following:

- Freestanding fireplaces—prefabricated metal, self-contained, and available in various designs. These fireplaces have an exposed flue that rises through either the ceiling or wall to the exterior. Freestanding fireplaces must be set on noncombustible bases.
- Open-front fireplaces—the most common fireplace. An open front fireplace is constructed of either masonry or prefabricated metal.
- Open-two-sided fireplaces—may be cantilevered or post-supported and are bidirectional.
- Open-three-sided fireplaces—may be cantilevered or post-supported and seen from multidirections.
- Open-four-sided fireplaces—have metal fireplace hood and flue. Depending on their form and proportions, open-four-sided fireplaces may be suspended from above and may be omnidirectional.
- Prefabricated fireplaces—have metal exteriors with heat-resistant insulating fibers and are used in all standard building construction systems. Prefabricated fireplaces are freestanding or open front.

Fireplace openings are 29″ or 33″ high. Hearth sizes are 30″ to 36″ wide and 16″ deep and the flue size is 12″ round. An inadequate flue size may cause malfunctions.

Masonry

Masonry fireplaces are constructed from solid masonry, bricks, stone, reinforced concrete, and mortar. Masonry fireplaces require a foundation. The fireplace is built after the foundation has cured. Masonry over a fireplace opening is supported by a lintel of noncombustible material, normally an angle iron. (See Figure 4.50.)

At or near the floor level, a hearth extension is constructed of brick, concrete, tile, stone, or other noncombustible material. The hearth extension must extend at least 16″ in front of a standard fireplace (30″ to 36″) opening and at least 8″ on either side of the opening.

Wood framing and combustible materials must be at least 2″ from the outside face of the fireplace and from the back surface of the fireplace. Combustible materials must be at least 6″ from the inside surface of the flue liner. All spaces between masonry fireplaces and wood beams, headers, joists, or trimming must be firestopped using noncombustible material.

The firebox must be constructed of firebrick. The flue should be centered over the fireplace to avoid uneven drafts. The flue sides and smoke chamber should be smooth to minimize warm air current and smoke drag. Flue sides should slope inward at about a 60° angle from the damper ends to the flue inner faces.

The flue front should slope inward. The smoke shelf should deflect downdrafts of cool air close to the flue walls upward to mix with rising hot air. The damper

■ **FIGURE 4.50**

Masonry fireplaces require a concrete foundation.

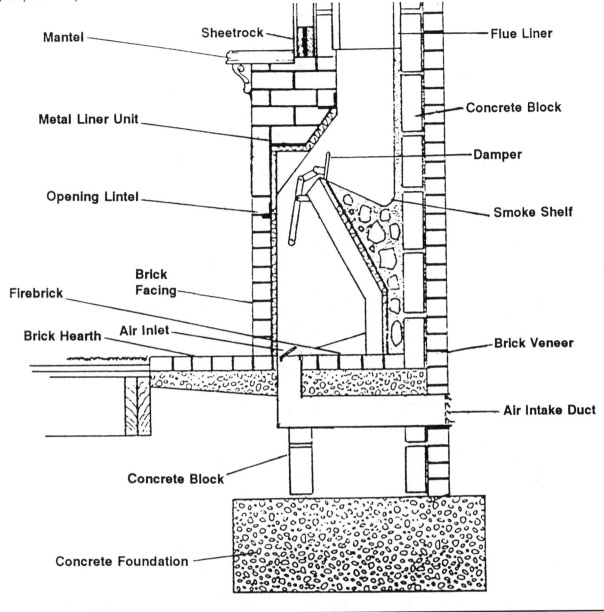

should regulate fireplace draft and be placed forward to form a smoke shelf.

Fireplace walls should not be less than 8″ thick and not less than 12″ thick if built from stone or hollow masonry units. All wall faces exposed to fire should be lined with firebrick or other fire-resistive material.

The back width of the fireplace is usually narrower than the front by approximately 6″ to 8″ to guide smoke and odors toward the rear of the firebox. The back wall of the firebox should be vertical for approximately 12″

to 14″ and taper forward toward the upper section of the fireplace. The throat area should be about 1⅓ times the flue area to promote draft.

Heat loss up the chimney is reduced if an adjustable damper is used to control the opening. The smoke shelf prevents backdrafts. The smoke shelf is concave to retain any slight amount of rain that may enter the chimney. To function properly, the smoke shelf should be 8″ above the top of the fireplace opening.

Prefabricated fireplaces are often used in new residential structures to provide high-energy-efficient heating.

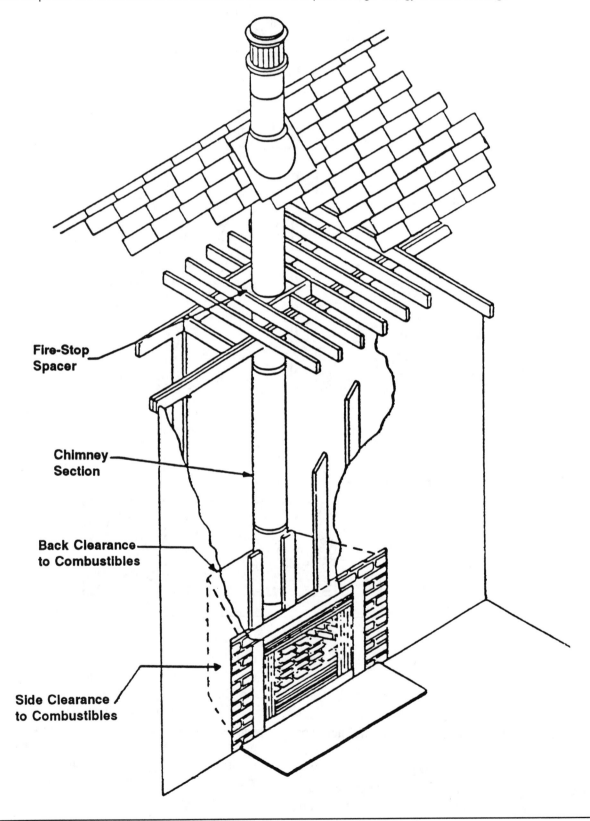

Fire-Stop Spacer

Chimney Section

Back Clearance to Combustibles

Side Clearance to Combustibles

Prefabricated

Factory-built metal fireplaces consist of a fire chamber assembly and roof assembly. The fire chamber assembly (firebox) is installed to provide clearance to combustible materials. If the fireplace chimney extends through floors and ceilings, factory-furnished firestops or firestop spacers must be installed. Hearth extensions should be hollow metal, tile, brick, stone, or other noncombustible material.

Prefabricated metal fireplaces are available in freestanding, built-in and insert designs. Prefabricated metal fireplaces emit either radiant heat or convection heat. Radiant heat is infrared energy that is emitted from outer surfaces of a solid-fuel-burning fireplace. When this energy encounters physical objects, it is transformed into heat and absorbed by the objects. Convection heat is heated air; when air molecules are heated, the radiant energy is given off. Convection heat fireplaces have a firebox separated from the outer surfaces by an air space or a convection chamber. (See Figure 4.51.)

The convection chamber collects cool air at the bottom and forces heated air to reenter rooms from the top. The convection fireplace may also be equipped with a blower and vents to adjacent rooms.

All prefabricated metal fireplaces must be approved by Underwriters Laboratory (UL). Prefabricated fireplaces require approved noncombustible material to line firebox walls and floors. All prefabricated fireplaces must be properly sealed for fire safety.

Chimneys

Chimneys and vents must permit proper draft. Chimneys and vents must be structurally safe, durable, smoke-tight, and capable of withstanding the action of flue gases. Mortars used in chimneys may erode, causing cracks to open in the masonry and allowing flue gases to be diverted. Flue linings provide a smoother flow and greater protection from leakage.

The greater the temperature differences between chimney gases and outside atmosphere, the better the draft. The interior chimney has better draft because masonry retains heat longer. The chimney height and the flue size are important factors in providing sufficient draft.

Masonry chimneys must be constructed of solid masonry units or reinforced concrete walls not less than

4" in thickness. All chimneys are required to extend at least 3' above the point where they pass through the roof of the building and at least 2' higher than any portion of the building within 10'. (See Figure 4.52.)

Masonry chimneys must be lined with fireclay flue liners at least ⅝" thick, unless the chimney wall is 8" thick. To prevent moisture from entering between the bricks or between the bricks and its flue liner, a mortar cap is usually placed over the top course of brick. The chimney exterior brick should be inspected through the attic and roof section. Masonry chimneys are often not constructed properly through the attic.

Fireplace flues must not be smaller in diameter than recommended by the manufacturer. Flue size is based on the fireplace face opening (width × height) and the flue shape. For example, a 36" × 44" fireplace opening has an 11 sq. ft. or 1,584 sq. in. area. A chimney with a round flue liner must have a 15" diameter flue or provide an area of 176 sq. in. A square flue liner must be 13" × 18" or provide an area of 234 sq. in. If the chimney is unlined, the flue must be 12" × 18" or have an area of 216 sq. in.

■ **FIGURE 4.52**

Chimney height must extend 3' above the point where it passes through the roof of the building and be at least 2' higher than any portion of the building within 10'.

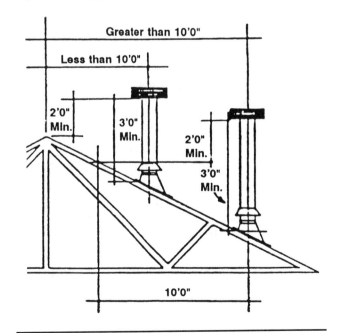

■ REVIEW QUESTIONS*

Wood

1. Softwood trees include

   A. pine.
   B. fir.
   C. cedar.
   D. All of the above
   E. None of the above

2. Decay and dry rot develop when moisture conditions exist.

   A. True
   B. False

3. Musty smells are associated with high humidity and decay.

   A. True
   B. False

Construction

1. In building a frame or wooden skeleton, studs rest on the sills, which are secured to the foundation wall.

   A. True
   B. False

2. Plugging vents in a pier-and-beam house

   A. is a desirable way to lower heating and cooling bills.
   B. helps dry out the crawlspace.
   C. may cause moisture and mildew problems in the crawlspace.

3. Exterior walls of a frame residence include wooden members called

   A. studs.
   B. stringers.
   C. Neither A nor B

4. A 2″ × 4″ board used as a stud would be ⅝″ × 3½″ because of surfacing operations.

   A. True
   B. False

5. The top horizontal board that aligns and receives the rafters is called the _____.

6. Which of the following items should an inspector write on the inspection report?

   A. Beam that does not rest on a pier
   B. Twisted floor joist
   C. Signs of wood rot
   D. All of the above
   E. None of the above

7. The truss roof system has four parts.

   A. True
   B. False

8. Name the four parts of a truss roof.

   _____

   _____

   _____

   _____

9. Windows and doors do not require flashing on homes with contemporary wood siding.

   A. True
   B. False

10. What are the two basic types of fireplaces?

    _____

    _____

11. Minimum chimney height above the roof line is three feet.

    A. True
    B. False

---

*Answers to all of the chapter review questions are located in Appendix C at the back of this book.

12. Water penetration into a home may be caused by

    A. a leaking roof.
    B. improper drainage.
    C. windows and doors not properly flashed.
    D. All of the above

13. All wood contains water.

    A. True
    B. False

14. Fungi and termites are often found together because they require similar environmental conditions.

    A. True
    B. False

15. A real estate inspector must be familiar with registered grade trademarks.

    A. True
    B. False

16. A nonpressure wood preservative process is acceptable for lumber used in contact with the ground.

    A. True
    B. False

17. Decay fungi cannot seriously damage wood that has a moisture content below what percentage?

    A. 8 percent
    B. 20 percent
    C. 25 percent
    D. None of the above

18. The system of construction in which studs are continuous from foundation to roof is generally termed

    A. balloon framing.
    B. western framing.
    C. platform framing.
    D. pole framing.

19. The board that rests on the perimeter of a concrete slab floor would be the

    A. floor joist.
    B. stud.
    C. sill plate.
    D. subfloor.

20. The maximum allowable moisture content of seasoned lumber is

    A. 8 percent.
    B. 14 percent.
    C. 19 percent.
    D. 24 percent.

21. Rafter boards pulling away from the ridge board may indicate foundation movement.

    A. True
    B. False

22. Some woods demonstrate a natural resistance to fungus attacks.

    A. True
    B. False

23. Floor systems using steel channels require bridging to prevent racking.

    A. True
    B. False

24. The metal channel that supports the metal studs is called

    A. sole plate.
    B. track.
    C. sill plate.

25. Where would you find the heel-joint connections?

    A. Header joist connection
    B. Ceiling joist connection to rafter
    C. Blocking connection

26. Cold form steel has a galvanized coating to protect it from corrosion.

    A. True
    B. False

EIFS

1. The most common areas where failures develop in EIFS are:

   A. chimneys.
   B. roof rakes.
   C. around windows and doors.
   D. All of the above.
   E. None of the above.

2. EIFS should be a minimum of _____ inches above finish grade.

   A. 4 inches
   B. 2 inches
   C. 8 inches

3. Sealants used to repair EIFS walls should be approved by the manufacturer.

   A. True
   B. False

4. Ladders can dent, puncture, or scar EIFS.

   A. True
   B. False

5. Backwrapping onto the back side of the insulation board should be a minimum of 2½″.

   A. True
   B. False

■ INSPECTION CHECKLIST

Wood and Construction

BRICK VENEER

Yes No

- ☐ ☐ Is mortar soft?
- ☐ ☐ Is there brick separation around mortar joints or windows?
- ☐ ☐ Are walls buckled?
- ☐ ☐ Are there missing bricks?
- ☐ ☐ Are windows caulked properly next to brick? Check for water penetration inside the residential structure.
- ☐ ☐ Are mortar joints damaged? Check for signs of a previous fire.
- ☐ ☐ Do brick walls have weep holes? Check that weep holes are not caulked over. If walls do not have weep holes, inform the purchaser that there may be a mildew odor.
- ☐ ☐ Was Mexican adobe brick used? Describe brick damage on the report.

WOOD SIDING

Yes No

- ☐ ☐ Is wood siding securely fastened and not buckling or pulling away?
- ☐ ☐ Does wood siding have missing knots?
- ☐ ☐ Is flashing missing around windows or doors on contemporary wood siding structures? Check for water penetration on the inside of the residential structure.
- ☐ ☐ Is rough cedar siding used?
- ☐ ☐ Is fiber board or Masonite siding used?
- ☐ ☐ Is plywood siding used? Check plies for separation and proper grade stamp.
- ☐ ☐ Is asbestos siding used? Check for broken pieces.

ROOF

Yes No

- ☐ ☐ Are there dips or sags in the roof? Check roof structure in sag areas.
- ☐ ☐ Is plywood used for roof decking?
- ☐ ☐ Does plywood have proper grade stamp (if visible)?

METAL FRAMING

Yes No

- ☐ ☐ Is the metal joist properly supported?
- ☐ ☐ Are the bridging and web stiffeners and are all connections made using the proper angle plates or gussets and screws?
- ☐ ☐ Are roof rafters properly supported?
- ☐ ☐ Any evidence of thermal bridging such as streaking on drywall?
- ☐ ☐ Is there any evidence of moisture and mold forming?

CORNICE

Yes No

- ☐ ☐ Is there damage to fascia board? Check for boards pulling away at corners.
- ☐ ☐ Are soffits wet and buckled?
- ☐ ☐ Are soffit vents open and securely fastened?

WOOD SHUTTERS

Yes No

- ☐ ☐ Are wood shutters securely fastened to the residential structure? Check shutters for damage.

RAFTERS AND TRUSSES

Yes No

- ☐ ☐ Are rafters pulling away from ridge board? A structural engineer must be consulted for structural problems.
- ☐ ☐ If there are splices, is every splice supported?

  Note: *A splice that is overlapped 3' on either side and properly nailed does not necessarily need to be supported.*

- ☐ ☐ Is furnace hung from a rafter? If so, the furnace must be properly supported, including purlins and supports.
- ☐ ☐ Is there a crack or a split in a rafter?
- ☐ ☐ Is there a metal fireplace with a brick chimney on the roof? If the chimney is not bricked

through the attic, rafters must be properly supported.

Yes No

☐ ☐ Has a new roof been applied over an existing roof covering? Check for cracks in the rafters.

☐ ☐ Is a collar beam missing? Check whether rafters are pulling away from the ridge board.

☐ ☐ Is a ridge board scabbed? Check that rafters are tightly connected.

☐ ☐ Are supports cut on a trussed roof? Indicate these deficiencies on the report.

SOFFITS AND SKYLIGHTS

Yes No

☐ ☐ Is there insulation in the soffit? Insulation holds moisture and could cause rotting.

☐ ☐ Is the skylight tunnel insulated?

☐ ☐ Are there signs of water penetration?

☐ ☐ Is skylight flashed properly?

☐ ☐ When roof pitch is under 4/12, is skylight on a 4″ curb?

CEILING JOISTS

Yes No

☐ ☐ Are there cracks or splits? Ceiling joists will probably be covered with insulation and will not be visible. Indicate damage on the report.

☐ ☐ When trusses are present with a pull-down stair, were trusses cut?

☐ ☐ Is the roof built without trusses? If so, it is common to splice ceiling joists over an inside load-bearing wall. Splices must overlap and be securely fastened to joists.

☐ ☐ Are there signs of a sagging roof? If so, recommend that a structural engineer inspect the roof.

DRAINAGE

Yes No

☐ ☐ Is water standing around or under the house?

☐ ☐ Is soil sloped away from foundation?

☐ ☐ Is there movement in the water meter with all water turned off in house?

☐ ☐ Any evidence of a sewer line leak?

☐ ☐ Is condensate drain line from HVAC properly terminated?

VENTILATION

Yes No

☐ ☐ Is the crawlspace vented? Mildew problems develop without proper ventilation. Residential structures with additions require careful attention.

☐ ☐ Is there a vapor barrier?

☐ ☐ Is the crawlspace used as a return air chamber for the heating and air-conditioning equipment?

☐ ☐ Are vent openings covered? Vent openings must be open to allow circulation.

☐ ☐ Are vent screens in place?

☐ ☐ Are there vents within 3′ of each corner of foundation wall?

FLOOR JOISTS, GIRDERS, AND SILL PLATES

Yes No

☐ ☐ Is there a musty odor present in the crawlspace, basement, or house?

☐ ☐ Have the girders been notched?

☐ ☐ Have the floor joists been notched?

☐ ☐ Are floor joists warped or twisted?

☐ ☐ Is there water damage to sills and floor joists under exterior doors, sliding doors, patios, and windows?

SUBFLOORING

Yes No

☐ ☐ Is the subflooring warped or damaged?

☐ ☐ Is the subflooring loose or in need of repair?

☐ ☐ Is there evidence of a leak under bathrooms, kitchen, or utility room?

WINDOWS

Yes No

☐ ☐ Are windowsills and casings damaged? Improperly flashed windows can allow water penetration.

☐ ☐ Do windows have gaps along casing?

☐ ☐ Are windows damaged?

☐ ☐ Are windows equipped with burglar bars?

☐ ☐ Do burglar bars open? At least one in each room should be able to be opened to the outside without the use of keys or tools.

Yes No

☐ ☐ Is there condensation or fogging between the glass layers of Thermopane windows? This indicates a broken seal, and the window should be replaced.

☐ ☐ Does the home have wooden windows? Check that windows are operable. Note windows that are painted shut. Recommend that at least one window operate in each bedroom. Also check the condition of the glazing, rope pulleys, and locks.

☐ ☐ Does the residential structure have crank windows? Check operation of windows.

☐ ☐ Does the residential structure have leaded windows? Check flatness of glass panels.

☐ ☐ All windows should be properly screened.

DOORS

Yes No

☐ ☐ Is veneer in good condition? Note weather damage.

☐ ☐ Are there paneling cracks in solid doors?

☐ ☐ Do doors have leaded glass? Check for buckling.

☐ ☐ Do exterior doors lock or latch properly?

☐ ☐ Do exterior doors have weather stripping?

☐ ☐ Is there physical damage, such as holes?

☐ ☐ Do doors fit properly? Wear at the top of a door or a striker plate that is repositioned could indicate foundation problems.

☐ ☐ Are doors equipped with burglar bars?

GLASS SLIDING DOORS

Yes No

☐ ☐ Do glass sliding doors roll and lock easily?

☐ ☐ Do sliding screens operate?

☐ ☐ Is the weather seal between frame and glass intact? Check both sliding and stationary sides.

☐ ☐ Is there visible damage?

FLOORING

Yes No

☐ ☐ Is there a fall in rooms? It could indicate foundation problems or girder problems.

☐ ☐ Are there squeaky wooden floors in a pier-and-beam or screeded slab foundation? Squeaks indicate lack of nailing on sub-flooring, particularly on plywood subflooring.

WALLS

Yes No

☐ ☐ Are there horizontal cracks in sheetrock or exterior brick? Cracks could indicate foundation or structural problems.

☐ ☐ Is sheetrock pulling away and gaping in the corners of rooms or closets? This could indicate either foundation or structural problems.

☐ ☐ Are there diagonal cracks at windows or doors?

☐ ☐ Are walls buckled?

MILDEW

Yes No

☐ ☐ Are there indications of mildew? Mildew will leave black spots on sheetrock. Check closets and laundry rooms, particularly along the baseboard next to the washer. Mildew inside a residential structure is caused by water penetration, saunas, laundry-room leaks, and humid climates (lack of dehumidification).

WATER PENETRATION

Yes No

☐ ☐ Check for water penetration by examining tackstrip and carpet. Report signs of water penetration. Water penetration is caused by improper drainage, windows and doors that are not flashed properly, a leaky roof, or sunken rooms not sealed properly.

Yes No

☐ ☐ Is the earth grade against the outside brick? Check carpet along the wall in area for water penetration.

☐ ☐ Are there sunken rooms? Check carpet.

☐ ☐ Do you suspect water penetration along windows and doors?

☐ ☐ Is there a prefab fireplace on an outside wall? There may be water penetration if it is not sealed properly.

FIREPLACE

Yes No

☐ ☐ Does the fireplace have a damper?

☐ ☐ Does the damper operate properly?

☐ ☐ Does the fireplace have an operable gas starter?

☐ ☐ Does the fireplace have gas logs?

☐ ☐ If gas logs are present, does the fireplace damper have a damper block?

☐ ☐ Is the smoke shelf positioned properly?

☐ ☐ Is the firebrick securely in place?

Yes No

☐ ☐ Is the lintel sealed? Check the condition of the facebrick or stone and the condition of the hearth.

☐ ☐ Is the chimney in the attic sealed?

☐ ☐ Does the metal chimney use a triple-walled vent pipe?

☐ ☐ Is there proper clearance between combustibles and metal pipe?

☐ ☐ Is the fireplace metal? Has it been over-heated? Check the metal liner for buckling.

☐ ☐ Is the chimney height adequate? Check the chimney height over the roof line. If the chimney is within 10′ of the peak, the chimney must extend 2′ above the roof.

☐ ☐ Is there a buildup of creosote?

☐ ☐ Is there an exterior mounted glass door?

☐ ☐ Is the mortar cap solid and sloped away from the brick? This prevents water from seeping through and damaging the mortar.

☐ ☐ Is the brick chimney pulling away from the house? This is a sign of foundation problems.

☐ ☐ Does the residential structure have a coal fireplace? If so, inform the purchaser.

■ REPORTING GUIDELINES

Inspection reporting guidelines for structural system (construction—walls, doors, ceilings, floors) and fireplaces incorporating the above checklist:

Interior walls, doors, ceilings and floors. The inspector shall

- report as in need of repair deficiencies of the surfaces of walls, ceilings and floors as related to structural performance or water penetration that are present and visible;

- report as in need of repair accessible doors that do not operate properly, excluding locks and latches;

- report as in need of repair deficiencies in steps, stairways, balconies, and railings;

- report as in need of repair spacings between intermediate balusters, spindles, or rails for steps, stairways, balconies, and railings that permit passage of an object greater than 4″ in diameter; and

- report as in need of repair the absence of safety glass in hazardous locations.

■ REPORTING GUIDELINES *(Continued)*

Specific limitations for interior walls, doors, ceilings and floors. The inspector is not required to do the following:

- Determine the condition of floor, wall, or ceiling coverings unless such conditions affect structural performance or indicate water penetration
- Report obvious damage to floor, wall, or ceiling coverings
- Determine the condition of paints, stains, and other surface coatings
- Determine condition of cabinets

Exterior walls and doors, windows and door glazing. The inspector shall

- report as in need of repair present and visible deficiencies of exterior walls that are related to structural performance and water penetration;
- report as in need of repair deficiencies in the condition and operation of exterior doors and garage doors, including door locks and latches when present;
- report as in need of repair damaged glazing in windows and exterior doors;
- report as in need of repair any insulated windows that are obviously fogged or display other evidence of broken seals;
- report as in need of repair the absence of safety glass in hazardous locations;
- report as in need of repair missing or damaged window and door screens;
- report as in need of repair in homes having burglar bars the absence of functional keyless burglar bars in appropriate locations;
- report as in need of repair inoperable windows at burglar bar locations of sleeping rooms or egress areas and any inoperable windows at other randomly sampled accessible burglar bar locations; and
- report as in need of repair spacings between intermediate balusters, spindles, and rails that permit passage of an object greater than 4″ in diameter.

Specific limitations for exterior walls and doors, windows, and door glazing. The inspector is not required to do the following:

- Report the condition or presence of storm windows or doors, awnings, shutters, or security devices or systems
- Determine the condition of paints, stains, or other surface coatings
- Determine the presence of, or extent or type of, insulation or vapor barriers in exterior walls

Fireplace and chimney. The inspector shall

- report as in need of repair deficiencies in the visible components and structure of the chimney and fireplace;
- inspect the interior of the firebox and the visible flue area, and report as in need of repair built up creosote in visible areas of the firebox and flue (the inspector is not required to determine the adequacy of the draft or perform a chimney smoke test);

■ REPORTING GUIDELINES *(Continued)*

- report as in need of repair a damper that does not operate;

- report as in need of repair the absence of a noncombustible hearth extension;

- report as in need of repair deficiencies in the lintel, hearth, and material surrounding the fireplace, including clearances from combustible materials;

- report as in need of repair the absence of firestopping at the attic penetration of the chimney flue, where accessible;

- report as in need of repair any gas log lighter valves that do not function or that leak gas;

- report as in need of repair any circulating fan that does not operate, if present;

- report as in need of repair deficiencies in combustion air vent, if present; and

- report as in need of repair deficiencies in chimney coping or crown, caps, or spark arrester (inspected from ground level at a minimum).

5 Roofing

This chapter covers some of the various styles and types of roofs and roofing materials. There are many different roofing systems and many combinations of component materials. The home inspector should become familiar with the types of materials and specific roofing practices that are common to his or her area of practice. The associated equipment, such as flashings (cap flashings, valleys), roof jacks, vents, and chimneys, also are discussed. We cover information that is important to the real estate inspector, such as the testing of materials (ASTM—American Society for Testing and Materials), ventilation, and reroofing.

The roof of a building serves primarily as an enclosing surface between the interior and exterior environments. Its structural loads result from external forces (wind, rain, and snow) and the weight of materials used in the construction. Any equipment mounted on the roof, such as air conditioners and solar panels, is additional weight. As an external surface of a building, the roof may be required to have a fire resistance rating to prevent fire from spreading to adjacent buildings.

A roof is constructed similarly to the floor of the house. It has framework, rafters that support the sheathing, and underlayment, which is called *roof deck*. The roof deck is the nailing base for the roofing material. The roof should provide a barrier against weather and control the flow of air, moisture, water vapor and heat. Thermal expansion and contraction can sometimes be a problem for the various connections and the durability of the material used. Solar radiation (sun) is a major feature. In areas subject to high winds and hurricanes, the roof construction becomes critical in preventing uplift.

The roof must be structurally sound and maintained to prevent rain or dampness in the building.

The shape of the roof may be flat, sloping, or arched. For example, the shed-type roof slopes in only one direction; the gable roof slopes in two directions; the hip roof slopes in four directions. A mansard roof is a combination of sloping sides with a flat top surface, while a gambrel roof has two slopes in one direction with one slope steeper than the other. A "built-up" roof is a type of flat roof. It may be contained within an extended wall (parapet), overhang the wall, or end at the edge of the wall. Each of these types of roofs has different problems with different solutions.

Consider the type of roof when choosing a roofing product. One of the most critical is the slope of the roof. It affects the surface drainage, thereby dictating the limits within which certain types of shingles or rolled roofing may be used. Free drainage is essential to the total performance of all roof coverings; it can make the difference between a weathertight roof and one that leaks. The slope of a roof is the very function of the style of a roof. (See Figure 5.1.)

Coverage is an indication of the amount of weather protection the roofing provides and depends on the number of plies or layers of material that lie between the exposed surface of the roofing and the deck. The material is designated single, double, or triple coverage. The number of plies varies, and coverage is usually considered to be that number of plies that exists over most of the roof area. For example, where no significant roof area has less than two thicknesses of material, the installation would be considered double coverage. Some roll roofing material is generally considered single coverage because it provides a single layer of material over the greater part of the roof area.

Exposure is the portion of the roofing exposed to the weather. The exposure for various roof materials is specified by the manufacturers.

The style of type of roof is a significant feature of the building's appearance and character.

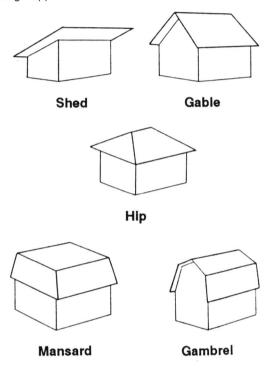

Shed   **Gable**

Hip

Mansard   **Gambrel**

■ MEASUREMENTS

Regardless of the type or style of roof or the roofing material used, roofing is measured by the square, which equals 100 sq. ft. of roof area. A roof slope that measures 15′ at the rake and 40′ at the eave is 600 sq. ft. or 6 squares (15 × 40 = 600 ÷ 100 = 6). (See Figure 5.2.)

Slope and pitch describe the same roof characteristic (incline), expressed two different ways. (See Figure 5.3.) Pitch is the ratio of the rise of the roof to the span of the roof expressed as a fraction. For example, if the span of a roof is 24′ and the rise is 8′, the pitch is 9/24, or 1/3. Slope is the ratio of the rise of the roof to the run of the roof. (See Figure 5.4.) The run is half the length of the span. Expressed as slope, the same roof as described above is said to rise 8″ (inches) per ft. of horizontal run. If the rise of a 24′ roof span were 6′, the pitch would be 1/4 and slope would be 6″ per ft. of run (6/12). The rise is measured from the center or the highest peak of the ridge. It is not necessary to know the span to determine the slope.

To determine the roof slope, a carpenter's level and a measuring tape are required. (See Figure 5.5.) Form a right triangle with the level, roof and tape. The tape and level should intersect 12″ from the point where the level and roof meet. Measure the vertical distance from the roof surface to the bottom of the level. The number of inches followed by 12 gives the slope. The slope is very critical because certain kinds of roofing materials have limitations on the various slopes with which they are compatible. For example, asphalt shingles cannot be used on a flat roof, and a built-up roof cannot be used on a 4/12 and steeper slope. A roof with a 21/12 slope is not suitable for asphalt shingles unless special precautions are used when the shingles are installed. Whether a particular roof incline is expressed in pitch or slope, the results of area calculations will be the same.

Various types of materials and accessories are required to complete a typical roof installation. This includes shingles (wood, asphalt, tile, or metal) or roll roofing, underlayment, starter strips, and hip and ridge shingles. The accessories include drip edges, valley flashings, roof jacks, and vents. Estimates must be made of the required quantities of each material before the contractor can start the job. These estimates are based on calculations made from the dimensions of the roof. Although roofs come in a variety of shapes and styles, virtually all roofs are composed of plane surfaces that can be subdivided into simple geometric shapes—squares, rectangles, trapezoids, and triangles. Thus, nearly all roofing area calculations all simply area calculations for these basic shapes. (See Table 5.1.)

Area/Rake Conversion Table	
Slope (inches per foot)	Area/Rake Factor
4	1.054
5	1.083
6	1.118
7	1.157
8	1.202
9	1.250
10	1.302
11	1.356
12	1.414

Hip/Valley Conversion Table	
Slope (inches per foot)	Hip/Valley Factor
4	1.452
5	1.474
6	1.500
7	1.524
8	1.564
9	1.600
10	1.642
11	1.684
12	1.732

■ **FIGURE 5.2**

Calculations are required to determine the dimensions of a roof.

Square :   A unit of measure equaling 100 sq. ft.
              Used as a basis for measuring roof area.
              (10 × 10 = 100 sq. ft. equal 1 sq.)

Example :   Rake = 15'
              Eave = 40'

              40 × 15 = 600 sq. ft.
              600 ÷ 100 = 6 squares.

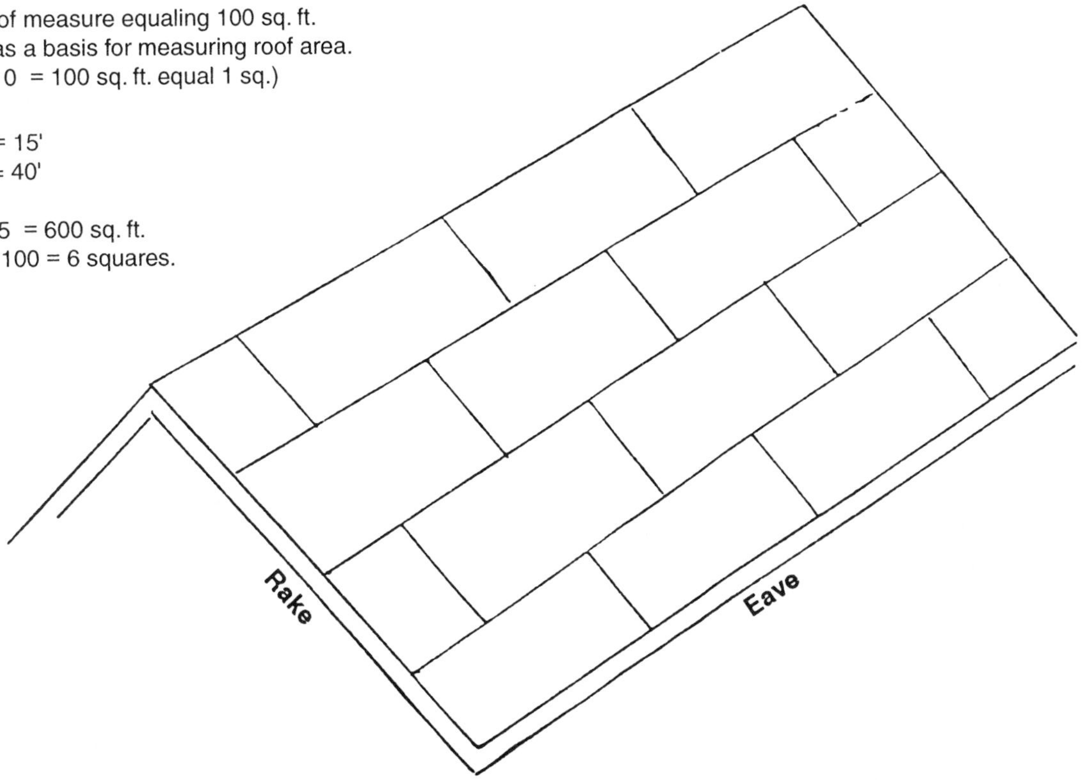

The simplest roof to estimate is one with unbroken planes, such as a shed roof that is only one rectangle.

The area is found by simply multiplying the rake line by the eave line, or A × B. (See Figure 5.6.) The gable roof is composed of two rectangular planes. Its area is found by multiplying the rake line by the eave line, if the two rectangular planes are the same, then multiplying the product by 2 (A × B × 2 = total roof area). The total roof area divided by 100 (A × B × 2 ÷ 100) equals the number of squares of roofing (round off the answer to the next highest number) required to complete the installation.

Roofs that have projecting dormers or intersecting wings through the various roof planes use the same basic calculation approach as simple roofs. This equation involves many subdivisions of the roof surface, which are calculated separately, then added together for total roof area. No matter how complicated a roof may be, its projection onto a horizontal plane will define the total horizontal surface the roof covers. (See Figure 5.7.)

A typical roof is complicated by valleys, dormers and ridges at different elevations. The lower half of

Figure 5.7 shows the projection of the roof onto a horizontal plane. In the projection, the inclined surfaces appear flat and intersecting surfaces appear as lines. Measurements for the horizontal projection of the roof can be made from the plans, the ground, or inside the attic. The actual area is a function of the slope. Calculations must be grouped in terms of roof slope. Those of different

■ **FIGURE 5.3**

Pitch and slope relationships.

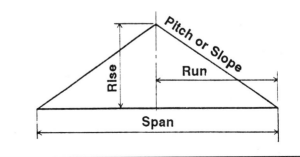

■ **FIGURE 5.4**

Minimum pitch and slope requirements for various asphalt roofing products.

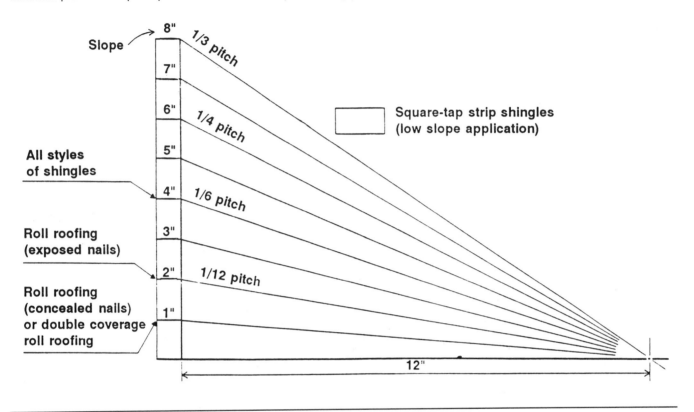

slopes are not combined until the true roof areas have been determined. The term ell refers to roof slopes that vary from the main roof, such as dormers and ridges that are at different elevations.

The horizontal area under the 9″ slope roof is

$$26 \times 30 = \quad 780$$
$$19 \times 30 = \quad 570$$
$$\text{Total} \quad = \overline{1,350} \text{ sq. ft.}$$

From the gross figure, deductions must be made for the area of the chimney. For the triangular area of the ell roof that overlaps and is sloped differently than the main roof, calculate the following:

Chimney $\quad 4 \times 4 = \quad 16$
Ell roof $½ (16 \times 5) = \quad \underline{40}$ (triangular area)
$\qquad\qquad\qquad\qquad \overline{56}$ sq. ft.

The net projected area of the main roof is

$$1,350 - 56 = 1,294 \text{ sq. ft.}$$

■ **FIGURE 5.5**

Procedure to measure roof slope.

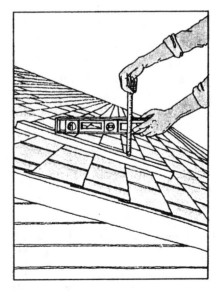

■ FIGURE 5.6

Multiply A × B to find square feet.

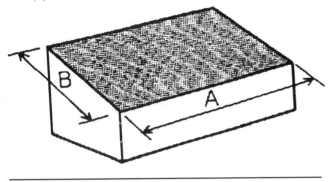

The horizontal area under the 6″ slope roof is

20 × 30   = 600
½ (16 × 5) =   40
Total   = 640 sq. ft.

Using the area/rake table (Table 5.1) to compute the roof area and the 1,294 sq. ft. with 9″ slopes, the area/rake factor is 1.250. Multiply 1,294 × 1.250 = 1,617.5 sq. ft. To compute the roof area of 640 sq. ft. with 6″ slope with the area/rake factor as 1.118, multiply 640 × 1.118 = 715.52 sq. ft. The total roof area is 1,617.5 + 715.5 = 2,333 sq. ft.; divided by 100, the roof area computes to 23.3 squares, rounded to 24 squares.

Include in the estimate the requirements for ridge and hip shingles, rake shingles if using tile, lengths of flashings and drip edge, underlayment, and either nails or staples. Ten percent of the number of squares of roofing material required should be added to allow for waste for double-covered shingles or tile at the eaves.

An inspector should recognize a 2/12 slope as being a very low slope and not suited for wood shingles or built-up construction. A mineral surface rolled roof or self-sealing shingles are recommended for low sloped roofs. This type of roof can be found on small homes, sheds, carports, garages, and patios. It is not necessary to determine the slope unless there appears to be the possibility of a problem with the roof being too flat or too steep.

When inspecting the roof, especially an older roof, it is important to walk on it. Do not walk on the roof if it is wet. Roofs get very slippery when wet and become very dangerous. Additionally, steep roofs 8/12 or more and decorative type roofs (tile, slate, metal) can be damaged when walked on. These roofs should not be walked on unless the inspector has been trained to walk on these types of roofs.

■ MATERIALS

Materials used for pitched roofs are wood, fiberglass, asphalt, tile, slate or concrete. Sheet materials such as roll roofing, aluminum, copper, tin, or galvanized iron also are used. The most common roof covering for flat or low-pitched roofs is built-up roofing with an aggregate topping or a cap sheet.

Materials used as roof coverings must be either Class A, B, or C roof coverings. These materials are tested in conformance with the ASTM code (ASTM E-108 Standard Method of Fire Tests of Roof Coverings).

Decking

Flat roofs, often called *built-up roofs,* are covered with alternating layers of roofing felt and asphalt with a gravel layer on top. There are built-up roofs surfaced with an insulating polyurethane foam that is sprayed on and painted with a protective coating. The principal function of the roof material is to shed a drop of water and move it until it falls to the gutter or ground.

The type of material used for roof decking depends on the roof material used on the house. Most decks have both sheathing and underlayment. The sheathing provides the nailing base for the roof surface. Flat and sloping roofs, built-up or asphalt shingle roofs usually have plywood or wafer board nailed directly to the rafters. Older homes may have 1″ × 6″ or 1″ × 8″ lumber nailed to the rafters for roof decking. Wood shingles or wood shakes are often laid over 1″ × 4″ lumber spaced over the rafters. This sheathing style is called *open sheathing* because it permits air circulation.

The underlayment is sandwiched between the sheathing and roof surface. Roofing felt is a thick, fibrous black paper made from wood chips and paper and saturated with asphalt. It is thick enough to resist outside water penetration and thin enough to allow moisture to escape from the inside. Extra waterproofing is necessary in hurricane areas, and tile roofs often have underlayment consisting of built-up layers of roofing felts and hot mopped asphalt. Most sloping roofs are covered with overlapping layers of asphalt shingles, wood shingles or shakes, tile, metal, or molded plastics.

Wood/Cedar

Wood roofing materials are made from western red cedar. Western red cedar is characterized by fine, even grain and exceptional strength in proportion to weight.

■ **FIGURE 5.7**

Horizonal projection of a complex roof.

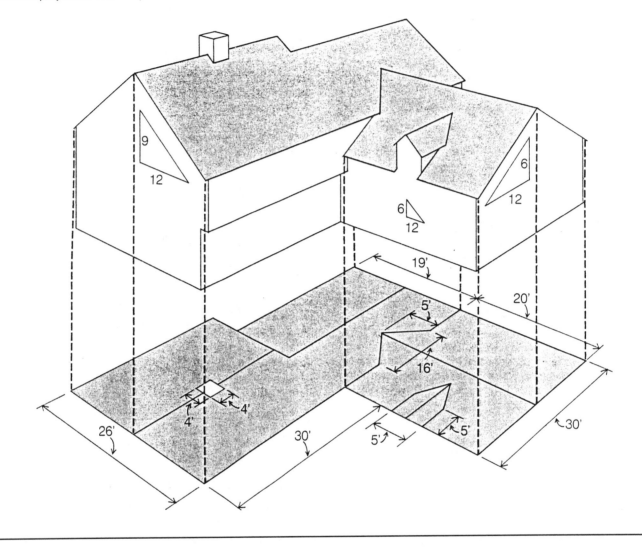

This cedar has a low ratio of expansion and contraction rates. It changes with moisture content and has a high permeability to liquids. The cellular composition of western red cedar—millions of tiny air-filled cells per cubic inch—provides a high degree of thermal insulation. The wood has outstanding rigidity in hurricane winds and resilience under the pounding of hail.

In low-humidity climates where moss, fungus, and mildew are not prevalent, wood preservatives will prevent excessive dryness and prolong the life of the cedar roof. In the South, heat and humidity will destroy the cedar roof if it is not maintained and treated.

Cedar roofs will begin to show their age in five years. In hot, humid climates, the sun depletes the natural oils in the roofs. It is recommended that wood preservatives be applied every three to five years to help maintain the oil content and make the cedar shingles last longer. When the oil is depleted, the shingles begin to crack and curl. This is the natural aging process and the beginning of a potential roof leak.

Wood roofing materials are produced as shingles and shakes. Cedar shingles are sawed so both surfaces are smooth with a uniform thickness at the butt of the shingle. (See Figure 5.8.)

Cedar shakes have split faces and sawn backs. Cedar logs are first cut into desired lengths. Blanks or boards of the proper thickness are split and then run diagonally through a bandsaw to produce two tapered shakes from each blank. (See Figure 5.9.)

■ **FIGURE 5.8**

Different grades of shingles.

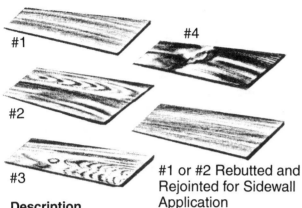

#1

#4

#2

#3

#1 or #2 Rebutted and Rejointed for Sidewall Application

Description

The premium grade of shingles for roofs and sidewalls. These top-grade shingles are 100% heartwood, 100% clear, and 100% edge-grain.

A proper grade for some applications: Not less than 10" clear on 16" shingles, 11" clear on 18" shingles, and 16" clear on 24" shingles. Flat grain and limited sapwood are permitted in this grade.

A utility grade for economy applications: Not less than 6" clear on 16" and 18" shingles, 10" clear on 24" shingles.

Same specifications as above for No. 1 and No. 2 grades but machine trimmed for parallel edges with butts sawn at right angles. For sidewall application where tightly fitting joints are desired. Also available with smooth sanded face.

■ **FIGURE 5.9**

Different types of shakes.

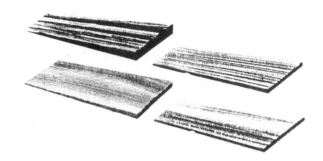

Description

These shakes have split faces and sawn backs. Cedar logs are first cut into desired lengths. Blanks or boards of proper thickness are spilt and then run diagonally through a bandsaw to produce two tapered shakes from each blank.

These shakes are sawn on both sides.

Produced largely by hand, using a sharp-bladed steel froe and a wooden mallet. The natural shingle-like taper is achieved by reversing the block, end-for-end, with each split.

Produced in the same manner as taper-split shakes except that by splitting from the same end of the block, the shakes acquire the same thickness throughout.

Shingles have a smooth surface, whereas shakes have at least one highly textured, natural-grain split surface. Shingles and handsplit shakes are generally used for roofs and some walls in the natural state.

If not treated, red cedar will eventually weather to silver, dark gray, or dark brown. Bleaching agents may be applied, which encourage a silver-gray result.

Most of the older cedar roofs are not treated and do not have any Underwriters Laboratories (UL) rating. Now most building codes require shingles and shakes to be pressure treated with chemical solutions for UL recognition. Normally, a treated shingle or shake with fire-retardant qualities has a Class C UL rating.

Cedar Shingles

Cedar shingles have four grades. Number 1 cedar shingle is 100 percent heartwood, 100 percent clear and 100 percent edge grain. Each shingle is normally 18″ in length with no knots. The grain of the wood from the butt to the end will veer only ¾″. There will be very little curling with number 1 shingles. Number 2 cedar shingles are the same length, vary in grade with at least 11″ clear of knots, and have flat grain with a limited amount of sapwood from the butt end. Number 3 cedar shingle is a utility grade for economy applications and will not have less than 6″ clear. Number 4 cedar shingle is utility grade for undercoursing, interior use, and sidewall applications.

The labels on the bundles will disclose the grade of shingles in the bundle. A bundle of number 1 wood shingles has a blue label, number 2 shingles have a red

■ **FIGURE 5.10**

Split in flatgrain cedar shingle and missing shingle; shingles eroded and broken causing water penetration.

label, and number 3 shingles have a black label. Number 4 cedar shingles are rarely encountered in an inspection.

Cedar shingles are applied on slopes of 4/12 or greater. The exposure, that is the portion of the shingle directly exposed to the elements, is 5½″. Sometimes cedar shingles will be installed on a 3/12 slope. When the slope is lower than 4/12, the exposure must be decreased to 4½″ for number 1 shingles. On number 2 shingles, the exposure has to be decreased to 4″.

Most splits observed in cedar shingles and cedar shakes are due to grain pattern of the wood and repeated shrink/swell cycles induced by changes in moisture content, referred to generically as *natural weathering*. Long-term net shrinkage, which initiates and extends

splits that develop in the wood, is greatest tangential to the growth rings of the wood. Natural weathering splits are distinguishable from hail-caused splits by their color, shape, and pattern. Splitting of wood caused by natural weathering will be more common in shingles or shakes with flatgrain-cut wood as opposed to edgegrain-cut woods. (See Figure 5.10.)

Hail impacts in wood leave recognizable impact marks. A hail-caused split in wood is indicated by an impact mark coincidental with a fresh split in the wood. (See Figure 5.11.) Wood splits from hail impact occur at the moment of impact. Wood that is not split by an impact and that shows only spots, dents, and gouges is not considered damaged.

■ **FIGURE 5.11**

Hail-caused broken and split cedar shingles plus exposed nails.

A wood shingle roof should never be less than three layers thick.

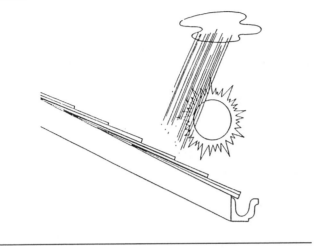

Splits that have developed from natural weathering will grow in a tapered fashion, typically, from the butt edge of the shingle or shake toward the head. The edges of the split tend to be rounded from being smoothed by water erosion. Splits from weathering also tend to be V-shaped in cross-section because the top surface of the wood dries more quickly and shrinks more than the bottom surface. The owner may have had inspections made by contractors and adjusters who walked on and broke some shingles or shakes. A recent split caused by footfall will resemble the hail-caused split in its having sharp edges and bright color on the fracture surfaces, but it will not have the coincident initiating impact mark. The skill of the inspector must determine whether a split is caused by an impact or a footfall and whether a split is severe enough to present a problem. Shingles or shakes that have cupped, curled, or are worn thin are most susceptible to footfall damage, and foot traffic generally is heaviest near valleys and ridge areas.

A properly installed cedar shingle roof will always be three shingles thick. (See Figure 5.12.) In other words, it takes three cracks in a row to cause a leak. On number 2 cedar shingles, it takes two cracks in a row to cause a leak.

Cedar Shakes

Cedar shakes have only one grade. Number 1 implies that there are no knots or defective shakes allowed. They are hand split and they are available in two lengths: 18″ and 24″. The most common is the 24″. The exposure for an 18″ shake is 7½″ and for a 24″ shake, 10″.

Installation procedures for cedar shakes vary by locality. In some areas, when properly installed, shake roof felt will be visible only from the attic, with none showing on the exterior. From the attic, there should be no daylight seen through the shakes, as can be observed with the cedar shingle roof. From the outside there should be only shakes showing, without any visible felt when observing from the roof. This allows for breathing. (See Figure 5.13.) In other areas of the country, the shakes are installed over a plywood subroofing. Always check the roofing styles for your area.

Asphalt

Asphalt is a dark brown to black cementitious material consisting primarily of bitumens, which occur in nature or are obtained in petroleum processing. Asphalt roofing is classified in three groups: shingles (see Figure 5.14), roll roofing (see Figure 5.15) and underlayment.

Shingles and roll roofing are outer roof coverings designed to be exposed to the weather and withstand the elements. Underlayments are underroof coverings, meaning that the saturated felts provide the necessary protection for the exposed roofing materials. The asphalt coating provides the long-term ability to resist weathering and remain stable under severe service temperatures.

Asphalt/Fiberglass

All asphalt shingles have a base material of fiberglass or organic felt, which provides the matrix that supports the other components. They also provide the strength to withstand the handling, manufacturing, and service conditions after installation.

The surfacing of ceramic-coated mineral granules shields the asphalt coating against the sun's rays. It also adds color to the products and provides fire resistance. The ceramic-coated mineral granules applied to the top surface of the shingles during the manufacturing process come in a wide range of colors.

Asphalt shingles are the most common roofing used today and are manufactured as strip shingles. Strip shingles are rectangular, measuring 12″ wide by 36″ long, and may have as many as five cutouts along the 36″ dimension. Cutouts separate the shingle tabs that are exposed to the weather and give the roof the appearance of being composed of a larger number of individual unit strip shingles. The most popular shingles are three-tab strip shingles.

Cedar shakes require felt underlayment between each course.

ROOFS

Double starter course

18-inch 15 lb. felt laid over top portion of each course

VALLEYS

Metal valley sheets should be 20-inch minimum width

HIPS AND RIDGES

Double starter course

Alternate overlap

Most shingles are available with strips or spots of factory-applied, self-sealing adhesive. This adhesive is a thermoplastic material that is activated by the heat of the sun after the shingles are on the roof. Exposure to the sun's heat bonds the shingles and provides greater wind resistance. This sealing process takes place within a few days, depending on the geographic location, roof slope, and orientation of the house on the property. Another

fact involved is whether it is spring, summer, fall, or winter. In winter, early spring, and even late fall, the self-sealing process is slower than in the warmer times of the year.

Tabs of strip shingles may be trimmed or offset to obtain straight or staggered buttlines. They are embossed or built up from several laminations of base material to give a three-dimensional effect. Staggered buttlines, embossing, and laminations, combined in various ways, create textures on finished roofs that resemble wood, slate, or tile.

Interlocking shingles are designed to provide strong wind resistance. There are various shapes and types of locking devices that provide a mechanical interlock on the roof.

Most shingles manufactured since the early 1980s have a fiberglass mat and are called *fiberglass shingles*. The advantages of fiberglass include a UL Class A rating and life expectancy of 20 to 40 years, depending on the type of installation and weight of the shingle.

Organic shingles have a felt mat made of wood and paper (cellulose) fibers. Both fiberglass mat shingles and organic mat shingles are commonly referred to as *comp* (short for composition) *shingles*. The organic shingles will have a UL Class C rating and a 15-year to 25-year warranty. The fiberglass mat shingles will have a UL Class A rating and a 25-year-plus warranty.

Roll Roofing

Roll roofing is manufactured, packaged, and shipped in rolls. The roofing is 36″ wide and 38′ long with various weights. Roll roofing can be purchased with either a mineral granule embedded in the top or with a smooth surface. (See Figure 5.16.)

Some mineral-surfaced roll roofing is manufactured with a granule-free selvage that suggests the amount each succeeding course should overlap the preceding course. The manufacturer's recommendations concerning top, side, and end laps should be followed. The amount of overlap determines how much of the material is exposed to the weather and the extent of coverage of the roof surface. Roll roofing is also used as a flashing material. Roll roofing should not be installed when the temperature is below 45°F.

Inspecting Asphalt

When inspecting composition shingles or rolled roof material, be mindful that whether asphalt or fiberglass, these materials react the same to hail, wind, and

■ **FIGURE 5.14**

Various types of asphalt shingles.

| PRODUCT | Configuration | Per Square | | | Size | | Exposure | ASTM* fire and wind ratings |
		Approximate Shipping Weight	Shingles	Bundles	Width	Length		
Self-sealing random-tab strip shingle 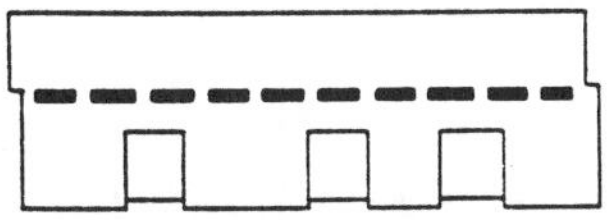 Multi-thickness	Various edge, surface texture and application treatments	240# to 360#	64 to 90	3, 4 or 5	11½" to 14"	36" to 40"	4" to 6"	A or C - Many wind resistant
Self-sealing random-tab strip shingle 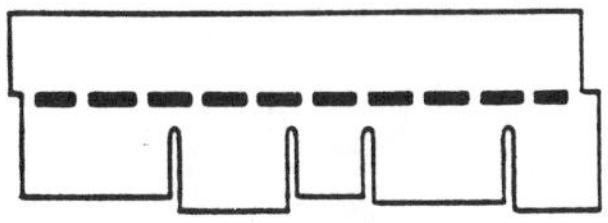 Single-thickness	Various edge, surface texture and application treatments	240# to 300#	65 to 80	3 or 4	12" to 13¼"	36" to 40"	4" to 5⅝"	A or C - Many wind resistant
Self-sealing square-tab strip shingle 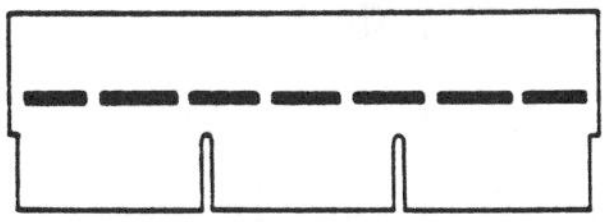 Three-tab	Three-tab or Four-tab	200# to 300#	65 to 80	3 or 4	12" to 13¼"	36" to 40"	5" to 5⅝"	A or C - All wind resistant
Self-sealing square-tab strip shingle 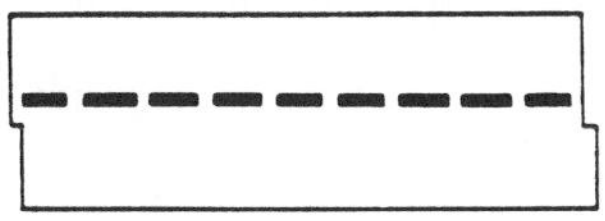 No-cutout	Various edge and surface texture treatments	200# to 300#	65 to 81	3 or 4	12" to 13¼"	36" to 40"	5" to 5⅝"	A or C - All wind resistant
Individual interlocking shingle 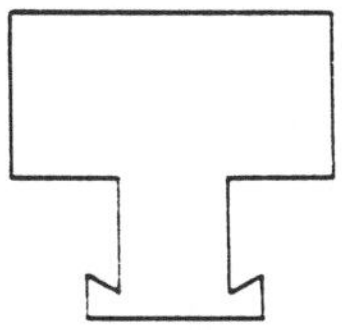 Basic design	Several design variations	180# to 250#	72 to 120	3 or 4	18" to 22¼"	20" to 22½"	—	A or C - Many wind resistant

SOURCE: American Society for Testing and Materials.

■ **FIGURE 5.15**

Various types of asphalt rolled roofing material.

PRODUCT	Approximate Shipping Weight		Squares Per Package	Length	Width	Selvage	Exposure	ASTM[1] fire and wind ratings
	Per Roll	Per Square						
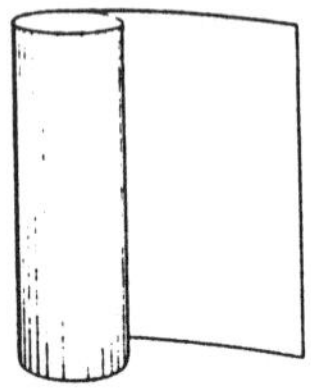 Mineral surface roll	75# to 90#	75# to 90#	1	36' to 38'	36"	0" to 4"	32" to 34"	C
 Mineral surface roll (double coverage)	55# to 70#	110# to 140#	½	36'	36"	19"	17"	C
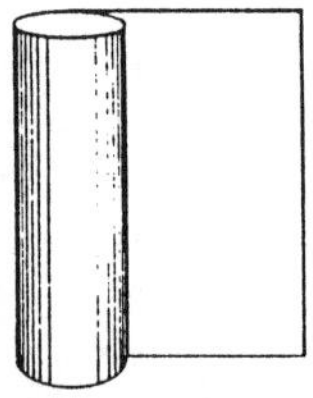 Smooth surface roll	50# to 86#	40# to 65#	1 to 2	36' to 72'	36"	N/A	34"	None
 Saturated felt underlayment (non-perforated)	35# to 60#	11# to 30#	2 to 4	72' to 144'	36"	N/A	17" to 34"	2

1. American Society for Testing and Materials.
2. May be component in a complete fire-rated system, check with manufacturer for details.

■ **FIGURE 5.16**

Application of double coverage roll roofing parallel to the rake.

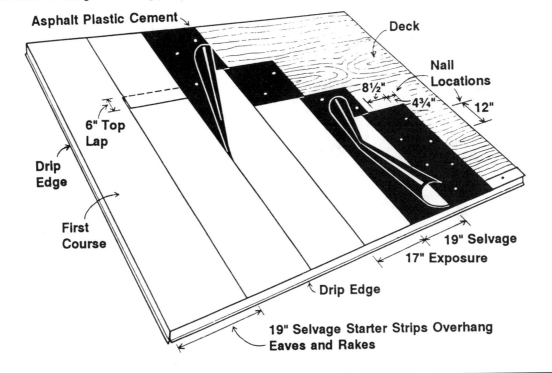

■ **FIGURE 5.17**

Shingles are cracked, curled, and the mineral surface is deteriorating from weathering exposure.

other types of damage. The first step is to be able to differentiate hail damage from nonhail damage. Functional damage to roofing materials from hail has been defined as the diminution of water shedding capability or reduction of the expected service life of the roofing material.

Hail-caused damage to an asphalt shingle in roofing is rupture of the reinforcing mat or displacement of granules sufficient to expose underlying shingle or underlayment. Penetration of the shingle, in effect, removes a ply of roofing and has the potential for allowing water to reach the fasteners or butted joints in the underlying shingle. (See Figure 5.17.)

Mechanically caused damage to shingles during shipping, handling, and installation can disturb the granule surface enough to displace and expose the mat. This is true particularly for warm fiberglass shingles subject to foot traffic on the roof. Patterns of weathering or manufacturing deficiencies can result in areas of little to no granule coverage on the shingles. Bundle variations should be relatively easy to detect because the affected shingles will be arranged in diagonal or vertical columns. In contrast, exposed areas of asphalt caused by hailstone impact will be roughly circular in shape and

randomly distributed in the shingles. Blistering may appear as small, bubbled features in the granule crust whose tops weather away to leave pits in the shingles.

■ **FIGURE 5.18**

Bruises in a fiberglass composition shingle caused by mechanical abuse.

The pits have steep sides and often extend to the mat. Therefore, an inspector must evaluate the overall condition of the shingles on the roof and differentiate between hail damage and other types of damage. (See Figures 5.18, 5.19, and 5.20.)

Tile

Tile roofs are popular throughout the South and Southwest. Tile roofing is available as both clay and concrete tile. Clay tile is kiln-dried and made to last the life of the building. Barrel-shaped clay tile is commonly called *mission tile,* a name derived from the architecture of California's Spanish missions. Concrete tile and shingles are manufactured from cement, sand, and water and then extruded in various configurations, such as S-shaped, ribbed, and flat. (See Figure 5.21.)

Tiles measure 12″ × 17″ with ½″ thickness. Concrete tile is available in several colors, such as earth tones and shades of green, black, or red, while clay tile is red.

An inspector should not attempt to walk on a tile roof unless he or she has been trained to do so. Only a professional should attempt to repair one. (See Figure 5.22.)

Slate

Slate is a hard, fine-grained, metamorphic rock that cleaves naturally into thin, smooth-surfaced layers.

Slate for roof shingles is mined in quarries in Vermont and Virginia or imported.

Slate has a long service life with little or no repair. The most common problem with slate roofs is replacing broken slate shingles. Slate shingles are brittle, and it requires a professional roofing contractor who is experienced in installing a slate roof to repair or install the shingles. (See Figure 5.23.)

Slate roofs require not less than two layers of 15-lb. felt or one layer of 30-lb. felt underlayment. The nails for slate shingles should be number 14 gauge copper or number 14 gauge corrosion-resistant nails. The slate roof will not deteriorate like asphalt and wood, although the underlayment will deteriorate after 20 to 30 years. At that time, the slate shingles will have to be removed, new underlayment put down, and the slate shingles reinstalled.

Both tile and slate are heavy shingles. Slate weighs 7 to 10 lb. per sq. ft. dead load. It is important that the roof

■ **FIGURE 5.19**

Asphalt shingles damaged by tree limbs hitting the roof.

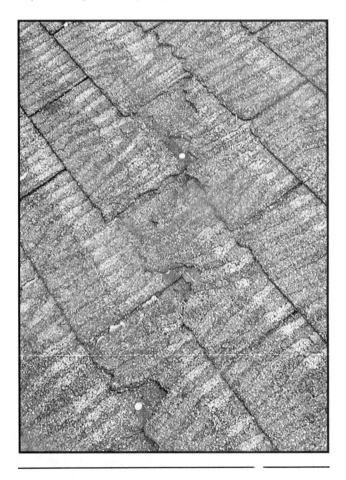

■ **FIGURE 5.20**

Asphalt shingles are old, and granules are falling into the gutter.

framing be constructed to carry the weight of the roof without sagging. (See Figure 5.24.) The slate roof should not be walked on by anyone not experienced in walking on slate and tile roofs. Slate roofs should not be installed on any roof with a slope of less than 3/12.

The inspector should observe the condition of the roof by first putting a ladder up in several places around the outside perimeter of the house. Second, inspect the attic for any evidence of water penetration.

Metal

Metal roofs are becoming more popular on new homes and many older homes. Homeowners are now able to make the decision of what kind of new roof to buy. If there were asphalt shingles on the old roof, that's most likely what the homeowner bought for a new roof. Wood shakes, slate, or Spanish tile is likely to be replaced by the same material.

More recently, a very old material has appeared in new shapes and colors. It is metal, and the reasons for its

growing acceptance are many. New technology has allowed metal to be shaped, textured, stamped, and colored to emulate the look of other roofing material. There are metal simulations that cost less, weight less, and last longer. The metal roof is outstanding as a barrier to weather; it doesn't contribute to fire, isn't eaten by insects, and doesn't promote algae growth. The metal roof requires very little maintenance and can last virtually as long as the building. Some of the newer versions of metal roofs carry a 50-year limited warranty.

If an old roof consists of one or two layers of asphalt or fiberglass shingles, the lightweight metal roof can often be installed over the shingles, saving the cost of tear-off. The old roof will serve as a condensation barrier and added insulation. Because most metal panels have a raised profile, there will be natural ventilation between the roof and the roof deck. In addition, metal does not store heat but reflects it, and many of the coatings used on metal roofing materials have high reflective ratings.

Steel roofing coated with zinc is called *galvanized steel* and usually consists of corrugated galvanized steel panels. These panels will not rust until the zinc coating wears off or is damaged. They should be painted with a zinc-rich paint to increase their durability. Steel coated with aluminum or an aluminum-zinc combination will resist corrosion even if unpainted. Stainless steel is the most expensive of all but it is maintenance free. Terneplate is steel coated with an alloy of lead and tin, and its durability depends on paint. New terneplate should be coated on both sides with red iron-oxide linseed oil paint. The exposed side should get two coats of oil-base paint.

Corrugated panels of galvanized steel, known for their ease of installation, have spawned variations made of aluminum, terneplate, or aluminum coated steel that come in corrugations as well as being shaped in ribs. The roof panels can be furnished in various lengths (up to 24 feet that in most cases eliminate end lap seams and overlapping side seams that are designed to prevent water from being siphoned under a panel. When installing a metal roof, it is important that the roofing contractor be familiar with installing metal roofs.

Galvanized steel roofs are usually galvanized steel panels applied to permanent structures. Galvanized steel roofs are popular for certain installations because they are easy to install and they can be painted. The maintenance that is required includes removing rust and keeping the roof well painted with a good metal paint. Leaks can be repaired by renailing, caulking, or replacing all or part of the panel.

■ **FIGURE 5.21**

Various types of clay and concrete shingles and tiles.

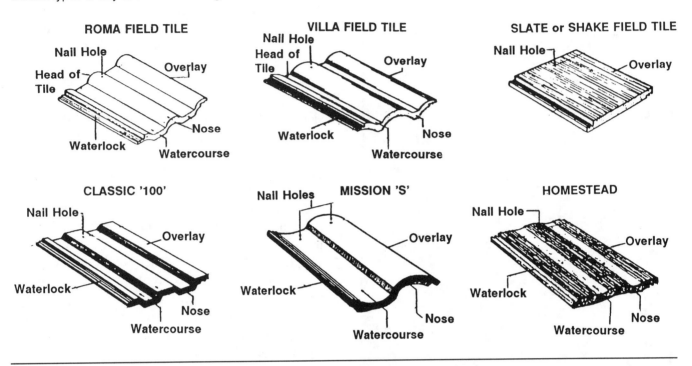

■ **FIGURE 5.22**

Proper roof installation using concrete shingles.

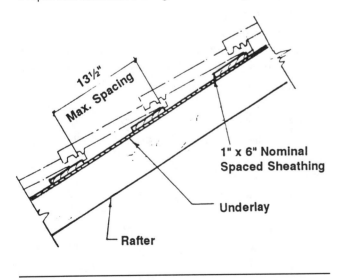

■ **FIGURE 5.23**

The construction of a slate roof requires special contractor attention.

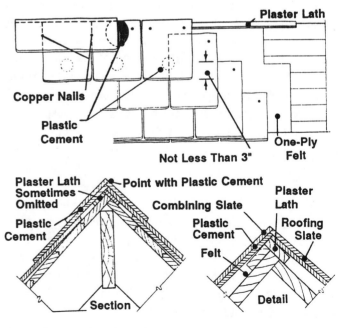

■ **FIGURE 5.24**

Framing for various types of shingles.

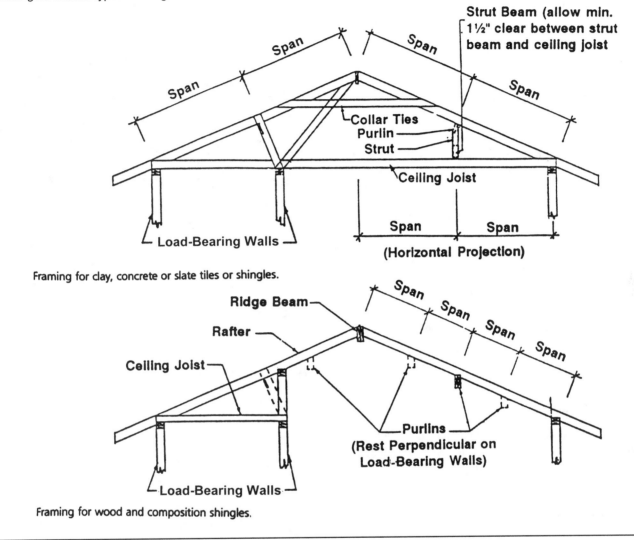

Framing for clay, concrete or slate tiles or shingles.

Framing for wood and composition shingles.

Aluminum is lightweight and is ideal for roofing; however, it is a soft material and easily damaged. Aluminum roofing does not require painting, but because aluminum is a lightweight material, the surfaces can be embossed and colored. Hail and objects falling on them such as tree limbs usually damage aluminum roofs.

Aluminum shingles are shaped to interlock with each other for wind resistance. Because they are durable and lightweight, they are sometimes preferred in areas where there is heavy snowfall. The aluminum roof should not be walked on because it is easily damaged. Instead, it should be inspected by placing a ladder against the house in several areas so the total roof can be observed. The attic should be inspected for water

penetration. Aluminum shingles should be installed over an underlayment of not less than 30-lb. felt applied for a base sheet. Aluminum shingles should not be installed on a roof with a slope of less than 3/12.

Copper roofs are usually 16-oz. copper sheeting and are applied to permanent structures. When they are properly installed, they require very little maintenance or repair. Proper installation allows for expansion and contraction with changes in temperature.

It is not recommended that an inspector walk on a copper roof. The roof should be inspected by placing a ladder against the house in several areas so the total roof can be observed, and the attic should be inspected for water penetration.

Copper roofs require very little maintenance. Copper will weather to a greenish copper oxide that can be prevented or removed by wiping the surface with linseed oil. Flashings for metal roofs should be made of the same material as the roof. If different kinds of metals are used, they should be insulated so the two surfaces cannot touch, avoiding corrosion.

Inspecting Metal Roofs

When inspecting a metal roof, the inspector who has not been trained to walk a metal roof of that type, should not walk on the roof but should inspect it using a ladder at eave height and/or binoculars. The inspector should take particular care to check the following:

- Rib roof—gable ends, filler strip to seal edges at the eave and ridge
- Roof flashings
- Proper nails used for nailing panels; nails prefitted with washers for leakproof fastening; copper roofs nailed with copper nails
- Dents or damaged spots caused by hail or falling or rubbing tree limbs

■ INSTALLATION

Proper installation of roofing materials is critical for long-lasting use. The following sections suggest important steps to consider for different roofing materials.

Wood/Cedar

Wood shingles should not be butted too close to each other. The recommended spacing between cedar shingles is ¼″ and no more than ⅜″. (See Figure 5.25.) Shingles swell when wet. If nailed too close, the shingles will cup and crack. They should be installed with two nails per shingle 1″ above the exposure line and ¾″ from the edge. On any roof, the exposure of the ridge should be the same as for the shingles.

The proper exposure of the wood shingle roof is determined by two factors. One factor is the slope of the roof, and the other is the length and grade of shingle.

Wood shakes must be laid down with felt paper. The shakes should not be butted too close to each other. The recommended spacing between shakes is ½″. (See Figure 5.26.)

■ FIGURE 5.25

When applying wood shingles to a roof, shingles are to be spaced ¼″ to ⅜″ apart to allow for expansion.

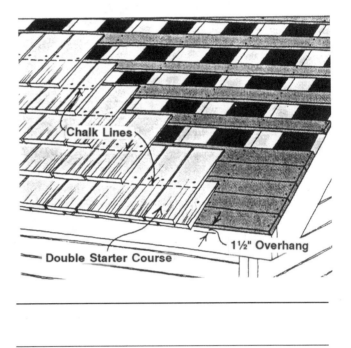

■ FIGURE 5.26

When applying a wood shake roof, shakes are spaced ½″ apart to allow for expansion.

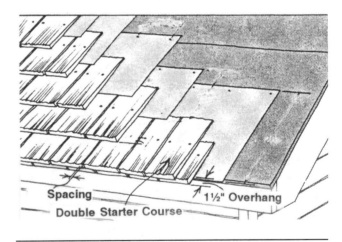

Tile and Slate

Tiles have lugs on their underside to hook over furring strips on the roof and then are nailed or wired in place. The furring strips can be nailed either to a solid deck or to the rafters. (See Figures 5.27 and 5.28.)

■ **FIGURE 5.27**

Tile used for roofing.

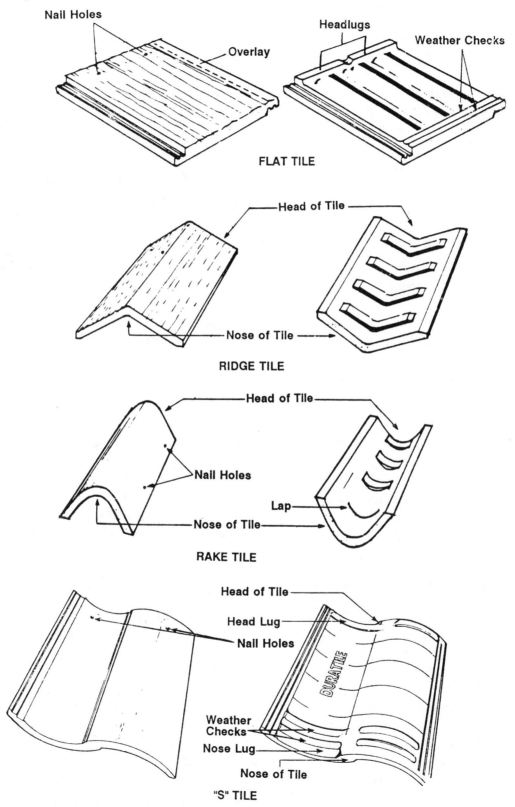

FLAT TILE

RIDGE TILE

RAKE TILE

"S" TILE

■ **FIGURE 5.28**

Tile application at hip and ridge.

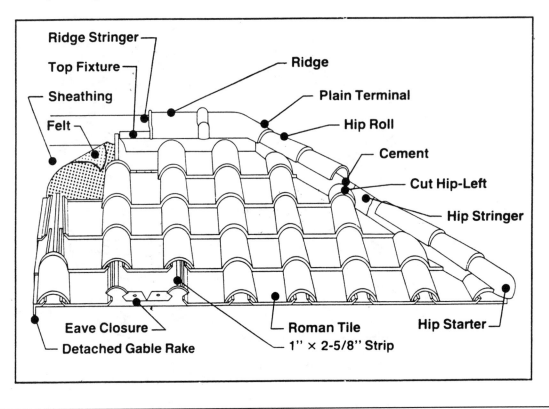

Tile roofs should have two layers of 15-lb. felt or one layer of 30-lb. felt. The minimum slope for a tile roof is 3/12. The weight of the tile requires that the roof structure be supported with additional structural bracing. Tiles range in weight from 8 lb. per sq. ft. to as much as 19 lb. per sq. ft. By comparison, asphalt shingles weigh 2 lb. per sq. ft.

The S-type and mission tile must have bird stops installed at the eaves. Sheet lead is recommended for flashings for tile roofs because it can be easily formed to fit the contour of the tile for better sealing qualities. The fascia should be raised 1½″ for the starter course of tile.

Asphalt Shingles

Asphalt shingles are most commonly material used today for roofing. The average asphalt shingle is 36″ in width and 12″ in depth. The exposure on an asphalt shingle roof is determined by the manufacturer. Installation and nailing instructions are noted on the bundles of shingles. The exposure normally ranges from 5″ to 6″.

On the asphalt shingle, the butt edge is called a *tab* and the spacing between the tabs is called a *cutout*. The portion of the shingle that is above the exposure line is called *top lap*. The head lap is the only portion of the shingle that has three thicknesses. The bulk of the roof has two thicknesses. (See Figure 5.29.)

■ **FIGURE 5.29**

A schematic of an asphalt shingle roof.

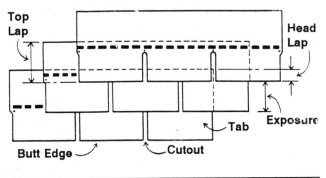

Nailing

Roofing nails are made of steel or aluminum. Steel nails should be zinc-coated because they need to be corrosion resistant. Roof nails made from copper are also available. Roofing nails should have barbed or deformed shanks and should be 11 to 14 gauge with large heads ³⁄₁₆″ to ³⁄₈″ diameter. The nails should be long enough for the shank to penetrate the roofing material completely and extend at least ¾″ into the roof decking. (See Figure 5.30.)

Staples should be zinc-coated for corrosion protection and should be 16-gauge minimum with a minimum crown width of ¹⁵⁄₁₆″ and a shank of sufficient length to penetrate ¾″ into the roof decking. It is important for the entire crown of the staples to bear tightly against the surface of the shingle. (See Figure 5.31.)

When the roof has been properly installed, no nails or staples should be visible. If nails or staples do show, the roof has been improperly installed.

Underlayment

Underlayment is used on composition roofing for three reasons: (1) Underlayment is a necessary component to complete the fire-rated assembly; (2) it keeps the deck dry before the application of the shingles; and (3) if some shingles are lifted or torn loose by high winds during a storm, the underlayment will shed some water for a short period and prevent damage to the interior of the house. (See Figure 5.32.)

Underlayment is not always required when reroofing a composition roof, on a slope of 6/12 or greater or when the shingles are three thicknesses. When inspecting a composition roof, the underlayment will not be visible to the inspector.

Underlayment is required on other types of roofs, such as wood shake, slate, and other decorative roofs. On wood shake and tile-type roofs, the underlayment should be visible from the attic, but it should not be visible from the exterior.

It is important that asphalt-saturated felt be used as underlayment. Coated felts, tar-saturated materials, polyethylene, laminated waterproof papers, or other plastics are vapor barriers. These barriers could trap moisture between the roofing materials and the roof deck, causing them to deteriorate prematurely.

■ FLASHINGS

Any intersections or penetrations of a roof's surface by vertical walls, soil stacks, chimneys, skylights, etc.,

■ **FIGURE 5.30**

Correct and incorrect methods for nailing shingles and shakes.

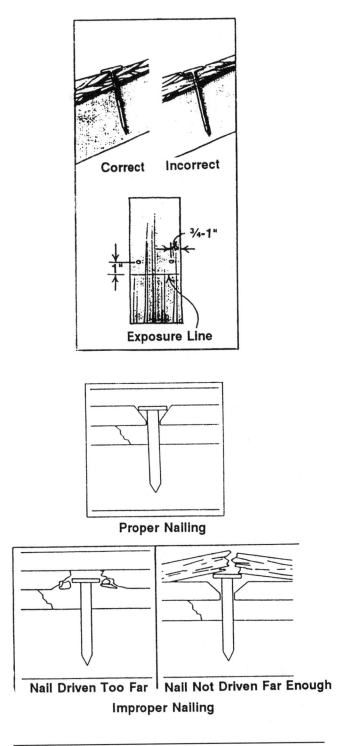

create opportunities for leaks to occur. These places must be protected if the roof is to function properly. Pieces of metal or rolled roofing is used to prevent

■ **FIGURE 5.31**

Correct and incorrect applications of staples.

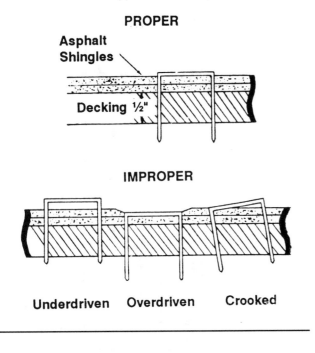

seepage of water into a building around any intersection or penetration in the roof. Flashings are the system used to seal the edges of a membrane at walls, expansion joints, drains, gravel stops, and other areas where the membrane is interrupted or ends. Base flashings cover the edges of the membrane, while cap flashing or counterflashing shields the upper edges of the base flashing.

Drip Edge

Drip edge, also called *metal eave* or *eave flashing,* is installed both on the rake and on the eave. It is manufactured in 10′ lengths. It is partially nailed through the roof and overhangs the trimmer fascia board. The purpose of the drip edge is to shed water past the decking material and protect the fascia and cornice board from moisture penetration. (See Figure 5.33.)

The drip edge is not required on all roofs, but is required when reroofing with composition shingle over wood shingle. When doing so, the wood shingle roof becomes the roof decking. The old wood shingles must be trimmed back and drip edge used to cover exposed decking material.

For maximum protection against ice dams, eaves flashings must be installed wherever there is a possi-

■ **FIGURE 5.32**

Application of underlayment on low slopes.

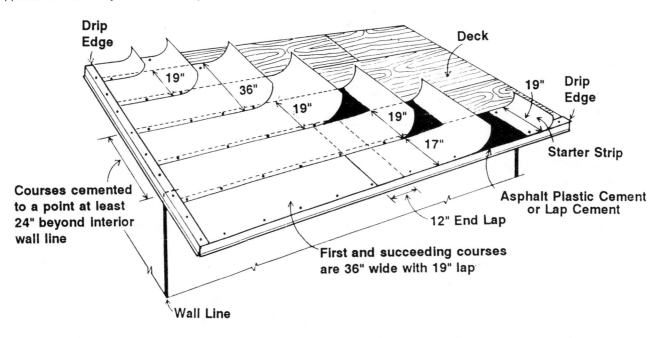

Installation of a drip edge.

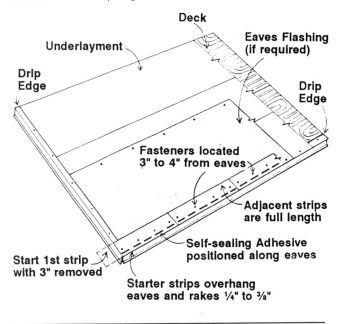

flashing. Cap flashing is used to cover the shingle flashing, which is often installed in sections and inserted in open mortar joints, penetrating 1½" into the mortar joint. The flashing strip may be either a metal strip or asphalt-saturated felt underlayment. The strip is a continual piece that lies over the last course of shingles. The flashing strip should be bent to extend 5" up the vertical wall and at least 4" onto the last shingle course. (See Figure 5.35.)

■ FIGURE 5.34

Application of step flashing and step flashing against a vertical sidewall.

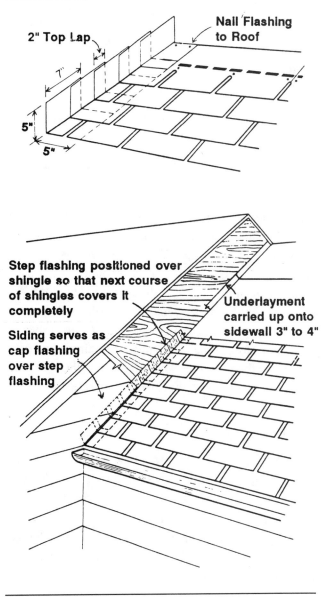

bility of icing along the eaves. The flashing material and width of the flashing strip depend on the severity of the icing conditions that could occur. The eaves flashing should overhang the drip edge by ¼" to ⅜".

Step Flashing

Other types of flashings include base and step flashing. When the roof butts against a vertical wall, the end of each shingle course is protected by metal flashing shingles that are rectangular. These tin or galvanized metal shingles are bent at a 90° angle and extend up the side wall over the sheathing a minimum of 4".

When roofing felt is used under the wall finish, it is turned up on the wall and covered by the flashing. One piece of flashing is used at each shingle course. When the siding is installed over the flashing, there should be a 2" space between the bevel edge of the siding and the roof shingles. This type of flashing is called *step flashing*. (See Figure 5.34.)

Counterflashing

When the roof intersects a brick chimney or wall, step flashing is used at the end of each shingle course. The step flashing is covered by counterflashing or cap

■ FIGURE 5.35

Installation of counterflashing or cap flashing.

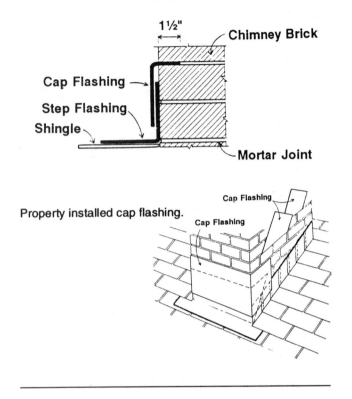

Property installed cap flashing.

■ FIGURE 5.36

Roof shingle applications around vent pipes.

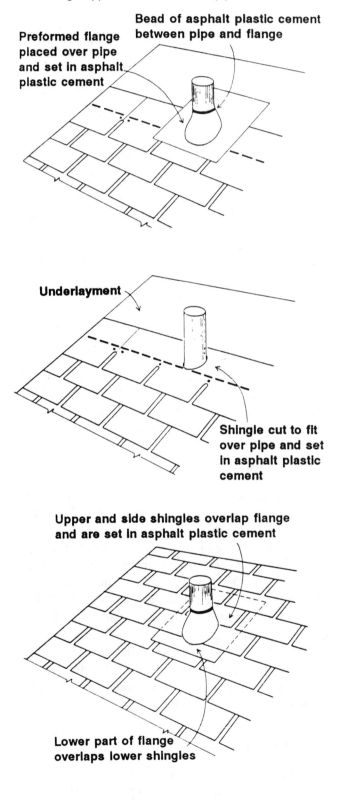

An additional row of shingles is required over the flashing strips and trimmed to the width of the strips. The siding over the vertical flashing serves as the cap flashing or counterflashing. There should be a 2″ space between the bottom edge of the siding and the roof. All dwellings have circular vents and ventilators, pipes, or stacks projecting through the roof that require a special type of flashing. The next course of shingles usually butts up to the vent pipe. The shingle over the vent pipe area is cut out to fit the diameter of the pipe.

Flashing Flange

Usually, the shingle is set in asphalt plastic cement over the pipe and nailed down. A preformed flashing flange assembly (also called a *roof jack*) that fits snugly around the pipe is placed over the vent pipe. The assembly is set in asphalt plastic cement. The flange should lie flat on the roof. After the flashing is in place, the installation of shingles will continue. (See Figure 5.36.)

Cricket

Flashings around chimneys have been discussed under step flashing and counterflashing. However, when flashings are installed around chimneys, it is often necessary to install a cricket at the intersection of roof deck and back face of the chimney. (See Figure 5.37.)

A cricket consists of two triangular pieces of plywood joined to form a level ridge that extends from the center of the chimney back to the wood deck. (See Figure 5.38.) When roofing is installed, the same procedures are followed as for flashing a vertical wall. Cap flashing or counterflashings must be placed over all base flashings to prevent water penetration between base flashing and chimney. The metal flashing should extend into the mortar joint of the brick 1½", then should be sealed with mortar and bent over the top of the base flashing. The flashing covering the base flashing should overlap 3".

■ VALLEYS

Valleys require a sturdy flashing because they have excessive water movement and weight due to the natural dam effect (particularly on a low-sloped roof) caused by debris such as leaves, branches, and buildups of snow and ice. Excessive water passes through the valleys to the gutters rather than to any other area of the roof. Valleys, formed by two intersecting roof lines, are usually covered with metal flashing or mineral-surfaced roll roofing. The width of the valley between shingles should increase from the top to the bottom. When adjacent roof slopes vary, such as a low-slope roof intersecting with a steeper roof, a crimped standing seam should be used. This diverts the water and protects the roof with the lower slope in heavy rains.

There are different ways of treating valleys, such as open valleys, woven valleys, and closed-cut valleys. Woven and closed-cut valleys are used for strip shingles. For any type of valley treatment used, the valley flashing should be installed before the shingles are installed. The fire rating of the completed roof determines the valley construction techniques used.

Open Valleys

Open valleys can be composed of either metal or composition roll roofing. If metal is used, it must be not less than 28-gauge, corrosion-resistant, galvanized sheet metal. Depending on the type of roof and slope, the sections of flashing should have an end lap of 4" to 6".

The width of the flashing varies with the slope, load, and type of roof. On some roofs, a flashing 12" wide might be adequate, while other roofs might require that the flashing be 36" wide. When rolled roofing is used for a valley, there is usually underlayment under the rolled roofing or a double ply of rolled roofing. Although it is not always necessary to have underlayment under metal valley flashing, most roofing contractors use underlayment. Open valleys are used with wood shingles; wood shake roofs; slate, tile, metal, other decorative roofs; and some asphalt shingle roofs. (See Figure 5.39.)

Woven Valleys

The valley flashing is already in place along with the underlayment. The shingles on the intersecting roof surfaces are applied toward the valley from both roof areas simultaneously. Each roof area may be worked separately up to a point about 3" from the center of the valley, which can be enclosed later. (See Figure 5.40.)

Whichever procedure is followed, either woven or cut valley, the last shingle should extend at least 12" onto the intersecting roof. This includes the first course along the eaves of one roof area up to and over the valley. The first course of the intersecting roof along the eaves should extend across the valley over the top of the shingles crossing the valley. Again, the shingle should extend at least 12" on the other roof surface. Each shingle should be pressed tightly into the valley. The woven valley sometimes is preferred for its appearance and excellent weather protection.

Closed-Cut Valleys

The valley flashing is already in place along with the underlayment. The first course of shingles is along the eaves of one intersecting roof plane and across the valley. The shingles on the roof plane that has the lower slope or lesser height and the end shingle should extend at least 12" onto the adjoining roof. All succeeding courses should be laid in the same manner, with the end shingles extending across the valley and onto the adjoining roof. The shingles should be pressed tightly into the valley. The first course of shingles should be placed along the eaves and cross the valley onto the adjoining roof plane. The shingles being installed should be trimmed no less than 2" back from the valley centerline. (See Figure 5.41.)

For the proper flow of water over the trimmed shingle, the upper corner of each shingle should be

■ FIGURE 5.37

Installation of base flashing at front, side, and rear of chimney.

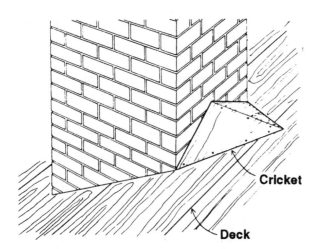

Location and configuration of a chimney cricket.

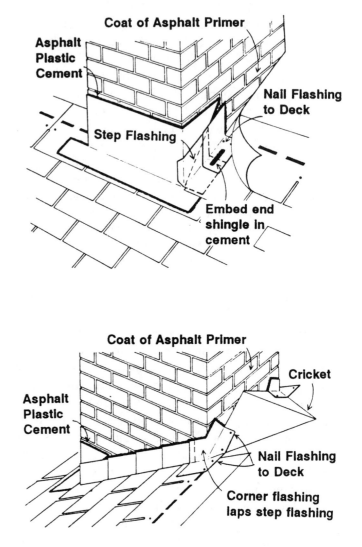

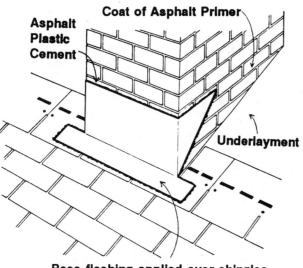

Base flashing applied over shingles and set in asphalt plastic cement

trimmed 1″ on a 45° angle to direct the water in the valley. The trimmed end of the shingle should be embedded in a 3″-wide strip of asphalt plastic cement.

■ TESTING

Fire resistance is an important safety consideration and the main concern behind many local building codes. The Federal Housing Administration (FHA) and Depart-

ment of Veterans Affairs (VA) require that roofing materials conform to certain standards. Asphalt roofing manufacturers submit materials to independent testing laboratories for testing against established standards.

Fire Resistance

The most widely accepted standard for building materials is ASTM E-108. If the material being tested meets the standard, the product will carry the testing lab-

FIGURE 5.38

Application of base flashing over cricket.

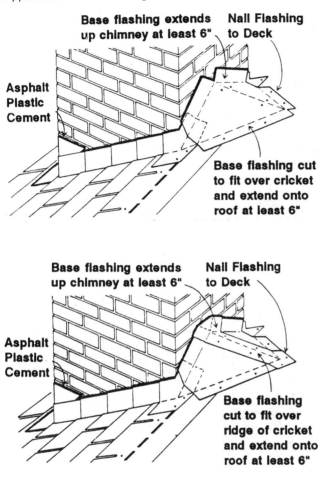

oratory's label. (See Figure 5.42.) This indicates its class of fire resistance in agreement with the named standard. There are three classes, which are listed below.

1. Class A—Severe exposure to fire. Roof coverings include slate, tile, concrete, corrugated asbestos cement, fiberglass, or other coverings approved by the testing agency.
2. Class B—Moderate exposure to fire. Roof coverings include corrugated iron sheets, galvanized iron sheets, galvanized iron shingles, sheet copper, or other coverings approved by the testing agency.
3. Class C—Light exposure to fire. Roof coverings include asphalt shingles, asphalt roll roofing, pressure-treated cedar shingles, pressure-treated cedar shakes, or other coverings approved by the testing agency.

Most asphalt roofing materials are Class C or better. The label is evidence that the material will provide the fire resistance for which it is rated.

Not all types of roofing materials have a fire-resistance rating. For example, untreated wood shingles and wood shakes are unrated. Most building codes now require wood shingles and wood shakes to be pressure treated with a fire retardant to give them a Class C rating. Fiberglass and most of the decorative roof materials such as slates, tile, and metals have a Class A or B rating. Flat roofs also have minimum performance requirements when exposed to external fire situations.

External Fire Ratings

Most building code agencies require that flat roofs have minimum performance requirements when exposed to external fire situations. The recognized test procedure for evaluating this performance is Underwriters Laboratories' UL 790 (Tests for Fire Resistance of Roof Covering Materials). This test is approved by the code agencies and is virtually identical to the ASTM E-108 procedure.

Under the UL 790 test procedure, roof coverings are rated Class A, B, and C. Class A is the highest rating, and such roofing materials are defined as being effective against severe fire exposures. Materials with Class B and C ratings are defined as being effective against moderate and light fire exposures, respectively. These ratings reflect tests completed on assemblies, not individual components. The assemblies consist of the type of roofing system (adhered, ballasted, or mechanically attached), membrane, insulation, and deck. The type of roof deck on which the membrane and insulation are to be applied determines the number and types of tests required under the UL 790 procedure.

Noncombustible decks (concrete, gypsum, or steel) require only the spread of flame test. Combustible decks (plywood, wood, or tectum, i.e., roof structure or covering) require spread of flame test, intermittent flame test, and burning brand test. The basic criteria for determining the performance rating under each of these tests follow.

Spread of Flame Test
- Class A (10 min. exposure) 6'0" max flame spread
- Class B (10 min. exposure) 8'0" max flame spread
- Class C (4 min. exposure) 13'0" max flame spread

■ FIGURE 5.39

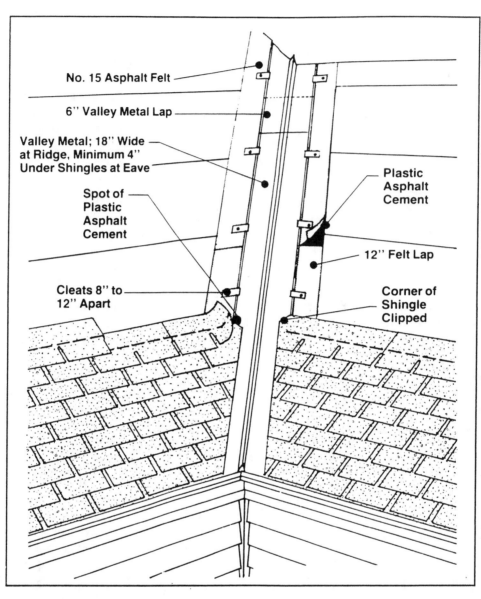

No. 15 Asphalt Felt

6" Valley Metal Lap

Valley Metal; 18" Wide at Ridge, Minimum 4" Under Shingles at Eave

Spot of Plastic Asphalt Cement

Cleats 8" to 12" Apart

Plastic Asphalt Cement

12" Felt Lap

Corner of Shingle Clipped

Use of roll roofing material for typical open valley using valley metal flashing.

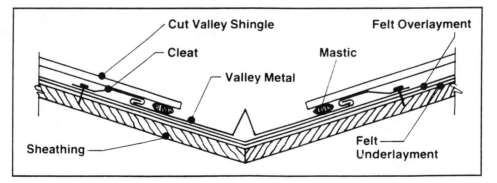

Cut Valley Shingle

Cleat

Felt Overlayment

Mastic

Valley Metal

Sheathing

Felt Underlayment

Section through valley.

■ **FIGURE 5.40**

Installation of shingles in a woven valley.

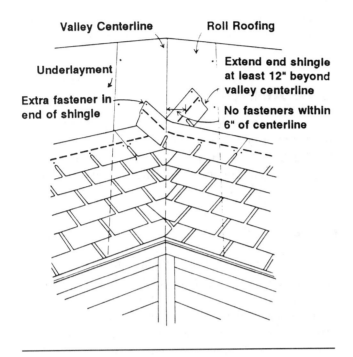

■ **FIGURE 5.41**

Installation of shingles in a closed-cut valley.

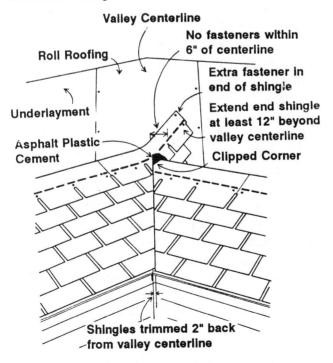

Failure occurs if the spread length is exceeded, if the flame travels laterally off both sides of the deck, if the top surface of the deck is exposed, or if flying brands are produced that continue to burn on the floor.

Intermittent Flame Test
- Class A (15 cycles, 2 min. on, 2 min. off)
- Class B (8 cycles, 2 min. on, 2 min. off)
- Class C (3 cycles, 1 min. on, 2 min. off)

The intermittent flame test is continued until all evidence of flame, glow, and smoke has disappeared from both the exposed surface and the underside of the test deck. Failure occurs if the deck sustains a flame, if the

■ **FIGURE 5.42**

Typical labels from an independent testing laboratory.

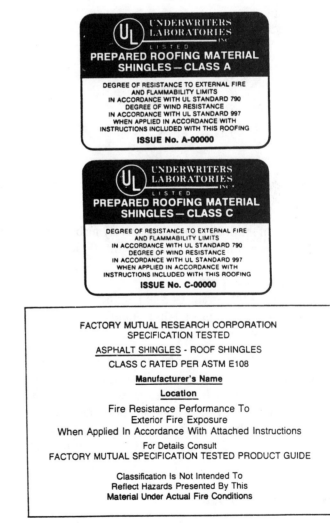

■ FIGURE 5.43

Diagram of a typical gutter and downspout system.

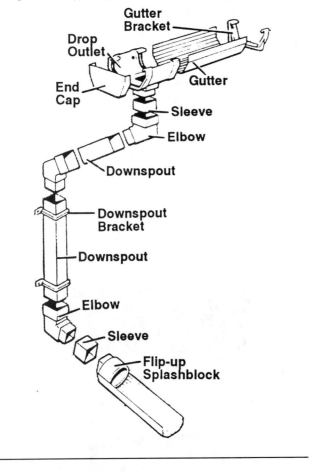

top surface of the deck is exposed, or if flying brands are produced that continue to burn on the floor.

Burning Brand Test
- Class A—2,000-gram (4.5-lb.) brand
- Class B—500-gram (1.1-lb.) brand
- Class C—9¼-gram (3-oz.) brand

The brand test is continued until the brand is consumed and until all evidence of flame, glow and smoke has disappeared from both the exposed surface and the underside of the test deck. Failure occurs if the deck sustains a flame, if the top surface of the deck is exposed, or if flying brands are produced that continue to burn on the floor.

Wind Resistance

Asphalt roofing shingles are tested for performance in high winds. The testing laboratory tests shingles applied to a roof deck in agreement with the manufacturer's specifications. They are also subjected to a 60-mile-per-hour wind for two hours with no single tab lift during the test according to ASTM D-3161 or a similar standard. In some hurricane or wind-prone areas in the country, the uplift requirements are greater.

■ DRAINAGE

It is important that all roofs drain, regardless of the slope of the roof. If the water is allowed to fall next to the foundation, serious damage may result. Therefore, gutters and downspouts are installed to carry water away from the foundation.

Gutters

Gutters are a good investment, provided they are properly installed and maintained. Gutters properly installed will slope to the downspouts to allow them to carry the water away from the roof. (See Figure 5.43.) A gutter that does not drain properly can cause water damage to the roof structure (fascia, soffit, and rafters). Gutters and downspouts are manufactured from various materials, such as aluminum, copper, galvanized steel, vinyl, and wood.

Aluminum gutters are popular because they are lightweight and can be installed in continual lengths. They have a baked enamel finish for low maintenance and are more durable and weather resistant. Aluminum gutters are available in different sizes and various gauges of metal (thickness of material). The aluminum downspout also is available in various sizes and gauges of metal.

Copper gutters are very expensive. They are larger than other types of gutters. All splices have to be soldered to seal them. Copper gutters will usually be found on larger, more expensive homes.

Galvanized gutters are probably the least expensive gutters to install. Galvanized gutters are sold in 10′ lengths. It is important to seal each splice to prevent leaking and corrosion. It also is important to keep these gutters cleaned and painted. They can be purchased with baked-on enamel, which is a good investment. If left unpainted, galvanized metal deteriorates quickly. Galvanized gutters and downspouts are available in various sizes and gauges of metal.

Vinyl gutters are low-maintenance. They also are sold in 10′ lengths. The splices need to be sealed. Vinyl gutters will not corrode, rot, or blister, but will have some expansion or contraction.

Wood gutters, if available, would be very expensive. Currently, some old homes have wood gutters. Wood gutters need to be cleaned, sealed, and painted to prevent deterioration.

Gutters and downspouts have various brackets, straps, spikes, and ferrules to attach the gutters to the fascia. The aluminum gutter requires a bracket to give it the required support, but the galvanized metal gutter uses the spike and ferrule for hanging support. The spike and ferrule method is the easiest and quickest way to hang guttering. The drawback is that spikes work loose through normal wear, allowing the gutter to come loose from the fascia board. Copper gutters have their own brackets. These gutters are heavy and require more support than the other gutters. When gutters are installed in sections, it is important that the overlapping follows the water flow and not the reverse.

Downspouts

Downspouts need to be sized correctly to carry the water from the roof to a desired area away from the foundation. They should be strapped securely to the wall or post and there should be at least one downspout for every 40′ of gutter. The downspout should dump onto a splash block sloped to drain away from the foundation or drain into a tile to carry the water away. (See Figure 5.44.)

When inspecting, it is wise to recommend that water from a downspout not be allowed to drain directly onto a roof below. The upper story downspout should connect to a lower level gutter on the lower roof. (The home may have been originally constructed that way, so be sure to state this as only a recommendation.)

Gutters and downspouts are sized according to the area of the roof they are to drain. Gutters are sized in diameters. The smallest are 4″, 5″, and 6″. Downspouts are sized 3″ × 3″, 3″ × 4″, and 3″ × 5″. The downspout has to be sized to drain the gutter.

■ VENTILATION

Proper ventilation of the attic is not easily understood but is a very helpful method of controlling heating and cooling costs. Ventilation also aids in obtaining the maximum life from the building materials used in the roof construction and the roof covering itself. Some of the possible problems include premature failure of the roofing,

■ FIGURE 5.44

Downspouts consist of a concrete or plastic splash block, a leader extension, or a drywell.

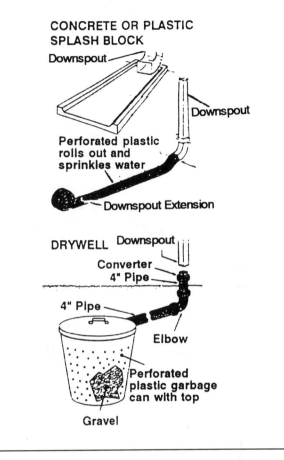

including blistering and buckling caused by deck movement. Moisture accumulation in insulation and rotting of wood members are also reasons for failure.

During summer months, radiant heat from the sun can cause very high roof deck temperatures. Gradually, the entire attic space is heated, and the entire dwelling feels the effect of the hot roof. The heat buildup can be short-circuited by ventilating the underside of the roof deck. Prolonged exposure to high heat levels will accelerate aging and shorten the service life of roofing materials. For example, asphalt products will dry out and become brittle, curl and crack. Wood shingles and shakes also will curl and crack. Having a properly ventilated air flow through the attic between the roof deck and a layer of insulation will offer protection against heat buildup.

Cold-weather problems are different. Heavier insulation and tighter construction help seal the side walls more effectively against air migration. Large volumes of

■ **FIGURE 5.45**

Various types of roof vents used in construction.

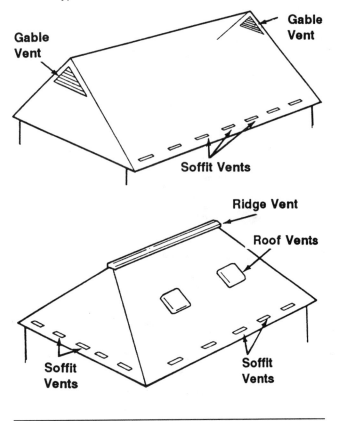

occupancy-generated water vapor are pushed toward the drier outside air. Vapor retarders will reduce the flow, but will not stop it. Condensation forms when the vapor comes in contact with the cold surface, such as the underside of the roof deck. The water can soak the insulation, rendering it useless, and can cause wood rot, ceiling damage, and peeling paint. Proper ventilation will guide water vapor to circulate freely under the roof deck, where it can be removed before condensation occurs. Proper ventilation allows air to carry away water vapor before it can condense.

There are minimum ventilation requirements for all attics with several effective methods for ventilating attics. (See Figure 5.45.) Some of the best methods are combinations of soffit vents and ridge vents, which provide a natural draft from the bottom to the top of the attic space. Another combination is soffit vents and gable vents. If the soffit vents are not used, properly sized gable vents alone will be adequate. Attic ventilation can be improved by adding turbine vents to the roof. The turbines can be either wind driven or power

driven. The power-driven turbine is usually equipped with a thermostat that controls the operation of the power vent. The thermostat can be set to a desired temperature for operation. Turbine vents can improve attic ventilation by 50 percent. The minimum specifications are 1 sq. ft. net free ventilating area for every 150 sq. ft. of attic floor space.

Louver and vent openings should not be covered during winter. Soffit vents should not be blocked by insulation. Structures with bath and kitchen vents must be vented to the exterior of the dwelling and not into the attic to prevent excess moisture. Many times, bathroom vents can cause roof damage in isolated areas.

Built-up roofs should have good cross ventilation to protect the roof structure and roof from the underside. When the roof decking and roofing are nailed to the top side of the rafter and the ceiling is nailed to the bottom, it is necessary to have ventilation.

Roofs with an attic also require ventilation and need to be insulated. Both are important. There should be at least 2″ between the top of the insulation and the underside of the roof deck. (See Figures 5.46 and 5.47.)

■ DAMAGE

Built-up roofs are difficult to inspect because most have no attic. So unless the water has penetrated the

■ **FIGURE 5.46**

A schematic drawing indicating the importance of proper attic ventilation.

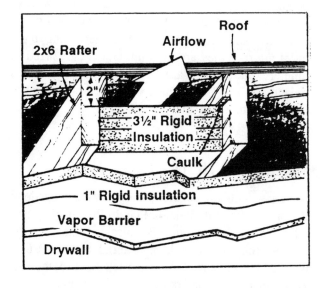

■ **FIGURE 5.47**

A cross-sectional diagram of proper ventilation and airflow.

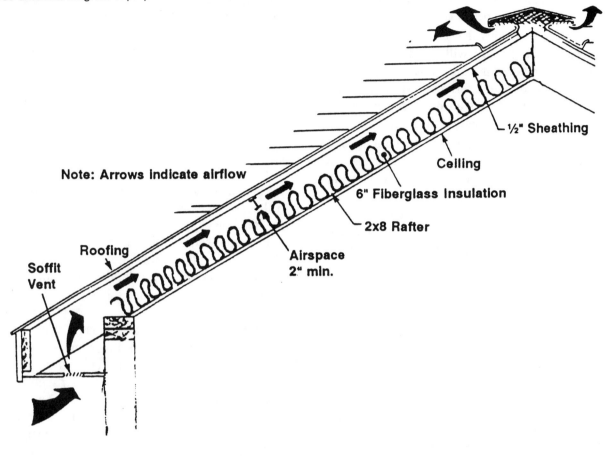

Note: Arrows indicate airflow

½" Sheathing

Ceiling

6" Fiberglass Insulation

2x8 Rafter

Airspace 2" min.

Roofing

Soffit Vent

ceiling, small leaks could go undetected. There are several signs the inspector should observe when inspecting a built-up roof:

Alligatoring is the cracking of the surfacing bitumen on a built-up roof, producing a pattern of cracks similar to alligator hide. The cracks may extend through the surfacing bitumen.

Blistering is a spongy, raised portion (bubble) of a roof membrane ranging from 1″ to a barely noticeable height.

Delamination is the separation of the plies in the roof membrane system, which usually appears as a blister.

An *expansion joint* is a structural separation between two building elements.

A *fishmouth* is a half-cylindrical or half-conical opening formed by an edge wrinkle.

A *strawberry* is a small bubble or blister in the flood coating of a gravel-surfaced roof membrane.

The inspector should observe the bare areas (exposed felt) and separation between roof surface and drip edge.

Roof discoloration can be caused by algae, also called *fungus growth*. This is a frequent problem. It is often mistaken for soot, moss, dirt, or tree droppings. The algae that causes this discoloration does not feed on any of the roofing materials, so it does not affect the life of the roof. The algae may cause a light-colored roof to turn dark brown or black in a few years.

Algae discoloration is very difficult to remove from the roof surface. The roof surface can be lightened with a diluted solution of chlorine bleach, which should be sponged on the roof gently. Do not scrub the roof because scrubbing will loosen and remove the granules, causing damage to the roof. It is important to use caution when using this solution so other parts of the dwelling, including the shrubbery, are not damaged or destroyed. After the solution has been sponged on the roof, the roof should be thoroughly rinsed off with a garden hose to remove the solution. The cleaning usually is only temporary, and the discoloration could recur. The roofing industry has now developed algae resistant roofing.

There are other stains that are encountered with roofs. Dirt and soot normally will not damage the roof, only discolor it. However, there are certain types of moss that can cause a roof to deteriorate. Moss indicates moisture, and prolonged moisture on the roof can cause the roof to leak and, eventually, can destroy the roof.

There are stains that are inherent in certain types of roofing, such as cedar shingles. Some cedar shingle roofs are installed over 1″ × 4″ furring strips, allowing the underside of the shingles to be observed from the attic. There will be dark stains on the shingle. These are not water stains, but rather the oils bleeding out of the cedar shingle. A roof leak would appear as a stain, but it would also stain the furring strip and run down a rafter. The inspector should look for excessive light (direct light) coming through the roof.

■ WARRANTIES

The inspector should never discuss the warranty of a roof or roofing material because the manufacturer's warranty might not be transferable to the new owner. Many manufacturers' warranties are transferable, but they can be voided if the interior has been remodeled or if walls have been moved.

The manufacturer's warranty should be read very carefully by the inspector's customer if there is a valid warranty on the roofing material. Many times, when a home is inspected, the inspector will find that the roof needs replacing. If the inspection is done pursuant to a real estate contract for sale, the inspector can recommend that the seller obtain a valid contract from a reputable roofing contractor. The roof can be installed after the change of ownership to allow the warranty to be in the new owner's name.

The life expectancy of a cedar shingle roof depends on the grade of shingle, the slope of the roof and the maintenance of the roof.

■ REROOFING

One question that is often asked of an inspector is what the condition of the roof is and whether it should be replaced. A roof should be replaced when it is no longer economically feasible to repair it.

Regular maintenance is required on all roofs. Some roofing materials require more maintenance than others. Cedar shingle and cedar shake roofs, after three to five years, are considered high-maintenance roofs. Lignin, a molasses-like substance that cements the wood cells together, bleeds out of the shingles and shakes, which become brittle, crack, and curl. Wind then blows them off the roof. Once a year, the roof needs to be inspected and repaired.

The built-up roof is also a high-maintenance roof because of the flat surface. It is necessary to remove any tree branches and other debris and clean the roof drains to allow water to drain off the roof. There should not be any standing or ponding of water on a built-up roof. A built-up roof should completely drain within 24 hours after a rain. Other roofs also should be inspected annually; however, as a rule, they will not require as much maintenance as cedar shingle, cedar shake, and built-up roofs.

When the roof approaches the end of its economic life, the cost of repairs becomes as expensive as replacing the roof. Before the contractor replaces the roof, it is important that the company be familiar with the local codes on roofing materials. It should also be aware of the number of roofs allowed before they must be stripped. For example, some cities allow three asphalt shingle roofs on a dwelling before stripping, and other cities allow only two asphalt shingle roofs. (See Figure 5.48.)

When asphalt shingles are installed over a cedar shingle roof, it becomes the decking. It is not wise to install a cedar shingle roof over asphalt shingles because the asphalt shingles have a tendency to deteriorate faster. Due to uneven surfaces of cedar shakes, it is very difficult to install asphalt shingles over them. When composition shingles are installed over another roof, whether composition or cedar shingle, it is called an *overlay*. In some areas, when composition shingles are the overlay on a cedar shingle roof, some insurance companies will not insure the roof.

To replace a cedar shingle roof or a cedar shake roof with the same kind of roof, the old roof should be removed first. This is important in warmer climates where there is high humidity, which causes the roof to deteriorate prematurely.

Composition shingles may be used over an old wood shingle roof if certain precautions are taken. When placing a composition shingle over a wood shingle, the wood shingle roof becomes the decking for

■ **FIGURE 5.48**

Bridging and nesting are two reroofing methods that may be used when replacing asphalt shingles with asphalt shingles.

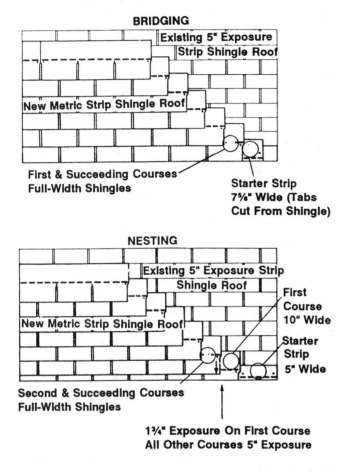

■ **FIGURE 5.49**

Reroofing with asphalt shingles over an old wood shingle roof.

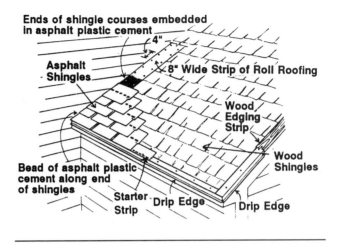

the composition shingle roof. The rough edges of the old roof must be trimmed and the edge treated as a new deck by installing a metal strip that is called the *drip edge*. (See Figure 5.49.) Many government and other lending agencies will not make loans on properties that have exposed decking material.

Decorative roofs have to be removed before a new roof can be installed. This includes slates, tiles, clay, concrete, and metals. Another determination the inspector must make is whether the condition of the existing roof deck is sound and undamaged. The roof structure must be adequate for the style of roof the customer wants installed.

The homeowner may want a different style of roof than he or she currently has. For example, the dwelling may have a cedar shingle roof that the homeowner wants replaced with a tile roof. The roof structure

would have to be reinforced because of the weight of the tile. (See Figure 5.50.)

Each built-up reroof or re-cover project has its own specific problems that require individual assessment. The roofing contractor needs to prepare for reroofing by thoroughly checking the existing roof system and the reasons why the roof deteriorated.

The existing roof deck must be sound and undamaged. A sample of the existing membrane should always be removed down to the deck. The insulation should be inspected for wetness and, if damaged, it should be replaced. If the existing insulation is dry and undamaged, it may be possible to salvage it. Some insulation products cannot be salvaged; removing the membrane causes delamination of the insulating boards. A single minimum layer of insulation should be installed over the existing insulation to provide a suitable surface for the new membrane. This should be done regardless of the style of roof or whether it is a wood shingle, an asphalt shingle, a decorative (slate, tile, or metal), or a built-up roof.

■ BUILT-UP ROOFS

Flat roofs have several types of coverings. The most common is a built-up roof with a gravel surface. Built-up roofs are constructed by building ply (layer) upon ply of organic or fiberglass felt. A mopping of asphalt or coal tar pitch is used between plies to produce a monolithic slab of waterproofing. The felt serves only to rein-

■ **FIGURE 5.50**

Roof structure must be reinforced when replacing a wood shingle roof with a tile or slate roof.

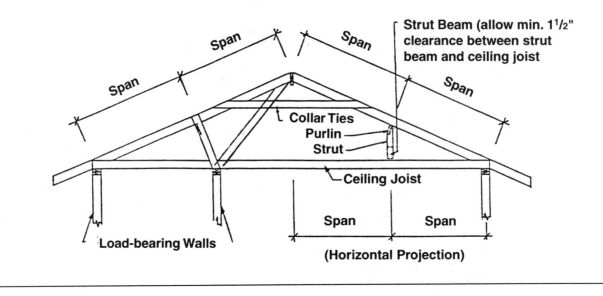

force the bitumen and keep it in place. Mineral aggregate surface on built-up roofing consists of three layers of 15-lb. felt applied only to solid-surface roofs with slopes not greater than 2/12. (See Figure 5.51.) When gravel makes initial contact with the hot bitumen flood coat, it should become embedded in the bitumen. The balance of the gravel serves as ballast and protection for the roof membrane surface.

Other flat roofs are modified bitumens. They are applied either with hot asphalt or with torches that melt the bitumen and weld the laps together to make a complete roof. This type of roof may have a gravel surface. It also may be unsurfaced or have a surface coating of gray emulsion or aluminum. Other types of flat roofs are EPDM, CPE, PVC, or CPSE. Some of these will be mineral surfaced. Some are laid loose and have large rocks for ballast (to hold them down) (See Figure 5.52.) while others are mechanically attached. The color will be black, gray, or white.

EPDM is an elastomeric compound synthesized from ethylene, propylene, and drene monomer. EPDM is generally used for roofing as a vulcanized material. It is also possible to formulate EPDM membranes that are not vulcanized. EPDM sheets range in thickness from 30 to 60 mils. These membranes are usually white or black; resist ultraviolet rays, weather, and abrasion; and have low temperature flexibility. The membranes also retain their properties of resilience and tensile strength in aging tests at high temperatures.

CPE (chlorinated polyethylene) may be formulated for roofing membranes, which range in thickness from 40 to 50 mils. CPE membranes are flexible and strongly

■ **FIGURE 5.51**

Asphalt glass fiber felt roof membrane with aggregate surfacing is installed over an insulated roof deck.

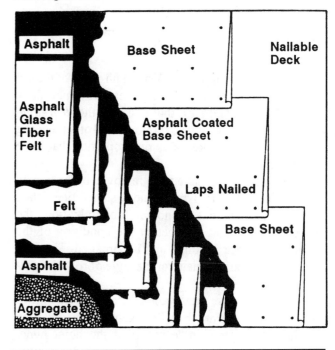

■ **FIGURE 5.52**

Mechanically fastened Versigard roof installation.

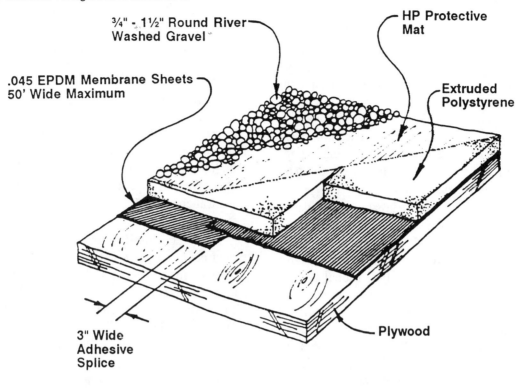

¾" - 1½" Round River Washed Gravel

.045 EPDM Membrane Sheets 50' Wide Maximum

HP Protective Mat

Extruded Polystyrene

3" Wide Adhesive Splice

Plywood

resistant to oils and chemicals. They are resistant to bitumen and can be installed directly over asphalt or coal tar pitch roofs. CPE is excellent in all climates and is ozone resistant.

PVC (polyvinyl chloride) in its basic form is a hard material. It requires the addition of other compounds (plasticizer and stabilizers) and ingredients to produce the desired physical properties. PVC membranes can be produced by calendering, extruding, or spread-coating. They may be either reinforced with fiberglass or non-reinforced and are usually 40 to 48 mils in thickness. When properly formulated, PVC has excellent fire resistance and seaming capabilities. It is chemically incompatible with bituminous materials.

CSPE (chlorosulfonated polyethylene) is a synthetic rubber under the name of *hypalon*. It is a self-curing, nonvulcanized elastomer, available as a liquid coating or in sheet form for single-ply application. CSPE may be reinforced with polyester scrim or laminated to felt backing materials with a finished thickness of 30 to 60 mils. CSPE is a nonvulcanized product that exhibits thermoplastic qualities during field installation. It is resistant to ozone, weathering, pollutants, and most chemicals.

The most vulnerable part of any roof system for leaks is at flashing locations. These are roof penetrations and points at which the horizontal roof deck joins a vertical surface.

Premature roof failures are caused by both economic and technical factors. Economically, the building's roof system normally falls far behind the more glamorous building systems competing for construction money. Many poor decisions underlie many premature roofing failures. Many designers and builders fail to build in a slope to avoid water ponding.

Technical factors that contribute to premature roof failures include expanding roof dimensions, complex roof design, field application, proliferation of new materials, and the trend toward more flexible buildings.

Roofs must withstand a much broader attack from natural forces than do other building components. Roof surfaces experience annual temperature changes exceeding 200°F. Some temperature changes occur rapidly as solar radiation heats the roof to 180°F. This heat accelerates photochemical deterioration. Snow, sleet, rain, hailstones, acid mists, pollutants, and fungi attack the roof.

Expanding roof dimensions also may cause roof problems. A large roof is more complex and subject to more problems than a small roof. Larger roofs must have expansion joints to accommodate thermal expansions and contractions. Membrane splitting is caused by movement of unanchored insulation boards. The major cause of splitting occurs more frequently on large roof surfaces because the boards have greater area to move, thus producing membrane stress concentrations. Peripheral venting is less effective in relieving vapor pressure within a large roof system because roof area quadruples as its perimeter doubles.

Level built-up roofs also run a greater risk of inadequate drainage, a major cause of roof failure. Long structural spans deflect more than short spans. These deflections increase ponding probability. Large roof plans increase the inaccuracies in dimensional variations in decking, insulation, and membrane thickness. Other construction inaccuracies are humps and depressions and fabricated column heights. Still other hazards include water ponding on the roof that causes membrane delamination when freezing water penetrates the plies. Fungal growth caused by standing water may deteriorate organic roofing materials. Irregular ponding creates a warping pattern of surface elongation and contraction, wrinkling the membrane. Water penetration into organic or asbestos felts reduces their strength.

Despite problems of poor roof design, most roof failures are caused by poor workmanship. Many roofing contractors fail to read roof specifications. A built-up roof should be inspected at least twice a year. This avoids clogged drains, which cause water to pond to excessive depths and may cause the roof to collapse. Other areas to check are the flashings and membrane. Splits, blisters, bare areas, and other repairable defects must be repaired before they leak. If not, water penetrates the building and causes the roof to degenerate to the point of an expensive tearoff-and-replace situation.

Roof Components

A built-up roof system has three basic components: structural deck, thermal insulation, and membrane. A vapor retarder is required for roofs over humid interiors in cool climates. Flashings are a basic part of a built-up roof assembly. It is indispensable to seal joints where the membrane is either pierced or terminated at gravel stops, expansion joints, vents, drains, walls, and curbs. The built-up roof assembly functions as a system, that is, the performance of each component depends on the performance of the other components. The waterproof membranes' integrity depends on the security of the components' anchorage. The shear-strength between the deck and vapor retarder, insulation, and between the insulation and membrane must be secure for roof soundness. The insulation's thermal resistance can be drastically reduced by moisture, and it also depends on the effectiveness of the vapor retarder and membrane. The integrity of the vapor retarder, insulation, and membrane depends on the stability of the structural deck, which transmits gravity, earthquake, and wind forces to the roof framing. The four major design factors are component anchorage, dimensional stability, deflection, and fire resistance.

Decks are classified as nailable or nonnailable for the purpose of anchoring the insulation, vapor retarder, or membrane to the deck. Timber or plywood decks should be nailed only because of the threat of heated bitumen dripping through the joints. Concrete is limited to nonnailed deck.

Vapor retarders are made of various materials. The common vapor retarder, known as a vapor seal, comprises three bituminous moppings with two plies of saturated felt or two bituminous moppings enclosing an asphalt-coated base sheet. Vapor-retarder materials also include various plastic sheets, aluminum foil and laminated kraft paper sheets used with bitumen sandwich filler or bitumen kraft paper. The vapor retarder may cause problems that outweigh the benefits.

For example, if the insulation contained moisture when installed, the vapor retarder will prevent the moisture from escaping. The vapor retarder is not always incorporated in the roof design. If it is required, it must be designed with either edge venting or stack vents. Large roof areas may have stack vents, allowing moisture to escape and reducing damage from vapor pressure buildup.

Thermal insulation increases interior comfort, prevents condensation on interior building surfaces and reduces operating costs for heating and cooling. Thermal insulation also relieves the concentrated stresses transferred to the built-up membrane from movement in the structural deck, and provides an acceptable substrate for membrane application on the deck. Insulation is available in several forms: rigid insulation prefabricated into boards, dual-purpose structural deck and insulating planks, and fiber board insulation. Fiber board insulation is most vulnerable to moisture

■ **FIGURE 5.53**

A satisfactory method of joining the two-piece flashing system.

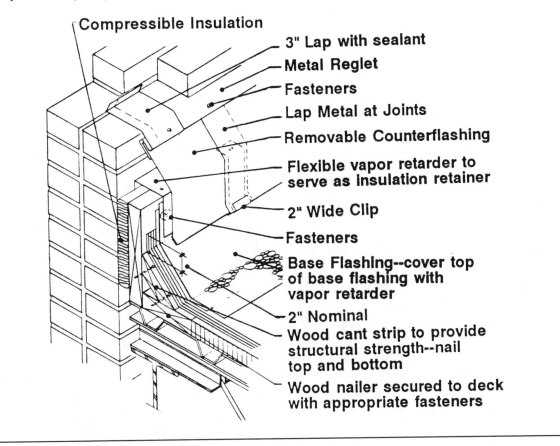

Compressible Insulation

- 3" Lap with sealant
- Metal Reglet
- Fasteners
- Lap Metal at Joints
- Removable Counterflashing
- Flexible vapor retarder to serve as insulation retainer
- 2" Wide Clip
- Fasteners
- Base Flashing--cover top of base flashing with vapor retarder
- 2" Nominal
- Wood cant strip to provide structural strength--nail top and bottom
- Wood nailer secured to deck with appropriate fasteners

and eventually rots and weakens fibrous organic board or organic plastic binder. All insulation materials are vulnerable to moisture or freeze-thaw damage.

The built-up membrane, which is the weatherproofing component of the roof system, has three basic elements: (1) felts, (2) bitumen alternated like a multideck sandwich, and (3) a surfacing, usually an aggregate. The membrane forms a semiflexible roof covering with as few as two plies or up to four or five plies of felt contoured to fit the deck. The waterproofing agent is the bitumen, which is asphalt or coal tar pitch. The felts stabilize and strengthen the bitumen and prevent excessive flow when the bitumen is semifluid. They also distribute contractive tensile stress when bitumen is cold.

Mineral aggregate—normally gravel, crushed rock, or slag—is used to protect the bitumen flood coat from life-shortening solar radiation. Aggregate permits the use of heavy uniform bitumen coating for greater waterproofing and longer membrane life. Aggregate also

serves as a fire-resistant skin preventing flame spread, and it protects the bitumen from wind, rain, and other physical damage. Surfacing aggregate is not used on smooth-surfaced asphalt roofs such as asbestos or fiberglass felts. The advantage of a smooth-surfaced membrane is that it allows early detection and repair of leaks through membrane fissures that would be obscured by the aggregate. Smooth-surfaced roofs require more frequent maintenance than aggregate-surfaced roofs.

Flashings may be classified as base flashings, which form the upturned edges of the membrane where it is pierced or terminated, and as counterflashings or cap flashings, which shield the exposed joints of base flashings. Base flashings are constructed of bitumen, impregnated felts, fabrics, plastics, or nonmetallic material. Counterflashings or cap flashings are constructed of sheet metal, galvanized or stainless steel, copper, lead, or aluminum. Flashings are generally the major source of roof leaks. (See Figure 5.53.)

Roof Drainage

It is important that all roofs drain properly and a *necessity* that a flat roof drain properly. A flat roof that is well drained will give much more trouble-free service than one that does not drain properly. All flat roofs require some slope to cause the roofs to drain. Roofing experts recommend a minimum ⅛″ per foot of slope. Flat roofs should completely drain in 24 hours to have proper drainage. Flat roofs that allow water to pond can be very dangerous. This adds to the roof structure weight that it was not designed to carry and could cause structural failure and shorten the life of the roof. For example, a roof pond that is 40′ × 70′ with a depth of ⅞″ adds 3.3 tons to the weight of the roof. Problems that can be caused from ponding are many.

- Roof structural members fail, causing the roof to collapse.
- Ponding water is the cause of moisture invasion into the membrane and through any imperfections in the membrane: bare felt (no protective coating), fishmouth, splits, cracks. Liquid moisture can leak into insulation or into the building. Heated by the summer sun, the entrapped moisture accelerates growth of an interply void into a blister. Ice can delaminate the membrane as water freezes and expands. Continued freeze-thaw cycles can enlarge the delaminated areas.
- Moisture in insulation reduces the thermal resistance drastically and causes the organic fibers to rot.
- Standing water causes the growth of vegetation and fungi. Plant roots and fungi penetrate the membrane and spread into the insulation, creating objectionable odors and ideal breeding areas for insects.
- The roof surface temperature between the dry and ponded areas of the roof will have wide variations. In the summer, these temperature differences can range as much as 70°F or more. These differences cause warping patterns of surface elongation and contraction; entrapped water changing from cold to hot and vice versa creates condensation that causes further damage.
- Ice has a very high coefficient of thermal expansion-contraction. When ponded water freezes, the thermal movement of ice erodes the aggregate surface.
- Ponding or evidence of ponding can void some roofing manufacturers' warranties.

These are not all the problems poor drainage can cause. The real estate inspector should be aware that when there is evidence a roof has poor drainage, there could be serious consequences.

There are two different drainage systems: interior and peripheral. Depending on the size of the structure and roof design, one or both of the systems could be used. In the interior system, water flows from elevated peripheral areas to interior drains. Leaders conduct the water through the building interior to a storm sewer or to the exterior away from the building. The peripheral drainage system has a roof that is sloped slightly from the center of the roof to the peripheral low points. The slope continues to the scuppers and leaders located on the outside of the building.

The interior drainage system has advantages over the peripheral drainage system. With drainage pipes passing through the interior of a heated building, the interior system will continue to move water and melting snow during cold winter months. The operation of the peripheral drainage system depends totally on the outside temperature. In mild climates where temperatures seldom drop below freezing, the peripheral system functions very well. But freezing weather will cause the scupper areas and gutters to freeze and not function. This causes major roof damage. Peripheral drainage systems require more elaborate flashings. The gutters and scuppers also need to be protected. The peripheral system may have ice damming and metal flashing distortion from freeze-thaw cycles. Irregularly shaped roofs require extra drains for proper drainage. Water normally requires a straight flow from the elevated areas to the drain.

Poor drainage, especially on a flat roof, is probably the most common problem in inadequately sloped or dead-level decks. Other problems that interfere with the drainage system are gutters not properly installed. Gutters should be installed a little below the roof elevation. Other obstacles are scuppers not large enough or not properly flashed and sealed and strainers missing or clogged on drain inlets. There are other problems that can influence the drainage that a real estate inspector might find, but the ones mentioned are probably the most common.

Improper drainage, the main problem with built-up roofs, shortens the life span of a roof up to 50 percent. Therefore, roof design is very important. A dead-level roof may be essentially uncorrectable. Providing proper slope for drainage may require raising peripheral or wall flashings to impractical elevations, forcing a compromise on proper drainage. If ponding water invades the insulation, moisture will raise heating

Crickets should be located in low valleys between roof drains and on the high side of all curbs.

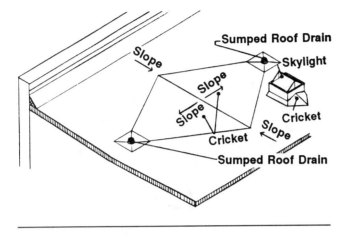

and cooling bills. Water absorption will triple heat loss through a roof system.

There is a way slopes may prove more practical and economical and provide positive drainage. Crickets and saddles are formed with tapered board insulation or poured fill. Flashing elevations are very important. Flashings should be located at the roof's high points, never in the low areas. (See Figure 5.54.)

The toughest roof drainage problem occurs with an existing roof that ponds water. Ponding water is a common problem with failed, dead-level, or inadequately sloped roofs. All roofs should be designed and built to ensure positive drainage. Ponding water is detrimental to roof membranes and causes problems such as

- deck deflections (may cause structural failure);
- membrane deterioration;
- debris accumulation;
- water-weakened felts splitting, causing leaks; and
- ice formation and membrane damage.

Every roof has its own specific set of drainage requirements. To ensure positive drainage, flat roofs should have at least the standard 1/4" slope per foot. Roof deflections are critically important in providing roof drainage. They should be limited to no more than 1/240 of the roof span to accommodate stresses of the concentrated or uniform loading. Drains must be located at points of maximum deflection in the roof. Because drainage must occur under both minimum and maximum loading conditions, an additional minimum

slope of 1/8" per foot must be added to positively drain the roof. Precast concrete decks or long-span prestressed concrete decks incorporate camber. Depending on structural design of the roof and drain placement, the camber may assist or restrict drainage. Drains should be recessed below the roof surface. Sufficient insulation must remain around the drain to prevent condensation. This is accomplished by setting the drain head below the insulation level and tapering the insulation down to the drain. Regular maintenance must be performed to prevent clogged drains. To avoid water buildup dangers from clogged drains, auxiliary drains or through-wall scuppers are recommended. (See Figure 5.55.)

Expansion Joints

Roof expansion joints are used to minimize stress and movement effects of the building's components. Expansion joints also prevent the stresses from splitting or ridging the roof membrane. The expansion joints in the roof assembly must be in the same location as the building's structural expansion joints. Every building component has varying coefficients of expansion and contraction, and each is subjected to varying temperature changes. Expansion joints must extend the entire

Membrane plies, metal flashing, and flash-in plies extend under clamping ring.

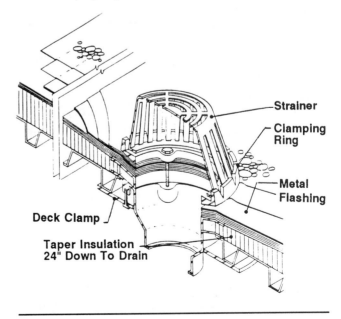

■ **FIGURE 5.56**

Expansion joint allows for building movement in both directions.

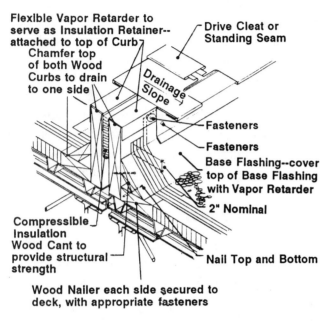

Flexible Vapor Retarder to serve as Insulation Retarder-- attached to top of Curb
Chamfer top of both Wood Curbs to drain to one side
Drive Cleat or Standing Seam
Drainage Slope
Fasteners
Fasteners
Base Flashing--cover top of Base Flashing with Vapor Retarder
2" Nominal
Compressible Insulation
Wood Cant to provide structural strength
Nail Top and Bottom
Wood Nailer each side secured to deck, with appropriate fasteners

■ **FIGURE 5.57**

Area dividers should be located between the roof's expansion joints.

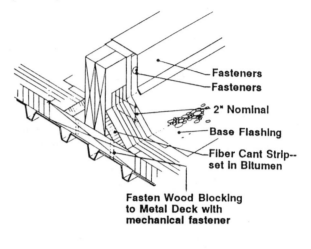

Fasteners
Fasteners
2" Nominal
Base Flashing
Fiber Cant Strip-- set in Bitumen
Fasten Wood Blocking to Metal Deck with mechanical fastener

width of the roof and never terminate short of the roof edge or perimeter. The expansion joint must accommodate contraction as well as expansion. Water must never drain through or over an expansion joint. (See Figure 5.56.)

Expansion joints are required

• when expansion or contraction joints are provided in the structural system;
• where steel framing, structural steel, or decking changes directions;
• where separate wings of L, U, T, or similar configurations exist;
• when the decking type changes, for example, when precast concrete deck abuts a steel deck;
• when additions are connected to existing buildings;
• at junctions where interior heating conditions change, such as when a heated office abuts an unheated warehouse; and
• where movement between vertical walls and roof deck may occur.

Area Dividers

Where expansion joints are not provided, area dividers help control thermal stresses in a roof system.

Area dividers minimize stress transmission from one area of the roof to another by dividing the entire roof area into smaller sections. These sections should be rectangular and uniformly spaced. An area divider is designed simply as a raised double wood member attached to a properly lashed wood base plate anchored to the roof deck. Depending on climate and area practices, area dividers for attached membrane systems are generally required at 150' to 200' intervals. They should be located between structural roof expansion joints and should not restrict water flow. (See Figure 5.57.)

Mechanical Curbs

The structural roof design must always allow for concentrated loading of mechanical equipment. Vibrations from roof-mounted or joist-mounted mechanical equipment must be isolated from the membrane and flashings. Some equipment may allow moisture to enter the building either from the exterior or from condensation. Mechanical equipment housings must be watertight. Water discharge from mechanical equipment must not be allowed on the roof surface.

Large mechanical units use drainage crickets to provide adequate drainage. Mechanical units should not restrict water flow. (See Figure 5.58.)

■ **FIGURE 5.58**

The concentrated load can be located directly over columns or heavy girders in the structure of the building.

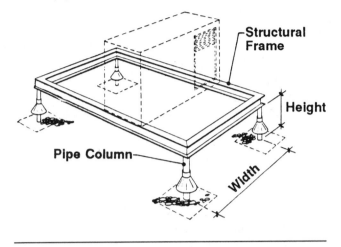

■ **FIGURE 5.59**

Clearances for multiple pipes are required to seal the penetrations.

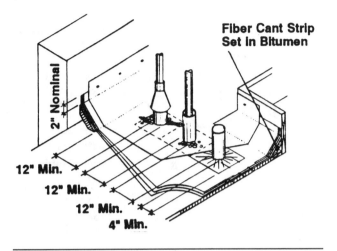

Penetrations

Penetrations around pipe projections may be flashed into the membrane using soft metal or lead flashing with integral flashing flanges stripped into the membrane. Dependable practice dictates that curbs be placed around all penetrations. Pitch boxes or pitch pockets around penetrations should not be used because they are a constant maintenance problem. Projections should not be located in valleys or drain areas. Adequate space should be allowed between pipes, curbs, and walls for installation of roofing materials. (See Figure 5.59.)

All curbs, penetrations, roof drains, and plumbing pipes must be in place before the roof is installed. Openings for curbs cut through the roof membrane after roof installation may cause serious bitumen drippage problems when the membrane is constructed of low-softening-point bitumen. All curbs must be fastened to the roof deck or building structure. (See Figure 5.60.)

Roof drains and vent pipes must be in place and restrained prior to roofing. This prevents damage to the flashings or membrane if mechanical devices are installed over the completed membrane. (See Figure 5.61.)

Heavy loads such as large mechanical equipment should not be rolled over the completed membrane because they may damage the roof. These loads may cause failure in horizontal shear between the membrane insulation or deck.

Preformed Roof Insulation

Roof insulation provides insulation for the building and a substrate on which the built-up roofing materials are applied. Roof insulations used for heat flow control are installed in two layers with all joints offset between the upper and lower layers. Over steel decks, mechanical fasteners are used to attach the first insulation layer. The

■ **FIGURE 5.60**

The curb, wood nailer, insulation, and seal strip.

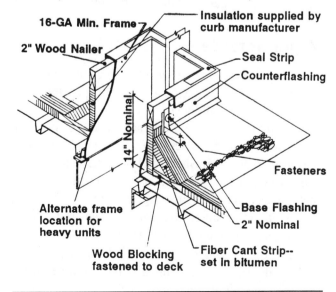

■ FIGURE 5.61

A satisfactory method of grouping pipe that must be above the roof surface.

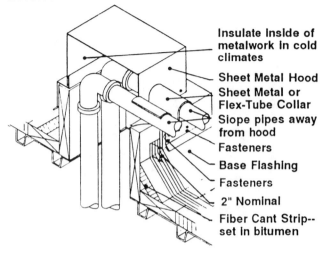

- Insulate inside of metalwork in cold climates
- Sheet Metal Hood
- Sheet Metal or Flex-Tube Collar
- Slope pipes away from hood
- Fasteners
- Base Flashing
- Fasteners
- 2" Nominal
- Fiber Cant Strip-- set in bitumen

second insulation layer is laid in moppings of hot asphalt with the greater insulation value. All roof insulation must be protected from the elements before, during, and after installation. During and after installation, protection is provided by immediate roof membrane installation. Proper membrane application on low-sloped roofs requires roofing felts laid perpendicular to the water flow, beginning at the drain points in the deck. All roof membrane plies must be installed in an unbroken time period. Phased construction is not recommended. The long dimension of the insulation boards is laid perpendicular to the water flow.

Vapor Retarders

The term *vapor retarder* refers to a broad range of roofing materials used to control water vapor flow from the interior of the building into the roof system. Moisture in the form of water vapor originates from construction processes. These processes include interior concrete and masonry, plaster finishes, fuel-burning heaters, and cementitious roof fills. Occupancy-generated sources include such areas as swimming pools; textile, food, and paper plants; or other wet-process industrial plants.

In temperate climates of the United States during the winter months, water vapor generally flows upward through the roof system from a heater. In more humid interiors, the vapor flows to the colder, drier exterior.

Vapor retarders are required more often in northern climates than in the South. In southern regions, downward vapor pressure is expected and the roof membrane becomes the vapor retarder. Vapor retarders are installed at locations where they will be warmer than the winter dew point temperature. The dew point should fall within the insulation. It is recommended that moisture relief vents, preferably one-way vents, be incorporated into the roof system. There should be one vent per 1,000 sq. ft. of roof area.

Roof system vapor retarders generally fall into two classifications:

1. Bituminous membranes—This typical two-ply installation using three moppings of steep asphalt provides a vapor retarder with a permeability rating of less than 0.005 perm.
2. Nonbituminous sheet systems—These include PVC, films, kraft paper and aluminum foil combinations that may provide vapor retarders having permeability ratings ranging from 0.10 to 0.50 perm. PVC films and associated cold-applied adhesives are not recommended. Whenever vapor retarders are used, they should be constructed of materials compatible with other roof system components.

Bitumens

Asphalt and coal tar are the bitumens used for roofing purposes. They are versatile waterproofing materials whose properties are desirable for use in built-up roofing practice. They are thermoplastic, changing to fluid with heat and to solid material with cold.

Roofing bitumens are not the glue with which roofing felts are cemented together. Actually, the process is more of a welding or fusion than a gluing. The heated mopping bitumen melts and fuses with the saturate bitumen in the roofing felts and welds the plies together. Correct application temperatures are vital to the high-quality roof membrane system. High bitumen temperature must be maintained to create the welding process. The bitumen properties are such that heating it at extreme temperatures for long periods may reduce the softening point of asphalt and raise the softening point of coal tar pitch. This bitumen property has produced the false impression that temperatures ordinarily employed in bituminous heating are damaging to the material. In the past, this impression has led to restrictive heating criteria that have substantially contributed to poor roof installations. Bitumens may be heated at high temperatures for short periods of time without damage. In fact, they must be heated to high temperatures to achieve complete fusion and strong bonding to the plies.

Temperature affects the viscosity or flow of the bitumen and mopping weight. High temperatures may lead to light moppings, incomplete film coverage, voids, and a potential lack of waterproofing. Temperatures too low lead to heavy moppings, poor adhesion, potential slippage problems, high expansion properties, and low tensile strengths, contributing to roof splits. There is an optimum viscosity range; an optimum temperature range at the point of application for achieving complete fusion; and optimum wetting and mopping properties that result in desirable interply bitumen weight. Equiviscous temperature (EVT) is the optimum application temperature of asphalt. It is the temperature range at which a viscosity of 125 centistokes is attained plus or minus 25°F. This is the practical and optimum temperature for wetting and fusion at the application point. A tolerance range is added in the field to accommodate effects of windchill, sun, or ambient temperature. This range is expressed as a temperature plus or minus 25°F. Asphalt bitumen should be sufficiently heated in the kettle/tanker to achieve the optimum viscosity temperature range (EVT) at the application point. Heating bitumen is subject to two restraints: (1) bitumen should not be heated to or above the actual Cleveland Open Cup (COC) flash point and (2) bitumen should not be heated and held above the finished blowing temperature (FBT) for more than four hours.

Coal tar roofing bitumens have fewer material variations than asphalt. EVT has not been applied to coal tar bitumen for this reason. The same concept is applicable: heating and application temperatures for coal tar are slightly lower than for asphalt bitumens. Most manufacturers recommend a kettle temperature of 425°F, with application temperatures ranging from 325°F to 400°F. Higher temperatures may be necessary to attain the proper application temperature, but they should be maintained for only short time periods.

Flashings and Cants

Flashing is required wherever water is likely to collect or where it must be directed to prevent roof surface penetration. These areas are around chimneys, around roof vents, and where two roof planes meet. Flashings are usually made of metal; however, there are flashings constructed of plastic as well as rolled asphalt roofing material.

The most vulnerable part of any roof system is the point at which the horizontal roof deck and a vertical surface meet. Most roof leaks occur at the flashings. Flashings are divided into two groups: composition flashing (base flashing) and metal flashing (counterflashing and cap flashing).

For parapet wall and expansion joint locations, one ply of No. 15 asphalt-saturated organic felt shall be installed on top of all roofing ply felts, extending 2″ above the top of the roofing ply felts. Reinforced base flashing shall then be applied. It shall extend 4″ beyond the toe of the cant strip, up the face of the cant strip, and to a minimum of 8″ and a maximum of 14″ above the roof surface. A separate piece of wall covering is required above this height. Both flashing plies shall be set in a full mopping of hot steep asphalt or asphalt roof cement. Expansion joint flashings allow expansion and contraction. The wood curbing is placed against the wall and secured to the deck because building components are subjected to thermal movements at different rates and in different directions from the roof membrane.

Metal flashings have a high coefficient of expansion. Metal flashings are isolated from the roof membrane wherever possible to prevent metal movements from splitting the membrane. Flashing details that require metal flanges sandwiched into the roof membrane are to be avoided. All walls and protections with composition base flashing or metal counterflashing must be installed in the wall above the base flashing. The installation of the counterflashing takes place after that of the base flashing. Single-piece installations cannot be flashed properly, nor can roofing maintenance and reroofing be performed without damaging the metal. Sheet metal must never be used as base flashing.

Metal wall cap flashing instead of masonry coping is often used to cover the top wall. Gravel stops are raised above the water line by the use of tapered cants and wood blocking. Metal flanges for low-profile gravel stops are set in mastic on top of the completed roof membrane and nailed at close intervals to the wood nailer. The metal flange then must be primed with asphalt primer and felt flashing strips applied. Interior drainage is recommended. Edges should be raised if possible, and metal edging never should be used as a water dam or water stop. Connecting sheet metal to the roof membrane should be avoided. Pipe projections through the membrane require metal flashing or roof jack insertion into the membrane. Metal flanges are set in mastic over the completed membrane and primed and stripped in with flashing strips.

Surfacing and Aggregate

Roof membranes, if not presurfaced, require some type of wearing surface. This surfacing is applied as soon as possible after membrane installation. Gravel, slag, and marble chips are aggregates used for aggregate-surfaced roofs. Asphalt and liquid surface coatings are used on smooth-surfaced roofs. Gravel or aggregate surfacing is set in hot bitumen.

Occasionally, on well-applied roofs, small black globules known as raspberries or blueberries will form in the roof surface. These are not detrimental to the roof and simply indicate that large quantities of bitumen flood coat were applied and bubbled around the aggregate. Aggregate surfacing should not be applied to roofs with slope greater than 3″ per foot.

Smooth-surface coatings should be applied as soon as possible after the membrane is installed. Some coatings must be applied over a previously applied thin coating of hot asphalt. Emulsions must be protected from freezing and must not be applied in freezing temperatures or when precipitation is occurring or expected. Frozen material must be discarded. Foot traffic on the roof is highly detrimental in extremely cold or warm temperatures and must be controlled.

Reroofing

Each reroof or re-cover project has its own specific problems that require individual assessment. The existing roof deck must be sound and undamaged. A sample of the existing membrane should always be removed down to the deck. The insulation is carefully examined, and wet or damaged insulation should be replaced. It is possible to salvage existing roof insulation if it is undamaged and dry. Some insulation products cannot be salvaged because removing the membrane causes delamination of the insulation boards. If doubt exists about the adequacy of attachment of the first insulation layer, the first layer must be mechanically attached before the second layer is applied. When removing the membrane causes minor damage to the existing insulation, a single minimum layer or re-cover board is used over the existing insulation to provide a suitable new membrane surface. Installing a new roof membrane directly to the existing roof is discouraged. Changes in wood blocking heights and additional expansion provisions may be required at reroofing time. Existing drainage provisions must be examined and revised as needed.

Inspection and Maintenance

All roofs require periodic maintenance. Some maintenance and complex repairs must be completed by qualified roofers. The owner can help maintain the roof by ensuring that regular cleanup procedures are performed.

Owner inspection and maintenance recommendations follow:

- Inspect the roof at least twice a year (spring and fall) and after any severe storm. Perform frequent inspections on buildings containing manufacturing facilities that evacuate exhaust debris onto the roof. Clean roof drains of debris. Remove leaves, twigs, cans, and balls that plug roof drains. Bag and remove all debris from the roof.
- Note conditions resulting in leakage, such as heavy or light rain, wind direction, temperature, and time of year leaks occurred. All these are important clues used to trace roof leaks. With all the facts, the diagnosis and repair of roof problems proceed more rapidly.
- Do not allow foot traffic on the roof in very cold or very hot weather. Do not allow the installation of radio and television antennas or mechanical equipment without notifying a roofing contractor. Allow only authorized personnel on the roof.
- Do not puncture blisters or spread coatings or mastic that cover up evidence that may be necessary to determine the problem.

■ REVIEW QUESTIONS*

1. Which roof has four sloping surfaces to the eaves?

   A. Gable
   B. Hip
   C. Mansard
   D. Gambrel

2. How many square feet in a square of roofing?

   A. 10
   B. 50
   C. 100
   D. 500

Use the following diagram to answer questions 3 through 5.

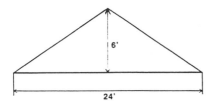

3. What is the rise of this roof structure?

   A. 6'
   B. 12'
   C. 24'
   D. None of the above

4. What is the span of this roof structure?

   A. 6'
   B. 12'
   C. 24'
   D. None of the above

5. What is the slope of this roof structure?

   A. 6/24
   B. 6/12
   C. 1/4
   D. Cannot determine from this drawing

6. Older untreated cedar shingles have what class UL fire rating?

   A. A
   B. B
   C. C
   D. No fire rating

7. An individual should observe sunlight through a wood shingle roof.

   A. True
   B. False

8. A wood shingle roof must be at least three layers thick.

   A. True
   B. False

9. A cedar shake roof requires no underlayment.

   A. True
   B. False

10. Granules in asphalt shingles protect the shingles from the sun's rays.

    A. True
    B. False

11. What type of decking may sustain asphalt composition shingles?

    A. Old wood shingles
    B. Old composition shingles
    C. Solid plywood decking
    D. All of the above

12. Built-up roofing should not be used on roof slopes of 4/12 or steeper.

    A. True
    B. False

13. Slate and tile roofs require underlayment.

    A. True
    B. False

14. What is the UL classification of slate and tile roofs?

    A. A
    B. B
    C. C
    D. Do not have a UL classification

---

*Answers to all of the chapter review questions are located in Appendix C at the back of this book.

15. A galvanized steel roofing panel does not require painting.

    A. True
    B. False

16. A stainless steel roof is all but maintenance free.

    A. True
    B. False

17. The metal roof panels can be furnished in various lengths up to

    A. 8'.
    B. 18'.
    C. 24'.

18. When a metal roof is installed over a composition shingle roof, the old roof serves as

    A. a condensation barrier.
    B. added insulation.
    C. natural ventilation.
    D. All of the above
    E. None of the above

19. When inspecting a metal roof, the inspector should report all

    A. dents or damaged spots.
    B. hail damage.
    C. improper nailing.
    D. All of the above
    E. None of the above

■ INSPECTION CHECKLIST: ROOFING

Preliminary

Identify the type of roofing. Note on the inspection report:

Yes No

☐ ☐ Wood shingle
☐ ☐ Composition
☐ ☐ Composition over wood shingle (reroof)
☐ ☐ Wood shake
☐ ☐ Built-up roof
☐ ☐ Tile or slate
☐ ☐ Metal roof
☐ ☐ Shingle, other

> **Note:** *Indicate on the inspection report if weather or access conditions are unfavorable to perform a thorough inspection.*

EXTERIOR

Yes No

☐ ☐ Are there sags in the roof or ridge?
☐ ☐ Are brick chimney and walls properly flashed and counterflashed?
☐ ☐ (a) Step flashing must be used for wood shingles.
☐ ☐ (b) Is counterflashing pulled away?
☐ ☐ (c) Is flashing rusted through on back side of fireplace?
☐ ☐ Is flashing properly installed where a roof intersects a wall? Flashing should be behind siding. Be careful of room additions.
☐ ☐ Do turbine vents rotate freely?
☐ ☐ Do furnace flues, hot water heater flues, and metal fireplace flues have rain skirts?
☐ ☐ Do furnace flues, hot water heater flues, metal fireplace flues, and roof ventilators have rain caps?
☐ ☐ Are metal flue vents rusted through?
☐ ☐ Are all roof penetrations flashed?
☐ ☐ Are skylight covers secured?
☐ ☐ Are vinyl plumbing vent roof jacks cracked or torn?
☐ ☐ Do soffits or fascia boards have wood damage?

Yes No

☐ ☐ Are valleys in acceptable condition?
☐ ☐ (a) Are metal valleys rusted through?
☐ ☐ (b) Are asphalt valleys deteriorated?
☐ ☐ (c) Do valleys need to be cleaned?
☐ ☐ Evidence of wear, deterioration, lifting shingles, tiles, or flat roof materials?

INTERIOR

Look at the ceiling in each room, including closets. Be particularly alert on flat roofs without attics. Identify each ceiling that shows evidence of a leak.

Yes No

☐ ☐ Is there evidence of leaks? If so, where are they located?
☐ ☐ Is ceiling sagging?
☐ ☐ Do skylight shafts show evidence of leaks?
☐ ☐ Does the house have a gas furnace? Check the furnace closet for evidence of leaks at the vent flashing.
☐ ☐ Is the house without eaves? Water penetration can occur where the roof ends at the outside wall. Pull the carpet at random spots along the inside wall to check for stains.
☐ ☐ Does the house have dormers? Carefully check the dormer areas (ceilings and walls) for leaks.

> **Note:** *On a two-story house, remember that stains on lower ceilings could be caused by plumbing leaks. Other common causes of ceiling water stains include the following:*

☐ ☐ (a) Attic drain pans that overflow.
☐ ☐ (b) Suction refrigerant lines in the attic that are not insulated.
☐ ☐ (c) Copper condensate lines in the attic that are not insulated.
☐ ☐ (d) Ductwork in the attic that does not have a vapor barrier.
☐ ☐ (e) Water lines in the attic that have frozen and burst. Example: icemaker line to refrigerator, line to humidifier.

> **Note:** *Be alert where you see that ceilings are freshly painted or that ceilings are painted with a high-gloss enamel. A gloss enamel paint will not show water stains.*

ATTIC

Yes No

☐ ☐ Do any of the roof penetrations show evidence of leaks?

☐ ☐ Furnace flue vent(s)?

☐ ☐ Metal fireplace flues?

☐ ☐ Plumbing vents?

☐ ☐ Attic ventilators?

☐ ☐ Do roof lines with dormers show evidence of leaks?

☐ ☐ From valleys above?

☐ ☐ At flashings at the sides and bottom of dormer?

☐ ☐ Do valleys show evidence of leaks?

☐ ☐ Decking stained, rotted, or delaminated?

☐ ☐ Valley rafters stained?

☐ ☐ Are there leaks in areas where items are secured to the roof? For example, solar panels and basketball hoops.

☐ ☐ Do rafters sag?

☐ ☐ Are rafters cracked?

☐ ☐ Are splices supported?

☐ ☐ Are ceiling joists supported by load-bearing walls?

☐ ☐ Are valley rafters supported?

☐ ☐ Is it a truss roof? If so:

☐ ☐ Are the gusset plates loose?

☐ ☐ Are any diagonal supports missing or cut?

☐ ☐ Are the cords cut?

☐ ☐ Is there sufficient bracing where items, such as furnaces, are supported from rafters?

☐ ☐ If the roof has been reroofed with a heavier material, is there bracing?

WOOD SHINGLES

Yes No

☐ ☐ Is there direct light into the attic?

☐ ☐ Is the slope 4 on 12 or greater?

☐ ☐ Is there evidence of leaks in the attic? Remember that as shingles age, the oil naturally turns dark on their underside.

☐ ☐ Are shingles missing?

☐ ☐ Are shingles loose?

☐ ☐ Has felt paper been used under ridge shingles?

☐ ☐ Is there evidence of recent repairs? For example, tin shingles or replaced shingles.

☐ ☐ Are there split shingles?

☐ ☐ Are there excessively curled shingles?

☐ ☐ Is the roof weatherworn?

☐ ■ Excessive cracks?

Yes No

☐ ☐ Soft shingles?

☐ ☐ Damaged shingles?

☐ ☐ Feels soft when walking around?

☐ ☐ Are there soft spots on the roof? Check to see whether the lath is broken or not secured to the rafter.

☐ ☐ Are there exposed nails? If an area of shingles has been replaced, there will be exposed nails on the top course.

☐ ☐ Are the shingles staggered? Do splits and gaps align from one course to the next?

☐ ☐ Are there defective shingles?

WOOD SHAKES

Yes No

☐ ☐ Is the slope 4 on 12 or greater?

☐ ☐ Is felt paper visible from roof?

☐ ☐ Are wood shakes visible from attic?

☐ ☐ Are shingles missing?

☐ ☐ Are there split shingles?

☐ ☐ Are there damaged shingles?

☐ ☐ Is there evidence of recent repairs? For example, tin shingles or replaced shingles.

☐ ☐ Is the roof weatherworn?

☐ ☐ Excessive cracks?

☐ ☐ Soft shingles?

☐ ☐ Are there exposed nails?

☐ ☐ Are shingles staggered?

COMPOSITION SHINGLES

Yes No

☐ ☐ Does the roof hump? The decking could possibly be coming up. Some slight sags and high points are common with roofs using 3/8 decking.

☐ ☐ Is the slope 4/12, or greater? If 30-lb. felt or double underlayment is used, 2/12 is allowed.

☐ ☐ Is drip edge at rake and eave?

☐ ☐ Are shingles missing?

☐ ☐ Are tabs broken?

☐ ☐ Are shingles installed correctly in relation to cutouts and nails?

☐ ☐ Are nails exposed between cutouts?

☐ ☐ Are nails and staples breaking through the surface of shingles?

☐ ☐ Is there hail damage?

☐ ☐ Are granules missing, exposing asphalt?

Yes No

☐ ☐ Are shingles weatherworn?
☐ ☐ Are tabs puffy?
☐ ☐ Are tabs curled?
☐ ☐ Are shingles brittle?
☐ ☐ Is the amount of missing granules excessive?
☐ ☐ Does the roof feel springy? Check for a broken rafter or truss, damaged decking, or a lack of bracing.
☐ ☐ Is the reroof over wood shingles? Be sure the shingles are properly sealed where the roof intersects with the wall.
☐ ☐ Are there defective shingles?

SLATE ROOFS

Yes No

☐ ☐ Exercise care when inspecting slate roofs. Only knowledgeable roofers should walk on these roofs.
☐ ☐ Are there broken slates? For example, foot traffic around antenna and chimney.
☐ ☐ Are there rust streaks? Nails that have backed out and are rusting leave streaks on the slates.
☐ ☐ Is the felt underlayment deteriorating?
☐ ☐ Is there proper flashing around all penetrations?
☐ ☐ Is there evidence of leaks in the attic?

TILE ROOFS

Yes No

☐ ☐ In a reroof application, is there extra roof bracing?
☐ ☐ Are there cracked or broken tiles?
☐ ☐ Is there flashing around chimney and at walls?
☐ ☐ Is there roof mastic or mortar under all hips and ridges?
☐ ☐ Are bird stops installed at eaves on S-type and mission tile?
☐ ☐ Identify the type of fastening:
☐ ☐ (a) Nail.
☐ ☐ (b) Wire and nail. Attach wire to tile and nails to wood member.
☐ ☐ (c) Wind lock. Looks like a fish hook that fastens to a nail or another fastening device and hooks over butt end of tile to hold tile in high-wind areas.
☐ ☐ (d) Tile nail. Nails into deck and acts as both tile nail and wind lock.
☐ ☐ (e) Storm lock. A strap device for side edge of all tiles.
☐ ☐ (f) Twisted wire method. Uniform Building Code (UBC) approved for all tiles.
☐ ☐ (g) Brass strip tile tie. Like twisted wire, but made of a brass strip.
☐ ☐ (h) Single line tile tie. Runs from tile to tile, fastened under head lap, up the length of the roof.
☐ ☐ (i) Foam adhesive.

ALUMINUM SHINGLES

Yes No

☐ ☐ Is there evidence of leaks in the attic?
☐ ☐ Is there evidence of leaks on the ceilings?
☐ ☐ Are any shingles bent from foot traffic?
☐ ☐ Does the bottom of the gable edge have cutouts?
☐ ☐ Is there evidence of recent repair?
☐ ☐ Are hips and ridges loose?
☐ ☐ Are flashings around openings sealed?
☐ ☐ Is counter flashing around chimney nailed and caulked?
☐ ☐ Are there weep holes (1″ square) on the bottom of the shake directly below the vent pipe and turbine flashing?

BUILT-UP ROOFS

Yes No

☐ ☐ Is water standing or is there evidence of previous ponding?
☐ ☐ Does the roof sag?
☐ ☐ Is there evidence of blisters?
☐ ☐ Are there bald spots where aggregate is missing?
☐ ☐ Is aggregate loose on the roof?
☐ ☐ Are there any fishmouths?
☐ ☐ Are seams visible?
☐ ☐ Are all penetrations flashed and counter-flashed?
☐ ☐ Is the asphalt alligatoring?
☐ ☐ Is the gravel guard damaged?
☐ ☐ Does the decking feel soft?
☐ ☐ On roofs with slopes, is the asphalt moving? It will appear as waves or wrinkling along the ply lines.

Yes No

☐ ☐ Are the gutters obstructed?
☐ ☐ Are the drains sized and located properly?
☐ ☐ Is there standing water around drains, indicating the drains are set too high?
☐ ☐ Is there plant growth on roof covering?

DOWNSPOUTS AND GUTTERS

Yes No

☐ ☐ Are there rust spots/holes in the metal?
☐ ☐ Are gutters loose and sagging?
☐ ☐ Is there evidence of wood rot in fascia boards?
☐ ☐ Are downspouts damaged?
☐ ☐ Do downspouts drain at foundation wall?

■ REPORTING GUIDELINES

Here are inspection report guidelines for roofs incorporating the above checklist.

Roof, roof structure and attic. The inspector shall:

- Report the type of roof covering and report as in need of repair

  - a roof covering that is not appropriate for the slope of the roof;

  - fasteners that are not present or that are not appropriate (where it can be reasonably determined); and

  - roof jacks, flashing, and counterflashing that are not present or not properly installed;

- inspect the general condition of, and report evidence of previous repairs to flashing, skylights, and other roof penetrations;

- report as in need of repair inadequate attic space ventilation;

- report as in need of repair deficiencies in the roof covering, structure, and sheathing;

- report any visible evidence of moisture penetration;

- report as in need of repair the lack of or inappropriate installation of components such as purlins, struts, collar ties or rafter ties, where necessary;

- report as in need of repair excessive deflections or depressions in the roof's surface relating to the performance of the framing and the roof deck;

- enter and inspect attic space(s) except when inadequate access or hazardous conditions exist, as reasonably determined by the inspector, and report the method used to inspect the attic if the inspector did not enter the attic;

- report the method used to inspect the roof if the inspection is performed from other than roof level;

- inspect for the presence and report the approximate depth of insulation where visible; and

- report as in need of repair deficiencies in visible installed gutter and downspout systems; and

- report if felt has been cut off at ridge vent

Specific limitations for roof, roof structure and attic. The inspector is not required to do the following:

- Determine the remaining life expectancy of the roof covering

- Inspect the roof from the roof level if the inspector reasonably determines that he or she cannot safely reach or stay on the roof or that damage to the roof or roof covering may result from walking on the roof

6 Plumbing

Plumbing involves the installation, maintenance, and alteration of piping, fixtures, appliances, and accessories in connection with sanitary or storm drainage facilities, venting systems, and public or private water supply systems. A plumbing system consists of three systems: (1) aseptic, an adequate potable water supply system; (2) septic, a safe and adequate drainage system; and (3) mechanical, ample fixtures and equipment.

■ ASEPTIC SYSTEMS

Aseptic systems include all potable water lines originating from the city tap or well unit and extending to the last faucet or valve in the residential structure. Aseptic systems are considered clean systems.

Water Service

Water pipe in a residential structure should be as short and straight as possible. Pipe bends reduce water pressure to fixtures in the house.

The residential service line should be buried under 2' to 4' of soil to prevent freezing. The local or state plumbing code should be consulted for recommended depth in specific areas of the country.

A corporation stop is connected to the water main and is used to shut off the municipal supply. A corporation stop is located under the street and necessitates breaking the pavement to reach the valve. A valve in the corporation stop permits pressure in the water main while service to the building is completed.

A curb stop is a valve that isolates a residential structure from the main water supply for repairs, nonpayment of water bills, or flooded basements. A long-handled wrench is used to reach the valve in the curb stop.

A meter stop is a valve placed on the street side of the water meter to isolate the meter for installation or maintenance. Local codes often require a gate valve to shut off water for residential plumbing repairs. Curb and meter stops should be used only when necessary because they are easily damaged.

A water meter is a device that measures the amount of water used in a residential structure. Water meters are usually the property of the city or water provider. Also, some meters may belong to homeowners. Most meters come with a yoke to maintain electrical continuity even if the meter is removed. If not, the water line was used as the ground for the electrical service, and a grounding loop device must be installed around the water meter. (See Figure 6.1.)

Potable Water Supply

A potable water supply system transfers water from the community distribution system to various areas of the residential structure. Water is distributed through the residential structure by a system of piping. (See Figure 6.2.) A potable water supply system requires a water meter, a water heater, and various fixtures and appliances, such as water softeners and other water treatment equipment. Many cities now require backflow prevention devices (check valves) on the inbound side of the water meter. When check valves are required, it is necessary to install an expansion tank on the water heater to absorb the shock when water is turned off or there is thermal expansion of the water.

Water in potable water systems often has corrosive effects and causes deposits to form in piping. These deposits ultimately reduce the capacity of the pipe to transport water. Proper water treatment can prevent deposits from forming in pipe.

■ **FIGURE 6.1**

A jumper must be installed around a water meter if the house ground connection is made on the house side of the water meter.

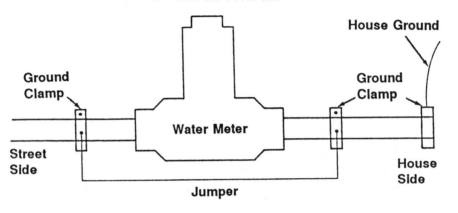

WATER METER JUMPER

Water Wells

Homes beyond city or utility company water mains use ground water. It offers the advantage of being relatively clean. However, this is true only if the well is properly located and installed. If a private well is a source for the potable water system, the residential inspector should recommend that the homeowner have the water tested. The well should be equipped with a

■ **FIGURE 6.2**

A potable water supply system transfers water from the community distribution system to various areas of the residential structure by means of a piping system.

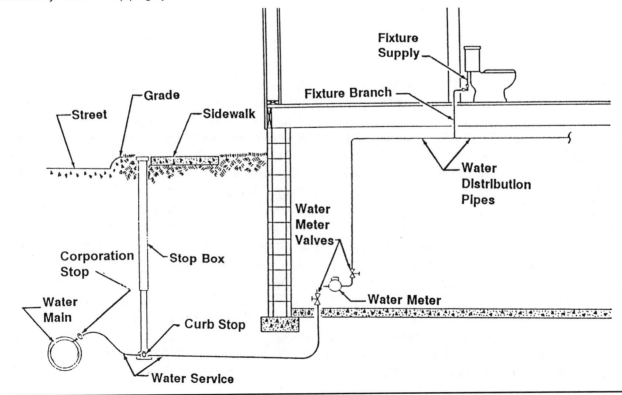

chlorinator, or other filtration system, and be approved by a testing laboratory.

The depth of the water table below the earth's surface will vary from a few feet to hundreds of feet. It tends to follow roughly the contour of the earth. As a general rule, depth is not particularly important in determining where to locate the well. Other factors, such as the relative position of potential sources of contamination and how near the well is to the place where the water will be used, are more important. The well must be a minimum of 100 feet from pollution sources such as septic tank and leach fields, abandoned storage tanks, etc. The well should be located on higher ground so surface water will flow away from it. A deep well is preferred because the greater depth allows the water to filter through more soil before it is pumped out of the well.

Well depth and water demand rate are important factors in determining the best type of pump to use in a well. Wells deeper than 25 feet require a pump device installed within the well casing. Although all the parts of the pump do not need to be in the well casing, the primary functioning element of the pump must be installed near the water table. Several of the deep well pumps operate exactly like a shallow well pump, except part or all of the pump is installed in the well casing. So the pump might not be visible to the inspector, who will have to depend on checking the water flow at the faucets. The submersible centrifugal pump is a popular pump because it has low starting torque, is self-priming, and provides uniform flow. (See Figure 6.3.)

The capacity of a submerged centrifugal pump depends on two features of the pump. The first is the width and diameter of the impeller, and the second is the number of stages in the pump. Regardless of the pump that is used in a private well, there must be a pressure tank.

Water supply systems must provide water instantly while maintaining constant pressure. To do this, some type of storage tank is required. Municipal water systems generally depend on water towers to store water and use gravity to provide the required pressure.

It is not feasible for an individual to construct a water tower for a private system. However, it is necessary with a private well to have a pressure tank. Water is incompressible, so it is necessary to introduce air into the tank. The air compresses, providing the force necessary to cause the water to flow through the plumbing system. If the water in the tank falls below a predetermined level, the pump is automatically started by the low-pressure switch. The pump refills the tank with water. As the water fills the tank it compresses the air in the tank until

■ **FIGURE 6.3**

Each stage of a centrifugal pump increases water pressure.

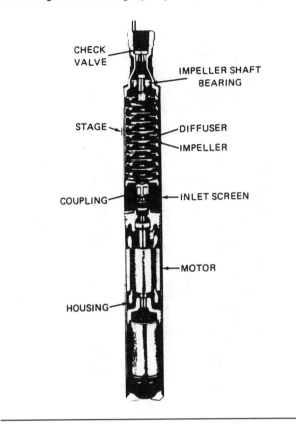

the high water level is reached and the high-level pressure switch turns off the pump. (See Figure 6.4.).

After sizing the pump for the well the next important item is sizing the pressure tank. To size the pressure tank, you must know the pump capacity vs. maximum demand. If the pump capacity is greater than the maximum demand for water, the minimum size tank can be selected. The tank must be large enough to supply the maximum demand that is not supplied by the pump.

If the system will operate satisfactorily at lower pressure, a larger volume of water can be obtained from a given size tank. Increasing the supercharge on the tank increases the volume of water that can be drawn from the system. For sizing tanks, the usable capacity should be twice the pump capacity in gallons per minute. Controlled amounts of chlorine should be added to the water supply to act as a disinfectant. Chlorine will not only kill bacteria but it will also remove iron, manganese, hydrogen sulfide, and bad odors from the water by oxidization. Chlorine is added automatically with a chlorinator.

■ **FIGURE 6.4**

Operation of a hydropneumatic pressure tank. As water volume builds up, so does pressure. A separator prevents tanks from becoming "waterlogged."

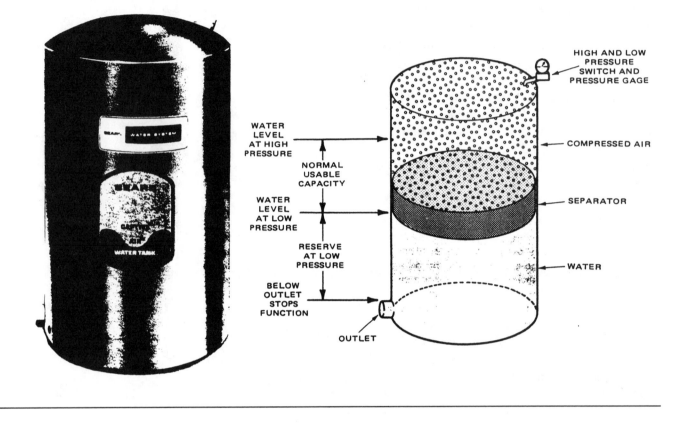

When inspecting private water wells, the inspector usually adds an extra fee for the additional time and expense involved to have a coliform analysis of the water. Recommend that all tests be performed as required by the Clean Water Act.

A residential structure must have an adequate supply of hot and cold potable water for drinking, cooking, and bathing. Each dwelling must have equipment capable of heating water in adequate amounts to serve the appropriate plumbing fixtures.

Plumbing Systems

The plumbing system in a residential structure should (1) supply hot and cold water to users and (2) drain wastewater and sewage discharged from these fixtures to a public sewer or private disposal system without allowing backflow of water or sewer gases into the system. Water distribution systems consist of piping and equipment within residential structures that transfer water from community distribution or private water

systems to points of use throughout a dwelling. Equipment and fixtures within a common residential structure include hot and cold water lines, valves, faucets, air chambers, circulating pumps, commodes, bidets, bathtubs, and showers to provide access to the water at the point of use.

Pipe

The size of basement mains and risers depends on the number of plumbing fixtures in the residential structure. A ¾" pipe is the minimum size used from the meter. A ½" pipe connects various fixtures and appliances. A ½" pipe is reduced again to ⅜" at connections to faucets for lavatories, kitchen sinks, bathtubs, showers, and commodes. Proper water pressure to these fixtures must be maintained.

Copper water pipe will not corrode and deteriorate. Galvanized iron pipe corrodes from the inside out. Various factors, such as the hardness of water, determine how fast pipe will deteriorate. Water with a high iron content will cause galvanized pipe to develop a buildup on the inside walls of the pipe and reduce water flow and pressure. Iron pipe is susceptible to leaking at thread joints because of corrosion due to electrolysis. Electrolysis produces chemical change through an electric current generated by a chemical reaction between the iron pipe and minerals in the water. All potable water pipe located above ground and in attics should be insulated and protected from freezing and physical damage.

Plastic pipe used in a residential structure includes polyvinyl chloride (PVC), chlorinated polyvinyl chloride (CPVC), polybutylene (PB), and acrylonitrile-butadiene-styrene (ABS). PVC pipe is used only with cold water because it becomes soft when exposed to heat or hot water. CPVC pipe can be used with either hot or cold water. PB piping, generally colored gray or blue, is used for both hot and cold water and is used in areas where potential for freezing water exists. PB pipes will accommodate expansion due to freezing water. A class action lawsuit has been filed over past problems with leakage at the joints, but PB is still in use today. Verify with local jurisdiction if allowable for installation today. ABS pipe is used for drains, waste, and vent piping.

Copper pipe is available in three wall thicknesses: K (thick), L (medium), and M (thin). All three types have

the same exterior diameter. Copper piping is color coded for ease of identification. Rigid copper pipe is available in 10′ to 20′ lengths, and soft copper pipe is available in 30′, 60′, and 100′ coils. Drainage, waste, and vent (DWV) pipe is used for drainage and venting systems.

Black iron pipe is used to carry gas through the residential structure. Copper should not be used for natural gas installations because the chemical reaction between the two causes corrosion. A stop should be located within 3′ of the gas valve on a water heater, a furnace, or any other gas appliance.

Hot and Cold Water Main Lines

Hot and cold water main lines are usually hung from the basement ceiling, in the crawlspace or found under the slab. Main lines are attached to the water meter and hot water tank on one side and to fixture supply risers on the other side. These pipes should be neatly installed and supported by pipe hangers or straps of sufficient strength and number to prevent sagging.

Hot and cold water lines should be approximately 6″ apart unless the hot water line is insulated. This distance ensures that heat is not transferred from the hot water line to the cold water line. (See Figure 6.5.)

■ **FIGURE 6.5**

Hot and cold main lines are attached to a water meter and hot water tank on one side and fixture supply risers on the other side.

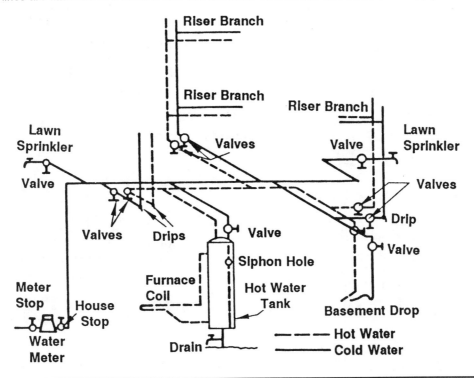

■ **FIGURE 6.6**

Fullway (gate) valves control the water flow by means of a wedge disc that fits against a smooth surface.

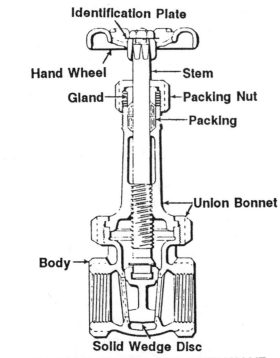

RISING STEM, SOLID WEDGE DISC GATE VALVE

RISING STEM, SPLIT WEDGE DISC GATE VALVE

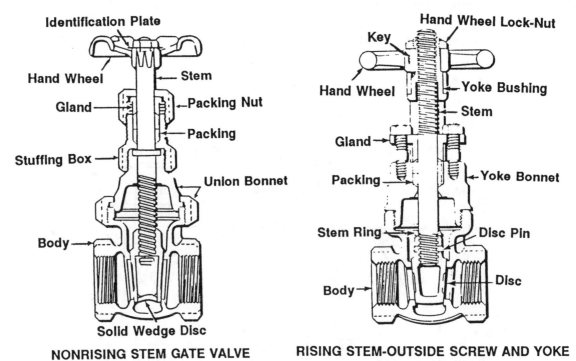

NONRISING STEM GATE VALVE

RISING STEM-OUTSIDE SCREW AND YOKE (OS&Y GATE VALVE)

Supply mains should have a drain valve or stop waste valve to remove water from the system for repairs. These valves should be on the low end of the line or on the end of each fixture riser. Fixture risers start at the basement main and rise vertically to fixtures on upper floors of the residential structure. In a one-family dwelling, riser branches usually proceed from the main riser to each fixture grouping. Fixture risers should be supported with a pipe bracket and not depend on the branch risers for support.

Each fixture is connected to a branch riser by a separate line. The last fixture on a line is usually connected directly to the branch riser.

Valves

A fullway or gate valve controls the flow of water by means of a wedge disc that fits against a smooth surface. A fullway valve offers minimum water flow resistance. The discharge side of the water meter as well as an unmetered water supply must have fullway valves installed. A fullway valve is also installed on the cold water supply pipe to the water heater. (See Figure 6.6.)

Compression or globe valves permit water to flow through an annular ring seat on which a circular disc is forced. Compression valves are frequently used in water supply lines inside residential structures because they are reliable and easy to repair. Compression valves are used for water cutoffs to the various plumbing fixtures. (See Figure 6.7.)

The compression valve is spherical and has a partition that closes off the inlet side of the valve from the outlet side, except for a circular opening. The top side of the circular opening is ground smooth. A neoprene washer (flat or contoured) is connected by a screw to the disc located at the end of the stem. The stem has threads so that when the valve is closed, the washer is compressed against the annular ring seal, which shuts off the water supply.

Check valves allow water to flow in only one direction. Check valves include lift check (usually used in vertical pipe) and swing check (usually used in horizontal pipe) valves. (See Figures 6.8 and 6.9.) Lift check valves and swing check valves are designed in such a way that when the water flow tries to reverse itself, the check valve closes. Check valves (backflow preventers) are required on all fixtures (e.g., flush valves, hose bibs,

■ **FIGURE 6.7**

Compression (globe) valves permit water to flow through an annular ring seat upon which a circular disc is forced.

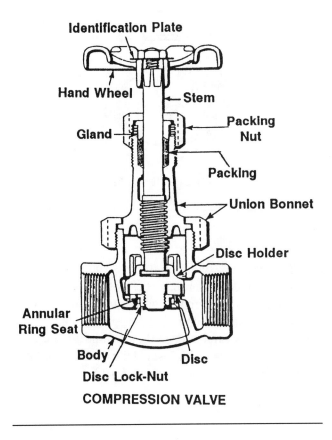

COMPRESSION VALVE

■ **FIGURE 6.8**

Performing the same functions as lift check valves, swing check valves are used in horizontal pipe.

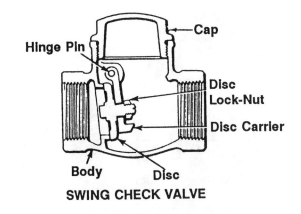

SWING CHECK VALVE

Faucets

Compression faucets have replaceable neoprene washers and are commonly found on outside hose bibs. This faucet is also used in bathroom, utility room, and kitchen fixtures. Compression faucets found in kitchens and bathrooms usually indicate two compression faucets with a mixer in the center and the water discharging through a single spout. (See Figure 6.11.)

Noncompression faucets (washerless faucets) require less maintenance than compression faucets because there is no neoprene washer to wear. Washerless faucets control water flow with two discs in the body of the valve. (See Figure 6.12.) One disc is stationary while the other disc rotates with the handle. A hole is drilled in each disc so the holes are aligned when the handle is in the open position and water is allowed to flow. In the closed position, the disc rotates the hole away from the hole in the stationary disc, cutting off the water flow.

Single-control faucets control both hot and cold water by using either a rotating cylinder or a rotating ball. The faucet with a rotating cylinder is a cartridge faucet. As the cylinder rotates, it controls water temperature and the rate of water flow. This type of valve is easy to maintain.

A cam or cartridge faucet has a screwtop with O-rings on the body. Another single-control faucet has a replaceable rubber washer and seat; it can be found in bathrooms, utility rooms, and kitchens. (See Figure 6.13.)

Other single-control faucets use a rotating plastic or metal ball. This ball has openings that align with hot and cold water openings as the lever is rotated to the right or left. The ball also aligns with respective hot or cold water ports to produce desired water temperature as well as flow rate. Noncompression faucets have neoprene O-rings used for seals that are occasionally replaced.

Kitchen and bathtub faucets can have a combination valve. Kitchen sinks equipped with a vegetable sprayer will have a diverter in the base of the faucet spout. The diverter valve diverts water from the faucet spout to the vegetable sprayer. Bathtubs with an overhead shower also have a diverter. The bathtub diverter can be a stem on the spout lifted to divert water or it can be a button depressed to cause the shower to operate.

Air Chambers

Air chambers are pressure-absorbing devices that are located close to valves or faucets at the end of long-

■ **FIGURE 6.9**

Check valves allow water to flow in only one direction and are used on hose bibs, sprinkler systems, swimming pools, and spas.

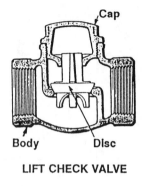

LIFT CHECK VALVE

sprinkler systems, swimming pools, and spas) where backflow could contaminate the potable water.

Gas valves, referred to as *ground valves* or *stop valves,* are usually found on gas appliances and main cutoffs. The gas valve is open if the handle is parallel to the pipe. The gas valve is closed if the handle is perpendicular to the pipe. (See Figure 6.10.)

■ **FIGURE 6.10**

A gas valve has a core that allows gas to pass through when the passageway is in line with the inlet and outlet openings.

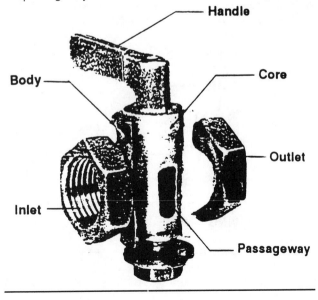

■ FIGURE 6.11

Compression faucets for combination bath and shower fittings use a valve or knob to divert water to the shower head.

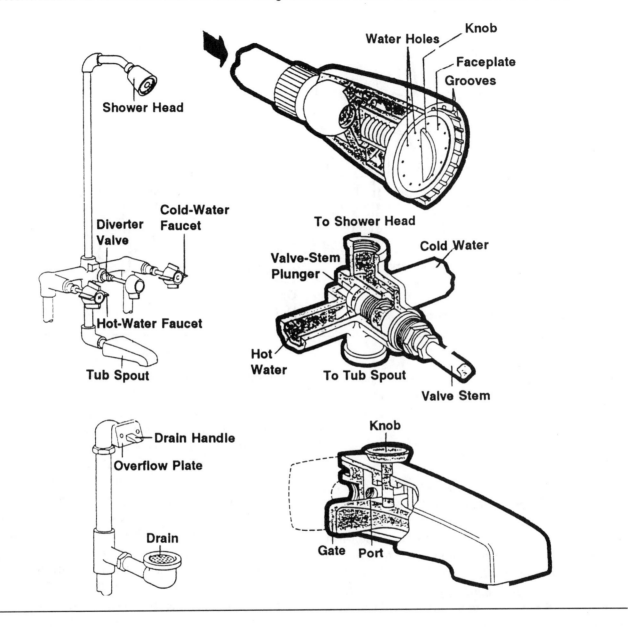

runs of pipe. (See Figure 6.14.) Air chambers are usually found on the hot side of the water heater and may be located under sinks or in bathroom walls. Air chambers are used to remedy water hammering, the rattling of plumbing pipes that occurs when water flow is suddenly reduced, causing a shock wave. Water hammering is caused by improper sizing of the water pipes.

Air chambers can be purchased or fabricated on site from copper pipe approximately 15″ to 18″ long with a cap soldered on the top to trap air. If water hammer

occurs, the shock can cause leaks at the joints when associated with the excessively high water pressure.

Circulating Pumps

Circulating pumps are commonly used in large residential structures and commercial buildings. Circulating pumps provide instant hot water to plumbing fixtures at the farthest outlet from the water heater. A return line must be added to complete the loop for recir-

■ **FIGURE 6.12**

Noncompression faucets control water flow through the alignment of openings in both a stationary and a movable disc.

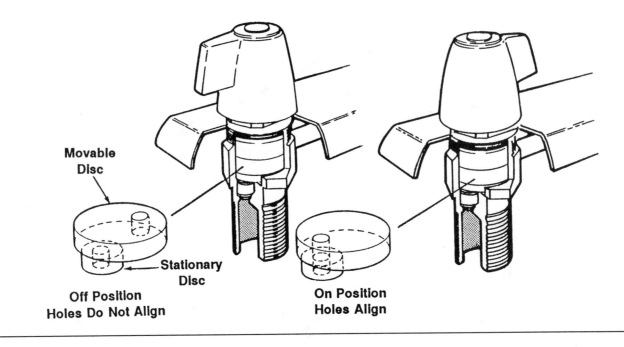

Movable Disc

Stationary Disc

Off Position
Holes Do Not Align

On Position
Holes Align

culating water through the drain valve at the bottom of the heater. Circulating pumps are operated by a thermostat, timer, or manual switch.

Commodes

Commodes are designed to carry away liquid and solid organic wastes. Water required to carry wastes to the sewer can be under pressure or gravity flow. Water directed through passages causes a scouring action in the bowl to move solid wastes through the trap into the sewer. As water and solids move through the trap, the flowing water causes a siphoning action. The movement of the water through the trap causes a drop in atmospheric pressure at the trap outlet. The partial vacuum, along with water from the bowl, removes the waste. The siphoning action draws the water from the bowl and slows the flow of water through the trap, allowing air to enter the trap. As air enters the trap, it breaks the vacuum. This process equalizes pressure on both sides of the trap. The flush tank supplies water to reseal the trap.

The two flushing mechanisms are pressure flush and gravity flow. The pressure flush mechanism is a valve that permits a pre-established amount of water to enter a commode or urinal for the purpose of flushing away solid or liquid wastes. A tank is not required with a

pressure flush valve. Gravity flow flushing has the tank mounted on the commode bowl with the flush valve located at the bottom of the tank. There is also a seal between the tank and bowl. The gravity flow tank has a fill valve connected to the water supply line and allows the tank to refill each time the commode is flushed.

Four commodes used in residential structures are wash down, reverse trap, siphon jet, and siphon action. (See Figure 6.15.) A separate trap is not required because all of these commodes have a built-in seal.

Tanks used with these commodes are generally separate, but supported on the bowl. Usually, the commode is supported on and anchored to the floor. The drain from the bowl penetrates the floor construction.

The commode is connected to the drain through a closet flange anchored to the subfloor. The flange has two elongated slots for the bolts that hold the commode. When the commode is installed, a wax toilet bowl seal is installed on the commode discharge opening. After the wax seal is installed, the commode is set on the closet flange and bolted to the floor. The commode should be tight to the floor. Loose commodes will leak at the bowl seal and damage the floor. Leakage also creates conditions conducive to termites and other wood damage.

The reverse trap commode is similar to the siphon jet commode. It has a smaller water area and a smaller

■ **FIGURE 6.13**

Single-control faucets control water flow by permitting a rubber sleeve to flex away from hot and cold water ports.

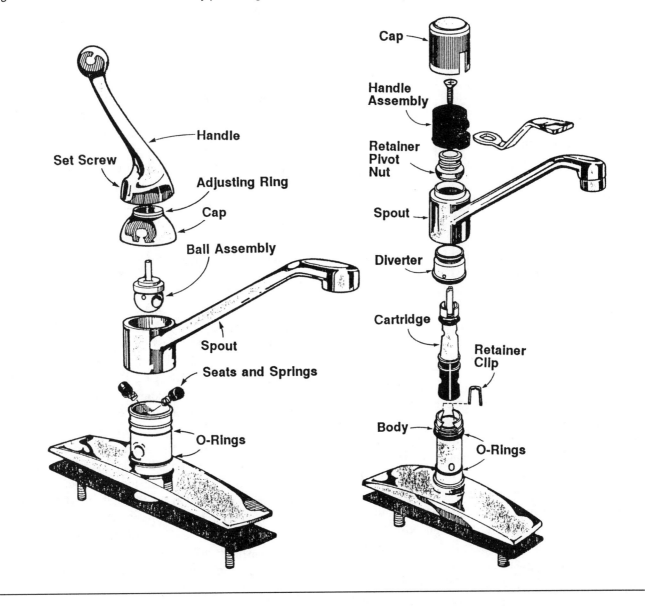

seal than the siphon jet commode. The siphon action commode is usually a low-profile, one-piece commode with a larger water surface area and quieter flushing action than the reverse trap commode or the siphon jet commode.

The National Energy Act went into effect January 1, 1994, and requires that all commodes manufactured for residential use have a capacity of no more than 1.6 gallons per flush.

Commode design has not changed much for almost 100 years with the exception of reducing tank size from 7.5 gallons to 3.6 gallons. Most water in standard commodes is used to create the siphoning action needed for a complete sanitary flush. Commode tank water, displaced during the flush cycle, pressurizes the tank to create a vacuum pull on the water. The vacuum helps the push force of gravity in the toilet bowl passageway.

Most 1.6 gallon commodes operate under the same principles. However, they have considerably less tank water, less water surface area, smaller traps, and water seals. The design often results in problems such as incomplete flushes. To compensate for smaller capacity, tanks

■ **FIGURE 6.14**

Air chambers are used to absorb pressure in piping assemblies.

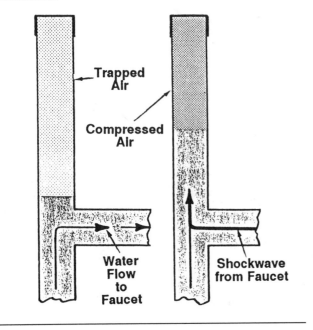

were made taller and narrower to increase the head. Bowls have steeper sides to increase the gravitional pull, and the water spot is smaller. A *water spot* is the water standing in the bowl that acts as a trap seal for the sewer. To achieve complete and efficient waste removal, the toilet had to be completely redesigned, including the sump, passageway, jet, and angle of rim holes, to make the most efficient use of a smaller volume of water. The design must provide a positive thorough-flushing action. With smooth contours and a glazed vitreous china surface on the inside, the trapway siphons quickly. Fast-moving water provides quick and complete waste removal.

There are several different new designs. Kohler has designed a pressure-clean system. The pressure-clean tank operates by using 1.6 gallons or less of pressurized water for each flush. The backflow preventer, pressure regulator, and aspirator are mounted directly on the pressure-clean tank. These components work with the incoming pressurized water supply to provide a controlled, efficient flush. A minimum water supply pressure of 25 psi is required. (See Figure 6.16.)

One prime concern about the small volume of water used is the possibility of clogged sewer lines. However, it has been discovered that the 1.6-gallon commodes, whether gravity or pressurized tank, provide adequate

sewer line removal for residential use. The pressurized tank modes have a more forceful flush and a larger water spot and tend to perform more satisfactorily. The small-volume commodes can help extend the life and efficiency of wells and septic systems in rural areas by placing less water demands on these systems.

While manufacturers made similar design changes to meet the National Energy Policy Act of 1992, the National Energy Act also affected other plumbing fixtures beginning January 1, 1994. It affected the flow rate on shower heads and kitchen and lavatory faucets, which are now set at 2.5 gallons per minute with 80 psi line pressure. These fixtures must be permanently marked with their actual or maximum flow rate.

When inspecting the commode, the inspector should check the inside of the tank for defective or deteriorating parts. The flush valve (flapper) should be checked to be sure it seals the bottom opening of the tank so water is not seeping out. Then inspect the fill valve to ensure that the tank fills properly and the water in the tank is at the proper level. *Note:* The inside of the tank is often stamped with the date of manufacture. The commode should be flushed several times to check for water leakage and to be sure only cold water is connected to the commode. Check the connection between the tank and bowl for leakage. Check the bowl to be sure it is securely fastened to the floor by rocking the commode gently.

(When checking this be very careful because if the commode is loose, it can leak.) Be sure to check around the base of the commode for water leaks and water damage to the floor. If the foundation is a concrete slab and the commode is not tight to the floor, it should be reset with a new wax ring. Where the underside of the floor can be observed for leakage, it is possible to tighten the commode without replacing the wax ring.

Bidets

Bidets have long been popular in South America and Europe and are becoming widely accepted in America. The bidet is used for personal hygiene. The bidet is fitted with faucets and a pop-up stopper that permits filling of the bowl, and it is rinsed through a rim flushing action similar to that of a commode. The bidet is connected to a drain with a P-trap. Hot and cold water supply lines should be connected in the same manner as for the lavatory. The bidet must be bolted to the floor. When inspecting a bidet, the inspector should check to see if the bidet is secure to the floor and that both the hot

■ **FIGURE 6.15**

Four water closets used in residential homes are washdown, reverse trap, siphon jet and siphon action.

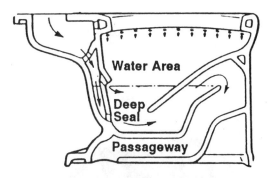

Washdown water closets spill water into the trap from around the rim, and from two larger openings near the trap.

Reverse trap water closets have a trap outlet at the back of the bowl.

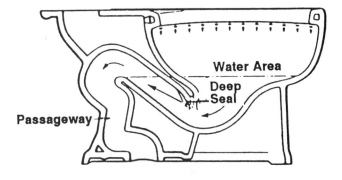

Siphon jet water closets do not require a head of water in the bowl to flush solids. Water is delivered from the closet spud to the trap outlet.

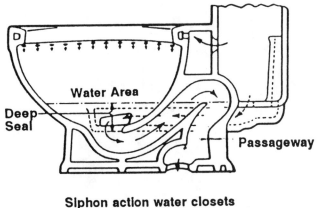

Siphon action water closets combine the closet and flush tank in one unit.

and cold water supplies to the faucets have adequate pressure. Bidets do not have wax rings but are connected to the sewer by a P-trap. (See Figure 6.17.)

Sinks and Lavatories

Sinks may be free standing or built into cabinets. Lavatories may be wall mounted, pedestal mounted, or built into cabinets. Most kitchen sinks are porcelain on steel or stainless steel. Sinks must have hot and cold water supplied to them and a drain system that passes through a P-trap. The drain opening should be equipped with a stopper. Most kitchen sinks have a disposal attached to the sink in at least one drain before waste-

water enters the P-trap. Disposals are not recommended with on-site sewage systems.

When inspecting sinks and lavatories, the inspector should check the condition of the sinks; is the porcelain or enamel chipped? This should be noted because the underlying steel will rust, causing the sink to leak. The faucets should be turned on to verify that the hot water is on the left and the aerator is in place. The drain stop should be closed and the sink filled to the flood rim. There should be at least a 1″ air gap between the water and the aerator on the faucet. Then turn the faucets off and open the drain. If the sink drains slowly, it is an indication of a partially clogged drain or that the system is not vented properly. When checking under the sink, check

■ **FIGURE 6.16**

The gravity flush system (left) and the pressurized water flush system (right).

the condition of the cabinet as well as the condition of the drain line. Does the cabinet have water stains or water damage? If the P-trap is metal, carefully check the bottom of the trap for leaks. The inspector should note any defects, whether they are cosmetic or functional.

Bathtubs and Showers

Bathtubs are available in enameled cast iron, steel, or gel-coated fiberglass. Occasionally, they are fabricated on site and lined with ceramic tile. Bathtubs may be recessed into surrounding walls at both ends and back. Joints between the bathtub and surrounding surfaces should be waterproof. The water overflow must be connected to a fixture drain line on the inlet side of the

trap. The bathtub may have a shower. When the shower is over the tub, the tile or tub enclosure should be sealed to prevent water penetration. (See Figure 6.18.)

When inspecting the bathtub, if the tub is fiberglass or plastic, always step into the tub to check for cracks in the bottom because they may not be visible except under pressure. If the tub is tile and/or there are tile walls, tap the tile with the handle of a screwdriver to check for loose tile, and check the grout. Loose tiles will have a hollow sound when tapped. Always check the tile wall around the faucets for a soft wall caused by leaking faucets. Check the condition of the tub. If the tub is porcelain or enamel on steel, check for chipped porcelain or enamel. The plumbing fixtures should not be loose in the

■ FIGURE 6.17

Bidets require a P-trap.

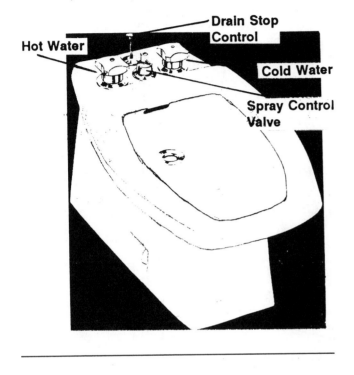

wall. If the shower is over the tub, the shower head should not be loose in the wall.

The floor around the tub should be checked for damage from leaking or from not being supported properly. If the bathroom has a tile floor, the inspector should tap the tile around the tub and commode with a screwdriver handle to check for loose tiles. Turn on the faucets, close the drain stop, and fill the tub approximately half full. Check the water from the faucets to verify that hot is on the left and cold is on the right. If the shower is over the tub, check the diverter valve function by operating the shower, and check all valves and the shower head for leaks.

If the shower is over the tub, the tub walls have to be protected from water. This can be done in many ways. A fiberglass tub and wall may be molded in one piece, and there may be fiberglass sectional walls, ceramic tile, or plastic walls made from high-impact-resistant plastic.

If there is a whirlpool tub, the inspection of the tub is the same as a regular tub. The inspector should close the drain stop and fill the tub so the water is approximately 2″ above the jets, then turn on the pump and check the jets. If black water comes from the jets when first turned on, this is an indication that the pump and lines are not draining, and this should be noted as a defect. The pump

should be on a dedicated circuit and GFCI (ground fault circuit interruptor) protected. When operating the jets, the air vents should be opened to give full pressure to the jets. It is important to locate the access panel to the pump and motor. After checking the jet action, turn off the pump and open the drain stop to check for slow drainage.

Stall Showers

Showers may be separate from the bathtub. The shower may be manufactured from fiberglass or porcelain enamel-on-steel, or built on the site from ceramic tile or marble. The fiberglass shower is usually one piece and the porcelain enamel-on-steel shower has to be assembled at the building site. The ceramic tile and marble showers are built on the site and require shower pans fabricated from sheet lead, plastic, or copper.

When inspecting a fiberglass shower, first step inside onto the shower base and inspect for cracks. Cracks might not be visible without weight on the base. Porcelain enamel-on-steel showers require that the joints be sealed with a waterproof grout.

Ceramic tile and marble require that all joints be sealed with grout to prevent leaking. When inspecting a shower, be sure to check the tile by tapping with a screwdriver handle. The loose tile will have a hollow sound. All tile and marble joints should have grout in them. If tiles have not been properly grouted, they can look fine but the joints will leak. If the tile has not been thoroughly cleaned before grouting, the grout might not adhere to the tile. (See Figure 6.19.)

The shower may have either a glass door enclosure or a curtain. In a shower with a glass door enclosure, the glass should be tempered glass. The inspector should check the glass and enclosure to be sure they are sealed properly and not leaking. A window in a shower is susceptible to leaking, causing water damage in the wall below. If there is a seat in the shower it is susceptible to leaking. Inspect the seat to ensure the water will not pool on top.

The inspector also should check the plumbing fixtures to be sure they are not loose in the wall and that the hot water is on the left. When inspecting, the water should be run with it hitting the walls, and the drain should be stopped. Fill the base with approximately 4″ of water, and check the faucets and shower head for leaks. Turn the water off, let it stand for 30 minutes, and then check for leaks around the base and, if possible, under the bathroom. If the shower is on an outside wall, check outside for water seepage. In all cases, walls along tubs, commodes and showers should be checked for water damage.

■ **FIGURE 6.18**

Bathtubs are available in enameled cast iron, steel, or gel-coated fiberglass.

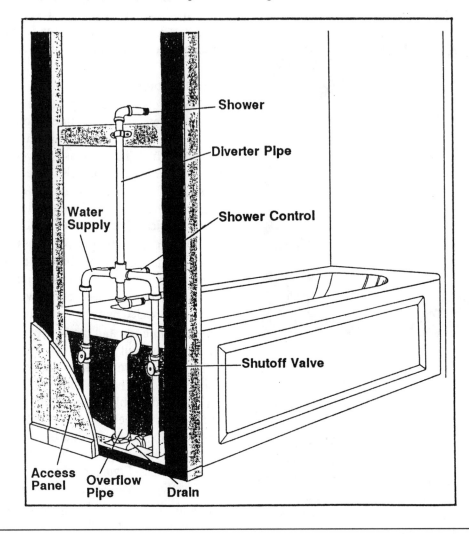

■ SEPTIC SYSTEMS

Septic systems include sewers and drain lines from the flood rim of all fixtures to the entrance of the city sewer or the septic tank and absorption field. The septic system contains harmful bacteria and methane gas. Sanitary drainage and vent piping systems extend from the sanitary sewer to fixtures in the residential building. (See Figure 6.20.)

Sewers and Drains

The water supply brought into a residential structure must be discharged quickly and quietly from the dwelling through the drainage system. To avoid health risks, a residential structure may have two drainage systems: one for sanitation and one for storm drainage.

These two systems must be separate within the dwelling.

In addition to discharging water, the drainage system disposes of organic fluids and solid wastes. Waste is susceptible to rapid decomposition and must be disposed of to public or private sewage disposal systems.

Drainage systems must be properly sized to transport water and waste at sufficient velocity and to prevent clogs. Because drainage flows under gravity, drainage pipe must be considerably larger than water supply pipe, and the layout of the piping must be as direct as possible. Residential drainpipe must be sloped toward the sewer to ensure scouring of the drain. The usual pitch

■ FIGURE 6.19

One-piece fiberglass shower stalls are manufactured and installed in residential structures.

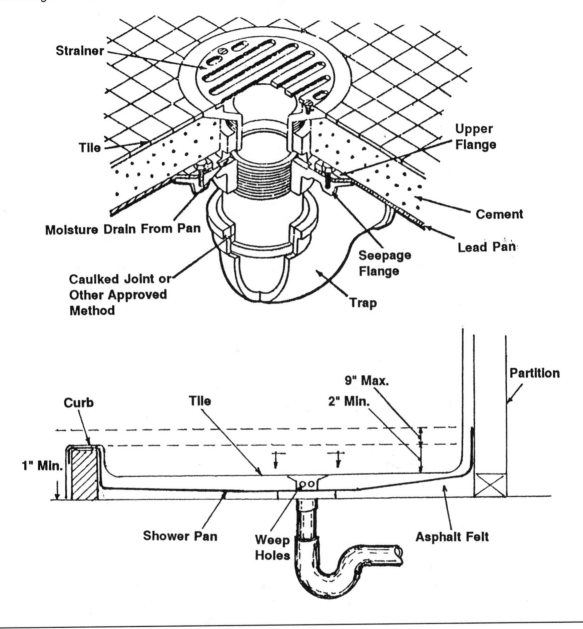

of drainpipe is ¼" fall for every 1' of length. If the pitch is too steep, liquid wastes will fail to carry solids. If the drainpipe is too flat, no scouring occurs and solid waste is deposited. Blockage will occur if solid wastes remain in the drain pipe. Accessible cleanouts are installed on drainpipes at each change of direction. (See Figure 6.21.)

Individual branch pipes from each fixture are connected to horizontal branches leading to vertical stacks (soil or waste), which in turn connect to a horizontal building drain at the lowest level. The diameter of the horizontal drain pipe must be increased in accordance with the number of fixtures served.

The drainage system must prevent waste decomposition gases from passing through the plumbing fixtures back into living areas. In residential structures, the principal assembly of drainpipe is installed within partitions and connects lavatory, commodes, bathtubs, and showers. The main line is a soil stack that runs vertically

■ **FIGURE 6.20**

Sanitary drainage and vent piping systems extend from the sanitary sewer to fixtures in the residential building.

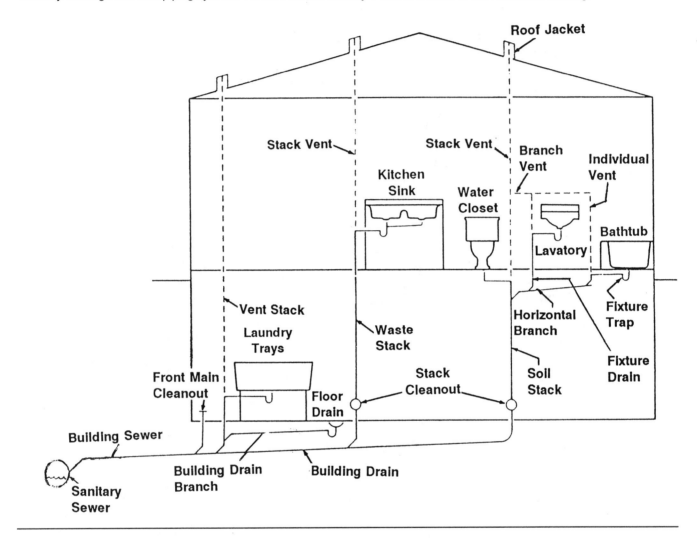

from the building drain, which is the lowest horizontal piping in the drainage system, up through the structure to the roof. Waste lines are connected to this main soil stack. Vent lines are connected to a separate vent stack, which acts as a main source of air to and from the roof or to the upper portion of the soil stack. Stack vents are an extension of a solid or waste stack above the highest horizontal drain connected to the stack. (See Figure 6.22.)

The building drain receives and conveys discharge from soil, waste, and drainage pipes in the residential structure to the building sewer. The building sewer conveys wastes to a city sewer, a septic tank, or another means of disposal.

While the size of a public sewage system is the responsibility of the community, the size and type of a private disposal system are the responsibility of the site owner and are based on soil, site conditions, and the probable quantity of waste. If there is a possibility that sewage could flow back into the residential drain, a backflow preventer should be installed.

Cross Connections

Cross connection is back siphonage of contaminated water or other unwanted materials into the potable water system. Back siphonage can be attributed to several conditions that can cause a cross connection, such as negative pressure (vacuum) in the potable water plumbing system or improperly installed vents. Back siphonage can also be caused by plumbing fixtures

■ **FIGURE 6.21**

Improper pitch in horizontal drainage pipes leads to a buildup of solid deposits while a proper pitch ensures an adequate flow of waste materials.

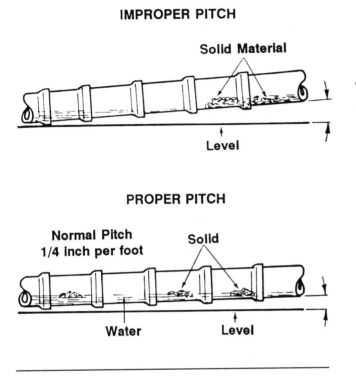

IMPROPER PITCH

PROPER PITCH

■ **FIGURE 6.22**

Stack vents consist of interconnected vents extending throughout all levels or floors of a residential structure.

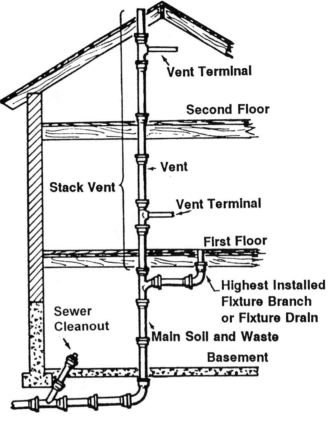

where water exits below the flood rim or physical connections between the drinking water supply and another piping system that cause one system to flow to the other, for example, a private water well connected to the potable water supply by a valve. Contaminated water can enter the potable water if the valve is opened, if the valve fails, or if negative pressure is created in the potable water supply. The most common backflow prevention devices are air gaps that prevent a cross connection between the water supply pipes and a sink. There should be a gap of at least 1″ between the end of the faucet where water exits and the flood rim of the sink to keep wastewater from entering the potable water supply if the sink overflows. (See Figure 6.23.)

Vacuum breakers are backflow prevention devices that are required on hose bibbs or any potable water outlet with a hose connection. (See Figure 6.24.)

There are other ways to control back siphonage, such as installation of check valves that will allow the potable water to travel in only one direction. They are often referred to as *backflow preventers*. Backflow

preventers are required by National Codes on all lawn sprinkler systems whose source of water is the potable water system. Many cities now require backflow preventers on the house side of water meters. When backflow prevention is required on the house side of meters, it is necessary to install an expansion tank on the water heater to allow for expansion and contraction of the water. Inspectors should be familiar with code requirements pertaining to controlling cross connections because cross connections can be found on nearly every inspection.

Traps

A plumbing trap is used in a waste system to prevent passage of sewer gas into a structure without affecting the fixture's discharge. All fixtures connected to a household plumbing system except toilets, which have integral traps, should have a trap installed in the line.

■ **FIGURE 6.23**

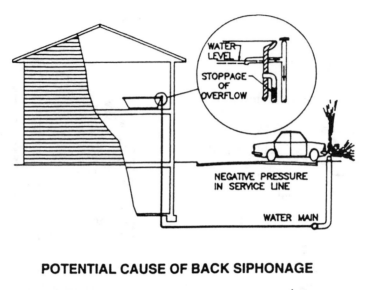

POTENTIAL CAUSE OF BACK SIPHONAGE

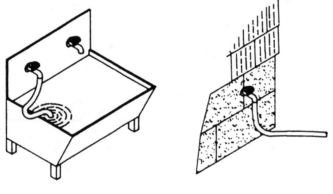

Because a plumbing system is subject to wide flow variations that originate from different sections of the system, there is a wide variation in waste-line pressures. These pressure differences tend to destroy the water seal in a trap.

The P-trap and the drum trap are traps approved for use by plumbing codes. P-traps are used with lavatories, sinks, drinking fountains, showers, and other installations that do not discharge an abundance of water. P-traps have a 2″-deep water seal. A deep seal trap has a 4″-deep water seal. (See Figure 6.25.)

Drum traps have a water seal trap that passes large amounts of water quickly. Drum traps are commonly connected to bathtubs, foot baths and sitz baths. They normally are located within 2′ of the fixture. (See Figure 6.26.)

The full S-trap, ¾ S-trap or bag trap should not be used in plumbing installations. These traps are almost

■ **FIGURE 6.24**

Vacuum breakers are mounted on an existing sill cock and used to prevent back-siphoning.

■ **FIGURE 6.25**

P-traps are commonly used with lavatories, sinks, drinking fountains, and showers.

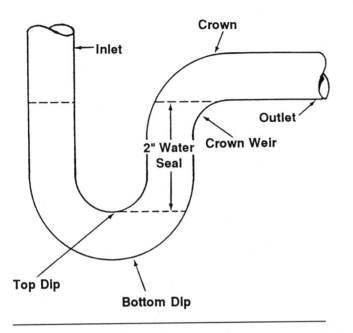

■ **FIGURE 6.26**

Drum traps are commonly used with bathtubs, footbaths, and stiz baths.

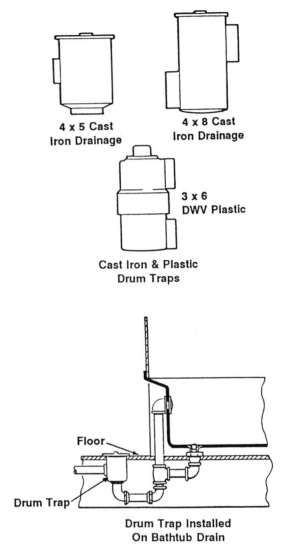

impossible to vent properly. The ¾ S-trap forms a perfect siphon. The bag trap, an extreme form of an S-trap, is seldom found in residential structures. (See Figure 6.27.)

Traps that depend on moving parts for effectiveness and traps with internal partitions are usually inadequate and have been prohibited by plumbing codes. (See Figure 6.28.)

Vents

When venting is properly installed, system air is allowed to circulate through the waste piping. The function of a vent is to maintain air inside waste and drainage piping at a constant pressure. Wind and drain load can have an effect on the air pressure in the waste and drainage line. Venting also allows sewer gases to exhaust above the roof line of the dwelling. Without proper venting, waste and drainage systems will not function. (See Figure 6.29.)

Sewer gases are harmful to the human body. A trap is a fitting that provides a liquid seal to prevent emission of sewer gases without physically affecting the flow of wastewater or sewage. Traps are installed in waste drainage piping to prevent sewer gas from entering the residential structure by providing a water seal.

The seal in a plumbing trap may be lost due to siphonage (direct or indirect momentum), back pressure, evaporation, capillary attraction, or wind effect. Back pressure and evaporation are the primary causes of seal loss.

Direct siphonage causes seal loss if a vacuum is created in the waste piping. The water that forms the seal can be sucked out of one or several traps. This problem results from inadequate venting. (See Figure 6.30.)

Indirect or momentum siphonage occurs when the discharge of one fixture causes water to be siphoned from another fixture. Negative pressure at a lower trap

The full S-trap, ¾ S-trap, and bag trap are almost impossible to vent properly and should not be used in plumbing installations.

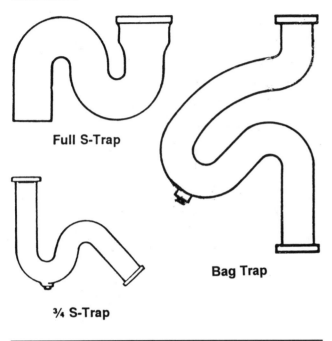

Full S-Trap

Bag Trap

¾ S-Trap

Traps with moving parts and traps that have internal partitions are prohibited by local plumbing codes.

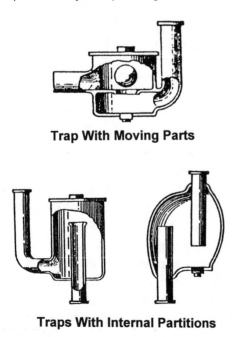

Trap With Moving Parts

Traps With Internal Partitions

causes the water flow to draw air through the vertical pipe. This improper venting results from vent pipe that is too small or in the wrong location. A vent located near the lower trap would bring in air to protect the trap seal. (See Figure 6.31.)

Back pressure is the result of air pressure blowing through one or more traps, causing the loss of a trap seal. Back pressure is usually a problem in multistory structures. A problem can result if the water flowing through the waste and drainage piping completely fills the stack, allowing air pressure to build ahead of the water. Unless there is a vent located near a fixture trap, the pressure will blow through the trap. (See Figure 6.32.)

Evaporation of water in traps will induce trap seal loss. If the drain is not used for extended periods of time, water will evaporate, causing trap seal loss. If a trap serves a fixture that might not have water flowing often enough to maintain the water seal, a deep trap should be installed or some method of maintaining a water seal in the trap.

Capillary attraction can also cause trap seal loss. This seldom happens; however, string, lint, or rags lodged in the trap can cause capillary attraction to occur. These foreign materials absorb and siphon water. Usually, the next time the fixture is used, the water will clear out the foreign material.

Wind blowing across a stack can cause a downdraft that will act as back pressure. The location of the vent stack on the roof can control the downdraft problem. To avoid downdrafts, vents should not be installed in roof valleys or at the roof ridge.

Water flow in soil pipes varies according to the number and type of fixtures used. A lavatory provides a small water flow, and a water closet provides a large water flow. Small water flows tend to cling to the sides of pipe, and large water flows form a waste slug as they drop. Air in front of the water slug becomes pressurized as it falls down the pipe. As the pressure builds, air escapes through a vent or a fixture outlet. If the vent is plugged or no vent exists, the only escape for air is the fixture outlet.

If a waste pipe is placed vertically after the fixture trap, as in an S-trap, wastewater continues to flow after the fixture is emptied and clears the trap. The action of the water discharging into the waste pipe removes air from the pipe and causes negative pressure in the waste line.

Plumbing systems are ventilated to prevent trap seal loss, material deterioration, and flow retardation. Venting in the plumbing system maintains equal

■ **FIGURE 6.29**

Vents maintain constant pressure in waste and drainage piping in a residential structure.

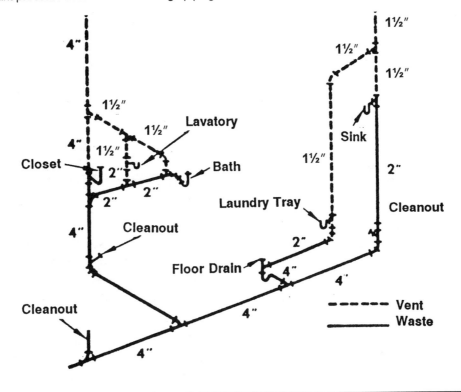

■ **FIGURE 6.30**

Siphonage by direct momentum is one cause of plumbing trap seal loss.

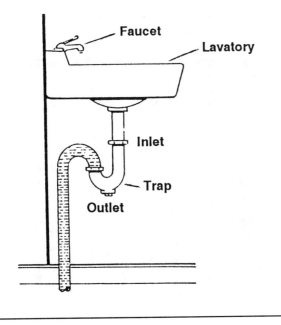

atmospheric conditions on both sides of the trap. Pressure developed in front of a column of moving or falling water in a drain line can create great enough pressure to blow the water seal through the fixture trap and into the building interior. Pressure behind moving water in a drain can be low enough to suck a water seal into the drainage system. Venting systems provide a free-flowing air connection to the outdoors.

Venting maintains pressure throughout the waste and drainage piping system of a residential structure. Residential plumbing may use one or more of the following venting methods:

- Individual fixture vents are installed as close to the trap as possible. Individual fixture vents are not widely used on residential construction because of cost. (See Figure 6.29.)
- Circuit vents are installed on two or more fixtures that discharge into a horizontal waste and drain branch line. These vents are located between the last two fixtures on the branch line. (See Figure 6.33.)
- Unit vents are installed where two similar fixtures discharge into the waste and drainage piping. Unit

■ **FIGURE 6.31**

Siphonage by direct momentum can induce loss of the plumbing trap seal.

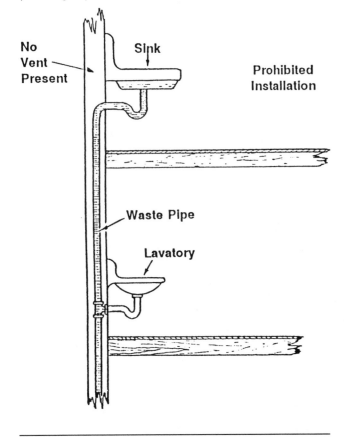

■ **FIGURE 6.32**

Back pressure can cause the loss of a plumbing trap seal.

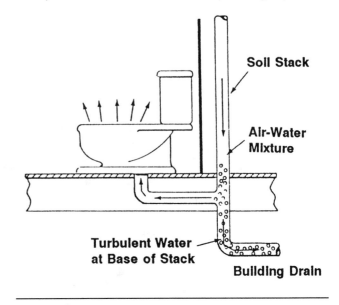

a lower fixture that could empty the lower trap seal. Combination waste vents are permitted in residential bathrooms because drainage from a lavatory and bathtub at the same time is unlikely to occur.

Vent pipe installation is similar to soil and waste pipe. The vent pipe extensions through the roof must ter-

■ **FIGURE 6.33**

Circuit vents are installed on horizontal branches serving two or more fixtures.

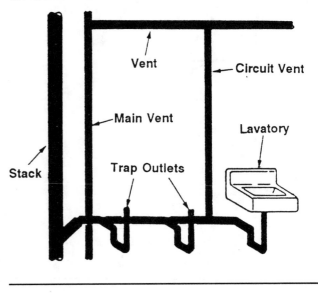

venting is commonly used where fixtures are installed back to back in separate rooms. (See Figure 6.34.)

- Wet venting is used when a vent from a fixture is remote from a wall. When wet venting is used, the fixture drain is oversized and used as a vent as well as a drain. Wet venting is common in bathroom fixture groupings. Wet venting uses the vent pipe as the waste line. Wet venting is used only for lavatories, bathtubs, and showers and should not be used for commodes, washing machines, dishwashers, or kitchen sinks. (See Figure 6.35.)
- Loop venting is venting that protects several traps adequately without requiring a separate vent stack for each fixture. Plumbing codes have limitations on the allowable distance from a trap to vents. (See Figure 6.36.)

A separate vent stack is normally required for two-story residential structures because it serves as a vent for

■ **FIGURE 6.34**

Unit vent installation is used for wall-hung fixtures, water closets, and bathtubs.

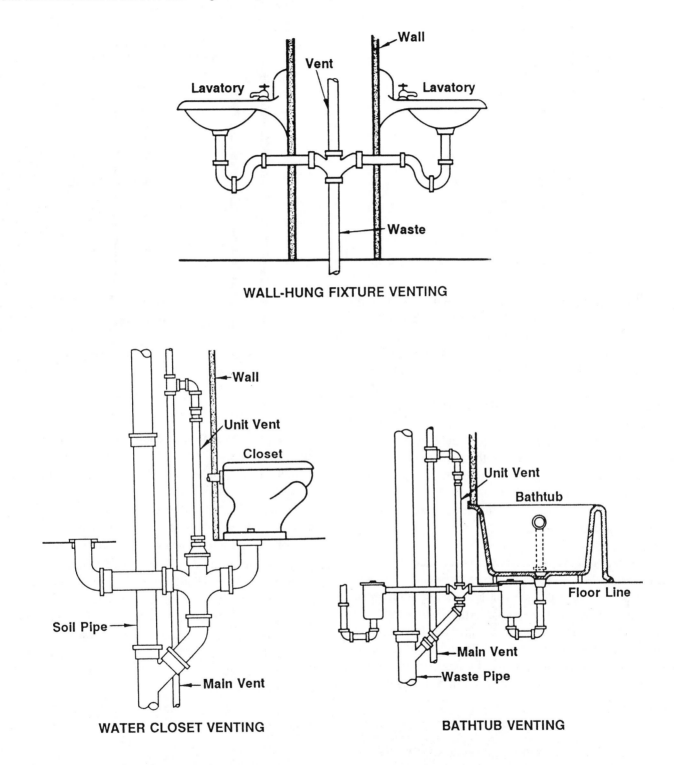

WALL-HUNG FIXTURE VENTING

WATER CLOSET VENTING

BATHTUB VENTING

■ **FIGURE 6.35**

Wet vents are installed to serve fixtures (e.g., lavatory and bath) that discharge water only.

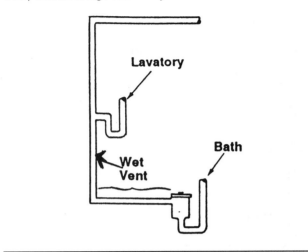

■ **FIGURE 6.36**

Looped vents are installed when vertical stacks would be objectionable. Bleeder connections are used to drain collected moisture.

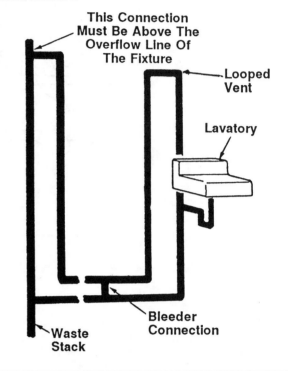

minate at least 6″ above the high side of the penetration. Where the roof is to be used for any purpose other than weather protection, vent extensions shall run at least 7′ above the roof. Vents must not terminate beneath doors, windows, or other openings. A vent terminal shall not be within 5′ horizontally of an opening to the interior unless it is at least 2′ above the top of the opening.

An air admittance valve is a one-way valve designed to allow air to enter the plumbing drainage system when negative pressures develop in the piping system. The device must close by gravity and seal the vent terminal when the internal pressure is equal to or greater than atmospheric pressure. The air admittance valve is designed to act as a substitute for vent piping extending to the open air.

Air admittance valves may be used as sewer vents in areas where it is impossible to vent a fixture, such as a sink installed on an island in the kitchen. Air admittance valves are permitted for single fixtures or for multiple fixture traps. The air admittance valve must be installed to permit free movement of air. It should not be less than 4 inches above the trap arm of the fixture served and must be accessible for periodic inspection or replacement.

Drains

Water brought into the residential structure is discharged through a drainage system. The drainage system is a sanitary system carrying primarily interior wastewater or a combined system carrying interior wastewater and roof run-off water. (See Figure 6.37.)

Proper sizing of the sanitary drain depends on the number of fixtures served. Minimum drain size is 3″ in diameter to the sanitary sewer. Materials used for drains are cast iron, vitrified clay, plastic, copper and, in rare cases, lead. Drainpipe is sized so waste flows while the pipe is approximately one-half full, ensuring proper scouring action so solids will not be deposited in the pipe.

The Uniform Plumbing Code Committee has developed a method for the sizing of residential drains in terms of fixture units. One fixture unit equals approximately 7½ gallons of water per minute. This is the surge flow rate of water discharged from a wash basin in 1 minute. Tables 6.1 and 6.2 show fixture unit values and the minimum number of fixture units attached to a sanitary drain.

A fixture drain is the drain from the trap of the fixture to the junction of that drain with other drains. The size of the trap and fixture drain must be sufficient to drain the fixture rapidly. The trap and fixture drain must be the same size. (See Figure 6.38.)

A branch drain is a waste pipe that collects waste from two or more fixtures and conveys it to the building

■ **FIGURE 6.37**

Storm water drainage systems carry primarily interior wastewater or interior wastewater and roof run-off water.

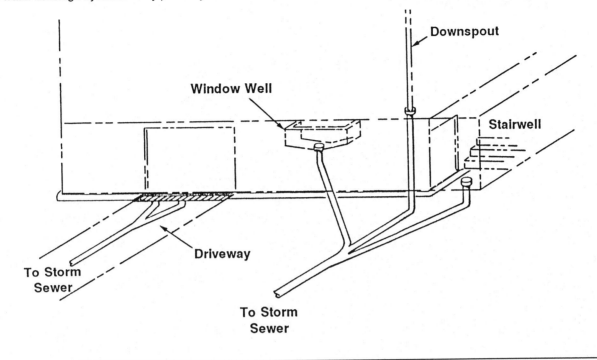

■ **FIGURE 6.38**

Fixture drains are connected to a single fixture.

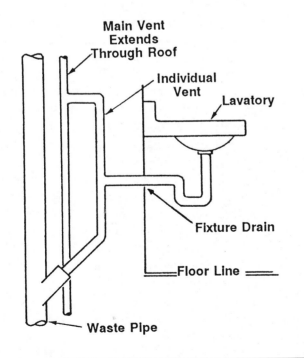

drain. Water closets must have a minimum 3″ diameter drain, and only two water closets may connect into the one drain.

All branch drains must join the building drain with a Y-fitting. The Y-fitting is used to eliminate solid deposits in or near the connection. A buildup of solids will cause a drain blockage.

Sewage Ejectors

Sewage ejectors are designed for sanitary systems that are below the city sewage system or when a drain field is higher than the septic tank. Sewage ejectors use an electric sump pump with a float switch to pump sewage into the city sewer and effluent to the drain field. (See Figure 6.39.)

The pump used to discharge waste into the city sewer must be capable of pumping solids. The pump used to discharge waste into a septic system need only be capable of pumping liquids. The ejector tank must be vented for proper operation and to prevent odors from seeping into the residential structure. The ejector is usually located in the basement or in a closet. A check valve is located on the discharge side of the ejector as well as on the inbound sewer line to prevent raw sewage backup.

■ **TABLE 6.1**

Fixture Unit Values

REQUIRED CAPACITIES AT POINT OF OUTLET DISCHARGE

FIXTURE AT POINT OF OUTLET	FLOW RATE (gpm)	FLOW PRESSURE (psi)
Bathtub	4	8
Bidet	2	4
Dishwasher	2.75	8
Laundry tub	4	8
Lavatory	2	8
Shower	3	8
Shower, temperature controlled	3	20
Sillcock, hose bibb	5	8
Sink	2.5	8
Water closet, flushometer tank	1.6	15
Water closet, tank, close coupled	3	8
Water closet, tank, one-piece	6	20

MAXIMUM FLOW RATES AND CONSUMPTION FOR PLUMBING FIXTURES AND FIXTURE FITTINGS

PLUMBING FIXTURE OR FIXTURE FITTING	PLUMBING FIXTURE OR FIXTURE FITTING
Lavatory faucet	2.2 gpm at 60 psi
Shower head	2.5 gpm at 80 psi
Sink faucet	2.2 gpm at 60 psi
Water closet	1.6 gallons per flushing cycle

■ **TABLE 6.2**

Minimum Fixture Service

Fixture	Supply Line	Vent Line	Drain Line
Bathtub	½″	1½″	1½″–2″
Kitchen sink	½″	1½″	1½″
Lavatory	⅜″	1¼″	1¼″
Laundry sink	½″	1½″	1½″
Shower	½″	2″	2″
Water Closet (tank)	⅜″	3″	3″

Sump Pumps

Sump pumps are used to remove ground water and/or surface water from a structure. Sump pumps keep a basement or a crawlspace dry and prevent mildew and moisture problems. (See Figure 6.40.)

Drain tile is buried in gravel around the perimeter of the foundation and under the basement floor or below the surface of the crawlspace. The tile is run to the sump that collects ground water. The sump is simply a closed container that will collect water until a predetermined depth is reached. The sump pump is located in the sump and pumps the water from the sump to the storm sewer, depending on local codes, or away from the structure to an area far enough away from the foundation that it will not return. The sump pump is activated by a float switch. The discharge pipe used with a sump pump should have a check valve to prevent backflow.

When inspecting a sump pump, the inspector should check the installation for the check valve on the discharge pipe and run the pump to be sure it works. Putting water in the sump to check pump operation is sometimes necessary. Check the sump for debris and damage.

On-Site Sewage Facility
Septic Tanks

A septic tank is the most widely used on-site treatment option. Approximately 25 percent of all new homes use septic tanks. One of every four persons in the United States depends on a septic system for treatment and disposal of household water. The septic system is used for residential property without access to municipal treatment plants. A residential septic system requires periodic maintenance to continue functioning effectively. Plumbing codes require that septic tanks be sized according to the residential structure. For example, a two-bedroom home must have a minimum septic tank capacity of 750 gallons, and a three-bedroom home must have a minimum septic tank capacity of 1,000 gallons.

Research shows that most septic tank systems fail within 10 to 20 years due to lack of regular maintenance. The most common oversight is failure to have septic tanks pumped out. Pumping out a tank costs between $75 and $150, while replacing a system may cost between $3,000 and $10,000 or more. Preventive maintenance of a septic system will outweigh the cost of replacement.

Septic tanks are buried, watertight tanks designed and constructed to receive wastewater from a home or business. They separate solids from liquids, provide limited digestion of organic matter, store solids, and allow the clarified liquid to discharge for further treatment and disposal. Settleable solids and partially decomposed sludge settle to the bottom of the tank and accumulate. The scum of lightweight material, including fats and greases, rises to the top. The partially

■ **FIGURE 6.39**

Sewage ejectors use an electric sump pump that pumps waste into the city sewer and effluent to the drain field.

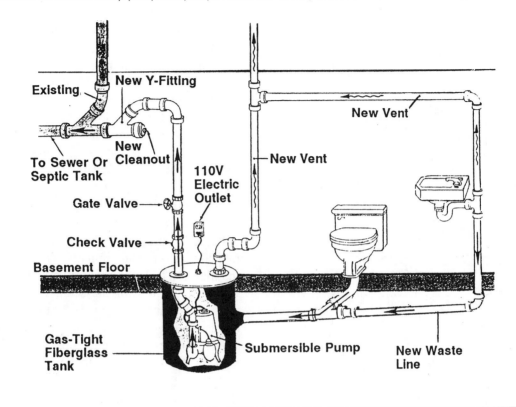

clarified liquid is allowed to flow through an outlet structure below the floating scum layer. Proper use of baffles, tees, and ells protect against scum overflow. Clarified liquid can be disposed of through soil absorption systems. Septic tanks cannot remove disease-causing organisms. Septic tank effluent receives a greater degree of treatment in the soil absorption system than in the tank.

A typical septic system consists of the septic tank (usually made of concrete) and soil drainfield. Effluent flowing from the tank is distributed throughout the drainfield by perforated drainpipe in graveled trenches. Effluent is purified as it is absorbed through the underlying soil. (See Figures 6.41 and 6.42.)

An alternative septic system consists of a septic tank combined with a seepage pit or leaching pool. Seepage pits and leaching pools are used on sloping sites; however, they should never be installed in semi-impervious or impervious soil. Soil must be sandy gravel, which may require digging 40′ to 50′. The pit or pool requires a location where the normal groundwater level

is at least 8′ below grade or 2′ below the bottom of the pit or pool. The pit or pool must be located at least 100′ away from the potable water supply and at least 15′ away from the residential structure.

Seepage pits or leaching pools are underground tanks made with hollow tile, stone, or brick walls, without mortar and with open joints to permit effluent to seep into the soil. The roof is concrete with manholes, while the bottom is earth. Precast reinforced concrete rings are also available that can be set directly in proper soil conditions.

Septic tanks are settling basins that prevent floatable solid materials (greases or oils) from entering the soil drainfield. If solid materials get into the drainfield, effluent backs up in the trenches and might break through to the lawn surface or back up into the house.

Gradually, the septic tank accumulates thick layers of sludge and scum, which decrease effectiveness. These layers should be removed every two to four years. Regular pumping of the septic tank ensures optimum operating condition. The inspector must find the

Submersible sump pupmps remove ground water and/or surface water from a residential structure.

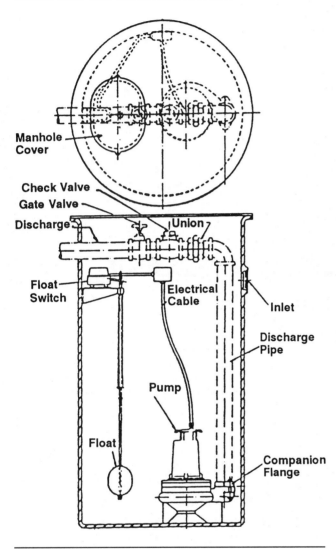

Manhole Cover

Check Valve
Gate Valve
Discharge
Union
Float Switch
Electrical Cable
Inlet
Discharge Pipe
Pump
Float
Companion Flange

location of the buried tank. This should be indicated on the property survey. If it is not, consult previous owners or neighbors. If they do not know, go to the basement or crawlspace and trace the sewer pipe out through the wall. This will indicate where to look outside.

Late winter and early spring are the best times to locate a septic tank. The warm water that flows into the tank warms soil and causes snow to melt or grass to green earlier than it does in other parts of the yard. Other clues to the tank's location are where grass grows poorly or exceptionally well or where soil is either slightly mounded or depressed from excavation during installation. In some parts of the country, county health officials may have a map showing the tank's location on the lot.

The inspection of the septic tank itself should be done only by a professional. After a likely spot has been found, the soil should be probed when it is moist with a thin metal rod. Once the tank has been located, the professional digs farther away from the house to find the manhole over the outlet baffle.

The professional refers to the cross section of the septic tank and notes the location of the outlet baffle. Most tanks use either concrete dividers or cast iron pipe fittings for baffles. The lower end of the outlet baffle will be used as a reference point in the measuring process. To find this point, the professional lowers a stick with a hinged flap into the tank. The stick is then moved around and raised, feeling for the firm resistance of the bottom of the baffle. This depth then is marked on the stick.

The stick again is lowered into the tank in front of the outlet baffle and pushed through the scum, allowing the hinged flap to fall horizontally. The professional raises the stick and feels for increased pressure, which reveals where the bottom of the scum layer is; the stick is marked. The distance between the two marks on the stick represents the distance between the bottom scum layer and the bottom of the outlet pipe. If this distance is less than 3″, the tank needs to be pumped.

The professional now tests the sludge depth. He or she tacks or ties some old bath towels or sturdy paper towels to the bottom of the stick. The scum layer is avoided by lowering the stick between the baffle and the bottom of the tank and twirling it. After a minute or two, the stick is carefully removed. The depth of the sludge layer is determined by noting the distinct black layer on the towel. If the top of the sludge layer is less than 12″ from the mark on the pole showing the bottom of the outlet baffle, it is time to pump the tank. If not done properly, the pumping may wash solids into the drainfield and damage it.

The entire contents of the tank, not just the liquid, should be removed. Agitation is required to get the solids in suspension. There is no need to leave anything in the tank to act as a "starter" for the bacterial population, which the tank needs to work properly. Such bacteria are present in the household wastewater sewage and rapidly reestablish themselves. There is no need to wash, scrub, or disinfect the tank. Some chemicals used to clean septic tanks are extremely toxic compounds that could contaminate the surrounding drinking-water wells.

Eventually, every septic tank needs to be pumped. Additives that claim to eliminate the need for pumping do not help; some can even interfere with the regular operation.

■ **FIGURE 6.41**

A typical septic system consists of a septic tank and soil drainfield.

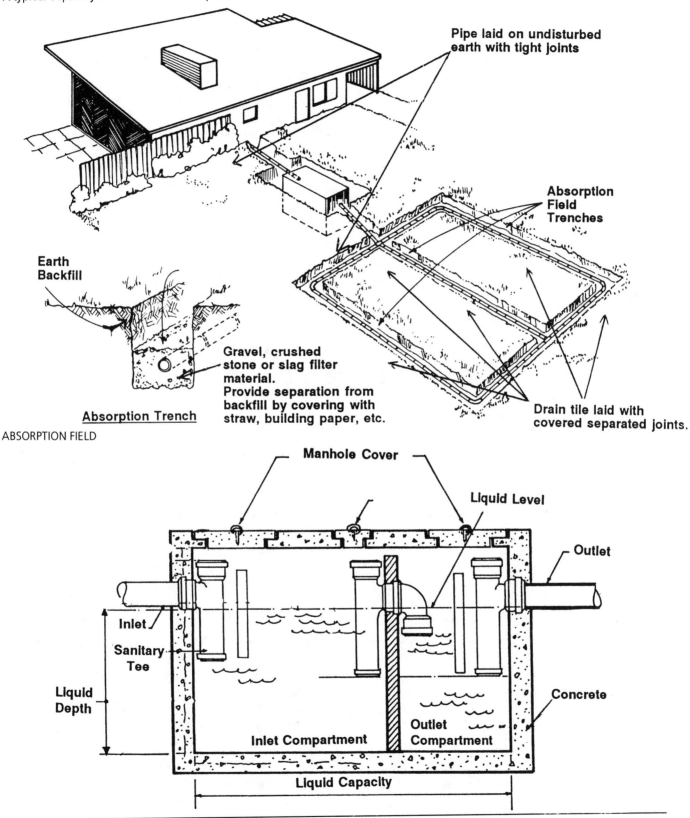

Pipe laid on undisturbed
earth with tight joints

Absorption
Field
Trenches

Earth
Backfill

Gravel, crushed
stone or slag filter
material.
Provide separation from
backfill by covering with
straw, building paper, etc.

Drain tile laid with
covered separated joints.

Absorption Trench

ABSORPTION FIELD

Manhole Cover

Liquid Level

Outlet

Inlet

Sanitary
Tee

Liquid
Depth

Inlet Compartment

Outlet
Compartment

Concrete

Liquid Capacity

■ FIGURE 6.42

Aerobic systems are designed to quietly, efficiently, and automatically treat all household wastewater within 24 hours.

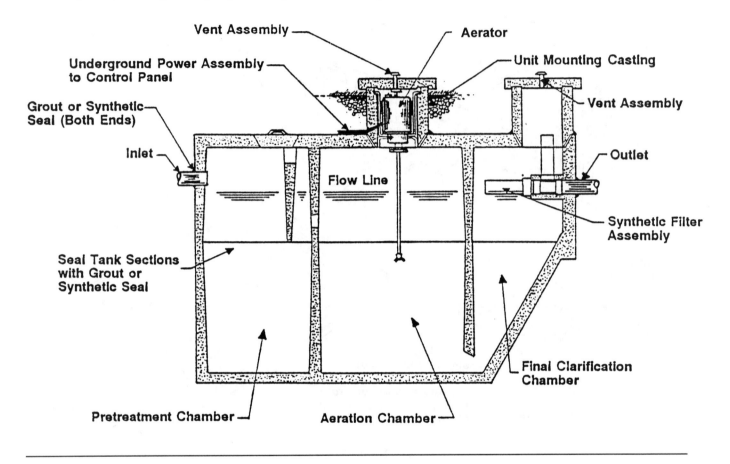

After pumping, inspect the inside of the tank for deterioration, especially of the concrete inlet or the outlet baffles. If anything needs replacement, use plastic or cast iron sanitary tees. Unless repairs have to be made inside the tank, NEVER ALLOW ANYONE TO ENTER A SEPTIC TANK. The poisonous gases that may remain in the tank can cause asphyxiation quickly. The homeowner should have recent records as to when the tank was last pumped. By giving the septic system the periodic maintenance it requires, the unpleasant and costly inconvenience of a failed or poorly operating system can be avoided. For a water-well system, it is recommended that the quality and volume of water be checked by a qualified authority.

The basic function of the septic tank is to serve as a settling basin to prevent solid materials from reaching the drainfield. By decreasing the amount of solids entering the tank, the interval between pumpings can be increased to ensure a properly operating system.

Only human waste should be disposed of in the septic system. Disposable diapers, sanitary napkins, paper towels, rags, coffee grounds, and grease should never enter a septic tank. These items degrade slowly and increase the fill rate of the septic tank.

Inside the septic tank, millions of bacteria break down organic substances and contribute to the treatment process. Disposal of strong chemicals such as household cleaners, paints, varnishes, solvents, garden pesticides, and photographic chemicals can kill these bacteria and disrupt the treatment process. These chemicals also damage the solid drainfield and may contaminate local wells. Ordinary use of sink and toilet bowl cleaners will not cause problems; however, excessive use can be detrimental.

Several common household appliances greatly affect the operation of the septic system. Garbage disposals are discouraged because these waste materials fill the septic tank faster. Furthermore, the finely ground solid

■ **FIGURE 6.43**

Grease traps and interceptors.

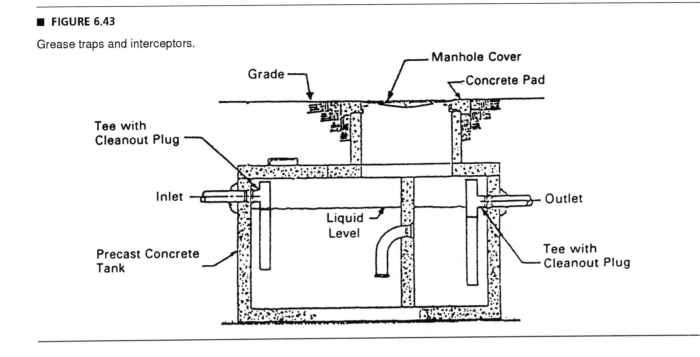

wastes may not settle in the septic tank, but may flow into the solid drainfield and clog soil pores.

A water softener is another appliance that can threaten a septic system. The very nature of chemical treatment of water results in an increase in sodium in household wastewater. Over a period of time, this extra sodium physically changes the soil, decreasing permeability and causing premature drainfield failure. It is beneficial for homeowners with water softeners to flush coarse gypsum down the toilet each month. The calcium in gypsum neutralizes the effect of added sodium and keeps soil permeable. Recharging water softeners adds several hundred gallons of water to a septic system each week. Water of this nature can be drained to an alternate disposal location.

One of the best ways to extend septic tank life is to decrease the amount of water used. Most homeowners can decrease water consumption by 20 to 30 percent. Besides being beneficial for the septic system, such conservation saves the well pump and is cost-effective on hot water heating expenses. Leaky faucets and toilets that run continuously should also be repaired.

Holding Tank

Holding tanks are allowed only on a very limited basis. They are not intended to be a treatment process, but a temporary means of handling sewage until a permanent disposal method can be implemented. Limited occupancy structures with no other acceptable method of sewage disposal might be allowed holding tanks.

Grease Traps

A grease trap or interceptor, like a septic tank, is a chamber where gravity is used to separate solids from the water, providing primary treatment. Grease traps are often referred to as *flotation chambers* because more floating solids are expected than settleable or suspended solids. Settleable solids should be excluded as much as possible from a grease trap. No garbage disposal wastes should be discharged to a grease trap.

Interceptors are multicompartment grease traps. If a septic tank system is properly designed, grease traps are not needed or recommended for individual home kitchens. Interceptors are required on kitchen waste lines from institutions such as restaurants, schools, hospitals, etc. Factors affecting the performance of grease traps and interceptors are

- temperature of wastewater,
- solids,
- concentration,
- retention time, and
- maintenance.

Grease trap/interceptor design is similar to that of a septic tank. (See Figure 6.43.) The major difference is that the outlets are deeper to allow a larger volume for grease builddown. The minimum size of the tank is

100 gallons. When sizing a grease trap or interceptor, the volume in gallons should be a minimum of four times the total gallons per minute from all fixtures discharging to the trap.

The inlets and outlets must be within 12" of the bottom of the tank. Inlets and outlets must be accessible, and each compartment must have a port for grease removal.

Like septic tanks, grease traps and interceptors are gravity separation chambers. However, they require more frequent maintenance. If a grease trap fails to do its job and large amounts of grease reach the disposal field, the system will fail. Therefore, it is important to ensure that only a minimum amount of grease enters the wastewater line. A maintenance program should include removal of grease and any settleable solids whenever 60 percent to 70 percent of the grease retention capacity has been obtained. Depending on the usage, the frequency or removal could be once a week or every two or three months.

Inspect the soundness of the tank, connections, and baffles at every pumping. Use a licensed hauler who can document proper disposal of grease.

Aerobic Systems

Most of the proprietary on-site sewage treatment plants are small aerobic plants that use a form of extended aeration. They treat or stabilize both suspended and dissolved wastes using aerobic bacteria that require the continual presence of free oxygen. The free oxygen is added by mechanical pumping or by mixing atmospheric air, which contains approximately 19 percent free oxygen, into the wastewater being treated.

The aerobic biological treatment process used in on-site units is basically the same as that found in municipal activated sludge sewage treatment plants that are permitted to discharge their effluent to surface waters. The process is highly effective when properly designed and operated. Daily monitoring and solids dissolving are not expected with on-site units. Therefore, effluent quality is more variable with home treatment units. Typical problems associated with home aerobic systems include mechanical failures, inadequate dissolved oxygen, foaming, bulking, and solids washout. When properly designed and operated, aerobic systems treat home wastes more completely than anaerobic septic tank systems because aerobic treatment more efficiently removes dissolved organic matter. By definition, proprietary units are those units that have been designed, tested, and approved. This list includes Class I systems, which require effluent quality below 30 mg./L. TSS (total suspended solids) and Class II units which require effluent quality below 60 mg./L. BOD (biochemical oxygen demand) and 30 mg./L. TSS. Class I units may be considered for surface application, while Class II units may be used only for subsurface disposal. Aerobic plants can have higher initial costs as well as higher operating and maintenance costs when compared with septic tank systems using conventional soil absorption systems.

Aerobic systems are designed to quietly, efficiently, and automatically treat all household wastewater within 24 hours. Aerobic systems use an extended aeration process for wastewater treatment. (See Figure 6.42.)

Tank fluctuations in daily wastewater flow do not affect the performance of an aerobic system. The tank has a total capacity of 1,200 gallons, which consists of 475 gallons in the pretreatment chamber, 600 gallons in the aeration chamber, and 125 gallons in the clarification chamber. Two classes of aerobic systems are rated by the National Sanitation Foundation (NSF): the Class I system, which has a home wastewater treatment plant and an upflow filter, and the Class II system, which has the home wastewater treatment plant without an upflow filter. Both systems require a drainfield similar to that of a septic system.

Wastewater enters the pretreatment chamber of the plant and is retained in this chamber long enough to allow an aerobic biological action to physically break down and pretreat the wastewater before passing it to the aeration chamber. Once the wastewater has been conditioned, it flows into the aeration chamber of the treatment plant, which is equipped with aerobic bacteria. The aeration chamber is designed to hold wastewater and bacteria that destroy organic material. To complete treatment, it is necessary to provide the right environment for the bacteria by controlling the introduction of oxygen into the chamber through use of an aerator.

The aerator is installed in the aeration chamber center to provide even distribution of oxygen into the chamber. The unit draws fresh air into the tank while circulating the contents. Stimulated by the supply of oxygen, bacteria multiply rapidly and are thoroughly mixed with the tank contents to ensure complete oxidation of organic materials.

Finally, wastewater flows into the settling, clarifying chamber, where activated sludge and organic particles are removed so only purified effluent is discharged from the plant. Unlike liquid in the aeration chamber, liquid in the clarification chamber is still, which allows the sludge and organic particles to settle to the lower

■ **FIGURE 6.44**

Upflow filter aerobic systems are required when the residential structure is located near a lake, river, or water well.

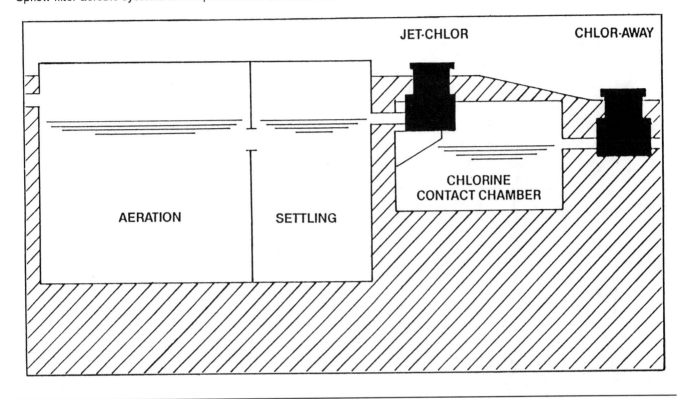

sidewalls of the clarification chamber. The clarification chamber is designed to allow sludge and organic particles to return through the opening at the bottom of the inner wall into the aeration chamber. This allows only the clear, highly treated water at the top of the chamber to flow into the final discharge line through the baffled outlet. Effluent disposal is simplified because the highly treated water extends the life of the leach field and filters.

Aerobic plants need to be checked periodically by trained personnel to ensure that all mechanical equipment is operational and that the process is functioning properly. Most maintenance policies call for site visits at least once every four months.

A two-year service contract is required to be provided, as part of the basic purchase price, by manufacturers and distributors of on-site aerobic plants. An additional fee is charged for renewal of the service contract after the initial two-year period.

The maintenance and operational checks or evaluations at a minimum should include the following:

• Lids and covers need to be removed and all mechanical equipment checked for proper operation.

These checks include activating each motor, pump, etc. Schedule lubrication and clean per specifications.

• Filters on aerators checked for replacement.

• Screens or strainers on pump intakes checked for cleaning or replacement.

Upflow Filters

An upflow filter added to an aerobic system produces pure effluent. Many properties, such as lake resorts or properties that have wells and septic systems, require a Class I aerobic system to reduce lake, river, or well contamination. The upflow filter is housed in a rectangular concrete tank. Plant effluent is channeled to the bottom of the tank. A thick concrete grate supports a 6" layer of 1/4" to 1/8" smooth gravel, pebbles, or inert aggregate above the bottom. Effluent flows through the filter medium, enters a concrete trough, and flows out of the tank. Fluid flow through the filter is achieved by hydraulic displacement—incoming fluid dropping to the bottom of the tank causes fluid to flow through the stones into the effluent channel. The oxygen-rich effluent from the plant promotes growth on the filter medium of the bacteria that treat effluent. (See Figure 6.44.)

■ FIGURE 6.45

Chlorinators reduce bacteria produced from effluent.

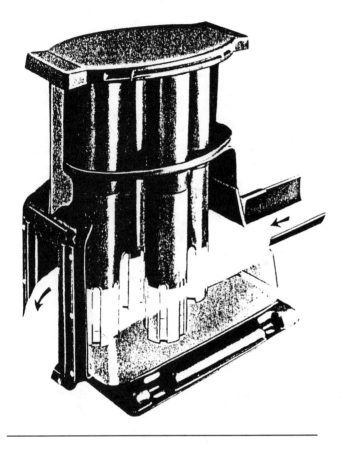

Chlorinators

Treated wastewater flows through the chlorinator. The water contacts chlorine tablets that gradually dissolve and slowly release controlled amounts of active chlorine into the wastewater. As the water flow rate increases, the liquid level in the chlorinator rises and more tablets are immersed. As the water flow rate decreases, the liquid level drops and fewer tablets are immersed.

Chlorination rate and chlorine residual can be adjusted and will remain constant in proportion to water flow. Adjustments are made by varying the number of tablet feed tubes that are filled. Home chlorinators require restocking approximately twice a year for the average family. (See Figure 6.45.)

Little maintenance is required on the aerobic system. It is recommended that only maintenance people familiar with the system service it. Maintenance rules the inspector should be aware of follow:

- Never remove the aerator.

- The air intake vent cap in the manhole cover and the screen inside the vent cap must be kept clear and unrestricted for a free flow of air to the aerator.
- Only the pretreatment and aeration compartments should be pumped. The clarification compartment on the outlet end should be hosed out through the aeration compartment.
- The finished grade of the lawn or garden should be kept at least 1″ below the manhole top to permit access to the plant.

The inspector may find the following options on aerobic systems:

- Warning buzzer—The warning buzzer sounds if the circuit breaker trips and the aerator warning light is activated.
- Aerator silencer—If the sound of the aerator is audible, a silencer may be installed.
- Upflow filter—The upflow filter is required for the Class I system and available as an option for the Class II system.
- Chlorinator—The chlorinator is installed on the discharge line of new or existing systems and is above or below the ground. The chlorine tablets in the chlorinator complete bacteria killing and inhibit bacterial growth.

■ MECHANICAL SYSTEMS

Mechanical systems include gas piping, flue and vent piping, water softeners, and water heaters. Mechanical systems also include furnaces, air conditioners, fireplaces, swimming pools, and spas. However, this equipment requires licensing by various agencies and does not fall under plumbing.

Water Softeners

A water softener is installed at the entrance of the potable water line for the purpose of extracting minerals, removing odors, changing the taste, and softening water. Water softeners clear cloudy water and create more desirable and usable water. (See Figure 6.46.)

Most water softeners have clocks that are set to recycle or regenerate automatically at regular times. Regenerating requires four to six hours to complete. If the unit is installed properly, outside faucets should bypass the softener to prevent wasting treated water.

■ **FIGURE 6.46**

Water softeners extract minerals, remove odors, change taste, and soften water used in residential structures.

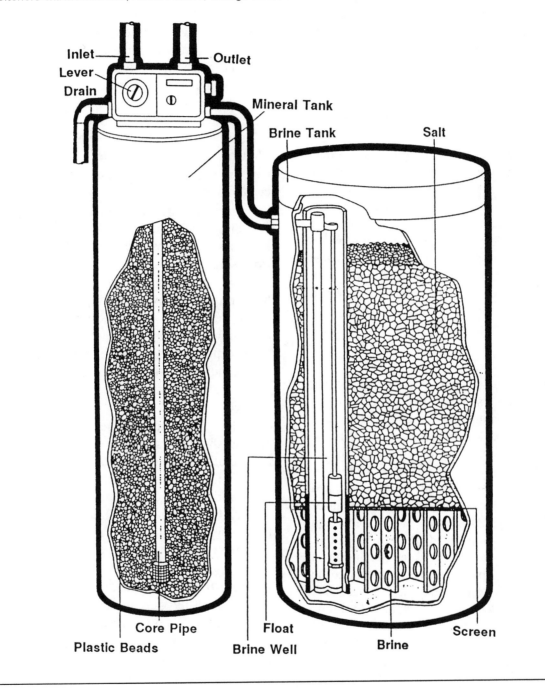

Water softeners are a necessity in approximately 80 percent of residential structures in the United States because of hard water, which contains calcium and magnesium. Hard water forms insoluble scale and scum from soap or detergent.

Soap scum is deposited on fabrics when they are washed, dulling the colors. Dishes washed in a dishwasher will have spots on them caused by the minerals. Scale is formed when hard water is heated. Hard water also stains sinks, tubs and toilets. Water pipes can become clogged with the scale buildup, resulting in low water pressure and damage to dishwashers, water heaters, and miscellaneous appliances.

Water softeners consist of a resin tank, brine tank, and control valve. The resin tank contains a resin bed made of $\frac{1}{32}''$ diameter styrene and divinylbenzene beads. The resin beads hold positively charged ions. As hard water passes through the resin bed, the calcium and magnesium bond to the resins. After a period of time, the resins become saturated with minerals and it is necessary to recharge the system. The brine tank holds water and dissolved salt solution (brine) used to recharge.

Recharging is accomplished by the control valve, which determines the direction of water flow through the resin tank. During recharging, the control valve reverses the flow of the dissolved salt solution (brine) through the resin bed to clean and recharge the resin beads. The calcium and magnesium ions are discharged as waste during the backwashing cycle. Because an ion exchange unit replaces chemicals that cause hard water with sodium, it is not advisable for those on sodium-restricted diets to drink water from this kind of softener.

Water Heaters

Water heaters are powered by electricity, fuel oil, gas, or solar energy. Water heaters consist of storage tanks for heating water and providing hot water over a limited period of time. Water heaters are available in various sizes and shapes. They are found in cabinets under kitchen counters, utility rooms, closets, attics, or garages. When a water heater, gas or electric, is installed in a garage, the inspector should be sure that the point of ignition, which is the pilot light or the bottom element on electric water heaters, is installed 18″ above the floor. Water heaters installed in attics or on a second floor must set in a drain pan and the pan must have a drain line to the exterior. Water supply systems may have devices such as pressure-reducing valves, check valves, backflow preventers, etc., installed to control certain types of problems such events as high line-pressure, frequent cutoffs, and the effects of water hammer. When these devices are not equipped with an internal bypass and no other measures are taken, the devices cause the water system to be closed. As the water is heated, it expands (thermal expansion), and closed systems do not allow for the expansion of heated water.

Thermal, or heat, expansion takes place because when water is heated, it expands approximately 2½ percent in volume for every 100°F of temperature rise. If for some reason the hot water cannot expand within the water supply system, such an increase in pressure within the system could cause damage.

Of the two conditions just described, high temperature and high pressure, high temperature is far more dangerous in a water heater. If a water heater storage tank ruptures from high pressure, a stream of water will pour from the tank until the pressure is relieved. However, if the tank ruptures from high temperature, it may go through the roof of a building. If the relieving point of the water heater's temperature and pressure (T-P) relief valve is reached, the valve relieves the excess pressure. The temperature-pressure relief valve is not intended for constant relief of thermal expansion, which is unacceptable and must be corrected.

Any devices installed that could create a closed system are recommended to have a bypass and/or an expansion tank to relieve pressure built up by thermal expansion in the water system. Possible noises due to expansion and contraction of some metal parts during heat-up and cool-down do not represent harmful or dangerous conditions. In some areas, scale or mineral deposits will build up on the heating elements and tank. These deposits cause a rumbling sound. In areas where such conditions exist, it is recommended that water heaters be drained and flushed as part of routine maintenance.

All water heaters have the built-in safety high-temperature shut-off system. The electric water heater has a high-limit shut-off system with a reset button located on the thermostat. Gas water heaters are equipped with an automatic gas shut-off system. High-temperature shut-off is built into the gas control valve and cannot be reset. If the high-temperature shut-off activates, the gas control valve must be replaced. (See Figure 6.47.)

Temperature and Pressure Relief Valves

Water heaters are considered pressure vessels. All water heaters must be equipped with a temperature and pressure (T & P) relief valve, which operates when water becomes too hot due to an interruption of the water supply or a faulty thermostat. (See Figure 6.48.) The temperature and pressure relief valve must be installed in the top 6″ of the tank. If the water heater gets too hot or builds too much pressure, the relief valve opens to relieve pressure. Water heater manufacturers recommend that temperature and pressure valves be tested at least once a year for proper operation. The water heater should have a water shutoff valve on the cold water side of the heater.

■ **FIGURE 6.47**

Water heaters found in most residential structures are powered by electricity or gas.

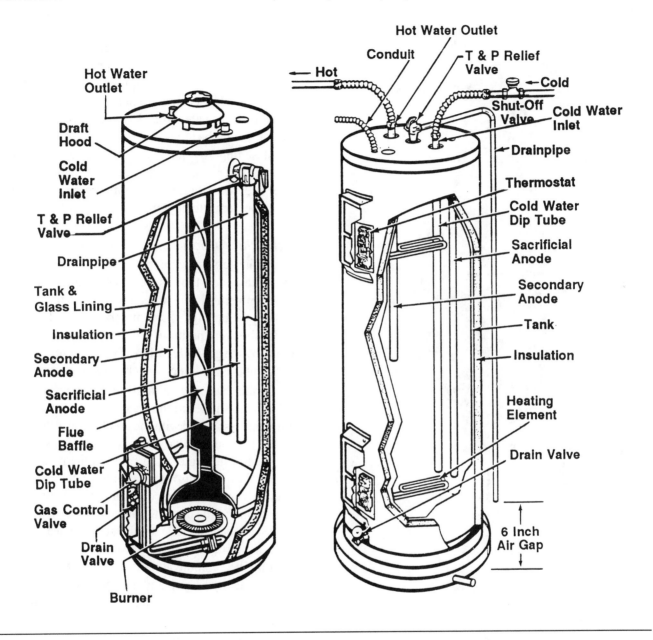

The temperature-pressure relief valve must be installed directly into the fitting of the water heater designated for the relief valve. The drain line from the temperature and pressure relief valve must gravity drain to the exterior. The temperature and pressure relief valve drain line should terminate outside maximum 24″ and minimum 6″ above the ground and point down. The drain line cannot be reduced in size. It must be the same size as the valve; for example, if the valve is ¾″, the drain line must be ¾″. (See Figure 6.47.)

Excessive length of more than 15′ or using more than two elbows may cause restriction and reduce the valve discharge capacity. No valve or other obstruction is placed between the relief valve and tank. (See Figure 6.48.)

■ **FIGURE 6.48**

Temperature and pressure relief valves guard against excessive water pressure or temperature.

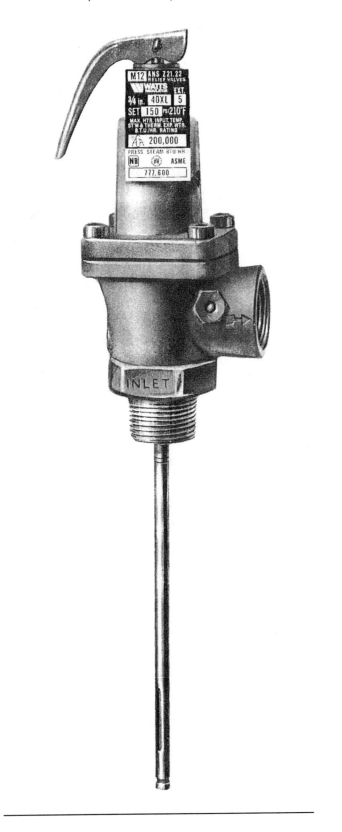

Thermostats

Water temperature in the water heater must be controlled by a thermostat to maintain desired temperature. The thermostat is a heat-sensitive switch that controls an energy source. The thermostat has a sensing element that is heat-activated. The expansion or contraction of the sensing element causes the thermostat to open or close the switch or valve. When temperature drops in the water heater tank, the sensing element activates the energy source to heat water to a desired temperature. Thermostats should be at normal setting, 120°F. This is the lowest setting for hot water supply to dishwashers. Electric water heaters are equipped with adjustable upper and lower thermostats; both thermostats must be set at the same temperature.

Sacrificial Anode Tubes

All heaters are equipped with a sacrificial anode tube. The anode tube is made of magnesium, which attracts minerals in the water and protects the tank from electrolysis damage. The minerals will destroy the anode tube over a period of time, and it eventually will be eroded by the galvanic action of water. If the sacrificial anode tube is missing, water may have an odor.

Certain water conditions will cause a reaction between this anode rod and the water. The most common complaint associated with the anode tube is "rotten egg smell." This odor is derived from hydrogen sulfide gas dissolved in the water. The smell is the result of four factors, all of which must be present for the odor to develop. They include a concentration of sulfate in the water supply; little or no dissolved oxygen in the water; sulfate-reducing bacteria within the water heater; and an excess of active hydrogen in the tank. The excess is provided by the cathodic action of the anode. With these factors, the hydrogen and sulfur combine to form hydrogen sulfide gas, which releases the rotten egg smell to water.

Active use of the water heater reduces the problem, but idle water heaters (due to vacancies, vacations, etc.) allow the accumulation of hydrogen sulfide gas and add to the odor problem. Water-softening equipment also aggravates the odor problem by eliminating chlorine and increasing bacteria in the water supply. In many situations, the smelly water condition is not experienced until after a water softener is installed. Smelly water can easily be eliminated or reduced by replacing the anode tube with one of less active material (magnesium to aluminum) and chlorinating the water heating system.

When homes are vacant and utilities off, the water heater should be drained. It is also important that if utilities are on, gas to the water heater should be turned off, as should the circuit breaker for an electric water heater.

Dip Tube

The cold-water inlet is the opening that is connected to the cold water supply pipe; it contains the inlet or dip tube extending toward the bottom of the tank. The purpose of the dip tube is to carry the incoming cold water through the stored hot water to the bottom of the tank. This way, the cold water does not mix with the hot water and is delivered to the bottom of the heater where it is heated very rapidly.

Each dip tube has a small hole, *called an antisiphon hole,* located near the top end of the tube. The antisiphon hole prevents the hot water in the tank from being siphoned out during an interruption in cold water supply.

Sometimes certain conditions will cause a reaction between the dip tube and the water. When this condition occurs the water gives off an odor that often smells like rotten eggs, which also occurs with the anode tube. The inspector must report the odor and call for repair or replacement of the water heater.

Gas

When gas water heaters operate normally, the pilot light heats the thermocouple and produces an electric current, measured in millivolts. This current, in turn, produces a magnetic field in the solenoid coil, which opens the solenoid valve. If the thermocouple fails, the pilot light will not burn, which stops the electric current to the solenoid valve coil and turns off the gas. The thermostat is controlled by expansion and contraction of the heat-sensing unit. As water temperature decreases, the sensing unit opens the gas valve.

A safety cutoff thermostat is a fail-safe device because it cuts off current to the solenoid valve if water temperature exceeds a predetermined limit. The safety cutoff is an electric thermostat connected to the solenoid and thermocouple. Gas water heaters must be installed near a flue or chimney for proper venting to ensure proper draft.

A gas water heater cannot operate properly without the correct amount of combustion air. Failure to provide proper amounts of combustion air may result in a fire, an explosion, or generation of deadly carbon monoxide gas. Many water heaters are installed in confined spaces such as closets. A confined space is a space whose volume is less than 50 cubic feet per 1,000 British thermal units

(Btus) per hour (hr.) of the aggregate input rating of all appliances installed in that space. The confined space must have two permanent openings for combustion air. One opening must commence within 12" of the top and one must commence within 12" of the bottom of the enclosure. The dimensions of each opening must be a minimum of 1 square inch (sq. in.) per 1,000 Btus per hr. of the total input rating of all gas utilization equipment in the confined space, but not less than 100 sq. in.

Gas water heater tanks have a flue baffle, extending from just above the burner to the top of the tank, that is visible below the draft hood. The baffle collects heat from burned gases as they travel through the flue and transfers the heat through the water in the upper portion of the tank. The cold water dip tube has a small hole at the top, or a vacuum relief valve, installed in the cold water supply line above the heater top. This prevents siphoning of water from the heater or tank in the event of negative pressure on the potable water supply.

Many gas-fired water heaters are diagnosed as leaking when the heater is not actually leaking but condensation has fooled the inspector and homeowner. A certain amount of condensation forms on all gas-fired water heaters whenever the tank is filled with cold water and the burner is on. Moisture from the combustion products condenses on the cooler tank surfaces and forms water drops, which may fall onto the burner or other hot surfaces to produce a sizzling or frying noise. This condition is most prevalent in winter months when incoming water temperatures are cooler. Condensation is present only when the burner flame is on and water in the tank is heating. It should not be confused with a leaking tank. Excessive condensation due to undersizing and/or improper venting will cause a number of problems, including pilot light outage and premature corrosion of the burner area and tank itself.

Venting

Gas and oil water heaters require an abundance of combustion air and must be vented through the roof. Gas and oil water heater vents must operate properly or carbon monoxide could be released in the residential structure and pose a dangerous situation. The length of the vent should be as short and straight as possible. Horizontal vent pipe runs should slope toward the roof ¼" per foot. The diameter of the vent pipe from the water heater must be no less than the diameter of the draft hood outlet and terminate to the outdoors through approved vent piping. When the vent from the water heater is connected directly into the furnace vent, a Y-connector

■ **FIGURE 6.49**

Direct vent water heaters must vent horizontally to the outside.

Outer Channel

Inner Channel

a relatively low flue gas temperature. Such temperatures may not be high enough to properly open thermally operated vent dampers. This causes spillage of flue gases and may cause carbon monoxide poisoning. All vent dampers must bear evidence of certification complying with the American National Standards.

When determining location for a direct vent water heater, snow accumulation and drifting should be considered in areas where applicable. When the water heater vent cap is low enough to touch or is accessible to small children, installation of a protective vent cover is recommended. Care should be taken to maintain adequate ventilation around the vent cap. Failure to have required clearances between vent piping and combustible material may result in a fire hazard. Obstructions and deteriorated vent systems may present serious health risks or the danger of asphyxiation. Direct vent water heaters will not have a draft hood.

The vent must vent out horizontally to the exterior and through a double wall pipe. The inner channel vents excess combustion products into outside air. The outer channel extracts outside air to fuel combustion. (See Figure 6.49.)

A power vent water heater requires its own separate venting system. It cannot connect to an existing vent pipe or chimney. It must terminate horizontally to the outdoors. Whenever possible, the vent terminates on the leeward side of the building. Condensation may be created, at times, as combustion gases exit the vent cap. Discoloration of surfaces in proximity to the vent cap may occur. (See Figure 6.50.)

The vent piping cannot exceed a total of 35', including vertical and horizontal runs, and can have no more than three elbows. It cannot slope downward, and horizontal runs require ¼"-per foot rise. All horizontal runs require adequate support at 3½' intervals. The power vent operates on a 110/120 volt power source and should be within 5' of the water heater. No extension cord should ever be used. (See Figure 6.51.)

To ensure proper venting of gas-fired water heaters, the correct vent pipe diameter must be used. Any additions of other gas appliances to the vent of this water heater will adversely affect the operation of the water heater. The combustion and ventilation air flow must not be obstructed. Obstructed or deteriorated vent systems may present serious health risks, including asphyxiation.

Vent pipe from the water heater must be 3" in diameter PVC schedule 40 or metal pipe and must slope upward ¼" per foot. The vent pipe must extend a minimum of 1½" through the exterior wall. There is a

should be used. The connection should never have a T-connector because it will not allow the heater and/or the furnace to draft properly.

Any vent damper, whether operated thermally or otherwise, must be removed if its use inhibits proper drafting of the water heater. Gas-fired water heaters with thermal efficiency in excess of 80 percent may produce

■ FIGURE 6.50

Power vent water heaters use PVC piping.

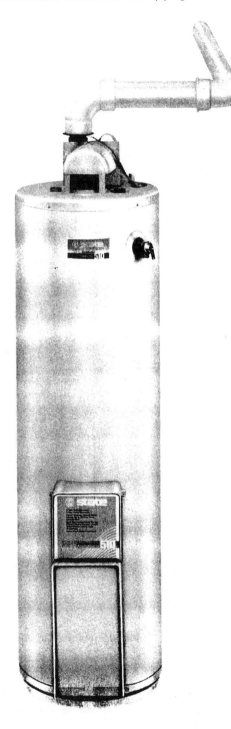

■ FIGURE 6.51

Proper venting for a power vent water heater is required.

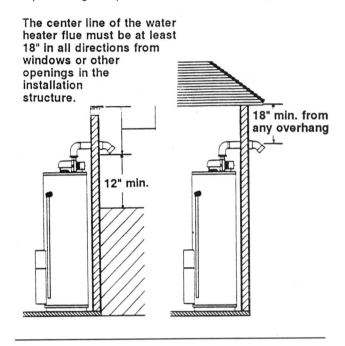

The center line of the water heater flue must be at least 18" in all directions from windows or other openings in the installation structure.

12" min.

18" min. from any overhang

venting manual reset switch located on the draft hood. If the venting manual reset switch is activated, it will not reset itself. Before resetting this reset switch, check for flue blockage and propriety of the venting system. To reset the venting manual reset switch, press the red reset button. The inspector should look for (1) obstructions that could cause improper venting (the combustion and ventilation air flow must not be obstructed), (2) damage or deterioration that could cause improper venting or leakage of combustion products, and (3) rusted flakes around the top of the water heater.

Electric

Electric water heaters are the same basic unit as gas water heaters, except that the energy source is electricity rather than gas. Normally, electric water heaters have elements in both the upper and the lower sections of the tank. Each element has a separate thermostat. Electric water heaters have a high-limit protector at the top of the upper thermostat identifiable by a red reset button. Single-element heaters are also available. Single-element heaters have the element located at the tank bottom.

Instant Water Heaters

Instant water heaters have been used in Europe for years. Tankless water heaters may be installed at the point of use. Each unit consists of a heat exchanger, a gas or an electric heater, and a control mechanism. The mechanism that controls water temperature at the faucet is an important difference among products on the market. There are small units intended to heat water for one faucet and large units to replace a conventional whole-house water heater. Generally, instantaneous water heaters are considered more practical for nonresidential use, low-use areas such as guest bedrooms, weekend cabins, etc. The larger gas units are thermostatically controlled, eliminating their sensitivity to inlet water temperature. Regardless of the water supply temperature to the house, these units produce water at a constant outlet temperature.

Electronically controlled electric units are available. These units allow the user to set the temperature and adjust the flow rate at the faucet. A tankless water heater may reduce costs and save energy because it eliminates the standby losses associated with conventional tanks. *Standby losses* refers to energy wasted during the time water is maintained hot in the tank waiting to be used. The amount of savings for elimination of standby losses depends on many variables, including size and efficiency of the tank being replaced, cost of energy used to heat water, and frequency and amount of hot water used. Standby losses are not the huge waste they may seem.

Solar

Solar water-heating systems are basically the same as other water-heating systems, except for the use of solar energy. The two basic solar heating systems are passive and active. Passive solar heating is a solar system using natural means of heat collection, storage, and distribution. Active solar heating uses pumps or blowers to move either air or a water/antifreeze mixture.

The major components in a solar heating system include the storage vessel, piping system, and controlling mechanism. The storage vessel can be a box of rocks used in an air system or a tank of water used in a water system. A typical piping system consists of copper water pipes or an air duct system. All materials in the piping system must be well insulated. The controller is an electronic device that uses thermistors to monitor temperature at the collectors and in the storage vessel. When the collectors are warmer than the storage vessel, the controller activates pumps, which move fluids through the system and bring solar heat into storage or the residential structure.

The most common use for solar heat is domestic water heating. Solar water-heating systems consist of one or two tanks. Two-tank systems use a standard water heater storage tank. One-tank systems use only a standard water heater.

In both the one-tank and two-tank systems, collectors are mounted on the roof of the residential structure. The storage tanks are inside with the transport module. The transport module consists of a pump(s), a compression tank, an electronic controller, a pressure relief valve and a check valve.

The two solar collector types are concentrating and flat plate collectors. Concentrating collectors are concave mirrors or convex lenses that focus the sun's energy onto a pipe to collect heat.

Such collectors generate high temperatures, but require expensive fluids and have high heat losses. Concentrating collectors use a direct beam of radiation and require a tracking mechanism to keep the collector pointed at the sun.

Flat plate collectors are less expensive to operate than concentrating collectors. These collectors are usually mounted at the same angle as the roof and do not move. Flat plate collectors make use of direct, reflected, and diffuse solar radiation and use a water/antifreeze mixture or air that will produce temperatures less than 200°F. Flat plate collectors vary in size and weigh approximately 120 pounds (lb.) to 200 lb. per collector.

A check valve should be in the solar fluid line going from the pump to the collectors. The check valve prevents nighttime *thermosiphoning,* the backward flow of solar fluid through the piping system caused by convection when collectors cool at night. The large solar storage tank keeps the glycol-water antifreeze fluid in the heat exchanger hot. The hot fluid has a tendency to rise to the collectors on the roof. The cool glycol fluid in the collectors falls as the hot fluid rises. This process takes the heat gathered during the day and uses it for nighttime heating. The check valve prevents backward migration of fluid at night.

There should be two relief valves in a solar system. One relief valve is in the glycol fluid piping on the discharge side of the pump. Its relief pressure ranges from 30 pounds per square inch (psi) to 90 psi, depending on the manufacturer. The relief valve discharge on the glycol piping must not be routed to a sanitary sewer. The second relief valve must be on the storage tank. This is the same relief valve as found on a standard water heater. Because the storage tank relief valve carries only water, it can be routed to the drain from the water heater. This relief valve is a safety device that relieves pressure inside the storage tank.

A pump controlled by an electronic controller circulates fluid through the collectors to the heat exchanger in the storage tank. The pump and electronic controller must be on a dedicated electrical circuit and properly grounded. The system switch should be in the automatic position. The system must never be in the off position unless the collectors are covered. If fluid is not allowed to circulate, collector fluid will boil and blow out through the relief valve. The pump is checked by operating the manual switch located on the electronic controller and by measuring fluid temperatures entering and leaving the collectors. If the pump is moving fluid through the collectors, there will be a temperature differential. The manual switch should be repositioned to the automatic position when checking is complete.

The tempering valve must be in the water line between the storage tank and standard water heater. The tempering valve is a temperature-sensitive valve that mixes cold water with hot water from the storage tank and delivers the mixture to the water heater. The temperature of the tempering valve is manually set at the same temperature as the water heater thermostat. The tempering valve is checked by running hot water and measuring the temperature with a thermometer. The water temperature should be the same as the tempering valve set point.

Air vents must be at high points of the glycol piping system. To fill the system with fluid, air must be removed from the piping. Air vents located at high points allow air to escape as the piping system is filled with glycol fluid. Air vents can be used to check the level of glycol fluid in the system. Liquid should come out of an opened air vent at the highest point in the system. The system is probably short of glycol fluid if no liquid discharges from the air vent at the highest point. Air trapped in the system, with the pump running, will produce gurgling or swishing sounds. Air bubbles trapped in a pipe can overheat the system and cause the relief valve to bleed off glycol fluid.

With the solar water-heating system, the sun heats fluid in the collectors that is pumped inside to heat water in a storage tank. Cold water from the main water source replaces hot water from the solar storage tank and, in turn, is heated by the collector fluid, which keeps the conventional heating system from operating.

The sun heats collectors on the roof, and a thermistor relays the storage tank temperature to the controller. If the collectors are warmer than the tank, the controller activates the pump that moves fluid through the collectors to a heat exchanger in the bottom of the storage tank. The controller stops the pump when the collector sensor cools to within 2° or 3° of the storage tank sensor.

Water Heater Safety Tips

Use caution when inspecting water heaters. They can be explosive. Check the flashing, venting materials, and installation through the attic. In addition, the cold water inlet valve should be on the cold water side. Newer tanks have insulating nipples made from material that should be dielectric (nonconducting) to prevent corrosion. Corrosion indicates possible water leaks. Check for dents or water stains on the tank. When inspecting a solar system, the inspector should pay careful attention to how the collectors are mounted on the roof. Improper mounting can cause roof leaks that are not immediately visible.

Four tips for the safe operation of a water heater include the following:

1. Never operate a water heater (gas or electric) without water or a temperature and pressure (T & P) relief valve. The T & P relief valve protects against excessive water temperatures and pressures.
2. T & P relief valves indicate a maximum set pressure not to exceed the marked hydrostatic working pressure of the water heater.
3. T & P relief valves and discharge piping should adhere to the following local codes:
   - Valves must not be blocked, plugged, or reduced in size.
   - Discharge pipe must be capable of withstanding 250°F without distorting.
   - Water heaters must be installed to allow drainage of the T & P relief valve and discharge pipe. Valves that cannot completely drain after discharge will eventually corrode and cease to function.
   - Water heater drains must terminate at an approved location, usually at the exterior, between 6″ and 12″ above the ground for it to be visible.
   - Valves must not be installed between the relief valve and tank. The temperature-sensing probe must be immersed in the top 6″ of the tank where water is the hottest.
   - There must not be a thread, plug, or cap at the end of the discharge line.
   - The termination should have an elbow installed to direct the discharge toward the ground.

■ **FIGURE 6.52**

Designers use a plot plan to place sprinkler heads so lawn or garden areas are adequately watered.

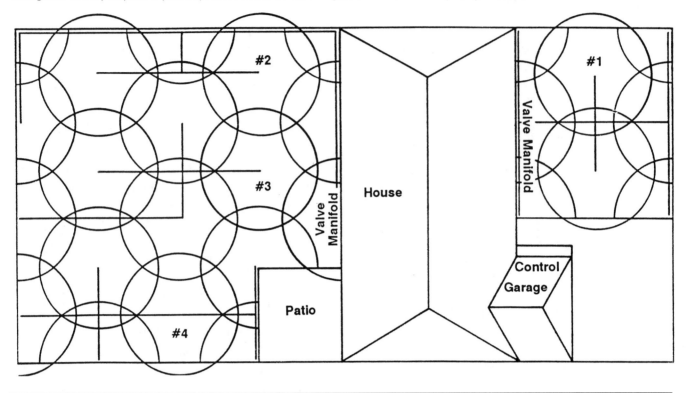

- Tank maintenance should include draining a small amount of water from a gas-fired tank at least twice a year and manually operating the relief valve at least once a year. If, after manual operation, the valve fails to completely reset and continues to release water, immediately close the cold water inlet and follow the tank's draining instructions for replacing the valve.

4. The following conditions produce water heater noises:
   - Expansion and contraction of metal parts during periods of heat-up and cool-down do not represent harmful or dangerous conditions.
   - Sediment buildup in the tank bottom of gas water heaters will create varying amounts of noise and will cause premature tank failure.
   - When a gas water tank is filled with cold water, there will be a certain amount of condensation formed while the burner is on. Moisture from the products of combustion condenses on the cooler tank surfaces and forms drops of water that may fall onto the burner or other hot surfaces and produce a sizzling noise in the burner area. Condensation is normal and should not be confused with leaking.

Sprinklers

Lawn sprinkler systems have recently become popular because new materials (e.g., PVC piping) used for these systems have lowered cost.

Water pressure has a major effect on sprinkler head operation and is used to determine sprinkler head types and styles. Water pressure affects pipe size, pipe length, and distance between sprinkler heads. Water pressure is also used in determining the timing device that is required for an automatic system.

When checking water pressure, the faucet must be on an unregulated water supply line from the meter. If water pressure exceeds 80 psi, a pressure regulator should be installed in the manifold supply line between the main water supply line and shutoff valve to the sprinkler manifold.

Controlled coverage must be considered when installing a sprinkler system. Controlled coverage is a

■ FIGURE 6.53

Sprinkler systems are protected against freezing by using an automatic drain valve located at the lower end of the circuit.

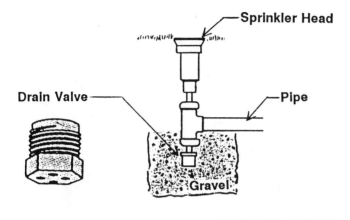

■ FIGURE 6.54

Pop-up spray valves are installed in sprinkler systems for residential lawn areas.

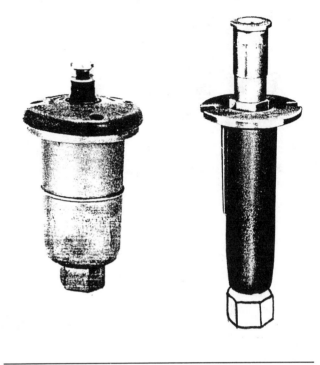

plot plan of the area to be sprinkled. This plan should show boundary lines and an outline of the house, driveways, patios, walls, etc. The plan should also show all planter boxes and lawn areas as well as the location of the water meter and service line. (See Figure 6.52.)

Other important considerations for controlled coverage include

- soil (sand, clay, sandy loam, etc.);
- topography (level, sloping, etc.);
- plant life to be watered;
- amount of water desired; and
- location of sprinkler heads to ensure that desired areas are completely covered without wasting water on drives, patios, walks, or the structure.

Sprinkler systems also should be protected against freezing. Freezing damages sprinkler heads, pipes and valves. The sprinkler system should be protected with an automatic drain valve located at the lower end of the circuit or station. The automatic drain valve closes when the water pressure is on that particular circuit or station. When the water pressure is off, the valve is open and the line drains. (See Figure 6.53.)

All sprinkler head operation is measured in gallons per minute (gpm) at a given water pressure in psi. For example, pop-up spray heads have a 3.2 gpm rating at 25 psi. Rotary and wave heads have a gpm rating and are adjustable.

The three different sprinkler heads used in a sprinkler system are (1) spray, (2) rotary and (3) wave. Each type of sprinkler head is available in several models to meet specific requirements. Installation

depends on plant life to be watered, head capacity, head location, and water pressure.

Pop-up spray heads are popular in residential sprinkler systems. These sprinkler heads are installed flush with the ground and the spray nozzle pops up to spray above grass or flowers. When the water is shut off, the spray nozzle drops down in the sprinkler head. With the sprinkler flush with the ground, an unobstructed use of the lawn is allowed without damaging the heads. (See Figure 6.54.)

Fixed spray heads are designed for flower beds and shrubs. These spray heads are fixed heads that do not have pop-up features. Fixed spray heads are available to water most configurations. (See Figure 6.55.)

Fixed spray heads can be configured to water in a circular (e.g., 360°, 180°, 90°) or in a square pattern. Patterns can also be configured for narrow strips of lawn. The spray nozzle will extend from 3″ to 12″. Fixed spray heads do not require high water pressure to operate. If designed properly, fixed spray heads will provide adequate coverage with water pressures ranging from 20 psi to 25 psi.

Rotary spray heads cover larger areas than fixed spray heads. Rotary heads also require more water

■ **FIGURE 6.55**

Fixed spray heads are designed for flower beds and shrubs.

pressure for operation. Pop-up rotary heads are used when the system is installed on large property areas. (See Figure 6.56.)

Wave sprinkler heads are designed to cover large rectangular areas. Wave heads can be adjusted for various sizes of coverage and are installed above ground. (See Figure 6.57.)

There are several different valves that can be used on a sprinkler system. These include the following:

- The antisiphon valve allows fluid to travel in only one direction. This valve will not allow foreign matter to return to the household water supply. Antisiphon valves are controlled electronically with a solenoid or are operated manually. (See Figure 6.58.)
- The angle valve is at a 90° angle to both the inlet and outlet openings. This allows the supply line to be used at the bottom of the valve and discharge out the side. The valve offers less resistance to the water flow. This valve is controlled electrically with a solenoid or can be manually operated.
- The in-line valve allows the water supply to enter from one side and discharge out the other side. In-line valves are used above or below ground. This valve can be controlled electronically or operated manually.
- The check valve allows fluid to flow in only one direction. (See Figure 6.59.)

All automatic sprinkler systems require a control timer. Control timers are sized by the number of circuits (stations) they control. Control timers can be 120V (volts) or 240V and are solid state or use a clock. Clocks

■ **FIGURE 6.56**

Pop-up rotary spray heads are installed below ground. Rotary heads are installed above ground.

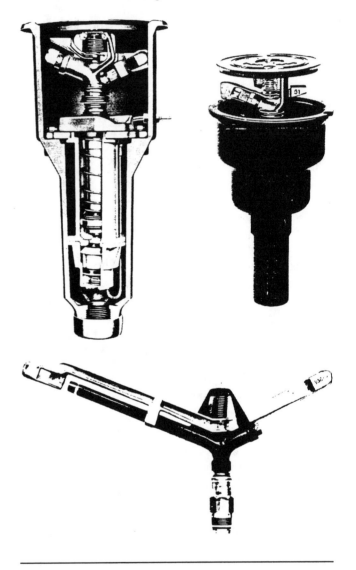

must be set for time of day and programmed to operate the system through its cycles. Control timers also control the length of time each circuit will operate.

An antisiphon device must be installed between the main shutoff valve for the sprinkler system and the manifold or 6″ above the highest head, whichever is higher.

The residential inspector should operate the sprinkler system only when the ambient temperature is above freezing. The inspector should check the sprinkler system in the manual mode and inspect each circuit (station) for broken heads and broken water lines. The sprinkler system must also be checked for an antisiphon

■ **FIGURE 6.57**

Wave sprinkler heads distribute water over a rectangular area.

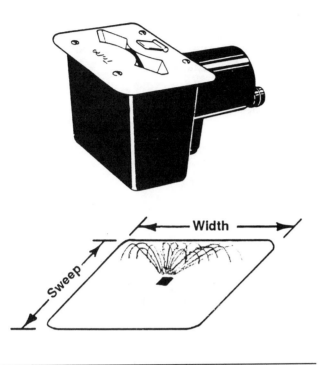

or a backflow prevention device. The inspector should verify that the sprinkler system does not backsplash on the exterior walls.

■ **FIGURE 6.58**

Antisiphon valves allow fluid to travel in only one direction.

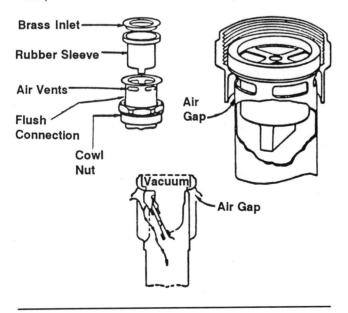

■ **FIGURE 6.59**

Check valves prevent backflow.

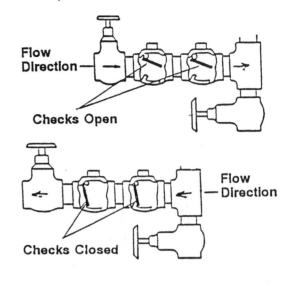

Whirlpool Tubs

Most whirlpool tubs have two jets. One is located on each end of the tub, which causes water to swirl around the tub in a whirlpool fashion. Other whirlpool tubs force water into the tub through three or more jets located on the tub sides or ends. (See Figure 6.60.)

The motors used in whirlpool tubs usually are from ⅓ horsepower (hp) to 1 hp and operate on a 120V/20 amp (ampere) circuit, which should be grounded and GFCI (ground fault circuit interrupter)-protected. The switch or timer must be located in an area where it cannot be operated from the tub unless an air pressure switch is used. It is recommended that the motor be connected to a timer rather than a toggle switch. The pump should never be operated with water below the jets in the tub. The motor, pump, and plumbing should be easily accessible. Most whirlpool tubs have venturi jets, which control the amount of air that is pulled through the jets. The amount of air entering through the venturi controls the jet water action.

The size of the pump and motor controls the flow of water in a whirlpool tub. Larger pumps and motors produce more water movement. The whirlpool system, including the pump, should be drained when the tub is drained. Standing water in lines allows bacteria to grow, causes odors, and contaminates the water used for the next bath.

When inspecting the whirlpool tub, the water level should be 2″ to 3″ above the ports before operating the

■ **FIGURE 6.60**

Whirlpool tubs have jets that cause water to swirl around the tub.

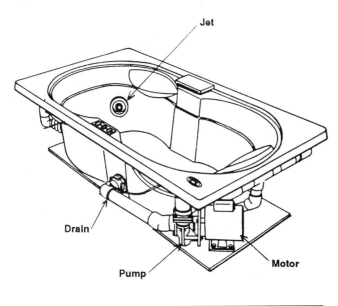

pump. When the water level is below the ports, the pump will spray water out of the tub like a hose nozzle. Operating the pump without water will destroy the pump seals. When operating the pump, it is important, when turning on the pump, to observe if any discolored water comes from the returns. If discolored water appears, the inspector needs to report it as in need of repair because the system is not draining as it is designed to do.

■ REVIEW QUESTIONS*

1. What are the three categories of a house plumbing system?

   _____

   _____

   _____

2. Potable water lines belong in which of the three plumbing categories?

   _____

3. Real estate inspectors may open any seals or locks on city water meters.

   A. True
   B. False

4. All water heaters must have a temperature-pressure relief valve installed.

   A. True
   B. False

5. What material cannot be used for the temperature-pressure relief valve line?

   A. Copper
   B. Galvanized steel
   C. PVC plastic
   D. All can be used.

6. What part of the water heater neutralizes hot water corrosion and protects the tank interior?

   _____

7. A plumbing trap prevents which of the following from entering the house?

   A. Mice and small animals
   B. Sewer gas
   C. Water backup
   D. Municipal plumbing cleaning tools

8. What type of plumbing trap would you expect to find under a sink?

   A. P-trap
   B. Drum trap
   C. Mechanical trap
   D. S-trap

9. A trap may lose its water seal by

   A. siphonage.
   B. back pressure.
   C. evaporation.
   D. All of the above

*Answers to all of the chapter review questions are located in Appendix C at the back of this book.

10. A commode has a built-in trap.

 A. True
 B. False

11. A commode that is loose on the floor should be re-set with a new wax seal.

 A. True
 B. False

12. An inspector should test the tile around the shower for loose spots or leaks.

 A. True
 B. False

13. In which of the following may a cross connection occur?

 A. Swimming pools
 B. Sprinkler systems
 C. Outside faucets
 D. All of the above

14. Fiberglass and steel showers require shower pans.

 A. True
 B. False

15. The sprinkler system is required to have a backflow prevention device at the potable water supply conection.

 A. True
 B. False

16. Gas water heaters are required to have a flue baffle.

 A. True
 B. False

17. A private well used for potable water should be equipped with a chlorinator or other filtration system.

 A. True
 B. False

18. Gas water heaters are dangerous if

 A. the gas pressure is low.
 B. they are too small for the home.
 C. they are not vented properly.

19. Water lines running through the attic should be

 A. ¾″ in diameter.
 B. insulated and protected.
 B. equipped with expansion loop.

20. A power vent water heater requires its own separate venting system.

 A. True
 B. False

21. Water that travels to the absorption field is called *scum*.

 A. True
 C. False

22. The capacity of a submersible centrifugal pump is determined by the

 A. width of the impeller.
 B. diameter of the impeller.
 C. number of stages.
 D. All of the above

23. When sizing pressure tanks, the usable capacity should be twice the pump capacity in gallons per minute

 A. True
 B. False

24. All water heaters installed in a garage must be elevated above the floor _____ at the point of ignition.

 A. 12 inches
 B. 16 inches
 C. 18 inches

25. Aerobic systems, if equipped with filters and chlorinators, can discharge effluent to the surface.

 A. True
 B. False

26. If property has a well and septic system, it is not required that an inspector locate well and septic and field lines.

 A. True
 B. False

27. When inspecting a property with a private water well, the inspector should recommend a coliform analysis of the water.

    A. True
    B. False

28. By definition, an OSSF (On-Site Sewage Facility)

    A. consists of a treatment and disposal process.
    B. is any system on less than ten acres.
    C. is any wastewater system producing less than 5,000 gallons per day.

29. A legally sized septic tank

    A. is 1,000 gallons or larger.
    B. provides two to three days detention time.
    C. provides one to two days detention time.
    D. must have steel reinforcing.

30. Minimum size of a grease trap interceptor is

    A. 100 gallons.
    B. 500 gallons for commercial establishments.
    C. four times the gpm of all fixtures discharging to it.
    D. Both A and C
    E. All of the above

31. The difference between a Class I and Class II aerobic treatment plant is

    A. cost.
    B. weight.
    C. that Class I must always utilize low pressure closing.
    D. that Class II cannot be used for surface application.

32. Site service visits for aerobic plants should include

    A. removal of lids and cover for access to plant chambers and equipment.
    B. activation of all mechanical equipment and evaluation while running.
    C. checking if all filters, screens, and strainers are clean or to be replaced.
    D. an evaluation of the process operation.
    E. All of the above

■ INSPECTION CHECKLIST: PLUMBING

Preliminary

The water supply piping used within the residential structure is

Yes No

- ☐ ☐ Galvanized
- ☐ ☐ Copper
- ☐ ☐ Plastic
- ☐ ☐ Cast iron

KITCHEN SINK

Yes No

- ☐ ☐ Does the vegetable spray hose have low water pressure?
- ☐ ☐ Is the vegetable spray hose leaking or disconnected?
- ☐ ☐ Do faucets leak around the stems?
- ☐ ☐ Does the swing spout on the sink leak?
- ☐ ☐ Is the sink chipped or damaged?
- ☐ ☐ Are faucets loose?
- ☐ ☐ Do faucets have low water pressure?
- ☐ ☐ Are plumbing connections leaking under the sink?
- ☐ ☐ Is there an inappropriate plumbing repair? For example, epoxy, glue, duct tape, etc.
- ☐ ☐ Is the P-trap missing?
- ☐ ☐ Is an S-trap being used under the sink?
- ☐ ☐ Is the trap located in a crawlspace?
- ☐ ☐ Has leaking caused cabinet damage?
- ☐ ☐ Is the drain stop inoperable?
- ☐ ☐ Is the hot water dispenser leaking and/or inoperable?
- ☐ ☐ Are hot and cold water available?
- ☐ ☐ Are metal sinks rusted?
- ☐ ☐ Does water drain slowly?
- ☐ ☐ Check dishwasher drain. Does it have air gap and discharge on trap side?

LAVATORY

Yes No

- ☐ ☐ Do plumbing vents terminate in the vanity?
- ☐ ☐ Is the sink damaged?
- ☐ ☐ Do faucets leak?
- ☐ ☐ Are faucet stops broken?
- ☐ ☐ Are faucets loose?

Yes No

- ☐ ☐ Are hot and cold water available?
- ☐ ☐ Is hot water on the left and cold water on the right?
- ☐ ☐ Is there an air gap (back siphonage)?
- ☐ ☐ Are wall-mounted sinks firmly secured to the wall?
- ☐ ☐ Is there a water-hammering sound?
- ☐ ☐ Is the lavatory sealed to the countertop?
- ☐ ☐ Do faucets have low water pressure?
- ☐ ☐ Are drain parts missing or not operating?
- ☐ ☐ Does water drain slowly?
- ☐ ☐ Is there excess faucet corrosion?
- ☐ ☐ Are connections leaking under the sink?
- ☐ ☐ Is there an inappropriate plumbing repair?
- ☐ ☐ Is the P-trap missing?
- ☐ ☐ Is an S-trap being used under the sink?
- ☐ ☐ Is the trap located in a crawlspace?
- ☐ ☐ Has leaking caused cabinet damage?
- ☐ ☐ Are handles damaged or missing?

BATHTUB

- ☐ ☐ Are there cracks in the fiberglass tub? (Step into the tub to check.)
- ☐ ☐ Is tub surface damaged?
- ☐ ☐ Is there an air gap (back siphonage)?
- ☐ ☐ Does tile require grout?
- ☐ ☐ Are tiles loose or missing?
- ☐ ☐ Are tiles damaged?
- ☐ ☐ Are walls soft?
- ☐ ☐ Is plumbing loose in walls?
- ☐ ☐ Are hot and cold water available?
- ☐ ☐ Are hot and cold faucets reversed?
- ☐ ☐ Do faucets have low water pressure?
- ☐ ☐ Is there a water-hammering sound?
- ☐ ☐ Are faucet stops broken?
- ☐ ☐ Do faucets leak?
- ☐ ☐ Are drain parts missing or not operating?
- ☐ ☐ Is strainer in place?
- ☐ ☐ Does water drain slowly?
- ☐ ☐ Is there excess faucet corrosion?
- ☐ ☐ Does tub base leak?
- ☐ ☐ Does the shower diverter valve operate properly?
- ☐ ☐ Are handles damaged or missing?

WHIRLPOOL

In addition to bathtub checks, fill the tub to 2″ to 3″ above the nozzles and make the following inspections:

Yes No

- ☐ ☐ Are there leaks?
- ☐ ☐ Does the pump have sufficient pressure?
- ☐ ☐ Is the pump connected to a timer?
- ☐ ☐ Are the location and accessibility of the pump and motor convenient?
- ☐ ☐ Do pump and lines drain?

SHOWER

Yes No

- ☐ ☐ Are there cracks in the fiberglass shower? (Step into the shower to check.)
- ☐ ☐ Does tile require grout?
- ☐ ☐ Are tiles loose or missing?
- ☐ ☐ Are tiles broken?
- ☐ ☐ Are walls soft?
- ☐ ☐ Are handles damaged or missing?
- ☐ ☐ Is plumbing loose in the walls?
- ☐ ☐ Is there a water-hammering sound?
- ☐ ☐ Are hot and cold water available?
- ☐ ☐ Are hot and cold faucets reversed?
- ☐ ☐ Do faucets have low water pressure?
- ☐ ☐ Are faucet stops broken?
- ☐ ☐ Is shower head damaged or missing?
- ☐ ☐ Does the shower head need a seal?
- ☐ ☐ Do faucets leak?
- ☐ ☐ Is strainer missing?
- ☐ ☐ Does water drain slowly?

  Operate shower for approximately 20 minutes or place stopper in shower and fill to threshold and hold for entire inspection.

- ☐ ☐ Are there signs of an epoxy repair?
- ☐ ☐ Are there leaks around the shower exterior?
- ☐ ☐ Is there water or signs of a previous leak under the carpet?
- ☐ ☐ Is water leaking outside the residential structure with showers located on exterior walls?
- ☐ ☐ Are there leaks or wood damage under the house with a crawlspace?
- ☐ ☐ Is shower enclosure broken?
- ☐ ☐ Does shower enclosure leak?

COMMODE

Yes No

- ☐ ☐ Is commode loose at the floor?
- ☐ ☐ Is bowl or tank damaged?
- ☐ ☐ Is tank lid damaged or missing?
- ☐ ☐ Is seal leaking between the tank and bowl?
- ☐ ☐ Is refill tube missing or improperly installed?
- ☐ ☐ Is flush mechanism inoperable?
- ☐ ☐ Does a cross connection exist at the fill valve?
- ☐ ☐ Is ball cock valve leaking?
- ☐ ☐ Are there base leaks?
- ☐ ☐ Does water shut off?

OUTSIDE FAUCET

Yes No

- ☐ ☐ Are handles damaged or missing?
- ☐ ☐ Are faucets leaking?
- ☐ ☐ Does a cross connection exist?
- ☐ ☐ Cap off the faucet and turn on the water. Is there a leak behind the wall?
- ☐ ☐ Is piping loose in the wall?
- ☐ ☐ Is there evidence of an underground leak?
- ☐ ☐ Are faucets frostproof?

UTILITY ROOM

Yes No

- ☐ ☐ Do faucets leak?
- ☐ ☐ Does sheetrock have water damage?
- ☐ ☐ Does subfloor have water damage?
- ☐ ☐ Is hot water on the left and cold water on the right?

  Note: On vacant homes, use hose to check faucet operation.

SPRINKLER SYSTEM

Note: State in the inspection report that sprinkler system checks are on manual mode only. Do not check the sprinkler system if temperatures are near or below freezing. If the sprinkler system is not inspected, note the reason in the inspection report.

Note the system control on the inspection report.

Yes No

- ☐ ☐ Manual
- ☐ ☐ Automatic

Is a backflow prevention device present? Provide water to zone 1. If nothing happens:

Yes No

☐ ☐ Is unit powered?
☐ ☐ Is control set to "rain" position in wet weather?
☐ ☐ Is unit controlled by a rain gauge?
☐ ☐ Are controls set?
☐ ☐ On digital controls with clock timers, is the time set?
☐ ☐ Is water on to the system? (Check for a partially closed valve.)

Complete the following checks for every zone:

☐ ☐ Is water present in the zone?
☐ ☐ Are sprinkler heads damaged or missing?
☐ ☐ Do sprinkler heads require adjusting?
☐ ☐ Is there evidence of underground water leaks?
☐ ☐ Does water shut off?
☐ ☐ Is there exposed pipe in the yard?
☐ ☐ Are risers slit or damaged?

WATER HEATER

Note the size of the water heater on inspection report.

Yes No

☐ ☐ Is the cold water cutoff valve leaking?
☐ ☐ Are there leaks or excessive corrosion at water connections?
☐ ☐ Are water lines installed properly (hot to hot, cold to cold)?
☐ ☐ Is the drain valve leaking?
☐ ☐ Is the water tank leaking?
☐ ☐ Is the T-P valve drain line reduced?
☐ ☐ Is the T-P valve corroded?
☐ ☐ Is the T-P valve drain line manufactured from proper materials?
☐ ☐ Is the T-P valve drain line unobstructed? (The valve must be operated in order to test this.)
☐ ☐ Does the T-P valve drain line terminate in an approved location?
☐ ☐ Does water have an odor?
☐ ☐ Does flooring indicate wood damage?
☐ ☐ Is there an adequate amount of hot water?
☐ ☐ If installed in the attic or on second floor, is a drain pan under the unit?
☐ ☐ If installed in garage, is it 18″ from the floor?

ADDITIONAL GAS WATER HEATER CHECKS

Yes No

☐ ☐ Date if possible. *Note:* serial number will help to date.
☐ ☐ Is a gas odor present?
☐ ☐ Are clearances adequate?
☐ ☐ Is there adequate combustion air supply?
☐ ☐ Any evidence of flashback?
☐ ☐ Is the thermostat damaged?
☐ ☐ Does the pilot flame light?
☐ ☐ Does the pilot flame need adjustment?
☐ ☐ Is the burner inoperable?
☐ ☐ Is the burner excessively rusty or dirty?
☐ ☐ Is the vent pipe improperly installed or disconnected?
☐ ☐ Does the vent pipe terminate in the attic?
☐ ☐ Does a single wall vent pipe pass into the ceiling?
☐ ☐ Are two diverters installed?
☐ ☐ Is the baffle in proper position (located in the flue)?
☐ ☐ Do copper gas lines pass through the wall, floor, or ceiling?
☐ ☐ Is there a dripleg on gas line?

ADDITIONAL ELECTRIC WATER HEATER CHECKS

Yes No

☐ ☐ Are wires burned or damaged?
☐ ☐ Are wires to the element disconnected?
☐ ☐ Are there leaks in the jacket?
☐ ☐ Are thermostats set at the same temperature?
☐ ☐ Are wiring connections made inside cabinet?
☐ ☐ Is wiring secure at cabinet?

SOLAR WATER HEATER

Yes No

☐ ☐ Are collectors facing a southerly direction?
☐ ☐ Are collectors shaded?
☐ ☐ Is the tilt angle of collectors acceptable?
☐ ☐ Can property damage or hazard result from the installation?
☐ ☐ Is the collector glass damaged?
☐ ☐ Has the collector mounting framework been weather treated to prevent corrosion?
☐ ☐ Have all mounting penetrations been caulked or sealed?
☐ ☐ Have collector vent holes been opened?

Yes No

- ☐ ☐ Has piping been insulated?
- ☐ ☐ Have sufficient pipe hangers been installed?
- ☐ ☐ Does the piping system have visible leaks?
- ☐ ☐ Have necessary air vent valves been properly installed?
- ☐ ☐ Have dielectric unions been used between dissimilar metals?
- ☐ ☐ Have additional isolation valves been provided for major system components?
- ☐ ☐ Has the water heater and/or solar storage tank been insulated?
- ☐ ☐ Has temperature-pressure relief plumbing been completed?
- ☐ ☐ Have potential freezing problems been considered with pipes in an unconditioned space?
- ☐ ☐ Is the power outlet grounded?
- ☐ ☐ Are collector and storage sensors attached?
- ☐ ☐ Are tempering valves in place and controlling water temperature?
- ☐ ☐ Does the pump move fluid?
- ☐ ☐ Does the system have the proper fluid level? (Check the highest air vent.)
- ☐ ☐ Are all surfaces with running temperatures of 120°F or higher isolated?
- ☐ ☐ Have all temperature and pressure relief valves been installed?

CIRCULATING PUMP

Yes No

- ☐ ☐ Do connections leak?
- ☐ ☐ Does the pump leak?
- ☐ ☐ Is cord damaged?
- ☐ ☐ Is the pump adequately supported?

ADDITIONAL CRAWLSPACE OR BASEMENT CHECKS

Yes No

- ☐ ☐ Is there a visible sewer line leak?
- ☐ ☐ Are cleanouts accessible?
- ☐ ☐ Is there a shower leak?
- ☐ ☐ Any evidence of a water supply piping leak?
- ☐ ☐ Is there a leak at the commode connection?
- ☐ ☐ Are there other leaks under kitchen and bath areas?

Yes No

- ☐ ☐ Is there wood damage associated with a plumbing leak?
- ☐ ☐ Is sewer piping capped off?
- ☐ ☐ Are bathtub, shower, washer, and other drains trapped correctly?
- ☐ ☐ Have any joists or girders been cut, notched, or drilled improperly?

ADDITIONAL ATTIC CHECKS

Yes No

- ☐ ☐ Are water lines insulated?
- ☐ ☐ Does the plumbing vent terminate through the roof?
- ☐ ☐ Are plumbing vents sloped correctly?
- ☐ ☐ Are plumbing vents damaged?
- ☐ ☐ Do plumbing vents terminate in attic?
- ☐ ☐ Does gas hot water heater flue terminate in attic?

ADDITIONAL OUTSIDE CHECKS

Yes No

- ☐ ☐ Are plumbing vents flashed correctly at roof?
- ☐ ☐ Do plumbing vents have adequate clearance from roof?
- ☐ ☐ Do drains terminate outside?
- ☐ ☐ Are drain cleanout covers missing?
- ☐ ☐ Does the water meter move?

SEPTIC SYSTEM

Yes No

- ☐ ☐ Does the system back up, indicating a blockage?
- ☐ ☐ Is there adequate drainage?
- ☐ ☐ Any evidence of drainfield pooling?
- ☐ ☐ Does water rise to the surface of the drainfield?
- ☐ ☐ Is the septic system an anaerobic system or an aerobic system?
- ☐ ☐ Is aerobic system effluent discharge subsurface to field lines?
- ☐ ☐ Is aerobic system effluent surface discharge?
- ☐ ☐ Is the filter and chlorinator in place?
- ☐ ☐ Is the service contract current on the aerobic system?
- ☐ ☐ Does the home have a water softener?
- ☐ ☐ Is there a garbage disposal?

POTABLE WATER SUPPLY

Yes No

☐ ☐ Does the area require a backflow preventer (check valve) on the water meter for household use only?

☐ ☐ If the area does require a backflow preventer on the water meter, is an expansion tank in place on the water heater.

☐ ☐ Is the potable water supplied by an outside source?

☐ ☐ Is the potable water supplied from an on-site well?

☐ ☐ Is there a septic system on the property?

☐ ☐ If both a septic system and potable water well are on the property, is there a minimum of 100′ separation between any part of the septic system and well?

☐ ☐ Is the well equipped with a chlorinator?

☐ ☐ Is the pressure tank adequate to meet demand?

☐ ☐ Is the pump accessible?

Yes No

☐ ☐ Is the water pressure constant when operating multiple plumbing fixtures at the same time?

☐ ☐ Is the electrical wiring done properly with circuit protection?

Note: *The following is a list of disclaimers that should be included in the inspection report on plumbing.*

A list of items not responsible for when a house sits vacant:

Yes No

☐ ☐ Sewer and drain lines stopping up

☐ ☐ Leaks at faucets—seals and washers dry out

☐ ☐ Leaks at dishwasher—seals dry out

☐ ☐ Disposal locks up

☐ ☐ Water heater leak at drain valve

☐ ☐ Electric water heaters—water drained and power on can cause damage to heating elements and thermostats

☐ ☐ Gas water heater—if gas has been off—thermocouples can fail

■ REPORTING GUIDELINES

Inspection reporting guidelines for plumbing systems (including gas lines, septic systems, private wells, and lawn sprinklers) incorporating the above checklist.

Plumbing systems. The inspector shall

- inspect and report as in need of repair deficiencies in the type and condition of all accessible and visible water supply and waste-water and vent pipes;

- inspect and report as in need of repair deficiencies in the operation of all fixtures and faucets where the flow end of the faucet is not connected to an appliance;

- report as in need of repair the lack of backflow devices, antisiphon devices, or systems or air gaps when applicable;

- report as in need of repair incompatible materials in connecting devices between differing metals in the supply system, where visible;

- report as in need of repair deficiencies in water supply by viewing functional flow in two fixtures operated simultaneously;

- report as in need of repair deficiencies in functional drainage at accessible plumbing fixtures;

- report as in need of repair deficiencies in installation and identification of hot and cold faucets;

■ REPORTING GUIDELINES (Continued)

- report as in need of repair mechanical drainstops that are missing or do not operate if installed on sinks, lavatories, and tubs;

- report as in need of repair commodes that have cracks in the ceramic material, are improperly mounted on the floor, leak, or have tank components that do not operate;

- report as in need of repair accessible supply and drain pipes that leak;

- report as in need of repair the lack of a visible vent pipe system to the exterior of the structure or improper routing or termination of the vent system;

- report as in need of repair a shower enclosure that leaks; and

- report as in need of repair any exterior faucet attached or immediately adjacent to the structure that does not operate properly.

Specific limitations for plumbing systems. The inspector is not required to do the following:

- Operate any main, branch or shut-off valves

- Inspect any system that has been shut down or otherwise secured

- Inspect any components that are not visible or accessible

- Inspect any exterior plumbing components such as water mains, private sewer systems, water wells, sprinkler systems, or swimming pools

- Inspect fire sprinkler systems

- Inspect or operate drain pumps or waste ejector pumps

- Inspect the quality or the volume of well water

- Determine the potability of any water supply

- Inspect water-conditioning equipment, such as softeners or filter systems

- Inspect solar water heating systems

- Determine the effectiveness of antisiphon devices on appropriate fixtures or systems

- Operate free-standing appliances

- Inspect private water supply systems, swimming pools, or pressure tanks

- Inspect the gas supply system for leaks

- Inspect for sewer clean-outs

Inspection guidelines for gas lines. The inspector shall

- inspect and report as in need of repair deficiencies in the condition and type of all accessible and visible gas piping; and

- test gas lines by using a local or an industry-accepted procedure.

Specific limitations for gas lines.

- The inspector is not required to inspect sacrificial anode bonding or check for its existence.

■ REPORTING GUIDELINES *(Continued)*

Inspection guidelines for lawn and garden sprinkler system. The inspector shall

- operate all zones or stations on the system manually

- report as in need of repair deficiencies in water flow or pressure at the circuit heads

- report as in need of repair surface water leaks, the absence or improper installation of antisiphon valves and backflow preventers or the absence of shut-off valves;

- inspect and report as in need of repair deficiencies in the condition and mounting of the control box and visible wiring;

- report as in need of repair deficiencies in the operation of each zone and associated valves, spray head patterns and areas of non-coverage within the zone; and

- check for backsplash.

Specific limitations for lawn and garden sprinkler system.

- The inspector is not required to inspect the automatic function of the timer or control box, the rain sensor, or the effectiveness and sizing of antisiphon valves or backflow preventers.

Inspection guidelines for private water wells. The inspector shall

- operate at least two fixtures simultaneously;

- report the type of pump and type of storage equipment;

- report as in need of repair deficiencies in water pressure and flow and operation of pressure switches;

- inspect and report as in need of repair deficiencies in the condition of visible and accessible equipment and components;

- report as in need of repair wiring that is improper or lacks circuit protection;

- report as in need of repair deficiencies in the well head, including improper site drainage;

- recommend, or arrange to have performed, a coliform analysis; and

- report the proximity of any known septic system.

Specific limitations for private water wells. The inspector is not required to do the following:

- Open, uncover or remove the pump, heads, screens, lines, or other component parts of the system

- Determine water quality or potability or the reliability of the water supply or source

- Locate or verify underground water leaks

Inspection guidelines for individual private sewage systems (septic systems). The inspector shall

- report as in need of repair deficiencies in accessible or visible components of the system at the time of the inspection;

- operate plumbing fixtures and report as in need of repair deficiencies in functional flow;

- walk over the area of tanks and fields or beds and report as in need of repair any visual or olfactory evidence of effluent seepage or flow at the surface of the ground;

■ REPORTING GUIDELINES *(Continued)*

- report as in need of repair areas of inadequate site drainage around or adjacent to the system;

- report the proximity of any known water wells; underground cisterns; water supply lines; streams, ponds and lakes; sharp slopes or breaks; easement lines; property lines; soil absorption systems; swimming pools;or sprinkler systems;

- inspect the operation of the system;

- report the lack of visible access to tanks;

- report the type of the system, if possible, and the location of the drainfield; and

- report as in need of repair aerators or dosing pumps that do not operate or equipment that is improperly wired.

Specific limitations for individual private sewage systems (septic systems). The inspector is not required to do the following:

- Excavate or uncover the system or its components to determine the size, adequacy or efficiency of the system

- Determine the type of construction used unless readily known without excavation or destructive examination

7 Electricity

One of the largest single influences on our lives today is electricity. It affects our lives in many different ways every day. For any person, it would be hard to imagine life without electricity. Although it is very important, the average person has very little knowledge or understanding of electricity.

As a real estate inspector, this knowledge is essential to perform an adequate and thorough inspection. Successful real estate inspectors must acquire electrical knowledge and skills if they are to meet the demands of their profession.

The use of electrical energy for lighting, appliances, heating and cooling, tools, and equipment has increased rapidly in the past few years. Electricity is a valuable source of energy. It can, however, be a severe safety hazard. An inadequate electrical system containing overloaded circuits or defective wiring and outlets can be a fire hazard as well as a safety hazard to animals and humans.

Electricity is a form of energy generated by friction, induction, or chemical change. It can also be produced by magnetic, chemical, and radiant effects. Energy, in general, can be neither created nor destroyed; it merely changes from one form to another. Electrical energy is a form of light, mechanical, and heat energy.

Providing electrical energy to a dwelling is the last stage in the power flow and the beginning of another. For the electricity to flow, it must travel from a higher to a lower potential voltage.

■ CONDUCTOR

A conducting metal or wire permits an easy flow of electrical energy. For electricity to work, it must be transported from one place to another. Electricity can be made to flow in all matter; however, this flow is easier in some kinds of matter than in others. Materials that permit easy flow of electricity are referred to as *conductors* Electricity flows over the conductor, with relative ease (little resistance) in some materials, such as copper, and with substantial resistance in others, such as iron. Good conductors are silver, copper, aluminum, and mercury. Conductive materials are usually formed into wire. The quantity of electricity that can safely be transferred by a conductor depends on the size of the conductor. For, example, iron wire would have to be ten times as large as copper wire to carry the same current.

If an excess of electricity is pushed through a small conductor, large amounts of heat are generated and can create a hazardous situation. Therefore, correct sizing of the conductor is vital. Conductors are sized according to gauge numbers. The lower the gauge number, the larger the wire. The National Electric Code sets the standards for the safe sizing of conductors.

Copper

Copper wire is the most popular conductor used for residential properties because, next to silver, it is the best conductor. Corrosion does not cause copper conductors to deteriorate, and the corrosion product is as good a conductor as the copper itself. Copper does not have as great an expansion/contraction rate as aluminum.

Wire sizes are indicated by a number. The smaller the number, the larger the wire. For example, number 14 copper is the smallest wire permitted by code for use on a branch circuit with a 15-ampere (amp) capacity circuit breaker or fuse. Number 8 copper wire is permitted by code for use with a 40-amp circuit breaker or fuse. Proper wire size and type are very important.

■ **TABLE 7.1**

Amps	Copper	Aluminum
15	14 ga	12 ga
20	12 ga	10 ga
30	10 ga	8 ga
40	8 ga	6 ga
60	4 ga	4 ga

When current flows through a wire, it creates heat. The greater the amount of flow, the greater the amount of heat generated. Doubling the amperage without changing the wire size increases the amount of heat by four times. In addition to heat generation, there will be a reduction in voltage as a result of attempting to force more current through a wire than it is capable of carrying. The common sizes of copper wire found in dwellings are 14, 12, 10, and 8. (See Table 7.1.)

Aluminum

Aluminum wire is found in dwellings built after 1965 to the present time. In 1972, manufacturers modified both aluminum wire switches and outlets to improve the performance of aluminum-wired connections. The switches and outlets are labeled "CO/ALR." CO indicates that the device is acceptable for copper wire, and ALR means it is acceptable for aluminum wire. Aluminum wire does not behave the same as copper wire because aluminum wire has approximately a 30 percent higher expansion/contraction rate than copper. When aluminum wire is exposed to the atmosphere, a film of aluminum oxide forms on the metal surface. The oxide is an insulator, not a conductor of electricity. Aluminum wire, like copper, is a good conductor of electricity.

Most of the high-voltage transmission lines in the United States are made of aluminum or aluminum reinforced with steel. Aluminum wire is also used as the service entrance wire that connects the dwelling service to the power line in the street. Aluminum wire weighs less than copper wire, which makes it attractive for transmission lines. The oxide is not a problem for transmission because of the high voltages that are involved. However, oxidation is a problem with residential wiring because the current is supplied at much lower voltage. As the oxide continues to build up on the wire, it builds up the resistance. Heat comes with the resistance, thereby reducing the voltage. Aluminum wire or metal will start

oxidizing almost immediately when exposed to the atmosphere. Therefore, it is important that the exposed surfaces be protected from the atmosphere. Because of the expansion/contraction rate of aluminum, an electrical system using aluminum that is installed properly can have problems due to the movement of the wire, causing loose connections. These loose connections cause arcing and short circuits, in turn causing fires.

When the aluminum wire is be attached to the terminal screws, the wire should be stripped to allow from ⅔ to ¾ wrap around the screw. The wire should not be nicked from stripping and should be placed on the screw so that the wrap of the wire is in the clockwise direction. After the screw is snug on the wire, a torque-reading screwdriver should be used to tighten it to 12"-lb. (inch-pounds). After tightening the screws on the device, a coating of a good antioxidant compound such as Alnox or Penetrox A13k or some other antioxidant should be used on all exposed terminals (See Figure 7.1.)

One recommended method of connecting copper to aluminum is by splicing. However, when splicing copper to aluminum, it is important that the proper material be used at the splice. Proper repair for splicing copper to alu-

■ **FIGURE 7.1**

Correct method of terminating aluminum wire at wire-binding screw terminals of receptacles and snap switches (Underwriters Laboratories, Inc.).

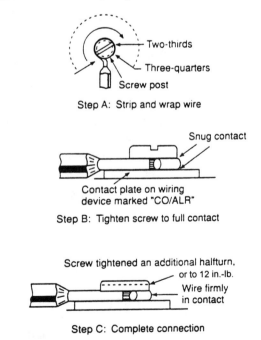

Step A: Strip and wrap wire

Step B: Tighten screw to full contact

Step C: Complete connection

minum wire is known as the *crimp connector repair method*. Crimp connector repair consists of attaching a piece of copper wire to the existing aluminum wire branch circuits with a specially designed metal sleeve and powered crimping tool. The metal sleeve is called a *Copalum parallel splice connector*. To properly make a reliable crimp connection, the powered crimping tool develops approximately 10,000 lb. of necessary force. This type of connection is a permanent connection that is, in effect, a cold weld. An insulating sleeve is placed around the crimp connector to complete the repair.

Aluminum wire is still approved in the National Electric Code. Some cities have passed an ordinance restricting aluminum wire use, but the ordinance affects only construction from the date the ordinance went into effect. All homes built before that date are grandfathered. If a real estate inspector observes a problem, he or she should report it, but an inspector does not have the authority to determine the type of repair. The inspector should refer problems to an expert—in this case, a licensed electrical contractor.

Other areas of concern are wire splicing and pigtailing the receptacles and switches. It is important that a real estate inspector be familiar with the various signs of problems associated with electrical systems, such as warm-to-the-touch face plates on receptacles and switches, flickering lights, and the smell of burning plastic at the electrical panel, switches, and receptacles. These same warning signs may appear with copper wire. When inspecting receptacles, switches, and electrical panels, the inspector should touch the face plates and panel with the back of the hand.

Insulators

Insulators are materials that have extremely low conductivity. Some good insulators are rubber, plastic and glass. Conductors put electricity where it is desired; insulators isolate the flow of electricity. Insulation prevents the metallic conductor from coming into contact with other materials and also prevents contact with the metal conductor by people. Each type of approved insulation has been tested for the highest permissible temperature at which it can operate safely. Other materials are used in the jacket, which provides physical protection for the assembly of conductors. These materials protect against heat, corrosive liquids, moisture, oil, gas, and rodent attack and offer some degree of fire resistance.

Wire insulation under the sheathing has different colors that indicate the use of the wire. A wire with green

■ **TABLE 7.2**

Color	Function
Black	Hot wire
Red	Hot wire
Blue	Hot wire
White code black*	Hot wire
White	Neutral wire
Green	Grounding wire
Green and yellow	Grounding wire
Bare copper	Grounding wire

*White is always a neutral wire, with the exception of a switch loop, where it must be identified as hot with a dab of black paint or wrapping at the end with black electricians' tape.

insulation, or green with a yellow stripe, is always a ground wire. If it has white insulation, it is a neutral wire. Black, red or blue insulation indicates a hot wire. (See Table 7.2.)

The inspector must ensure that the correct wire size is used in the home. This includes not only the correct wire size for intended use but also the correct insulation where visible.

There are four types of insulation: rubber (*R* or *RU*), mineral (*M*), asbestos (*A*) and thermoplastic (*T*). Other designations indicate the physical protection: for example, *U* designates approval for underground usage; *H* designates that the insulation is heat-resistant; and *W*, that the insulation is water- or moisture-resistant. However, in residential construction, nonmetallic cable is more commonly used. The nonmetallic sheathed cable is a manufactured assembly of two or more insulated conductors having a nonmetallic sheath. Nonmetallic sheathing, identified as type *NM*, is flame-retardant and moisture-resistant. Type *NMC* sheathing, in addition to being flame-retardant and moisture-resistant, is fungus- and corrosion-resistant. The service entrance cable can be a single conductor or a multiconductor assembly that is flame-retardant and moisture-resistant. The service entrance cable is designated type *SE* or type *USE* for underground use. Underground cable for branch circuits should be designated *UF*. The overall covering must be moisture-, fungus-, and corrosion-resistant and flame-retardant. Type *UF* can be buried underground.

Nonmetallic cable, also called *Romex cable*, is a set of insulated electrical conductors and may have a bare grounding conductor held together and protected by a plastic cover. Nonmetallic cable is used in residential

■ **FIGURE 7.2**

Cable with ground wire.

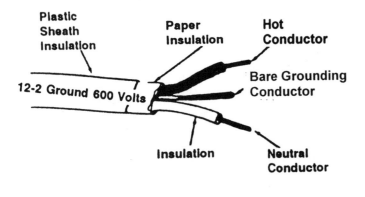

wiring throughout the country because it is inexpensive and easy to install.

Important information is printed on the plastic cover to help the inspector ascertain that the proper wire size and type of nonmetallic cable are used for the environment. The numbers printed first give the wire size, such as 12 gauge (ga) or 14 ga. Following the wire size is the number of conductors (wires), such as two or three. Following the number of conductors is the word *ground,* which indicates that a bare ground wire is present, and letters indicating the plastic cover type. Some non-

metallic cable also has maximum voltage stamped on the cover. Nonmetallic cable must have a ground wire to properly ground outlets and appliances. It is important that the correct insulation be used in any given area. (See Figure 7.2.)

Knob and Tube Wiring

When inspecting a home built in the early 1900s, if the inspector finds a fuse box, it is a good possibility the home will have knob and tube wiring. The tube is the insulator where the wire passes through the joists and studs. The knob supports the wire where it runs along a flat surface. (See Figure 7.3.) In older homes where the electrical system has not been updated, there will be a two-wire 120-volt system. The inspector can check this by observing the number of wires at the weatherhead. Two wires can only be 120 volts, and three wires are 240-volt service.

The inspector should inspect the wiring in the attic and crawlspace or basement carefully. It is possible that the wiring will be covered with insulation, so it may be necessary to pull back the insulation to observe the condition of the wire. It is important to be careful because the insulation may be brittle and broken or the insulation may have fallen off. If knob and tube wiring is observed, the inspector should recommend evaluation of the electrical system by an electrical contractor.

■ **FIGURE 7.3**

Old knob and tube wiring.

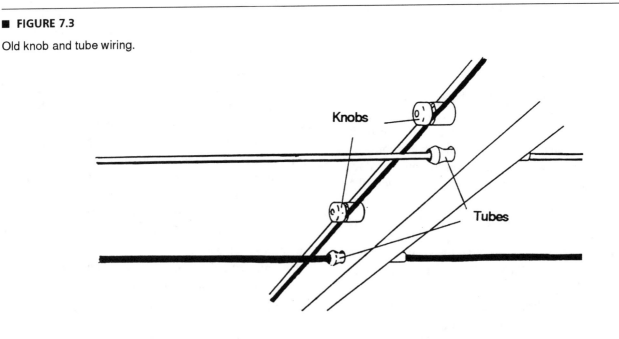

■ **FIGURE 7.4**

A generator or battery is considered a typical source.

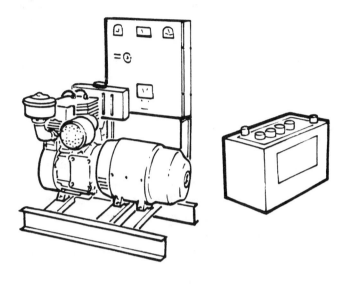

■ ELECTRICAL CIRCUIT

Three items that are required for an electrical circuit are a source, a path, and a load.

Source

For electrons to do work, an excess of electrons must accumulate at a particular location. The source could be an electric power plant or an automobile battery. A battery always has two terminals—one negative and one positive. The excess of negatively charged electrons gathers at the negative terminal in a battery, leaving a deficiency of electrons or positively charged ions at the positive terminal. Because all electrons have like, negative charges, they repel each other. With the large number of electrons amassed at one location, tremendous electrical force is generated as the electrons repel. This force is called *electrical pressure* or *electrical energy*. The source is the supply of this electrical energy for all electrical circuits. (See Figure 7.4.)

Path

The path is usually in the form of a metal conductor or wire to transport the electrons from their source to the place where the electrons will be put to work. This wire from the source to the work area is called the hot leg of the circuit. (See Figure 7.5.)

■ **FIGURE 7.5**

Electrons must have a path to follow.

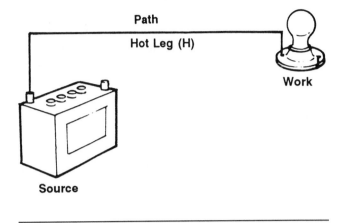

Load

The term *load* designates the point in an electrical circuit where electrical work is to be done. The load will always have resistance to electron flow as electrical energy is converted to other forms of energy. These other forms of energy are heat energy (e.g., toaster), light energy (e.g., lamp), and mechanical energy (e.g., fan). When electrical energy converts to other forms of energy, work is being done. The electrons flow through the load via an electrical path from the load back to the source. The wire that runs from the load to the source is the neutral leg of the circuit. (See 7.6.)

■ **FIGURE 7.6**

Completed circuit.

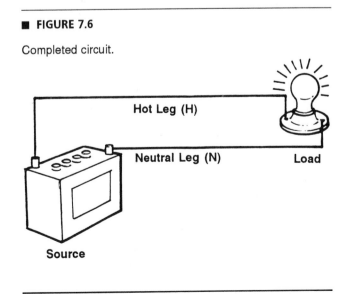

Voltage

Voltage is the measure of the force at which electricity is delivered. It is similar to the pressure in a water system. Voltage can best be explained by comparing electrical pressure to water pressure. Electricity will not flow through a circuit unless it is forced by electrical pressure. The force of electrical pressure is similar to the pressure exerted by water in a cylinder that has only one opening at the top. Pressure exists at all levels within the cylinder owing to the weight of the water. As the water level increases, the pressure that acts on the cylinder increases. If a hole is cut into the lower part of the cylinder, the pressure exerted by the weight of the water forces the water out of the hole. In an electrical circuit, the electrical pressure forces the electrons through the path or conductor to the load. Water flows, owing to the pressure difference, from the inside to the outside of the cylinder. For electrons to flow, there must also be a difference in electrical pressure between two points in a circuit. Electrons will always flow from high pressure (negative terminal) to low pressure (positive terminal) if a path is provided.

This flow can be represented with two cylinders of water connected at the bottom by a tube. One cylinder is full of water while the other cylinder is empty. The full cylinder has a greater volume of water, which induces a high pressure; the empty cylinder has a low pressure.

The potential to do work exists because of the pressure differential between the two cylinders. If the tube between the two cylinders is opened, allowing a path for the water to flow, the high pressure in the full cylinder will force the water through the tube to the empty cylinder. When the potential difference drops to zero, the water will stop flowing because the water levels in the two cylinders are equal.

The same situation happens at the source of an electrical circuit. As long as a potential difference exists, there is the capability to put electrons in motion to do work. The potential to do work is useless unless a load is added to the circuit.

Amperage

A measure of the amount of electrical current in a circuit at any given time is called the *amperage*. One method of measuring electrical flow would be to select a single point on the conductor and count the electrons that pass that point. However, the electrons are so small that it would be impossible to count the actual number. Instead, electrical flow is measured in amperes. This is analogous to sizing a water hose according to the amount of water that passes a given point in one minute. Conducting wire is sized according to the amperage. For example, a 14-ga copper wire is good for 15 amps; however, an aluminum wire must be 12-ga to be good for 15 amps. The difference is due to the varying capabilities of different materials to safely carry electricity without generating excessive heat due to the friction within the wire.

Watt

The watt is a measure of the amount of electricity flowing. It is expressed mathematically as volts × amps. A kilowatt is 1,000 watts. Usage of 1,000 watts for one hour is called a *kilowatt hour*. Electricity is sold in quantities of kilowatt hours.

Conductors capable of carrying 100 amps safely would provide 23,000 watts of power at 230V (volts) (230V × 100 amps = 23,000 watts) for a three-wire source; however, a two-wire source would provide only 11,500 watts at 115V (115V × 100 amps = 11,500 watts).

The watt is the unit of measure for power consumption. The rating of a lightbulb is expressed in watts; for example, a 75-watt lightbulb requires 75 watts of electric power to operate. Electric appliances also are rated in watts: an electric water heater rated at 4,500 watts requires 4,500 watts of electric power to operate.

Resistance

Resistance is the property of an electrical circuit that restricts the flow of current. Resistance is generally associated with a load. The greater the amount of resistance, the greater the amount of heat that is generated. The heat is electrical energy that has been converted into heat energy by the resistance of the wire. The heat developed in an electrical conductor is wasted and the electric energy used to generate it is wasted. If the heat generated by the flow of electricity through the wire becomes excessive, it can cause a fire. Therefore, the National Electric Code sets the maximum permissible electrical current that may flow through a certain type and size of conductor (wire). In addition to heat generation, there will be a reduction in voltage as a result of attempting to force more electrical current through a conductor than it is capable of carrying. (See Figure 7.7.) Certain appliances, such as induction-type motors, may be damaged if operated at too low a voltage. Resistance is measured in ohms.

■ **FIGURE 7.7**

■ **FIGURE 7.7**

Excess of electrons through a small conductor causes high resistance.

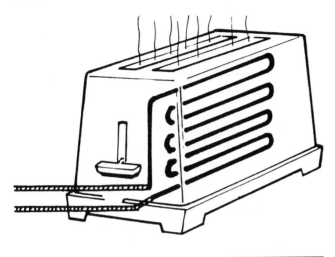

■ **FIGURE 7.8**

Transmission lines function for a distance to the distribution lines.

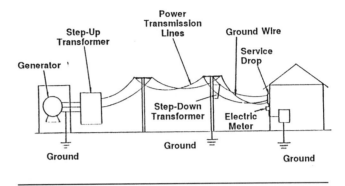

Ohms

The ohm is a measure of electrical resistance or electrical friction. Ohm's Law describes the relationship between voltage, current, and resistance in an electric current. Current is directly proportional to voltage and inversely proportional to resistance. Three components can be found in any complete electric circuit: current (amps), potential difference (volts) and resistance (ohms). Therefore, if any two values are known, the third can be determined by the mathematical formulation of Ohm's Law: $A = V/R$. For example, if the volts and ohms are known, the amps can be determined by dividing the volts by the ohms (120 volts ÷ 12 ohms = 10 amps). If the volts and amps are known, the ohms can be determined by dividing the volts by the amps (120 volts ÷ 10 amps = 12 ohms).

■ GENERATING ELECTRICITY

To use electric current, the current must travel from the source through the path to the load and back to the source in a complete cycle or circuit. The source produces one of two basic types of electrical current: alternating current (AC) or direct current (DC). Each type of electric current has unique properties, which can make it more desirable than the other under certain circumstances. (See Figure 7.8.)

Direct Current

Direct current flows constantly in one direction. This is based on the fact that electrons always flow from the negative terminal to the positive terminal. A chemical reaction inside a battery maintains the potential difference by depositing electrons on the negative terminal. If a wire is connected from the negative terminal to a lightbulb, then to the positive terminal, a circuit has been created. This is direct current. The direct current will continue to flow until the circuit is broken or the source stops supplying electrons.

Alternating Current

Alternating current is current that flows through a conductor in one direction for a split second, then flows in the opposite direction for a split second. (See Figure 7.9.) The direction alternates because of a technique used at the power plant called *electromagnetic induction*. This technique is based on power generated by passing a conductor through magnetic lines of force. A power plant uses an AC generator consisting of a stator (a large coil of conductor wire) and a rotor (a large magnet) to produce alternating current.

The magnetic lines of force are cut by the conductor (stator) every 1/120 of a second. As the lines of force are cut, AC current correspondingly flows in one direction for 1/120 of a second, then in the other direction for 1/120 of a second. This completes one *cycle,* which cycle is also referred to as a *hertz* (hz). In the United States, power is generated at 60 cycles or hz per second. In most foreign countries, the power is generated at 50 cycles or hz per second.

Alternating current flows through a conductor in one direction for a split second, then flows in the opposite direction for a split second.

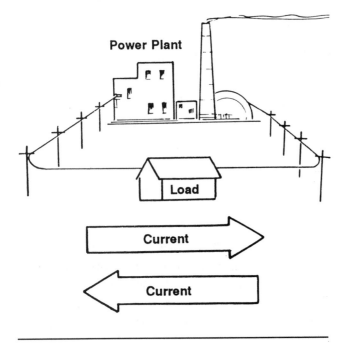

After the electricity is mechanically generated at the power plant, the voltage from the generator is connected to a step-up transformer immediately outside the power plant. This transformer increases the voltage to a level at which it can efficiently be transmitted over the transmission line. The power from this location is then carried over transmission lines (often many miles) to transmission substations, where the voltage is reduced by a step-down transformer to a subtransmission voltage, which is still greater than distribution voltage. The subtransmission voltage serves industrial and commercial customers that have their own transformers. Subtransmission voltage is also used to supply the distribution substation with power. Voltage is reduced to the distribution primary voltage by another step-down transformer at the distribution substation, and distribution primary lines carry this voltage to residential and rural areas. The primary distribution voltage is then reduced to the 120/240V secondary distribution voltage, which serves residential and rural properties. The final reduction in voltage occurs at the step-down transformers mounted on the distribution poles or buried underground throughout these areas. The secondary distribution voltage enters the homes through the service drop and house entrance.

Transformers

Transformers are electrical devices used to convert AC voltage to either a higher or a lower AC voltage. A transformer used to change 120-voltage alternating current (VAC) to 24 VAC is called a *step-down transformer,* and a transformer used to change 120 VAC to 240 VAC is called a *step-up transformer.* Transformers are available in a variety of capacities for stepping up or stepping down. Construction of a transformer is simple. Windings of conductor wire are placed around one side of an iron ring and connected to the power source. This is called the *primary winding.* Another winding of conductor wire, called the *secondary winding,* is placed on the opposite side of the ring. There is no physical electrical connection between the primary and secondary windings of the transformers. Electrical energy is transferred from the primary windings to the secondary windings by the process of induction. (See Figure 7.10.)

Induction

Whenever electricity is in the conductor, a magnetic field surrounds the conductor. Whenever a con-

Transformers are available in a variety of capacities for stepping-up or stepping-down AC voltage.

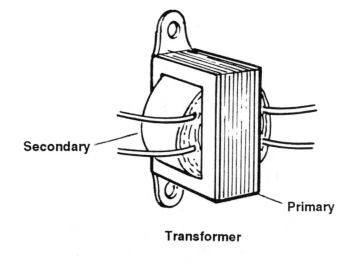

ductor cuts magnetic lines of force, or the magnetic lines of force cut the conductor, electrons are excited in the conductor and voltage is generated. These statements explain the process of induction.

The AC voltage output of the secondary winding of a transformer is determined by the number of windings that exist in the secondary compared with the primary. A greater number of windings in the secondary implies that more electrons are excited and thereby more voltage is produced by the secondary. When there are fewer windings in the secondary, fewer electrons are excited and the voltage produced is less. The secondary side of a 24V transformer will have approximately ⅕ the number of windings that the primary side has and also ⅕ the voltage output of the primary side of the transformer (24V ÷ 120V = ⅕). Transformers are sized according to the amount of power the secondary windings can handle. The power capability is expressed as VA (voltage × amperage). For example, if the secondary voltage of a transformer is 24V and the amperage capacity of the secondary is 2 amps, the VA rating or size of the transformer is computed as follows: VA = 24V × 2 amps = 48 VA. The transformer is rated at 48 VA. A transformer should never be replaced with a transformer with a smaller VA rating because, in time, the transformer will burn out and malfunction. A transformer can be replaced with one that has a larger VA rating.

A DC power source cannot be used with a transformer because direct current flows constantly in one direction. The electrons always flow from negative to positive. A magnetic field must remain in motion if a continuous voltage is to be induced in the secondary windings. As the electrons flow in the primary winding, the magnetic field builds in intensity. When the electron flow stops, the magnetic field collapses. As the electron flow changes direction, the magnetic field intensifies.

Ampacity

Ampacity is the measured current a conductor can carry continuously under the conditions of use without exceeding the conductor's temperature rating. Ampacity is given in units of amperes. The ampacity rating is equivalent to 125 percent of the actual amperage draw of the electrical component. If an electric motor draws 5 amps, the ampacity can be calculated the following way: 5 amps × 125% = 6.25 amps. The extra 25 percent is to ensure that the wiring will not catch fire in the event of an electrical overload. If the circuit is properly fused, an overload will blow the fuse before the wire generates enough heat to cause a fire.

Circuit

A circuit is a path of electrical flow from a power source through a load, returning to neutral charge or ground. The circuit enables a clock to keep time and a radio to play music. All of the electrical energy is used at the load. Electrical energy is converted to heat energy, light energy, or mechanical energy.

Series Circuit

A series circuit is a circuit in which electricity flows in only one path. The loads are wired from end to end, forcing the electricity to pass through the first load to get to the second and on through all loads connected in the circuit to return to neutral charge or ground. (See Figure 7.11.) In circuits that are connected in series, all loads are required to operate or none of them will operate. This can be seen, for example, in the old-fashioned strings of Christmas-tree lights. If one bulb is defective, none of the bulbs will operate; each bulb has to be checked to find the defective bulb. A break in any part of the circuit cuts off the flow of electricity throughout the circuit. Amperage throughout the circuit is constant. The amperage flowing through each of the loads is the same as the amperage flowing through the entire circuit. Consider a circuit that has a total amperage of 2 amps. Because the amperage throughout a series circuit is constant, the loads within the circuit will each have an amperage reading of 2 amps.

■ **FIGURE 7.11**

Loads are wired end-to-end.

■ **FIGURE 7.12**

A parallel circuit is a circuit in which electrons have two or more paths to follow.

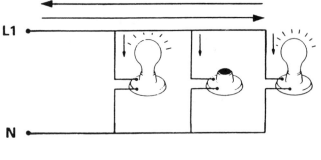

The total or equivalent resistance of the circuit is equal to the sum of the individual resistances. For example, if two 20-ohm loads are wired in series, the total or equivalent resistance of the series circuit is 40 ohms. The amperage of a circuit is directly related to the total or equivalent resistance of the circuit: If the equivalent resistance is increased, amperage is decreased; if the equivalent resistance is decreased, amperage is increased. The total voltage of a series circuit is equal to the sum of the voltage drops across all loads in the circuit. Voltage drop is directly related to the resistance of the load: If resistance is high, the voltage drop is high; if resistance is low, the voltage drop is low.

Parallel Circuit

The parallel circuit is a circuit in which electricity has two or more paths to follow. If two or more paths with loads are wired in parallel, electricity can pass through all or any one of the loads. (See Figure 7.12.)

Unlike the series circuit, if one of the loads is removed, the other loads remain energized. In a parallel circuit, the voltage across each path equals the voltage potential of the entire circuit. If the voltage potential between the hot and neutral legs of the circuit is 120V, the voltage across each load is 120V. Voltage is the same across each load in a parallel circuit because the same source potential is supplied to each of the loads. Not all loads in a parallel circuit are necessarily of equal resistance. If two loads of unequal resistance are wired in parallel, the amperage passing through each is different. Because electricity always flows through the path of least resistance, the portion of the parallel circuit with high resistance will have a low amperage draw, while the portion of the circuit with low resistance will have a high

amperage draw. Consider a circuit where the resistance of load A is 60 ohms and the resistance of load B is 10 ohms. Load A has six times the resistance to electrical flow than load B. Therefore, more amps flow through load B than through load A, while the voltage remains the same across both loads. Because load A has six times more resistance to electrical flow than load B, six times as many amps will flow through load B than through load A. Load A draws 2 amps and load B draws 12 amps. To arrive at the total circuit amperage draw, add the amperage of loads A and B together for a total of 14 amps. The amperage is measured with an amprobe.

The total or equivalent resistance of a parallel circuit is always less than the smallest of the individual resistances. The equivalent resistance of a parallel circuit will decrease as more new paths with loads are added to the circuit. The total amperage of a parallel circuit is equal to the sum of the amperages of all loads in that circuit. Amperage within a parallel circuit is directly related to the resistance. The voltage across each path of a parallel circuit is equal to the voltage potential of the entire parallel circuit.

Switch

A switch is a device that opens and closes an electrical circuit. A switch has at least two positions: open and closed. When the switch is deenergized, in the open position, no electricity flows through the circuit. When the switch is energized, in the closed position, the electricity flows through the circuit.

Switches are used to isolate loads. For this reason, switches are always located on the hot leg of the circuit. A switch should never interrupt the neutral leg of a circuit. The simplest switch is a single-pole, single-throw (SPST) switch, which means it has one pole (moving mechanism) and one throw (position) in which the pole can make contact. A single-pole switch will operate only one circuit from one location.

If a second contact is added to an SPST switch, the switch becomes a single-pole, double-throw (SPDT) switch. The pole can be thrown to one of two positions to energize one of two different circuits or loads. Appliances that require 240V use a switch called a *double-pole, single-throw (DPST) switch*. A DPST switch is required on appliances such as window air conditioners. SPST switches and DPST switches are marked "off" and "on".

Three-way switches are used when it is desired to operate a load from two different locations. Two three-way switches are required to accomplish the operation.

■ **FIGURE 7.13**

Switches that control lighting fixtures from a single location or multiple locations.

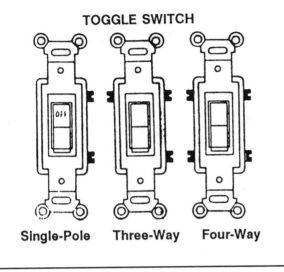

TOGGLE SWITCH

Single-Pole   Three-Way   Four-Way

The three-way switch is a DPST switch. The three-way switch can be identified by the three terminal screws. The single terminal screw at one end of the switch is called the *common*. The hot leg is connected to this terminal. The two bottom terminals are called the *traveler terminals*. The traveler wires are connected to the traveler terminals on both three-way switches. The three-way switch will not have any *on-off* markings.

Four-way switches may be used with two three-way switches to control a load from three or more locations. Four-way switches are connected between two traveler wires. The four-way switch can be identified by the four terminals. There are no on-off markings. If it is desired to operate a load from five different locations, it would require two three-way switches and three four-way switches. The four-way switches must be connected to the traveler wires that connect the two three-way switches. (See Figures 7.13 and 7.14.)

There are other types of switches, such as dimmer switches and motion switches. A dimmer switch is also called a *resistor switch*. It has on-off markings and a resistor built into the switch to allow resistance to be increased, which in turn lowers the voltage, causing the lights to dim. Resistance causes heat and because of this, the dimmer switch will feel warm to the touch, but it should not be hot. Motion switches are designed to operate with movement. When a person enters a room, the switch senses the movement and turns on the light.

■ **FIGURE 7.14**

Switches usually control lighting fixtures and/or receptacles.

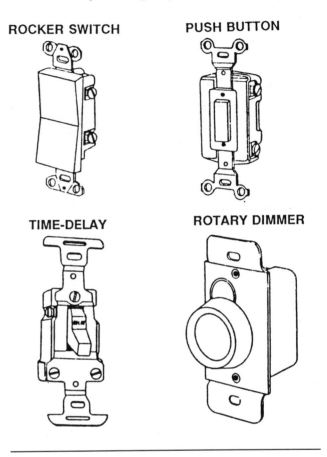

ROCKER SWITCH   PUSH BUTTON

TIME-DELAY   ROTARY DIMMER

■ CIRCUIT PROTECTORS

Excessive current flowing through a circuit can be very dangerous. It can damage components and cause a circuit to overheat and start a fire. To prevent excessive current flow, circuit protectors are installed on each circuit. There are two major types of circuit protectors: circuit breakers and fuses.

Circuit Breaker

A circuit breaker is a circuit protector that is heat sensitive when in the on position. The current flows through a thermal device within the breaker. If the sensor detects excessive heat, the sensor turns off the current. This is called *tripping the circuit breaker*. The circuit breaker can be reset and continue to be used. To reset a circuit breaker it must be moved to the off position before being moved back to the on position. (See

■ FIGURE 7.15

The circuit breaker may be reset by simply flipping the switch.

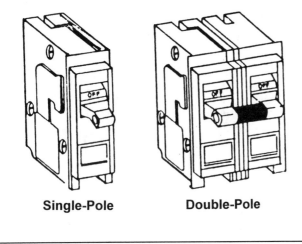

Single-Pole   **Double-Pole**

■ FIGURE 7.16

Fuses come in many different amperage ratings.

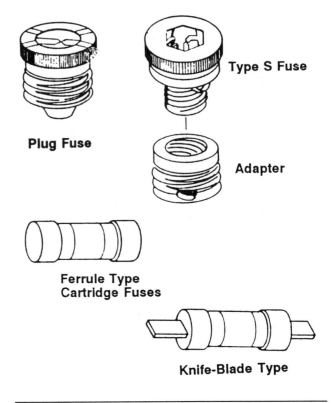

Plug Fuse

Type S Fuse

Adapter

Ferrule Type Cartridge Fuses

Knife-Blade Type

Figure 7.15.) The circuit breaker is always connected to the hot leg of the circuit, and it can be used on a 120V or a 240V circuit.

Fuse

The fuse is the other type of circuit protector used to protect a circuit from an overload of excessive current. Fuses are sized according to the amperage they will carry without breaking the circuit. One of the problems that is encountered with the standard plug-type fuse is that a fuse with a higher rating than the circuit is designed for can be installed or a piece of foil or a penny can be used behind a blown fuse. When this occurs, the circuit and loads have no protection.

There are three different types of fuses. The plug-type fuse is interchangeable regardless of the amperage rating. The S-type or T-amps (tamperproof) fuse has an adapter that screws into the fuse box. The inside thread on the adapter will accept only one size of tamperproof fuse. For example, the adapter for a 15-amp fuse will fit only a 15-amp fuse. Time-delay fuses are designed to withstand the initial current loads caused by starting motors. These fuses are called cartridge fuses and are sometimes found on air-conditioner compressors. There are two types of cartridge fuses: the ferrule contact cartridge fuse and the knife-blade contact cartridge fuse. Normally, the ferrule fuse will be on circuits from 30 amps to 60 amps and the knife-blade fuse will be on circuits above 60 amps. (See Figure 7.16.)

Receptacles

Receptacles or electrical outlets are contact devices installed at the outlet for the connection of a single attachment plug. A multiple receptacle is a single device containing two or more receptacles. Receptacles are rated by their voltage and amperage rating, which will determine the configuration of the device. Receptacles are designed to accommodate straight-blade and locking-type plugs. Locking-type receptacles are sometimes used for power tools. The 120V receptacles are polarized. (See Figure 7.17.)

It is recommended that all conductors be connected to the screws, whether the conductors are copper or aluminum. The inspector should be certain that all three-prong receptacles are grounded. (See Figure 7.18.)

Polarized Receptacles

These are easily identified because the neutral slot is longer than the slot on the hot side. The polarized receptacle has been designed so plugs on certain equipment and appliances can be inserted only one way. Recep-

■ **FIGURE 7.17**

Three-wire rounded receptacles.

20-A Grounded

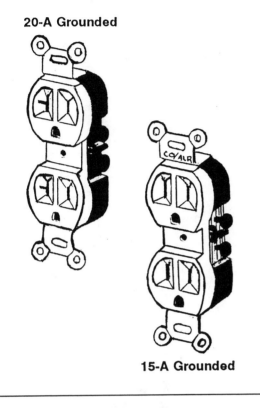

15-A Grounded

tacles that are designed for 240V will not accept a 120V plug and vice versa. It is important that the receptacle be connected properly. In other words, the neutral conductor should be connected to the chrome screw or neutral terminal and the hot conductor connected to the brass screw or hot terminal. If the receptacle has a ground terminal, which would be a green terminal, the bare conductor should be connected. If the conductors were reversed, the receptacle would be connected with reverse polarity. Because the current flow has been reversed, making the neutral side the hot and the hot side the neutral, it has caused a dangerous condition because it can cause shock as well as damage to an appliance or a tool. (See Figure 7.19.)

The receptacles will have information printed on them as to their rating, whether they are UL approved, and the types of conductors that can be used safely with them. An example is CO/ALR, which can be used with copper, aluminum, or copper-clad conductors only. This is the receptacle that should be used with aluminum wire.

Ground Fault Circuit Interrupter

Three types of ground fault circuit interrupters (GFCIs) may be used in residential properties: circuit breaker, receptacle, and portable plug-in. The circuit

■ **FIGURE 7.18**

Branch-circuit extension to existing installation illustrating a separate grounding conductor connected to the main grounding electrode. This method is also permitted to ground a replacement 3-wire receptacle in the existing ungrounded box on the left, where no grounding conductor is available.

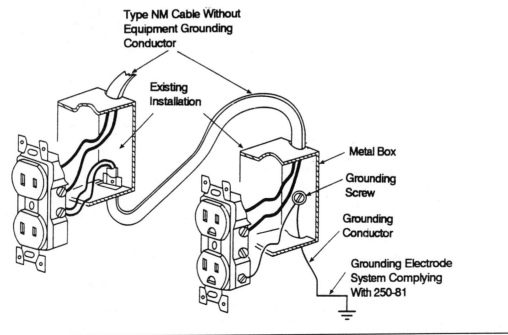

■ **FIGURE 7.19**

Polarized appliance receptacle.

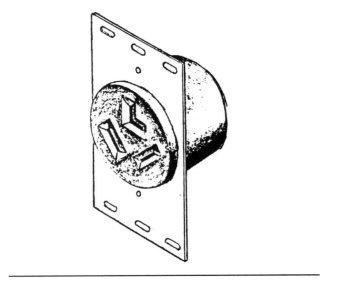

■ **FIGURE 7.20**

GFCI (ground fault circuit interrupter) devices.

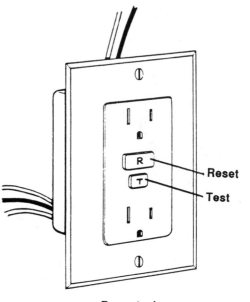

Receptacle

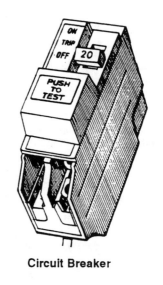

Circuit Breaker

breaker type is installed in the service panel that protects selected circuits. The circuit breaker GFCI serves a dual purpose. It shuts off electricity in the event of a ground fault, but it also trips when a short circuit or an overload occurs. Protection covers the wiring and each receptacle, lighting fixtures, etc.

The receptacle type is used in place of a standard duplex receptacle found throughout the house. The receptacle GFCI protects against ground faults whenever an electrical product is plugged into an outlet. Some receptacle GFCIs may be installed so they also protect other outlets downstream in the branch circuit.

The portable plug-in GFCI may be used in areas where permanent GFCIs are not practical. One portable type contains the GFCI circuitry in a plastic enclosure with plug blades in back and receptacle slots in front. It can plug into a receptacle. The electrical tool or appliance is plugged into the GFCI.

A GFCI is a safety device that senses any shock hazard and interrupts the flow of electricity in the circuit. The GFCI can be a circuit breaker located in the electrical panel. If it is in the form of a circuit breaker, it will have a push-button marked "test" that one can push, and if it is functioning properly, the button should trip the circuit breaker. The other type of GFCI is a receptacle with the test and reset buttons in the center of the receptacle. (See Figure 7.20.)

The GFCI is designed to trip and interrupt the circuit at approximately 5 to 8 milliamps (MA). The standard fuses and circuit breakers are not as sensitive as the GFCI

and are therefore slower in reacting. Receptacles requiring GFCIs are outdoor receptacles that are below 6'6", bathroom receptacles, kitchen receptacles located on countertops and wet bar sinks, and garage receptacles, except one receptacle for a garage door opener and one receptacle for a refrigerator/freezer. GFCIs are also required on swimming pool and spa lights. The receptacle-type GFCI must be connected properly to operate. For the GFCI to operate, the conductors from the panel have to connect to the line side of the receptacle.

Arc-Fault Circuit Interrupter

Arc will not be protected by GCFIs or circuit breakers. The arc-fault circuit interrupter is a circuit breaker that will be mounted in the panel box with the other breakers. The arc-fault circuit interrupters are only available in circuit breaker form. At the present time, they are required on bedroom outlets and fixtures.

Multicircuit Receptacles

Multicircuit receptacles are used in the kitchen for small appliances such as a dishwasher and a disposal, where one side of the receptacle needs to be hot all the time for the dishwasher and the other side needs to operate from a switch for the disposal. The break-off fin has to be removed on the hot side of the receptacle. Multicircuit receptacles can be dangerous because they have two circuit breakers.

■ ELECTRIC SERVICE

Electric service entrance can be from either an overhead power line or an underground power line. If overhead, the conductors will loop down from a utility pole to an entrance head, also called a *weatherhead*. If underground, a conduit with the conductors in it will attach to the meter base at the bottom. (See Figure 7.21.)

The service drop should be properly secured. The service entrance conductors should be installed either below the level of the entrance head or below the termination of the service entrance cable sheath. Drip loops must be formed on the individual conductors. If the conductors pass over other roofs, they must clear a flat roof by 8' and a roof with a 4/12 slope by 3'. All electrical conductors must clear residential driveways by at least 12'. For public streets, alleys, and driveways, other than residential property, the clearance must be 18'. These clearances vary from city to city and state to state. It is wise for the inspector to be familiar with the various requirements in the areas to be inspected.

Underground service requires different inspections. When wires are underground, they must be protected from moisture and physical damage. The opening in the dwelling foundation where the underground service enters the building must be moistureproof. The local codes concerning allowable materials and methods for this type of service entrance should be referred to.

Typical service entrance to residential dwelling with grounding to water pipe.

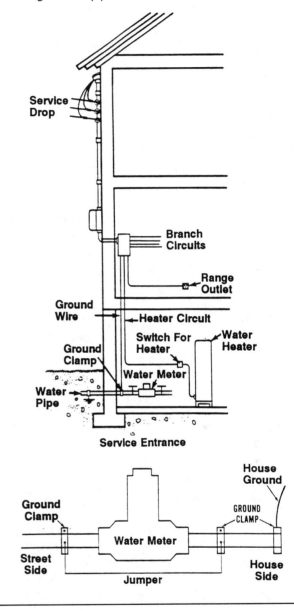

Wires on conductors should be of sufficient size to carry the load and should never be smaller than number 8 copper wire or the equivalent.

Electric service consists of two or three conductors. Regardless of the number of conductors to the weatherhead, one of the wires in every installation is grounded. This neutral wire is always white. The hot wires will be black, red, purple, or some other color other than white or green. The potential difference or voltage between the hot wires and the ground of a normal residential electrical system is 115V where there is a two-wire installation. If there is one hot wire and one neutral wire, there is 115V of service available. When there are three wires, two hot and one neutral, there is either 115V or 230V service.

In a three-wire system, the voltage between the neutral and either of the hot wires is 115V; between the two hot wires, it is 230V. The advantage of a three-wire system is that it permits the operation of heavy equipment such as air-conditioning, electric ovens and cook tops, and electric clothes dryers. The majority of these appliances require 230V circuits. Also, the three-wire system can be split at the service panel into two 115V systems to supply the power for the electric lights and other small appliances. The National Electric Code recommends a minimum of 100 amp, three-wire service. This type of service is adequate for a single-family dwelling and provides a safe electric supply for the lighting, the refrigerator and an 8,000-watt cooking range, plus other appliances that total 10,000 watts.

Two-wire service, supplying 115V, is restricted to only small appliances and lighting because it is not capable of producing 230V for operating heavy electrical equipment. Dwellings with two-wire service are inadequate by today's standard. Normally, this type of service is only 30 amps.

Grounding Conductor

A grounding conductor is a conductor used to connect equipment or the grounded circuit of a wiring system to a grounding electrode or electrodes. In addition to the ground connection provided by the utility company, every building is required to have an independent ground, called a *system ground*. The system ground provides for limiting the voltage on the circuit, which might be necessary when the circuit is exposed to lightning, or limiting the maximum potential to ground due to normal voltage. The system ground's main purpose is to protect the electric system itself and provide limited protection to the user. The system ground should be a continuous conductor of low resistance and of sufficient size to conduct current from lightning and overloads safely so that the overcurrent protection can trip, breaking the circuit. (See Figure 7.22.)

The equipment ground consists of grounding the metal parts of the service entrance, such as the service switch, as well as the service entrance conduit, armor, or cable. The usual ground connection is to a cold water pipe of a city water system or a rod driven into the ground. If the cold water pipe is used as a ground, it must be grounded within 5′ of where the water enters the

Grounding the electrical system.

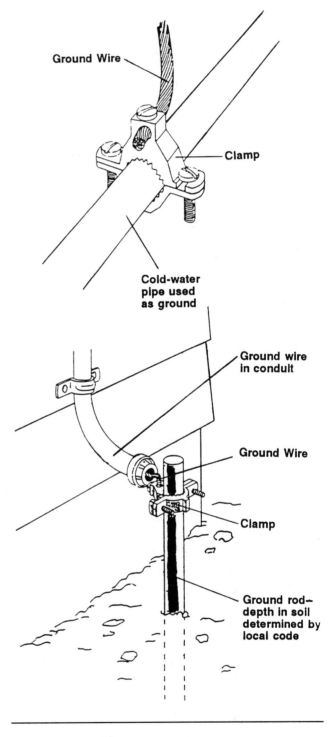

structure. The connection should be made to the street side of the water meter. If the connection is made on the house side of the water meter, a jumper wire should be attached on both sides of the water meter. In the event the water meter is removed, the electrical system will maintain its equipment ground.

Electric Meter

The electric meter may be located inside or outside the dwelling. The meter itself is weatherproof and is plugged into the meter base, which is also a weatherproof socket. When the electric meter is plugged in, it is sealed by the power company, and it is unlawful for the seal to be broken by any unauthorized person.

Electrical Service Panel

The electrical service panel is the distribution center from the utility company to the dwelling. The electrical panel provides the means to safely service the lighting, mechanical, and heating systems of the dwelling. The electrical panel contains the main disconnect switch or breaker that will turn off the total electrical system to the dwelling. It also contains the individual circuit breakers or fuses to the individual circuits such as lighting, appliances, heating, and cooling. When circuit breakers are used instead of fuses, the use of a main circuit breaker may or may not be required. A house with seven or more branch circuits or a house that uses fuses requires a separate disconnect means or main circuit breaker ahead of the branch circuit breakers or fuses. (See Figure 7.23.)

The inspector should remove the electric panel cover to observe the conductors and circuit breakers or fuses. Conductors should be observed for proper sizing to circuit breakers or fuses. Observe the condition of insulation on the conductors. If insulation is blistered and/or discolored, this indicates a problem with that circuit and the inspector should refer it to a licensed electrician. For panels with fuses, it is extremely important that the inspector correlate conductor size with fuse capacity. These panels, as well as circuit breakers, do not allow double wiring. (See Figure 7.24.)

The electric panel should be located in an area where there is adequate space to service the panel. The panel should always be accessible and not hidden from view. Panels should not be in bathrooms, clothes closets or kitchens. When inspecting an electrical panel, the inspector should touch the panel with the back of the hand before removing any screws. Alternating current will cramp the hand if touched with the palm side and could cause serious injury. (See Figure 7.25)

The electrical panel will have two bus bars that have screw terminals for the two hot wires to be connected. A neutral bus bar has a screw terminal to connect the ground wire. Often, the ground and neutral bus bars are contiguous. The two hot bus bars are designed to accept the circuit breakers or fuses.

There should never be more than one wire to any circuit breaker or fuse. This includes the two main screw terminals. The neutral and ground bus bar should have only one wire under each individual screw. If more than one wire is under one screw, it is referred to as *double wiring.* This practice is dangerous because the wires can work loose from vibration and cause a fire hazard and/or overload the circuit breaker. If additional electric panels are required, they must be protected in the same manner as the main panel. The main disconnect for the subpanel should be located in the main panel.

The inspector should observe the wire size in relation to the circuit breaker or fuse. When two single circuit breakers are connected to a 230V circuit, the breakers need to be tied together to cause both breakers to trip.

Every switch, receptacle, and wire splice must be in a junction box, which must be anchored to a stud or joist. The wire should be secured to the stud or joist to prevent pulling the joint loose. All junction boxes need to be covered for safety. All fixtures must be mounted in a junction box. The boxes are metal or plastic and are manufactured for outdoor use or for use around water. This box is referred to as a *weathertight box,* to be used as an outside receptacle.

■ THREE-PHASE POWER

Commercial power usually consists of three-phase circuits and loads. Three-phase circuits have three power conductors and one circuit ground. Commercial electrical service transports these conductors into a switchboard. At the switchboard, three pole breakers distribute power to various three-phase circuits and loads.

Two of the three power conductors may be used to feed a single-phase power supply for single-phase loads. This provides high-voltage single-phase power. One of the two power legs and a ground provide a circuit with 120V power.

Other transformers may be located on the property. The inspector checks that they are protected and operate properly. He or she looks for full voltage and makes sure

■ FIGURE 7.23

Wiring a service panel.

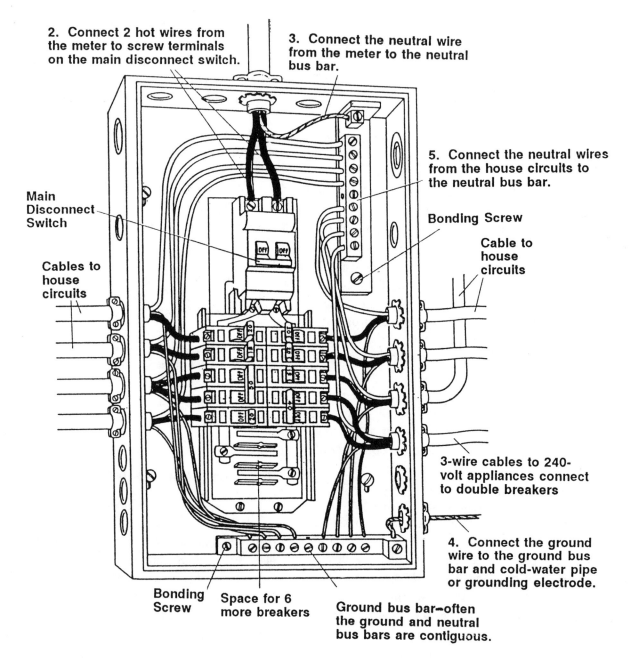

1. **Bring the cable from the meter into the service panel.**

2. **Connect 2 hot wires from the meter to screw terminals on the main disconnect switch.**

3. **Connect the neutral wire from the meter to the neutral bus bar.**

5. **Connect the neutral wires from the house circuits to the neutral bus bar.**

Bonding Screw

Cable to house circuits

Main Disconnect Switch

Cables to house circuits

3-wire cables to 240-volt appliances connect to double breakers

4. **Connect the ground wire to the ground bus bar and cold-water pipe or grounding electrode.**

Bonding Screw

Space for 6 more breakers

Ground bus bar—often the ground and neutral bus bars are contiguous.

■ **FIGURE 7.24**

Service entrance, armored cable.

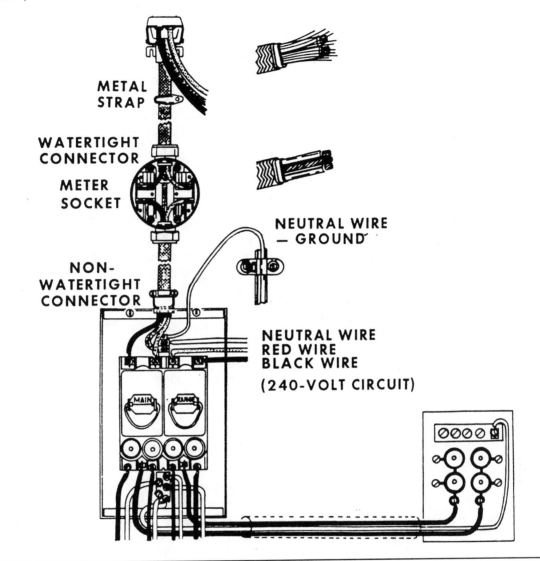

METAL STRAP

WATERTIGHT CONNECTOR

METER SOCKET

NON-WATERTIGHT CONNECTOR

NEUTRAL WIRE — GROUND

NEUTRAL WIRE
RED WIRE
BLACK WIRE
(240-VOLT CIRCUIT)

the transformer does not leak. Any motors on the property are checked for proper operation. The inspector ensures that the equipment they control operates as intended.

Commercial power lines are usually contained in conduit. Conduit protects the conductors from damage and protects the environment from fire by containing any electrical sparks or arcing. There are several types of conduit in use. Some are rigid and made of metal, others are metal and flexible, while still others are made of plastic. Each type has its own use and advantages.

All power stations generate three-phase electric power. Even though most homes use single-phase power, commercial establishments require three-phase power. They need it for several reasons. Large horsepower motors use only three-phase power. Commercial and industrial locations have many 240V and 120V circuits. Three-phase power provides these circuits.

■ CONDUIT

Conduit is a raceway containing electrical conductors that protects the conductors from external damage. Conduit confines any arcing and sparks inside the conduit to protect the building and anything nearby from fire damage. There are several types of conduit, all of which have advantages and uses. Most commercial

Minimum dimensions for electrical panel.

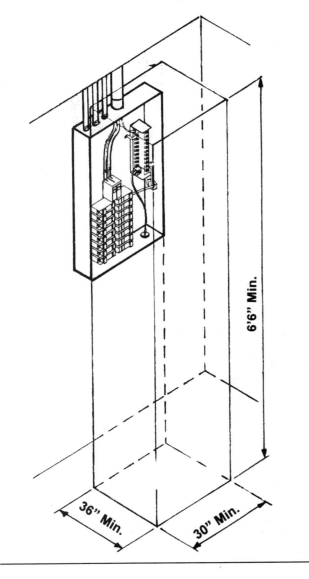

6'6" Min.

36" Min.

30" Min.

establishments are required to have electrical conductors in conduit for fire safety reasons.

Metal Conduit

There are several types of metal conduit, all offering excellent protection to the conductors. Some types of metal conduit are for inside use only, while others may be used outside the building. Some conduit may be used in damp or hazardous environments.

Junction boxes and fittings must be of the same material as the conduit to prevent electrolysis. Conduit must be supported at proper intervals.

Rigid Metal Conduit

Galvanized steel or aluminum conduit is considered rigid metal conduit. It provides the best protection to conductors and may be used inside or outside the building, either exposed or concealed, and in hazardous areas. Because any arcing and sparks are contained, it offers fire protection. And because it is solid metal, it has the best strength and, if installed properly, makes an excellent equipment ground.

The inspector checks that rigid metal conduit is supported every 10' and within 3' of any box or fitting. He or she also looks for proper connections using proper fittings. Any rust or corrosion should be called out.

Intermediate Metal Conduit

This is also a metal conduit, but it has a thinner wall and is about 25 percent lighter than rigid metal conduit. It may be installed in any atmospheric condition, including hazardous areas. Because it is a strong conduit, it can withstand severe mechanical abuse.

Electrical Metallic Tubing

This is a metallic conduit that is 40 percent lighter than rigid metal conduit. It uses set screw and compression couplings. Because it is made lighter and has a thinner wall, it cannot withstand severe mechanical abuse.

Flexible Metal Conduit

Flexible metal conduit is a jointed metal conduit, also known as *greenfield*. It may be used in applications where other metal conduit is used, but not in wet areas, hazardous areas, hoistways, or battery rooms. Greenfield is used as fixture whips in 4' to 6' lengths.

In some applications, it is also used as grounding material. However, the flex cannot exceed 6' and the conductors must be protected by a fuse or circuit breaker of 20 amps or less. Flex conduit requires support every 4½' and within 12" of a fitting.

Liquidtight Flexible Conduit

This is a weatherproof flexible conduit. It is sometimes known as *sealtight*, and it comes with a plastic outer jacket. The outer jacket is waterproof, greaseproof, and oilproof and withstands chemicals. This type of conduit is suitable for fixed wiring applications. It cannot be used as a separate grounding conductor when used in fixed wiring. Like other flexible conduit, it must be supported every 4½' and within 1' of a fixture or fitting.

■ FIGURE 7.26

Total bends (offsets) in a raceway system are limited to a total of 360° between enclosures, outlets, or pull boxes.

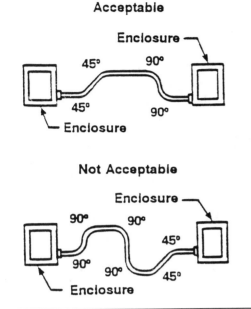

Nonmetallic Conduit

Nonmetallic conduit is usually plastic conduit. It is lightweight, it can be cut with a hacksaw, and joints or fittings are glued together. It cannot be used for a grounding conductor.

Rigid Nonmetallic Conduit

There are two basic types of rigid nonmetallic conduit and both are usually polyvinyl chloride (PVC). One is schedule 40 PVC and the other is schedule 80 PVC.

Schedule 40 PVC

Schedule 40 PVC is plastic PVC. As such, it is waterproof and does not corrode. Thin-wall PVC is not as strong as metal conduit; therefore, it must be protected from damage. Heavy-wall PVC may be used for the same applications as rigid metal conduit.

Schedule 80 PVC

Schedule 80 PVC is plastic PVC and is much stronger than schedule 40 PVC. It may be used in locations where schedule 40 cannot be used.

The inspector must look for any breaks in the plastic conduit or for lack of proper support. All plastic conduit must have tight, solvent, welded joints. There must be a separate grounding conductor inside plastic conduit.

Conduit Design and Sizing

Conduit size must be large enough so the allowable fill area the conductors occupy does not exceed that prescribed by the National Electric Code. This is usually 40 percent for like-sized conductors. If conductors are of different sizes, National Electric Code requirements vary.

There should be a total of no more than 360° of bends in a run of conduit. If there are more than 360° of bends, damage may occur to the conductor insulation when the installer pulls the conductors through the conduit run. (See Figure 7.26.)

■ REVIEW QUESTIONS*

1. In an electrical circuit, voltage forces electricity to flow to all appliances.

   A. True
   B. False

2. Amperage is a flow of electrons required to produce operation of an electrical appliance.

   A. True
   B. False

3. A complete electrical circuit must have

   A. voltage.
   B. load.
   C. path.
   D. All of the above

4. The service entrance is where electric power lines enter the house.

   A. True
   B. False

* Answers to all of the chapter review questions are located in Appendix C at the back of this book.

5. Electrical wires must clear all flat roofs by how many feet and driveways by how many feet?

   A. 6; 15
   B. 8; 12
   C. 10; 12

6. Two-wire service will be only _____ service.

   A. 115V
   B. 230V
   C. 440V

7. The electric service panel delivers power only to 240V appliances.

   A. True
   B. False

8. Name two types of electrical circuit protectors designed to interrupt electricity in the case of a short circuit.

   _____

   _____

9. Name two acceptable grounding sources for the electrical panel.

   _____

   _____

10. What is the color of the insulation around a hot wire with voltage?_____

11. What is the color of the insulation around a neutral wire?_____

12. Copper is a better conductor of electricity than aluminum.

    A. True
    B. False

13. What is the amperage of 14-ga copper wire?

    A. 15
    B. 18
    C. 20
    D. 30

14. What is the amperage of 12-ga aluminum wire?

    A. 15
    B. 20
    C. 25
    D. 30

15. GFCI-protected receptacles are found in

    A. bathrooms.
    B. swimming pool areas.
    C. outside receptacles.
    D. All of the above
    E. Only A and B

16. Voltage is the measure of force at which electricity is delivered.

    A. True
    B. False

17. Electricity is sold in quantities of

    A. volts.
    B. amperage.
    C. kilowatt hours.

18. Three-prong outlets do not require grounding

    A. True
    B. False

19. The inspector should remove the electrical panel cover to observe

    A. proper wire size per circuit breaker.
    B. condition of insulation on the conductor.
    C. type of wire.
    D. All of the above

20. If the house has only two wires that run from the power pole, the service is limited to

    A. 230 volts.
    B. 115 volts.
    C. 100 amps.

■ INSPECTION CHECKLIST: ELECTRIC

Service Entrance

Yes No

☐ ☐ Is the clearance over roofs and driveways proper?

☐ ☐ Is the clearance around the service head adequate?

☐ ☐ Is the weatherhead loose?

☐ ☐ Does the weatherhead turn down?

☐ ☐ Is there a drip loop?

☐ ☐ Is the service entrance cable damaged?

☐ ☐ Are any temporary wire connections at the weatherhead?

☐ ☐ Are all visible conduit connections sealed tightly?

☐ ☐ Does the size of the service entrance match or exceed the size of the main circuit breaker disconnect at the service panel (if equipped)?

☐ ☐ Does a branch circuit feed off the meter base?

☐ ☐ Is the service entrance adequately sized?

Minimum capacity:

☐ ☐ 1. 100-amp, three-wire service—This type of service is sufficient in a one-family house or dwelling unit to provide safe and adequate electric supply for the lighting, refrigerator, iron, 8,000-watt cooking range, plus other appliances requiring a total of up to 10,000 watts.

☐ ☐ 2. 60-amp, three-wire service—This system is safely capable of supplying current only for lighting and portable appliances such as a cooking range and regular dryer (4,500 watts) or an electric hot water heater (2,500 watts); it cannot handle additional major appliances.

☐ ☐ 3. 30-amp, two-wire service—This system can safely handle only a limited amount of lighting, a few minor appliances, and no major appliances. Therefore, this size service is substandard in terms of modern household needs for electricity. Furthermore, it constitutes a fire hazard and a threat to the safety of the home and the occupants.

SERVICE PANEL

Yes No

☐ ☐ Check for proper screws. No Phillip heads.

☐ ☐ Using the back of your hand, is the service panel cabinet hot to the touch?

☐ ☐ Is the panel loose in the wall?

☐ ☐ Is the panel cover in place?

☐ ☐ Before removing the cover, check to see:

☐ ☐ Is there an odor of burnt plastic?

☐ ☐ Are the circuit breakers hot to the touch?

☐ ☐ Is access restricted or blocked?

Carefully remove the cover. If breakers start falling out or there is evidence of sparking, put the cover plate back on and recommend an electrician. With the cover removed, identify the type of wire used:

☐ ☐ Copper

☐ ☐ Aluminum

☐ ☐ Combination

If it is safe to proceed, make the following checks:

☐ ☐ Is there evidence of arcing at the power bus bars?

☐ ☐ Antioxidants on all exposed aluminum wiring connections?

☐ ☐ Are the service entrance conductors burned or damaged?

☐ ☐ Are the service entrance conductors loose at the main lugs? Be very careful when putting your hand inside a hot panel.

☐ ☐ Is there double wiring off the main lugs to feed a branch circuit? (Branch circuit is not protected.)

☐ ☐ Can all power be shut off with six throws of the hand (6 breakers) at a centralized location?

☐ ☐ Is the neutral wire from the meter connected to the neutral bus bar?

☐ ☐ Is the box bonded into the ground bus bar and the neutral bus bar at the main service panel?

☐ ☐ If there is a subpanel, are the ground bus bar and neutral bus bars isolated?

☐ ☐ Is the grounding electrode properly connected?

☐ ☐ Are any neutral wires loose or not connected?

Yes No

☐ ☐ Are any neutral wires burned, or oxidized (aluminum)?

☐ ☐ On grounded systems, are all ground wires connected?

☐ ☐ Is there double wiring at circuit breakers or fuse connections?

☐ ☐ Is the circuit protector correctly sized for the wire?

☐ ☐ On 220V circuits or split-circuit wiring, is a double breaker used or are two single breakers installed so that a tie breaks both legs together?

☐ ☐ Is there evidence that the ground wire has been used for a neutral on split-circuit wiring?

☐ ☐ Are any hot wires nicked, burned or damaged?

On GFCI-type circuit breakers, check the test function. Each outlet reviewed to be GFCI should also be checked with a tester and tripped.

☐ ☐ Does the breaker trip? Be sure to reset the breaker.

RECEPTACLE

Yes No

☐ ☐ Are any receptacles missing face plates?

☐ ☐ Are any receptacles painted over?

☐ ☐ Are any receptacles loose in the wall?

☐ ☐ Is there any evidence of arcing?

☐ ☐ Are outside receptacles missing weatherproof covers?

☐ ☐ Is aluminum wiring used in the home? If so, remove the face plate from at least one receptacle in every room and make the following checks:

☐ ☐ Are there any burned wires?

☐ ☐ Are any connections loose?

☐ ☐ Does aluminum wiring stab to the back of the receptacle?

☐ ☐ Is aluminum wiring pigtailed to copper?

☐ ☐ Is aluminum wire secured correctly to the receptacle connection?

☐ ☐ Is aluminum wire oxidized at receptacle connection?

Note: Switches and receptacles made before 1971 and rated at 15 or 20 amps were not marked if they were intended for copper wire only. If they were to be used for copper or aluminum, they were marked "CU-AL." After 1971, the National Electric Code forbade the use of aluminum wire with these devices. The new devices for use with aluminum were then stamped "CO/ALR." Consider the age of the house and check receptacle identification to see whether it is approved for aluminum wiring.

Yes No

☐ ☐ Are any receptacles the 120V grounded type? If so, use a circuit analyzer and check for:

☐ ☐ Open hot (dead plug)

☐ ☐ Open neutral

☐ ☐ Open ground

☐ ☐ Hot/neutral reversed (reverse polarity)

☐ ☐ Hot/ground reversed

☐ ☐ Poor ground (feedback)

Note: If the check at the service panel shows that an older house is not grounded, remove several face plates and check the ground connection.

☐ ☐ Does the neutral wire wrap around the ground screw?

☐ ☐ Does a ground wire go to a water pipe?

☐ ☐ Are any receptacles the 120V ungrounded type? If so, use a circuit tester and check for:

☐ ☐ Open hot (dead plug)

☐ ☐ Hot/neutral reversed (reverse polarity)

Note: If a receptacle is dead, make sure it is not controlled by a wall switch.

On GFCI type receptacles, check the "test" function.

☐ ☐ Does the receptacle trip? Be sure to reset the receptacle.

Note: Consider the age of the house and local code requirements (past and present); then determine whether receptacles are GFCI protected as required. Regardless, identify all swimming pool lights and receptacles at the pool that are not GFCI protected.

☐ ☐ Are there any exposed 220V receptacles? If so, check them with the circuit tester:

☐ ☐ Is each hot terminal powered?

SWITCHES AND LIGHT FIXTURES

Yes No

- ☐ ☐ Are any switches missing face plates?
- ☐ ☐ Are any switches loose in the wall?
- ☐ ☐ Are any switches warm or hot to touch?
- ☐ ☐ Do outside switches have weatherproof covers?
- ☐ ☐ Flip each switch on. If the receptacle or light does not come on, make the following checks:
- ☐ ☐ Are outside lights controlled by a cad cell?
- ☐ ☐ Are bulbs burned out at the fixture or is the fixture bad?
- ☐ ☐ Does the two-way switch work?
- ☐ ☐ Is the switch a dummy?
- ☐ ☐ Are bulbs missing?
- ☐ ☐ Are any fixture covers missing?
- ☐ ☐ Are all fixtures securely fastened?
- ☐ ☐ Does any fixture or ceiling fan sag at the ceiling? Does ceiling fan operate at all speeds?
- ☐ ☐ Does ceiling fan reverse switch operate?
- ☐ ☐ Are any wiring connections exposed at the fixture?
- ☐ ☐ Does the doorbell operate?
- ☐ ☐ Do fluorescent lights buzz or flicker?
- ☐ ☐ Is the house equipped with low voltage lights? If so, make the following checks:
- ☐ ☐ Do the lights operate? If not check the following:
- ☐ ☐ Is the unit plugged in?
- ☐ ☐ Is the timer in the manual position?

Yes No

- ☐ ☐ Is the circuit protector tripped?
- ☐ ☐ Are any bulbs burned out?

ADDITIONAL ELECTRICAL

Yes No

- ☐ ☐ Is the grounding electrode securely fastened to a copper cold water line (if visible)?
- ☐ ☐ Is temporary wiring used (zip cord)?
- ☐ ☐ Do any electrical cords run under rugs?
- ☐ ☐ Do any electrical cords run through walls or doorways?
- ☐ ☐ Are there any octopus outlets?
- ☐ ☐ Are there any wire splices in the crawlspace, attic, garage, or outside that are not in the junction box?
- ☐ ☐ Are junction boxes covered?
- ☐ ☐ Is there evidence that metal junction boxes are not grounded?
- ☐ ☐ Are wires lying on the ground under the house?

Yes No

- ☐ ☐ Are any wires touching or lying on metal (water pipe, vent work, etc.)?
- ☐ ☐ Is single-strand wire used in the attic or crawlspace?
- ☐ ☐ Are any wires bare or frayed?
- ☐ ☐ Are any wires too low between the house and the garage?
- ☐ ☐ On swimming pool applications, are circulating pumps bonded properly?

■ REPORTING GUIDELINES

Inspection reporting guidelines for electrical systems incorporating the above checklist.

Service entrance and panels. The inspector shall

- inspect service entrance cables and report as in need of repair deficiencies in the integrity of insulation, drip loop, separation of conductors at weatherheads, and clearances;
- report as in need of repair a drop, weatherhead, or mast that is not securely fastened;
- report as in need of repair the lack of a grounding electrode conductor in the service where visible, or the lack of secure connection to the grounding electrode or grounding system;

■ REPORTING GUIDELINES *(Continued)*

- report as in need of repair accessible main or subpanels that are not secured to the structure or appropriate for their location (weather-tight if exposed to weather, appropriate clearances and accessibility), do not have inside covers (dead fronts) in place, do not have conductors protected from the edges of metal panel boxes, do not have trip ties installed on labeled 240-volt circuits, do not have proper fasteners, or do not have knockouts filled;

- inspect and report as in need of repair deficiencies in the type and condition of the wiring in the panels, in the compatibility of overcurrent protectors for the size of conductor being used, and in sizing of listed equipment of overcurrent protection and conductors, when power requirements for listed equipment are readily available and breakers are labeled;

- report as in need of repair a panel that is installed in a hazardous location, such as a clothes closet, bathroom, or kitchen;

- report as in need of repair the absence of appropriate connections, such as copper/aluminum approved devices, pigtailed connections, or crimp connections, and the absence of antioxidants on aluminum conductor terminations; and

- report as in need of repair the lack of main disconnect(s).

Specific limitations for service entrance and panels. The inspector is not required to do the following:

- Determine service capacity amperage or voltage or the capacity of the electrical system relative to present or future use

- Determine the insurability of the property

- Conduct voltage drop calculations

- Determine the accuracy of breaker labeling

Branch circuits, connected devices and fixtures. The inspector shall

- report the type of branch circuit wiring

- inspect all accessible receptacles and report as in need of repair a receptacle in which

  - power is not present,

  - polarity is incorrect,

  - the unit is not grounded, if applicable,

  - there is evidence of arcing or excessive heat,

  - the unit is not secured to the wall,

  - the cover is not in place, or

  - ground fault circuit interrupter devices are not properly installed as set forth by the current edition of the National Electric Code, publication 70A of the National Fire Protection Association International Residential Code, or do not operate properly as shown by use of a separate testing device;

- operate all accessible wall and appliance switches and report as in need of repair a switch that:

  - does not operate or is damaged,

■ REPORTING GUIDELINES *(Continued)*

- displays evidence of arcing or excessive heat, or
- is not fastened securely with cover in place;

- inspect installed fixtures including lighting devices and ceiling fans;

- report as in need of repair an inoperable or missing fixture;

- report as in need of repair deficiencies in exposed wiring, wiring terminations, junctions and junction boxes, boxes without covers;

- report as in need of repair deficiencies or absences of conduit in appropriate locations or conduit that is not terminated securely;

- report as in need of repair appliances and electrical gutters that do not have proper bonding;

- report as in need of repair subpanels that are not properly bonded and grounded;

- report as in need of repair the lack of disconnects in appropriate locations;

- inspect (if branch circuit aluminum wiring is discovered in the main or subpanels) a random sampling of accessible receptacles and switches and report as in need of repair the absence of appropriate connections, such as copper/aluminum approved devices, pigtailed connections, or crimp connections;

- report as in need of repair the improper use of extension cords; and

- report as in need of repair the absence of or deficiencies in the installation and operation of smoke or fire detectors not connected to a central alarm system.

8 Heating and Ventilation

■ HEATING AND VENTILATION SYSTEMS

Heating and ventilation equipment covers a broad line of well-engineered heating and cooling equipment and accessories to provide ultimate comfort at maximum efficiency and economy.

Consumers demand more efficient heating and cooling units to lower operation costs, which lowers monthly utility bills. Utility companies want the public to purchase more efficient equipment because they benefit by not requiring additional power plants. As an incentive, utility companies issue rebates to their customers for installing high-efficiency units. Manufacturers of heating, ventilating, and air-conditioning (HVAC) equipment are aware of this problem and compete to produce high-efficiency equipment. The U.S. government also has a role in this scenario. Because low-efficiency equipment uses more energy and increases our reliance on foreign energy sources, the Department of Energy dictated minimum energy efficiencies beginning January in 1992. After this date, no equipment could be produced with season energy efficiency ratio (SEER) and EER cooling efficiencies of less than 10.0 and annual fuel utilization efficiency (AFUE) gas heating efficiencies of less than 80.0 percent. The government edict creates high-efficiency heating and cooling equipment standards.

Consumers demand more reliable heating and cooling units for two reasons. First, installation costs have risen. Considering the escalated cost, consumers need their equipment to last. Manufacturers build quality into their products, which manifests itself in longer warranties. Furnace heat exchanger warranties used to be guaranteed for ten years. Today, some warranties on high-efficiency gas furnace heat exchangers are for the lifetime of the furnace buyer. The standard

warranty on air-conditioning compressors used to be five years. It has now increased to ten years and may include the condensing coil.

The second reason for improved reliability is competition with foreign manufacturers. To compete for the U.S. consumer, domestic products are now more reliable. Manufacturers have made many technological advances. They use microprocessors extensively, enabling them to use variable-speed motors.

Heating systems may be nonducted or ducted. Nonducted systems center mainly on heating but also on wall unit air conditioners. Heated air in a nonducted system is transmitted naturally from a heat source located in each room. As heat is emitted from the source, hot air rises and is replaced with cooler air in the lower part of the room. This pattern of air movement caused by uneven temperatures is called *convection*. With nonducted systems, a separate cooling system or window units must be installed.

Ducted systems are centrally located to treat air for temperature, humidity, and cleanliness. Provisions for outdoor fresh air and quiet operation are incorporated into the system. Treated air is moved by a blower and is forced through a network of ducts to strategic points throughout the house. (See Figure 8.1.)

There are six components or properties composing the comfort system: temperature control, filtration, noise reduction, outside air, humidity control, and air circulation.

1. Temperature control is the most important element in the system. The controlled temperature of a conditioned space creates a comfortable environment. The human body is aware of temperature variations of 1½°F (degrees Fahrenheit). An individual can endure fluctuating temperature but would not be comfortable. Controlled temperature does not indicate that every room in the

■ **FIGURE 8.1**

A Typical furnace may be gas, oil, or electric.

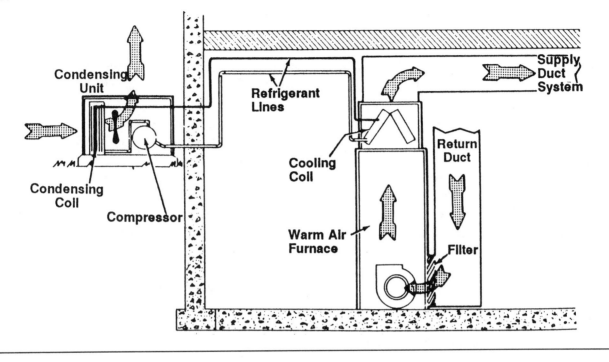

house must be the same temperature. For example, bedroom temperatures vary from those in other rooms such as the living room or kitchen. However, the controlled temperature of each room should remain constant throughout the heating and cooling seasons. Air circulation is the controlled, gentle movement of air throughout the house during both the heating and the cooling seasons.

2. Filtration must be provided to filter the air in the conditioned space to remove lint, dust, dirt, and other organic materials.

3. Noise reduction. Noises from a heating and cooling system are of two types: air and mechanical noises. Air noise is directly related to air velocity. As air moves faster, more noise can be produced from components. Less noise is produced as the air moves slower. The installation is important to eliminate noise-producing air leaks at joints in the duct system. Mechanical noises within the heating and cooling system are caused by metal components. Metal components include the mechanical components that produce and distribute the warm and cool air, the control components, and the duct.

4. Outside air. With well-constructed homes, it is essential that provisions be made to introduce fresh outdoor air into the home to prevent staleness and stuffiness and to provide necessary combustion air.

5. Humidity control. The moisture content of the air must be controlled during the heating and cooling seasons. During winter months, cold outdoor air introduced into the system lowers the moisture content of the air. The moisture content of the air must be increased. With a higher humidity level, the thermostat may be set at a lower temperature while maintaining comfort.

6. Air circulation. Humidity (moisture) can be maintained at a desirable level in a conditioned space only when air is in motion.

Heat Transfer

Heat is a form of energy and, as such, cannot be created or destroyed. It can be moved or transported from one place to another through varied mediums. To understand how a heating and cooling system operates, it is necessary to understand the forms of heat transfer. Just as water always flows downhill, from a high level to a low level, heat always flows in one direction, from a high temperature to a low temperature. There are three main forms of heat transfer: conduction, radiation, and convection.

Conduction

Conduction is the transfer of heat from particle to particle. For example, if a rod is heated over an open flame, heat travels by conduction from the hot to the cooler end. Conduction heat transfer also occurs between different substances in contact with one another. An example is house construction. There are combinations of wood, insulation, plaster, brick, and concrete. These different materials often touch each other. If the temperature inside is hotter than that outside, conduction heat will pass outward through these materials. If the outdoor temperature is hotter than indoors, heat will flow into the house.

Radiation

Radiation is the transfer of heat through space. As light travels through space, radiant heat passes through air without warming it. While the ambient temperature is 80°F, the sun's rays can heat a roof to 160°F. All objects radiate heat. Depending on time and surface type, higher temperatures increase the quantity of radiant heat. At the same temperature, a rough, dark surface will radiate more heat than a smooth, light-colored surface.

Convection

Convection is the transfer of heat with the movement of fluid. The definition of fluid is any substance (liquid or gas) that can flow. Air is a mixture of several gases. As air flows or moves, it carries heat from one place to another.

In a gas furnace, heat energy is released by the combustion process inside the heat exchanger. The heat exchanger is designed so the air passes over its entire surface, transferring a large amount of heat energy to the air. The air carries the heat energy to the conditioned space, where it mixes with the cooler room air. In a forced warm air system, air is the fluid used to move heat from the heat exchanger to the room to be heated. A forced warm air system is also considered a direct fired system.

Heating unit applications can be called *up-flow, down-flow* or *horizontal-flow.* The flow is the direction in which the blower forces the air from the unit. Air flow

direction relies on heating unit placement and location of the duct. A central location in the structure is selected for unit placement. This placement minimizes long spans of duct. For example, a home with a basement uses an up-flow heating unit. The duct is installed above the furnace near the floor joists. In homes without basements, heating units may be installed in a utility room/closet, a crawlspace, or an attic with duct installed in the attic or crawlspace.

If the home is built on a concrete slab, the heating unit is normally in a utility closet or in the attic. A utility closet installation in colder climates is usually down-flow. The duct is embedded in the concrete and warms the floor during the heating season. In warmer climates, the heating unit is often up-flow, with the duct above the ceiling. This application accommodates cooling (cool air falls, promoting air circulation) and requires less material and labor cost for installation. Attic applications normally employ horizontal-flow units, with the duct in the attic.

Cooling

The cooling section consists of an outdoor unit that contains a condensing coil, a compressor, and other essential components. Refrigerant lines connect the outdoor unit with the indoor evaporator coil that is located in the supply plenum of the furnace. The cooling unit pumps cool refrigerant through the evaporator coil, which removes heat from the air. This type of indoor/outdoor arrangement is called a *split system.*

Packaged cooling systems and packaged combination heating/cooling systems are viable options for residential installations. In both systems, all components are contained in a single outdoor unit, either on a slab at grade level or on a rooftop. Both types of packaged units are self-contained systems with their own blower and duct. Air flow is horizontal for a slab unit and down-flow for a rooftop unit.

Another type of combination heating/cooling unit is a heat pump. Heat pumps are popular for energy efficiency reasons. The heat pump is basically a cooling system with the capacity to reverse its system operation to produce heat. Similar to split-system cooling, heat pumps can be incorporated into the home heating system. The heat pump transfers heat from outdoors to indoors. The furnace is the auxiliary heat source. Heat pumps are also made in packaged outdoor units.

■ **FIGURE 8.2**

Warm air perimeter radial system for crawlspace.

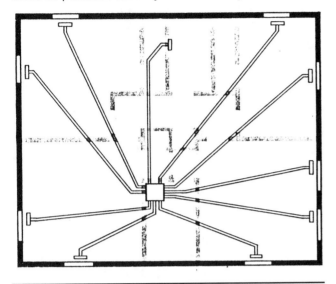

Duct

A duct is a network of tubes that carries treated supply air to the conditioned space and return air back to a blower for recirculation. Air movement in the duct works on the principle of air pressure difference; air moves from higher to lower pressure areas. (See Figure 8.2.)

Because air pressures in the duct are relatively low, the duct can be made from various materials. Galvanized sheet steel is the most common material. Aluminum, plastic, fiber board and fiberglass also are used. Duct is either round or rectangular in shape and rigid or flexible in configuration. Insulating material is applied to the duct (either inside or outside) to reduce heat transfer and sound. This is important on ducts running through attics or crawlspaces.

When the ducts provide both heated air and cooled air, it is necessary to clean and/or change the filter regularly. In the cooling season, when the air conditioner is operating, the blower may be blowing 50°F to 60°F air through a duct that is in a 100°F-plus space. In such conditions condensate forms on the inside of the ducts. Dust particles that filter in through cracks in splices and through the filter mix with the condensate. This can cause mold and mildew to form. This mold and mildew will appear on the supply grill when it is severe. One of the signs of this condition is a dirty filter. Also when checking the air-conditioned air across the evaporator

coil and there is a high return temperature and a low supply air temperature, this is an indication not moving enough air-conditioned air. Check a grill close by; it might have condensate on it. This could be a costly repair because some ducts might have to be replaced. If it isn't visible on the grills or on the other checkpoints, it is not in the scope of a visual inspection.

Blowers

The blower consists of a wheel with scoops called *scrolls* and a motor to drive the wheel. The blower is designed to move the treated air across the heat exchanger and throughout the house. There are two types of blowers: a belt drive and a direct drive.

Belt Drive Blower

In a belt drive blower, a belt runs from a pulley mounted on the motor to a pulley mounted on the blower wheel. All moving parts are anchored on a rigid U-frame, which is fastened by resilient mountings to the furnace. The design of this frame ensures easy adjustment and alignment of pulleys and belt for optimum performance.

Depending on the motor pulley adjustment, varying amounts of air are moved by a belt drive blower. The pulley can be enlarged by screwing one side inward toward the other side, which causes the blower wheel to rotate faster. The pulley's effective circumference may be reduced by screwing one side outward from the other side to reduce blower wheel speed. (See Figure 8.3.)

Direct Drive Blower

The direct drive blower motor is mounted inside the blower and is directly linked to the blower wheel. Air volume changes are electrically modified by varying the speed of the motor, using a speed controller or speed tap. (See Figure 8.4.)

Two to five speeds can be obtained by wiring the hot wire to the desired speed tap lead and the neutral wire to the common motor lead. The unused hot wire leads must be taped separately to prevent contact with an electrical ground. The rotating motor produces a back voltage (emf) of approximately 200 VAC (voltage alternating current) through electromagnetic induction. Extreme caution should be exercised when handling leads with 200 VAC electrical potential. If not taped, the leads could cause arcing to ground, shorts or serious electrical shocks.

■ **FIGURE 8.3**

Volume of air moved depends on motor pulley adjustment.

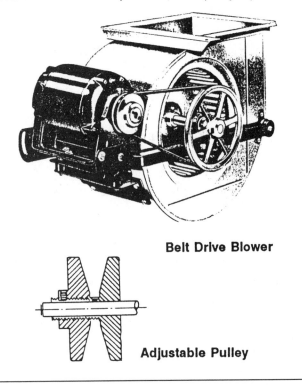

Belt Drive Blower

Adjustable Pulley

■ **FIGURE 8.4**

A direct drive blower electronically adjusts air volume changes.

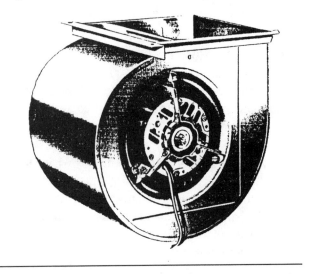

Filters

A filter is the device in a forced-air heating or cooling system that mechanically screens out dust, dirt,

lint and other impurities from the system's airstream. The filter is located upstream from the blower in the return air side of the system. Air contaminants come in different sizes. Some air contaminants are large enough to see with the naked eye, while others are not visible. The unit of measure for air contaminants is the micron. A micron is an extremely small unit of measurement. For example, 1 inch (″) equals 25,400 microns. The eye of a needle is approximately 787 microns.

Two types of filtering systems or devices are available, the mechanical filter and the electronic filter. Many differences exist between these two filter types.

Mechanical Filters

The mechanical filter is a fiberglass medium that commonly acts as the screen; it cleans the air before the air is recirculated through the system by the blower. A mechanical filter removes particles larger than 50 microns. It effectively removes larger particles of dust and lint to protect the heating and cooling equipment. However, it cannot remove smaller particles of pollen, spores, and bacteria.

A dirty filter reduces the system's airflow, which reduces operating efficiency of the heating and cooling system. There are two types of mechanical filters: slab and hammock. Most slab filters are disposable and are square or rectangular fiberglass screens with a cardboard frame. Although there are many different sizes, the proper size must be used and installed to filter the system's airflow. When the filter becomes dirty, it should be replaced with a new one. The nondisposable slab filter is a polyurethane medium encased in a metal frame. When this filter is dirty, the medium is washed and reused. (See Figure 8.5.)

The hammock filter is mounted on a wire frame and allows two to three times more filter area than the slab. The frame slides in and out of the blower compartment on guide rails. Hammock filters are disposable; when the filter becomes dirty, it is removed and the new medium must be sized for the wire frame. The medium is attached to the wire frame and installed in the blower compartment. A dirty filter causes several problems with the heating or cooling system. Problems include dirty coils, ductwork restrictions, restricted air flow and heat exchanger hot spots or burnout. (See Figure 8.6.)

Electronic Air Filters

Electronic air filters remove particles larger than 0.1 micron. They may help relieve allergies by removing dust, dirt, lint, pollen, and fungus spores. They

Slab-type filter.

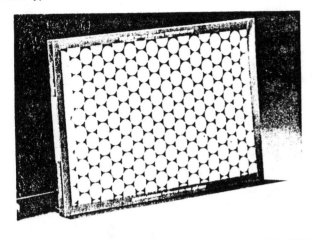

also effectively remove bacteria, smoke, and odors associated with organic materials. They cannot remove odors caused by vapors, such as tobacco smoke, fuel oil fumes, etc.

The electronic air cleaner consists of four major sections: the prefilter, the charging section, the collecting section, and the power pack, also called the *voltage supply*. Its method of operation begins with the prefilter screening the larger particles before they enter the electrostatic field. The electrostatic field is constructed of fine wire mesh, expanded aluminum or a foam medium

■ FIGURE 8.6

Filter medium is mounted on wire frame.

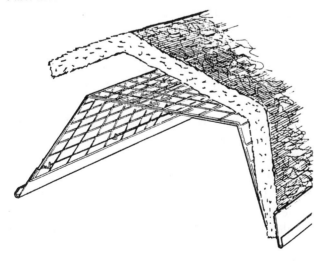

that serves the same purpose as the mechanical filter in the blower compartment. (See Figure 8.7.)

The charging section, sometimes called the *cell*, consists of a band of wire filaments (ionizing wires). Supplied with high direct current (DC) voltage from the power pack, the ionizer wires create an electrostatic field. When smoke, dust, dirt, and smaller airborne particles pass through this field as they enter the cell, they are positively or negatively charged. The collector cell contains alternating negatively and positively charged plates that capture the contaminant particles of the opposite charge.

The power pack consists of a step-up transformer and a rectifier circuit. The step-up transformer provides the necessary charge in the ionizer and collector sections by increasing the incoming 120-volt (V) alternating current (AC) to 3,000V to 4,500V DC at the collector. The cells and the rectifier circuit (also called a *voltage doubler*) boost the 3,000V to 4,500V DC to approximately 6,000V to 9,000V DC at the charging cells. The power pack connected to the bus bar is the surge resistor. Its function is to protect the power pack against a high electrical surge, which occurs if there is a short in the high-voltage section. The surge resistor absorbs any sudden surges, protecting the power pack components from damage.

When properly installed, the electronic air cleaner is electrically and/or mechanically interlocked with the furnace or cooling system blower circuit. The electronic air cleaner should operate only when the furnace blower is energized. To test the power pack, most electronic air cleaners have a test button on the front by the on-off switch. In performing this test, the test button should be pushed in, causing a short. This shorts out the power pack, causing the capacitors to discharge. A snapping noise will indicate that the power pack is operating normally.

The location of a humidifier is very important when used in conjunction with an electronic air cleaner. The humidifier must be installed downstream of the electronic air cleaner. The reason is that the air leaving the humidifier has enough moisture to cause an electrical high-voltage short in a downstream electronic air cleaner. The electronic air cleaner must be cleaned at least twice a year, in the spring and fall.

A properly operating electronic air cleaner produces a slight odor. A person who has never had this type of filter might be concerned, but the slight odor is normal. The electronic air cleaner removes smoke and odor associated with organisms (pollen, etc.), but normally it will not remove vapor odors (tobacco smoke,

■ **FIGURE 8.7**

Components and operation of an electronic air filter.

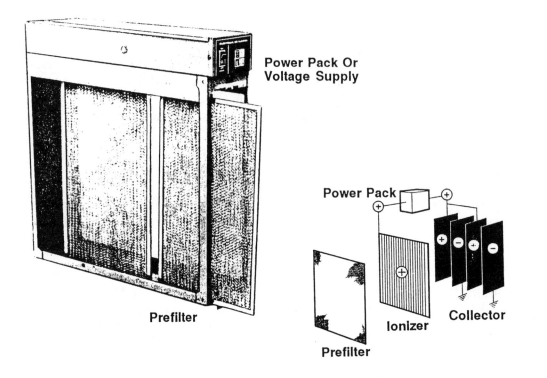

etc.). Some activated carbon filters filter these odors; however, most carbon filters are combustible. Care must be taken to install them upstream of the electronic air cleaner to ensure that the filter is not exposed to the high voltage of the air cleaner.

Filter Inspection

Minimum inspection steps are recommended. A heating and cooling system requires either a mechanical filter or an electronic air cleaner. When inspecting the electronic air cleaner, it is important that the cover be removed. (On some air cleaners, the power pack is a part of the cover; on others, the power pack is located inside the front cover.) After the cover and power pack have been removed, the prefilter, collecting cell, and charging cell should be in full view. The inspector must observe filters and the bottom of the case for debris. The air cleaner should be reassembled and the thermostat adjusted to energize the blower and power the air cleaner. Inspectors must be certain it operates. Usually, when the blower is operating, it is not necessary to push the test button because dust and dirt activate the col-

lecting and charging cells. This, in turn, activates the snapping noise and may cause emission of a slight odor.

If the electronic air cleaner is operating and there is television or radio interference, there may be several reasons for this interference. Poor contact between the power door and the cell or between the cells may be one reason; another may be an improper ground or a loose electrical component. Other possible reasons include ionizer wires that may be loose, broken, or close to the ground plate; dirt lodged in the ionizer section; or dents in the collector plates.

If the electronic air cleaner makes a humming sound, several factors may be responsible. These include excessive dirt in the ionizer or collector sections in the cell, loose wires in the ionizer, and improper wire connections. If the electronic air cleaner is not cleaning, several possible causes of this include the cell, the power door, and problems outside the unit.

Other areas of the electronic air cleaner also require maintenance, but inspectors need not become involved with them. If any of the above are observed, it is recommended that a service company be called and noted on the inspection report.

Thermostat

The thermostat is a heat-sensitive switch and is the automatic control center for the heating and cooling operation. It automatically turns the heating and air-conditioning equipment on and off to maintain controlled temperatures within a dwelling. The thermostat allows the homeowner to control the temperature. Thermostats come in several different shapes. Many thermostats have thermometers incorporated in their covers, to be used as a heating or cooling guide.

Bimetal

The material used within the thermostat, called *bimetal,* reacts quickly to temperature change. Bimetal is made by bonding two dissimilar metals with different rates of expansion and contraction. The two metals are usually brass and invar, an alloy of iron and nickel. Bimetals work on the principle that two dissimilar metals expand and contract different amounts when heated or cooled. Thus, when heated or cooled, the bimetal warps. The amount of warpage depends on the materials used and the temperature of the bimetals. The metal that expands the most becomes the outside of the curve while the other metal becomes the inside. When the room temperature is 72°F, the bars of brass and invar are the same length. When heated, the brass and invar expand, increasing their lengths at different rates. Brass expands more than invar when heated and becomes the outside metal. When cooled, the bimetal will warp in the opposite direction because brass contracts more than invar. Different bimetal shapes are used in various other heat-sensitive, electrical switching devices such as limit overloads and relays. (See Figure 8.8.)

Temperature Indication

With one end of the bimetal anchored, the other end moves up and down as the temperature fluctuates. When a temperature scale is placed at the free end, this bimetal can be used to indicate room temperature. The thermostat uses the bimetal coil for both the temperature control setting and the room temperature indicator (thermometer). The bimetal coil used in the thermostat for controlling the heating and cooling system has the advantage of being compact and extremely sensitive to small changes in temperature.

Switching Mechanisms

If an electrical contact is placed on the end of a bimetal strip, the contact touches a fixed contact as the

■ FIGURE 8.8

Bimetals operate on the principle that two unlike metals expand and contract by different amounts when heated and cooled.

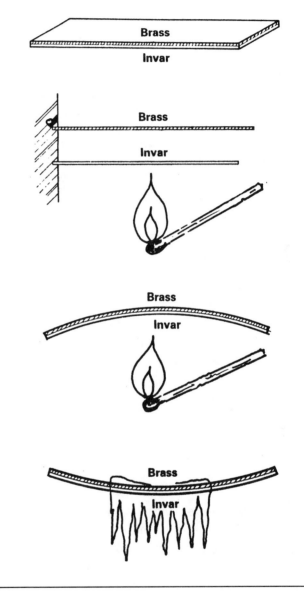

bimetal warps, and the bimetal becomes a switch. Bimetal has the ability to automatically activate electrical devices as the temperature changes. The contacts are exposed openly on the surface. Disadvantages with exposed contacts that affect conductivity and cause arcing include dust, oxidation, and corrosion.

Enclosed Contact Switch

The switch contacts are sealed in a glass tube to protect them from dust and moisture. The contacts open

■ **FIGURE 8.9**

Enclosed contact switch.

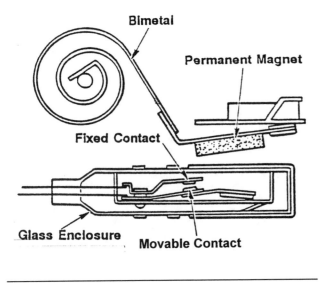

■ **FIGURE 8.10**

Mercury switch.

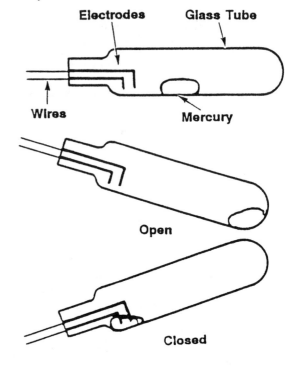

and close, depending on movement of a magnet attached to the movable end of the bimetal coil. The bimetal response controls the position of the magnet. The disadvantages of this kind of switch include the possibility of a cracked glass tube and damaged movable parts. (See Figure 8.9.)

Mercury Switches

Mercury switches are sealed glass tubes containing two electrodes and a small droplet of mercury, which is an excellent electrical conductor. When the tube is tipped in one direction, the mercury flows to the lower end. If the mercury is at the end opposite the electrodes, the switch is open and no current can flow. If the tube is tipped in the opposite direction, the mercury flows to the electrodes, makes contact with both, and causes current to flow, thus closing the switch and completing the electrical circuit. The glass tube is mounted on the outside of the bimetal coil, allowing the switch to turn on and off as temperature changes. (See Figure 8.10.)

The mercury thermostat switch must be level and secured to the wall. Mercury conductivity can be adversely affected if the glass tube becomes cracked or if the switch is wired into line voltage circuit. In either case, oxidation or mercury distortion occurs. When mercury is contaminated, the resulting film causes insulation on the electrodes, and the thermostat malfunctions.

Differential

The thermostat holds a room at a preset temperature. Vibration from a person walking can bounce the mercury bulb, causing the furnace to cycle on and off rapidly. To overcome this problem, the glass bulb inside the thermostat has a small hump in the center. The mercury must run over the hump when the bulb is tilted. It takes more tilt in either direction for the mercury to flow from one end to the other. The weight of the mercury works with the shape of the bulb to control the effects of vibration. The weight of the mercury also delays the movement of the bimetal. The bulb and weight of the mercury cause the thermostat to turn the furnace off. The built-in temperature difference is 2° F and is called the *differential*. If the temperature control is set for 68°F, the furnace will turn on when the temperature falls approximately 1°F lower than the set point.

Heat Anticipator

To compensate for thermostat override, a thin wire resistor called the *heat anticipator* is located near the bimetal coil. The amperage causes the anticipator to heat and warm the bimetal coil faster than it is warmed by

■ **FIGURE 8.11**

The heat anticipator is connected in series with the gas valve in a gas furnace, with the primary control in an oil furnace, and with the heat sequencer in an electric furnace.

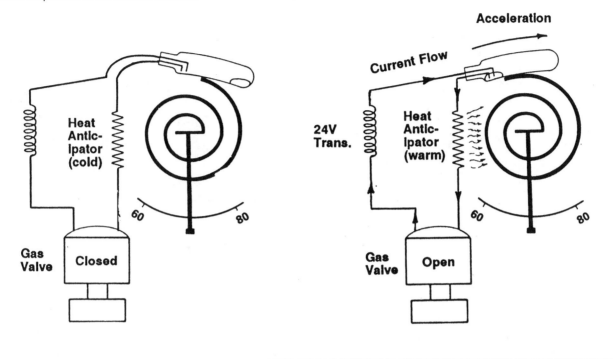

room temperature. When the anticipator is properly adjusted, room temperature is controlled within 1°F. Some heat anticipators have fixed resistance, while others have adjustable dials. The adjustable heat anticipator has a slide wire adjustment with a pointer scale marked in tenths of an ampere (amp). This sets the anticipator to coincide with the type of furnace used: gas, oil, or electric.

The anticipator is set according to the amperage draw of a control circuit. The resistance and amount of heat generated by the anticipator are needed for precise control of the furnace and room temperature. The heat anticipator adjustment determines the length of the heat cycle. As more heat is directed to the bimetal coil, a shorter heating cycle occurs. Longer heating cycles occur with less heat directed at the bimetal coil. (See Figure 8.11.)

Heating-Cooling Thermostat

For year-round comfort, heating and cooling system controls are combined in one thermostat. Two mercury bulbs are mounted on the same bimetal coil to avoid bulk and the expense of two separate coils. The heating and cooling anticipators are mounted near the

coil. Two mercury bulbs are combined into one by using a common electrode, a heating electrode and a cooling electrode. (See Figure 8.12.) When the bulb tilts in one direction, it closes the cooling contacts. The opposite direction closes the heating contacts.

■ **FIGURE 8.12**

Heating-cooling thermostat.

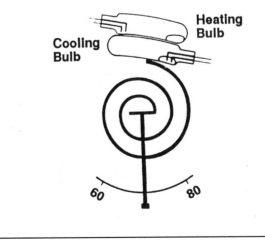

■ **FIGURE 8.13**

Thermostat, heating mode.

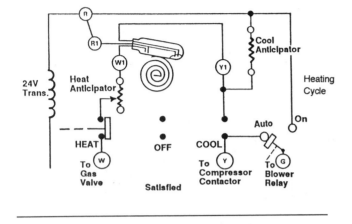

System Switch

The thermostat must provide a switch to prevent continuous cycling between heating and cooling. The switch throws the control to the heating circuit and disconnects the cooling. When the switch is in the off position, neither the cooling nor the heating circuit is energized. Thermostats are equipped with a fan switch. When the fan switch is placed in the *auto* position, the blower operates only when the thermostat calls for heating or cooling. When the thermostat is satisfied, the blower shuts off. If the switch is placed in the *on* position, the blower operates continuously. (See Figures 8.13 and 8.14.)

■ **FIGURE 8.14**

Thermostat, cooling mode.

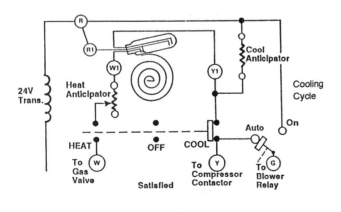

■ **FIGURE 8.15**

Two-stage thermostats use one bimetal coil.

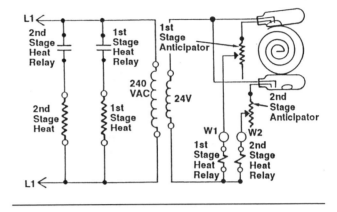

Two-Stage Thermostat

The two-stage thermostat has two bulbs mounted on the same bimetal coil. Mounted at a slightly different angle, one mercury switch closes before the other. One bulb energizes the first stage. On continued demand, the second bulb energizes the second stage. The first stage of heat satisfies the thermostat demand when heat delivered is greater than heat loss of the structure. As the outside temperature drops, heat loss in the structure increases and room temperature decreases to the differential between stages of heat—approximately 2°F. The second stage of heat is energized when the second mercury switch closes its contacts. The second stage of heat is de-energized once the demand is satisfied. Each thermostat bulb has its own anticipator that has its own settings. The amperage draw for each anticipator must be measured separately and set accordingly. (See Figure 8.15.)

The two-stage cooling thermostat is used with the two-speed cooling unit. When there is a cooling demand, the thermostat energizes the first stage (low speed of the unit) as the outdoor temperature increases. When the inside temperature surpasses the low-speed cooling capability, the second mercury switch closes the contacts, energizing the second stage (high speed of the unit). An interlock prevents the first stage from running simultaneously with the second stage. Cooling in this manner matches the unit's capacity with the outdoor temperature. A single speed and stage unit uses more energy and operates at peak capacity continuously.

Outdoor Thermostat

The outdoor thermostat is used with either a single-stage or a two-stage indoor thermostat to match the heat

■ **FIGURE 8.16**

Outdoor thermostat.

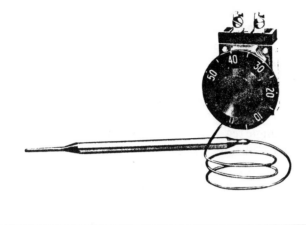

output of an electric furnace to heat loss of the conditioned space, based on outdoor temperature. The outdoor thermostat monitors the outside temperature. More heat is required with a colder outside temperature. The outdoor thermostat is 24V, bellow switch. (See Figure 8.16.)

The manually adjusted thermostat is normally set at a temperature at which heat loss in the conditioned space is not satisfied by the previous heating stages. The function of the outdoor thermostat is similar to that of the two-stage heating thermostat. If the outside temperature is above the setting of the outdoor thermostat, the previous stage satisfies the heating demand. The outdoor thermostat cannot energize the additional heat elements.

Setback Thermostat

The automatic setback thermostat is an energy-saving device that permits selection of temperatures for certain periods of low demand during the day. The setback thermostat saves fuel and energy in both the heating and the cooling seasons. The thermostat has a rechargeable battery and maintains full power by a 24V AC thermostat circuit. The quartz clock allows changing temperature periods up to three times every 24 hours. The setback thermostat operates for both heating and cooling. This type of thermostat should not be used with a heat pump. The heat produced is at a lower temperature, about 90°F versus 130°F or more for a fossil-fueled furnace. As a result, the unit takes longer to heat the house and may take hours of running to satisfy the thermostat or make it comfortable. For most climates, it may be less expensive to set a comfortable temperature and leave it there.

Digital Thermostats

Digital thermostats can be programmed for up to two 10° periods a day, for example, 10° lower while you sleep and 10° degrees lower while you are at work. Digital thermostats are available that can automatically calculate when the heating/cooling system needs to begin operating to reach the desired temperature at the preprogrammed time. Most digital thermostats have a battery backup so if the power is interrupted, the programming is not lost. These thermostats can be totally automatic so that the most comfortable temperatures for winter and summer can be programmed and set for automatic operation. The thermostat will maintain the selected temperatures winter and summer with no adjustments required. These thermostats are also available for heat pump operation.

Thermopile Thermostat

The thermopile thermostat generates direct current (DC) millivoltage (mV) by gas pilot and thermocouples. These systems produce either 500mV or 750mV. The thermocouple thermostat must be selected to match the electric outputs. When the temperature falls, the thermostat completes the circuit to the gas valve, initiating the heat cycle. The thermopile must never be connected to a power source other than an mV pilot generator. (See Figure 8.17.)

Subbases

The subbase operates as a thermostat mounting plate and also contains wiring control connections for the thermostat. The thermostat is fastened to the subbase and completes the electrical connections.

Gravity Warm-Air Heating System

In gravity warm-air furnaces, the air is heated and transferred to the space to be heated. Air is the heat carrying medium. The furnaces are made from cast iron or steel and can burn various types of fuel.

Gravity warm-air furnaces are different from forced air furnaces because they do not have fans or blower. These warm-air heating systems operate because of the difference in specific gravity of warm air and cold air. Warm air is lighter than cold air and rises if cold air is available to replace it. Satisfactory operation of a gravity warm-air heating system depends on three factors; size

■ **FIGURE 8.17**

Thermopile thermostat.

Millivolt Thermostat

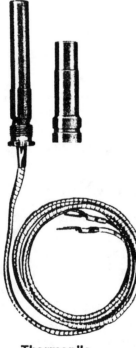

Thermopile

of warm and cold air ducts, heat loss of the building, and heat available from the furnace.

The most common source of trouble in these systems is having insufficient duct area, usually in the cold air return duct. The total cross-sectional area of the cold air return duct or ducts must be equal to or greater than the total cross-sectional area of all warm ducts. (See Figure 8.18.)

The simplest type is the floor furnace suitable for small homes where all rooms can be grouped around a large single register. The most common difficulty experienced with this type of furnace is supplying a return air opening of sufficient size in the floor. Most gravity warm-air furnaces are large units and will be located in the basement, and most of them are either wood burning or coal burning unless they have been converted to burn some other type of fuel.

When a home is inspected that has one of these furnaces, the inspector must be very thorough because if the furnace has been burning coal or wood there could be soot build-up in the fire box and chimney. This build-up could be creosote and be very dangerous. Other areas that should be observed are the firebox for warping, cracks, and the grates that the coal or wood sits on in the firebox.

■ GAS FURNACES

Heating equipment has undergone remarkable changes, including pulse combustion and radical designs in heat exchangers. Induced draft blowers are used extensively. These advances are coupled with variable-speed indoor blower motors. Modern furnaces extract so much heat from the burned gas that water vapor condenses. The furnaces' AFUE efficiencies range to more than 97 percent.

In gas furnaces, fuel is either natural or liquefied petroleum (LP) gas. The combustion process consumes oxygen obtained from surrounding air or air supplied to the combustion chamber by a small blower.

Natural gas is odorless, colorless and accumulates in upper portions of oil and gas wells. Raw natural gas is a mixture of methane (55 percent to 98 percent), high hydrocarbons (primarily ethane), and noncombustible gases. The composition of natural gas varies with location. Heat values of natural gas can vary from 900 Btus (British thermal units) to 1,200 Btus per cubic foot (cu. ft.), but the usual range is 1,000 to 1,050 Btus per cu. ft. Odorants are added to natural gas for safety purposes.

■ **FIGURE 8.18**

Gravity warm-air furnace.

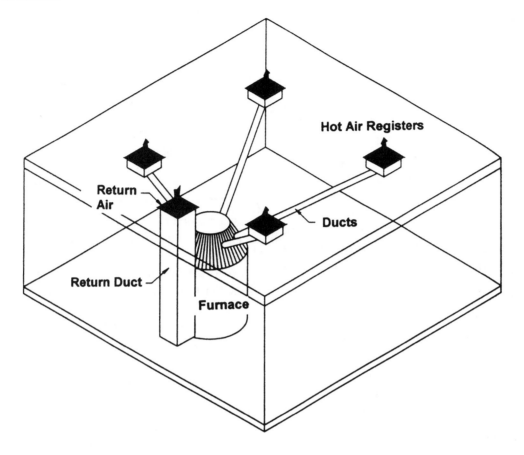

LP gas consists of propane and butane, which are normally obtained as by-products of oil refinery operations. Propane and butane are gaseous under atmospheric conditions, but can be liquefied by moderate pressures at normal temperatures. Three LP gases are commercially available as fuels: propane, butane, and a mixture of the two.

Commercial propane has a heat value of approximately 2,500 Btus per cu. ft. of gas. At atmospheric pressure, propane has a boiling point of –40°F. The low boiling point enables use in subfreezing climates. Propane is available in cylinders, bottles, tank trucks, or tank cars.

Commercial butane has a heat value of approximately 3,200 Btus per cu. ft. of gas. At atmospheric pressure, butane has a relatively high boiling point of 32°F. Butane cannot be used in cooler climates unless the gas temperature is at or above 32°F. Butane pressure is decreased by diluting with lower-boiling-point gases.

Butane is available in bottles, tank trucks, or tank cars, but not in cylinders. Commercial propane-butane mixes are available in differing ratios of propane to butane. Their properties fall between propane and butane values.

Propane-air and butane-air mixtures are used in place of natural gas in small communities and during peak loads by natural gas companies. This practice is called *spiking*. Natural gas companies spike the gas to maintain adequate line pressure during peak-load conditions.

Combustion, Dilution, and Ventilation Air

Until recently, there was no problem in bringing in sufficient amounts of outdoor air for combustion—infiltration provided all the air that was needed and then some. In today's homes, built with energy conservation in mind, tight construction practices make it necessary to bring in air from outside for combustion. Consideration also must be given to the use of exhaust fans, appliance vents, chimneys, and fireplaces because they force out of the house additional air that could be used for combustion. Unless outside air is brought into the home for combustion, negative pressure (pressure outside greater than pressure inside) will build to the point that a downdraft can occur in the furnace vent pipe or chimney. Combustion gases can enter the living space creating a potentially dangerous situation. Special consideration must be given to combustion air needs as well as requirements for exhaust vents and gas piping.

All gas-fired appliances require air for the combustion process. If sufficient amounts of combustion air are not available, the furnace or other appliance will operate in an inefficient and unsafe manner. When fireplaces, exhaust fans, or clothes dryers are used at the same time as the furnace, much more air is required to ensure proper combustion and to prevent a downdraft.

Insufficient amounts of air cause incomplete combustion, which can result in production of carbon monoxide (CO) gas. In addition to providing combustion air, fresh outdoor air dilutes contaminants found in indoor air. These contaminants may include bleaches, adhesives, detergents, solvents, and other contaminants that are corrosive to furnace components. (See Figure 8.19.)

The Combustion Process

Combustion is a chemical reaction that occurs when fuel gases combine with oxygen and ignite. The combustion triangle is composed of three elements: fuel, heat, and oxygen. All three elements must be present to ignite and sustain a flame. Fuels are a form of potential energy. They follow the Law of Conservation of Energy, which states one form of energy can be neither created nor destroyed but can be converted into other forms of energy. When fuel burns, it transforms into two other forms of energy—light and heat. Heat energy is measured in Btus.

The products of combustion are the same for both LP and natural gas. However, the amount of by-products emitted will vary. Energy is released in the process as heat, and certain by-products are formed. Hydrogen contained in the fuel gas combines with oxygen to form water vapor (H_2O). Oxygen also combines with carbon from the fuel gas to form carbon oxides, including carbon dioxide (CO_2) and carbon monoxide (CO). CO_2 is formed with a sufficient oxygen supply, while CO may form with an inadequate oxygen supply. Nitrogen in combustion air passes through the combustion process virtually unchanged, although some nitric oxide (NO) is produced.

The nature and makeup of the combustion products depend on the ratio and conditions during combustion. Complete combustion of 1 cu. ft. of natural gas requires 10 cu. ft. of air (about 2 cu. Ft. of oxygen) plus heat for ignition and yields by-products consisting of 1 cu. ft. of CO_2 and 2 cu. ft. of H_2O. Because, air is 80 percent nitrogen and 20 percent oxygen, approximately 8 cu. ft. of nitrogen passes through the reaction unchanged. Complete combustion for 1 cu. ft. of LP gas requires 18 cu. ft. of air (about 3½ cu. ft. of oxygen) and a flame for ignition. The products of combustion are 2 cu. ft. of CO_2 and 3 cu. ft. of H_2O, with 14½ cu. ft. of nitrogen.

The combustion ratio assumes an ideal condition, under which all oxygen is used. Additional air must be supplied to ensure that the oxygen required for complete combustion is available. The additional air is called *excess air*. When the excess air supply produces adequate oxygen, combustion is complete. H_2O and CO_2 are produced, and full heat value is released. Complete combustion utilizes fuel gases efficiently and creates harmless by-products.

If the excess air supply is insufficient, the oxygen content is inadequate, incomplete combustion results, and the full heat value is not released. In addition, incomplete combustion produces harmful by-products, including CO, aldehydes, and soot. CO is odorless, colorless, tasteless, and deadly when it contaminates the blood. It is toxic at low concentrations. The American Gas Association (AGA) allows only 0.4 percent of the vent products to consist of CO. The vent products are flammable and explosive in a wide range of mixtures with air.

Aldehydes are toxic combustion products with an acrid odor, which makes them immediately detectable. Aldehydes irritate the eyes, nose, and throat. If aldehydes are present, CO always is present. However, the absence of aldehydes does not ensure that CO is not present.

The products of complete combustion are

- carbon dioxide (CO_2),
- water vapor (H_2O), and
- nitrogen (passes through the flame unchanged).

The products of incomplete combustion are

- carbon dioxide (CO_2),
- water vapor (H_2O),
- carbon monoxide (CO),
- aldehydes (irritate eyes, nose, and throat), and
- soot (unburned carbon).

■ **FIGURE 8.19**

Air for combustion is supplied in various ways.

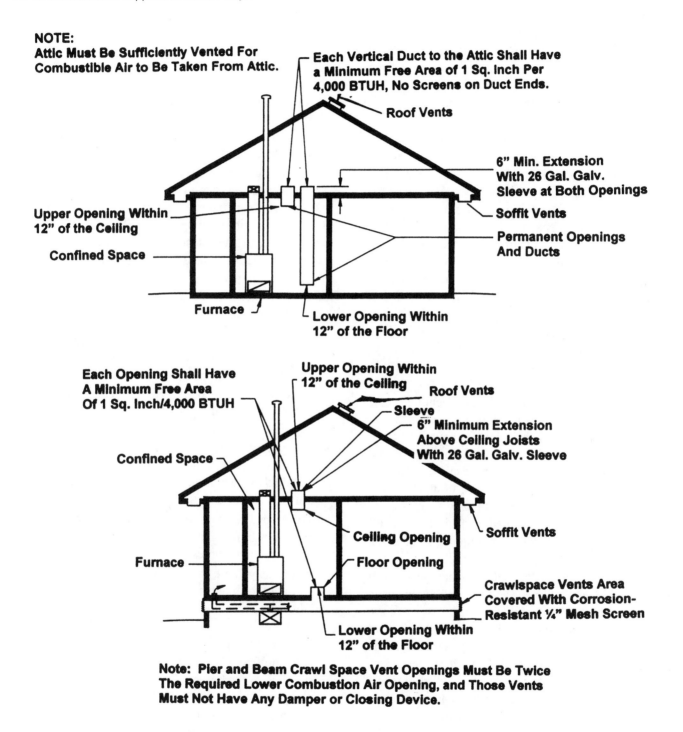

NOTE:
Attic Must Be Sufficiently Vented For Combustible Air to Be Taken From Attic.

Each Vertical Duct to the Attic Shall Have a Minimum Free Area of 1 Sq. Inch Per 4,000 BTUH, No Screens on Duct Ends.

Roof Vents

6" Min. Extension With 26 Gal. Galv. Sleeve at Both Openings

Upper Opening Within 12" of the Ceiling

Soffit Vents

Confined Space

Permanent Openings And Ducts

Furnace

Lower Opening Within 12" of the Floor

Each Opening Shall Have A Minimum Free Area Of 1 Sq. Inch/4,000 BTUH

Upper Opening Within 12" of the Ceiling

Roof Vents

Sleeve

6" Minimum Extension Above Ceiling Joists With 26 Gal. Galv. Sleeve

Confined Space

Ceiling Opening

Floor Opening

Soffit Vents

Furnace

Crawlspace Vents Area Covered With Corrosion-Resistant ¼" Mesh Screen

Lower Opening Within 12" of the Floor

Note: Pier and Beam Crawl Space Vent Openings Must Be Twice The Required Lower Combustion Air Opening, and Those Vents Must Not Have Any Damper or Closing Device.

Consider Combustion Air during an Inspection

When performing the inspection of a dwelling, part of what is inspected are the gas-fired appliances. Some of these appliances include furnaces and water heaters that draw combustion air from within the structure.

The codes and standards are written to allow some latitude for interpretation. That allows inspectors to use their own style to accomplish the intent of the codes and standard.

When observing these gas-fired appliances, we look at their condition and how they perform when tested using normal operating controls. All inspectors have their own styles, methods, and devices to help them feel confident that they are thorough and accurate in their assessments.

Prior to removing the first panel from the furnace or getting ready to fire up the water heater, the inspector should size up and evaluate the areas that these appliances are in, noting the type and number of stored items. Now, in an area that gave these gas-burning, air-gulping appliances plenty of space, what is called a *confined space* has been created. A confined space, by definition of SBCCII Standard Gas Code, is "A space whose volume is less than 50 cu. ft. per 1,000-Btus per hour of the aggregate input rating of all appliances installed in that space." What that is saying is that a 100,000-Btu input furnace alone requires a minimum of 5,000 (100 x 50) cu. ft. of clear space to supply it with the proper amount of combustion air within that space. A room with an 8' ceiling would have to be 625 sq. ft. in size.

Now that the furnace is supplied with enough combustion air, add a 40,000 Btu (about a 40-gallon) water heater into this utility space. This would require a room with an area of 875 sq. ft., which is a good sized room. The larger the Btu rating, the more air is required. Therefore, a furnace could easily cause a water heater to downdraft. A lone water heater can have a combustion air problem when it is installed in a closet by itself because a 40,000 Btu water heater requires a 250 sq. ft. room with an 8′ ceiling.

When inspecting older homes that have been updated and in which furnace and air conditioning have been relocated, keep in mind that originally both the water heater and furnace shared the same chimney, and now only the water heater uses the large chimney. This can cause a definite drafting problem for the water heater. The inspector may want to make note on his or her report that "combustion air supply is questionable for existing gas fired appliances," or use a CO detector to test.

Burner Flame

Dust, lint, or carbon deposits obstruct burners and shutters, causing an uneven, yellow-tipped flame. The burners must be cleaned.

Gas burners have a blue flame when primary and secondary air adjustments are correct. Combustion occurs in two distinct and well-defined zones. Oxygen contained in primary air combines with gas (hydrocarbons). The initial combustion and primary air combustion occurs on the extremely thin surface of the bright blue inner cone. The air and gas mixture contained inside the cone is composed of unburned gas and primary air. The secondary air combustion takes place on the outer shroud surface. A yellowish flame indicates insufficient primary and secondary air. A collection of soot indicates inadequate secondary air.

Flame propagation (speed of burning) is important. The primary air and gas mixture must flow faster than the burner flame consumes it. Otherwise, flashback occurs and the gas begins burning at the orifice. Flashback also occurs if gas pressure is too low. If the primary airflow is too fast, the flame blows away from the burner (lifting).

Flame characteristics provide evidence of air/gas mixture problems that cause incomplete combustion. (See Figure 8.20.)

- The yellow flame has a small blue portion near the burner port. The large outer portion is yellow and frequently accompanied by smoke. Soot commonly collects in the heat exchanger and vents. The yellow flame indicates incomplete combustion caused by insufficient primary air.
- The yellow-tipped flame is similar to the yellow flame and also is caused by insufficient primary air supplied to the burner. The yellow tips appear on the outer portion of the flame.
- The orange/red color in flames is observed as streaks caused by burning dust in the combustion air. This is not a problem unless streaking is excessive.
- A soft, lazy flame occurs when enough primary air is admitted to the burner to eliminate the yellow tips. With this flame, the inner and outer portions are not clearly defined, as in the sharp flame. It is caused by low gas pressure to the burner.
- A lifting flame occurs when too much primary air is supplied to the burner. This flame results in incomplete combustion and can be recognized by separation from the burner ports. A blowing noise can occasionally be heard.
- A floating flame indicates insufficient secondary combustion air, caused by restricted airflow, inadequate venting, or both. The flame appears as a flickering cloud. A sharp odor may be noticed due to the unburned combustion by-products.

■ **FIGURE 8.20**

Flame characteristics provide evidence of air/gas mixture problems, which cause incomplete combustion.

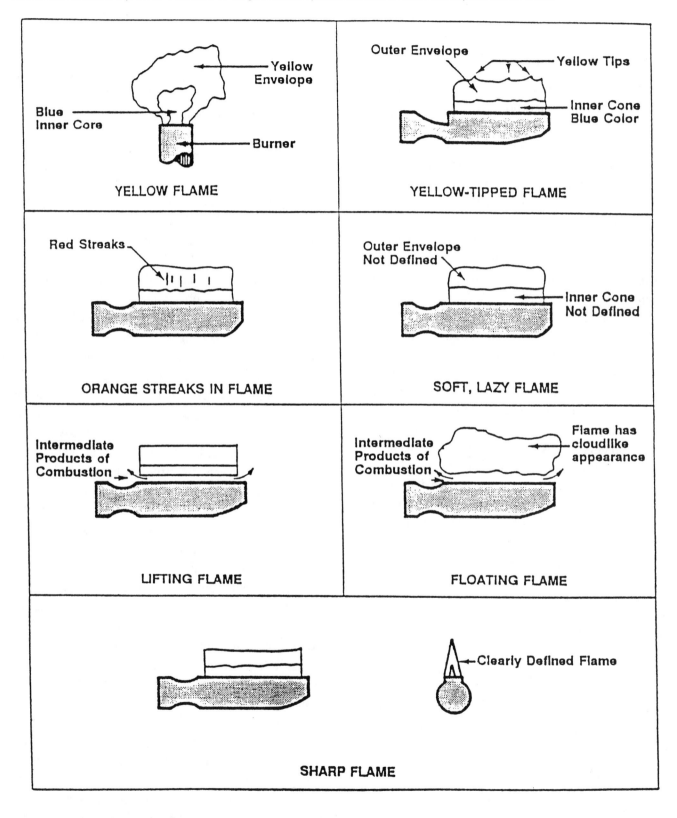

- A sharply defined blue flame indicates proper gas, and primary and secondary air mixture. Both the outer portion and inner cone are pointed with straight sides. The flame rests directly on the burner ports.

Atmospheric Burners

Gas burners used in conventional gas furnaces are atmospheric. Atmospheric burners use air within the house for combustion and venting. Gas is routed to the burner, where it flows through the orifice, which meters gas to the burner. Air mixes with gas at the burner intake owing to atmospheric pressure. A power burner uses an air blower to supply combustion air.

The gas and air mixture ignites at the burner. The combustion gases rise through the heat exchanger, where heat transfers to the conditioned space. The combustion gases pass through the flue pipe and exhaust through the chimney.

Gas burners control the air/gas mixture for combustion and determine the character and shape of the flame. Aerated burners mix air with gas prior to discharging the mixture for combustion. This burner is often called a *Bunsen* or *blue-flame burner.* Aerated burners provide complete combustion of fuel gases over a wide range of gas pressures and flow rates.

Air mixed with gas prior to exiting the burner port is called *primary air.* Aerated burners provide an adjustment for the primary air flow to achieve desired flame characteristics. Additional air is required for complete LP combustion. This air enters the flame from the burner area and is called *secondary air.*

If the primary air is introduced to the burner at atmospheric pressure, the burner is an atmospheric burner. The primary air is thoroughly mixed with gas inside the atmospheric burner head. Most burners incorporate a venturi tube, a throat that forces the air/gas mixture to accelerate and then quickly decelerate.

The turbulence effectively mixes the air and gas. Primary air enters the burner instantly when gas flows through the burner orifice. Secondary air is introduced to the flame by the heat exchanger draft. (See Figure 8.21.)

Heat Exchanger

In a gas furnace, combustion takes place inside a heat exchanger. Air passing over the outside surface

Primary and secondary air are required for atmospheric burners.

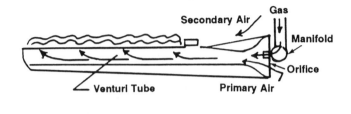

absorbs heat from the flame. The heat exchanger provides total separation of the combustion area and treated air to ensure that combustion products do not mix with the warm air to the dwelling.

The heat exchanger is divided into several sections, called *clamshells,* to obtain a greater heating surface. The term *clamshell* evolved from the process of manufacturing heat exchangers by stamping two metal sheets, one left and one right. (See Figure 8.22.)

The metal shells are welded along a common vertical seam to form a clamshell design. The cavity at the bottom of the heat exchanger is designed to accept burners. At the top of the atmospheric-type heat exchanger are a draft diverter and a vent connector. They direct combustion products from the heat exchanger into a draft diverter and into the vent. (See Figure 8.23.)

Nonuniform heating of the heat exchanger results in high-temperature areas called *hot spots.* Hot spots damage the heat exchanger structure and can burn through the metal wall.

Most combustion by-products exit through the flue, but some of the flue gases can pass through the hole and leak into the conditioned air supply. A leaking heat exchanger causes burners to operate improperly. The leakage causes incomplete combustion and forms CO and other harmful by-products. Heat exchanger leaks must be promptly corrected. This involves replacing the exchanger or the entire heating appliance. (See Figure 8.24.)

The heat exchanger is designed for air to pass over the outside of the exchanger and to pick up the maximum amount of available heat energy from the surface. The heat exchanger is constructed of light-gauge metal. A possible malfunction is deterioration of the exchanger

■ **FIGURE 8.22**

Duracurve Heat Exchanger is usually divided into several sections.

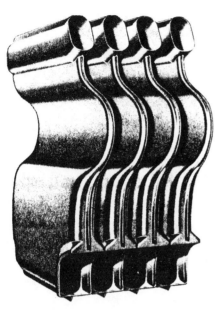

Duracurve Heat Exchanger

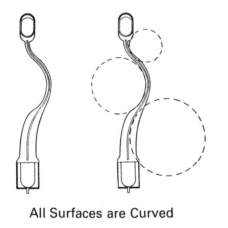

All Surfaces are Curved

■ **FIGURE 8.23**

Draft is required to remove combustion by-products from the heat exchanger.

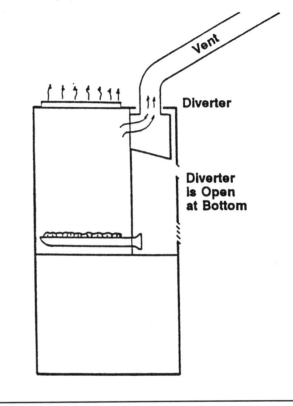

wall. The breakdown may be due to expansion and contraction over years of use.

Some heat exchangers are coated with a protective ceramic layer that resists deterioration from corrosion or acids. Age may cause this ceramic coating to break down, especially in the seam area. With the absence of the protective ceramic coating, the metal body of the exchanger is exposed to the elements and will rapidly rust or corrode. Dripping water causes rust. When the furnace is connected to the air conditioner, the heat exchanger will rust more quickly than in a furnace

without air-conditioning. The heat exchanger usually fails during the cooling season.

With burners properly adjusted, combustion products are relatively harmless because they contain primarily nitrogen, H_2O and CO_2. When the main burner is improperly adjusted and combustion is incomplete, the products may include CO, aldehydes and soot. Although other incomplete combustion products can be harmful and damaging, CO is the primary health hazard. Serious health hazards develop if even small concentrations of CO accumulate in the conditioned air. Unless the dwelling has an abundant supply of fresh air ventilation, asphyxiation (death by insufficient oxygen) or actual CO poisoning (death by blood contamination) occurs.

For this health reason, a positive outside fresh air supply must circulate within the dwelling during the heating season. This supplies fresh air while reducing or eliminating odors within the dwelling.

There are several methods to detect a leak in heat exchangers. However, the only sure method to detect leaks is to dismantle the appliance and visually inspect

■ **FIGURE 8.24**

Combustion by-products are improperly released during heat exchanger failure.

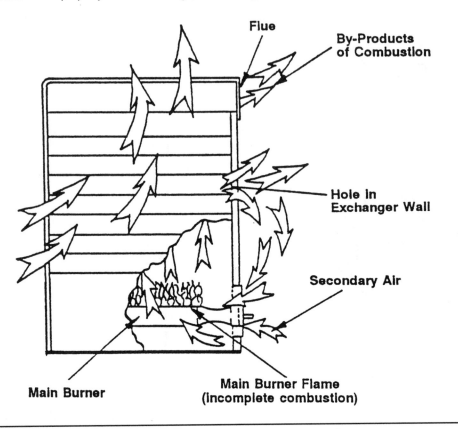

the heat exchanger. Because of the potential liability to the inspection organization, this method is not recommended for detecting heat exchanger leaks, unless performed by a professional. Because of the required time, expense, and expertise, other methods of leak detection are used.

Visual inspection of the main burner flame characteristics may indicate faulty heat exchangers. This procedure is applicable to appliances that use a blower to distribute heat (forced-air heating systems). If the main burner flame has normal characteristics with the blower off, check with the blower on. If the characteristics change or the flame lifts from the burner ports, the heat exchanger is faulty.

Smoke bombs have been used with limited success to test for heat exchanger leaks. The smoke bomb is inserted into the heat exchanger cavity. If smoke is detected in the supply air to the dwelling, the exchanger is leaking. In many cases, however, the smoke drifts out of the exchanger and into the supply air even if the exchanger is not leaking. This is caused by a smoke

bomb that develops more smoke than the system can adequately vent.

The last popular method of testing is called the *odor test*. A small quantity of wintergreen, liquid peppermint, or another aromatic substance is deposited in a small metal container (bottle cap). The cap and substance are placed on each main burner. As the substance is heated, it generates a distinctive odor. If the odor is detected in the supply air of the dwelling, a leak exists. This method has only limited success.

Some HVAC reference materials mention a salt spray test. The test consists of spraying a saltwater mixture into the heat exchanger while the burners are operating and the blower is off. A propane torch is inserted into the plenum. If the blue propane flame turns yellow or red, this may indicate a heat exchanger leak. Dust or dirt carried in the supply airstream will turn the flame yellow and indicate a bad heat exchanger. Most manufacturers do not recommend using this test. The heat exchanger may check out properly, but the salt spray solution will cause corrosion and shorten the life of the exchanger. With proper tools, a heat exchanger leak can be detected by measuring CO and CO_2 levels. Despite all alternatives, the only reliable method is to visually inspect the exchanger.

Venting

Venting adequate air supply is essential for safe and efficient gas furnace operation. To maintain safe operating conditions within a home using vented gas appliances, combustion products must be exhausted and the air supply continually replenished. With inadequate combustion air supply, the combustion gas venting is incomplete. Some gases may remain in the home and be recycled through the furnace.

As previously discussed, The combustion process uses oxygen in the air and produces CO_2 and H_2O. If combustion products are not removed and fresh air supplied, the oxygen supply is depleted. Under these conditions, harmful by-products such as CO form.

In older homes with loose construction, combustion air is replenished by infiltration through cracks around doors and windows. New homes with tight construction and older homes remodeled for energy conservation must provide fresh air to the furnace room. Ducts or louvered grills that connect to the outside are used. Exhaust fans, clothes dryers, or fireplaces compound the ventilation problems of tightly constructed homes.

A gas furnace properly vented safely exhausts combustion products to the outside and provides adequate oxygen to the furnace. An effective venting system removes all combustion products from the furnace. It ensures that sufficient air is drawn through the heat exchanger to provide complete fuel gas combustion.

Conventional gas furnaces use two venting systems: natural draft and power vents. Natural draft systems use convection, which is caused by the temperature difference between combustion products and outside air. This method is popular and common. Power vents utilize mechanical blowers to draw or force combustion products out the vent. If the fan is positioned to draw flue gases through the heat exchanger, draft is induced. Many manufacturers use induced draft in high-efficiency furnaces. If the fan is positioned to push flue gases through the heat exchanger, the draft is forced. Commercial rooftop units use forced draft.

■ **FIGURE 8.25**

Common symptoms of poor vent system operation are condensation, spillage, and chronic pilot outage.

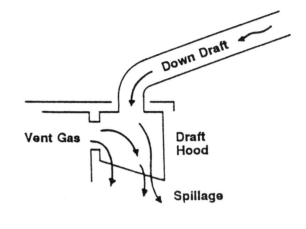

Natural Draft

Heat energy is the power source that operates the vent in natural draft systems. Combustion gases rise in vents because they are hotter and lighter than surrounding air. As combustion gases move upward through the chimney, cooler air is drawn into the combustion area. The air movement establishes a draft, which replenishes required oxygen for combustion and exhausts by-products from the home.

A conventional gas furnace depends on the chimney effect created by the heat exchanger to replenish combustion air. The heat exchanger is a small chimney. It is factory designed to match the burner and provide draft necessary to draw the correct amount of combustion air. In most cases, vent system problems are due to one of three conditions: incorrect sizing of the vent system, improper installation or inadequate air supply. Troubleshooting is accomplished more easily if symptoms are observed. (See Figure 8.25.)

If flue gases cool to dew point, condensation occurs in the flue pipe. The condensate is acidic and can literally eat away the metal pipe. Condensate flowing back to the flue pipe can damage the furnace. If a severe condensation problem is apparent, check for rust, at the furnace vestibule panel and heat exchanger. On a conventional furnace installation, condensation is usually caused by long horizontal runs. Condensation can be a problem on new high-efficiency furnaces (those with conventional furnace designs) where flue temperatures border on the dew point.

■ **FIGURE 8.26**

The draft hood is a box that is open at the bottom.

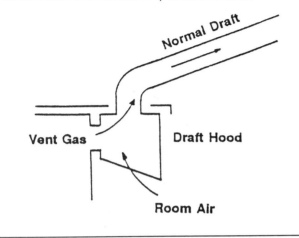

To prevent chimney draft from upsetting the balance between the heat exchanger and gas burner, a relief device is used between the furnace and vent. The relief device is designed and built as part of the furnace. The device is called a *draft hood* or *diverter*.

Vent gases from the furnace pass into one side of this box. The vent pipe may be connected to either the opposite side or the top of the box, depending on its design. (See Figure 8.26.)

The draft hood performs two functions. First, it provides the gas furnace with additional air supply for draft hood dilution. In the absence of a draft hood, excessive draft pulls an abnormal quantity of air into the heat exchanger and removes heat from the furnace. In extreme cases, excessive draft lifts the flame from the burner, causing incomplete combustion. The added heat lost up the chimney results in inefficient operation. Second, the draft hood acts as a relief opening to prevent any changes in the chimney draft from affecting normal heat exchanger combustion.

Hot vent gases pass into the draft hood and into the vent pipe without spillage at the bottom opening. The gases stay toward the top of the draft hood and are removed by the vent pipe and chimney draw. Chimney draft is greater than the draft required to remove combustion gases. Additional furnace room air is drawn into the bottom opening and passes through the vent with the combustion gases.

Certain conditions upset chimney draft. The draft hood relief opening offers an escape for combustion products. When there is backdraft, blockage, or no draft,

the opening is used. The exit prevents combustion products from collecting in the heat exchanger, smothering the burner flame, or causing incomplete combustion.

Spillage occurs when combustion gases are discharged from the draft hood bottom opening. The gases discharge into the home and create high-humidity problems. Spillage can deplete the oxygen supply to the burner flame.

Momentary draft hood spillage, occurring when wind conditions cause a momentary downdraft, is no cause for alarm. But prolonged spillage from the draft hood is drawn to the burner. The flue products deplete the oxygen supply at the flame and cause incomplete combustion. CO and other incomplete combustion products spill through the draft hood. Prolonged spillage is extremely dangerous and can be fatal if not corrected.

Appliance draft hood spillage causes condensation on windows and walls or creates odors. A vent system incorrectly sized, improperly installed, blocked, or with a downdraft can cause spillage. Flue gases and spillage result when the height of the vent is short or small in diameter. If the vent is large in diameter, excessive amounts of dilution air will enter the vent. The combustion products cool and reduce the draft in the vent, which causes spillage.

Lengthy lateral runs without upward pitch or sags cause extra flow resistance. Small amounts of sagging lower the draft where slight spillage occurs. Elbows in vent piping increase flow resistance of gases passing through the vent. Two 90° elbows are permitted in a vent system. If more than two are used, the system will not perform properly.

In cases where occasional spillage results, the flow resistance in the vent is marginal. A slight reduction of the resistance solves the problem. If a lateral run is not properly pitched upward at least ¼″ per ft. from the appliance, excess resistance results.

When several appliances connect to an improperly sized common vent, spillage occurs. Spillage occurs if the smaller appliance (water heater) in the multiple-vent system has a short connector rise or a long lateral run. When the appliance operates alone, it generates insufficient draft to overcome resistance and displaces cooler air in the common vent. Because the heat exchanger surface of a water heater is water backed, the flue gases require more time to reach normal operating temperature.

Spillage can be a problem in tight construction with no air infiltration. This is true when tight construction is coupled with an open fireplace or exhaust fans.

To test for spillage, after the appliance has been operating for five to ten minutes, hold a lit cigarette or smoking match near the appliance draft hood opening. If the smoke is drawn into the opening, the vent is performing satisfactorily. If the smoke is not drawn into the vent, spillage is occurring at the appliance draft hood.

To determine which appliance vent is spilling within the dwelling, check each appliance separately for spillage. If some appliances vent improperly, spillage is due to vents or vent connector problems immediately above the appliance. If all appliances vent properly, leakage is occurring in the vent system, and a smoke test should be performed. If none of the appliances vents properly, the highest vent system connection should be investigated.

To test for vent system leakage, a smoke gun is often used. The smoke gun cartridge discharges a chemical into the vent, which gives off a smoky vapor. For best results, the venting system is pressurized (capped) during the test. As the smoke rises through the vent system, the smoke leaks out and is visually detected. Smoke testing should start from the lowest point of the vent section.

The volume of combustion by-products the chimney can draft depends on two factors: (1) the temperature difference between the vent gas and outside air and (2) the diameter and height of the chimney.

Little or no draft occurs when the outside air is the same temperature as the flue gases. If H_2O formed in the combustion process remains heated, it continues in its vapor state and is discharged into the atmosphere outside the dwelling. If the vent pipe temperature drops to the dew point, the H_2O condenses into a liquid. The typical dew point temperature in a high-efficiency furnace is between 135°F and 140°F, subject to CO_2 content, relative humidity and barometric pressure. As combustion gases cool, draft is reduced. This disrupts the combustion products exhaustion and creates insufficient combustion air supply.

As combustion gases cool in the chimney, moisture condenses on the chimney walls. Because of compounds in the fuel gas, reactions to condensate form mild carbonic, carbolic, and sulfuric acids. These acids damage most chimneys, particularly masonry.

Many masonry chimneys were designed to vent combustion gases of solid fuels such as wood or coal. These gases reach a temperature between 600°F and 1,000°F. The draft generated at these temperatures is strong enough to overcome the high resistance of an unlined chimney. Gas-burning furnaces produce flue gases at a much lower temperature (400°F to 550°F) for both conventional furnaces and high-efficiency furnaces. Unlined masonry chimneys are marginal vents for gas furnaces.

Fan Control

One of the major controls in the line voltage circuit is fan control. The fan control switch is a heat-actuated switch equipped with open contacts. It contains a bimetal heat-sensing probe that senses air temperature passing from the furnace into the system.

The furnace illustrated in Figure 8.27 shows the location of the fan control in an up-flow type furnace. The probe is a spiral type and is installed in the heating unit on the front side of the cabinet. The bimetal probe is inserted through the cabinet into the heat exchanger portion of the furnace. The bimetal probe must be positioned to sense the temperature of air passing over the heat exchanger. When the temperature reaches the preset point, the bimetal probe closes the open contacts, completing the circuit and starting the blower motor.

■ **FIGURE 8.27**

Heat exchanger temperature is monitored by the fan control.

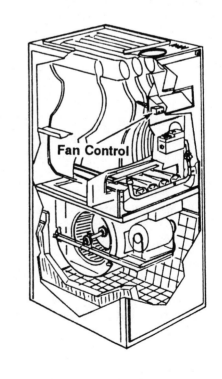

There are two types of fan controls: combination control and single fan control. With the combination control, the fan control portion has two adjustable levers to set the blower's on and off temperatures. The fan control settings are field adjusted and designed to turn on at approximately 100°F. When the air passing over the heat exchanger reaches 100°F, the switch closes the contacts and the fan turns on.

The off position on the switch is field adjusted and set at approximately 25°F below the on position. If the switch is set below the return air or room temperature during the normal heating season, continuous blower operation is accomplished.

The difference between the fan's on and off positions is called *fan control differential*. The temperature difference between these two positions is set from 15°F to 25°F. If the differential is set lower than 15°F, the control will cycle with very slight temperature fluctuations. This causes undesirable fan cycling. If the differential is set higher than 25°F, the blower waits too long before coming on. Heat loss from the furnace increases, reducing efficiency.

The other fan control is the single fan control. It has one adjustable lever to control the blower-off temperature. This is a fixed differential control with a built-in differential of 25°F. The blower-on temperature will always be 25°F higher than the blower-off temperature.

The down-flow and horizontal units require a different type of fan control. If the up-flow control is used in a down-flow or horizontal unit, the following undesirable situation would occur: On a call for heat, the burners would ignite, causing heat to migrate naturally to the top of the unit. This heat would cause a secondary safety limit (located near the top of the down-flow and horizontal units) to shut off the burners before the fan control bimetal became hot enough to turn on the blower. The unit would cycle on and off secondary limit and result in inefficient operation.

To alleviate this problem, down-flow and horizontal units use a timed-start fan control to initiate blower operation. The timed-start control uses a thermal timing mechanism to energize the blower. The timing mechanism is a 24V heater. When the furnace burners ignite on a heat call, the heater begins to warm a bimetal probe. (The probe is located in the heat exchanger portion, the same as in an up-flow unit.) The bimetal probe eventually warps and closes line voltage contacts, turning on the blower. The timing mechanism cannot be field adjusted and normally takes less than one minute to initiate blower operation. Unlike the up-flow fan control,

the timed-start control is not dependent on sensing heat from the burners to actuate the blower. The blower is energized before the burner heat increases sufficiently to shut the unit down on the secondary safety limit.

When the heat demand has been satisfied, the burners shut down and the 24V timed-start heater is dropped out of the circuit. The residual heat from the heat exchanger causes the bimetal probe to maintain blower operation until the furnace has sufficiently cooled. This off-time normally takes about one and a half minutes. The off temperature set point can be adjusted on the control.

Limit Control

The limit control is a safety device wired into the low voltage circuit. The high temperature limit control monitors air temperature passing over the heat exchanger and is combined physically with the fan control.

The limit has a set of normally closed contacts actuated by a heat-sensitive bimetal probe and switching action called *SPST* (single-pole single-throw). The limit control protects against blower failure or restrictions such as dirty filters, which reduce airflow over the heat exchanger. If the heat exchanger overheats, the passing air temperature increases. This is detrimental to the heat exchanger. The limit control senses the air temperature passing over the heat exchanger. If the limit control becomes hot, the bimetal probe opens the closed contacts. The open setting is approximately 200°F. This breaks the thermostat control circuit, shuts down the gas valve, and turns off the burners. The limit automatically resets or closes the contacts at 25°F cooler (175°F) than its opening point. The difference between the opening and closing temperatures is the differential. The limit control break and make set points are factory set and should never be field calibrated. (See Figure 8.28.)

An additional limit control is used for reverse-flow and horizontal heating units. The secondary limit is installed either in the blower outlet or between the blower outlet and the heating section. The lower limit's bimetal probe is not located to sense the air temperature surrounding the heat exchanger. Because heated air rises, the second safety device is necessary.

The secondary limit monitors the heated air temperature that rises by gravity and determines whether the heat exchanger is hot. Contacts and switching operate the same as the limit control and are installed in series with the control circuit. The limit is set to trip at a lower

■ FIGURE 8.28

Combination fan and limit control.

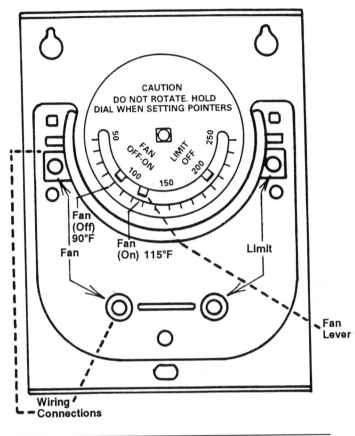

temperature than the primary limit and is used for blower failure protection.

Main Gas Valve

The main gas valve controls the gas flow into the furnace burners. The main gas valve is a combination gas valve, which incorporates the pilot safety and gas pressure regulator functions. (See Figure 8.29.)

The main valve consists of two parts: a manual valve and an automatic valve. The manual valve is upstream from the automatic valve and stops gas from reaching the unit. Once the manual valve is on, the automatic gas valve controls gas flow into the burners. The automatic valve electrically opens and closes through the heating circuit terminal of the thermostat. When the thermostat calls for heat, the automatic valve opens. When the heat demand is satisfied, the valve closes.

The automatic valve contains a valve disc attached to an iron core plunger. The spring-loaded plunger holds the valve disc closed against a valve seat. A coil is located at one end of the valve plunger. When the thermostat calls for heat, voltage travels through the terminal and energizes the coil. A magnetic field created around the coil attracts the plunger. The plunger overcomes the spring tension and lifts into the magnetic field. The valve disc lifts off the valve seat, allowing gas flow to the burners. When the heat demand is satisfied, the terminal contacts open and the coil de-energizes, discontinuing the magnetic field. The spring forces the plunger down, sealing the valve disc to the valve seat. The gas flow to the burners stops and the burner flame goes out.

Note: Units manufactured after January 1, 1980, include a redundant gas valve to satisfy AGA requirements. These valves incorporate two 24V solenoids, both of which energize on heating demand. The solenoids are wired in parallel, but are piped in series. If one solenoid sticks open, the other ensures gas shutoff at the end of the cycle.

Furnace Ignition

Standing Pilot

A standing pilot flame burns constantly to ignite the main burner flame. A pilot is a miniature gas burner that uses primary and secondary air for combustion. A crossover igniter, a piece of metal used as a bridge between the burners, is used to ignite several burners. As gas flows from the main burners, a portion flows through the igniter slot until it contacts the pilot light. (See Figure 8.30.)

If the pilot light is extinguished and the burner fails to ignite, raw gas collects in the furnace, causing an explosive hazard. A method to detect an extinguished pilot light is provided by a thermocouple. The pilot flame constantly heats the thermocouple. Pilot flame heat on the thermocouple generates a minute amount of electricity, measured in millivolts. The electricity holds open a small pilot valve that permits gas to enter the burners. If the pilot flame goes out, the pilot valve closes and stops the gas flow to the burners.

To properly generate electricity for the thermocouple, the pilot flame must envelop the hot-junction tip from $3/8''$ to $1/2''$. If the pilot flame does not burn or is misaligned with the thermocouple, electricity generation either is insufficient or stops completely. (See Figure 8.31.)

The load-connection end of the thermocouple is electrically connected to an electromagnet (similar to the automatic main gas valve) powered by millivoltage.

■ **FIGURE 8.29**

Combination gas valve.

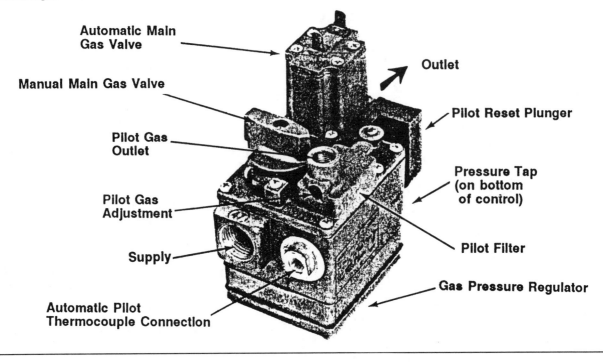

■ **FIGURE 8.30**

The crossover igniter alignment is critical. Misalignment causes a noisy, delayed ignition.

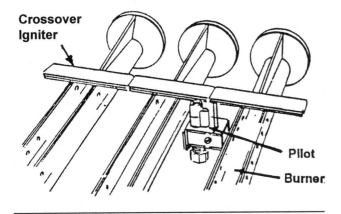

■ **FIGURE 8.31**

The pilot sensor or thermocouple proves the existence of the pilot flame and its size.

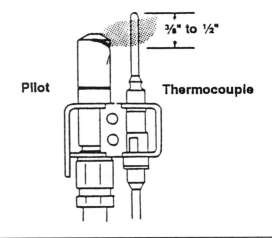

The electric main gas valve cannot be opened unless the gas pilot is lit and sufficient flame lights the main burner.

Most manufacturers provide 100 percent safety shutoff on both natural and LP gas furnaces. LP gas furnaces require 100 percent safety shutoff, even though it is not required by code on natural gas units. When the pilot flame goes out on LP units, the pilot valve must close, preventing any pilot gas from entering the heat exchanger. LP gas is heavier than air and will not dissipate up the flue. Instead, LP gas puddles in the bottom of the heat exchanger, causing hazardous conditions when relighting the pilot.

■ **FIGURE 8.32**

The pilot assembly includes a pilot burner, spark electrode, and sensing probe.

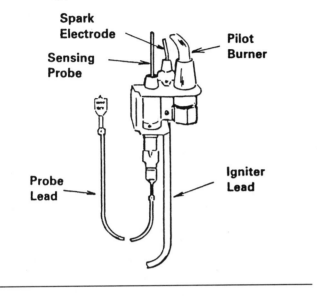

Electronic Pilot Ignition

Most furnace manufacturers have introduced electronic ignition and vent damper options to improve efficiency and energy conservation. Until the mid-1970s, gas furnaces used standing pilots to ignite the burners. Electronic ignition systems eliminate standing pilots and light the pilot at the beginning of the on cycle. This implies a savings in pilot light gas. Vent dampers prevent heated air contained in the house from drafting up the chimney during off cycles. Both electronic ignition and vent damper provisions improve the efficiency of the traditional atmospheric burner without affecting the natural draft of combustion by-products.

Three popular electronic ignition systems used in residential furnaces include Penn-Johnson, Robertshaw, and White-Rodgers. The Penn-Johnson electronic pilot ignition system consists of a solid-state ignition control unit and pilot assembly. (See Figure 8.32.)

When the thermostat calls for heat, the spark electrode and pilot burner gas valve automatically energize, producing a pilot flame. The sensing probe proves the presence of the pilot flame. Once the pilot flame is proved, the spark electrode de-energizes and the main burner gas valve is energized. The main burner gas is ignited by the pilot flame, as on a conventional gas furnace. When the thermostat is satisfied, the main burner valve and pilot valve are de-energized, shutting off the gas supply.

If the pilot burner does not light within 30 seconds after the call for heat has been initiated, a lockout timing device provides 100 percent pilot gas shutoff and de-energizes the ignition system. If the pilot flame goes out while the main burners are operating, the sensing probe detects flame absence. This causes the main gas valve to close, energizing the spark electrode to relight the pilot flame. The entire sequence takes approximately 8/10 of a second. If the pilot then fails to light, the ignition control will lock out.

The ignition control stays locked out until power to it is broken. This is accomplished by switching the system subbase at the thermostat from heating to off and back to heating. If a heating demand still exists, the system immediately attempts to light the pilot for another ignition trial. The ignition control may also be reset by flipping the disconnect switch at the unit off and on.

The electronic ignition system uses a sensing probe to verify flame conditions through flame rectification. The sensing probe functions differently from a thermocouple in a standard furnace.

Flame rectification is the gas flame property that permits it to act as a DC current path between two metal objects. The current path is established when AC voltage is applied between two objects enveloped in a gas flame. AC voltage is applied to the flame sensor and pilot burner tip by G60 circuitry. G60 is the Penn-Johnson name for the ignition control.

Electrons are discharged from the pilot tip to the flame sensor and back. More electrons hit the pilot tip than the flame sensor because the grounding area is much larger. The end result is a pulsating DC current flowing through the flame in one direction (flame sensor to pilot tip), which has much larger magnitude than DC current flowing in the opposite direction (pilot burner tip to flame sensor). The pulsating DC current is the only type of signal the G60 sensing circuitry accepts as proof of flame. Both the rectified DC current and current path must exist before the G60 allows the main gas valve to open.

The Robertshaw electric ignition system uses internal relays and thermal sensing to automatically light the pilot on heating demand. It permits main gas valve operation only after the pilot has been proven. If the ignition control detects an unsafe condition, gas flow to the furnace is shut off and electrically locked out. The control must be manually reset before attempting another restart.

Together, the ignition control and flame sensor light the pilot during each running cycle (intermittent pilot). The main burner and pilot are extinguished during the

■ **FIGURE 8.33**

The thermal lockout switch must be manually reset before the system is placed back into operation.

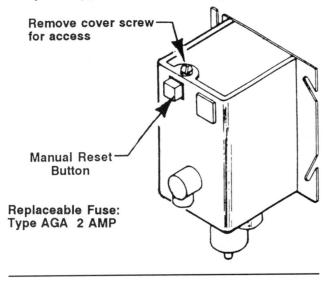

Remove cover screw for access

Manual Reset Button

Replaceable Fuse: Type AGA 2 AMP

off cycle. On heating demand, the ignition control energizes the pilot valve and a relay that initiates sparking and also powers the lockout circuit. The sparking stops after the pilot is lighted owing to electronic sensing. If burner ignition is not established within 90 to 180 seconds (sec.), the thermal lockout switch opens to de-energize the entire system. A waiting period of 5 minutes (min.) is required to allow the thermal heater to cool. (See Figure 8.33.)

A flame sensor is secured directly to the ignition control. It consists of an internal switch and a mercury sensing probe, which is located in the pilot flame. The switch changes position only after the pilot flame has been proven; then the switch energizes the main gas valve and relay. The relay de-energizes the thermal lockout circuit to maintain system operation while also energizing another relay. The second relay locks out the sparking circuit for the remainder of the cycle. This feature prevents the possibility of a reignition attempt with unburned gas in the heat exchanger. In the event of gas failure, the flame sensor cools, switches back to the cold position, then incorporates relay functions to energize the thermal lockout switch. This, in turn, de-energizes the entire system.

The gas valve body uses two 24V valves to control gas flow to the furnace. The pilot valve is located in front of the main valve and controls both the pilot and burners. Pilot gas is taken from the two valves. The main valve controls only gas flow to the burners.

The gas valve features a gas cock, pilot adjustment, regulator adjustment and gas outlet pressure tap. Pilot flame should envelop ⅝″ to ¾″ of the mercury probe.

The pilot burner assembly consists of a burner, a pilot hood, an electrode and a mercury sensing probe. As the pilot valve energizes, the electrode begins sparking until the pilot flame is established. The pilot gap is ⅛″. The Robertshaw electric ignition uses a mercury sensing probe to verify pilot flame conditions.

The thermal-sensing probe and capillary tube that connect to the flame sensor are both filled with mercury. As mercury heats, it exerts pressure through the capillary tube. At a predetermined pressure point, the flame sensor switch moves to the hot position. This action verifies that a sufficient pilot flame exists.

With the White-Rodgers electronic ignition system, the thermostat calls for heat and energizes both the igniter/safety timer and gas valve pilot-gas solenoid. The igniter/safety timer creates sparks, igniting the pilot gas at the burner, and the safety timer begins its timing sequence. Once a pilot flame is established, the igniter/safety timer stops generating sparks.

The pilot flame heats the mercury flame sensor. Once sufficient heat is sensed (in about 45 sec.), the mercury flame sensor switches the main valve on, allowing main burner gas flow. The pilot flame then ignites the main burner gas and the system is in full operation mode. When the room thermostat is satisfied, its contacts open, de-energizing both the pilot valve and the main valve and ceasing all gas flow.

The solid-state control performs two functions: (1) generating ignition sparks and (2) timing pilot burner ignition through the mercury flame sensor. When the room thermostat (or vent damper) energizes the igniter/safety timer, it begins generating ignition sparks and feeds power to the gas valve pilot-gas solenoid, causing it to energize and allow gas to the pilot burner. The safety timer circuit is designed to lock out and interrupt power to the gas valve if the main valve has not been energized by the mercury flame sensor within approximately 2 min.

To reset the igniter/safety timer, the thermostat circuit must be opened for 5 min. to allow the timer to cool and close its contacts. A five-wire harness connects the igniter/safety timer to the gas valve and is not repairable.

After the igniter/safety timer energizes the pilot valve, a pressure switch internal to the gas valve confirms gas presence and energizes the pilot circuit. Once pilot flame is established, the flame sensor switches to

■ **FIGURE 8.34**

The flame sensor switches from cold to hot only when the mercury has vaporized, proving pilot flame existence.

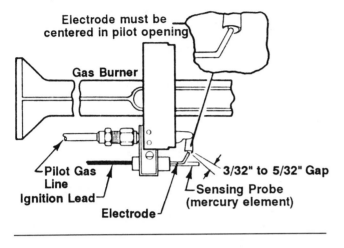

the hot position to energize the main valve. The pilot flame ignites the main burners.

Should a gas failure occur, the pressure switch opens to de-energize the pilot valve, ceasing all gas flow. The sensing probe cools and the flame sensor switches to the cool position. The system automatically attempts a restart before it locks out.

The flame sensor is a mercury-filled temperature sensor consisting of a sensing element, a capillary tube, an expansion diaphragm and a switch mechanism. As the pilot flame heats the sensing element, the mercury in the element begins to expand. When mercury is heated to its vaporization temperature, a large amount of expansion occurs. The capillary tube transmits the expansion to the diaphragm, which moves and trips the snap-switch mechanism. The sensor switches to the hot position in approximately 45 sec. if an acceptable pilot flame is present. The sensor requires approximately 20 sec. to cool. (See Figure 8.34.)

The pilot burner assembly consists of a burner, a pilot hood, an electrode, and a sensing probe. As the pilot energizes, the electrode begins sparking until pilot flame is established. The electrode is installed to ensure that sparks jump from the electrode, through the pilot gas stream and to the pilot burner hood. The electrode gap is $^3/_{32}''$ to $^5/_{32}''$, and the electrode tip must be centered in the pilot opening.

Automatic Vent Damper

The automatic vent damper feature of quickly reacting by electronically proving the pilot makes it well-suited for the heating system. The automatic vent damper is an energy conservation device designed to reduce heat loss up the vent. The damper automatically opens to expel combustible products when the furnace is on and closes to block heat loss when the furnace is off. The automatic damper is used only on AGA-certified gas units.

The automatic vent damper consists of a damper actuator unit and a damper assembly. The damper assembly is mounted in the furnace vent pipe, and the actuator is attached to the damper assembly. An interlocking plug electrically connects the damper actuator to the electronic pilot control inside the furnace. The damper rotates in one direction; the actuator is energized to both open and close the damper. The energized actuator rotates the damper in 90° increments. A set of microswitches inside the actuator automatically de-energizes the actuator at the end of a 90° opening or closing rotation. The damper and actuator are factory calibrated and do not require field adjustments. A plastic pointer on the shaft between the damper and actuator indicates damper blade position.

When the thermostat calls for heat, the damper actuator energizes and the damper is driven to the fully opened position in 15 sec. When the damper is fully open, the actuator de-energizes, the electronic pilot ignition system energizes, and the main burners ignite. The actuator is electrically interlocked with the electronic pilot control. The damper must be fully open before the ignition system is energized. When the call for heat is complete, the thermostat contacts open, the ignition system and main burners are de-energized, and the damper actuator is again energized. The actuator drives the damper fully closed in 15 sec. This is sufficient time to vent all harmful combustion gases from the heat exchanger. After dampers are fully closed, the actuator is de-energized. The system is now ready for the next heating cycle.

Types of Furnaces

High-Efficiency Furnace

Many high-efficiency furnaces are available. They vary in heat capacities, efficiency, installation costs, and operation methods. Most high-efficiency furnaces operate by fundamental principles associated with conventional atmospheric burners. These furnaces use similar burners and heat exchangers. They depend on draft both to exhaust combustion by-products and to draw combustion air to the open flame.

Lack of oxygen in the combustion process may create harmful by-products such as CO. Holes in the heat exchanger interfere with burner operation, causing incomplete combustion and harmful by-products. Most high-efficiency furnaces depend on air within the home for combustion air. Because this air has already been heated, an additional heat loss exists that lowers furnace efficiency. On tightly constructed homes with little infiltration, outside air must be introduced into the home to ensure an adequate oxygen supply. As in conventional atmospheric burners, heat is required to produce natural draft. When combustion gases cool, natural draft is hindered. As the temperature drops to the dew point, condensation occurs.

Spiraling energy costs of the 1970s mandated higher efficiency heating and air-conditioning equipment. In 1975, the United States Congress passed the National Energy Policy and Conservation Act (NECPA). The efficiency of each furnace is tested using Department of Energy (DOE) procedures. This efficiency rating is called an AFUE rating and is required for every model furnace up to 225,000-Btu input.

Many furnace manufacturers chose to alter the basic design of the atmospheric burner to slightly increase efficiency ratings. The design changes are described by terminology specifically associated with high-efficiency furnaces.

Condensing Furnace A condensing furnace is a furnace that includes provisions to drain condensate that has formed in the combustion process. The following quotation defines condensing furnaces according to DOE standards:

A condensing furnace means a furnace or boiler which condenses part of the water vapor generated by the burning of hydrogen in fuels and is equipped with a means of collecting and draining this condensate. A furnace or boiler shall be considered a condensing furnace only if the latent heat loss coefficient is less than 1. Latent heat loss coefficient means the coefficient which is the fraction of the total heat remaining in the flue gases after any condensing has occurred, as calculated.

The latent heat loss coefficient compares the percentage of heat remaining in the flue with the percentage of heat recovered during condensation. For example, if 50 percent of the normal flue heat content is regained during condensation, the other 50 percent is lost to the vent. The ratio of the flue heat percentage to the condensation heat percentage gives the latent heat loss coefficient. In this case: 50% Flue ÷ 50% Condensation = 1.

Recuperative A recuperative device, such as the recuperative coil and recuperative stainless steel cell, is a device in which combustion gas passes through to recoup and reduce the flue gas temperature before venting. The term *recuperative furnace* is not defined by the AGA or DOE, but is generally used to describe an additional stainless steel coil or clamshell.

Latent Heat of Combustion Before water can go through a physical change of state, heat must be added or subtracted. For example, once water temperature is at its boiling point, additional heat is needed to convert the water into vapor. This heat is termed *latent,* or *hidden,* because it cannot be measured as sensible heat. Each pound of water requires 960 Btus to convert from liquid to vapor state. Conversely, before water vapor can change to liquid, 960 Btus must be released for each pound of water condensed. Latent heat of combustion refers to this hidden heat that must be *released* or added before the water vapor or liquid changes.

Induced Draft An induced draft system consists of a mechanical blower that draws combustion products from the heat exchanger and discharges them into the vent. Because mechanical energy helps move vent gases, less heat energy is required for draft.

Pressurized Vent Venting systems incorporating induced draft use the fan's mechanical energy to force combustion gases through the vent. The fan thus pressurizes the vent pipe, which may create problems with ordinary vent pipe. Combustion gases may spill through the vent seams, where they cool and condense. This promotes rusting, which penetrates through the vent lining and destroys the pipe. Only a sealed flue should be installed in a pressurized vent.

One advantage of a pressurized vent is that the vent pipe may run horizontally and discharge through the side of the house. This system is not dependent on natural draft to exhaust flue gases.

Zero-Pressure Vent *Zero-pressure vent* is a term that describes venting characteristics of some high-efficiency furnaces. These furnaces incorporate an induced fan, which must overcome the resistance of only the heat exchanger. The fan pulls combustion products through the heat exchanger into the flue. The flue products then are exhausted by natural draft.

The only method to improve efficiency on furnaces using conventional burners and heat exchangers is to extract additional heat from the combustion gases, which lowers the flue temperature. Typically, flue temperatures range from 400°F to 550°F on a conventional furnace, with lower temperature ranges for high-efficiency furnaces. Because less heat is available for venting, provisions must be included to mechanically vent flue gases. This is accomplished with an induced draft fan designed to draw certain quantities of combustion air to the burners, through the heat exchanger, and out the vent. The motor must be designed to withstand high temperatures encountered at the furnace. Additional electrical energy is consumed in the venting operation.

High-efficiency furnaces using induced fans do not include draft hoods. The heat exchanger, induced fan and vent are sealed in most designs. The furnace draws in air only at the burner. This design eliminates the amount of usable heat lost up the vent through a draft hood during the cool-down period at the end of each heating cycle. Because induced fans draw the oxygen supply required to sustain complete combustion, safety controls are needed to detect fan failure. These controls are sail or pressure switch devices that open on fan failure to de-energize the gas valve. If the safety control fails to shut off the gas supply on motor failure, incomplete combustion occurs, forming deadly by-products.

An induced fan venting system must be dedicated and not interconnected with vents of naturally vented appliances. Such venting systems also must not terminate in a masonry chimney. Because of these restrictions, the vent is often run through the nearest outside wall. This is possible because of low flue gas temperatures requiring smaller clearances to combustible construction. Low flue temperatures may allow the use of venting materials unsuitable for conventional gas furnaces. For example, polyvinyl chloride (PVC) plastic may be used up to 140°F, and chlorinated polyvinyl chloride (CPVC) plastic is stable to approximately 180°F.

An increase in furnace efficiency above 80 percent to 84 percent induces H_2O formed during the combustion process to condense on cool surfaces in the heat exchanger. It is possible for heat exchangers, even on standard atmospheric burners, to have some condensation form along the outside walls. This is called *chilled surface condensation* and occurs as the heat exchanger

initially warms on heating demand. This problem is compounded on high-efficiency furnaces, where flue gas temperatures are much lower. Many heat exchangers used in high-efficiency furnaces are constructed of aluminized steel to help resist corrosion. Although the aluminized coating provides some protection, the material is permeable. Moisture works into the steel clamshell, causing corrosion—particularly where the coating has been disturbed, such as at weld spots or scratches.

Condensate, which is mildly acidic, forms in a heat exchanger with efficiency greater than 84 percent. The condensed water from the furnace contains small amounts of sulfuric, nitric, or carbonic acid, depending on the fuel burned. The portion of the heat exchanger where condensation occurs must use materials resistant to condensate effects. An extra measure of corrosion protection is required because acids have a higher dew point than H_2O and condense first in the heat exchanger. This small amount of acid is then diluted before leaving the furnace. Condensate is removed by pipes or hoses, similar to condensate from the air-conditioning system. Most manufacturers use stainless steel to withstand corrosion.

As combustion gases cool below the dew point, condensation releases the latent heat of combustion. For each pound of water that drains, an additional 960 Btus are recovered from the flue gases. The latent heat of vaporization amounts to approximately 9 percent of the fuel input.

Although mildly acidic, condensate will not harm plastic, cast, or tile pipe or affect septic tanks. Condensate has a pH of 3.5 to 6.5 on a pH scale from 0 (strongly acidic) to 14 (strongly alkaline), where 7 is considered neutral. Many fruits, soft drinks, and wines exhibit similar pH levels. For example, the carbonic acid formed by mixing water and CO_2 in the combustion process has no greater corrosive qualities than a soft drink carbonated with CO_2. Condensate may be safely disposed of in any ordinary drainage, septic, or sewage system. This has been confirmed by a study of condensing furnaces conducted by Battelle Laboratories and commissioned by the Gas Research Institute.

Even the most efficient furnace using conventional burners and heat exchangers may reclaim only a small percentage of the latent heat of combustion. The H_2O remaining in combustion gases is routed to the vent. Because H_2O is close to the dew point temperature, it continues to condense as it travels out the vent. The furnace should include provisions to drain the condensate flowing back out of the vent. Otherwise, condensate collects at the cabinet, vestibule panel, and electrical makeup box, where it promotes rust and may damage furnace controls. The venting should be water-tight to prevent rust at the seams.

G26 Up-Flo High-Efficiency Furnace

The G26 series high-efficiency up-flow gas furnaces are manufactured with Duralok Plus® aluminized steel clamshell-type heat exchangers. They are available in heating capacities of 50,000 to 125,000 Btu per hour and cooling applications up to five tons. Units can be equipped for either natural gas or LP gas, and all units use electronic (intermittent pilot) ignition. The G26 high-efficiency up-flow gas furnaces are manufactured to meet California standards for emission of the various oxides of nitrogen and California seasonal efficiency requirements without any modifications. All units use a redundant gas valve required by AGA or CGA to ensure safety shutoff.

The G26 series high-efficiency gas furnace has energy efficiency ratings (AFUE) of 90.4 to 92.4 percent. The Duralok Plus® aluminized steel heat exchangers have a limited lifetime warranty. All other covered components have a limited warranty for a full five years.

The Duralok Plus® aluminized steel primary and stainless steel secondary heat exchanger assembly consists of a primary heat exchanger and secondary condenser coil assembly. The main three-pass clamshell-type heat exchanger is constructed of heavy gauge aluminized steel and is designed for normal expansion and contraction without metal fatigue. Its crimped seam design and construction provides long service life, maximum efficiency, and minimum resistance to airflow. The condenser coil is constructed of aluminum fins fitted to stainless steel tubes, and the coil is factory tested for leaks. The combined flue vent and condensate drain header box assembly is located on the front of the coil. The compact size of the complete heat exchanger assembly permits a low overall design of the furnace cabinet.

The flue assembly connects to the flue pipe with connector and hose clamps and to the induced draft blower. It vents combustion products and collects condensate. A flue trap drain hose runs from the assembly to the header box condensate trap. The header box on the end of the condenser coil contains a built-in internal trap and a removable boot on the bottom for easy cleaning and servicing of the header and trap. The header box trap also collects flue condensate from the flue trap for disposal through one single drain pipe.

Aluminized steel inshot burners provide efficient trouble-free operation. The burner venturi mixes air and gas in correct proportions for proper combustion. Burners are completely enclosed in a heavy gauge steel burner box, which has a sight glass for flame observation. The burner assembly is removable from the unit as a single component for service.

A solid-state electronic spark igniter provides positive ignition of the pilot burner on each operating cycle. Pilot gas is ignited and burns during each running cycle (intermittent pilot) of the furnace. (See Figure 8.35.)

The main burners and the pilot are extinguished during the off cycle. This system permits the main gas valve to open only when the pilot burner is proven to be lit. The pilot is a fully automatic operation on demand for heat. Should a loss of flame occur, the main gas valve closes, shutting down the unit. The ignition module has a light-emitting diode (LED) display to indicate the status and as an aid in troubleshooting. Its WatchGuard circuit automatically resets ignition controls after one hour of continuous thermostat demand after unit lockout to eliminate nuisance calls for service.

Automatic gas control provides a 100 percent safety shutoff. A 24V redundant combination gas control valve combines automatic safety pilot, manual shutoff option (on/off), pilot filtration, automatic electric valve (dual), and gas pressure regulation into a compact combination control. The dual valve design provides double assurance of 100 percent shutoff of gas to the pilot and main burners on each off cycle. The gas valve is automatically regulated with a pressure switch to maintain even gas flow, regardless of the type of venting installation.

A factory-installed induced draft blower prepurges the heat exchanger and safely vents combustion products. The blower motor has ball bearings, is thermally protected, and operates only during a heat demand cycle. A pressure switch prevents unit operation in case of blockage of combustion air, of the flue outlet, or of the condensate drain.

Limit control is accurately located to give protection against abnormal operating conditions. The control box is located in the blower compartment. The thermostat connections are made at the control box, which also contains the safety interlock switch, blower control center, control transformer, and circuit breaker.

The blower control center has a solid state board that contains all necessary controls and relays to operate the furnace. The fan control consists of an adjustable blower timed-off delay (1½ min. to approximately 6 min.) and a fixed blower timed-on delay of 45 sec. For the air-con-

■ **FIGURE 8.35**

The combustion process sequence of the G26 heat exchanger assembly.

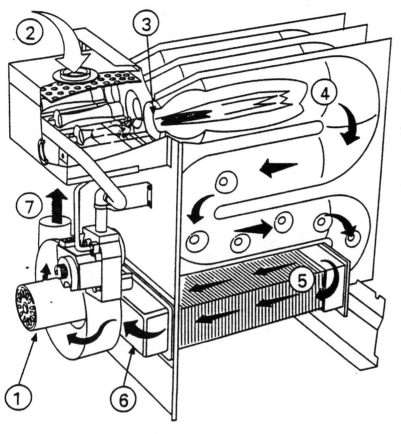

Combustion Process:
1. A call for heat starts the combustion air blower.
2. Outdoor air is drawn through pipe into the burner compartment where it mixes with gas in a conventional style inshot burner.
3. The pilot valve opens and a spark ignites the pilot. When flame is sensed the main valve opens and the pilot lights the burners.
4. Combustion products are drawn downward through the heat exchanger. Heat is extracted as indoor air passes across the outside surface of the metal.
5. Latent heat is removed from the combustion products as air passes through the coil. Condensate (water) is formed as the combustion products cool.
6. As the combustion products exit the coil, condensate is collected and drained away.
7. Combustion products are pulled from the heat exchanger and forced into the flue.

ditioning applications, the blower is automatically energized on thermostat demand for cooling. Also included on the board is a low-voltage terminal strip for thermostat connections. The terminal strip is a plug-in type for easy wiring and servicing. The solid-state board also has provisions for additional power supply requirements for 120V, 4-amp or less power humidifiers and electronic air cleaners.

The powerful blowers are quiet, multi-speed, and direct drive. Each blower assembly is statically and dynamically balanced. The multiple-speed leadless motor is resiliently mounted, and blower speeds are easily changed at the harness connector on the blower motor.

90 Plus Furnace

The 90 Plus furnace design is a radical change from the conventionally designed furnace. Circulating air travels through the furnace in the same manner as in the previous 90 Plus models. The difference is in the burner and heat exchanger. The heat exchanger is a cylinder

with holes in the rear where the flue gases move to a transition section. From this point on, the flue products move as in previous 90 Plus furnaces. The burner, which is entirely new, uses no secondary air. The burner is a 360° burner assembly, that is, the flame burns 360° around the burner, which is inserted into the center of the heat exchanger on the front.

This furnace uses one burner orifice. All the air for combustion is drawn from outside and enters the burner through a sealed combustion air pipe. The induced-draft blower draws in outdoor combustion air to the burner. This is primary air, which mixes with the gas and ignites at the burner head.

Primary Heat Exchanger The heat exchanger of the 90 Plus gas furnace utilizes a mechanically crimped seam instead of welded joints to assemble the components. The primary chamber is a horizontal cylinder that has a circular front. A rectangular transition section is attached to the rear of the cylinder. The heat exchangers are assembled and the joints are rolled mechanically.

The primary heat exchanger assemblies are built in two sizes, a 14″ diameter and an 18″ diameter. The primary heat exchanger is completely 409-HP stainless steel. The heat exchangers have an internal 185%R stainless steel flue baffle held in the rear seam between the cylinder and the transition section.

Secondary Heat Exchanger

The secondary heat exchanger is a single-pass coil using 3/8″ diameter 29-4C stainless steel tubes, each having internal tubulator strips. Aluminum fins are extruded over the tubes to enhance heat transfer. Flue gas condensation actually occurs in the secondary heat exchanger.

The 90 Plus furnace cannot be installed in a mobile home, trailer, or recreational vehicle.

Combustion and Ventilation Air

Combustion air must be free of acid-forming chemicals such as sulfur, fluorine, and chlorine. These elements are found in aerosol sprays, detergents, bleaches, cleaning solvents, air fresheners, paint and varnish removers, refrigerants, and many other commercial and household products. Vapors from these products, when burned in a gas flame, form acid compounds. The acid compounds increase the dew point temperature of the flue products and are highly corrosive after they condense.

Because this is a direct vent forced-air furnace, all combustion air is supplied directly to the burner through a special air-intake system. The maximum air intake pipe length is 40′ of straight pipe and four 90° DWV long sweep elbows plus the termination. No additional pipe is allowed to be added to the length if fewer than four 90° long sweep elbows are used. If less than 40′ of pipe is used, additional 90° long sweep elbows are not allowed. The minimum pipe diameter between the furnace and termination is 2″, up to and including the 75,000-Btu models. The pipe diameter between the furnace and the termination is 3″ for the 90,000-, 105,000-, and 120,000-Btu models. The horizontal combustion air inlet terminal is composed of a 2″ PVC coupling or elbow with a vertical wind deflector vane spaced 4″ to 6″ from the wall.

All units with horizontal air intakes must have a PVC drain tee in their air intake pipe at the furnace. A 1/2″ PVC loop trap catches any water in the air intake pipe and drains it into the furnace condensate drain through a flexible hose. This trap prevents any water from reaching the combustion air intake at the burner and disturbing furnace combustion. (See Figure 8.36.)

The combustion air for this furnace is supplied directly from the outdoors through the combustion air inlet system. When the 90 Plus is installed in a confined space, such as a utility room or closet, there must be 2″ of space at the front of the furnace to ensure proper ventilation.

When the furnace is installed in the same space with other gas appliances, such as a water heater, an adequate supply of combustion and ventilation air is necessary for all of the appliances. *Note:* An unconfined space must have at least 50 cu. ft. for each 1,000 Btus of the total input of all appliances in the space. If the open space containing the appliances is in a building with tight construction, outside air still may be required for the other appliances to burn and vent properly.

This furnace removes both sensible and latent heat from the combustion flue gases. Removal of latent heat results in water condensation. The condensed water drains from the secondary heat exchanger and out the drain trap.

Vertical Venting

This furnace must be vented to the outdoors with PVC schedule 40 pipe. The vent pipe is approved for 0″ clearance from combustible materials.

Drain line and overflow line can be 1/2″ flex tube or schedule 40 PVC with a discount union so the trap can be removed. The drain line should terminate at an inside drain. If no floor drain is available, a condensate pump that is resistant to acidic water must be installed. If a pump is used that is not resistant to acidic water, a condensate neutralizer must be used ahead of the pump. A condensate pump must have an auxiliary safety switch to prevent furnace operation in the event of pump failure, resulting in an overflow of condensate. A blocked or restricted drain line can flood the furnace heat exchanger. Hoses or tubes used should be low-density polyethylene, nylon or PVC.

Induced Draft Blower

The induced draft blower assembly uses a 115V single-phase motor. Lubrication is not required on the blower motor. The integrated furnace control initiates induced draft blower operation when the thermostat closes in the heat mode.

The furnace has a differential pressure switch to sense adequate flow of combustion air and flue products through the furnace and vent system. The pressure switch also shuts the furnace down if a blocked secondary heat exchanger drain condition exists. The 90 Plus furnace uses a 5- or 10-second pressure switch

■ **FIGURE 8.36**

Standard horizontal venting using accessory termination kits.

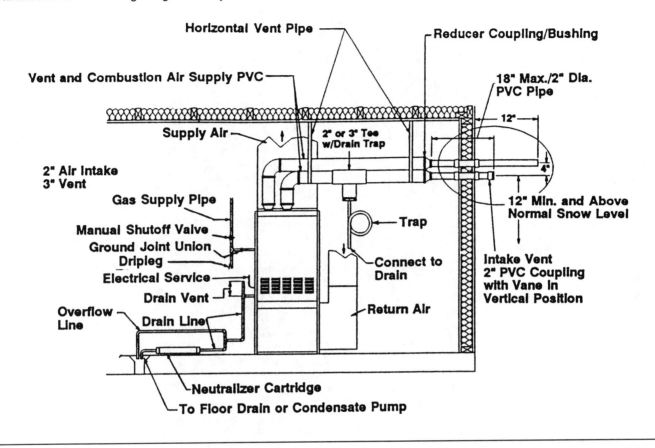

delay timer, which allows the pressure in the vent system time to stabilize during burner starting and avoids the nuisance of tripping the pressure switch.

The high limit control is preset by the manufacturer and cannot be calibrated in the field. It is set to prevent the circulating air leaving the furnace from exceeding the maximum outlet air temperature. It will automatically reset when the temperature returns to a point below its set point.

The vent temperature limit control is a manual reset control installed on the induced draft blower housing for sensing flue gas temperature. This control shuts off the main burners if abnormal flue gas temperatures occur.

Crusader

The Crusader up-flow and the 58DHC Crusader down-flow and horizontal-flow furnaces represent the middle-efficiency line with an 80.2 percent AFUE rating. The Crusader unit has a height of 40″ because of its S-shaped heat exchanger. A silicon carbide ignition

hot shoe lights the burners, which precludes a necessary pilot burner. Furnace operation is controlled by a solid-state microprocessor board. A draft-induced fan pulls combustion gases through the heat exchanger. The Crusader unit does not condense. (See Figure 8.37.)

On a heat demand, the microprocessor board starts the draft-induced fan. A pressure switch informs the board the fan is operating, and the board then energizes the silicon carbide hot shoe. When the hot shoe heats sufficiently to ignite the burners, the board opens the gas valve and gas ignites at the burners, using a solid-state sensor. After a time delay, the board starts the main blower. When the heat demand ends, the microprocessor board shuts down the gas valve, hot shoe ignition, and induced draft fan. The board waits a short time before stopping the main blower. (See Figure 8.38.)

With the burners at the bottom of the heat exchanger, the inspector views the flame and ensures proper combustion characteristics. He or she verifies that the burners do not light unless the induced fan starts.

■ **FIGURE 8.37**

Carrier Crusader furnace.

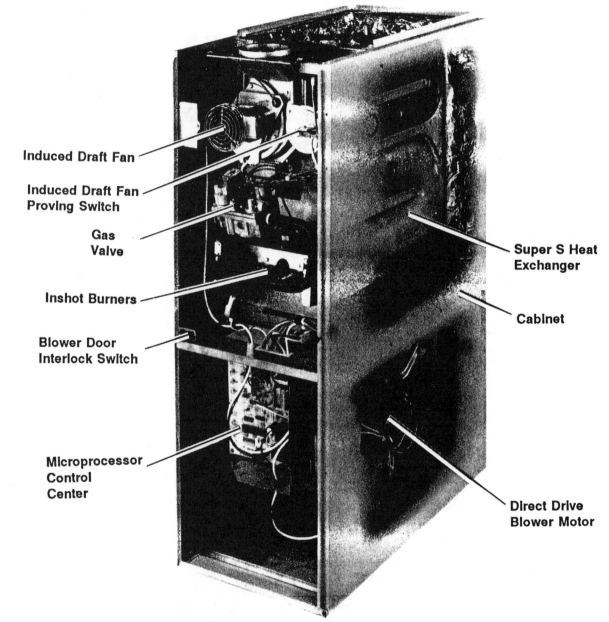

Induced Draft Fan

Induced Draft Fan
Proving Switch

Gas
Valve

Inshot Burners

Blower Door
Interlock Switch

Microprocessor
Control
Center

Super S Heat
Exchanger

Cabinet

Direct Drive
Blower Motor

Vent seams should be sealed with high-temperature tape from the furnace vent connection to the flue connection. Because of the heat exchanger S-design and the induced draft fan, it is difficult to determine whether a problem exists with the heat exchanger. If a yellow flame appears, or if carbon and corrosion exist at the heat exchanger bottom, the inspector should have a heating/cooling contractor further examine the furnace.

Weathermaker

The Weathermaker is the first condensing furnace. It uses an inverted heat exchanger with burners at the top. (See Figure 8.39.)

The combustion system is sealed with a small view port at the top for flame inspection. A microprocessor controls furnace operation. Both up-flow and down-flow models have efficiencies to 96.6 percent.

■ **FIGURE 8.38**

Crusader installation.

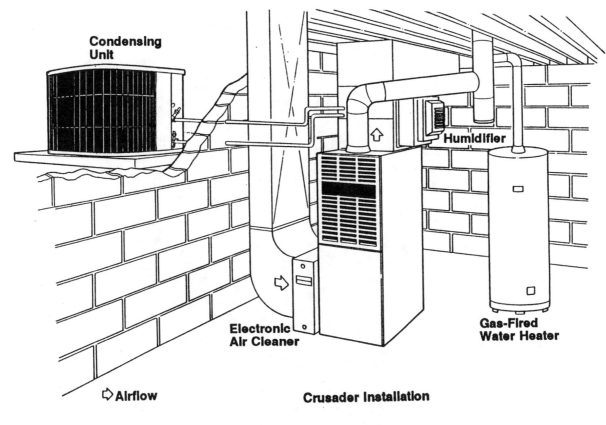

An induced draft blower pulls the gases down through the primary Super S heat exchanger into the Mini S condensing heat exchanger. Schedule 40 PVC pipe conveys outside combustion air to the burners and carries exhaust gases directly outside. Condensate flows through a plastic trap and pipe to a drain.

A heat call from the thermostat instructs the microprocessor to start the induced draft fan, which pulls combustion air directly from outside through PVC pipe. A proving switch informs the microprocessor board of induced draft fan operation. The board opens the pilot gas valve and electronically lights the pilot burner. After the pilot proves, the board opens the main gas valve and lights the main burners.

Combustion gases flow downward through the primary heat exchanger and into the condensing heat exchanger. The induced fan forces the cooled combustion gases through PVC pipe directly outside. Liquid formed in the condensing heat exchanger flows to a drain.

The microprocessor board delays main blower operation for several seconds after the unit starts. This allows the heat exchanger time to warm. After the heat call, the microprocessor board breaks power to the gas valve, ending the heat cycle. It terminates power to the induced draft fan. The main blower continues to operate for several seconds to deliver the maximum amount of heated air. Because the unit uses Super S and Mini S heat exchangers with sealed combustion, there is little for the inspector to observe in the heat exchanger. He or she should visually check for proper combustion characteristics at the view port. (See Figure 8.40.)

The induced draft fan must start and prove before the pilot lights. Inspect the PVC air intake and exhaust pipe for indications of overheating. This may include sags in the pipe or evidence of melting close to the furnace. Note any condensate leaks.

Caution! Do not set the thermostat greater than 3°F above room temperature to start the unit. Setting the temperature higher tells the unit that the demand is greater than the system can handle. The microprocessor

■ **FIGURE 8.39**

Weathermaker SXA furnace.

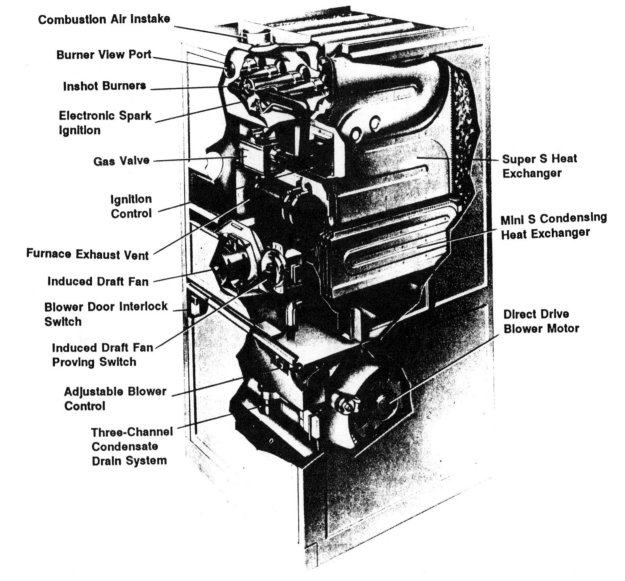

Combustion Air Instake

Burner View Port

Inshot Burners

Electronic Spark
Ignition

Gas Valve

Ignition
Control

Furnace Exhaust Vent

Induced Draft Fan

Blower Door Interlock
Switch

Induced Draft Fan
Proving Switch

Adjustable Blower
Control

Three-Channel
Condensate
Drain System

Super S Heat
Exchanger

Mini S Condensing
Heat Exchanger

Direct Drive
Blower Motor

"thinks" there is a malfunction in the unit and may set off alarms indicating immediate service is needed. This procedure should be followed with any furnace controlled with a microprocessor.

Weathermaker Infinity

The top-of-the-line Carrier furnace features the Super S heat exchanger with Mini S condensing heat exchanger and PVC pipe for air intake and exhaust. It is a sealed combustion system that uses a two-stage gas valve, allowing low and high fire at the burners. (See Figure 8.41.)

The major difference between the Weathermaker Infinity and other condensing furnaces is that both the induced draft fan and the main blower have variable-speed motors. A microprocessor controls complete furnace operation. The AFUE rating is 93.5 percent. Because of the variable-speed motors, the unit uses up to 80 percent less electric power than a standard furnace.

On a call for heat, the microprocessor starts the induced draft fan. The fan motor ramps up to the proper revolutions per minute (rpm). Two pressure switches monitor pressure differences in the exhaust system and shut down the system if the differences are not correct.

■ **FIGURE 8.40**

Carrier Weathermaker installation.

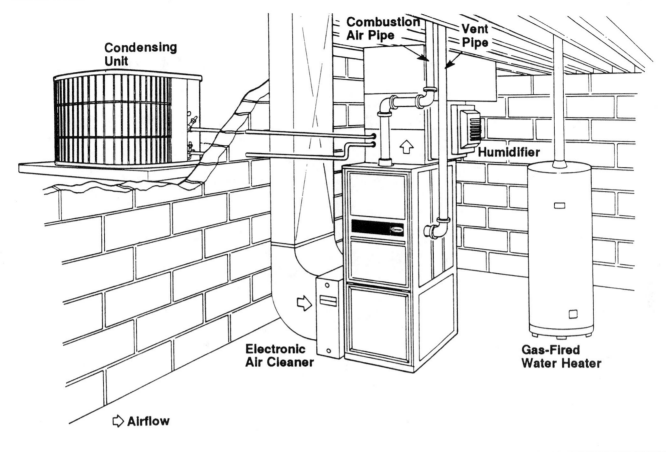

When the induced draft fan operates at the correct speed, the microprocessor board opens the pilot valve and electronically lights the pilot. With the pilot proved, the board opens the gas valve to light the main burners.

The microprocessor board monitors the time length of the last two burner firings and the time length between them. It uses this information to start the furnace on either high or low fire. To get the most efficiency from each operation, the board modulates the gas valve from high to low to keep the burners firing for at least 15 min. The board varies the rpm of the induced fan to deliver the proper amount of combustion air. The board varies the main blower rpm to deliver warm air to the living space.

After the heat call, the microprocessor closes the gas valves and stops the induced draft fan. The main blower runs for a set time to deliver the most warm air to the space. Do not set the thermostat more than 3°F above room temperature to start the unit. Because the unit uses sealed combustion, there is little for the inspector to observe in the heat exchanger. He or she visually checks for proper combustion characteristics at the view port.

The induced draft fan must start and prove before the pilot lights. Inspect the PVC air intake and exhaust pipe for indications of overheating. This could be sags in the pipe or evidence of melting close to the furnace. Check for any condensate leaks. Because of the variable speed of the main blower motor, the temperature rise of the furnace could vary considerably.

Trane

The XV 90 Variable Speed furnace is the Trane Company's high-efficiency condensing furnace. It is available in both up-flow and down-flow configurations. Because of its condensing feature, its AFUE rating is more than 90 percent. It uses an induced draft blower to draw combustion air through the heat exchanger. To further reduce operation cost, this unit uses a variable-speed blower motor. (See Figure 8.42.)

■ **FIGURE 8.41**

Carrier Weathermaker Infinity SXB furnace.

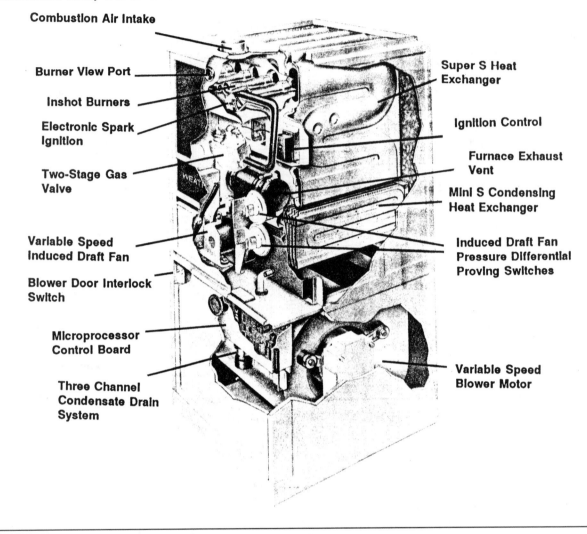

Combustion Air Intake

Burner View Port

Inshot Burners

Electronic Spark Ignition

Two-Stage Gas Valve

Variable Speed Induced Draft Fan

Blower Door Interlock Switch

Microprocessor Control Board

Three Channel Condensate Drain System

Super S Heat Exchanger

Ignition Control

Furnace Exhaust Vent

Mini S Condensing Heat Exchanger

Induced Draft Fan Pressure Differential Proving Switches

Variable Speed Blower Motor

On a call for heat, the unit's primary control starts the induced draft fan. The induced fan brings air into the combustion chamber as it exhausts air from the heat exchanger. A pressure switch detects fan operation. If the induced fan fails to start, the primary control stops furnace operation. When the primary control senses induced fan operation, it energizes a hot surface igniter and heats to approximately 2,000°F. No pilot flame is used with this furnace. When the hot surface igniter heats sufficiently, the primary control opens the gas valve, allowing gas to flow to the burners, where it ignites.

After the gas ignites, the hot combustion gases rise through the main aluminized steel heat exchanger cells. At the top of these cells, a manifold directs the gases to a stainless steel recuperative cell. The induced draft fan pulls the combustion gases down through the recuperative cell, and main blower air passing over this cell cools the gases to the point where H_2O condenses. This system recovers latent heat of combustion normally lost up a conventional flue.

The induced fan forces gases out through plastic vent pipe, which may vent either vertically or horizontally. Any liquid flows down clear plastic tubing to a vented trap and out to a drain. As the heat exchanger warms, a fan control brings the blower on after a short time period to move heated air throughout the home.

The inspector cannot visually inspect much of the main heat exchanger cells. The inspector can view the bottom of the main heat exchanger cells and the burner flame, which should be blue. As with any furnace using

■ **FIGURE 8.42**

The XV 90 components.

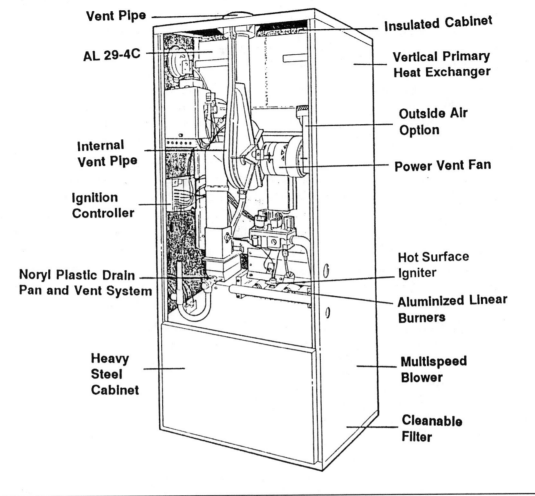

Vent Pipe — Insulated Cabinet

AL 29-4C — Vertical Primary Heat Exchanger

Outside Air Option

Internal Vent Pipe

Power Vent Fan

Ignition Controller

Hot Surface Igniter

Noryl Plastic Drain Pan and Vent System

Aluminized Linear Burners

Heavy Steel Cabinet

Multispeed Blower

Cleanable Filter

an induced draft fan, there is no draft diverter to check. The furnace should not fire unless the induced fan operates first.

The inspector checks the plastic vent pipe for sags or signs of overheating. The pipe should be well supported. He or she looks for any restrictions to water flow in the clear plastic drain from the bottom of the induced draft blower. This has been known to clog up with dust and airborne debris. If this tube does clog, the unit cannot fire.

Inspection of Gas Forced-Air Furnaces

The inspection of a conventional gas furnace begins when the inspector arrives at the property, if the furnace roof vent is visible on the roof. If the furnace is having a problem, the roof vent cap may be discolored. This can be caused by a cracked heat exchanger or incomplete combustion (dirty furnace). Sometimes the furnace has been replaced but the roof vent was not cleaned up.

When observing the furnace installation, it is important to check the gas line from the cutoff valve to the gas control valve. It is important that the proper type of gas line be used and protected at the entry through the furnace case.

Just because a furnace is only two to three years old, the inspector should never assume there isn't any problem with it. When a furnace has air-conditioning connected to it, the heat exchanger oxidizes faster than on a furnace that has no air-conditioning coils attached.

Inspecting a furnace is important; the results can be very serious if the inspector is not aware of proper operation of the furnace. An inspector should be aware that CO has no odor, but he or she should be sensitive to flue gas odors that might signify that CO also might be present.

When inspecting a furnace, it is important to have a copy of some standards of practice that can be used as a guide. When an inspector inspects any appliance, it should be operated in the normal operating mode. When starting the inspection, the access panels should be removed and the condition of the controls observed. Then the condition of the flue pipes, dampers, and the related components should be checked for safe operation. It is now time for the operational check. The thermostat should be set up to 90°F; if the furnace cycles, it is because the thermostat is not being satisfied and there may be a problem. Then shut the furnace off at the kill switch, which should be located where the power enters the furnace, to test the function of the switch. The heat shield (on mid-efficiency furnaces) should be removed so the heat exchanger can be inspected by using a mechanic's mirror and a good flashlight. Only part of the heat exchanger can be checked for excessive rust and cracks in the metal. Usually the heat exchanger will fail first around the pilot (if it is a standing pilot that is left on year round). Occasionally the inspector can reach in and feel a crack or look in and see the crack in the heat exchanger.

With the heat shield removed, the vestibule panel can be inspected for cracks. A crack here is common and usually is not as serious as a cracked heat exchanger. However, the crack or rust hole will get larger and the blower air can cause flame deterioration.

The ignition should be smooth, and all burners should light almost instantly. The inspector now checks the color and quality of the flame. The flame should be a sharp, clearly defined flame. The color of the flame should be predominantly blue, and the flame should rest directly on the burner ports. Any significant changes in the flame pattern, such as a yellow flame, a yellow-tipped flame, an orange/red color in flames, a soft lazy flame, a lifting flame, or a floating flame, are all indications of a problem and is creating CO that could be a hazard. When checking the burner for a flame pattern, you also should check the condition of the burner compartment for rust build-up on the burners. This can affect the gas flow to the burner ports and cause delayed ignition or floating flame patterns. The flame pattern should be the same on all burners.

When the blower turns on, there may be a slight discoloration in the flame, but the flame should settle down and return to the sharp blue flame. There should not be any change in the flame pattern. When the air chamber is pressurized by the blower air, a crack in the heat exchanger could let air impinge on the flame, which will cause disturbance of the flame on the burners. The furnace should run for a few minutes so the inspector can observe the operation of the furnace. With the thermostat set at 90°F the burner should cycle off for a brief period and then fire up again. When the burner cycles off and on, the high limit control is functioning properly. The high limit control is designed to prevent the furnace from dangerously overheating. The high limit control may shut down the burners anytime the heat exchanger temperature reaches approximately 200°F. The most common cause for the burners to shut down on a high limit is failure of the fan/limit control, but there are other things that the inspector should be aware of, such as clogged filters, a clogged evaporator coil on the air conditioner, or too many hot air registers that are closed or clogged.

The inspector should always check for gas leaks, at least around the equipment (furnace, water heater, range, etc.). Always be alert to a gas odor, particularly in the areas of the gas control valve, gas line, and pipe connections. Sometimes the control valve does not close tight when the system is off, and gas will leak into the burners. This is very difficult to catch, but with an electronic detector it is quite easy to pinpoint the location of the leak. Inspectors can use a liquid leak detector (soap bubbles) but should never rely only on smell when inspecting gas appliances. LP gas is heavier and denser than air. Leaking LP gas is difficult to detect because it has only a slight odor and collects near the floor.

When the furnace is operating, the inspector should check the draft at the draft hood. Also, check the vent pipe from the furnace through the roof. The flue pipe should be double wall, be as short a run as possible, have a positive slope, and the joints should be connected with screws. It is helpful for the inspector to be familiar with the local and national codes for venting gas appliances. When checking the draft, the burner and blower have to be operating. An easy way is to light a match and place the match under the draft hood. The draft should pull the flame up in the draft hood. If it blows the match out, the vent is blocked. This is what is called *spillage,* and flue gases are coming into the living spaces. When inspecting a furnace, if the inspector finds any areas that are not performing their function, he or she should note the problem on the report and recommend that a qualified technician evaluate the unit for safe and proper operation.

■ **FIGURE 8.43**

The purpose of the nozzle is to convert the liquid to a gaseous state.

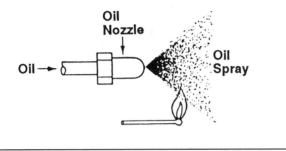

■ **FIGURE 8.44**

The barometric damper controls the draft.

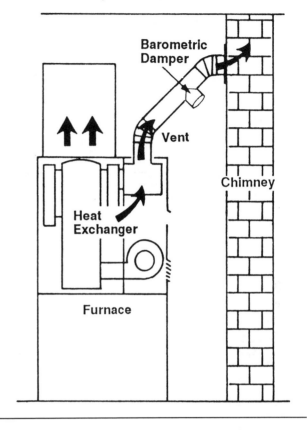

■ OIL FURNACES

Fuel oil is one of the heavier hydrocarbon fuels. It contains more carbon than lighter hydrocarbon fuels such as natural gas and LP gas. Oil must be converted from a liquid to a gaseous state for ignition and combustion in a process called *vaporization* of the oil. (See Figure 8.43.)

Several grades and/or weights of fuel oil are available, ranging from grade 1 through grade 6. Grade 1 fuel oil is a light distillate intended for use in vaporizing-type burners. High volatility is essential to ensure complete evaporation, which leaves minimum residue.

The most widely used residential heating oil is grade 2. Grade 2 fuel oil is heavier than grade 1 and is designed for use in pressure-atomizing-type burners found in oil furnaces. Such a burner sprays the oil under pressure into the combustion chamber, where it is heated, vaporized, mixed with air, and ignited. Grades 3 through 6 are heavier oils intended for burners designed to atomize oils of higher viscosity. The heavier grades of oil require preheating for greater atomization.

To maintain complete combustion, air is required, and an oil burner is supplied with a combustion air blower. For complete combustion, each pint of grade 2 fuel oil requires more than 14 lb. (215 cu. ft.) of air, which breaks down to approximately 3.3 lb. of oxygen and 11.1 lb. of nitrogen. This results in approximately 15 percent CO_2 in the flue gas.

An oil furnace cannot provide laboratory conditions for theoretically complete combustion. Therefore, excess combustion air is added to ensure complete combustion of the high-carbon fuel. As excess air is added, the percentage of CO_2 decreases. Approximately 10 percent of CO_2 in the flue gas shows adequate combustion air supply.

Venting

The venting system for an oil furnace is different from that of a gas furnace. One of the important differences is that the oil burner is supplied with a combustion air blower. It does not depend on secondary air for combustion. Although reasonable draft control is necessary for venting, draft conditions do not upset airflow when the oil burner blower is set for sufficient air amounts. Therefore, an oil furnace does not require a draft hood or diverter, as does the gas furnace. The oil furnace is vented directly into the chimney.

To regulate the oil furnace draft, a device called a *barometric damper* is installed in the vent pipe. (See Figure 8.44.) The barometric damper is hinged and weighted and opens to the furnace room. When chimney draft becomes too great, the damper swings partly open. The excess draft draws air from the room into the vent rather than drawing too heavily on the furnace. Less heat travels up the vent, causing an efficient system. The weight of the damper is adjustable to set the furnace draft at a desired point. This point is –0.03″ to –0.04″ water

The gun assembly, sometimes called the oil line assembly, includes the oil nozzle, oil pipe, and high-tension wire leads to the electrodes.

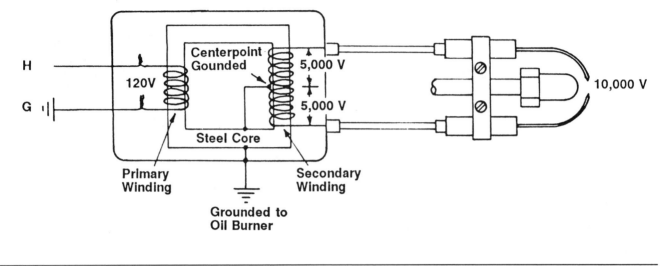

column into the draft water gauge. If there is too little vent draft, the furnace may force combustion products into the living space.

Oil Burner

An oil burner assembly consists of a burner motor, combustion air blower, pump, ignition transformer and gun subassembly, which includes electrodes. The oil burner motor supplies power to drive the pump and blower. The ignition transformer provides 10,000V to the electrodes, which creates a spark to ignite the oil. (See Figure 8.45.)

There are two types of pumps: a belt drive pump and a direct drive pump. (See Figure 8.46.) The oil pump pressurizes fuel oil and forces it through a metering orifice in the nozzle. The orifice in the nozzle is engineered and machined to provide proper oil flow and atomization at the recommended pressure (approximately 100 psi). The nozzle projects a cone-shaped, fine spray of oil droplets into the heat exchanger combustion chamber.

The blower provides combustion air, which mixes with the oil spray. The heat source required to vaporize and ignite the oil spray, which starts combustion, is provided by the high-voltage electrical arc that jumps between the electrode tips. When the burner starts, the arc is blown or fanned into the oil spray by combustion air velocity. The arc has sufficient heat to vaporize the oil in its vicinity and

ignite the vapor. The ignited vapor then ignites the remaining oil in the spray cone. (See Figure 8.47.)

The side view of the gun assembly in Figure 8.47 shows the position of the electrode tips in relation to the oil spray. The tips are not in the oil spray, but are fairly close to allow the arc to blow into the spray. Otherwise, the oil would form a carbon bridge across the tips and short them out like a spark plug. The shape of the electrode tip is important to produce a reliable arc. It is cone shaped with the cone end slightly flattened or dulled. In time, the cone burns away from electrical erosion and widens the electrode gap. It then must be reshaped with a file and the gap reset. The gap distance affects the spark temperature; the wider the gap, the cooler the spark.

The 10,000V to the electrodes are supplied by an ignition transformer. This is a step-up transformer that raises the voltage from 120V to 10,000V as required. Because the high voltage causes current to flow through resistances that will block the flow of 120V, insulated conductors are required. The insulation is provided by porcelain sleeves on the electrodes and high-tension noise conductors. The electrodes and conductors must be kept clean, or high voltage will force current to flow through a film of dirt, carbon, or oil on the surface of the porcelain and wire insulation.

There are two types of transformers. One is equipped with snap-on terminals for high-tension leads, and the other contains bus bar contacts for a spring-load bus bar. Some burners use a spring bus bar rather than

■ **FIGURE 8.46**

Oil burner pumps.

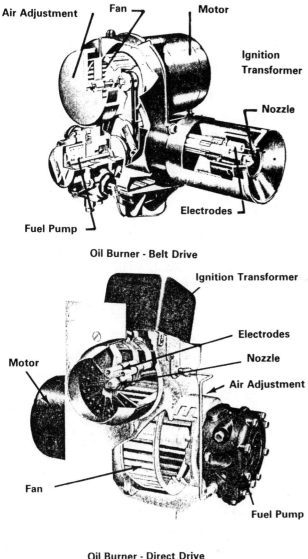

Oil Burner - Belt Drive

Oil Burner - Direct Drive

■ **FIGURE 8.47**

Gun assembly.

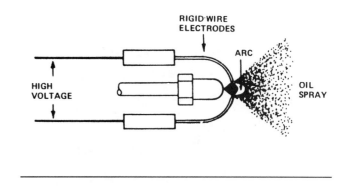

flexible wire cables. The bus bars contact the terminals on the transformer by spring tension. The transformer has 120V primary winding and 10,000V secondary winding on a steel core. The center of the secondary winding is grounded to both the core and the transformer case. They are also grounded to the burner and furnace and to earth ground. Each terminal of the secondary winding is 5,000V potential to ground even though the total between the electrodes is 10,000V.

The reason for center point grounding is to prevent more than 5,000V above ground, which may cause arcing to the nozzle or other burner parts. This would overcome the resistance of the porcelain and conductor insulation.

The 120V primary coil of the ignition transformer is connected in parallel with the oil burner motor. Therefore, the ignition spark is on when the burner is operating and remains on until the burner is turned off. This process is called *continuous ignition*. There are burner models that employ intermittent ignition. After a trial period for ignition and when the flame is established, the electrodes cease sparking by de-energizing the ignition transformer.

Burner motors used in most residential furnaces are manufactured in two types: the flange-mounted direct drive and the base-mounted belt drive. The motors used for residential burners are $\frac{1}{6}$ or $\frac{1}{8}$ hp single phase. The motor speed for the belt drive may be either 1,725 or 3,450 rpm. If the motor is 3,450 rpm, it may be reduced to 1,725 rpm, which is the correct pump operating speed. The direct drive motor must have an operating speed of 1,725 rpm because it is connected directly to the pump.

The oil burner pump motor is equipped with a manual thermal overload protector to protect the motor against overheating and/or overloading. The protector trips and locks out so the motor cannot restart. The reset button located on the motor case provides for manual restart of the motor.

Heat Exchanger

The heat exchanger on an oil-fired furnace has both primary and secondary heating surfaces. They are constructed of a combination of aluminized and cold-rolled steel. (See Figure 8.48.)

The primary heating surface is the area that surrounds the flame. The lower part of the primary section is

Oil furnace heat exchanger.

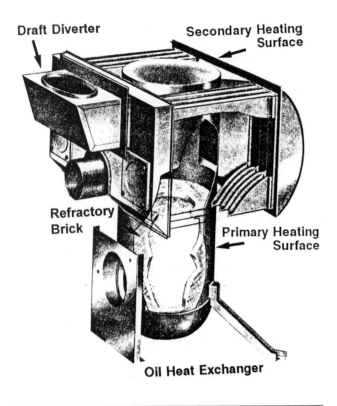

lined with refractory brick. The brick prevents the flame from approaching direct contact with the steel. The refractory brick quickly attains high temperatures and radiates heat, which enhances combustion characteristics.

The secondary heating surface is a series of steel sections that hot combustion gases must pass over before leaving the heat exchanger. Clean-out openings are located in the secondary heating surface, while clean-out access may be found in the primary section. The fire may be observed through the peephole in the cast iron inspection door.

Primary Control

Oil-fired furnaces are equipped with a central electrical control for the oil burner, to which the thermostat is connected and from which the burner and furnace are controlled. This control is called a *primary control* and is a combination ignition and safety control. Many older models refer to the primary control as a *stack control* or *protectorelay*. The function of the primary control is to supervise the operation of the burner and provide system safety by

- sensing the presence or absence of flame and shutting down the system if the burner fails to properly function and
- being subordinate to the system's temperature limit safety controls.

There are two basic types of primary control:

1. An intermittent ignition type that energizes the ignition system until the burner flame is proven, then turns off the ignition.
2. A constant ignition type that continues to energize the ignition system throughout the entire burner on cycle.

The primary control contains a 24V transformer; internal relays, including an oil burner relay; a flame detection circuit; and a safety switch that monitors the system. The line-voltage connections are made to pigtail wire leads and a junction box to which the control is attached. The low-voltage connections are made at the terminal block on the control.

There are four low-voltage connections on some primary controls; other controls have six low-voltage connections. Controls with four terminal connections are most common. The terminals are used in pairs and designated by letters for their intended use. For example, the terminals connected to the thermostat are designated as $T1$ and T or T and TA. A second pair of terminals is connected to the flame detector that monitors burner flame whether the burner is lit or not. These two terminals are designated S and S (sensor). Other primary controls may have other designations; for example, FD and FD (flame detector). The terminal control with six connections has a third pair of terminals. This third pair provides 24V to power the fan control on down-flow or horizontal-flow units. They energize whenever the thermostat calls for heat and de-energize when the thermostat is satisfied.

Flame Detectors

The flame detector is a device that senses the burner flame. When the flame detector senses the flame, it signals the primary control that transfers the information to the other circuits. Oil-fired furnaces are equipped with a flame detector. One type of flame detector is the stack-mounted thermal sensor. This control is mounted on the furnace stack or on the furnace front above the combustion chamber on equipment with low stack temperatures. It senses changes in stack temperature with a bimetal probe detector. The detector actuates a push rod to break a cold contact and produce a hot contact as the oil furnace fires.

The bimetal flame detectors or thermal flame sensors, also called *pyrostat detectors,* sense changes in stack temperature. A bimetal detector is used to actuate the push rod on temperature change to break a cold contact and produce a hot contact. This sequence de-energizes a safety switch and permits the burner to continue operation. As the bimetal moves in response to temperature changes, it makes or breaks a series of contacts. After a burner is shut down for weeks or months, pyrostat contacts may fall out of step, which prevents the burner from starting. The control must be placed back in step by the manual reset, which produces the cold contact. This is the normal start-up mode.

The pyrostat contacts may fail to produce contacts for three reasons: (1) the contacts may be contaminated, (2) the bimetal sensing element may be burned, or (3) the contacts are not receiving sufficient heat because of soot deposits. Clutch operation may be impaired by dirt buildup.

Another type of flame detector is the cadmium sulfide flame sensor, which is mounted in the oil burner. The newer model furnaces are equipped with the cadmium sulfide flame sensor, commonly referred to as the *cad cell.* The light-sensitive cad cell is mounted so it views the oil flame. The variable resistance of the cad cell in the presence of light is used to actuate a sensitive flame relay, which controls the burner. The swift response of the cad cell to light eliminates the lag found in bimetal sensors. This element is advantageous for large oil installations.

Fan Control

The fan control is one of the major controls. The fan control switch is heat actuated and has normally open contacts. It contains a bimetal type of heat-sensing probe that senses air temperature passing over the outer surfaces of the heat exchanger. The probe is a spiral type and is installed into the heating unit from the front side of the cabinet into the furnace's heat exchanger. Its position must be specific so the bimetal probe will sense the air temperature passing from the heat exchanger. When the temperature reaches the predetermined point, the bimetal closes the normally open contacts, completing the circuit, and starts the blower motor.

There are two types of fan controls. One is called a *combination control.* The fan control portion is provided with two adjustable levers. One lever is used to set the blower's on temperature and the other to set the off temperature.

The control settings are field adjusted according to the homeowner's desire, with the on or make point at approximately 100°F. Thus, when air passing over the heat exchanger reaches approximately 100°F, the switch starts the fan, delivering air to the living space. The off point on the switch may be set 15°F and 25°F below the make point. If the switch were set well below return air or room temperature during the heating season, continuous blower operation would result.

The difference between the fan on and off points is called the *fan control differential.* The temperature difference between these two points should be set between 15°F and 25°F. If the differential is too low (less than 15°F), the control cycles the blower motor. This is due to slight temperature fluctuations caused by residual heat from the heat exchanger. If the fan on setting is too high, the blower must wait too long before coming on. This increases heat loss from the furnace and reduces furnace efficiency.

The other type of control is the single-fan control. It has only one adjustable lever by which the desired blower off temperature is set. This is a fixed differential control with a built-in differential of 25°F. Therefore, the blower on temperature will always be 25°F higher than the blower off setting. If the homeowner wishes to maintain continuous air circulation, it is necessary to set the open or break point below normal return air temperature. This way, the air temperature passing over the heat exchanger remains above the break setting. Even though the burner is off, the blower continues to run.

When cooling is added to a standard furnace, an additive cooling relay is placed into the line circuit. This relay has a set of contacts that bypass the fan control and deliver power directly to the blower motor. The contacts are actuated by a coil that is run off the thermostat. The coil is energized on a cooling call or if the thermostat is set for automatic blower operation. This is necessary because on cooling, the air temperature circulated to the system would be below the off set point of the fan control. The fan control would shut off and not allow the blower to operate.

Horizontal and Reverse-Flow Furnaces

Reverse-flow (down-flow) and horizontal units present a different problem from the up-flow units. The fan control bimetal element for up-flow or down-flow and horizontal furnaces is located near the air discharge end of the heat exchanger. On a down-flow furnace, this element is near the heat exchanger bottom because the blower forces air downward.

At the beginning of a heating cycle, the blower does not operate unless the control is set for continuous blower operation. Because the blower is off, heat generated by the furnace rises upward and away from the fan control element. This prevents the element from sensing heat buildup and starting the blower when required. The same condition exists in a horizontal furnace because of the stack effect created by the ductwork. A special fan control is used to overcome this problem. The horizontal furnace is equipped with a timer that overrides the bimetal element. It turns on the blower within 30 sec. to 60 sec. after the thermostat calls for heat, regardless of air temperature. By this time, the heat exchanger is warm enough to deliver warm air to the register.

The fan control timer is directly controlled by the heating thermostat. Therefore, once the blower is timed on, it remains locked on by the timer until the heating thermostat is satisfied. When the thermostat opens, the timer is removed out of the circuit and causes the blower to operate until the discharged air temperature cools down to the blower off setting of the control.

Another control feature is its ability to automatically adjust the timer to turn on the blower sooner if the air is still warm from the previous cycle. Also, if the bimetal element senses air temperature at 65°F above the blower setting, it overrides the timer and turns on the blower. This 65°F differential eliminates any chance of the blower recycling when the burner is off. It also provides a safety override of the timer if excessive heat buildup should occur.

Primary Limit Control

Another safety device, called the *limit control,* is used to turn off the burner and control circuits if the air temperature becomes too hot. Some limit controls are combined with the blower control. In this case, one bimetal heat sensor actuates both the fan control switch and the limit control switch. As the temperature rises, the bimetal heat sensor first turns on the blower. If the heat sensor continues to overheat and the limit cutoff temperature is reached, the limit switch trips, causing the fuel valve to close and turn off the burner.

The limit control prevents furnace overheating, which may cause fire or damage furnace components. If the burner shuts off, one or more of the following conditions has occurred: blower failure, dirty air filter, duct system blockage, or any other condition that restricts airflow through the furnace.

The limit control is actuated by a bimetal element located on the discharge side of the furnace to monitor temperature of air leaving the heat exchanger. The bimetal sensor is connected to the closed contacts on the switch. When air temperature reaches the high-limit cutoff temperature, the bimetal sensor opens the contacts. This causes the line voltage to cut off the burners and controls.

The limit switch in the combination control is provided with an adjustable lever. A stop is installed that prevents the lever from being set above the safety cutoff temperature, which is 200°F.

On most furnaces, the limit control is calibrated to shut off the burner if discharged air temperature reaches or exceeds 200°F. The limit control switch automatically recycles and recloses the contacts when the air temperature drops 25°F below trip-out temperature. This 25°F differential is built into the switch. The limit control switch recycles the burner if the thermostat calls for heat, but trips out again if the air temperature exceeds 200°F. The trip-out temperature and differential are set by the manufacturer of the limit switch; therefore, neither should be changed or readjusted in the field. Tampering with these settings voids all equipment warranties and causes hazardous conditions.

When a separate limit control is used that is not combined with the blower control, it is located in a different area on the furnace from the blower control. It has its own bimetal element and operates the same as the combination control, except it does not have a dial setting. The 200°F limit setting and the 25°F differential setting are built in by the control manufacturer.

Secondary Limit Control

The secondary limit is an additional safety control on the reverse-flow and horizontal oil furnaces. Its function is to protect the blower motor from damage caused by high temperatures. The secondary limit switch is located in the furnace blower compartment and mounted on the blower housing. It continuously monitors temperatures around the motor.

Conditions that may cause the secondary limit to trip and open the circuit are a blower motor malfunction and abnormal restriction of return air. Without air movement to remove heat from the heat exchanger, heat builds up in the blower compartment.

The secondary limit contains closed contacts that are thermally operated. It uses 120V, or line voltage, and is connected in series with the primary limit control. If the blower compartment temperature reaches approximately 140°F during furnace operation, the secondary limit switch trips. This opens the normally closed contacts, which de-energizes the oil burner control. The flame goes out, allowing the unit to cool to safe levels. The temperature must drop 25°F before the limit control contacts close. This 25°F differential is built in by the control manufacturer.

The secondary limit switch may have single-pole, double-throw (SPDT) switching action. When normally closed contacts are opened, another set of normally open contacts closes simultaneously. These open contacts are connected in series with the blower motor. When the oil furnace cycles off, residual heat in the heat exchanger rises into the blower compartment. If the heat is great enough, the secondary limit opens. This causes the normally open contacts to close and energize the blower motor to move heat out of the blower compartment and away from the motor.

CompleteHeat

The CompleteHeat system is a highly efficient combination system for heating air and water, using either natural gas or propane as fuel. The unit consists of two components: (1) the heating module and (2) the air handling module. The heating module consists of a high-grade stainless steel burner, heat exchanger, and a 30-gallon water storage tank. The air handling module replaces the conventional furnace and contains a copper tube, an aluminum fin heating coil, and a water circulating pump. (See Figure 8.49.)

The homeowner selects the temperature of the water held in the storage tank. As the hot water exits the tank, cold replacement water enters the bottom of the tank. A thermistor mounted on the tank's side senses when the hot water supply is significantly depleted, and the burner ignites to reheat the water in the tank.

The CompleteHeat system operation is controlled in part by the tank thermostat/direct spark ignition control board (TDSI) control, which has many functions. It monitors the tank water temperature (through the use of a thermistor) and provides the main burner ignition on each operating cycle. The TDSI control monitors and controls the gas valve, combustion air blower, and the HM30 water circulation pump operation. It also shuts off the gas valve in case of abnormal operating conditions. The control is equipped with the WatchGuard circuit, which automatically resets the ignition control lockout after one hour of continuous tank thermostat demand. The hot water thermostat adjustment is located on the lower left side of the HM30 control box. It is factory set at 120°F.

The water temperature setting may be raised by turning the dial clockwise to the desired setting. Temperatures up to 140°F are marked on the control board. Each mark represents an increase of 10°F with a maximum of 170° F.

Local codes should be checked before raising the water temperatures because many local codes allow a maximum water temperature of no higher than 120 °F. If water temperatures above 140°F are required, a jumper located on the heat module control board must be removed. Adjusting the dials to any temperature above 140°F will not raise the water temperature unless the P1 jumper is removed. (See Figure 8.50.)

The HM30 tank is made of stainless steel and is fully insulated. All gas, water and vent connections are made at the top of the tank.

Access to the tank is through the removable top cover. Cold water enters the tank through a dip tube. Drain valves are provided at the bottom of the tank on either side and have a standard garden hose connection. The HM30 cabinet base serves as an auxiliary drain pan when the fittings are installed.

A 120-V $\frac{1}{40}$-horsepower circulating pump is factory installed in the HM30 tank assembly to prevent hot water stratification and sediment buildup. The pump operates when the gas valve is energized by a call for domestic hot water. The pump will not operate when the gas valve is energized by a demand for space heating.

Th'e HM30 is equipped with a low-pressure gas valve. The valve is internally redundant to assure safety shutoff. If the gas valve must be replaced, the same type valve must be used. The 24VAC terminals and gas control knob are located on top of the valve.

A room thermostat senses temperature changes and energizes the control system in the air-handling unit. When the room thermostat calls for heating, the system's circulating pump immediately begins circulating hot water from the storage tank through a heating

■ FIGURE 8.49

CompleteHeat ™ System (AM30 and HM30) arrangement.

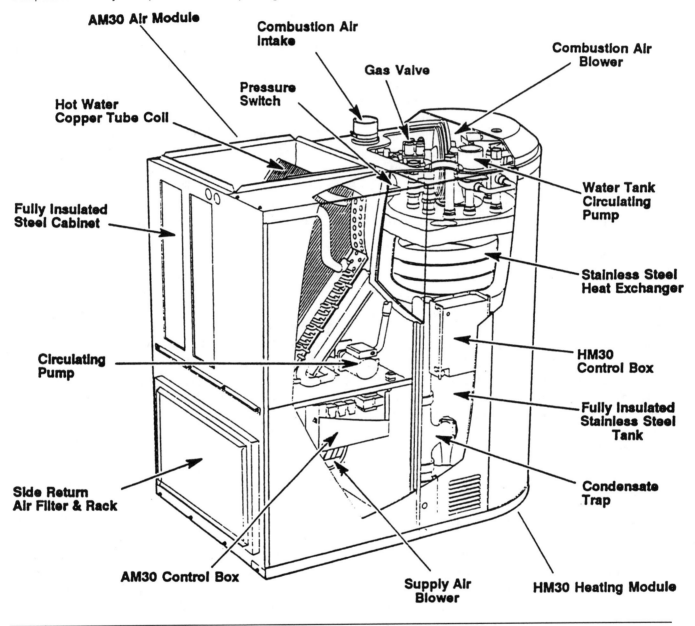

coil in the air-handling module. A time-delay circuit controls the circulating air blower to ensure air is fully heated before the air enters the ductwork. When the thermostat senses the space has reached the desired temperature, the pump stops circulating hot water and after a 30-sec. delay, the circulating air blower shuts off.

For the cooling function, controls operate the circulating air blower and the air conditioning system in the same manner as a standard furnace. The unique design feature combines advanced electronics with a water storage tank circulator to deliver hot water to the air-handling module. This results in warmer discharge air temperatures than most conventional high-efficiency gas furnaces.

The system's high heat input design insures that the amount of energy supplied is adequate to simultaneously heat both air and water, provided the unit installed in the home is properly sized to fit the appli-

■ **FIGURE 8.50**

Water temperature adjustment is made by turning the dial clockwise.

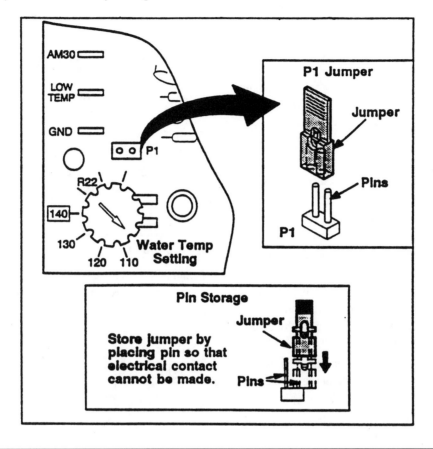

cation. If there is an unusually high demand for heating, however, water heating has priority.

Water left in the space heating coils during the summer months is circulated through the tank and heating coil for a short period of time four times a day, to ensure water does not lie in the system for protracted periods of time and to prevent the accumulation of mineral deposits. Intermittent circulation occurs only when air-conditioning is not operating.

The CompleteHeat system is quiet because of the sound reduction techniques, including fully insulated cabinets and super quiet blowers, that are used. CompleteHeat features a totally sealed combustion system. Its submerged heat exchanger muffles even the small noises generated in the combustion process.

The CompleteHeat system is engineered to work with air-conditioning coils and condensing units. Upflow and down-flow cooling coils fit directly on the supply air side of the air handling module and operate with standard ductwork connections. A short transition duct is required for horizontal installations. On the return side, air ducts connect directly to the cabinet or the external filter rack that is supplied with the unit. The system is designed to ensure that heat gain from the coil is introduced into the air-circulation system when the system is in the cooling mode and heating water.

The CompleteHeat system needs only a 30-gallon storage tank because it is designed as a high heat input system that can replenish its hot water supply in a fraction of the time required by conventional water heaters. The small tank improves efficiency by reducing standby heat loss and allows for a compact installation. Conventional water heating systems rely on relatively low Btu heat input coupled with larger storage tanks to maintain an adequate supply of hot water. The disadvantage of this method of water heating is that it requires significant recovery time to replenish its reservoir of hot water.

High heat inputs and fast recovery, combined with the comfort control technology, ensures a nearly constant supply of hot water (120°F to 140°F), even during peak demand.

High efficiency means lower fuel usage, which means lower fuel bills. The American Society of Heating, Refrigerating and Air Conditioning Engineers (ASHRAE) devised combined annual efficiency ratings to furnish information about the combined efficiency of air and water heating systems. The CompleteHeat system is certified under the Gama Certification Program in three efficiency categories: (1) CAE for combined efficiency, (2) AFUE for home heating, and (3) energy factor for water heating. CompleteHeat ranks among the most efficient systems in each of these separate rating systems.

The combustion air blower is located on top of the water tank and operates when the burner is required. The blower has a 120VAC single-phase motor and runs at 3400-3550 or 2600-3000 rpms. The speed varies depending on vent length. If the pressure switch trips because of blockage in the combustion air intake, flue outlet, or condensate drain, the gas valve will close and the blower will continue to operate. The burner is enclosed in a housing connected to the heat exchanger inside the tank. The burner uses 100 percent outside combustion air supplied by the combustion air blower.

The tubular heat exchanger is a single helix design on the HM30-100 unit and a double helix design on the HM30-150 unit. Both the single and double helix heat exchanger are made of stainless steel. The heat exchanger cannot be removed from the tank. (See Figure 8.51).

The flame sensor, located on the side of the spark electrode, uses flame rectification to sense combustion. The temperature/pressure relief valve is located on top of the water tank. The valve resets, once temperature and pressure return to normal.

The anode rod is a highly conductive aluminum alloy that protects the stainless steel tank from corrosion. The primary limit is a 24V SPST NC (single pole single throw normally closed) manual reset switch that actuates in case of excessive heat exchanger temperatures. The limit will trip on a temperature rise of 210°F degrees ± 12°F. The limit can only be reset after temperatures have dropped below 120°F.

The secondary limit is a 24V SPST NC auto reset switch, which actuates if the water supply is interrupted or if there is a pocket of air that requires purging. The limit will trip on a temperature rise of 350 degrees ± 12°F. The limit resets when temperatures drop to 10°F.

The HM30 thermistor monitors the tank temperature for the TDSI control board. The thermistor is factory installed on the left side of the tank.

The pressure switch interrupts gas flow under abnormal vent conditions. The switch is N.O. (normally open) and actuates at 0.4″ W.C. (water column) + .05 W.C. on a pressure fall. The pressure switch is an auto reset switch and will reset at 0.26″ W.C.

The flue/condensate trap assembly vents flue products and provides an internal condensate trap. The condensate trap is equipped with a removable boot to aid in servicing and cleaning. The condensate lien may exit either side of the tank.

■ **FIGURE 8.51**

Example of tubular heat exchange.

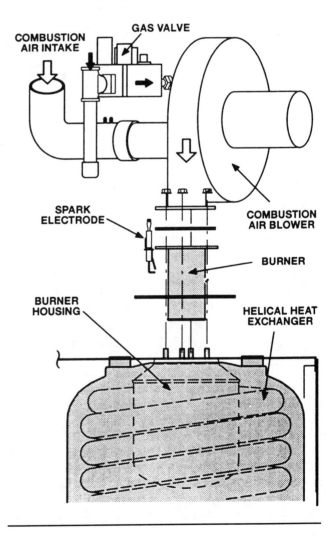

COMBUSTION ASSEMBLY

CompleteHeat uses 100 percent outdoor air for combustion air. Outside air contains far fewer contaminants than inside air, which ensures the integrity of the air supply and extends the life of the system's high-efficiency heat exchanger and burner. This method of combustion air allows CompleteHeat to be installed in tight, energy-efficient homes without experiencing operating or safety problems.

CompleteHeat is inherently safer than conventional furnaces and water heaters because of the completely sealed combustion system, which eliminates the open flame. CompleteHeat's flame rectification circuit closely monitors the combustion process, and the system's multiretry and watch-guard circuit institutes resumption of combustion following any temporary interruptions in the gas supply. In addition, the CompleteHeat system features high temperature protection by gas flow blockage protection and a standard temperature/pressure relief valve on the water storage tank.

The highest quality material is used in the CompleteHeat system, including stainless steel and brass, so water quality is not a problem. Additionally, the circulating action of the system combined with the top-mounted burner and heat exchanger dramatically reduces the effects of hard water. However, in regions where the water supply is extremely hard or contains impurities that affect taste, it may be desirable to install any standard water-conditioning or filtering equipment for residential installations.

The system is easily adaptable to zone heating with the installation of multiple air-handling units or radiant floor heating loops in parallel with the air-handling unit. The flexibility of the CompleteHeat system means it can be configured in numerous ways. Remote installation, where the air and heat modules are up to 30' apart, is achieved by simply adding additional copper piping between the two modules. Longer distances are possible, but require another circulating pump. With the exception of additional piping, remote installation procedures are identical to those provided for close-coupled units. The air-handling unit can be installed in upflow, downflow, or left/right horizontal positions. Because the heating module is design certified by the American Gas Association and the Canadian Gas Association, it can be used as a stand-alone water heater in applications requiring high-efficiency and large amounts of hot water.

CompleteHeat contains many operating features not available in other systems. These features include a 90 percent combined annual efficiency rating; a two-stage burner that ensures maximum efficiency and four times faster heating capacity over conventional water heaters; and electronic controls that assign priority to hot water heating that periodically circulates water through the system and maximizes comfort. Logical controls also make it easy to select continuous low-speed blower circulation and connect an optional freeze-guard thermostat. They also provide power supply connections for accessories commonly used in heating systems.

■ ROOM HEATERS

Vented Room Heaters

There are many types of vented room and space heaters. These heaters may be fired with natural gas, propane, fuel oil, kerosene, or wood. All heaters must comply with these listed clearances or the clearances specified in the code. Many units are designed to obtain their own combustion air through the adjacent exterior wall of the house to vent through the same wall. The primary inspection objective in this type of installation is to determine that room heaters are installed in accordance with the manufacturer's listed instructions.

The combustion air is drawn through a duct from the outside into the combustion chamber. After combustion of the fuel, the flue gases are vented through another duct passing through the wall to the outdoors. The flue gasses may be vented either by gravity or an induced draft. This is a direct vent room heater with a sealed combustion chamber. (See Figure 8.52.)

The unit must be located to provide adequate clearances from drapes, curtains, and combustible wall and floor materials. The unit must also be located to allow free movement of people in the room. Room heaters must be installed on noncombustible floors or approved assemblies that extend at least 18 inches beyond the heater on all sides. Heater installations that burn solid fuel are not allowed on the floor of a garage because of the possibility of sparks igniting gasoline fumes, oily rags, etc.

Room heaters are for heating rooms and similarly enclosed spaces, either in addition to or in place of a central heating system. They are desirable as a means of providing heat to small areas because of their simplicity of construction, low cost, and reasonable fuel consumption. (See Figure 8.53.)

These heaters are classified in accordance with the manner in which they transfer heat to the area to be heated, for example, by radiation and/or convection.

■ **FIGURE 8.52**

Direct vent room heater—sealed combustion-chamber type.

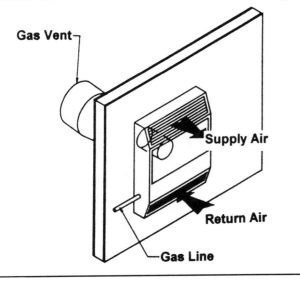

■ **FIGURE 8.53**

Room heater.

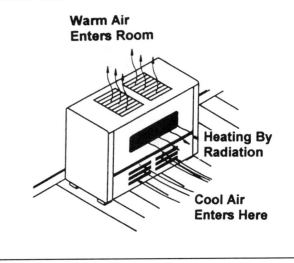

Some gas heaters are designed to be nonvented, and they are approved. However; use is prohibited in rooms generally kept closed, in bedrooms, and in bathrooms. The maximum size for nonvented heaters is 40,000 Btus, and they must be equipped with an oxygen depletion sensor.

There are several safety areas the inspector should be aware of when inspecting properties that have room heaters. An inspector needs to know what is considered combustible and noncombustible. A heater gives off radiant and convective heat. If a combustible material is too close to the stove, it will become hot and catch fire. For example, wood studs, even though covered with noncombustible sheetrock, can burn at abnormally low temperatures if exposed to constant heat. Clearances are usually specified by the manufacturer and by the mechanical codes to prevent overheating of combustible materials by keeping them at a distance. A wall or a ceiling is combustible if it is plaster on wood lath or sheetrock on wood studs.

If the wall is sheetrock on metal studs or joists or if the wall is entirely of concrete or brick, it is a noncombustible wall. All wood floors, carpet, and synthetic flooring materials are considered combustible and should be protected in an approved manner. Other combustible materials, including furniture, draperies, newspapers, and loose clothing, should also be kept away from the heater.

If the heater burns wood or coal, it is important when inspecting for the inspector to check the firebox thor-

oughly for creosote build-up, warped metal, cracks, and evidence of smoking caused by defective venting.

Vented Floor Furnaces

Vented floor furnaces are installed in small homes built with a crawlspace. They cannot be installed in a home with a basement because the floor furnace burner assembly cannot project into an occupied underfloor area. It is important to have access to floor furnaces for inspection, maintenance, and repair. If easy access is not available, the floor furnace will be less likely to receive these services and unsafe conditions could develop. Because service on floor furnaces must be performed from the crawlspace, access and working space requirements are similar to those required for horizontal furnaces in a crawlspace. (See Figure 8.54.)

Most manufacturers and codes have installation requirements for the floor furnace which are above the floor as well as below the floor. Below-the-floor requirements:

- Thermostats controlling floor furnaces must be located in the room in which the register of the floor furnace is located.
- Floor furnaces shall be supported independently of the furnace floor register.
- Floor furnaces must be installed not closer than 6″ to the ground. Clearance may be reduced to 2″, provided that the lower 6″ of the furnace is sealed to prevent water entry.

■ **FIGURE 8.54**

Floor furnace clearances.

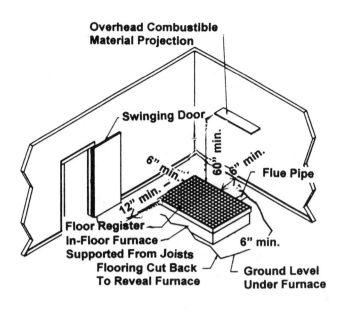

- When excavation is required for a floor furnace installation, the excavation should extend 30″ beyond the control side of the floor furnace and 12″ beyond the remaining sides. Excavations should slope outward from the perimeter of the base of the excavation.
- The vent must be securely connected and extend to the exterior of the building.

Above-the-floor requirements are:

- Floor registers of floor furnaces must be installed not less than 6″ from a wall.
- The furnace register must not be located within 12″ from doors in any position, draperies, or any combustible objects.
- The furnace register shall be located at a minimum of 5′ below any projecting combustible material. A clearance of 12″ must be maintained from items such as doors or drapes because these are combustible and could swing or blow over the hot air outlet. A minimum vertical clearance of 60″ is required above the floor furnace outlets because the hot air rises and could overheat combustible materials located above the outlet.

When inspecting a floor furnace, the inspector must check the following: From above the floor, check the heat exchanger carefully for warping and for trash that has fallen through the register. From the crawlspace, check that the furnace is vented and for possible water penetration in the burner compartment. Do not light the pilot light and/or burner if a potential problem is observed.

Vented Wall Furnaces

Wall furnaces are designed for installation in the studs of combustible walls with the furnace casing and other parts of the frame directly connected to components of the wall. This is possible because wall furnaces are designed to maintain proper internal clearances from the heated components and surfaces. A 6″ clearance must be maintained from inside room corners. Doors must be located to prevent swinging within 12″ of the furnace air inlet and outlet to avoid interference with the flow of circulating air and combustion air, as well as to maintain adequate clearance from a combustible door. An 18″ clearance from overhead projections is required because of the rise of heat from the wall furnace. (See Figure 8.55.)

Unlike forced-air furnaces, wall furnaces are not designed for the distribution of hot air through ductwork. Wall furnaces are often gravity types, with cooler air drawn into the bottom inlet by warm air that is rising out of the top inlet. This circulation of air does not have sufficient static pressure to force air through ductwork. Therefore, if ductwork were attached, the airflow would be reduced and cause potentially dangerous overheating. Certain models of wall furnaces are constructed with small blowers or fans to increase the circulation of air into the room. These small fans, however, are not designed to work with ducts. Some wall furnaces are also designed with hot air registers that open into the space on each side of the wall. This is not considered ductwork and does not create a problem of airflow.

■ NONDUCTED SYSTEMS

Heated air in a nonducted system is not circulated through a pipe or duct by an air mover such as a blower or fan. Heated air is transmitted naturally from a heat source located in each room. As heat is emitted from the source, hot air rises and is replaced by the cooler air in the lower part of the room. This air movement pattern, called *convection,* is caused by uneven temperatures.

A radiator heat source is the hot water or steam produced by a central boiler and piped to the radiator. Radi-

Vented wall furnace.

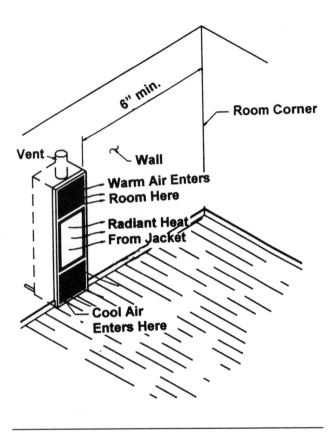

ators are placed near or under windows to reduce cold drafts and enhance the air movement. Modern radiators, called *convectors,* are encased in metal cabinets. The heat source may be hot water, steam or an electric coil. The metal cabinet is open or contains a grille that allows cooler air to enter the cabinet. Heat from the coil collects and rises out of the grille at the top of the cabinet. Rising heat is called *natural convection.*

Some nonducted systems are installed in floors or ceilings and may use water or steam (provided by a boiler) or electric coils. The coils are embedded either in the concrete floor or in ceiling plaster. With electric coils, because resistance changes as the coil heats, a correction factor of 1.065 is used on a cold coil to show calculations for both single-phase and three-phase applications.

The advantage of nonducted heat systems, whether water, steam or electricity, is room-by-room heating with individual thermostat control. One disadvantage of a nonducted system is a lack of provision for the installation of a controlled cooling system. Therefore, a separate

cooling system or individual window cooling units must be installed. Other disadvantages include no provision for humidity control, air stagnation, or air cleanliness, as well as space-consuming radiators or convectors in living areas and system inability to utilize passive solar heat gain in a room or control heat distribution.

Hot Water and Steam

All hot water systems are similar in design and operating principles. Boilers consist of a single heat source that supplies either steam or hot water and a combustion chamber for burning the fuel. Newer boilers are equipped with automatic fuel firing devices.

Boilers found in residential or small commercial buildings use either natural or LP gas. In some parts of the country, oil or coal is a suitable alternative. If coal is used as the energy source for the boiler, a check draft is required at the smoke pipe to control chimney draft. The gases pass from the combustion chamber to the flue passages, which are designed for maximum possible heat transfer.

Several different types of boilers are available, manufactured from cast iron, steel, or both. Their construction may be sectional, fire-tube, water-tube, or special. Domestic heating boilers are usually low pressure with a maximum operating pressure of 15 psi if steam and 30 psi if hot water.

The simplest hot water system is the one-pipe gravity heating system. Water is heated at the lowest point in the system and rises through a single riser or radiator branch from the top of the main to the radiator. After the water releases its heat in the radiator, it returns to the same main through return piping from the radiator. The cooler return water mixes with water in the supply main, causing the water to cool gradually. As a result, the next radiator in the system has a lower emission rate than the first radiator. The one-pipe system is not an efficient system for large homes. (See Figure 8.56.)

Another hot water system is the two-pipe system. The two-pipe system operates similarly to the one-pipe system, except the second pipe acts as the return to the boiler. The supply main allows water to enter the radiator, where it releases heat. The cooler water then enters the return main, which carries it back to the boiler. (See Figure 8.57.)

Most water-circulating systems are force-fed systems. A force-fed system contains a pump or circulator near the heater that circulates the water through the system. This system may operate at higher water tem-

■ **FIGURE 8.56**

Domestic heating boiler—one-pipe gravity system. .

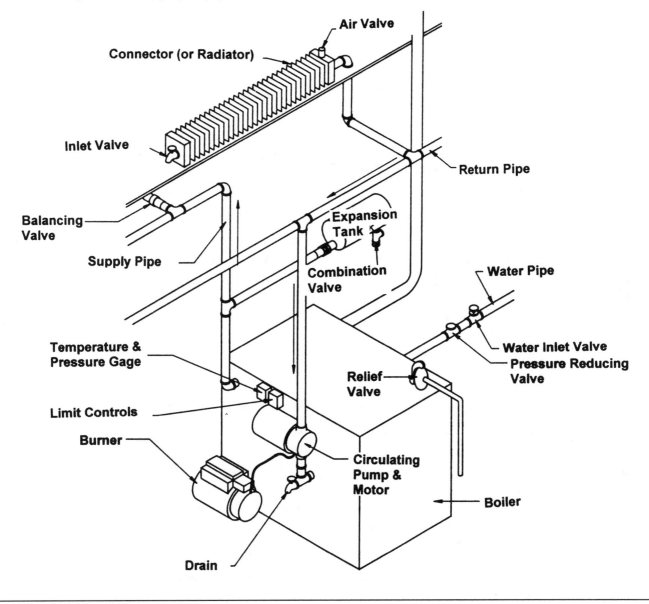

peratures. The fast-moving high-temperature water creates a responsive system with a smaller temperature drop through each radiator. Higher operating temperatures with lower temperature drops allow small-radiator use for the same heating loads.

Because heated water expands, a hot water system must be equipped with an expansion tank. The expansion tank may be either open or closed and must be of sufficient size to permit a water volume change within the heating system. An open expansion tank should be placed at least 3' above the highest point in the system. It

also requires a vent and an overflow. The usual location for the open tank is the attic. The enclosed expansion tank contains an air cushion that compresses and expands according to changes in system volume and pressure. The closed expansion tank is installed near the heater.

All boilers, whether hot water or steam, are subject to certain requirements that must be followed. The boiler must be placed in a separate room. The inspector must consider the physical requirements for a boiler, such as ventilation. A boiler room requires more circulating air

■ **FIGURE 8.57**

Domestic heating boiler—two-pipe gravity system.

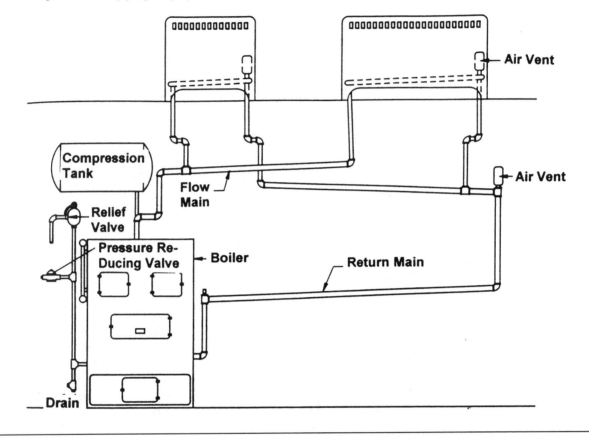

than a habitable room because the heat builds up from the boiler. Proper air circulation provides adequate combustion air for the boiler.

Most steel boilers are assembled with welded steel construction and are called *portable boilers*. Larger boilers are installed in refractory brick settings built on site. These include cast iron boilers shipped in sections and assembled at the site. Inside the combustion chamber, a group of tubes is suspended horizontally between the two headers. If flue gas passes through the tubes and water surrounds the tubes, the boiler is a fire-tube boiler. The boiler is water-tube when the water flows through the tubes and fire heats the tubes.

■ ELECTRIC HEAT

The heat produced by electrical resistance serves as the main heating source for heating applications or as auxiliary heat for heat pumps. One primary design consideration in heat pump systems is that the indoor coil must be located upstream from the heating elements. Both the heat pump and the electric elements may be energized simultaneously. The air is heated first in the refrigeration process as much as possible. The minimum amount of resistance heat is added to satisfy the thermostat. If the indoor coil were located downstream from the elements, damaging head pressure would occur when the heat pump and elements were energized together.

Electric heat relays or control sequencers within the equipment turn on the elements in steps to space out the amperage load. This process eliminates a large inrush or load on the electric system within the building.

Electric heat fundamentals are reviewed below.

1. Electric heat capacity is rated in kilowatts (kw), which is translated to British thermal units per hour (Btuh) output. The conversion relations are
   - 1 kilowatt = 1,000 watts (w)
   - 1 kilowatt = 3,413 Btuh
   - Btuh × 0.293 = watts

For example, a 5-kw element would expel 17,065 Btuh. Applying the above formula, the Btuh out-put of each element may be determined with a wattmeter. By dividing the wattage by 0.293, the actual Btuh is obtained.

2. Ohm's Law emphasizes that the kw output of an element may also be determined with an ohm-meter using the following formula (see also Figure 8.58.):

$$\text{Watts} = \frac{\text{Voltage}^2}{\text{Ohms}}$$

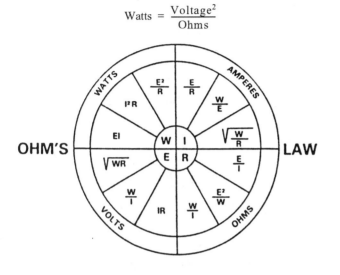

■ FIGURE 8.58

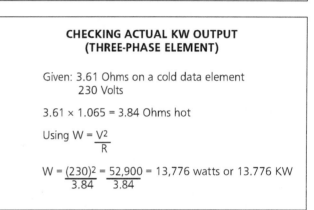

CHECKING ACTUAL KW OUTPUT (SINGLE-PHASE ELEMENT)

Given: 10.08 Ohms on a cold coil
220 Volts

$10.08 \times 1.065 = 11.53$ Ohms hot

Using $W = \dfrac{V^2}{R}$

$W = \dfrac{(220)^2}{11.53} = \dfrac{48,400}{11.53} = 4,195$ watts or 4.195 KW

CHECKING ACTUAL KW OUTPUT (THREE-PHASE ELEMENT)

Given: 3.61 Ohms on a cold data element
230 Volts

$3.61 \times 1.065 = 3.84$ Ohms hot

Using $W = \dfrac{V^2}{R}$

$W = \dfrac{(230)^2}{3.84} = \dfrac{52,900}{3.84} = 13,776$ watts or 13.776 KW

Supply Power

Line voltage entering an electric furnace at the main disconnect switch is 240V AC. Electrical service consists of two 120V hot wires and one neutral wire, which are all encased in conduit. Each hot wire is connected to a fuse or circuit breaker located where supply voltage enters the furnace. These serve as safety devices protecting the unit from wiring overloads or short circuits. If an overload occurs, the fuses blow or the circuit breakers trip, de-energizing furnace operation. A step-down transformer converts high voltage to 24V AC, which is necessary for the thermostat connection and associated control devices in the furnace.

Heat Elements

The function of the line-voltage heating element is to generate heat. An alloy of nickel and chromium metals, a typical nichrome wire heating element, is rated at 5.5 kw, although elements are available in other kw ratings. Given 3.412 Btus of heat per w, a typical element produces 18,766 Btus of heat per hr. The formula for computing heat output generated by wattage is w × 3.412 Btus/w equals total Btu output. Most electric furnaces have several elements, typically ranging between two

and six. The number of elements determines the unit heat capacity. The amperage draw per element ranges from 15 to 22 amps.

In a properly operating unit, energized heat elements must never glow red because the air routed over them by the blower absorbs heat. This indicates the furnace blower must always be energized before or at the same time a heat element is energized. If the blower is not moving adequate air volume across the elements, overheating occurs. Overheating causes the nichrome wire of the element to crystallize, owing to frequent metal expansion and contraction. Eventually, this induces a break in the nichrome wire. The blower is energized by an electric current sensing device called the *blower control,* by a blower relay, or by a control sequencing switch. These energize both the blower and element concurrently.

Safety Limits and Thermal Fuses

In addition to the circuit-sensitive fuses or circuit breakers, an electric furnace also contains heat-sensitive safety devices. These devices are temperature limits and thermal fuses, one for each heat element. The limit electrically de-energizes the heating element branch circuit when air temperature surrounding the element exceeds the setting (usually 120°F to 170°F). Possible causes may include restricted airflow from a dirty filter, an insufficiently sized and powered blower, or an electrical malfunction with the blower circuit. The safety limit switch automatically resets when the air temperature drops 15°F to 30°F below its break point, allowing the heat element to energize again. As long as a heat call exists from the thermostat, the elements continue to cycle on and off at their respective limits. It is undesirable to allow this to continue because the elements may receive crystallization damage. An additional safety device called a *thermal fuse* functions as a backup safety switch in the event of limit switch failure. A one-time safety device, a blown thermal fuse must be replaced before the element will operate.

Heat Relays and Control Sequencers

To space out the amperage load, electric furnaces are designed so elements cycle on one or two at a time. Spacing the load helps prevent an overwhelming, instantaneous electrical demand on the power company. The devices used to sequence the elements on or off are called *heat relays* and *control sequencers*. Both devices employ bimetals. A heat relay may sequence one element on or off in intervals of 15 sec. to 45 sec. The control sequencer works similarly to the heat relay, but may simultaneously control multiple elements and furnace blower operation.

Electric element staging is a popular energy-saving feature. This is accomplished by a two-stage heating thermostat or a single-stage or two-stage heating thermostat used in conjunction with a 24V outdoor thermostat.

To illustrate element staging, consider a five-element electric furnace. The first heat stage controls elements one, two, and three, and the second stage controls elements four and five. The first stage of heat, or three elements, operates when the thermostat calls for heat during moderate outdoor temperature periods. The second stage, or elements four and five, is engaged only during periods of extreme cold when the first stage cannot satisfy the heating demand. Energy savings result because not all elements are energized every time there is a call for heat. (See Figure 8.59.)

Due to the operation of different control sequencing devices, elements are engaged in sequence within each heat stage. Also, a two-stage thermostat used in conjunction with an outdoor thermostat may provide three heat stages. More than one outdoor thermostat may be necessary to deliver additional heat stages. For example, a six-element furnace with multiple thermostats may deliver six heat stages. Outdoor thermostats must be wired in the low-voltage circuit between the sequencers. Failure to use recommended installation procedures voids the Underwriters Laboratories (UL) nameplate.

Inspecting Electric Furnaces

Electric furnaces are referred to as *resistance heat*. The electric furnace will not have a heat exchanger as a gas forced air furnace has, so there is not a problem of flue gases (carbon monoxide) escaping to contaminate the air supply. The heat is supplied by a series of heating coils with each coil having a thermal fuse and temperature limit switch.

Most electric heat elements are rated at 240 volts. Depending on the power company, supply voltage will normally register 208-240V. As the supply voltage registers less than 240V, Btu output of the unit will decrease proportionately.

When inspecting the heating section, the inspector should be sure the power is off at the unit disconnect switch so the electrical wiring can be inspected for loose connections and damaged insulation. To make these checks, the vestibule panel has to be removed. This exposes all wiring and the fuse panel so their condition can be observed.

Next the inspector should check amperage draw as each heating element comes on. The inspector should snap the amprobe around one hot wire in the furnace vestibule. Be sure the face of the amprobe can be seen. Turn on the furnace disconnect and watch the indicator on the amprobe. *Note:* The blower must engage prior to or simultaneously with the first element. Each element, when it comes in, should have an amperage draw of 15-22 amps. If all the elements do not come on, there could be two possible causes: (1) an electrical malfunction of a control device of the element or (2) an outdoor thermostat that is holding out one or more elements (outdoor thermostat must be returned to initial set point).

When using the amprobe, be sure the amp draw reading is taken on all wires running from the power source to the elements. Replace vestibule panel and replace front door. Note: There is no limit switch check for basic maintenance electric, because of potential damage to the elements. With power on, check the temperature rise through the furnace. Make sure all doors are

■ **FIGURE 8.59**

Warm air electric furnace (up-flow-model).

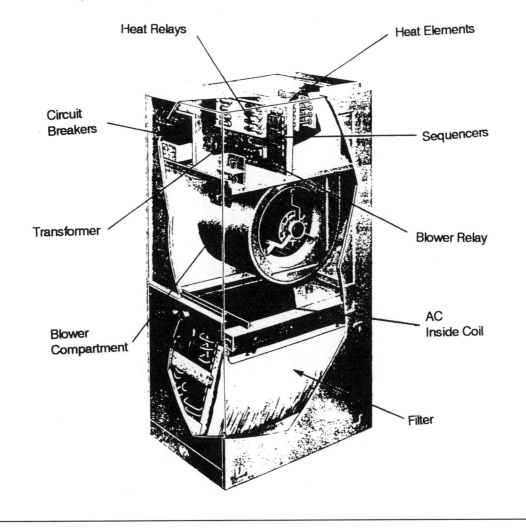

on the furnace; the proper temperature rise will be listed on the unit nameplate. To make this check, place another thermometer in the supply plenum, positioned out of direct line of the heating elements, and place a thermometer in the return air plenum close to the furnace. There should be a 40°F to 47°F difference between the thermometer in the return air duct and the thermometer in the supply duct. If the temperature difference is less than 40°F to 70°F, the blower is running too fast. If the temperature is more than 70°F, the blower is running too slow.

Check filter size and location and record all findings. If an outdoor thermostat is present, return it to its original setting. All other components are inspected in the same way as in other forced air furnaces.

■ SOLAR HEATING

A number of years ago, energy costs rose dramatically. People explored alternative energy sources to reduce their home- and water-heating costs. One of those methods included the use of solar heat. During the early 1980s, the U.S. government allowed tax credits for a percentage of the installation cost of an alternative energy source. At that time, many people took advantage of free solar heating to capitalize on tax advantages and reduce energy consumption.

High initial installation cost of solar heating equipment prevented most individuals from entering the solar heating market. The demise of tax credits in 1985

■ **FIGURE 8.60**

Passive hot water system.

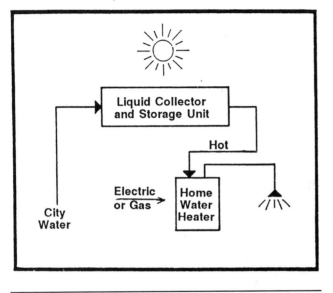

■ **FIGURE 8.61**

Active hot water system.

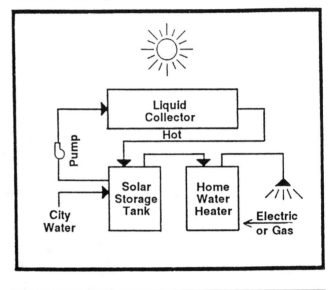

finished the solar heating business. Many homeowners did invest in solar heating systems for their domestic water and swimming pools. Some actually used solar heating to heat their homes in the winter. Homes are now sold with solar heating panels, and buyers require that they be inspected.

There are two basic types of solar heating: passive and active. In its simplest form, passive solar heating is defined as opening the drapes and allowing the sun to shine in. (See Figure 8.60.) Active methods use pumps or blowers to move working fluid, either air or a water/antifreeze mix. (See Figure 8.61.) In either case, there are four major components in a solar heating system:

1. Collectors
2. Storage vessel
3. Piping system
4. Controlling mechanism

The storage vessel is either a large box of rocks (See Figure 8.62.), used in an air system, or a large water tank, used in a water system. In some passive systems, storage is a large masonry wall that holds heat gathered during the day and slowly releases it at night.

The piping system is copper water pipes or an air duct system, and the pipes must be properly insulated.

The controller is usually an electronic device that uses thermistors to monitor the temperature at the collectors and in the storage vessel. When the collectors are warmer than the storage, the controller switches on the pumps to move fluid through the system to produce solar heat for either storage or the house.

Collectors

Collectors are usually mounted at the same angle as the roof and weigh approximately 120 pounds (lb.) per panel, while larger ones weigh about 200 lb. Collectors are available in various sizes, such as 3′ by 6′ or 4′ by 8′ and weigh about 6 lb. to 7 lb. per sq. ft.

Two types of solar collectors are concentrating and flat plate. The concentrating collector is either a concave mirror or a convex lens. It focuses the sun's energy onto a pipe to collect heat. The flat plate collector is a flat absorber plate mounted in a weatherproof box.

Concentrating Collectors

The great advantage of concentrating collectors is the high temperatures they generate. There are several disadvantages, including the use of expensive, exotic fluids; high heat loss; and the use of only direct beam radiation. Therefore, a tracking mechanism is required to move the collector array and maintain it pointed at the sun.

Flat Plate Collectors

Flat plate collectors should always face the southerly direction. These collectors are less expensive to build and use. They mount in one place and do not have to move,

■ FIGURE 8.62

Active air solar heating system.

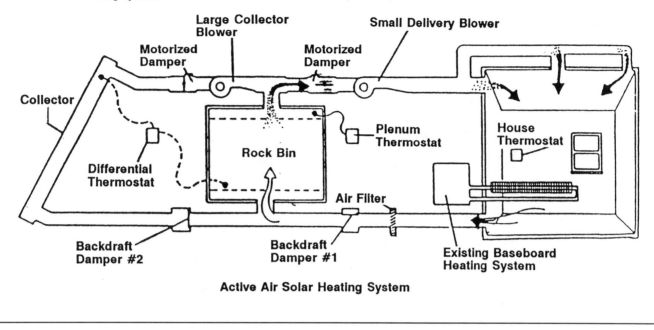

Active Air Solar Heating System

plus they utilize cheaper fluids—water or air. All kinds of solar radiation are used, including direct, reflected, and diffused. Temperatures generated are above 200°F.

Domestic Water Heating

Domestic water heating is probably the most common use for solar heat. The system consists of either one or two tanks. Two-tank systems use the standard water heater and a separate storage tank. One-tank systems use only the standard water heater as the tank.

In both cases, the collectors are outside on the roof. The storage tank(s) is inside with the transport module. The transport module consists of a pump(s), a compression tank, an electronic controller, a pressure relief valve, and a check valve. (See Figure 8.63.)

Operation

In a conventional water heating system, hot water is drawn from the water heater as needed. As it leaves the water heater, cold water replaces it from the main supplying the house. Gas burners or electric elements heat the water in the tank to a certain temperature.

With solar water heating systems, the sun heats fluid in the collectors, which is pumped inside to heat water in the storage tank. As hot water is used from the home water heater, it is replaced by water already heated by the

hot collector fluid. This prevents the conventional, more expensive heating system from operating.

If sun is present, it heats the collectors on the roof. A thermistor informs the electronic controller that the collectors are hot, and a second thermistor informs the controller of the storage tank temperature. If the collectors are warmer than the tank, the controller begins pump operation.

Fluid flows from the pump through the collectors to a heat exchanger located in the bottom of the storage tank in a two-tank system. Once there, it releases its heat to the water in the tank. The fluid flows back to the pump and around again for another heat load. When the collector sensor cools within 2°F or 3°F of the storage tank sensor, the controller stops pump operation.

Transport Module Components

There are several components of the transport module. Manufacturers may include all of the components or choose to use only a few.

Check Valves Check valves are one-way valves in the collector fluid piping. They are located between the pump and solar collectors and are designed to prevent nighttime thermosiphoning, the backward flow of solar fluid through the piping caused by convection.

■ **FIGURE 8.63**

Components of a domestic water heating system.

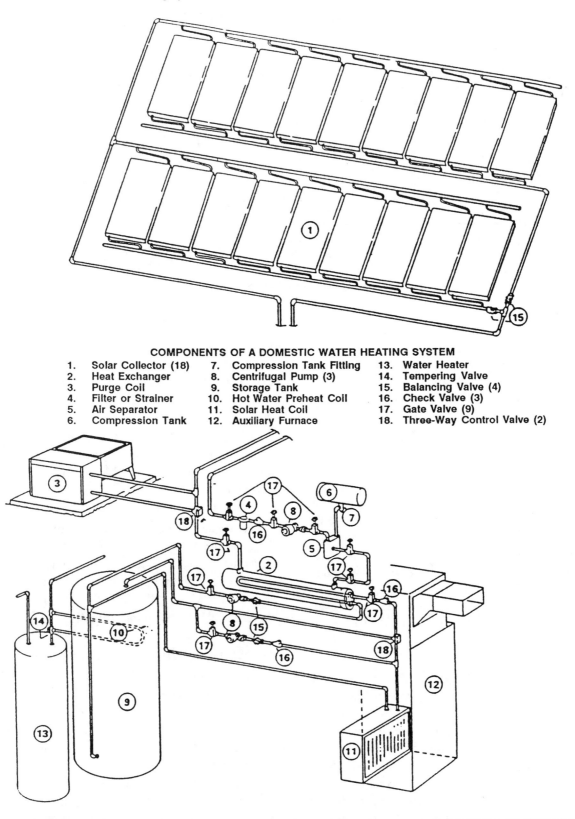

COMPONENTS OF A DOMESTIC WATER HEATING SYSTEM

1.	Solar Collector (18)	7.	Compression Tank Fitting
2.	Heat Exchanger	8.	Centrifugal Pump (3)
3.	Purge Coil	9.	Storage Tank
4.	Filter or Strainer	10.	Hot Water Preheat Coil
5.	Air Separator	11.	Solar Heat Coil
6.	Compression Tank	12.	Auxiliary Furnace

13.	Water Heater
14.	Tempering Valve
15.	Balancing Valve (4)
16.	Check Valve (3)
17.	Gate Valve (9)
18.	Three-Way Control Valve (2)

During evening hours, the collectors cool, and the storage tank must hold sufficient hot water for evening and early morning use. The hot water in storage maintains hot collector fluid in the heat exchanger. But hot fluid has a tendency to rise to the roof collectors and the cool fluid in the collectors will fall as the hot fluid rises. This process seizes heat gathered during the day and wastes it back to the cool night air. The check valves prevent this backward fluid migration at night.

Relief Valves   There should be two relief valves in the solar water heating system. One valve is in the collector fluid piping immediately after the pump. The relief pressure may be at many settings, depending on the manufacturer, such as 30 psi (pounds per square inch), 60 psi, 75 psi, or 90 psi. The relief valve discharge on the collector fluid piping must not route to a sanitary sewer or the environment. Most local codes prohibit dumping antifreeze fluid; it must route to a catch basin or pail.

The second relief valve must be on the storage tank and is similar to that found on a standard water heater. Because the storage tank relief valve carries only water, the valve can be routed to the same point as the relief valve from the water heater. It is a safety device to relieve pressure inside the storage tank.

Pump   A pump carries fluid from the collectors to the heat exchanger in the storage tank and back. Its operation is controlled by the electronic controller. To inspect the pump, turn the manual switch of the electronic controller to the on position and the pump should start. If you do not hear it operating, determine that line power to the system is on. To ensure the pump is pumping, measure fluid temperatures entering and leaving the collectors. If the pump moves fluid, there is a temperature change.

After checking the pump, be certain the system switch is in the automatic position. The system must never be left in the off position unless the collectors are covered. If fluid does not circulate, the collector fluid boils and blows out through the relief valve. The pump and electronic controller should be on their own electrical circuit. This way power cannot be interrupted if another device on the line blows a fuse. The circuit must be a properly grounded circuit.

Tempering Valve   There must be a tempering valve in the water line between the storage tank and water heater. This prevents scalding hot water from entering the water heater. The temperature-sensitive valve mixes cold water with hot water from the storage tank. It then delivers water into the water heater at the proper temperature.

The temperature setting of the tempering valve is manually set and must be set to the desired temperature, similar to the water heater thermostat. To check the valve, run a hot water tap in the house. Use a thermometer to measure the temperature of the water coming from the tempering valve. It should be no higher than the tempering valve set point.

Air Vents   To fill the system with fluid, air must be released. For this reason, air vents must be at the high points of the collector piping.

If air is trapped in the system, the pump will make a swishing or gurgling sound during operation. If an air bubble is trapped in a pipe, it may stop the flow of fluid. If fluid does not flow, the collectors overheat, and the fluid in the system will boil and build enough pressure to blow the relief valve.

Air vents may be used to check fluid level in the system. If a vent is opened at the highest point, liquid should come out. If no liquid appears at this highest point, the system is short of fluid.

■ ELECTRONIC AIR CLEANERS

Airborne impurities constantly circulate throughout a building. These impurities have detrimental effects on both occupants and HVAC equipment. Dirty indoor air may aggravate allergies or asthma and can shorten the life of heating and cooling equipment. A filtering device must be installed in the return air duct. (See the section on Filters, page 258.)

■ HUMIDIFIERS

A humidifier is a device that adds moisture to air when the air becomes too dry. During winter months, it may be necessary to add moisture to the indoor air for comfort. (The ideal relative humidity for the human body is 40 percent.) The process that uses a humidifier and humidistat to control the humidity or desired comfort level is called *humidification*. (See Figure 8.64.)

The actual amount of moisture the air contains is regulated by the temperature. Warm air holds more moisture than cold air. During the summer, humidity may become quite high. The weather, therefore,

■ **FIGURE 8.64**

Humidifiers increase the moisture content of heated air.

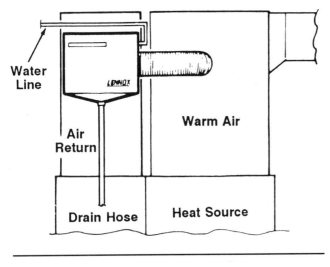

■ **FIGURE 8.65**

Humidifiers are used to add humidity to the conditioned spaces during the heating season.

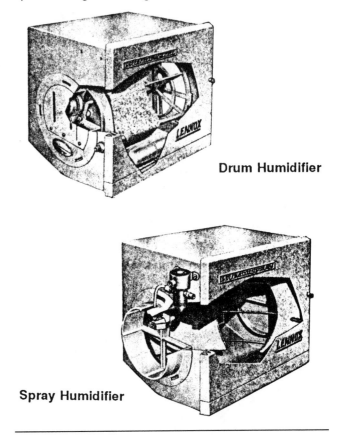

becomes humid and muggy, causing a hot and uncomfortable atmosphere, even though ambient temperature is not that high. To maintain comfort, moisture must be removed from the inside air, which is accomplished automatically during the cooling process. The cooling equipment lowers the indoor temperature and acts as a dehumidifier to lower the humidity level.

The air simulates a sponge, soaking up moisture from everything with which it comes into contact. As air is heated, it expands and occupies more space because warm air holds more moisture. Cool or cold air cannot hold much moisture, so as the air cools, the large "sponge" proceeds to shrink and occupy less space. If the temperature is sufficiently lowered, the moisture is squeezed out in a process called *condensation*. At temperatures below the saturation point, water vapor begins to condense. The temperature at which condensation occurs is called the *dew point*.

Relative humidity is defined as the ratio of the moisture amount actually in the air to the moisture amount the air is capable of holding at a given temperature. This ratio is expressed as a percentage. For example, a relative humidity reading of 100 percent means the air contains all the moisture it can hold at that temperature.

In cold climates, the outside air is dense and cannot hold much moisture. When the cold air outside infiltrates a home and is heated, it expands, and it draws additional moisture from the indoor environment. If no moisture is added, the relative humidity in the home lowers. Air with a low relative humidity is similar to a sponge wrung dry, and it will absorb moisture from

everything it contacts—furniture, carpet, people, etc. Low relative humidity may cause sore throats and respiratory discomfort as well as lowered resistance to diseases. It also produces static electricity and may damage house plants and furnishings. Humidifier use minimizes low relative humidity effects such as static electricity shocks, dry throat and nose, skin irritation, dry furniture, and dying house plants.

There are two types of humidifiers: the drum type and the spray type. Some models mount on the plenum on either the return air or the supply air side of the furnace. The other models, including freestanding models, have the appearance of a piece of furniture. Both drum-type and spray-type humidifiers are automatic and controlled by a device called a *humidistat*. The humidistat operates similarly to a thermostat. As the thermostat cycles heating and cooling equipment to maintain desired temperature, the humidistat cycles the humidifier to maintain desired relative humidity. (See Figure 8.65.)

The humidistat is adjustable, as is the thermostat. Some humidistats correlate the set point directly to the outside temperature. At 20°F or above, the humidistat should be set at 20°F. When it is –20°F or below, it should be set at –20°F, and for temperatures between –20°F and 20°F, the humidistat should be set accordingly. Some humidistats also contain an indicator that exhibits the approximate humidity level. The humidifier cannot be inspected during the cooling season because it is necessary to dehumidify or remove moisture from the air throughout the cooling season.

■ REVIEW QUESTIONS*

1. When soot is observed on the furnace vent or in the furnace, it indicates _____ combustion.

2. What are three causes of spillage?

   _____

   _____

   _____

3. The _____ control de-energizes a gas furnace when the output temperature is excessive.

4. The lack of primary air in LP gas furnaces causes a(n) _____ flame.

5. Natural draft systems operate according to the principle of _____.

6. Combustion gases are drawn out of the heat exchanger by _____.

7. A blocked orifice at the burner manifold _____ the Btu output at the furnace.

8. Too many elbows in the vent may cause _____.

9. The simplest method to check electric furnace heating elements is to use a(n) _____.

10. The heat exchanger in a furnace connected with an air-conditioner will oxidize faster than in a furnace having no air-conditioning coils.

    A. True
    B. False

11. A floor furnace can vent into the crawlspace.

    A. True
    B. False

12. The only sure method to detect a crack in a heat exchanger is to _____.

13. A cracked heat exchanger or rusty burners may cause the formation of _____.

14. It is good practice to turn off a gas furnace's pilot light in the summer.

    A. True
    B. False

15. If a gas furnace is equipped with a vent damper, you must check that the damper _____ on heating demand.

16. What component controls the operation of a power humidifier?

    _____

17. What are the three main forms of heat transfer?

    _____

    _____

    _____

18. There are two types of filtering systems or devices available.

    A. True
    B. False

_____

* Answers to all of the chapter review questions are located in Appendix C at the back of this book.

19. When an inspector is checking the draft, the burner and blower must be off.

    A. True
    B. False

20. The element(s) that must be present to ignite and sustain a flame is(are)

    A. fuel.
    B. heat.
    C. oxygen.
    D. All of the above

21. In the CompleteHeat system, the maximum water temperature by many local codes is

    A. 120°F.
    B. 140°F.
    C. 170°F.

22. The CompleteHeat system can also supply hot water to the house.

    A. True
    B. False

23. Which of the following are advantages of the flat plate collector?

    A. May use all types of light radiation
    B. Has less ambient heat losses than concentrating collectors
    C. May use less expensive transfer fluids, such as water
    D. All of the above

■ INSPECTION CHECKLIST: HEATING AND VENTILATION

DUCT

The following checks apply to ducts located in crawlspace, attic and closet.

Yes No

☐ ☐ Is supply duct insulated in unconditioned areas?

☐ ☐ On air-conditioning applications, is vapor barrier torn or missing in unconditioned areas?

☐ ☐ Does duct have kinks or restrictions?

☐ ☐ Is duct crushed in crawlspace or attic?

☐ ☐ Are all duct connections tight (no open seams)?

☐ ☐ Is duct sitting in dirt in the crawlspace?

☐ ☐ Is duct rusted or otherwise damaged?

☐ ☐ Is there airflow through supply registers?

☐ ☐ Duct leaks?

BLOWERS

Yes No

☐ ☐ Is blower belt drive?

☐ ☐ Is blower direct drive?

☐ ☐ Is squirrel cage clean?

☐ ☐ Are pulleys aligned properly?

☐ ☐ Is blower assembly secured properly in furnace cabinet?

☐ ☐ Is blower shaft loose in the bearing mounts?

☐ ☐ Is the blower compartment correctly sealed?

☐ ☐ Evidence of grease/oil bearing seepage?

☐ ☐ Does the blower produce rattling, noise, or excessive vibration?

FILTRATION

Yes No

☐ ☐ Is there a provision for a filter in the return air to blower?

☐ ☐ Does the filter need to be changed?

☐ ☐ What type of filter is used? _____

☐ ☐ Where is filter located? _____

Yes No

☐ ☐ What is the filter size? _____

☐ ☐ Is furnace equipped with electronic filters? Push the test button.

☐ ☐ Does filter make a popping sound? If not:

☐ ☐ Is blower operating?

☐ ☐ Is control switch in on position?

Note: *If filter is missing or extremely dirty, closely check air-conditioning operation. It may be advisable to recommend that evaporator coil be cleaned.*

THERMOSTAT

Yes No

☐ ☐ Is thermostat mounted level on the wall?

☐ ☐ Is thermostat securely fastened to wall?

☐ ☐ Any appearance of damage?

☐ ☐ Is thermostat subject to vibrations?

☐ ☐ Does thermostat suffer poor air circulation?

Remove cover.

☐ ☐ Is bimetal excessively dirty?

☐ ☐ Any evidence of a cracked or discolored mercury bulb?

☐ ☐ Is heat anticipator set at an extreme?

Flip fan selector switch to continuous position.

☐ ☐ Does indoor blower operate? If not:

☐ ☐ Is indoor unit disconnect off?

GAS LINE INSPECTION

Yes No

☐ ☐ Gas must be on at the meter. A real estate inspector is not allowed to remove any seals, plugs or locks to activate gas.

☐ ☐ Turn off all pilots but one during the normal inspection. This includes furnace(s), hot water heater(s), range, oven, gas lights, and pool heater. Shut gas off at meter. The pilot that is still lit will burn off gas in line. Turn off last pilot. Turn gas back on at meter. The surge of gas through the line will push against any corroded weak spots and allow the leak to appear in the test. Wait until meter stops moving and mark the smallest capacity dial. If meter keeps moving, make sure that all pilots are off and you are at the correct meter. Wait approximately 30 min. and check meter for movement. If leaks are observed, turn off gas at meter and notify gas company of address and location of leak (if known). The gas utility company will assume control from that point. If no leaks are observed, relight all appliances.

GAS FURNACE

Identify whether the house is zoned or central.

Yes No

☐ ☐ Are there adequate clearances?

☐ ☐ Is there sufficient combustion air?

☐ ☐ Any evidence of flashback?

☐ ☐ Are there burned or damaged wires?

☐ ☐ At the unit, is return air completely isolated from combustion air?

☐ ☐ Is furnace properly supported in attic?

☐ ☐ Any gas odor?

☐ ☐ Does pilot fail to light (standing pilot models)?

☐ ☐ Does pilot flame need adjustment?

☐ ☐ Is vent pipe improperly installed or disconnected?

☐ ☐ Any evidence of vent pipe rusting?

☐ ☐ Is the single-wall vent pipe in attic or through ceiling?

☐ ☐ Do copper gas lines or flexible connectors pass through wall?

☐ ☐ Through floor?

☐ ☐ Through ceiling?

☐ ☐ Are the copper or flexible gas lines kinked?

☐ ☐ Are crossover igniters aligned at burner?

☐ ☐ Any excessive rust and debris on burner or in burner compartment?

Yes No

☐ ☐ Is burner assembly missing?

☐ ☐ Any evidence of cracks within clamshell (bright light)?

Provide a full heating demand.

☐ ☐ Do burners ignite? If not:

☐ ☐ Is the thermostat set for heating?

☐ ☐ Is unit disconnect switch off?

☐ ☐ Is gas shut off?

☐ ☐ Do burners light smoothly?

☐ ☐ Does flashback occur? (It is not uncommon to have a slight flashback on startup, particularly in the summer.)

☐ ☐ Does the blower automatically begin after a short interval?

☐ ☐ Is there an excess of noise or vibration at the indoor blower?

☐ ☐ Does the furnace short cycle with a full heating demand?

☐ ☐ Does the limit control cycle off burner during a heating demand?

Allow burners to operate for a minimum of 10 min. and check burners for irregular flame patterns. Examples include:

☐ ☐ Flame burning at orifice or within tube?

☐ ☐ Flame burning through side of burner?

☐ ☐ Flame lifting from burner?

☐ ☐ Flame touching sides of clamshell?

☐ ☐ Flame dancing left and right?

☐ ☐ Flame being drawn under burner?

Note: Sight down each burner to check flame pattern.

☐ ☐ Identify other signs of burner or heat exchanger problems.

☐ ☐ Is there excessive buildup of indoor humidity?

☐ ☐ Any buildup of soot at furnace flue pipe outside?

☐ ☐ Any odor in house?

☐ ☐ Do headaches occur while furnace operates?

Yes No

☐ ☐ Are any orifices blocked off?

☐ ☐ Is there poor draft? (Make spillage check at draft hood. This is the most important gas furnace check.)

☐ ☐ Terminate the heating demand. Does the fan control cycle off indoor blower? If not:

☐ ☐ Is thermostat fan switch in continuous position?

☐ ☐ Does burner shut off?

Optional check—operate gas furnace without blower.

☐ ☐ Does limit control cycle off burners?

Note: If unit is electronic ignition, the sparking circuit lights the pilot and the pilot then lights the burner. If burner fails to light, turn disconnect off and on to recycle control. Some units have a manual reset button. If unit has an induced fan, there is no draft hood, and on a heating demand, the fan should operate before burners ignite.

Note: Remember to return thermostat to its original setting.

GAS FLOOR FURNACE

Yes No

☐ ☐ Is there debris in furnace area?

☐ ☐ Does pilot light? If not:

☐ ☐ Is gas shut off?

☐ ☐ Does pilot flame require adjustment?

☐ ☐ Are heat exchanger walls buckled?

☐ ☐ Is pilot access cap missing?

Note: It is desirable practice to note floor furnaces where the main burner operates independently from the pilot burner.

☐ ☐ Provide a full heating demand.

☐ ☐ Does burner operate?

While under the house, make the following checks:

☐ ☐ Is vent pipe connected?

☐ ☐ Are vent pipes rusted or holes present?

Yes No

☐ ☐ Does vent pipe have proper slope?

☐ ☐ Is furnace sitting on ground?

☐ ☐ In areas subject to water, is there a pan under unit?

GAS SPACE HEATERS

Yes No

☐ ☐ Are grates damaged?

☐ ☐ On heaters with pilots, does pilot light?

☐ ☐ Any unvented gas heaters?

☐ ☐ Any open flames in bedrooms or bathrooms?

☐ ☐ Does pilot need adjustment?

☐ ☐ Does burner operate correctly?

HIGH-EFFICIENCY FURNACE

Note: When a high-efficiency furnace is equipped with a microprocessor, the thermostat must not be advanced more than 3°F above room temperature. Setting the temperature higher informs the unit that demand is greater than the system can handle. The microprocessor "thinks" a malfunction in the unit exists and may set off alarms indicating immediate service is required. This procedure should be followed with any furnace controlled by a microprocessor.

CONDENSING FURNACE:

Yes No

☐ ☐ Is the PVC exhaust piping level?

☐ ☐ Does exhaust pipe discharge into drain?

☐ ☐ Is intake air properly plumbed?

VENT

Yes No

☐ ☐ Is single-wall metal pipe used in attic?

☐ ☐ Any evidence of rust on vent pipe in attic or on roof?

☐ ☐ Does vent pipe have correct slope in attic?

☐ ☐ Does vent pipe terminate in attic?

Yes No

☐ ☐ Is there sufficient clearance to combustible materials?

☐ ☐ Is vent pipe flashed correctly?

OIL FURNACES

Inspect the combustion chamber using a mirror and troublelight.

Yes No

☐ ☐ Is there carbon buildup?

☐ ☐ Are holes evident in the combustion chamber?

☐ ☐ Is burner head burned off?

☐ ☐ Does heat exchanger show excessive carbon or scale?

☐ ☐ Does high draft loss occur?

☐ ☐ Is fuel tank level checked by gauge?

☐ ☐ Does the fuel tank show evidence of water containment or sludge?

☐ ☐ Any damage to the tank?

☐ ☐ Is there oil seepage?

☐ ☐ Is tank secured to mountings?

☐ ☐ Is oil line equipped with a line filter?

☐ ☐ Does the fuel filter provide a shutoff valve?

☐ ☐ Are fuel lines between tank and burner damaged, loosely connected or broken?

☐ ☐ Is fuel line properly supported?

☐ ☐ Are all doors and panels on the furnace?

☐ ☐ Is furnace vent in place?

☐ ☐ Does the barometer damper operate?

☐ ☐ Is the combustion air blower operating?

☐ ☐ Does the oil burner motor operate?

NONDUCTED SYSTEMS

Type of nonducted system

Yes No

☐ ☐ Hot water?

☐ ☐ Steam?

☐ ☐ Electric?

☐ ☐ Is boiler equipped with operational pressure gauges?

Yes No

☐ ☐ Does boiler leak?

☐ ☐ Is boiler equipped with relief valves?

☐ ☐ Is circulating pump operable?

☐ ☐ Any leaks around shaft seals?

☐ ☐ Are heat coils located in floor or ceiling?

☐ ☐ Are heat coils located in radiator or base board?

☐ ☐ Is the heating system a hot water system?

☐ ☐ Steam system?

☐ ☐ One-pipe system?

☐ ☐ Two-pipe system?

☐ ☐ Four-pipe system?

☐ ☐ Is the source of energy natural gas?

☐ ☐ LP gas?

☐ ☐ Oil?

☐ ☐ Coal?

☐ ☐ Electric?

☐ ☐ Is expansion tank properly located?

☐ ☐ Does the boiler room contain proper ventilation?

☐ ☐ Is the boiler drafting properly?

ELECTRIC FURNACE

Remove electric heat access panel.

Yes No

☐ ☐ Are there any burned wires?

☐ ☐ Are wires disconnected from elements?

☐ ☐ Is furnace properly supported?

☐ ☐ Provide a full heating demand.

☐ ☐ Does blower begin immediately or within a few seconds?

☐ ☐ Is there amperage to each element? If not:

☐ ☐ Is thermostat set for heating?

☐ ☐ Are unit disconnects shut off?

Allow sufficient time for sequencers to cycle on all the elements.

☐ ☐ Is an outdoor thermostat being used?

☐ ☐ If a two-stage heating thermostat is used, is there a second-stage heating demand?

Yes No

- ☐ ☐ Does excessive noise or vibration exist at the indoor blower?
- ☐ ☐ Does unit cycle off properly?

  Some electric heat compartments are inaccessible. In this situation, perform a temperature rise check at the supply and return air systems.

- ☐ ☐ Is temperature rise acceptable?

  Note: *Remember to return thermostat to its original setting.*

SOLAR HEATING

The following checks should be conducted to test the solar water heating system.

Yes No

- ☐ ☐ Are there cracks in the collector glass?
- ☐ ☐ Is there water penetration of the collector weather stripping?
- ☐ ☐ Is there corrosion or damage to the collector box?
- ☐ ☐ Any evidence of leaks or damage in the roof or roof decking?
- ☐ ☐ Any system piping leaks?
- ☐ ☐ Are all pipes properly insulated?
- ☐ ☐ Test the highest air vent for proper fluid level. Is it acceptable?
- ☐ ☐ Does the pump run and move fluid?
- ☐ ☐ Is there a tempering valve?
- ☐ ☐ Does the tempering valve control the water temperature?
- ☐ ☐ Is the system's power supply properly grounded?
- ☐ ☐ Are collectors not mounted directly to the roof?
- ☐ ☐ Will collectors face south direction and not be subjected to shading?
- ☐ ☐ Is the collector tilt angle acceptable?
- ☐ ☐ Has roof stressing been considered?

Yes No

- ☐ ☐ Can any property damage or hazards result from the installation (ice dams on roof, standing water, leaks, etc.)?
- ☐ ☐ Has the collector mounting framework been weather treated to prevent corrosion?
- ☐ ☐ Have all mounting penetrations been caulked or otherwise sealed?
- ☐ ☐ Have collector vent holes been opened?
- ☐ ☐ Has all piping been insulated?
- ☐ ☐ Have sufficient pipe hangers been used?
- ☐ ☐ Are necessary air vent valves installed and located properly?
- ☐ ☐ Are all necessary charging and drainage ports provided?
- ☐ ☐ Have dielectric unions been used between dissimilar metals?
- ☐ ☐ Have additional hand isolation valves been provided for major system components?
- ☐ ☐ Has the water heater and/or solar storage tank been insulated?
- ☐ ☐ Has temperature/pressure relief plumbing been completed?
- ☐ ☐ Have potential freezing problems been considered when piping passes through an unconditioned space?
- ☐ ☐ Has a properly grounded power outlet been provided?
- ☐ ☐ Are the collector and storage sensors properly attached?
- ☐ ☐ Have water temperature control devices been set to prevent scalding?
- ☐ ☐ Has heat transfer fluid leak detection been considered?
- ☐ ☐ Is it impossible for any direct contact of heat transfer fluid and potable water?
- ☐ ☐ Are all surfaces with running temperatures of 120°F or higher isolated from pedestrian traffic to prevent burns?
- ☐ ☐ Have all temperature and pressure relief valves been installed properly?

FUEL SUPPLY TANK

Yes No

☐ ☐ Level and properly anchored?
☐ ☐ Correctly plumbed?
☐ ☐ Gauge?
☐ ☐ Excessive corrosion or leakage?

HUMIDIFIER

Yes No

☐ ☐ Any excess corrosion?
☐ ☐ Does medium require cleaning or replacing?
☐ ☐ Do cabinet or drain connections leak?

Provide a heating demand at thermostat and a humidity demand at humidistat. If humidifier does not operate:

Yes No

☐ ☐ Is blower operating?
☐ ☐ Is water supply turned off?
☐ ☐ Spray-type checks.
☐ ☐ Does the solenoid water valve open when energized by the humidistat?
☐ ☐ Does nozzle spray correctly?

Drum-type checks.

☐ ☐ Does the motor rotate when energized by the humidistat?
☐ ☐ Is the float valve operating properly?

■ REPORTING GUIDELINES

Inspection reporting guidelines for heating systems incorporating the above checklist.

Heating systems. The inspector shall

- report the type of heating system and its energy sources;

- report as in need of repair a system that does not operate properly using normal control devices;

- report as in need of repair deficiencies in the controls and accessible operating components of the system;

- In gas units, inspect the burner, and report as in need of repair deficiencies in the burner compartment, type, condition; draft, and termination of the vent pipe or proximity to combustibles; the lack of combustion and draft air or inappropriate location, or the lack of forced air in the burner compartment (full evaluation of the integrity of a heat exchanger requires dismantling of the furnace and is beyond the scope of a visual inspection);

- report as in need of repair gas units that display flame impingement, uplifting flame, improper flame color, or excessive scale buildup;

- report as in need of repair gas units that use improper materials for the gas branch line and the connection to the appliance;

- report as in need of repair in gas units deficiencies in materials used for the gas branch line and the connection to the appliance; the absence of a gas shut-off valve; or a valve that is not properly located, is inaccessible, or leaks;

- report as in need of repair elements in electric furnaces that do not operate;

■ REPORTING GUIDELINES *(Continued)*

- report as in need of repair a return chase or plenum that is not free of improper and hazardous conditions such as gas pipes, sewer vents, refrigerant piping, or electrical wiring; and

- report if the inspector deemed the furnace to be inaccessible.

Specific limitations for heating systems. The inspector is not required to do the following:

- Inspect accessories such as humidifiers, air purifiers, motorized dampers, heat reclaimers, electronic air filters, or wood-burning stoves

- Determine the efficiency or adequacy of a system

- Program digital-type thermostats or controls

- Operate radiant heaters, steam heat systems, or unvented gas-fired heating appliances

Ducts, vents (including dryer vents), and flues. The inspector shall

- report as in need of repair deficiencies such as damaged ducting or insulation, improper material, or improper routing of ducts where visible and accessible;

- report as in need of repair the absence of air flow at all accessible supply registers in the habitable areas of the structure;

- report as in need of repair deficiencies in accessible duct fans and filters;

- report as in need of repair deficiencies in installation such as gas piping, sewer vents, electrical wiring, or junction boxes in the plenum, returns, or chases or improper sealing, where visible;

- report as in need of repair deficiencies in the flue system components;

- report as in need of repair a flue or vent pipe that does not properly terminate; and

- report as in need of repair deficiencies in materials used for the venting systems.

Specific limitations for ducts and vents. The inspector is not required to do the following:

- Determine the efficiency, adequacy, or capacity of the systems

- Determine the uniformity of the supply of conditioned air to the various parts of the structure

- Determine the types of materials contained in insulation, wrapping of pipes, ducts, jackets, boilers, and wiring

- Operate venting systems unless ambient temperatures or other circumstances, in the reasonable opinion of the inspector, are conducive to safe operation without damage to the equipment

Evaporative coolers. The inspector shall:

- operate the motor and report as one or two speed;

- observe the electrical pigtail connection at the motor;

- inspect the power source in the unit;

■ REPORTING GUIDELINES *(Continued)*

- report as in need of repair a pump that does not function or deficiencies in the spider tubes, tube clips, and bleeder system;

- report as in need of repair deficiencies in the water supply line and float bracket;

- report as in need of repair the absence of a minimum one-inch air gap between water discharge at float and water level;

- report as in need of repair deficiencies in the fan (blower) and squirrel cage or rust build-up, deterioration, or corrosion;

- report as in need of repair deficiencies in the fan belt and pulleys;

- report as in need of repair deficiencies in the housing side panels, the water trays, the exterior housing, and the roof frame;

- report as in need of repair deficiencies in the roof jack or other mounting point and the location of the seasonal damper at the unit; and

- report as in need of repair deficiencies in the interior registers and the supply duct.

9 Air-Conditioning and Heat Pumps

■ AIR-CONDITIONING (COOLING)

When describing cooling equipment, inspectors often discuss the high side and low side of the system. The high and low sides of a cooling system refer to system pressure, not to physical location. High-side components include the condenser coil, condenser fan, and compressor. Low-side components are the evaporator coil and metering device. (See Figure 9.1.)

The two most common residential cooling applications are the matched remote or split system and the self-contained or packaged system. In the matched remote system, high-side components are housed inside the condensing unit cabinet. The cabinet is located outdoors, usually on a ground-level slab or base or on the rooftop. Low-side components are located indoors in the supply plenum of a furnace. No difference exists whether the furnace is an up-flow, a down-flow or a horizontal-flow supply. The low side (evaporator coil) and furnace may be located anywhere in the building, as long as sufficient access to condensate drainage and service exists.

All components (compressor, condenser, condenser fan, metering device, evaporator, and blower) in the self-contained system are located inside a common cabinet. The unit may be located outdoors (on a slab, base, or rooftop), in the wall, or anywhere the condenser has access to outdoor air. The self-contained system interconnects with the duct system to supply cool air to the conditioned space.

Compressor

The compressor is the most expensive and functionally important part of a complete refrigeration system. Its purpose is to circulate refrigerant through the system. The mechanical operation of a compressor is similar to that of a gasoline engine. A compressor has a cylinder, a piston, and valves. The driving force of the compressor is an electric motor.

The compressor motor is designed to operate at 208V AC to 230V AC or 220V AC to 240V AC. This motor contains internal run and start windings and an external run capacitor. The terminals for the motor are located on a terminal block outside the compressor and are labeled R for run, S for start and C for common. A voltage of 240V AC is supplied to R and C. The run capacitor is connected to R and S, with the potential across these terminals to reach 600V AC. A nonconductive plastic cover is placed over the terminal block for safety.

The compressor motor shaft is connected to a crankshaft, which moves pistons up and down in cylinders by a connecting rod. As the piston pulls down in a cylinder, vaporized refrigerant draws through a suction valve and drives the piston forward in the cylinder. The vapor is compressed, with an increase in pressure and temperature, and forced out of discharge valves. The high-pressure, high-temperature R-22 refrigerant then travels to the evaporator coil.

The compressor compresses the refrigerant and that turns to liquid and, at high pressure and high temperature, travels to the evaporator through the small liquid line which is hot. At the evaporator coil, the liquid refrigerant passes through an expansion valve or uses some other method that causes the refrigerant to expand and turn to a vapor, which absorbs the heat in the conditioned area. The vapor returns to the compressor in the larger cold line that completes the cooling cycle.

The compressor pumps only refrigerant in the vapor state. If liquid refrigerant should ever reach the compressor, a condition called *slugging,* the valves may be damaged, resulting in compressor failure. Refrigerant

■ **FIGURE 9.1**

Refrigerant flow for the cooling cycle of a heat-pump.

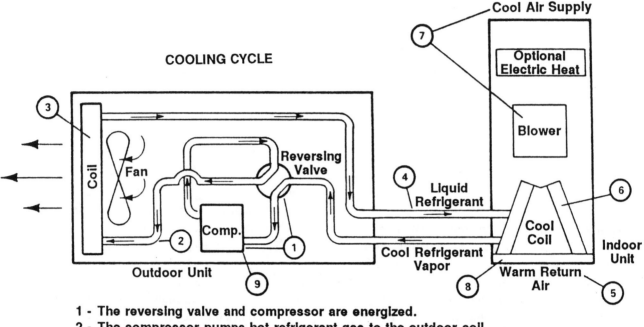

COOLING CYCLE

1 - **The reversing valve and compressor are energized.**
2 - **The compressor pumps hot refrigerant gas to the outdoor coil.**
3 - **The fan dissipates heat from the refrigerant and changes it into a liquid.**
4 - **The liquid refrigerant is sent on to the indoor coil.**
5 - **Warm air is drawn over the indoor coil by the blower.**
6 - **The refrigerant absorbs heat from the indoor air and changes into cool vapor.**
7 - **This lowers the temperature of the supply air which is distributed throughout the controlled space.**
8 - **This temperature change will remove moisture form the air and form condensate which must be piped away.**
9 - **The compressor suction pressure draws the refrigerant back into the compressor where its pressure is greatly increased. This completes one cooling refrigerant cycle.**

vapor is also used to cool the compressor motor windings. The compressor used in residential cooling is hermetically sealed and not field serviced or repaired. This indicates that all compressor components are housed in a steel shell that has been welded closed. Whether a compressor is operational may be determined by performing certain electrical and pressure checks.

Two-Speed Compressor

The two-speed compressor is the top-of-the-line condensing unit and heat pump. When operating on low speed, it reduces motor revolutions per minute (rpm) and capacity almost by half, which lowers energy consumption and operating cost. It raises the unit's efficiency, or SEER (Seasonal Energy Efficiency Ratio), to

almost double that at high speed. Units are available as 3-ton(t), 4-t, and 5-t units.

A two-stage thermostat controls compressor speed. When house temperature first exceeds the thermostat setting, the thermostat first-stage bulb calls for cooling and begins the compressor at low speed. If the outdoor temperature is not high, low speed satisfies the cooling demand with low-cost operation. (See Figure 9.2.)

If the outdoor temperature is high, low-speed operation cannot satisfy the thermostat demand and the house temperature increases. The thermostat second-stage bulb calls for additional cooling. The outdoor unit stops for one minute (min.), then starts the compressor at high speed. The compressor pumps refrigerant through the indoor coil to satisfy this greater load.

■ **FIGURE 9.2**

Two-speed compressor (single phase illustrated).

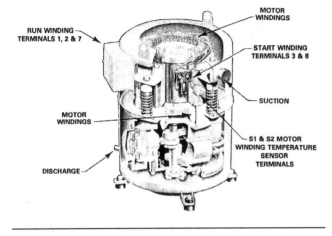

■ **FIGURE 9.3**

Detail of motor speed (cfm) plug-in connection.

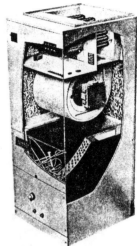

CB21 model—up-flow.

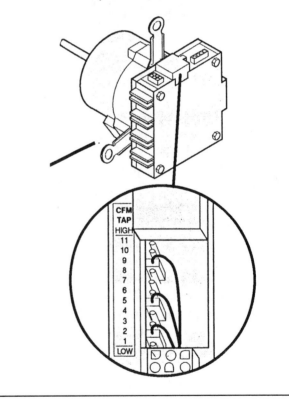

When the second-stage thermostat bulb is satisfied, the first stage continues to call for cooling. The unit stops for 1 min., then starts in low speed until either the first-stage bulb is satisfied or the second-stage bulb calls again.

The heat pump uses an outdoor thermostat to change compressor speeds. If the outdoor temperature drops below the thermostat set point, it automatically runs the compressor at high speed.

Efficiencies for two-speed compressor condensing units are in the 11 to 15 SEER range. Improved indoor air-handling units are on the market. These units are designed for maximum efficiency to complement high-efficiency outdoor units.

The unit is an indoor air handler, and its major components include an evaporator coil and a blower with the unique feature of a variable-speed blower motor. The motor is an electronically commutated motor (ECM). It varies its motor rpm to deliver correct airflow for both temperature and humidity control. (See Figure 9.3.)

Scroll Compressor

The scroll compressor offers many required features to meet heat pump requirements. Because of high energy and maintenance costs, consumers demand improved comfort from heat pump systems. This includes both improved indoor temperature control and warmer air during low-ambient operation. A scroll operates in an involute spiral. When matched with a mating scroll, it generates a series of crescent-shaped gas pockets between the two scroll members. During compression, one scroll is fixed (stationary), and the other scroll orbits (but does not rotate) around the fixed scroll. As this motion occurs, the pockets between the two forms are slowly pushed to the center of the two scrolls while simultaneously reduced in volume. When the pocket reaches the scroll form center, the gas is now at high pressure and is discharged through the port located at the center. Several pockets are compressed simultaneously, resulting in a smooth process. The suction and discharge process is a continuous flow.

■ **FIGURE 9.4**

The advanced scroll compressor sets new standards in heat pump efficiency.

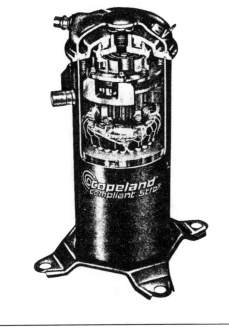

The scroll design offers several advantages. The scroll is simple and contains basically two components: a fixed scroll and an orbiting scroll. Only these two components are required to compress gas more efficiently than a piston compressor, which requires 12 to 15 components. (See Figure 9.4.)

Scroll compressors offer three advantages over the piston-type compressor. First, the suction and discharge processes of a scroll compressor are physically separated, which reduces heat transfer between the suction and discharge gas. The cylinder of the piston compressor is exposed to both suction and discharge gas, which reduces compressor efficiency. Second, the compression and discharge process of a scroll compressor is smooth. It compresses gas in approximately $1\frac{1}{2}$ revolutions compared with less than $\frac{1}{2}$ revolution for a piston. The discharge process occurs for a full 360° rotation versus 30° to 60° rotation for a piston. Finally, while the piston compressor requires both suction and discharge valves, the scroll compressor does not require any valves, which eliminates valve losses.

The scroll compressor is inherently 10 percent to 15 percent more efficient than the piston compressor, but has no reexpansion volume. All gas trapped in the outer pocket of the scroll members is compressed and released through the discharge port. This means the scroll compressor has a higher heat pump capacity than piston compressors.

Piston compressors in heat pump applications lack adequate capacity to heat in cold temperatures. The cause of this problem is the decrease in volumetric efficiency of piston compressors in low-temperature heat pump operation. The volumetric efficiency loss is due to reexpansion volume within the cylinder.

Reexpansion gas is gas compressed but not fully discharged during the discharge process, consuming part of the volume of the cylinder. The volume reduces compressor displacement and also reduces capacity.

The scroll compressor is durable and designed to yield to both liquid and debris by allowing the scroll forms to separate when liquid and debris are present. The scroll compressor maintains superior tolerance to liquid and debris. Because of extremely limited motion, the scroll compressor is quiet and perfectly balanced. The continuous suction and discharge flow produces low gas pulse. Because no dynamic valves are required, valve noise is not a factor, which allows quiet operation.

Scroll compressor advantages include a high-efficiency compressor that offers higher SEER levels than required. Design durability, particularly the scroll compressor liquid-handling feature, simplifies the system by eliminating the need for protection devices commonly required (accumulators and crankcase heaters). The scroll compressor may be started under any load without a start kit. The smooth, continuous compression characteristics of the scroll compressor and the elimination of valves produce an ideal compressor. (See Figure 9.5.)

Condenser Coil

A condenser coil is similar to an automobile radiator in both makeup and function. Copper tubing is laid in a winding or serpentine pattern. Attached to the copper tubing are thin aluminum fins spaced 10 to 20 per inch (in.) of tube. The purpose of the condenser is to remove heat from the refrigerant passing through the copper tubing. (See Figure 9.6.)

Aluminum fins provide a large surface area for heat transfer. Because condenser coil temperature is higher than that of surrounding outdoor air, heat transfer occurs. Heat transfer from high to low temperature is enhanced if large air volumes pass over the coil surface.

A condenser fan forces air through the condenser coil whenever the compressor operates. Air is blown or drawn through the condenser coil by the condenser fan.

■ FIGURE 9.5

Lennox heat pump with scroll compressor.

As heat is removed, the refrigerant condenses from gas or vapor to liquid. This occurs only because the refrigerant has been compressed. By forcing the R-22 molecules close together, the refrigerant condenses when heat is removed. The condenser, condenser fan, and compressor are usually mounted together in an outdoor unit. This group of components is called the *condensing unit.*

■ FIGURE 9.6

The condenser coil cools refrigerant.

Evaporator Coil

The evaporator coil, also called an *indoor coil,* is constructed similarly to the condenser coil. The function of the evaporator is to absorb heat from the air before the air travels to the conditioned space. (See Figure 9.7.) This is accomplished by running refrigerant, which has a lower temperature than the air blown over the evaporator coil, through the tubing. As the refrigerant absorbs heat from the air, it vaporizes or changes from liquid to gas. Frequently, the evaporator is mounted on a furnace to take advantage of an existing blower.

There are two basic types of residential-size evaporators. One is the slab-type evaporator, so-called because it is built in a rectangular shape. The other evaporator type is called an *A-coil.* (See Figure 9.8.)

The A-coil is constructed of two slab-type evaporators connected at one end and mounted at an angle to each other. A condensate drain is located at the evaporator bottom to catch moisture that condenses out of the air. Pipe is installed from the condensate drain connection to the floor drain.

Connecting Tubing

The components (compressor, condenser, and evaporator) are connected by copper tubing. Refrigerant travels through the tubing to these components. The tubing or line connecting the evaporator to the com-

■ FIGURE 9.7

The evaporator coil removes the heat from the structure.

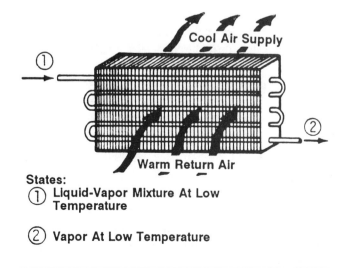

States:
① **Liquid-Vapor Mixture At Low Temperature**

② **Vapor At Low Temperature**

■ **FIGURE 9.8**

Evaporator coils used in cooling systems.

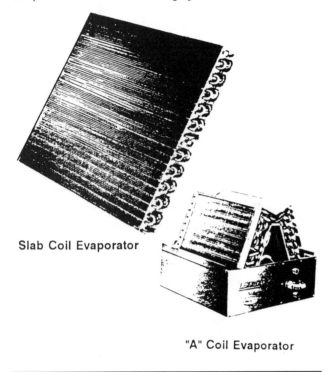

Slab Coil Evaporator

"A" Coil Evaporator

■ **FIGURE 9.9**

The metering device is used to meter refrigerant at the evaporator coil.

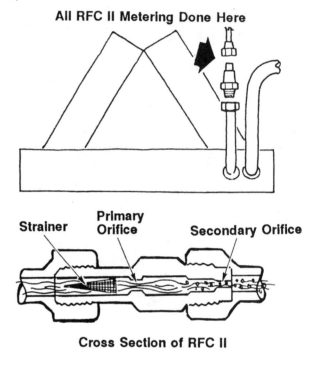

All RFC II Metering Done Here

Strainer Primary Orifice Secondary Orifice

Cross Section of RFC II

---

pressor is called the *suction line* and is larger in diameter than other lines in the circuit. The suction line carries refrigerant gas from the evaporator outlet directly into the upper part of the compressor shell. Temperature difference between the suction line and surrounding air (the suction line is cooler than the air) causes the line to sweat. Insulation placed around the suction line to prevent sweating also prevents the cool suction-line gas from extracting additional heat after leaving the evaporator.

Another line extends from the compressor discharge to the inlet side of the condenser. The line is called the *discharge* or *hot gas line* and is smaller than the suction line and quite hot to the touch. Because the compressor and condenser are located together, the discharge line is in the condensing unit. A third line extends from the condenser back exit to the evaporator inlet and is called the *liquid line* because it carries liquid refrigerant.

Metering Device

All mechanical refrigeration systems require a metering device. The metering device is located in the liquid line near the entrance to the evaporator coil.

Metering devices serve two functions: (1) they restrict refrigerant flow, thus maintaining the pressure drop necessary to produce low-temperature refrigerant for cooling, and (2) they regulate refrigerant quantity that may pass into the evaporator at any given time. The refrigerant amount admitted into the evaporator fluctuates according to the cooling load on the system. (See Figure 9.9.)

Two basic types of metering devices include the valve type (thermostatic expansion valve) and the restriction type (refrigerant flow control [RFC], capillary tube). The valve device contains moving parts that open and close while the restriction device consists of a small-bore (diameter) tube with no moving parts. Although metering methods of the two types differ, their function is the same.

The purpose of the thermostatic expansion valve is to control refrigerant flow to maintain an active evaporator coil under heat load variations. A thermostatic expansion valve meters liquid refrigerant into the evaporator coil at the same rate that the heating load boils the liquid within the evaporator. The RFC is another type of metering device. Like all restriction-type metering

■ **FIGURE 9.10**

A capillary tube is another method to meter refrigerants.

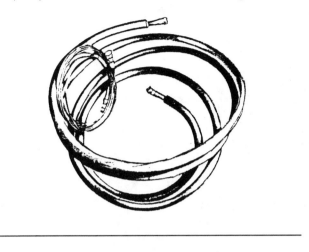

devices, the RFC has no moving parts. It consists of a small-bore copper tube that extends from the condenser to the evaporator, replacing the full-sized liquid line. Pressure differences in the system are maintained by the pumping action of the compressor. Refrigerant is metered into the evaporator by utilizing temperature/pressure vaporization effects on refrigerant in the small RFC line.

RFC II metering is accomplished by a small brass tube installed in the liquid line near the evaporator coil inlet. Small-bore orifices (primary and secondary) are precisely sized to the equipment.

A capillary tube is a restriction-type metering device. The tube is an extremely small-bore, short-length, seamless copper tube. Installed in the liquid line near the evaporator, the capillary tube acts as a constant throttle on the refrigerant. Several variables that affect refrigerant flow through the capillary tube include tube length, inside tube diameter, tightness of tube coils, and tubing temperature. (See Figure 9.10.)

The capillary tube works similarly to RFC and RFC II. As liquid flows through the tube, pressure decreases. At some point in the tube, the liquid begins to vaporize. The vapor formation in the capillary tube is called *vapor lock.* Vapor lock determines the amount of refrigerant metered to the evaporator coil.

Refrigerant Cycle

The liquid refrigerant leaves the condenser coil and travels to the metering device. The refrigerant pressure reduces, allowing some of the refrigerant to evaporate, which lowers the temperature of the remaining liquid-vapor mixture. After the expansion process, the lower refrigerant temperature allows the refrigerant to absorb heat at the evaporator coil.

The cooling effect and moisture removal occur at the evaporator coil. As air passes over the coil, propelled by the indoor blower motor, heat transfers from the air to the refrigerant and is absorbed by the refrigerant as it changes from liquid to vapor. Moisture is removed from the air when the cooling coil temperature drops below the dew point. Moisture condenses on the coil surface and drips into a pan that drains out. The conditioned air supplied to the room has both a lower temperature and lower moisture content. Combining this cooler, drier air and air within the living space maintains the comfort range selected by the occupant. (See Figure 9.11.)

The second step in the refrigerant cycle is the compression of vaporized refrigerant from a low-pressure/low-temperature vapor to a high-pressure/high-temperature vapor. At the compressor, electrical energy is converted to mechanical work, which increases both the pressure and temperature of the refrigerant vapor. The vaporized refrigerant from the compressor enters the condenser at a temperature above the outside temperature. Outside air passes over the coil to extract heat from the high-temperature vapor circulating through the coil. This results in a refrigerant change of state, and the vapor changes into liquid.

Run Capacitor

One or more run capacitors are wired in series with the compressor start windings and in parallel with the run windings. Capacitors are devices that store electrical energy. They are constructed of metal surfaces separated by insulating material that is nonconductive. This creates an electrostatic field in the motor windings and improves motor efficiency and power.

The run capacitor dampens voltage variation in the line and supplies constant voltage to the compressor motor. This allows maximum economy from voltage supplied by the power company. If the run capacitor bulges anywhere, it must be replaced.

Start Kit

A start kit consists of a start capacitor, also called an *intermittent duty capacitor,* and a potential relay. The start kit is a device that increases the starting torque of a

■ **FIGURE 9.11**

Refrigerant flow diagram.

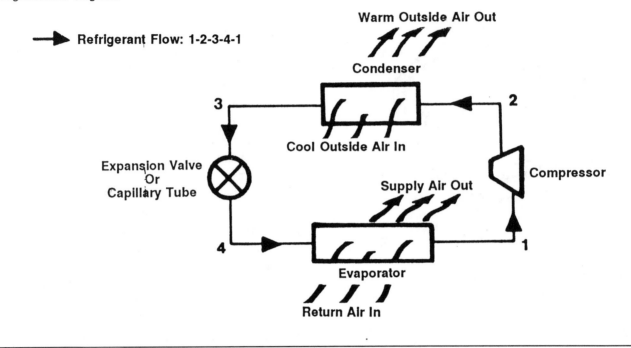

compressor and is sized according to the particular compressor.

Start kits are necessary when supply voltage is low, such as during extreme electrical demand periods common in metropolitan areas. Start kits may also be required when the compressor is tight or when an expansion valve metering device is used. Many expansion valves do not contain bleed ports to equalize pressure during the off cycle, which requires the compressor to start against strong head pressure. Under any of these conditions, the compressor may not start due to reduced starting torque and may shut off on internal overload.

The start capacitor is wired in parallel to the run capacitors to increase capacitance in the compressor circuit. This throws the start windings out of phase with the run windings, allowing the motor to start by itself. The start capacitor has a small, 15,000-ohm, 2-watt resistor wired across the terminals. The resistor is added to bleed off large voltages that may build up in the capacitor and cause problems in other components during the off cycle.

A wire extended from the disconnect switch is connected to one terminal on the start capacitor. The wire connected to the other terminal on the start capacitor is connected to the start terminal on the compressor.

The start capacitor is designed for short-term use only and burns out if not taken off line when the motor is at normal speed. When the compressor is at 75 percent of its full speed, the potential relay removes the start capacitor from the line. The potential relay includes a coil and normally closed contacts and is also called a *voltage relay* because it operates on back electromotive force (emf), or voltage generated by start windings.

The relay is connected in the wire leading from the start capacitor to the compressor start terminal. The wire from the start capacitor is connected to terminal number 1 on the relay. A wire is run from number 2 on the relay to the compressor start terminal. Terminals number 1 and number 2 are the normally closed contacts of the relay. The coil, number 5 on the relay, is connected to the common terminal on the compressor. The normally closed contacts are now in series with the start capacitor, and the potential relay is parallel to the start windings.

As the motor increases its speed, more voltage is developed across the relay coil. When the voltage reaches a predetermined value (back emf is around 370V AC to 400V AC), the relay coil energizes and opens the contacts, cutting the start capacitor from the circuit. The relay contacts are open whenever the compressor operates. When the compressor shuts off, the coil de-energizes and the contacts close.

■ FIGURE 9.12

The crankcase heater is used to maintain refrigerant temperature.

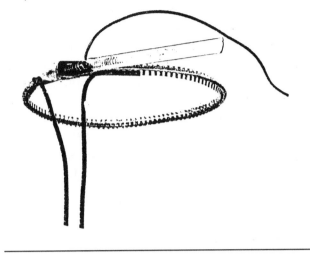

Crankcase Heater

When the cooling system is not operating, refrigerant migrates to the coldest part of the system, normally the compressor, and condenses. The refrigerant lies on the surface of the oil in the compressor crankcase. When the system begins to operate, the liquid refrigerant vapor pressure reduces and begins to boil off. The boiling refrigerant removes lubricating oil from the crankcase. The crankcase heater warms the oil, retaining the refrigerant in vapor state above the oil. Some manufacturers' compressors have internal, self-regulating crankcase heaters. (See Figure 9.12.)

Condenser Fan

The condenser fan is located outdoors as a condensing unit component. The condenser fan passes outdoor air, which is cooler than hot gas in the discharge line, over the heat transfer surface of the condenser. The air absorbs heat from the refrigerant and changes from gas to liquid. The condenser fan is wired in parallel with the compressor and operates with the compressor.

Two-Speed Condenser Fan Thermostat

New cooling systems are equipped with two-speed condenser fan motors. Speeds are controlled by a refrigerant temperature-sensing thermostat attached to the condenser coil. A heat-sensitive switch activates the motor into high or low speed, according to the rise or fall of ambient and refrigerant temperatures. (See Figure 9.13.)

■ FIGURE 9.13

Two-speed thermostat.

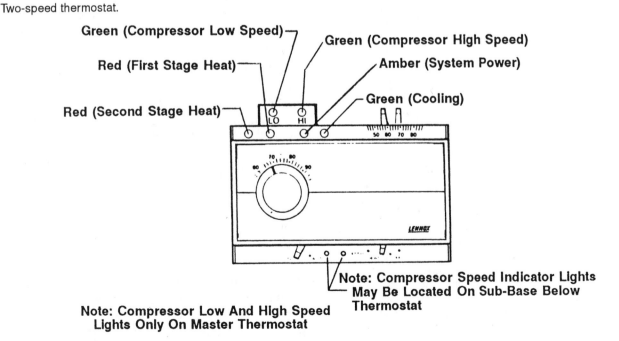

Low-Ambient Kit

The purpose of the low-ambient kit is to cycle the condenser fan to maintain head pressure in the outdoor unit. Under certain conditions, such as low-ambient outside temperature, the condenser fan should not operate because it lowers head pressure. The high-pressure switch, furnished in the kit, is wired in series with the outdoor fan, allowing it to cycle while the compressor operates. This maintains system cooling capacity. If head pressure falls to 140 pounds per square inch (psi) from cold outdoor air blowing across the condenser coil, the contacts de-energize the condenser fan. When head pressure builds to 285 psi, the contacts close and the condenser fan begins to operate.

High-Efficiency Cooling

Condensing unit efficiencies have traditionally been expressed as an energy efficiency ratio (EER). The EER is defined as the ratio of total cooling to power input, or Btuh Cooling Capacity) ÷ Total Wattage = EER [where Btuh represents British thermal units per hour].

As of January 1, 1979, all manufacturers are required to rate equipment by SEER. This is the ratio of total cooling output (Btuh) to power input in watts (w) for the season. It is determined by sizing a typical house so that at a 95°F outdoor temperature, the unit is 10 percent oversized. No load condition is assumed below 60°F. The SEER calculation penalizes for cycling losses at lower ambient temperatures. The SEER ratings are published semiannually in the Air Conditioning and Refrigeration Institute (ARI) directory.

Efficiency Improvements

Evaporator coil surfaces have increased in size. Because of the enlarged surface area, the evaporator absorbs heat more rapidly, increasing the flow rate. Enlargement of the coil surface also affects evaporator temperature. As the surface area increases, the evaporator temperature also increases (owing to better heat transfer capability).

Similar to the evaporator, the sizing affects coil temperature. In this case, however, the condensing temperature decreases. A larger coil releases system heat at a much lower temperature differential above the outdoor air. For example, the condensing temperature would vary between 110°F and 115°F at a 95°F outdoor temperature. This compares to a 130°F to 145°F condenser

temperature in earlier systems. The lower condenser coil temperature results in lower head pressure.

An increased flow rate through the evaporator and increased condensing unit efficiency cause suction pressures to increase, compared with earlier systems. With higher suction and lower head pressures, the refrigerant amount pumped per stroke increases. This directly affects the machine's SEER rating. In addition, more efficient compressors are continually engineered into the product line.

Some condensing unit models utilize a two-speed condenser fan motor. During light loads, the fan switches to a lower speed, reducing unit power consumption. A refrigerant temperature thermostat attached to a condenser coil return bend controls speed selection.

Operating Pressure

Each of the high efficiency compressor improvements affects system standard compressor pressures. The system operating pressures vary substantially between a superefficient machine and a conventional high side. Operating with a 75°F condenser-entering air temperature could expect a 70-psi-gauge (psig) suction and a 195-psig head pressure. In contrast, operating at the same 75°F outside temperature may expect an 82-psig suction and a 168-psig head pressure. This necessitates special consideration when charging these efficient machines. The operating cost increases, and the overcharge decreases compressor life.

In some systems, two-speed compressors shift speeds to match load requirements. While operating on low speed, the compressor may cut energy consumption by almost 50 percent over a single-speed compressor.

Compressor Contactor

The compressor contactor is a double-pole single-throw (DPST) relay device that closes or completes the circuit to the compressor whenever cooling is required. It is wired into the line between the compressor and the manual disconnect switch. A contactor has normally open contacts for each leg of the line and a magnetic coil, which, when energized, causes these contacts to close, allowing electricity to flow to the compressor.

High-Pressure Switch

High head or condensing pressure is destructive to a compressor. High pressures raise the vapor and oil temperature moving past the compressor exhaust valve to a point that may cause oil and refrigerant breakdown.

It is essential to stop the system before dangerous temperatures are reached. Therefore, many units are equipped with high-pressure safety cutout switches. If pressure exceeds a certain amount, the current from the control circuits shuts off, stopping the motor. The control senses discharge pressure, which may become too high from lack of condenser air, refrigerant overcharge, or a restriction in the coil.

Low-Pressure Switch

Many units are also equipped with a low-pressure safety cutout control. Frequently, units have both high and low controls packaged together as a dual control. Both sides operate independently of one another, but the linkage to the contacts is often combined.

The low-pressure safety control is located on the suction line. Motor compressor cooling depends on the amount and temperature of the suction vapor. If this vapor pressure is too low, the motor compressor may overheat and burn out. Low suction pressure may be caused by blower motor failure, low system refrigerant, or a restricted flow of refrigerant. If the blower is jammed so that it is unable to operate or if the belt slips, an insufficient air amount is delivered across the evaporator to maintain suction pressure. The low-pressure safety control stops the compressor motor before it is damaged.

Compressor Timed Interlock

The compressor timed interlock is a control device that prevents the compressor from fast cycling. This is caused if a thermostat demand for cooling is made before the system has time to equalize pressures from the previous cycle. By allowing these pressures to equalize after each cycle, the timed interlock helps prolong compressor life.

At the end of a compressor cycle, the solid-state control advances through a 5-min. timed interlock period. During this time, the compressor is de-energized. This process may occur up to 12 times an hour (hr). After the 5-min. delay, the compressor may start again. The delay period may differ among models and may be as short as 60 seconds (sec.). This is sufficient time for pressure equalization with bleed port thermostatic expansion valves. The compressor timed interlock is usually located on cooling units with no start kit and is wired in series with the other protective devices.

Two-Speed Compressors

Air-conditioning systems equipped with two-speed compressors are available in 3-t, 4-t, and 5-t capacities.

Two-speed compressors use energy only as necessary to remove heat and humidity by shifting speeds according to cooling demand. In the summer, cooling demand is actually light to medium nearly 80 percent of the time. The compressor runs on low speed, using half the energy of a conventional single-speed compressor. When demand is greater, the compressor shifts to high speed to maintain comfort levels. Single-speed units operate at high speed even when demand is light to medium, using more energy than necessary.

Reciprocating compressors are hermetically sealed with built-in protection from excessive current and temperatures. They are suction cooled and overload protected. Effective slugging protection is provided by large-housing, spring-loaded discharge valves, high-intake ports, and crankcase heaters. In addition, large-volume housing provides abundant oil reserve. Oil pumps are designed to ensure complete lubrication even during low-speed operation, using a special blended oil (natural and synthetic) that withstands high temperatures without breakdown. The crankshaft is statically and dynamically computer balanced. Low-clearance-volume pistons and cylinders yield increased volumetric efficiency, and strategically located discharge mufflers result in quiet operation. Immersible PTC (positive temperate coefficient) thermistor-type crankcase heaters are temperature actuated to operate only when required and ensure proper lubrication at all times. The motor is located within refrigerant flow patterns, resulting in low motor winding temperatures with twin solid-state temperature sensors embedded in motor windings to provide protection from excessive temperatures. Solid-state overload protectors are furnished in the unit control box and operate at 1,750 rpm during low speed and 3,500 rpm at high speed; a positive interlock between speeds prevents both speeds from energizing simultaneously. The entire running gear assembly is spring mounted within the sealed housing. In addition, the compressor is installed in the unit on resilient rubber mounts.

The latent load discriminator control is made possible with the use of the two-speed compressor and a dehumidistat (field installed) to sense relative humidity. The latent load discriminator kit controls the speed of the indoor evaporator unit blower motor to obtain maximum operating system efficiency. The kit contains a latent load control box and dehumidistat. The dehumidistat allows the indoor blower to stay in the high-speed and most-energy-efficient mode until humidity rises to a selected level. The blower then drops to low speed when the compressor is in low speed. This feature provides humidity control only when required and allows the system to operate in a high sensible heat removal, high-efficiency mode most of the year.

■ HEAT PUMPS

The heat pump is a total electric heating and air-conditioning unit. It cools similarly to conventional air conditioners, but in addition, it produces heat by reversing the refrigeration cycle. The advantage equals heat transferred instead of created.

More efficient than electric heat, a well-designed heat pump returns almost three times the amount of heat for every unit of electricity when operating in 40°F weather. The amount of heat transferred varies according to the outside temperature. As the temperature drops, the unit's efficiency drops. However, efficiency never drops below a one-to-one ratio when compared with straight electric heat.

The ratio between heat output and power input is known as the *coefficient of performance* (COP). For example, 1 kilowatt (kw) of straight electric heat provides 3,412 Btuh. If a heat pump's COP is 3.00, the same

kw delivers 10,236 Btuh. The COP ratio is calculated by dividing the total heat pump heating capacity by the total electrical input (w) and multiplying the result by 3.412.

The heat pump system may be either a split system with separate indoor and outdoor components or a single-package model with everything located outdoors. (See Figure 9.14.) On split systems, all major components must match the compressor to be covered under warranty. A misapplied system causes erratic operation and results in early compressor failure.

Heat pump terminology refers to indoor and outdoor coils rather than to condensing and evaporator coils. During the transition to the heating cycle, the outdoor coil changes from a condenser to an evaporator. The indoor coil changes from an evaporator into a condenser.

The piping from the reversing valve to the accumulator and on to the compressor is called the *vapor line*. During the summer, it transports low-pressure cool vapor; during the winter, it transfers high-pressure hot vapor.

Heat Pump Components

Previous heat pump thermostats were powered by only the transformer in the heat pump unit. This presented a problem for split systems because an electrical

---

■ FIGURE 9.14

Split or packaged systems require an ample air supply.

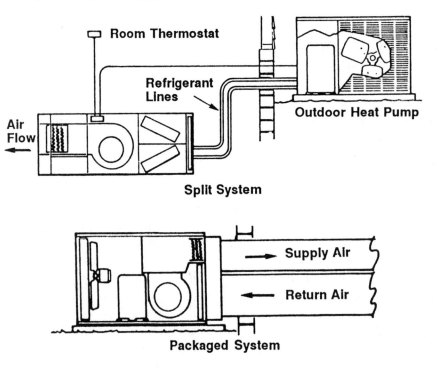

failure, such as a compressor burnout, would shut down the entire heating system. The heat pump transformer controls the indoor blower, compressor, and reversing valve, while the indoor transformer controls auxiliary and emergency heat.

Heat pumps today use one large transformer at the indoor equipment. An emergency heat function is designed into later thermostats. When placed into emergency heat, the compressor circuit is locked out, and auxiliary heat provides all the heating. When this feature is applied to systems using auxiliary heat staged by outdoor thermostats, field-provided relays bypass the outdoor thermostats. In emergency heat situations, an amber light appears at the thermostat to remind the homeowner that the heat pump is not operating; expensive auxiliary heat is being used.

In 1978, a new thermostat was introduced that featured an additional service light and a droop compensator. The service light is wired in series with the second-stage heat bulb of the room thermostat and a thermal sensor strapped to the compressor discharge line. The sensor monitors discharge temperature and closes on a temperature fall, which indicates that compressor operation has failed and that service is required.

The droop compensator lowers the degree of thermostat droop associated with heat pump thermostats. As the outdoor temperature falls below the balance point, the heat anticipator within the thermostat cycles more often. It consequently generates false heat, which deceives the bimetal into estimating the room temperature as greater than the actual temperature. As a result, room temperature may be maintained at a temperature several degrees lower than the actual thermostat setting.

To counteract the false heat, an additional resistor within the thermostat is wired in series with an outdoor thermistor located at the heat pump. The heat affecting the bimetal is maintained at a steady temperature so the equipment cycles in response to actual room temperature.

In addition to their improved efficiency, compressors have changed throughout the years. Copeland and Tecumseh compressors have an internal pressure relief valve that is spring loaded. The valve is designed to relieve discharge pressure at approximately 450 psi above the suction pressure.

When the relief valve is open, it may indicate defective valves (abnormally high suction pressure, low discharge pressure, and the inability to pump down the system). This occurs more frequently on new installation start-up and may be caused by minor slugging. When liquid refrigerant gets into the compressor, it is called *slugging* and could damage the compressor because compressors are designed to pump only vapor. The internal relief valve does not reset until system pressures equalize. When the valve is open, it reduces capacity so it cannot satisfy thermostat demand. The unit will operate in this condition until it is shut off and given sufficient time to equalize the system.

External compressor overloads have been replaced by internal overloads. In the case of the L7 compressor, they are replaced by a solid-state protector. There are many reasons why an internal overload may open. If the internal overload tripped because of an abrupt current increase, the motor has been slightly heated, and the protector should reset within a few minutes. If the compressor has been operating for a prolonged period and is thoroughly heat soaked, it may take two hours before the internal overload resets. Also, if the compressor shell exceeds 135°F, the internal overload opens. It is necessary to ventilate the compressor or cool it down by running water over it with the power off.

Crankcase heaters are used to prevent lubricant migration. Without the heater, lubrication loss and slugging occur. An integral part of some compressors, this type of heater is thermostatically controlled and temperature actuated to operate only when needed. This process is accomplished by improved compressor cooling and lubrication at low ambient temperatures.

Current heat pump split systems use a double expansion valve system. Some indoor coils are exclusively designed for heat pump usage and are factory equipped with expansion and check valves. Other indoor coils require a field-installed heat pump kit.

The reversing valve changes the refrigerant flow to either heating or cooling mode. On a call for cooling, the R-circuit of the thermostat actuates a solenoid coil, which moves a plunger in the reversing valve pilot control. (See Figure 9.15.) This changes the position of the main valve and reverses the refrigerant flow. The reversing valve moves into heating position whenever the solenoid is de-energized. The solenoid is a replaceable item on most reversing valves.

Never hit a reversing valve with a wrench or hammer. Hitting a valve rarely, if ever, solves a service problem. Permanent damage of the valve will result in failure.

On current production units, a liquid accumulator is welded into the suction line ahead of the compressor. The accumulator traps and prevents liquid refrigerant from flooding directly into the compressor during refrigerant cycle changes. This occurs primarily when changing from the heating cycle to defrost. The refrigerant con-

■ **FIGURE 9.15**

Reversing valve for conventional heat pump.

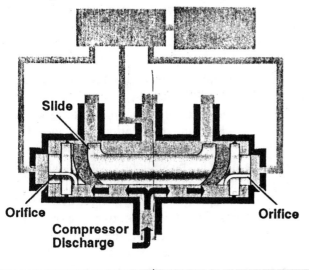

denses in the indoor coil, and liquid is suddenly pumped back through the suction line to the accumulator.

In addition, the accumulator helps prevent liquid refrigerant from migrating to the compressor during off cycles. The accumulator collects this refrigerant. A metering device within the accumulator feeds the refrigerant back to the compressor along with any oil. (See Figure 9.16.)

Refrigerant systems must be free of moisture. Under compression heat, moisture breaks down the oil,

■ **FIGURE 9.16**

An accumulator collects liquid refrigerant.

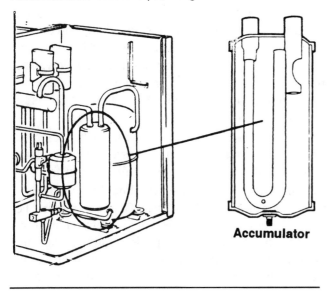

refrigerant and insulation into contaminants that cause compressor burnout. The drier uses a drying agent and a molecular sieve to extract damaging moisture and acid. The drier always must be replaced whenever refrigerant piping has been opened (such as during compressor replacement).

A check valve is used to bypass the expansion valve not in use. There are several types of check valves. Mechanical check valves consist of a disc and spring, permitting refrigerant flow in only one direction. Lennox is currently using special filter/driers that include check valves.

Thermistors within the solid-state system sense the difference between ambient air and refrigerant temperature. When the temperature difference exceeds the differential band (15°F to 25°F), the control board energizes the outdoor fan and defrost relay. This relay has a 24V DC coil energized through terminals R-R of the defrost board. The relay switches the reversing valve, stops the outdoor fan, and begins auxiliary heat.

The defrost pressure switch located in the liquid line terminates the cycle when pressure rises to 275 psig. This pressure corresponds to a 124°F coil temperature, which is sufficient to ensure complete defrost. After the unit returns to the normal heating cycle, the pressure switch resets at 200 psig, and the defrost control system is available for the next defrost cycle.

A pressure control senses the static pressure buildup caused by coil icing. When the static buildup exceeds a 0.5″ water column, the defrost cycle activates. This halts the outdoor fan and energizes the defrost control relay, which energizes the reversing valve and begins auxiliary heat.

The temperature-sensing bulb also affects the pressure control. Static pressure is exerted against the lever, which counteracts the force applied by air pressure. Changing the termination (diastat) screw changes the defrost cycle termination temperature.

This defrost control initiates defrost when pressure in the fan compartment reaches 0.5″ water column and when the temperature is at least 23°F below the defrost control temperature setting. This prevents the unit from preparing a false defrost due to wind blowing into the fan compartment. The control terminates the defrost cycle when the liquid line temperature reaches 65°F.

The clock timer combined with the defrost thermostat determines the necessity for a defrost cycle. The defrost thermostat is located near the outlet of the outdoor coil. When the coil temperature falls to 32°F, the contacts close. They remain closed until the coil temperature rises above 50°F. The clock timer motor runs whenever the compressor operates and the outdoor fan relay de-energizes. Every 90 min., this timer closes its contacts for a 20-sec. period. If the defrost thermostat and clock timer are closed at the same time, the defrost relay energizes. This stops the outdoor fan, energizes the reversing valve, and begins auxiliary heat. After the coil temperature rises to 50°F, the defrost cycle ends and the clock timer begins another 90-min. cycle. The clock timer motor is de-energized along with the outdoor fan motor during the defrost cycle.

If the 90-min. timer cycle allows the outdoor coil to become too heavily coated with frost, the cycle may be reduced to 30 min. To reduce the cycle, remove the clock timer cover. Loosen the lock nut or set screw holding the top cam and remove. Remove the bottom cam and replace the top cam, locking it so it is centered on the switch blade, and replace the cover.

The high-pressure control is located in the discharge line between the compressor and reversing valve. The switch has a cutout point of 410 psig and a manual reset. It protects the system from excessive pressures that may cause damage, and the switch is in series with the compressor contactor coil.

This low-pressure switch is used on packaged heat pumps. It is located in the liquid line and wired in series with the compressor contactor coil. The switch opens at 10 psig and automatically closes at 30 psig. Some packaged heat pumps are equipped with a low-temperature switch that terminates compressor operation when the outside temperature drops below the set point. The set point is field adjustable from 0°F to 20°F. The control automatically resets when the outdoor temperature rises 6°F above the set point. Compressors are designed for continuous low-ambient operation and are not equipped with the low-temperature shutoff switch.

Some compressors are equipped with a thermostat that checks the temperature of either the discharge gas or the crankcase. This switch is used in lieu of a low-pressure switch. The purpose of this control is to protect the compressor from a partial loss of charge. All hermetic compressors are suction-gas cooled. The suction gas returning to the compressor absorbs heat from the compressor windings to prevent overheating. Any reduction in the return gas volume may cause the compressor to overheat, which leads to early failure.

Traditionally, the low-pressure switch was used to shut off the unit when the charge became too low. With a heat pump, the pressure encountered during a defrost cycle was too low to protect the compressor during normal operation. Because the low-pressure switch was located on the liquid line, it took almost a complete loss of charge to open it. The internal compressor thermostat shut the compressor off when it overheated.

Now, there is a switch external to the compressor that also shuts off the compressor. This switch may be in two locations. Some units use a thermostat mounted on the discharge line of the compressor that shuts off the compressor when the discharge temperature exceeds 260°F. This switch must be manually reset after the discharge temperature drops to 225°F. Other units use a sensor clamped to the compressor bottom below the oil level. Because the compressor runs cooler at this point than does the discharge gas, the sensor is set to open at 190°F. It automatically resets at 110°F. The sensor should be mounted near the crankcase heater joint to minimize heater effects. While the primary function of the switch is to protect against a partial loss of charge, the switch also protects against reduced refrigerant flow. This function is similar to a restricted drier or an expansion valve that is not operating properly.

Heat Pump Operation

Basic operation considerations during the cooling cycle are the same as those for air-conditioning. Once the thermostat is placed in the cooling mode, the reversing valve energizes. At the reversing valve, the discharge line and the line traveling to the outdoor coil should be the same temperature. A cooling demand starts the compressor, which pumps hot, high-pressure gas to the outdoor coil, where heat is released by the outdoor fan. The refrigerant changes into a liquid and is transported to the indoor coil. Warm return air is drawn through the coil by the indoor blower. The refrigerant absorbs heat from the indoor air and changes into cool vapor that lowers the air-supply temperature. The cool vapor is then distributed throughout the controlled space. This temperature change removes moisture from the air and forms condensate, which must be piped away. The compressor suction pressure draws cool vapor back into the compressor, where the temperature and pressure are greatly increased. This completes the cooling refrigerant cycle.

As the subbase is switched from cooling to heating, there is a swooshing sound. The basic start-up is the same as it is for air-conditioning. In the heating cycle, the discharge line and line traveling to the indoor coil should be the same temperature at the reversing valve. In addition, the suction line and line traveling to the outdoor coil should be the same temperature. If testing the heat cycle on a warm day, the compressor may trip on high head pressure and cause compressor damage.

The thermostat's initial heating demand starts the compressor. The reversing valve de-energizes during the heating mode, and the compressor pumps hot refrigerant gas through the indoor coil, where heat is released into the indoor airstream. This warmed supply air is distributed through the conditioned space. As the refrigerant releases its heat, the refrigerant changes into a liquid and is transported to the outdoor coil, which absorbs heat from air blown across the coil by the outdoor fan. The refrigerant changes from liquid into vapor as it passes through the outdoor coil and then returns to the compressor, where it increases temperature and pressure. The hot refrigerant is then pumped back to the indoor coil to begin another cycle.

Heat pumps operating at temperatures below 45°F accumulate frost or ice on the outdoor coil. The relative humidity and ambient temperature affect the degree of accumulation. The ice buildup restricts airflow through the outdoor coil, which consequently affects system operating pressures. The defrost control detects this restriction and switches the unit into the defrost mode to melt the ice.

The reversing valve is energized and the machine temporarily transfers into the cooling cycle, where hot refrigerant flows to the outdoor coil. The outdoor fan stops at the same time, allowing an increase in discharge temperature to rapidly shorten the length of the defrost cycle. If supplemental heat exists, a defrost relay activates it to offset cooling released by the indoor coil. (See Figure 9.17.)

One common customer concern is vapor emerging from the outdoor unit. This is normal and occurs during the defrost cycle as ice buildup melts from the outdoor coil.

As the outside temperature drops, the heat pump operates for longer periods until it eventually operates continuously to satisfy the thermostat. The system balance point is where heat pump capacity exactly matches heat loss. The balance point varies among homes, depending on actual heat loss and heat pump capacity. However, the balance point usually ranges between 15°F and 40°F. Either electric heat or fossil fuels provide auxiliary heat.

Conventional heat pump applications use electric heaters downstream from the indoor coil. This prevents damaging head pressures when the heat pump and auxiliary heat run simultaneously. The indoor coil may be installed only downstream from auxiliary heat if a Fuelmaster control system is used. This control package uses a two-stage heat thermostat with the first stage controlling heat pump operation and the second stage controlling furnace operation.

■ FIGURE 9.17

Refrigerant flow for the heat pump cycle.

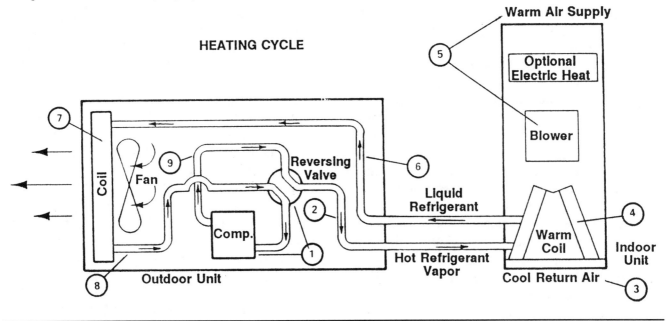

■ **FIGURE 9.18**

Typical Fuelmaster components.

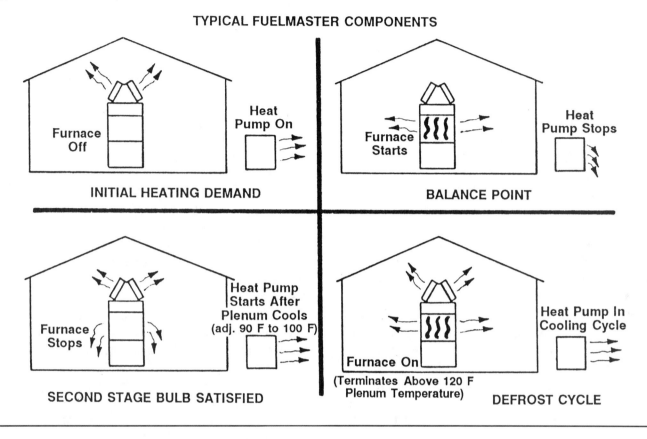

TYPICAL FUELMASTER COMPONENTS

Once the outdoor temperature drops below the balance point, the thermostat's second-stage bulb energizes the electric heat through the Y-terminal. Elements are sequenced on by heat relays. (See Figure 9.18.)

Many power companies require the use of outdoor thermostats to stage electric heat according to outdoor temperature. This prevents all the elements from energizing above the balance point. Emergency heat relays should be used in conjunction with outdoor thermostats to allow electric heat operation in the event of heat pump failure.

Outdoor thermostat set points are calculated according to structure heat loss and the heating capacity of each electric heat stage. An outdoor thermostat does not control all the electric heat because some heat is necessary for the defrost cycle.

A Fuelmaster system places the indoor furnace upstream from the indoor coil. The heat pump handles all heating until the outdoor temperature reaches the balance point. When the temperature drops below the balance point, the room thermostat closes its second-

stage bulb to start the furnace. It simultaneously energizes a relay to shut off the heat pump.

When the furnace satisfies the second-stage demand and plenum temperature cools to 90°F to 100°F, a heat pump delay turns on the heat pump. The heat pump controls the conditioned space until second-stage operation is required again. During the defrost cycle, the limit control cycles the furnace to prevent plenum temperatures exceeding 120°F.

When a heat pump system is installed, the customer should be informed of basic operating characteristics. This corrects any misconceptions and prevents unnecessary service calls.

One of the most common complaints from customers accustomed to gas or oil furnaces is the cool air discharged into the conditioned space. Supply air is actually warm and adequate to satisfy thermostat demand, but may appear cool when compared to supply air associated with fossil-fired heating equipment.

A heat pump system circulates equal air amounts in winter and summer. Because the balance point is frequently as low as 20°F on new homes, a low temperature rise occurs over the indoor coil. The lower the outdoor temperature, the lower the supply air temperature rise over the indoor coil, the lower the supply air temperature.

Heat pump systems operate longer on cycles than fossil-fired furnaces because of the lower temperature rise. The customer should evaluate his or her investment in monthly operating costs and total comfort rather than in operating time.

Many manufacturers currently use a thermostat with a red service light. The light warns homeowners that the compressor is not operating properly and that the heat pump requires service. As the heat pump cycles on by heating demand, this light may come on briefly until the compressor reaches its normal operating conditions. The customer should be informed that this short intermittent lighting is normal.

An amber light energizes whenever the thermostat is placed into the emergency heat position. The system should be placed into emergency heat mode only after the red service light warns of a heat pump malfunction. While the system operates on emergency heat, the thermostat locks out the heat pump and allows the electric heat to satisfy heating requirements. The amber light reminds the homeowner that he or she is not receiving heat pump benefits and is using expensive electric heat.

Unless filters are kept clean, the heat pump trips its high-pressure switch off. This is particularly true when outdoor temperatures are mild.

It is important that the customer be instructed how to restart his or her heat pump after a power outage. If power is off for more than 1 hr. and the outdoor temperature is below 50°F, the thermostat must be set to the off position. Do not restart the unit as soon as power is restored because the heat pump performs its job by circulating a refrigerant gas. This gas is constantly flowing in and out of the compressor when the unit is in operation. When the unit is not in operation, the gas tends to cool and liquefy inside the compressor. Because the compressor is designed to pump only gas, a low-wattage electric heater is located at the compressor to maintain refrigerant in a gaseous state. This heater is in the same circuit as the compressor motor and must be energized whenever needed.

When power is off for any reason, the heater cannot do its job, and liquid may collect in the compressor. If the unit is forced into operation at this stage, mechanical damage may result. Wait for 6 hr. after power has been restored before turning the thermostat to the on position.

The waiting period allows time for the heater to drive any liquid from the compressor.

To obtain temporary heat after a power outage, set the system selector on the room thermostat to emergency heat. This prevents the compressor from starting and actuates supplemental heat. At the end of the 6 hr. period, the thermostat may be reset to the heat position.

A mild weather kit may be used on heat pumps that must operate in the heating cycle during mild weather. Operating under these conditions may cause nuisance cutouts of the high-pressure switch. The mild weather control shuts off the outdoor fan motor when head pressure reaches 370 psig (before the high-pressure switch cuts out at 410 psig). This reduces the amount of heat captured from the outdoor air, which in turn reduces head pressure. This control automatically cycles the outdoor fan when pressure drops to 270 psig. It is wired in series to the outdoor fan motor. This kit is not recommended for use with all types of compressors owing to design and operating characteristics.

When high internal heat gains necessitate mechanical cooling during low-ambient conditions, problems arise in the basic refrigeration cycle. Low outdoor temperatures result in a low condensing temperature, which consequently lowers head pressure. As head pressure drops, the suction pressure also falls until it reaches 57 psig. At 57 psig, the equivalent saturated temperature is 32°F, and ice forms on the indoor coil. In addition, the low head pressure interferes with expansion valve operation.

Low-ambient kits consist of a pressure switch and thermal sensor. The pressure switch prevents icing at the indoor coil by cycling the outdoor fan to increase the evaporator temperature. The cutout point varies between RFC and expansion valve systems, but the cut-in point is 285 psig. The thermal sensor overrides the pressure switch when the heat pump operates in the heating cycle. Low-ambient kits are not offered or recommended for use with all types of compressors, owing to design and operating characteristics.

Two-speed compressors offer the same advantages on the cooling cycle as air-conditioning applications. On the heating cycle, the unit may be sized for larger tonnage than the cooling load. For example, if the home requires a 3-t unit for cooling, a 5-t two-speed heat pump may be used.

A ground water heat pump is a water source heat pump designed to operate at low water temperatures with various water qualities. It consists of two heat exchangers, a compressor, reversing valve refrigerant metering devices, and an indoor blower. One of the heat exchangers is a refrigerant-to-air exchanger and the other is a refrigerant-to-water exchanger.

Gaseous refrigerant is compressed by the compressor and pumped into the heat exchanger (condenser), where heat is removed. This allows the pressurized gaseous refrigerant to condense and liquefy. The pressure in the condenser forces liquid refrigerant through the metering device, which controls its flow into another heat exchanger (evaporator). This exchanger operates at lower pressure than the condenser, and the liquid refrigerant evaporates and absorbs heat. The evaporated refrigerant is then pulled into the compressor, compressed, and the cycle continues. The heat rejected in the condenser is discharged outside when the system is used for air-conditioning. However, when the system is used for heating, the heat rejected by the condenser is discharged into the conditioned space. To achieve the goal of having one unit that both heats and cools the conditioned space, a four-way valve, often called a *reversing valve,* is incorporated into the system. This allows the direction of the refrigerant flow to change according to the heating or cooling need. The indoor blower distributes conditioned air through the space.

Groundwater and Air-to-Air Heat Pump Differences

The primary difference between these two types of heat pumps is that air-to-air pumps use refrigerant-to-air heat exchangers as a means of sinking and sourcing heat pump requirements. The water source heat pump or groundwater heat pump uses water-to-refrigerant heat exchangers. It uses water sources as media to sink or source heat. (See Figure 9.19.)

Note: Although water is available from many sources, such as ponds, rivers, and lakes, only well water is acceptable as the supply source for groundwater heat pumps. The even temperature of well water ensures constant operating conditions for maximum efficiency and long equipment life. Because of surface water quality, including temperature changes and possible freezing conditions, surface water is not an acceptable supply water source for groundwater heat pumps.

■ **FIGURE 9.19**

Refrigerant flow for groundwater and air-to-air heat pump system.

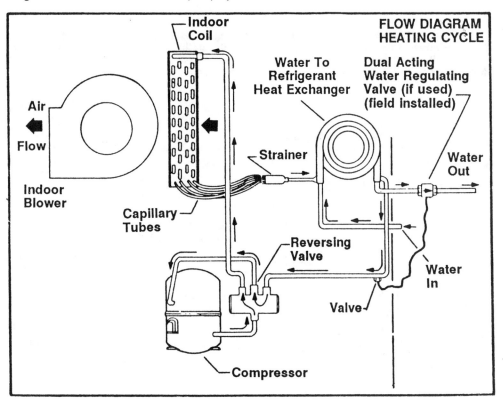

■ **FIGURE 9.20**

Operation principles for the water source heat pump.

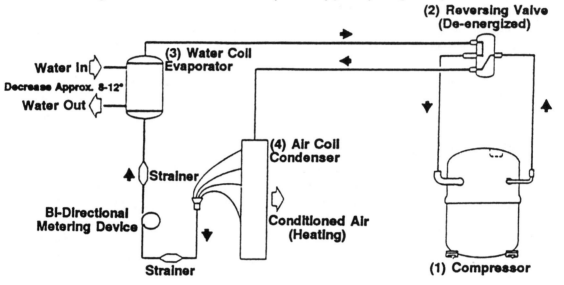

HEATING POSITION:
The reversing valve (2) directs hot refrigerant gas leaving the compressor (1) to air coil (4). Heat is transferred to the circulating room air by condensing the hot gas to a liquid. Liquid refrigerant flows to water coil (3) where it evaporates, absorbing heat from the water, to become a gas that flows back to the compressor (1) completing the cycle.

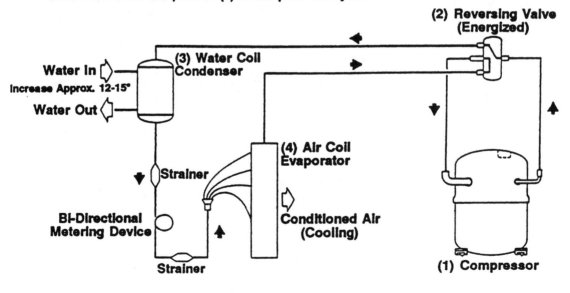

COOLING POSITION:
Compressor (1) pumps hot refrigerant gas through reversing valve (2) to water coil (3) where it is condensed to a liquid by giving up heat to circulating water. Liquid refrigerant flows into the air coil (4) where it evaporates, cooling the circulating room air. Refrigerant gas then flows back to the compressor (1) to complete the cycle.

Because groundwater heat pumps use water as their heat sink and source, there is never a freezing condition in normal operation. A defrost cycle is not required, and related efficiency defrost losses are not characteristic of groundwater heat pumps.

When groundwater, especially well water, is used as the heat sink and heat source for the groundwater heat pump, a constant efficiency level exists year round in either the heating or the cooling mode. The explanation for constant efficiencies is simple. Groundwater temperatures are constant. Because the water temperature flowing through the heat pump determines the pump's capacity and efficiency, constant water temperatures indicate constant capacity and efficiency throughout the heating season. This differs greatly from air-to-air heat pumps. With these, air temperature decreases from fall throughout winter, which decreases the capacity and efficiency of air-to-air heat pumps. Supplemental heat is then required to maintain desired temperatures in the conditioned space.

■ WATER SOURCE HEAT PUMP

Cooling Mode.   Heat is absorbed from the conditioned space by the refrigerant by circulating air over the air-to-refrigerant heat exchanger (plate-fin coil). While it is acting as an evaporator in the refrigerant circuit, heat is transferred via the refrigerant through the compressor, where it is highly compressed and forced into the water-to-refrigerant exchanger (chiller/condenser). Heat is absorbed by the circulating water from the hot compressed refrigerant and carried away at the same time, condensing the refrigerant to a liquid so that the cycle can be repeated. (See Figure 9.20.)

Heating Mode.   Heat is absorbed from the circulating water by the refrigerant heat exchanger (chiller/condenser), which in this mode is used as the evaporator by reversing the refrigerant flow. Heat is again transferred via the refrigerant through the compressor to the air to the refrigerant exchanger (plate-fin coil), which is now being used as the condenser. Here, heat from the refrigerant is absorbed by the room air that is circulated over the coil, thus transferring heat from the water to the air in the conditioned space.

Extreme care must be taken to prevent dirt or other foreign matter from entering the water pipes or piping components during installation. Pipes should be capped until they are ready to be connected into the system. The

water supply and return to the water-refrigerant heat exchanger should be marked. If the flow control device is installed in the supply water line to the heat pump, a suitable strainer must be installed ahead of the flow control device.

The equipment is designed to operate with water temperatures of 45°F to 90°F. To avoid condensation, it may be necessary to insulate piping if water temperatures will be lower than 60°F.

Condensate piping must be properly trapped with a continual slope a minimum of 1″ per 10′ to drain.

The water circulation system should be filled with clean water, and the air vents should be open during filling operation. With the air vents closed, start the circulating pump, then crack the air vents to bleed off any trapped air, thus ensuring circulation through all system components. Makeup water must be available to the system to replace the air that has bled off.

With the air vented and water circulating, the entire system should be checked for leaks. Operate the supplementary heat system during this operation. Visual checks should be made for leaks that may have occurred with the increased heat.

When inspecting the unit, the inspector should be certain of the following items:

- The water flow is established and circulating through all circuits.
- Water temperature is within normal operating range: 45°F to 90°F.
- Glycol has been added in the proper mix to prevent freezing in closed systems that can, under any condition, fall below the freezing point during either the heat pump operating cycle or the down cycle.
- All water valves are open and adjusted for proper water flow.
- Fuses and other protective devices are properly sized and in good working order.
- Belts are aligned and adjusted properly.
- Refrigerant tubing is not rubbing on cabinet or other tubing.
- Filters are installed and supply diffusers are open.
- If power is turned off to the unit, check to see why it is off before turning the unit on.
- Set room thermostat and other controls to operate in the cooling mode, with fan control to auto and temperature setpoint below room temperature.
- Check unit operation. It should be supplying cool air to the conditioned space. The reversing valve will be energized, the water leaving the chiller should be warmer than the entering water (approximately 12°F

to 15°F rise), the blower operation smooth, the compressor and blower amps within data plate ratings, and the suction line cool with no frost observed in the refrigerant circuit.

- Turn the thermostat to off, adjust temperature setpoint above room temperature, delay two min. before turning to heat with the fan on auto. The unit should run with the reversing.

Preventive maintenance is very important on these units, as on all HVAC systems. The heat pump should not be operated without the 1″ fiberglass filter in place. This filter should be replaced as often as necessary for efficient operation of the unit. The condensate drains should be checked and cleaned at least once a year to avoid the possibility of overflowing. For units that are on city water or well water, it is important to check the cleanliness of the chiller/condenser. Should the chiller/condenser become contaminated with dirt and scaling as a result of bad water, the chiller/condenser will have to be back-flushed and cleaned with a chemical that removes the scale. This service should be performed by an experienced service technician. Cooling towers of the closed type must be maintained and kept free of algae and contaminates, and they should have water treatment.

Direct-drive blower motors have sealed lubrication. The belt-drive blowers require oil twice a year with a few drops of #20 SAE nondetergent oil. Care should be taken not to use excess oil. Correct motor belt tension is set by pushing down on the belt half-way between pulleys. The belt should move or deflect from ¾″ to 1″. If the belt is excessively tight, excess heat will be generated in the bearings and will cause ultimate failure.

On a closed-circuit water system, there is auxiliary equipment, such as boilers, towers, and pumps, that also requires preventive maintenance.

Geothermal Heat Pump

According to the Environmental Protection Agency (EPA), geothermal systems are the most efficient of all available technologies resulting in low costs for space conditioning. Properly sized systems need little or no back-up resistance heat. In addition, these systems frequently have a desuperheater to supplement resistance water heating. (*Desuperheater* is a term for GeoExchange system's simple heat exchanger that is added to a water heater. GeoExchnage is Geothermal Heat Pump Consortium, operating under the EPA.) A geothermal system differs from a conventional heat pump in many

ways. Like heat pumps and air conditioners, geothermal systems make use of a refrigerant to help transfer or pump heat into and out of a building. The refrigerant is pumped through a closed loop that includes two heat exchangers and a condenser (hot zone in the winter). Geothermal systems take heat from the earth or ground water to warm the indoor air. The second part of the heat exchanger is an evaporator (cold zone in the summer). The process is reversed, in that the heat is removed from the building and transferred to the ground. There is no outside unit with a fan. Geothermal systems have a longer life compared with heat pumps because the sealed refrigerant system is not exposed to the outside environment.

A conventional residential heat pump is basically an air conditioner that adds a reversing capability so the condenser and evaporator can be switched, allowing it to extract heat from the outside air in the winter and transfer it inside. While being able to extract heat from cold winter air seems counterintuitive, the system is actually exposing the cold outside air to a refrigerant coil that is even colder than the refrigerant, and then to the building interior.

If the outside air gets extremely cold (below 20°F), a conventional heat pump cannot make the evaporator temperature low enough to absorb enough heat. That's when very expensive supplemental heating kicks in. Conventional heat pumps' operating efficiency is lowest when demand is highest; that is, they have to work hardest when the most is wanted from them. The colder the outside air, the more difficult is the task of extracting heat from it. The higher a building's rate of heat loss through windows, around doors, and through walls and roofs, the more heat is needed to be pumped inside to keep indoor temperatures comfortable. In summer, it's the same problem in reverse: The hotter the outside air, the harder it becomes to transfer heat to it.

The geothermal system eliminates this dilemma by using the relatively constant-temperature earth as a heat source in the winter and a heat sink in summer. Throughout the United States, the temperature of the ground below the frostline remains at a moderate temperature year-round, ranging from around 45°F in northern latitudes to around 70°F in the deep south.

So in the winter, a geothermal unit can extract heat from ground that is relatively warm compared with the cold outside air; in the summer, it can discharge heat to ground that is relatively cool, compared with the hot outside air. The geothermal system operates at much higher year-round efficiencies than a standard heat pump. A geothermal system transfers heat from the

■ **FIGURE 9.21**

Geothermal (GeoExchange) system.

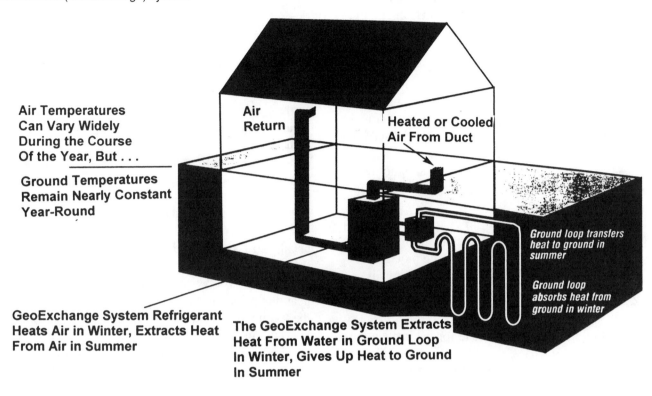

Air Temperatures Can Vary Widely During the Course Of the Year, But . . .

Ground Temperatures Remain Nearly Constant Year-Round

Air Return

Heated or Cooled Air From Duct

Ground loop transfers heat to ground in summer

Ground loop absorbs heat from ground in winter

GeoExchange System Refrigerant Heats Air in Winter, Extracts Heat From Air in Summer

The GeoExchange System Extracts Heat From Water in Ground Loop In Winter, Gives Up Heat to Ground In Summer

ground into the residence in winter. It doesn't burn any oil, natural gas, or propane. This makes the system an environmentally friendly, as well as safe and healthy, alternative to oil and gas furnaces and boilers.

The unique aspect of the geothermal system is the ground loop. The ground loop consists of several lengths of high-density polyethylene (HDPE) pipe, usually installed in horizontal trenches or vertical boreholes that are subsequently covered with earth and landscaping, driveways, and/or sidewalks.

Water or a water and nontoxic-antifreeze mixture is pumped through the ground loop piping and then to the geothermal unit inside the structure. In the summer, the liquid in the ground loop absorbs heat from the geothermal heat pump's condenser and carries it to the ground. In the winter, the liquid absorbs heat from the earth as it passes through the ground loop and then transfers that heat to the geothermal heat pump's evaporator. (See Figure 9.21.)

The type of soil and the building's heating and cooling loads determine the length of the ground loop. The loads are based on the building's size, design, con-

struction, orientation, and the local climate. Whether the ground loop will be most efficiently installed in horizontal trenches, in vertical boreholes, or even submerged in a pond, depends on the type of soil near the surface (rocky, sandy, clay-laden, etc.), the geology of the deeper terrain in the area, the amount of land, or the availability of a sufficiently deep body of water.

Generally, closed pond loops are less expensive than vertical loops, but they require more land area than the vertical loops. With the vertical loops, there is the cost of drilling the holes. Once the ground loop is installed, it can typically be forgotten. The polyethylene piping does not degrade, corrode, or break down in the ground or with water contact.

Most geothermal systems now include a designer heater that allows the ground loop to transfer some of its heat to the domestic hot water supply as it exits the geothermal unit, providing free hot water during the cooling season. Even in the winter, the geothermal unit can often help to reduce the amount of electricity or natural gas consumed by the water heater.

One of the complaints often heard from the owners of standard heat pumps is that the air coming from the vents in the winter is cool, creating a sense of draftiness. While the air is actually warmer than room temperature, it is cooler than the average person's skin temperature and that makes the air feel cold. The geothermal systems can produce much warmer air in winter because the ground temperature is much warmer than typical winter air temperatures. The geothermal system can make the air that flows from the vents into the room much warmer than a person's skin—typically well over 100°F making the occupants feel warm.

Because the air from the vents is at a higher temperature than the skin, heat flows from the air to our skin, making it feel warm.

Geothermal systems also provide superior year-round humidity control, and modular designs often make zoned heating and air-conditioning practical for even more comfort control throughout the entire house.

When inspecting a home with a geothermal system, the inspector should look for

- an ARI certification appropriate for the installation type. (Generally ARI-325 or ARI-330; ARI-320 may be acceptable for groundwater installations in the south.)
- a clean and professional installation; the contractor should be IGSHPA-certified or its equivalent. The contractor's label should indicate this.
- notification tags, which are needed if antifreeze was used in closed-loop systems.
- appropriate water disposal in an open loop system. Systems that are integrated with the domestic water supply well should have an expansion tank.

Note: Inspect a geothermal system like an air source system. It is not necessary to be concerned about the outside temperature. Following are some general guidelines:

- Testing an integrated (water heating) system: Drain some hot water from the system by opening a faucet. Turn it on and check that the circulating pump is running and the pipe to the water heater gets warm.
- Testing loop water flow: Some systems have in-line flow gauges, which should indicate a flow of more than 2 gallon/min. per ton of nameplate capacity. If there is no flowmeter and the system performs normally, further diagnostics are not generally required.
- Testing backup resistance heat (if installed): With a standard thermostat, raise the setting 5°F and check for current flow to the strips. Some thermostats may

delay 5 min. before activating. An "intelligent" thermostat may require other testing procedures.

For more information, visit Geothermal, Heat Pump Consortium, at www.geoexchange.org.

Heat Pump with Gas or Oil Furnaces

If heat pumps are to be matched with a gas or an oil furnace because the indoor heat pump coil must be located in the discharge air stream leaving the gas or oil furnace, they must have fossil fuel controls that will not allow gas or oil furnaces to operate when the heat pump is operating and vice versa. The heat pump is the most economical application in locations where it provides heat at a lower cost than gas or oil. The heat pump operates at temperatures where it is most efficient, usually 30°F and above. During a first-stage call for heat, the heat pump operates alone. When the outdoor temperature drops below the heat pump's balance point, the heat pump cannot supply all the heat required. During the second-stage heat call the fossil fuel control stops the heat pump and the fossil fuel furnace supplies all the heat required. During a heat pump defrost cycle, the fossil fuel control cycles the furnace to limit the air temperature entering the heat pump indoor coil.

Trane

The Trane Company manufactures high-efficiency heating and cooling equipment. It manufactures its own compressors. Trane's cooling equipment features standard compressors, scroll compressors, and now, variable-speed compressors and blower motors.

Trane's high-efficiency single-speed compressor unit is the XL 1200, which is both a condensing unit and heat pump. The TTX7 series indicates the condensing unit and the TWX7 series indicates the heat pump. Cooling efficiencies are from 11 to 13 SEER. Heat pump heating efficiencies are 3.0 to 3.5 COP, and the HSPF (heat season performance factor) ranges from 7.0 to 8.0. These units come in 1½, 2, 2½, 3, 3½, 4 and 5 t.

The unit features a high-efficiency single-speed compressor and a two-speed outdoor fan motor. It uses aluminum outdoor coil tubing with aluminum spine fins. The rest of the outdoor unit refrigerant piping is copper. A ten-year warranty is included with the XL 1200 and covers both the compressor and outdoor coil.

A top-of-the-line Trane condensing unit and heat pump is the XV 1500. It features a variable-speed compressor and a variable-speed outdoor fan and matches

■ **FIGURE 9.22**

Trane XV 1500 thermostat.

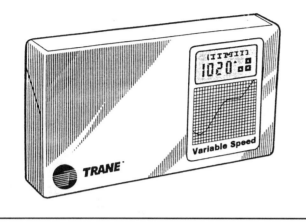

with an indoor unit having a variable-speed blower motor. The variable-speed motors are DC voltage motors and are controlled by a solid-state microprocessor. Trane has discontinued manufacturing the XV 1500 and replaced it with the XL 1800, which has up to 18 SEER. The XL 1800 has two compressors; one may be, for example, a 1½-t and the other a 3- or 3½-t. Only when the smaller compressor cannot satisfy the demand will the second compressor operate. The unit also has a two-speed fan motor. When inspecting, the inspector should be aware that the fan has two speeds and the unit has two compressors.

Thermostat

The thermostat for the XV 1500 is also a microprocessor. It displays the time and the indoor and outdoor temperature and shows an liquid crystal display (LCD) bar graph of the rpm of the compressor. The symbol for cool is an icicle and the symbol for heat is a small flame. A flashing flame is the symbol for auxiliary heat. The thermostat has a relative humidity sensor and responds both to indoor temperature and to indoor humidity conditions. (See Figure 9.22.)

Electronic Control Panel

The system has a solid-state electronic control panel that supervises the indoor and outdoor units. It gathers input from the thermostat and sensors in the outdoor unit and instructs the indoor blower, outdoor fan, and compressor to pump the correct amount of refrigerant, move the correct amount of indoor air over the evaporator, and move the correct amount of outdoor air over the condenser coil. This process allows excellent temperature

and humidity control with the best economical performance. The panel mounts on the wall near the indoor unit. (See Figure 9.23.)

When the thermostat calls for cooling, the microprocessor starts the compressor at a low rpm. The microprocessor changes the AC voltage to DC voltage for the compressor motor, and it also changes the frequency of the voltage going to the compressor motor. The rpm varies to pump enough refrigerant to control thermostat demand. The microprocessor changes the DC voltage and frequency to the indoor blower motor. The blower moves air to precisely maintain a comfortable temperature and humidity in the house.

As thermostat demand increases, the microprocessor ramps up the DC voltage and frequency to match demand. It may increase rpm by as little as 1 rpm. As the demand decreases, the system ramps down the compressor rpm. The change in compressor rpm is displayed on the thermostat bar graph. After the system satisfies the demand, the indoor and outdoor units continue to run at low rpm for 10 min. The low rpm ensures the most efficiency. The system then shuts off until the next thermostat demand.

Over a cooling season, the unit usually operates at approximately 35 percent of full rpm. This gives full rpm SEER efficiencies as high as 16.9. Heat pump HSPF ranges as high as 9.4, and COP ranges up to 3.2. The homeowner notices a lower utility bill and is comfortable with more even temperatures.

The inspector sets the thermostat 3°F to 4°F below room temperature to test the unit. Allow the unit to run for 5 to 10 min. This permits the unit to respond and ramp to a high rpm. The inspector checks the indoor and outdoor units, as with any condensing unit and evaporator. These condensing units come in 2½-, 3-, 4-, and 5-t sizes.

After the unit satisfies the thermostat, it runs for 10 min. Turning the thermostat to another mode stops this 10 min. run period. When the unit stops, there is a 5-min. time delay before it can run again. To best use this 5-min. delay, the inspector should test the operation of the auxiliary heat. Set the thermostat for auxiliary heat and check the operation of the electric heat elements. After checking the elements, set the thermostat back to its original setting.

To test the unit in the heating mode, set the thermostat for heat. Set the temperature 3°F or 4°F above room temperature. Allow the unit to operate for 5 to 10 min. and check that the large vapor line becomes hot.

■ **FIGURE 9.23**

Control wiring for the Trane XV 1500.

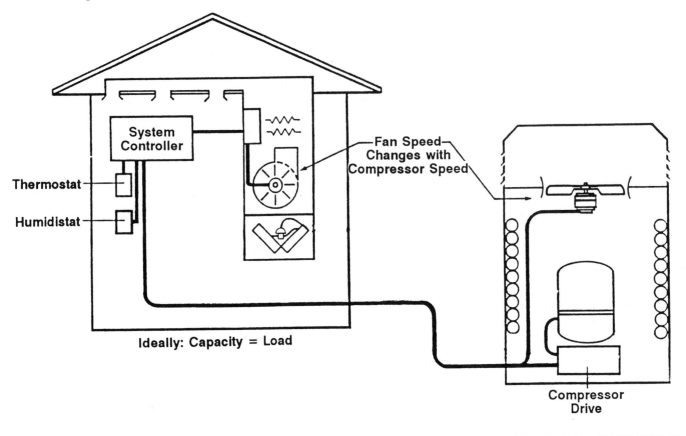

After testing the unit in the heating mode, set the thermostat heating temperature back to its original set point.

Carrier

The Carrier Company has been in the air-conditioning business longer than any other company. The founder, Willis Carrier, invented the air-conditioning process.

The Carrier 38TR and 38YR condensing units and heat pumps use Copeland compliant scroll compressors. These units have totally enclosed outdoor fan motors and copper coils with aluminum fins. Instead of the TXV metering device, Carrier uses its AccuRater piston, a restrictive metering device that uses a piston device to meter refrigerant. Its SEER efficiency is 11 to 12. The system should be inspected similarly to any single-speed condensing unit.

The 38YR heat pump also uses the scroll compressor. The heat pump uses expansion valves for metering devices. If the heat pump has a gas furnace for auxiliary heat, it must use the Optimizer II control to ensure that the furnace and heat pump do not operate at the same time. Cooling efficiencies are 10 to 12 SEER, with heat pump efficiencies at 7.0 to 8.0 HSPF and 3.0 to 3.5 COP.

Variable-Speed Condensing Unit and Heat Pump

The top-of-the-line Carrier condensing unit is the 38TV (also called the Infinity 2000). It has a variable speed compressor, an outdoor fan, and an indoor blower with a SEER ranging from 15 to 16. It comes in 2-t and 3-t sizes. The comparable Infinity 2000 heat pump is the 38YV.

Infinity

The heart of the Infinity condensing unit is a variable-speed compressor that uses a three-phase DC motor. An electronic controller called the *standard outdoor module* (SOM) gathers information from the indoor thermostat and outdoor conditions to vary the rpm of the compressor motor and outdoor fan motor.

A high demand for cooling causes the compressor and outdoor fan to run at a high rpm. If the demand for cooling is low, they run at a lower rpm. The compressor rpm varies from 1,900 to 3,000 or 5,000, depending on compressor size. The outdoor fan rpm varies from 400 to 900.

Indoor Unit. The Infinity 2000 must be matched with specific indoor units using a variable-speed indoor blower. The indoor unit uses a standard indoor module (SIM) to control the indoor blower. If the gas furnace does not have a variable-speed blower, a furnace interface kit is needed. The thermostat controls not only the speed of the compressor and outdoor fan but also the rpm of the indoor fan. (See Figure 9.24.)

The solid-state thermostat monitors both indoor temperature and humidity. It sends commands to both the SOM and the SIM. These modules command the compressor, outdoor fan, and indoor blower to pump refrigerant and move indoor air to maintain both the proper temperature and the proper humidity. The

outdoor unit operates only if the outdoor temperature is above 55°F.

Infinity Heat Pump. The Infinity heat pump is similar to the condensing unit. It uses variable-speed motors in the compressor, outdoor fan, and indoor blower. The same SOM and SIM control motor operation. The heat pump uses either electric heat strips or a gas furnace as auxiliary heat.

The outdoor temperature must be above 0°F for the heat pump to start. On heat demand, the outdoor fan and compressor ramp up to the proper rpm. The SIM delays indoor blower operation for 30 sec., allowing the indoor coil to warm. The outdoor fan and compressor stop when the thermostat reaches the set point. However, the indoor blower continues to operate for 3 min. to remove any residual heat from the indoor coil.

Pressing the emergency heat button on the thermostat locks out the outdoor unit and displays EH (emergency heat) on the thermostat. A heat call from the thermostat initiates indoor heating. The indoor unit then can be inspected. DO NOT SET THE THERMOSTAT MORE THAN 3°F ABOVE ROOM TEMPERATURE TO CHECK.

New O-Style Evaporator Coil

A different design of evaporator coil now is available. Conventional styles of evaporator coils have been the A-coil and the slab coil. The new one is a round design.

The coil is constructed first as a long, flat, conventional coil, then is rolled into a round shape. One of the round openings is closed with sheet metal, while the other is positioned in a condensate pan. The pan is open to allow air from the furnace blower to enter, and the air is forced through the coil and into the supply air plenum. Because of its design, the O-coil allows air through with less restriction than the A-coil. (See Figure 9.25.)

Evaporative Cooling

The evaporative or swamp cooler is an efficient means of air-conditioning for buildings in the arid regions of the West and Southwest. The evaporative cooler serves two purposes in controlling comfort within a living space. It provides both cooling and increased humidity levels in dry climates.

The evaporative cooler functions by lowering the dry-bulb air temperature entering the fan by saturating

■ **FIGURE 9.24**

Carrier variable speed indoor unit.

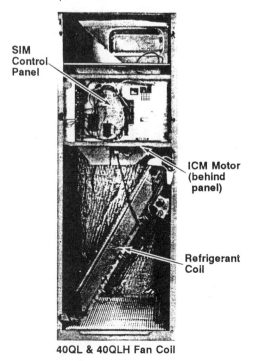

SIM Control Panel

ICM Motor (behind panel)

Refrigerant Coil

40QL & 40QLH Fan Coil

■ **FIGURE 9.25**

O-coil evaporator.

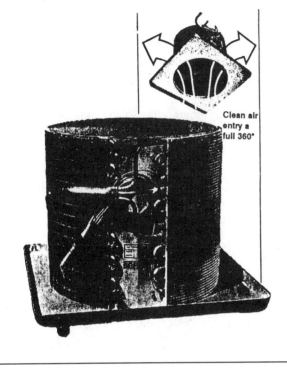

Clean air
entry a
full 360°

■ **FIGURE 9.26**

Evaporative cooler.

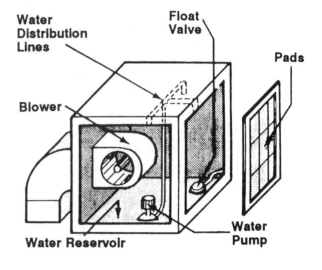

the air with moisture. As air passes through the wet chamber, its dry-bulb temperature lowers almost to the wet-bulb temperature for the given climatic condition. A large temperature reduction may be achieved in arid climates because of the low relative humidity and, thus, low wet-bulb temperatures in these regions. In some climates, conditioned or supply air may reach temperatures between 55°F and 65°F. (See Figure 9.26.)

The high relative humidity of the supply air helps produce comfortable relative humidity levels in the room. A suitable level of 30 percent to 50 percent relative humidity in the living space may be maintained.

■ REVIEW QUESTIONS*

1. Air-conditioning compressors should not be operated below _____°F.

2. The compressor pumps refrigerant only in the _____ state.

3. The condenser coil fins on air conditioners provide for heat transfer from high temperatures to low temperatures.

   A. True
   B. False

4. While condenser coils are located outside of a building, the evaporator coil would be an indoor coil.

   A. True
   B. False

5. When a heat pump is in the heat mode, the evaporator coil becomes the condenser coil. This process is accomplished through the _____ valve.

---

*Answers to all of the chapter review questions are located in Appendix C at the back of this book.

6. A heat pump should not be operated in heat pump mode when ambient temperature is above _____°F.

7. During heat pump operation, when heat pump capacity exactly matches heating loss, it is called _____.

8. The EER designation as applied to an air-conditioner refers to

   A. equal energy regulator.
   B. energy efficiency ratio.
   C. emergency energy rating.
   D. None of the above

9. To operate properly, evaporative coolers require a low relative humidity.

   A. True
   B. False

10. A conventional heating/cooling thermostat is acceptable for heat pumps.

    A. True
    B. False

11. A severely clogged condenser coil may cause the compressor to _____.

12. When a heat pump operates during the heating cycle, the vapor line should feel _____ to the touch.

13. One method of checking the air-conditioning system is by checking temperature drop across the _____.

14. When the heat pump is in the heat pump mode, if frost or ice accumulates on the outdoor coil, it usually indicates a defective _____.

15. When inspecting a high efficiency heat pump with an electronic control panel and thermostat, the thermostat temperature setting should never be moved more than 4°F in either direction.

    A. True
    B. False

16. A geothermal system is more efficient year-round than a standard heat pump.

    A. True
    B. False

17. In a geothermal system, the evaporator section absorbs energy and the condenser section releases energy.

    A. True
    B. False

18. The length of the ground loop is determined by the type of soil and the building's heating and cooling loads which are based on

    A. size.
    B. design.
    C. construction.
    D. climate.
    E. All the above

19. Whether the ground loop is most efficiently installed depends on the type of soil.

    A. True
    B. False

20. The ground loop consists of several lengths of _____ pipe.

    A. copper
    B. black iron
    C. polyethylene
    D. All of the above

21. The cost of installing the ground loop is the same for horizontal trenches, vertical boreholes, or submerged in a pond.

    A. True
    B. False

22. A geothermal system in heat mode can produce heated air in excess of 100°F.

    A. True
    B. False

Informational Internet Site for Geothermal Heat Pumps: www.geoexchanger.org.

■ INSPECTION CHECKLIST: AIR CONDITIONING AND HEAT PUMPS

AIR-CONDITIONING—INDOOR

Note: *If outdoor temperatures are below 60°F, state on the report that the air-conditioning system cannot be operated. Operating in low temperatures damages the compressor.*

Yes No

- ☐ ☐ Is evaporator case corroded?
- ☐ ☐ On gas furnace applications, does airflow first go through the heat exchanger and then the evaporator coil?
- ☐ ☐ Does excessive noise or vibration exist at the indoor blower?
- ☐ ☐ Is the primary condensate line blocked?
- ☐ ☐ Does the primary condensate line terminate in the crawlspace or next to a beam wall?
- ☐ ☐ Is the primary condensate line sloped correctly?
- ☐ ☐ Are the evaporator coil and suction line frosted or iced over?
- ☐ ☐ Does each supply air register have sufficient airflow?
- ☐ ☐ For attic installations or where unit is located above the living area:
- ☐ ☐ Is there an auxiliary condensate pan?
- ☐ ☐ Is there a secondary condensate line?
- ☐ ☐ Does the secondary condensate line terminate in a visible location?
- ☐ ☐ Is the secondary condensate line dripping water? (It should not drip water except when the primary line is plugged.)
- ☐ ☐ Does the evaporator coil have a provision for the condensate line or does a drain pan exist?
- ☐ ☐ Is the drain pan filled with condensate or debris?
- ☐ ☐ If the condensate lines are copper, are they insulated? (Even PVC condensate lines should be insulated.)
- ☐ ☐ Are the condensate lines sloped correctly?
- ☐ ☐ Is the suction line insulated?
- ☐ ☐ If an expansion valve is used, is the sensing bulb strapped to the suction line?

Yes No

- ☐ ☐ With a cooling demand, secure a temperature drop reading from the supply and return air systems. On a vacant house in the summer, it may take several minutes of operation before the system balances out.
- ☐ ☐ Is the temperature drop within 15°F to 20°F? If not:
- ☐ ☐ Are thermometers correctly calibrated?
- ☐ ☐ Does the temperature drop read slightly low on humid days?
- ☐ ☐ Does the temperature drop read high on very dry days (low humidity)?
- ☐ ☐ Has unit been allowed sufficient operating time in a vacant house during the summer?
- ☐ ☐ A low temperature drop matched with a less than cool suction line may indicate a low charge or refrigeration problem. A high temperature drop may indicate a dirty coil, a dirty filter or an air restriction such as a dirty blower.

AIR-CONDITIONING—OUTDOOR

Yes No

- ☐ ☐ Is the condenser coil plugged with debris?
- ☐ ☐ Any evidence of damage to the condenser coil?
- ☐ ☐ Are the fins damaged?
- ☐ ☐ Is there evidence of refrigerant leak?
- ☐ ☐ Does the unit sit level?
- ☐ ☐ Is the cabinet corroded?
- ☐ ☐ Is the electrical wiring acceptable?
- ☐ ☐ Is there adequate clearance around unit (airflow)?
- ☐ ☐ Does there appear to be an excess amount of insulation missing at the suction lines?
- ☐ ☐ Any kinks in the suction or liquid refrigerant lines?
- ☐ ☐ Do the condenser fan blades appear cracked or damaged?
- ☐ ☐ Provide a full cooling demand and perform the following checks:
- ☐ ☐ Do the indoor blower, condenser fan, and compressor operate? If not:
- ☐ ☐ Is the thermostat set for cooling?
- ☐ ☐ Is the disconnect switch off at either the indoor or the condensing unit?

Yes No

- ☐ ☐ Does the circuit breaker trip at the main electrical service panel?
- ☐ ☐ Is the compressor and/or condenser fan excessively noisy?
- ☐ ☐ Does either the compressor or the condenser fan cycle off during a full cooling demand?
- ☐ ☐ Does the system short cycle?
- ☐ ☐ Is there a temperature rise across the condenser coil?
- ☐ ☐ If the unit is equipped with a sight glass, are vapor bubbles visible?
- ☐ ☐ Does frost or ice appear at the suction line?
- ☐ ☐ Is the suction line cool to the touch?
- ☐ ☐ During a typical summer day, is the liquid line warm to the touch?

   Note: As the outside temperature drops, the liquid line temperature will also drop.

   Note: Remember to return thermostat to its original setting.

HEAT PUMP

Provide a cooling demand at the thermostat. Make all the same indoor and outdoor checks given in the air-conditioning section.

Yes No

- ☐ ☐ If installation includes auxiliary heat, does airflow first go through the indoor coil and then the heat source?

   Provide a heating demand at thermostat.

- ☐ ☐ Does installation include a heat pump thermostat?
- ☐ ☐ Do outdoor unit and indoor blower operate? If not:
- ☐ ☐ Is indoor unit disconnect off?
- ☐ ☐ Is outdoor unit disconnect off?
- ☐ ☐ Is thermostat properly set?
- ☐ ☐ Hold vapor line at indoor unit.
- ☐ ☐ Is vapor line hot?

   Switch thermostat to emergency heat and provide a full heating demand. This should cycle on only the auxiliary heat.

Perform heating checks as outlined in the electric heat section.

- ☐ ☐ Does unit cycle off properly?

Yes No

- ☐ ☐ During the winter season, is there an excessive amount of ice at the outdoor coil?

   Note: The cooling check verifies the compressor. Operate the heat pump only long enough to verify reversing valve operation. Placing the thermostat to emergency heat locks out the compressor to allow an auxiliary heat check.

   Note: Do not operate a heat pump in the heating mode at temperatures above 80°F (even for a short period). The resulting high head pressures will damage the compressor.

Carefully evaluate the supply and return air systems. Air restrictions such as a dirty indoor coil or dirty filter damage heat pumps.

   Note: Remember to return thermostats to original settings.

EVAPORATIVE COOLING

Yes No

- ☐ ☐ Is motor one- or two-speed?
- ☐ ☐ Is motor properly connected electrically?
- ☐ ☐ Is the pump operating properly?
- ☐ ☐ Are the spider tubes, tube clips, and bleeder system in acceptable condition?
- ☐ ☐ Are water lines installed properly?
- ☐ ☐ Is fan operating?
- ☐ ☐ Is squirrel cage blower operating properly?
- ☐ ☐ Does a minimum 1″ air gap exist between water discharge at float and water level?
- ☐ ☐ Any evidence of corrosion buildup or deterioration in the following:
- ☐ ☐ Fan or squirrel cage?
- ☐ ☐ Water trays or exterior housing?
- ☐ ☐ Supply ducts or interior registers?
- ☐ ☐ Is cooler properly installed?

■ REPORTING GUIDELINES

Inspection reporting guidelines for air conditioning and heat pumps incorporating the above checklist.

Cooling systems other than evaporative coolers. The inspector shall

- report the type of system and energy sources;
- operate the system using normal control devices except when the outdoor temperature is less than 60°F;
- inspect for proper performance, for example, by observing the temperature difference between the supply air and the return air or noticeable vibration of the blower fan, and report as in need of repair any deficiencies;
- report as in need of repair the lack or deficiencies in drainage of, condensate drain line and secondary drain line when applicable, including pipes made of inadequate material;
- report as in need of repair a primary drain pipe that terminates in a sewer vent, if the termination is visible;
- report as in need of repair a safety pan that is not appropriately sized for the evaporator coil or free of water or debris;
- report as in need of repair a return chase and plenum that are not free of improper and hazardous conditions, such as gas pipes, sewer vents, refrigerant piping or electrical wiring.
- report as in need of repair the lack of insulation on refrigerant pipes and the primary condensate drain pipe;
- report as in need of repair a condensing unit that does not have adequate clearances or air circulation, or that has deficiencies in the condition of fins, location, levelness and elevation above ground surfaces; and
- report as in need of repair conductor sizing and overload protective devices that are not appropriately sized for the unit.

Specific limitations for cooling systems. The inspector is not required to do the following:

- Inspect for the pressure of the system coolant or determine the presence of leaks
- Program digital-type thermostats or controls
- Operate setback features on thermostats or controls

10

Appliances

An appliance is a device that completes one or a series of designated household functions. Appliances are operated by either electricity or gas. Appliances cover a wide range of devices such as dishwashers, disposals, cooktops, ovens, ranges, microwave ovens, kitchen exhaust systems, refrigerators, freestanding ice makers, trash compactors, freestanding or built-in gas or electric grills, automatic washers and dryers, central vacuum systems, food centers, instant water heaters, and garage door openers. Freestanding appliances are considered personal property and a real estate inspector does not have authority to operate or inspect them *unless* the appliances are going to remain as part of the transaction. If they are part of the transaction, they become real property and the inspector must inspect them as if they were built-ins. The real estate inspector must have a working knowledge of appliances to complete an accurate and thorough inspection.

■ DISHWASHERS

Dishwashers are designed to wash, rinse, and dry dishes and utensils. The dishwasher is an electrical appliance that operates the pump, soap dispenser, rinse aid, spray jets, and rinse/dry cycle through an electric timer. The operation of a dishwasher requires hot water, usually 140 degrees Fahrenheit (°F) or hotter, according to the manufacturers' specifications; strong detergent; and water pressure. The dishwasher tub is either front loading or top loading. Dishwashers are built into a cabinet or are portable. If portable, the dishwasher should be on rollers and have a hose that attaches to the kitchen sink faucet. When the dishwasher cycle is complete, the faucet should be turned to release the pressure before detaching the hose. Built-in dishwashers are secured in a cabinet and connected to the hot water line. A dishwasher usually drains through the disposal. The hose must be higher than the dishwasher tub or be equipped with an air gap, which acts as a vacuum breaker to prevent a possible cross connection from the sink drain to the sewer line. This prevents contamination of the dishwasher or potable water supply. (See Figure 10.1.)

Timer

The timer controls all functions of the dishwasher so they operate at their designated times. The operating time of dishwashers ranges from 43 to 98 minutes (min.). Operating times depend on the dishwasher model and the selected cycle. The timer operates the solenoid valves that fill the tub with water, water drainage from the tub, the pump and motor, the soap dispenser, the rinse aid dispenser, and the heater. The timer also controls the length of time required to complete each selected cycle. (See Figure 10.2.)

Different timers are available, such as single knob, knob and push-button, push-button only, and digital. The timer should never be moved or changed while the dishwasher is in operation. To change the timer, move the door latch to the open position. The knob control timer should be turned in a clockwise direction. With a knob and push-button timer, the push-buttons are used to select the desired cycle and the knob operates the dishwasher. With push-button timers, the proper buttons are pushed for the desired cycle. A start button is pushed to activate the timer. The digital timer uses touch pads to select the desired cycle. Usually, the digital timer displays the length of cycle time for dishwasher operation. Digital timers on some dishwashers can be programmed to operate at a desired time.

■ **FIGURE 10.1**

Dishwashers are designed to rinse, wash, and dry dishes and utensils.

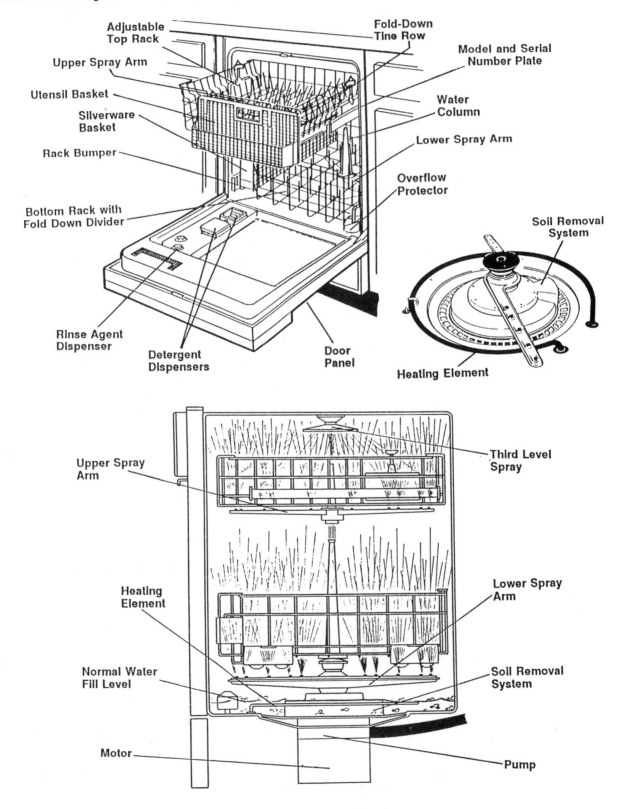

■ **FIGURE 10.2**

Dishwasher cycle times vary considerably—from 14 to 120 minutes.

DISHWASHER CYCLES

RINSE
HOLD

RINSE HOLD Cycle

For rinsing dishes that will be washed later.

To Operate: Before closing door, push selector button for RINSE HOLD. Turn Timer Knob to RINSE HOLD. Close door firmly until you hear it latch, the cycle will start.

Cycle Time: About 14 minutes

Water Usage: About 4.4 gallons

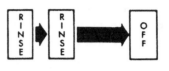

LIGHT
WASH

LIGHT WASH Cycle

For prerinsed or lightly soiled dishes and dishes that have been stored.

To Operate: Before closing door, push selector button for LIGHT WASH. Turn Timer Knob to LIGHT WASH. Close door firmly until you hear it latch, the cycle will start.

Cycle Time: About 58 minutes

Water Usage: About 6.6 gallons

WATER
MISER

WATER MISER Cycle

For medium soiled dishes. Saves energy by using less hot water than Normal Wash Cycle.

Cycle Time: About 66 minutes

Water Usage: About 8.7 gallons

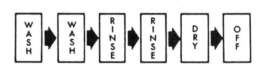

NORMAL
WASH

NORMAL WASH Cycle

For everyday heavily soiled dishes.

Cycle Time: About 74 minutes

Water Usage: About 10.9 gallons

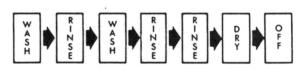

POTS
PANS

POTS PANS Cycle

For cleaning dishes, pots and pans with cooked-on or baked-on foods. Washing is delayed while water is automatically heated to the proper dishwashing temperature if your household water is not hot enough in both washes and the final rinse.

Cycle Time: About 90 to 120 minutes, depending on water heating time

Water Usage: About 10.9 gallons

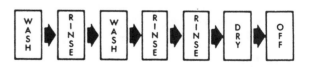

Inspection of the timer requires selection of the desired cycle while allowing the dishwasher to start and complete the cycle without touching the timer. If the timer fails to progress through the cycles, the timer is damaged. The cycle to select for inspecting the dishwasher is Normal Wash. The Normal Wash cycle is normally two washes, two rinses, and heated dry. It requires 75 min. to complete the full cycle. The short cycle completes a short wash in 68 min. More expensive dishwashers might have a sani-cycle, a pot scrubber cycle, and/or a plate warmer cycle. The sani-cycle and pot scrubber cycles require 98 min. A dishwasher that is programmed for the sani-cycle or pot scrubber cycle uses water with temperature from 160°F to 175°F. The timer controls the dishwasher operation by starting the cycle after the heater has raised the water to the operating temperature. The heater will heat water only 1°F per min. All cycles are controlled by the timer.

Pump and Motor

The pump and motor are operated by the timer through the wash, rinse, and pump-out cycles. A small amount of water should remain in the tub after the dishwasher has completed its cycle. This prevents the shaft seal from drying out and leaking. A leaking shaft seal should be replaced.

Soap Dispenser

At the precise time, the timer energizes the solenoid that opens the soap dispenser for the wash cycle. It is important for the soap dispenser to operate properly. Only approved detergents should be used in the dishwasher. Detergents approved for hand-washing dishes will damage the seals, gaskets, and pump.

Rinse Aid Dispenser

The rinse aid dispenser is operated by the timer and allows the rinse aid solution to mix with the rinse water to produce a sheeting action on dishes. Sheeting action prevents dishes from spotting, which is caused by hard water containing calcium, iron, and lime.

Drain/Disposal

The drain is connected by a rubber hose to the sink drain. While, the disposal is equipped to dispose of soft foods, hard food particles or objects will damage the disposer and the pump. Dishes should be rinsed before being placed in the dishwasher. The drain line should be connected to an air gap, or have a loop to act as an air gap, before it connects to the sewer drain.

Heater

The heater has two functions: (1) to heat water to the proper temperature and (2) to dry dishes by convection after the last rinse cycle. Some dishwashers have a heated blower for drying dishes. Whether the method of drying is by convection or blowing, the dishes will not be completely dry at the end of the cycle.

Spray Arms

The primary function of the spray arms is to spray detergent and water onto dishes under pressure through nozzles or jets located in the arms. The nozzles are positioned in the arms at an angle that allows the water pressure to rotate the arms to wash the dishes.

All dishwashers have an upper and a lower rack, but not all dishwashers have an upper spray arm. Many dishwashers are equipped with a spray head that is connected to the lower spray arm. The spray head has jets and, with water pressure, they extend up and rotate with the lower spray arm to wash dishes in the upper rack. The spray head raises up through the center of the lower rack. Another top spray arm has a pipe extending from the rear of the tub to the center. The pipe has jets and a pipe cap on the end at the center. The top rack is circular, and the rack rotates to wash the dishes. The spray arm will occasionally lose the end cap. If the cap is missing, the top spray will not wash dishes in the top rack. Hard water clogs the jets and nozzles with calcium deposits and causes malfunction.

Tub

Dishwasher tubs are constructed from steel with various finishes, such as stainless steel, porcelain on steel, or epoxy on steel. Regardless of the finish, all tubs will discolor and corrode if dishes are placed in the dishwasher without prior rinsing. Foods such as mustard, mayonnaise, lemon juice, vinegar, and salt can discolor and corrode tubs.

Stainless Steel

Stainless steel tubs will not chip, crack, or rust. The manufacturer may offer a longer warranty on a stainless steel tub than on another kind of tub. Discoloration may occur if the dishwasher is used only once or twice a week. Rinse dishes well with clear water before placing them in the dishwasher.

Porcelain

Tubs made of porcelain on steel have a tendency to chip. Corrosive foods and dishwashing detergents will attack the exposed steel, causing the tub to rust and producing leaks.

Epoxy

Tubs made of epoxy on steel have a softer finish than those with porcelain on steel. A slightly damaged finish, such as a scratch or cut, allows penetration of corrosive foods and detergents. The damaged area will form blisters in the finish, and these blisters will continue to grow, peel, and crack, exposing the steel. If the liner is not repaired, the tub will rust and leak.

Racks

Racks should have a protective finish without exposed metal. Exposed metal will corrode from foods and caustic properties of detergents, and the corrosion will stain glass, crystal, and china. Most racks are equipped with rollers. It is necessary that these rollers be in good operation and in proper location in relation to the spray bars. If the rollers are missing on the bottom rack, the spray arm will not operate properly. The top rack will not stay in place without rollers.

Door

The door is located either on the front or on the top of the dishwasher, and its interior finish will be the same as that of the tub. The top-loading dishwasher is portable. In the front-loading dishwasher, the soap dispenser and rinse aid dispenser are located in the door. The door should lay at a 90° angle to the opening; if it falls open or drops more than 90°, the hinges may be broken. The door should close and lock easily. Debris between the bottom edge of the door and the gasket may cause leaks. Below the door is a small, removable panel to allow access to the pump and the valves and to check for possible leaks.

■ DISPOSALS

Disposals are designed to pulverize food wastes. An ample amount of cold water flowing through the disposal flushes pulverized food wastes down the drain. Cold water helps solidify fatty or greasy wastes so they can be chopped and flushed down the drain. One of the dangers of using hot or warm water with a disposal is that fatty deposits or grease will not solidify in the disposal; rather they will solidify in the drain line and cause blockage. The disposal is designed to dispose of all normal kitchen food wastes and table scraps. Fibrous wastes such as corn husks, celery, and artichoke leaves will be disposed of more easily if mixed with other food wastes.

Cold water should be kept running through the disposal when disposing of fibrous wastes. Add only a small amount of waste at a time. The drain line should be purged periodically after disposing of fibrous wastes by filling the sink with 3 inches (") to 4" of cold water, turning on the disposal, and allowing the water to run through with no waste added.

The disposal should be clean before it is operated to allow the discharge water to drain freely. After operating the dishwasher, run the disposal briefly to remove food wastes and odors. These odors may be quickly dispelled by running orange or lemon peels or ice cubes through the disposal. All disposals are equipped with thermal overload protection to prevent the motor from burning up if the disposal jams. (See Figure 10.3.)

Disposals are also equipped with a reset button located on the bottom or on the side of the disposal. Some disposals have a provision at the bottom for a hex wrench to dislodge a jam. Other disposals have a switch to reverse the direction of the disposal to clear jams. If the disposal does not have either a provision for a hex wrench or a reversing switch, a piece of wood can be used to push the bottom of the grinding chamber in a counterclockwise direction. Never put hands in the disposal. *Be sure the power is off before attempting to dislodge any jam.* After the disposal is freed, push the reset button. If the reset button is ineffective, the motor may need time to cool.

A disposal is not recommended for use with a septic system.

Continuous Feed

A continuous feed disposal has a switch on the wall that controls the operation. This disposal is rated by motor size, which is usually $\frac{1}{3}$ or $\frac{1}{2}$ horsepower (hp). With this type of disposal, waste can be constantly fed in small amounts into the grinding chamber, with the disposal turned on and cold water flowing through the disposal. It is necessary to have a rubber splash guard to keep the waste from flying out during operation and to prevent utensils from falling into the grinding chamber.

■ **FIGURE 10.3**

Disposals are designed to remove normal kitchen food wastes and table scraps.

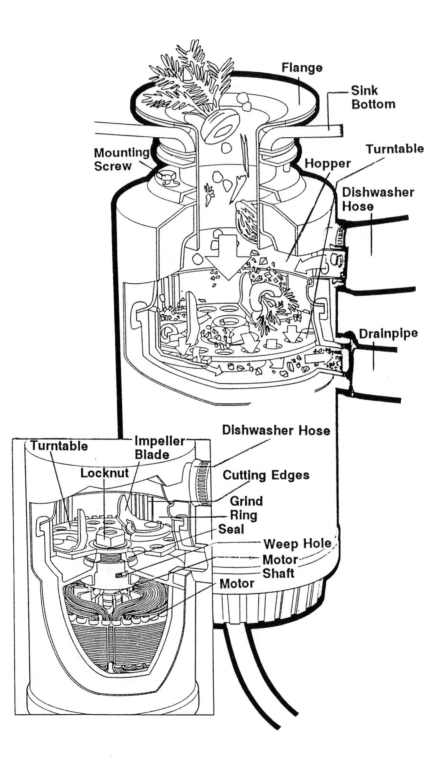

■ **FIGURE 10.4**

The disposal is not recommended for use with a septic system.

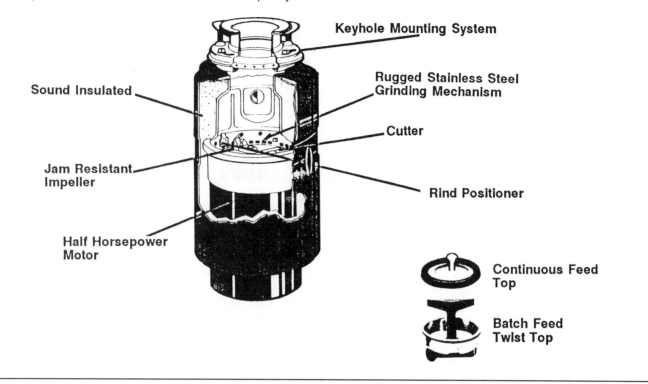

Batch Feed

The batch feed disposal is operated by a twist top that also takes the place of the splash guard. When waste is put in the disposal, the cold water is turned on. The twist top is placed in the mouth of the disposal and turned 90°. The twist top activates the switch and the waste is ground. The batch feed disposal is rated by size, such as 2-quart (qt.), 3-qt., etc. The twist top must be removed to feed in additional waste material.

Construction

Disposals may have a cast metal or stainless steel casing. Grinding chambers have stainless steel liners. The grind wheels are heavy cast iron with either swivel or fixed impellers that are a part of the grind wheel. Swivel impellers are held in place with rivets. These impellers direct the waste to the shredder ring, which shreds the waste. The swivel impellers are manufactured from cutlery steel and swing on the grind wheel. The impellers and rivets should not be loose on the grind wheel. If the impellers are frozen, the disposal may vibrate. (See Figure 10.4.)

Installation

The disposal must never have standing water in the grinding chamber. The drain from the disposal must be higher than the drain line to the sewer and discharge into a P-trap. It is very important that the disposal be on a grounded electrical circuit. If the disposal is continuous feed, the switch should be located on the wall.

■ COOKTOPS AND RANGES

Cooktops use gas, electricity, or both as the power source. A cooktop is a surface burner unit built into a countertop. Cooktops are available with various modules that allow flexibility in cooking; for example, a coil module can be removed and replaced with a griddle module. The module cooktop may have one side with two fixed or permanent burners and the other side may have a changeable module, or both sides can be modules.

Ranges can be freestanding, slide-in, or drop-in. The freestanding range is designed to stand by itself and has finished panels on both sides and the front. The slide-in range has unfinished sides. It requires a filler panel

Gas cooktops use natural, liquefied petroleum (LP), propane, or butane gas.

and backsplash to seal the range to the counter and cabinet. The drop-in range has no base or legs. It requires a base for support and also must be sealed to the cabinet and countertop. Ranges may have timers, clocks, and lights. The range also has an oven and a broiler with a modular or fixed burner cooktop. The oven in a range is usually larger than a built-in oven.

Gas

Gas cooktops and ranges are either freestanding or built-in. Gas can be natural, liquefied petroleum (LP), propane, or butane. When LP gas is used as the source of energy, a storage tank is present on the property. The cooktop surface (main top) may be brushed chrome, porcelain, stainless steel, or glass. (See Figure 10.5.)

Controls

The burner is controlled by a valve with the aid of a control knob. Some knobs must be pushed to adjust heat controls. Older cooktops and ranges have similar control valves.

Igniters

The gas cooktop and range has either an electronic igniter system or standing pilots. If the cooktop has a standing pilot, the pilot flame should stand 1/16″ and be blue in color. The burner should ignite from the pilot when the control valve is on. To adjust the pilot, lift the main top and adjust the screw at the gas manifold.

The electronic igniter should light the burner when the control valve is turned to "lite," which will be marked on the control knob. When the gas valve is in the lite mode, there should be a clicking noise and the burner should ignite. If there is no clicking noise and the burner fails to ignite, the unit may not be connected electrically or the circuit breaker could be off. When the igniter is functioning, with the main top raised a small spark should be visible at the igniter when the control valve is turned to lite. The igniter requires occasional cleaning with extreme care. Parts are delicate and should never be cleaned with liquids or abrasives.

Burners

Gas burners should ignite from the pilot. Older cooktops and ranges may not be equipped with a pilot. In the event the range is not equipped with a pilot, it should be noted on the inspection report. There have been many improvements made with gas burners in recent years. Original gas burners were subject to clogging from spills or boilovers, odors persisted from gas seepage, and the burners were difficult to clean and maintain.

Recent improvements in gas cooktops and ranges have all but eliminated complaints about gas. Early burners were inefficient; only about 40 percent of gas heat reached food. Heat loss was caused by the open flame that dissipated heat into the surrounding air. Proper air and gas mixture will eliminate problems with the open gas burner, such as a noisy or blowing flame, excessive flame height (greater than 3/4″), or smoking and soot.

Some new burners are sealed in cooktops, which eliminates spillovers into the burner box. New burners offer more efficient cooking—a 10,000 British thermal unit (Btu) burner is 15 percent to 20 percent faster than the old 12,000-Btu open gas burner. Depending on the manufacturer and the type of cooktop or range, burner sizes range from 5,000 Btus to 12,000 Btus. Newer gas burners have a control valve to sense flame presence when the valve is on. If the flame goes out, the burner will automatically spark until the flame is ignited. This ensures that the gas will ignite, even for low burner settings.

Grates

Grates are designed to give proper distance between the burner and cooking utensil and ensure even heat distribution. Grates can easily be removed for cleaning.

Electric

Electric cooktops and ranges require a minimum of 240 volts (V) of electricity to operate and, depending on the model, require a 30-ampere (amp) to 50-amp circuit breaker. The electric cooking unit is 75 percent more efficient than gas because the cooking utensil sits directly on the element. Electric ranges may have clocks, timers, and lights and also may have a center grill or cartridge cooktop. Cooktops normally have four elements. Elements vary in size from 6″ to 8″ in diameter. Most cooktops are equipped with two 6″ and two 8″ elements. Elements are either wired to a terminal block or plug in, which allows easy cleaning.

Controls

Elements are controlled by push-buttons or knobs. The knob turns an infinite control for flexibility in heat setting selections. For settings other than high or low, the control can be adjusted above or below the numbered settings. For example:

Low
2–4   Medium Low
5–6   Medium
7–9   Medium High
High

This applies to settings when using the cooktop cartridges or when using the grill. Care should be taken when removing control knobs.

Push-buttons do not have as much flexibility in adjusting the heat as the infinite control. Each push-button has a preset heat, such as simmer, low, medium, medium high, and high. The inspector should check the control by adjusting heat to low, medium, and high and allowing each element to reach the highest temperature for each setting.

Elements

There are several different elements and cooktops available. The conventional coil is the original burner element. The glass-ceramic cooktop has a black or a white surface with the element located below the surface. The cast-iron element is a solid element. The radiant element is sealed in a special ceramic glass. The induction element is flame-fast yet flameless. To provide a more concentrated heat, many new elements are sealed to the cooktop or located below the surface to allow easy cleaning. Whenever possible, each element should be inspected at all the various settings.

The conventional coil element has been the dependable burner element used for generations. (See Figure 10.6.) The two styles of coil elements are the dual element and the single element.

The dual element has two separate elements. A low setting operates the inner coil, producing no coloration. The medium setting operates the inner coil with slight coloration. The high setting operates both the inner and the outer coils which should heat to a cherry red. The dual element is connected with screws to a terminal located below the cooktop. The dual-element cooktop usually has push-button controls for preset heats.

The single element has an infinite control switch that allows any degree of heat. The single element is usually plugged into a receptacle under the cooktop at each burner opening. Plug-in elements can be removed for cleaning or replacement. Coils are sealed units, impervious to food and water spillovers. However, rough treatment can break the protective seal, allowing the element to fail. A failed element is identified by bubbles on the coil surface.

The glass-ceramic cooktop has elements located under the glass-ceramic surface at designated points so heat is in concentrated areas. The glass-ceramic material allows the areas surrounding the heating element to remain cool to the touch while cooking. The glass-ceramic cooktop retains heat for a longer period of time than the conventional coil element. The cooking element can be turned off several minutes before food is completely cooked, and retained heat will finish the cooking. If the glass-ceramic cooktop becomes damaged or broken, the cooktop should be replaced because burners mounted below the top are not sealed and spills could cause the element to short out. (See Figure 10.7.)

Cast-iron elements differ from other elements in cooking use, economy, cleaning, and safety. Cast-iron elements provide twice the surface area of coil elements,

■ **FIGURE 10.6**

Conventional coil element.

which allows heat to be distributed more evenly and provides better cooking control. Desired temperature is reached gradually (about one min. slower than with coil-type elements), and heat is retained for a longer period of time. (See Figure 10.8.)

Cast-iron elements are slightly elevated and are sealed in the cooktop. Spills flow to a cool area of the cooking surface. Heating coils are embedded in an insulating material and buried under the iron casting; they are not subject to temperature extremes and mechanical stress. Heat from cast-iron elements is conducted, rather than radiated, resulting in lower surface temperatures. Lower heat requirements result in reduced energy consumption. Because solid elements transfer heat evenly, there is no need for them to become red-hot to cook properly. Each cast-iron element has a built-in temperature limiter to protect it from excessive heat. The temperature limiter detects excess heat buildup and reduces power to the element.

■ **FIGURE 10.7**

Glass-ceramic cooktop is positioned over heating elements.

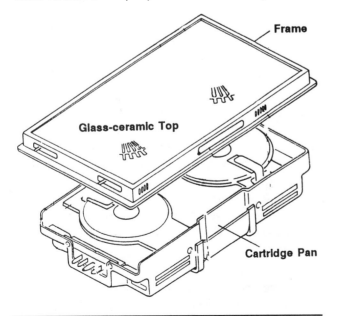

■ **FIGURE 10.8**

Cast-iron element.

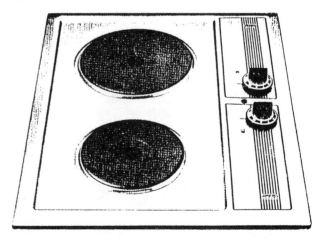

■ FIGURE 10.9

Radiant cooktop.

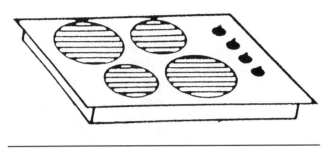

The physical characteristics of cookware influence the performance of the cooking system. The amount of surface contact the cookware achieves with the element will determine the time and energy needed to accomplish cooking. If cookware is warped from overheating, creating a space between the element and the cookware, the temperature limiter may detect excessive temperatures and automatically turn down the temperature. To ensure the best cooking performance, heavy flat-bottom cookware that conforms to the size of the element should be used. Undersized cookware will reduce cooking performance. Specialty cookware—woks, lobster pots, griddles, pressure cookers, canning vessels (6-qt. to 20-qt. capacity)—must achieve sufficient surface contact with the cast-iron element for maximum cooking performance.

Before cast-iron elements are used for the first time, they must be cured. To properly cure cast-iron elements, heat each element at its high setting. There will be some nontoxic smoke and odor; the rings around the elements will change to a gold color, which is normal. The kitchen exhaust should be operating to remove the smoke and odors. The elements should heat for 3 to 5 min. or until the smoking stops.

The operation of the radiant cooktop is based on the use of coil open resistant wires mounted below the glass-ceramic top. The glass-ceramic top produces infrared lightwaves that create heat over the radiant element while the rest of the surface remains cool. Radiant cooktops are attractive, easy to clean and provide quick-start heat. The radiant element is equipped with a temperature limiter, which limits cooking surface heat to 400°F. Radiant elements are as efficient as conventional coil elements. Most cookware can be used with a radiant cooktop. Cookware should be the proper size for the element and have a flat bottom for full contact. (See Figure 10.9.)

Induction cooktops use electric coils under a glass-ceramic cooking surface. Each electric coil generates a magnetic field that passes through the top and reacts with the iron in the cooking utensil, causing it to heat. In essence, the cookware becomes the heating element for the range. Benefits of induction cooktops are the cool, smooth cooking surface, attractive styling, cleanability, and safety. Induction cooktops have no open flame or hot element. The heat is confined to the cooking utensil. When the cooking utensil is removed from the cooktop surface, the elements shut off. If the cooking surface exceeds 400°F, the elements cycle down and a beep will sound. The elements are programmed to respond only to cookware with a minimum diameter of 4". Spoons and stirring utensils will not get hot if laid on a heating element that is on. Induction is the most efficient cooking process available and provides cooler room temperatures during summer months. The light-emitting diode (LED) control panel provides convenient electronic touch control settings. The sealed plastic control panel prevents food spillovers under the control pad. (See Figure 10.10.)

Cookware must have an iron content for the induction process to function. Glass or aluminum cookware is not suitable for this type of cooktop; however, most other cookware provides satisfactory results, including stainless steel, cast iron, and porcelain-on-steel.

■ OVENS

Gas or electric ovens may be located in a range or built into a cabinet. Ovens are available as conventional manual clean, self-clean, continuous clean, and microwave. Most ovens use radiant heat. The microwave oven and convection oven are electric. Convection ovens can also be combined with microwave ovens.

Oven features may include clocks, timers, and lights. Controls can be push-button, digital, or knobs. There are several different oven timers that control various functions of the oven. Ovens also must have a thermostat to maintain desired temperature. The thermostat probe should be placed in the oven brackets. If the thermostat probe is misaligned, false temperature readings result. A properly operating thermostat should read the actual oven temperature within 25°F of the desired setting. A mercury-filled thermometer is recommended for testing the thermostat.

■ **FIGURE 10.10**

Induction cooktop.

The oven door has a double wall with a cavity between the inner and outer panel. This cavity is filled with insulation and air. A glass window in an oven door has air space between tempered glass. The glass window will be cloudy if the two panels have not been sealed properly. The glass window should not be broken.

The oven door should open and close properly. When fully open, the door should be at a 90° angle to the opening. The door in an electric oven should have a stop to hold the door open at a 10° angle for broiling. Door gaskets and hinges should be checked for damage.

Oven lights normally operate with a switch on the door. When the door is closed, the light is off; when the door is opened, the light is on. Some ovens have a manual switch to operate lights without opening the door. Oven lights that do not function could indicate a bad bulb, broken wire, faulty socket, or bad switch.

Timers

A clock and an automatic timer are used to control the operation of the oven at a preset time. Ovens also have a minute timer that can be set from 0 to 60 min. The minute timer is not part of the clock or automatic timer. The clock must operate for the automatic timer to operate, but has no relation to the minute timer. The clock and timer must operate for the self-clean feature of an oven to function. A microwave in the top portion of a conventional oven has a separate timer that operates independently from the oven clock and timer.

Ovens with a single knob to control both the temperature and the various functions of the oven (bake, broil, clean) will not operate unless the automatic timer stop button is set for a specific cooking time or is disengaged. Ovens with one knob to control the temperature and another knob to select the other functions may be operated without the timer. Manual operation of an oven with separate knobs is not influenced by the automatic timer. (See Figure 10.11.)

Clock

The clock should be set to the correct time of day before the automatic cooking mode is set. To set the time on the clock, depress the minute timer and turn it in a

■ **FIGURE 10.11**

Conventional clock timer.

clockwise direction until the correct time has been reached. Turn the minute timer control to the off position.

To set an oven to start at a future time and shut off automatically, (1) depress and turn the start time control to the desired time, (2) turn the cooking hours control to the desired cooking time, (3) turn the selector control to timed bake, and (4) turn the thermostat to the desired temperature.

With double ovens, only one oven at a time can be set in an automatic mode unless the same length of time for each is desired. Clock-controlled baking is possible only in the radiant mode (timed bake setting). The convection oven setting on the selector is not controlled by the clock.

Electronic Range Control (ERC)

The ERC controls the thermostat, selector switch, and clock functions for bake, broil, timed bake and clean cycles. (See Figure 10.12.)

1. To set clock:
   a. Push CLOCK button.
   b. Turn SET knob to current time of day.

2. To set timer:
   a. Push TIMER button.
   b. Turn SET knob to desired amount of time (up to 9 hours [hr.], 50 min.).
   c. When time is up, a tone will sound. To cancel the tone, push the CANCEL button.

NOTE: The timer is a reminder only and will not operate the range. The timer can be canceled by pressing and holding the timer button until the time of day returns to the display.

3. To bake:
   a. Push BAKE button.
   b. Turn SET knob to select a baking temperature between 170°F and 550°F. After the bake temperature is set, the display will show the actual oven temperature as it rises (in 5°F steps). Push and *hold* BAKE button to show the temperature that has been selected. Once the oven temperature has stabilized at the elected temperature, the ERC will sound a single tone to signal that the oven has preheated. The preheat tone will sound as the oven bake relay cycles on for the second time.
   c. When finished baking, push CANCEL button.

■ **FIGURE 10.12**

The electronic range control (ERC) system controls the thermostat, selector switch, and clock functions for bake, broil, timed bake, and clean cycles.

4. To broil:
   a. Push BROIL button.
   b. Turn SET knob to HI or LO Broil.
   c. When finished broiling, push CANCEL button.

5. To use timed oven/delay start:
   a. To start now and stop later:
      1) Push COOK TIME button.
      2) Set length of baking time with SET knob.
      3) Push BAKE button.
      4) Set desired temperature with SET knob.
   b. To start later and stop later:
      1) Push COOK TIME button.
      2) Set length of baking time with SET knob.
      3) Push STOP TIME button.
      4) Set time of day when baking should be completed.
      5) Push BAKE button.
      6) Set desired temperature with SET knob.
      7) When STOP TIME is reached, three beeps will sound. To turn the tone off before the third beep, push CANCEL button.

6. To set a clean cycle:
   The self-cleaning cycle is preprogrammed for 3½ hr. The electronic range control can also be set for a delayed start of the clean cycle.
   a. To self-clean:
      1) Slide door lock handle to the right. By pressing lightly, the door locks properly. Never try to force the door lock handle. Forcing the handle may damage the locking mechanism.
      2) Push CLEAN button. The time at which the clean cycle will be finished can be determined by pushing STOP TIME button.
   b. To use delayed self-clean:
      1) Push STOP TIME button.
      2) Turn SET knob to time of day when the cleaning is to be completed (must be more than 3½ hr. later than current time of day).
      3) Slide the door lock handle to the right.
      4) Push CLEAN button.
   c. Important information:
      All controls must be set correctly for the

clean cycle to work properly. The stages of the cycle are noted.
   1) The controls are set and the door lock handle moved right into the lock position.
   2) The oven begins to heat. The broil burner will operate only the first 30 min. of the clean cycle and the bake burner will operate only from 30 min. to the end of the clean cycle.
   3) For safety, when the locking temperature is reached, the oven door cannot be opened. The lock indicator light will appear when the oven reaches 500°F.
   4) When the 3½ hr. clean cycle is over, the oven begins to cool.
   5) When the temperature has fallen below the locking temperature (about 20 min. to 30 min. after the oven goes off at the end of the clean cycle), the door may be opened. The lock indicator light turns off when the oven cools to 400° F.

7. To stop a clean cycle manually:
   a. Press CANCEL button.
   b. Wait for the oven to cool below the locking temperature (20 min. to 30 min.).
   c. Slide the door lock handle to the left to unlock the door. If the door lock handle does not move easily, wait a few more minutes, then try again. The oven will not unlock unless the oven temperature is below 560°F. Never force the door lock handle.

Note: The operation of the lock indicator light has no influence on the operation of the door lock.

When a timed function has been programmed, it can be recalled by pushing the corresponding function button. If a delay timed bake operation has been programmed, push STOP TIME to see when the cycle will stop or COOK TIME for the length of baking time entered. The messages at the left-hand side of the display show which operation the ERC is presently displaying.

8. Tones
   a. Function acknowledgment tone: Whenever a function button is pressed, the ERC will emit a tone to acknowledge the function. If this tone is not desired, press and hold CANCEL button

until a second tone is emitted, indicating the acknowledgment tone has been canceled. To restore the function acknowledgment tone, repeat the above procedure.

Note: Canceling the function acknowledgment tone will also cancel the preheat notification tone and the timer notification tone.

b. Attention tone: This tone sounds to indicate that temperature information has been omitted from a programmed delay start or timed oven function. The attention tone may sound during programming of an automatic oven function if the user takes more than 15 sec. to complete the programming operation.

c. Failure tone: If a detected component fails within the ERC or any of its related components or circuits, the ERC will emit a failure tone. One of the eight failure codes (–F1– through –F8–) will display the nature of the failure. Power to the oven relays will be removed during such a failure, ending cook or clean operations.

Gas

Three gas ovens are available: conventional cleaning, continuous cleaning, and self-cleaning. Older gas ovens do not have pilot lights and can be dangerous. New gas ovens have a standing pilot or an electronic ignition. (See Figure 10.13.)

Standing Pilot

Ovens with a standing pilot also may have a secondary pilot to conserve energy. The secondary pilot allows the flame to remain small until a demand is made from the oven to operate. When the demand is made, the secondary pilot opens, allowing the flame to enlarge and heat the thermocouple. This allows the gas valve to open and operate the burner. The gas valve will not open if the pilot is not on.

Electronic Pilot

The second pilot control is electronic. When the oven control is on, electricity heats a silicon carbide glow bar or coil beneath the burner. This bar or coil has to reach 2,000°F. When the safety valve opens, the gas will flow through the burner thermostat controls to the glow bar circuit, igniting the flow of gas until the oven reaches the preset temperature. The gas valve will not open if the silicon carbide glow bar or coil does not operate.

■ **FIGURE 10.13**

Gas ovens are available as conventional (manual) cleaning continuous cleaning, and self-cleaning.

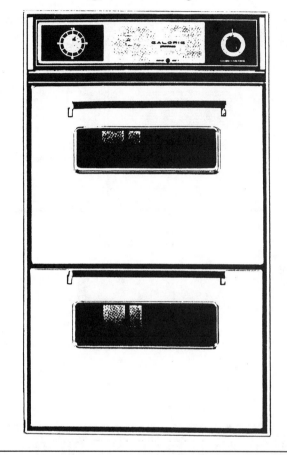

Electric

All electric ovens have two elements. The upper element is the broiling element, also used for preheating the oven on the bake cycle. The lower element is used for baking. Elements cover wide areas to provide even heat distribution throughout the oven. (See Figure 10.14.)

The thermostat operates both top and bottom elements; therefore, when broiling with an electric oven, it is necessary to have the oven door open. The oven door hinges have been designed to hold the door open at a 10° angle for broiling. If the door is closed when the oven is in the broil mode, the thermostat will cause the broiler to cycle on and off.

Electric ovens are available as conventional cleaning, continuous cleaning, and self-cleaning. Electric ovens have available more features than gas ovens. These features include a convection oven, a microwave oven, and a combination microwave and convection oven.

■ **FIGURE 10.14**

All electric ovens have an upper element for broiling and a lower element for baking.

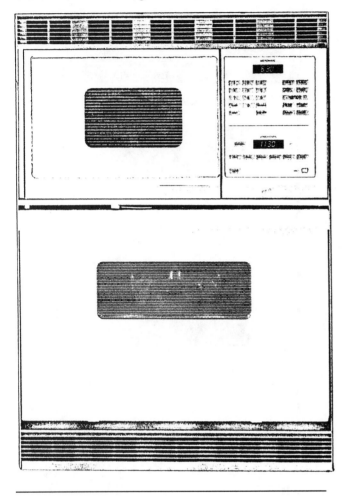

Self-Cleaning

Self-cleaning ovens are designed to clean the interior of the oven with heat. Cleaning temperatures vary from 900°F to 1,150°F, depending on the manufacturer. The high temperatures cause soil to burn off or become ash, which drops to the bottom of the oven. Racks and pans should be removed before cleaning; excessive heat will damage the finish. Areas outside the door gasket will not be cleaned by the self-cleaning cycle. These areas should be cleaned with nonabrasive detergents and hot water. It normally requires 2 to 3 hr. to complete the cleaning cycle. Oven cleaners should not be used on self-cleaning ovens.

The oven door has an interlock device that is activated when the oven temperature reaches 550°F. The lock light will remain on as long as the interlock device is activated. The lock is a lever located above the door that must be moved to the full right position for cleaning. Usually, there is a lock release button that must be pressed to move the lever. The lock lever should never be forced to lock or unlock. The oven may be equipped with an automatic door lock that will remain locked until the selector knob is turned off.

When a double oven or microwave/self-cleaning oven combination is in the self-cleaning mode, only the oven in the self-cleaning mode will operate. The oven timer must operate for the self-cleaning cycle to operate. Self-cleaning ovens have an exhaust fan to circulate air around the oven when cleaning. Some ovens have an exhaust system that vents to the exterior or an indoor vent with a catalyst to purify the air.

Preparation for a clean cycle:

- Soil on the oven front frame, under the front edge of the cooktop, on the door liner outside the door seal and on the front edge of the oven cavity (about 1″ into the oven) will not be cleaned during a clean cycle. During the cleaning process, use detergent and hot water with a soap-filled steel wool pad to clean the soil, then rinse the area well with a vinegar/water mixture. This will prevent a brown residue from forming when the oven is heated.
- DO NOT use commercial oven cleaners or oven protectors in or near the oven. These products, together with the high temperature of the clean cycle, may damage the porcelain finish.
- DO NOT clean glass ceramic cookware or any other cookware in the oven during a self-clean cycle.

Before the clean cycle:

- Remove the broil pan and grid, the oven racks, all utensils and any foil that may be in the oven. If oven racks are left in the range during a clean cycle, they will darken, lose their luster and become hard to slide.
- Wipe up excessive spillovers on the oven bottom. Too much heavy soil may cause smoking during the clean cycle.
- Clean the door seal by using a clean sponge to soak the soiled area with hydrogen peroxide. Repeated soaking may be needed, depending on the amount of soil. Frequent cleaning will help prevent excessive soil buildup. Do not rub the door seal excessively because the fiberglass material of the seal has a very low resistance to abrasion. Any cotton material (including cottonballs) can easily rub a hole into the seal; therefore, do not use any cotton materials to clean the seal. An intact and well-fitting oven door

seal is essential for energy-efficient oven operation and good baking results. If the seal becomes worn, frayed, or damaged in any way, or if it has become displaced on the door, the seal should be replaced.

Continuous Cleaning

Continuous cleaning ovens are designed to clean as they bake. The interior of the oven is coated with catalytic porcelain ceramic finish that enables cleaning while baking. The porcelain finish expands and contracts as the oven is heated and cooled, which prevents food from adhering to the sides of the oven. However, it is necessary to clean a continuous cleaning oven when large spills occur. Clean the interior with a mild detergent; never use oven cleaners on a continuous cleaning oven. The acid in oven cleaners breaks the bond between the metal and porcelain finish.

Jenn-Air manufactures a combination Jenn-Air and convection oven. This oven is a continuous cleaning oven, but has an accelerated cleaning mode option. The accelerated clean will operate only with the oven timer, and the operation should not exceed 2 hr. The selector knob has to be set on accelerated cleaning with the thermostat knob set at 550°F. In the accelerated cleaning position, the fan in the oven automatically turns on. To turn off the fan, turn the selector knob to off. The Jenn-Air oven interior has a catalytic porcelain ceramic finish that cleans itself while baking. The accelerated cleaning mode creates a higher heated airflow to speed the catalytic cleaning process.

Convection

The convection oven can be incorporated in either a conventional oven or a microwave oven. Both upper and lower elements in a convection oven cycle on and off during cooking, and a fan keeps the heated air circulating evenly around the food. As the hot air circulates, it strips away the layer of cooler air surrounding the food, allowing the heat to go directly into the food. This results in reduction of cooking time. When using a convection oven, the food must not be covered or wrapped. (See Figure 10.15.)

Jenn Air is working on another form of rapid cooking technology. This system will cook using microwaves assisted by jets of rapidly moving hot air that strike the food from above. A deflector under the food creates a vacuum effect that suctions air from below. This results in air being drawn across the top and

■ FIGURE 10.15

Convection ovens use one temperature and cook by cycling on and off while a fan keeps the heated air circulating evenly around the food.

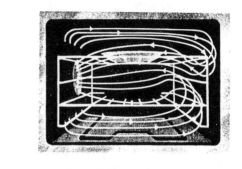

underside of the food in a constant heat-transfer relationship. The heat wraps the food, seals in moisture, browns, and cooks faster and more evenly, similar to the convection oven only with a different energy source.

■ MICROWAVE OVEN

Microwave energy is one form of high-frequency electromagnetic energy. Other forms are visible light and forms that cannot be detected without aid (radio waves, infrared rays, ultraviolet rays, X-rays, gamma rays, and cosmic rays). Microwaves are nonionizing energy and have a longer wavelength and less energy than ionizing energy. Microwave energy is not stored or retained and will not cause chemical changes in the human body. Microwaves stop immediately when production is stopped. There are no lingering microwaves; however, these waves can cause a rise in temperature. Because of combined length and strength, microwaves can penetrate a surface and create heat at or below the surface.

The magnetron tube is the source of microwaves in the microwave oven. The magnetron tube is a cylindrical cathode within a cylindrical anode surrounded by a magnetic field. The cathode of the magnetron is heated by a filament transformer and electrons are attracted to the anode. These electrons would normally travel in a straight line from cathode to anode, but their path is changed by the addition of the magnetic field. With permanent magnets surrounding the anode, the electrons take an orbital path from the cathode to the anode. As the electrons approach the anode, they pass by small, resonant cavities in part of the anode and the resulting interaction causes the resonant cavities to oscillate at

2,450 MHz (megahertz). This radio frequency (RF) energy is then radiated by the magnetron antenna into the wave guide. From the wave guide, the microwave energy passes the stirrer assembly into the oven cavity.

Microwaves react with objects in their path. The nature of the object in the path of microwaves determines which of three reactions will occur:

1. Reflection—Microwaves will reflect off metal objects, oven walls, or aluminum foil. The result is that no heat is produced inside the metal object, and arcing or sparks may occur.
2. Transmission—Microwaves will pass through glass, paper, or plastic. No heat is generated in these materials, although some heat can be transferred back from heated contents.
3. Absorption—Microwaves react to sugar, fat, or water molecules in food and heat is generated. High-speed oscillation causes friction between the molecules, converting the microwave energy into heat.

In the microwave oven, heating takes place on all sides of food. Because microwaves have only enough energy to penetrate ¾″ to 2″ from the surface, depending on the density, heating starts in outer layers of food. As heat builds in the outer layers, it is transferred inward, thus spreading the cooking process. Microwave cooking is much faster than conventional radiant cooking. As microwaves encounter a food object, the cooking process is immediate and no time is needed for oven preheating. Additional time is saved because the molecules within food are generating the heat through friction, as opposed to heat transfer from surrounding air.

A microwave oven has one level of heat, controlled by a timer that cycles the unit off and on. There is no thermostat that allows low, medium, or high temperature settings. The wave frequency remains the same for low as well as high settings. The only difference is the cycle speed. (See Figure 10.16.)

A variable power feature offers a choice of up to ten settings. The power is varied by turning the magnetron on and off. When set on low, the magnetron tube is at 10 percent. When set on high, the magnetron is at 100 percent. The defrost mode of the microwave oven allows the magnetron to be at 30 percent. The timer controls cycling.

■ **FIGURE 10.16**

Microwave ovens have one level of heat and are controlled by a timer that cycles the unit on and off.

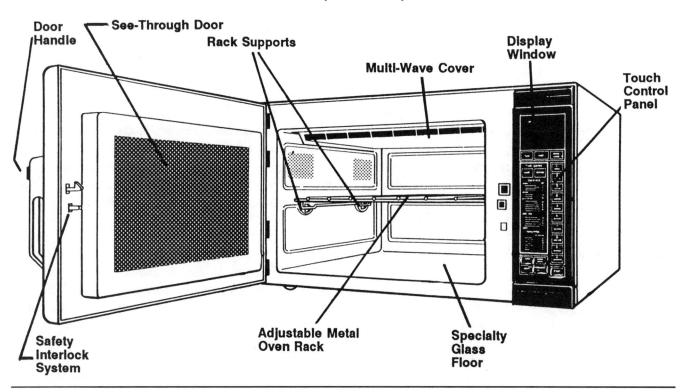

■ FIGURE 10.17

Temperature probe.

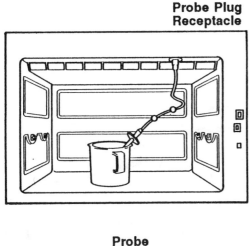

Probe Plug Receptacle

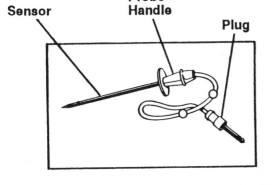

Sensor

Probe Handle

Plug

The microwave oven may have two methods of operation: a timer control that cycles the oven for the preset cooking time and a temperature probe. The temperature probe is set for a desired temperature. The microwave oven will turn off when the desired temperature has been obtained. The inspector should check both modes of operation. To check the timer control, place a nonmetal cup of cold water in the microwave, set the timer for 1 min. at the high setting and turn on the power. The water temperature should reach 100°F to 120°F. To check the temperature probe, place a cup of cold water in the microwave oven, insert the probe in the water, set the control to the desired temperature (120°F) and turn on the power. The microwave oven should turn off when water temperature reaches 120°F. (See Figure 10.17.)

The residential inspector does *not* check microwave ovens for radiation leaks. This should be stated on the inspection report. If clients are concerned about radiation leaks, the inspector should suggest that they consult an expert.

■ COMBINATION MICROWAVE AND HALOGEN LIGHT SOURCE OVENS

Amana's new wave oven cooks-using-light. The oven is small, and it grills, broils, bakes, and sears foods with infrared waves created by 12 halogen lamps, four in the floor and eight in the ceiling. These produce immediate, intense heat that can cook food in one-quarter of the time required by conventional ovens. A microprocessor cycles the lights on and off depending on the heat required. The oven has preprogrammed heat and time settings for several foods, and the individual can add more menus to its memory. The oven cooks at the speed of a microwave but with the performance of a thermal oven. However the wave oven requires a 240-V electric line to operate.

General Electric has developed a similar cooking-with-light oven. The Advantium oven uses halogen light from three 1,500-watt lamps. Depending on what's being cooked, it can also combine the light waves with microwaves. This oven converts into a fully functional microwave at the touch of a button. It bakes, broils and grills with no preheating. The oven can be preprogrammed with 100 menus on an LED display that's set up like a computer pull-down menu. An over-the-range unit that includes ventilation will also be available. The Advantium oven will also require a 240V electric line to operate.

■ KITCHEN EXHAUST SYSTEMS

The purpose of a kitchen exhaust system is to catch and dispose of cooking heat, odors, and steam and grease vapors. The ventilating hood should completely cover the cooking surface and remove heat, odors, and vapors.

Heat consists of expanded air molecules that move rapidly in an upward and outward pattern. One burner can create as much heat as a 1-t air-conditioner can remove in an equal length of time.

Water is a major component of the air and of food preparation. The act of cooking expands water molecules 1,800 times as they become steam vapor. As the steam vapor escapes the cooking surface, it carries with it grease and odors. If not captured by the exhaust system, the vapor can be absorbed into furnishings, walls, windows, and clothing. (See Figure 10.18.)

Vaporized cooking oil is the major problem in cooking. Cooking oil is organic matter that becomes

■ **FIGURE 10.18**

Kitchen exhaust systems dispose of heat, steam, odors, and grease vapors caused by cooking food.

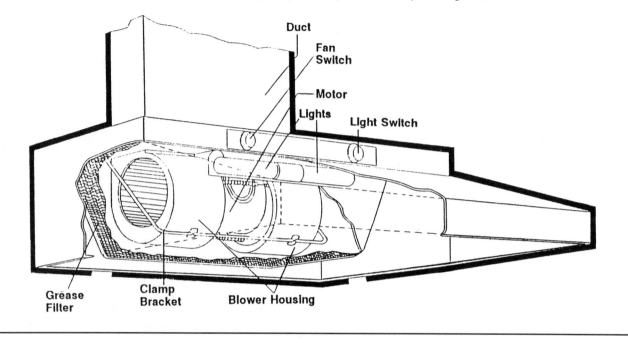

rancid, causes fungus growth, and glues dirt to whatever it contacts. Cooking one hour a day for a year will cause a gallon of grease to settle throughout a dwelling. Trapped oil particles become dangerous if they are allowed to adhere to airborne lint, which can easily be ignited.

Odors cling to walls, drapes and furnishings. Odors are acidic. If allowed to roam, they can fade and deteriorate wall and ceiling surfaces and damage furnishings. The only solution for removing odors is for the exhaust system to be vented to the outside.

Updraft Exhaust

There are three steps to control cooking pollutants:

1. Collection—Cooking vapors rise above the cooking surface. The hood should be placed above the cooktop to trap the rising pollutants before they expand or are blown into the home ventilation system by drafts.
2. Removal—Trapped vapors must be removed from the collection system by a centrifugal blower or a fan.
3. Venting—Vapors should be channeled outside. A vent system must allow the air to flow freely in the duct system and vent to the outside.

Hoods

The collection hood should cover burners completely and be as close to the cooking surface as possible (30″ or less). The hood should be tall enough to hold cooking vapors until they can be removed. The hood intake area should displace 50 cubic feet (cu. ft.) of air per min. per square foot (sq. ft.) for an average home. Heavier cooking requires an increased amount of air displacement.

Fans and Blowers

Fans have tremendous free air delivery ratings, but when forcing air through a duct, these ratings are meaningless. In an enclosed environment, fans create an effect that impedes airflow. An elbow or a duct size reduction causes a crosscurrent in the twisting air, often stopping the airflow completely. (See Figure 10.19.)

A centrifugal blower can provide positive air displacement through pipes and ducts. A 24″ diameter high-speed exhaust fan is required to remove the same amount of air as a 300 cu. ft. per min. (cfm) centrifugal blower.

Venting

Joints in ducts must be taped to produce tight seals. Hoods with more than one set of blowers may vent into a common duct. Ducts should never be smaller than 10″ in

■ **FIGURE 10.19**

Comparison of air removal between exhaust fans and blowers.

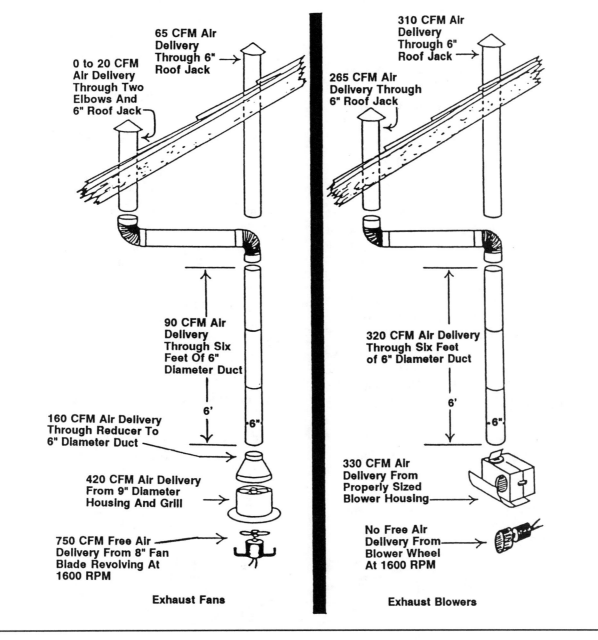

65 CFM Air Delivery Through 6" Roof Jack →

0 to 20 CFM Air Delivery Through Two Elbows And 6" Roof Jack

310 CFM Air Delivery Through 6" Roof Jack →

265 CFM Air Delivery Through 6" Roof Jack

90 CFM Air Delivery Through Six Feet Of 6" Diameter Duct

6'

6"

320 CFM Air Delivery Through Six Feet of 6" Diameter Duct

6'

6"

160 CFM Air Delivery Through Reducer To 6" Diameter Duct

420 CFM Air Delivery From 9" Diameter Housing And Grill →

750 CFM Free Air Delivery From 8" Fan Blade Revolving At 1600 RPM

330 CFM Air Delivery From Properly Sized Blower Housing →

No Free Air Delivery From Blower Wheel At 1600 RPM

Exhaust Fans

Exhaust Blowers

diameter for a 900-cfm blower or 12″ for a 1,200-cfm blower. Ducts should be brought together in the form of a Y-joint. All ducts should run in a straight line if possible because a duct system with extra elbows reduces efficiency up to 20 percent. For every 6 feet (′) of duct in runs longer than 20′, 20 cfm of air is lost. Duct size must be enlarged after the first 10′, and sharp turns should be avoided.

The kitchen exhaust system can be vented into a chimney as long as the size is adequate and neither the hot water heater nor the furnace is vented into the same flue. Kitchen exhaust systems should not be vented into the attic or under the house.

Indoor grills must be adequately vented to the outside. The hood must cover the grill completely and the control housing should be centered over the grill.

Cross drafts must be avoided because the smoke rises into the hood.

The cfm capacity of the hood ventilator will vary according to the location of the unit. For an indoor grill installed against a wall, a minimum of 100 cfm per sq. ft. of hood opening is required. If the hood opening is 2′ deep (front to back) and is 4′ long, multiply 2 by 4, which equals 8 sq. ft. of hood opening. Multiplying by 100 cfm equals 800 cfm. This hood would require a ventilator that would move 800 cfm of air through the vent system. Because of cross drafts, a hood located in an island or a peninsula may require a larger ventilator system to move air.

Filters

Grease filters are used in many kitchen exhaust systems. Grease vapor changes to a liquid form when cooled sufficiently or pressurized. The grease filter transfers some heat from the air passing through it, thereby affecting cooling of the vapors. The amount of pressure created is determined by the density of the grease filter and the volume of air being forced through the filter. If the volume of air is reduced, the amount of grease liquefaction will be drastically reduced. As grease is liquefied, it tends to fill the grease filter and reduce airflow substantially. The filter should be cleaned with detergent. Grease filters are manufactured with a fireproof material.

For the exhaust system to operate efficiently, the grease filters must be properly sized. The industry standard is to balance the filter area with the exhaust equipment. It requires 2 cu. ft. of air to pass through each square inch (sq. in.) of filter. The grease filter creates pressure and reduces the free air capacity of the blower so that the blower air rating is at 0.015″ of water column pressure. Static pressure of long duct runs also must be considered.

Vent-A-Hood manufactures the Magic Lung blower system, which does not have a grease filter. The Magic Lung liquefies cooking grease and vapors in the blower and exhausts purified air into the duct. The blower speed maintains suitable pressure to liquefy grease vapor and give maximum removal of heat-polluted air. The centrifugal action of the spinning squirrel cage blower separates grease from heated vapors. The pressure created by the squirrel cage blower prevents the entry of fire into the by-product reservoir or ducting.

Nonvented Exhaust

Nonvented exhaust systems must have a charcoal filter for filtering odors and grease vapors. The nonvented system will not remove heat or steam. Because the charcoal filter cannot be cleaned, after 6 hr. of cumulative operation, the filter should be replaced.

A nonvented hood, which is not as effective as a vented hood, is identified by louvers on the front of the hood. (See Figure 10.20.)

■ FIGURE 10.20

Nonvented exhaust systems use a charcoal filter to reduce odors and grease vapors.

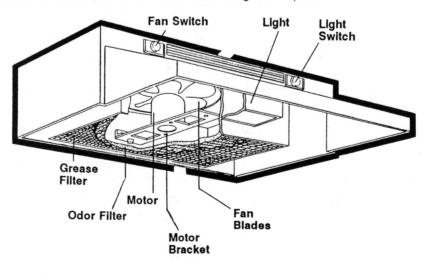

■ FIGURE 10.21

Downdraft exhaust systems remove cooking vapors, odors, and smoke from food prepared on a cooktop.

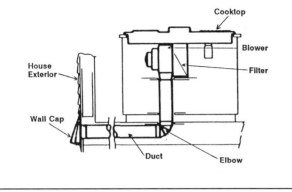

Downdraft Exhaust

Downdraft exhaust systems consist of an air-receiving chamber, a grease filter, and a blower. The system creates a high-velocity exhaust air pattern near the cooking surface that efficiently removes cooking vapors, odors, and smoke from foods prepared on a cooktop, from a grill, and from grill accessories. (See Figure 10.21.)

It is important that ducts are not damaged and joints are sealed. To ensure a full flow of air, there should be no restrictions in the ductwork. The thermal protector in the motor will overload and trip if airflow is restricted, and the motor has to cool before it can be restarted. Improper ducting may also result from or cause the following:

- Vent pipe is too small and/or not level.
- Filter placement—if the filter is not positioned properly, it restricts the airflow, causing the thermal overload protector to trip out.
- Tall utensils may cause odors in the kitchen because the taller the pot, the farther away it discharges odors, steam, etc., into the air. These vapors escape with sufficient velocity and energy to pass through the protective umbrella and release into the room. It is necessary to balance a lid across the top of the pot with the high side of the lid toward the center of the grill. This position directs odors and steam to where they can be trapped by the exhaust system.
- Smoke—Occasionally, puffs of smoke escape when grilling. Although there may be many causes, possible explanations include cross ventilation produced by opening or closing of doors, children running

through the kitchen, or raising the meat too high off the grill while turning it.

Jenn-Air

The Jenn-Air exhaust system ductwork is 5″ in diameter and has a maximum length of 10′ to 22′. When 90° elbows are used, 4′ has to be subtracted from the length of the duct for each elbow. Only two elbows should be used with 5″ diameter duct, and three elbows may be used with 6″ diameter duct. The maximum length for 6″ or 3¼″ × 10″ duct is 26′ to 30′. Flex ducting should be used only for short lengths. Ductwork should always end outside through the wall or roof, but never under the house or in the attic. The duct should exhaust through a surface wall cap. Laundry wall caps should not be used on a kitchen exhaust system.

In Jenn-Air cooktops and ranges with cartridge elements and a grill, the blower will operate when the grill is in place and on. If cooktop cartridges are in place, the blower must be activated with an on-off switch.

Regardless of the model, the grease filter is designed to be placed in the vent chamber at an angle. Facing the front of the cooktop or range, the top of the filter should rest against the left side of the vent opening. The bottom of the filter should rest against the right side of the vent chamber at the bottom. The Jenn-Air exhaust system should never be operated without a grease filter.

Roper

The Roper system is a downdraft system with a recommended 6″ diameter duct requirement. Duct length and number of elbows are the same for Roper and Jenn-Air systems. The Roper has two side vents and two grease filters. When the rear cooktop control is on, the blower will turn on automatically. The blower operates automatically when broiling uses a high or low setting. The bottom portion of the right vent switch operates the blower, and the top portion of the switch operates the oven light. The middle setting on the switch is the off position. Two jars (one for each well) are mounted behind the lower panel to catch grease drippings.

Cook'n'Vent

For gas or electric cooking, the Cook'n'Vent hoodless cooktop fits in islands, peninsulas, counters and pass-throughs. An adjustable speed control allows selection of the proper amount of ventilation. Dual controls raise the vent to the working position and lower the vent flush with the cooktop when not in use. (See Figure 10.22.)

■ **FIGURE 10.22**

Hoodless venting is used for cooktops in islands, peninsulas, and counters.

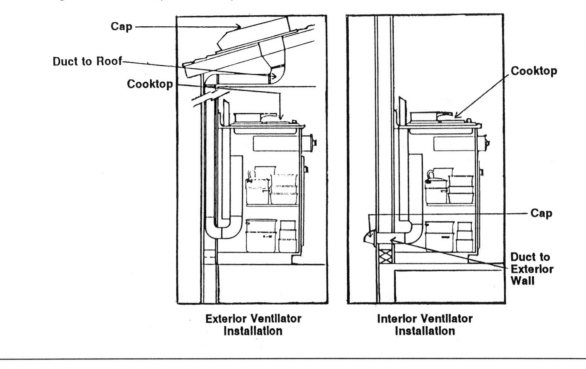

Exterior Ventilator Installation   **Interior Ventilator Installation**

In the raised position, the vent extends 7" to 8¼" above the cooktop to ventilate the entire cooking surface. The vent must be fully extended to operate. The Cook'n'Vent has a variable speed control to allow flexibility in speed adjustments for the blower. The ventilator is used in interior or exterior installations. For interior installations, the ventilator is mounted in the cabinet below the cooktop and pushes exhaust air from the vent directly outside. For exterior installations, the ventilator is mounted on the roof or outside wall as far as 65' above the cooktop.

Airflow is a function of duct size and length of duct run. Downdraft systems have specific draft specifications. The interior ventilator requires a wall cap or roof cap. The maximum length of duct run for the interior or exterior system is 40' using 3¼" × 10" rectangular duct or 65' using 10" round duct. Using 10" duct, the loss for each 90° elbow will be 2' of run length. The exterior venti-lator virtually eliminates all ventilator noise in the kitchen.

■ REFRIGERATORS AND FREEZERS

Refrigerators require inspection. Built-in refrigerators usually have the same 24" depth as the cabinets,

allowing the face to fit flush with base cabinets. A typical freestanding refrigerator protrudes into the room 4" to 6" beyond base cabinets. Built-in refrigerators include side-by-side units (freezer on one side, refrigerator on the other); over and under units (freezer below or above the refrigerator), all-freezer and all-refrigerator units, compact undercounter refrigerators, and ice makers. The width of these units ranges from 12" to 48" with a maximum of 40 cu. ft. of food storage.

Proper refrigerator temperatures range from 34°F to 38°F, while freezer temperature should be 0°F. Whether built-in or freestanding, frost-free refrigerators should never have frost buildup on the interior of the freezer or the refrigerator. Frost buildup usually suggests an air leak or a defective defrost heater.

Some built-in refrigerator/freezer units have removable exterior panels on the front and sides that allow the unit to coordinate with the decor. The removable panels can be changed whenever the decor is changed. Freestanding refrigerator/freezer units do not have removable front and side panels. Additional features of a freestanding refrigerator include door configuration, frost-free operation, automatic ice maker, and water and ice dispenser.

Doors

Refrigerator doors are designed for right-hand or left-hand opening by moving hinges to the opposite side of the door. Because of magnetic door gaskets, there are no latches or complicated hardware to relocate. Not all refrigerator/freezers have interchangeable doors; for example, the direction of the door opening cannot be changed on a side-by-side model.

Refrigerator doors are set at the factory for maximum swing of 90° to 137°. Doors are double walled with foam insulation between the walls. The outside surface of the door may be finished in stainless steel, porcelain on steel, glass, etc. The interior of the door has bins, which may be adjustable. The interior liner of the refrigerator/freezer is porcelain on steel or plastic. Shelves are glass or chrome racks, and the compartments for meat and the vegetable bins or drawers are porcelain on steel or plastic. Interior walls are insulated with foam insulation. Damage to the interior or exterior can allow cold air to leak, causing frost.

Components

The refrigerator/freezer unit consists of a compressor, a fan, an evaporator coil, and a condenser coil. The condenser coil is located on the back, top, or bottom of the exterior. Occasionally, the condenser coil requires cleaning. The refrigerator/freezer should always stand upright and, if moved, should have the compressor unit bolted down to prevent damage. The thermostat controls the temperature of the refrigerator and freezer. The higher the number on the temperature control, the colder the temperature. It is normal for temperatures to fluctuate slightly. (See Figure 10.23.)

Ice Makers

Refrigerator/freezer ice makers are automatic and require connection to a water supply, usually with a ¼" approved water line. A water turn-off valve is required at the water source if the water pressure exceeds 100 pounds per square inch (psi). A line filter is recommended when water has a high mineral content.

The ice maker automatically starts and replenishes the ice bucket. When the bucket is full, the stop arm cannot lower and the operation stops. During normal operation of the ice maker, sounds of water passing through the solenoid valve into the ice maker and ice dropping into the bucket can be heard. Ice production is influenced by conditions, frequency of door opening, or room temperature. Ice makers in refrigerator/freezers produce a maximum of 12 pounds (lb.) of ice in 24 hr. (See Figure 10.24.)

■ SELF-CONTAINED ICE MAKERS

Self-contained ice makers may be freestanding or built into cabinets. Ice maker units are manufactured similarly to refrigerator/freezer units: porcelain on steel, high-impact plastics, and changeable panels to match the decor. Self-contained ice makers have a compressor, fan, and thermostat and require water from the cold water line. (See Figure 10.25.)

Most ice makers require a drain for excess water. Models without a drain are also available. Self-contained ice makers can produce 50 lb. of ice in 24 hr. Cube thickness can be adjusted from ⅜" to ¾". Bins store 35 lb. of ice. Ice makers will not produce full-size ice cubes until the unit has had adequate time to reach the proper temperature.

■ TRASH COMPACTORS

Trash compactors reduce the volume of trash by compression to fit into a small container. Depending on the manufacturer and size, trash compactors develop pressures up to 5,000 psi. The trash compactor has a keylock that acts as a safety when the compactor is not in use. (See Figure 10.26.)

Door/Drawer

The trash compactor door or drawer must be closed and latched for operation. Some compactors have hinged doors instead of a drawer, with a bracket to hold the bin.

Bin

The trash compactor bin may be circular or rectangular, depending on the model. Trash compactors should use plastic bags specifically designed for that particular trash compactor.

Ram

The trash compactor ram fits the bin and usually has a screw drive. The screw drive allows the compactor to

■ **FIGURE 10.23**

Refrigerator/freezer units consist of a compressor, a fan, an evaporator coil, and a condenser.

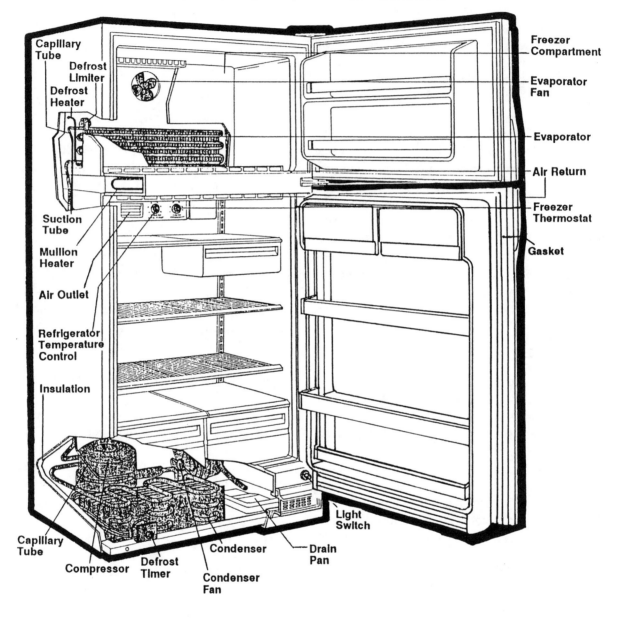

produce more force with a smaller motor. For example, a ½-hp motor can produce more than 3,000 lb. of pressure per sq. in. of ram force, reducing trash to one-quarter volume in 35 sec. When the start button is pushed, the motor drives the ram to the end of travel or until the back pressure of the ram exceeds the maximum pressure setting on the limit switch. When complete, the motor reverses itself and the ram is raised. Depending on the model, the ram has from 10″ to 18″ of travel.

Deodorizer

Garbage should not be placed in a trash compactor. Cans should be rinsed before being placed in the compactor. Even with these precautions, odors can develop. Manufacturers have designed deodorizers for compactors. Some trash compactors use a fan with a charcoal filter; others have a bracket in the top panel that holds an aerosol spray can for deodorizing the bin. A triggering

■ FIGURE 10.24

A refrigerator/freezer ice maker will produce a maximum of 12 pounds of ice in 24 hours.

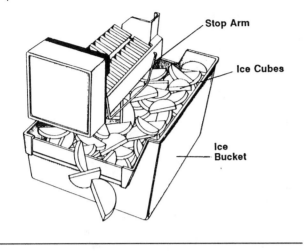

■ FIGURE 10.25

Self-contained ice makers have a compressor, fan, and thermostat.

device trips the spray can when the drawer is opened and closed.

■ WASHERS

A wide variety of clothes washers are available to the homeowner, including full-size, compact, and built-in. (See Figure 10.27.)

Tub

Full-size washers have a large-capacity tub that is porcelain on steel. Full-size washers may be equipped with a minibasket for small loads and delicate items. This basket is made of high-impact plastic and fits over the agitator post.

Lint Filter

A lint filter is in the tub. Some lint filters must be removed for cleaning, while others are self-cleaning.

Agitator

The agitator provides the multiaction needed for washing, regardless of load size. Front-loading washers do not have an agitator; a rotating drum lifts and drops clothes. Front-loading washers use less water and detergent than top-loading washers with agitators.

Pump and Motor

The pump circulates water through the filter and out to the drain. The motor operates the pump and the agitator. The motor operates at 115V.

Controls

Washer controls may be dials, push-buttons, or solid-state electronic pads to select water levels, water temperatures, cycles, and other options. The timer controls the time the machine is in the wash and rinse cycles. The timer also controls filling the tub, pumping the water from the tub, and the spin cycle.

Hoses

Water hoses connected to the washer should be approved for high pressure. The drain hose must be capable of handling the pressure and volume of water as the water is pumped out of the washer. The drain must have a P-trap large enough to accept the water without overflowing.

■ **FIGURE 10.26**

Trash compactors reduce the volume of trash by compression to fit into a small container.

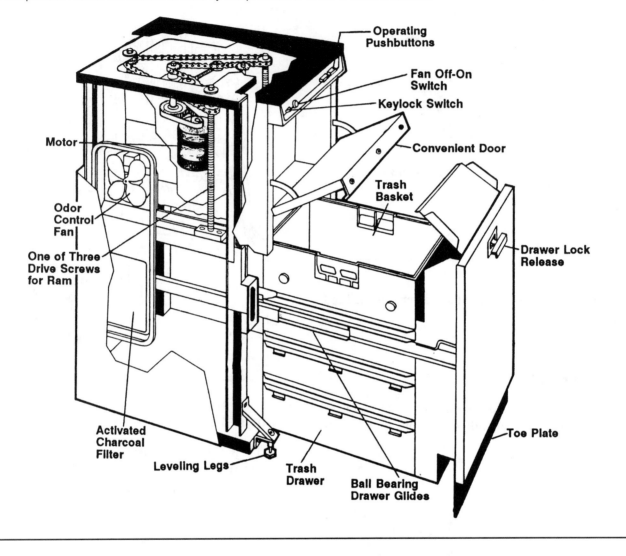

■ CLOTHES DRYERS

Dryers remove moisture from clothing with heat by tumbling the clothes in the drum. (See Figure 10.28.)

Timer

The timer controls the heat and length of time for tumbling. Three timer controls are available:

1. Dry cycle—provides a selection of preset time dry settings to match drying requirements. If the length of the dry cycle is short, clothes will not be dry. If the cycle is long, clothes will be overly dry, damaging some fabrics.

2. Automatic sense—measures the degree of dryness and turns off automatically when the selected degree of dryness is reached.

3. Automatic dry—thermostatically measures the exhaust air, automatically reducing tumbling temperature to its lowest setting during the final minutes of the drying cycle. The temperature control selections include regular, delicate fabrics (low heat), permanent press (with cool-down at the end of the cycle), and air only for cool tumbling (no heat).

The two sources of energy for dryers are gas and electricity. Gas dryers require a gas line, a 120V grounded outlet to operate the controls, an electronic

■ FIGURE 10.27

Washers have a large-capacity tub, a lint filter, an agitator, a pump and motor, a timer and controls, and hoses.

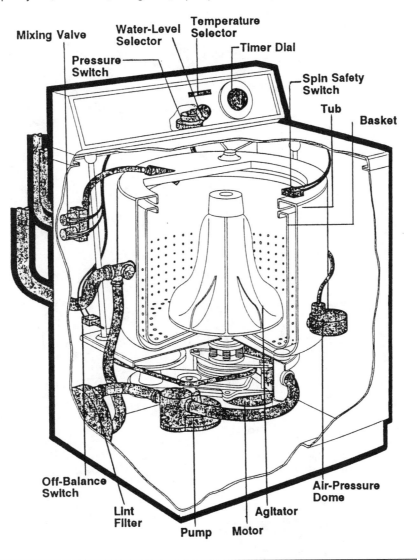

ignition system and lights. Gas dryers operate with natural gas or LP gas.

Electric dryers require a 208V or 240V single-phase power line connected to a minimum 30-amp. circuit breaker or fuse in the electrical panel. Small portable electric dryers may operate on 120V.

Venting

Both gas and electric dryers must be vented to the outside through a wall or the roof. Dryers vented under the floor or in the attic are fire hazards. Portable units do not require exterior venting.

Lint Filter

All dryers have lint filters to capture large lint particles. The lint filter should be kept clean for more efficient operation.

Door

The dryer door opens either from the top or from the side. All dryer doors must be closed and latched for the dryer to operate. Doors that open from the side must open a full 180° to allow full access to the dryer. Doors that open from the top are hinged on the bottom, which provides a shelf for loading and unloading clothes when open.

■ FIGURE 10.28

Dryers remove moisture from clothing by tumbling clothes in a drum.

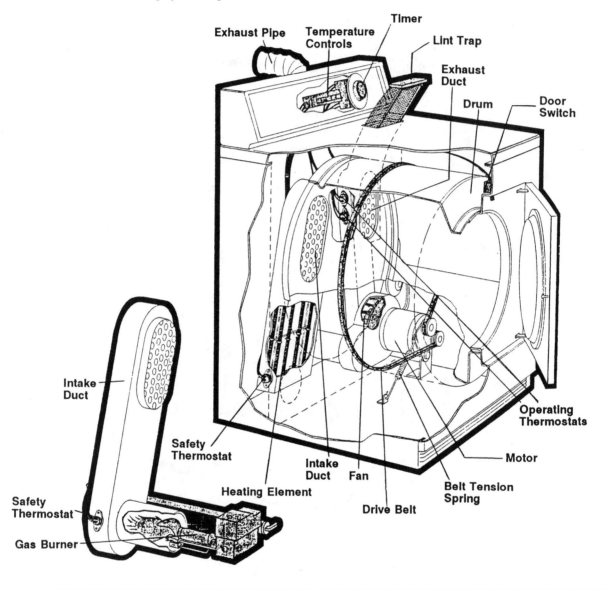

■ CENTRAL VACUUMS

Central vacuum systems are dry vacuums and should never be used to vacuum water or other liquids. Central vacuum systems are equipped with disposable soil bags that allow the air to pass through the special paper as soil is captured. A secondary filter is mounted around the motor to catch fine particles that escape through the bag. The air is exhausted to the outside. (See Figure 10.29.)

Central vacuum systems remove more dirt and dust than portable vacuums because they exhaust to the outside. Central vacuums are quieter because the power unit is usually located outside living areas.

Central vacuum systems are activated by inserting a lightweight, flexible hose into one of the inlets. The vacuum is instantaneous. Removing the hose deactivates the system. Attachments are available for all vacuuming jobs.

■ FIGURE 10.29

Central vacuum systems are dry vacuums usually installed in the garage or basement with tubes running behind walls, through the attic, or under floors to inlets throughout the house.

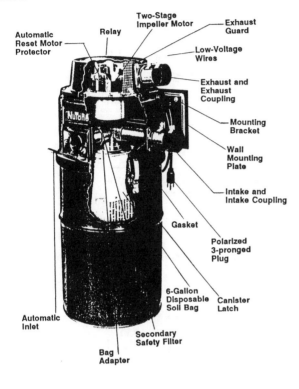

The vacuum hose is manufactured from soft poly-vinyl over steel wire interwoven with nylon cord. The soft polyvinyl is lightweight and allows coiling without backlash. The steel wire prevents the hose from col-lapsing, and the nylon cord provides strength and dura-bility. Hoses vary in length from 20' to 30' and are equipped with end couplings.

The central vacuum motor is usually installed in the garage or basement. Tubing from the power unit con-nects behind walls, in the attic, and under floors to unob-trusive inlets placed strategically throughout the dwelling.

The motor size of central vacuum systems will vary. Motors from 1¼ hp to 2 hp move 90 cu. ft. to 100 cu. ft. of air per min. through a 2″ opening. All motors are 120V and draw less than 15 amp. The built-in low-voltage switch controls the operation of the central vacuum. The central vacuum must be on a separate grounded circuit with at least a 15-amp. fuse or circuit breaker.

■ MISCELLANEOUS APPLIANCES AND EQUIPMENT

Food Centers

A food center is designed with a built-in motor located under the counter, preventing vibration or movement, and sitting flush with the countertop. The food center is composed of different appliances operated with the one motor. The food center has an infinite speed control dial that allows operation at the correct speed for each appliance.

The motor should be connected to a grounded appliance circuit. The food center may be found in kitchens and wet bars. Appliances available for use with the power unit are ice crusher, food processor, mixer, meat grinder, blender, shredder, slicer, can opener, fruit juicer, coffee grinder, and knife sharpener.

Instant Water Heaters

An instant hot water appliance is a small water heater with a capacity of 1 qt. that heats water to 190°F. It is equipped with a relief valve. The instant hot water unit is usually located under the kitchen sink with the faucet located on the sink.

Garage Door Openers

A garage door opener is an electrical device that opens and closes a garage door. It can be operated from inside the house by pressing a switch or from outside with a remote transmitter.

The size of the garage door opener motor is deter-mined by the size of the garage door. Larger motors are available for commercial overhead doors or doors larger than those commonly found on residential property.

The motor is connected to an adjustable slip clutch, which is electrically connected to a reversing switch. The reversing switch is a safety device that reverses door travel when the door comes in contact with an object in its path between the full open and full closed position. It is designed to prevent injury to people and damage to property. The remote transmitter is usually carried in the car and the receiver is in the garage. The receiver is mounted on the wall or on the garage door opener. The receiver and transmitter must be programmed with the same code.

The door track on one side has the receiver to the door operator installed and the other door track will have the

■ FIGURE 10.30

Two ways of performing garage door opener safety checks.

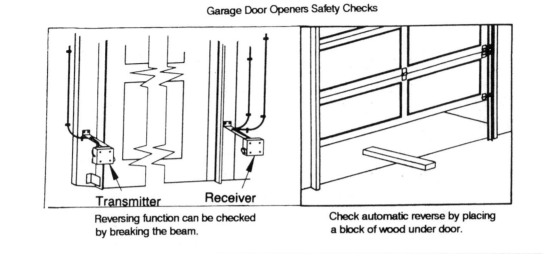

Garage Door Openers Safety Checks

Transmitter   Receiver

Reversing function can be checked
by breaking the beam.

Check automatic reverse by placing
a block of wood under door.

receiver to the transmitter installed. It is important that the two receivers be aligned or the door opener will not operate. Breaking the beam with the hand or some object can check the reversing function. (See Figure 10.30.)

The inspector should check the reversing function of all garage door openers and should inspect the door itself for damage (if wood, wood rot or other deterioration, and if metal, damaged panels). The homeowner should test the reversing feature at least every 30 days.

■ REVIEW QUESTIONS*

1. A kitchen exhaust using a blower is more efficient than one using a fan.

    A. True
    B. False

2. In a ductless kitchen exhaust system, the charcoal filter must be in place.

    A. True
    B. False

3. Name the two different types of kitchen disposals.

    _____

    _____

4. The batch disposal is energized by a

    A. switch.
    B. latch.
    C. twist top.
    D. lap top.

5. It is important that a disposal be grounded.

    A. True
    B. False

6. When inspecting a Jenn-Air system, it is important to locate the exhaust wall cap or roof vent.

    A. True
    B. False

---

*Answers to all of the chapter review questions are located in Appendix C at the back of this book.

7. When manually turning the timer control on a dishwasher, the door lock should be in the _____ position.

8. When inspecting an electric cooktop, the proper sequence for checking the elements is

   _____

   _____

   _____

9. Continuous clean ovens must never be cleaned with oven cleaners.

   A. True
   B. False

10. A convection oven cycles both upper and lower elements on and off, and the fan circulates heated air evenly around the food.

    A. True
    B. False

11. To check an oven thermostat, set the temperature for _____ degrees and allow the oven to cycle at least _____ times before collecting a thermometer reading.

12. When inspecting a microwave cooking center with a self-clean oven, if the oven is in the self-clean mode, the microwave should operate.

    A. True
    B. False

13. The proper refrigerator temperature is 34°F to 38°F, and the proper freezer temperature is 0°F.

    A. True
    B. False

14. Clothes dryers may be vented under the house or in the attic.

    A. True
    B. False

15. When inspecting a clothes washer, the inspector must move the washer.

    A. True
    B. False

16. If the dishwasher drains to the kitchen disposal, the inspector should check the connection at the disposal for _____ damage.

17. The vent pipe for a ducted kitchen exhaust system is limited as to size and number of elbows.

    A. True
    B. False

18. When venting a Jenn-Air with 5″ pipe, each elbow is equivalent to _____ feet of straight pipe.

19. The purpose of a kitchen exhaust blower is to remove _____, _____, and _____ from the home.

20. Self-cleaning ovens clean the interior of the oven using heat.

    A. True
    B. False

21. The Jenn-Air vent filter must be placed in proper position.

    A. True
    B. False

22. What are the two determining factors that control the operating time of a dishwasher?

    _____

    _____

23. What is the purpose of the small amount of water that remains in the bottom of the dishwasher?

    _____

24. When inspecting an electric cooktop, the top should be raised and the wiring inspected for any damage.

    A. True
    B. False

25. Before operating a microwave oven, what items of the microwave oven should you check first?

   A. Broken door hinges, seals, and broken glass
   B. Damaged case (interior and exterior)
   C. Outlet not grounded
   D. All of the above

26. What should you check when inspecting a central vacuum?

   A. Vacuum grounded
   B. No water in dust bag
   C. Check each outlet for proper operation
   D. All of the above

27. When inspecting a garage door opener, you should check the automatic reversing feature.

   A. True
   B. False

28. Inspectors should report any damage observed on the garage door.

   A. True
   B. False

■ INSPECTION CHECKLIST: APPLIANCES

DISHWASHER

Yes No

☐ ☐ Are door hinges damaged?
☐ ☐ Is door gasket damaged?
☐ ☐ Is door locking?
☐ ☐ Is interior damaged or rusted?
☐ ☐ Are front panels damaged?
☐ ☐ Are control buttons missing?
☐ ☐ If applicable, is cap on tubing of top spray bar?
☐ ☐ Is tub liner damaged and/or rusted?
☐ ☐ Is bottom or top rack damaged or in need of rollers?
☐ ☐ Is dishwasher drain looped?
☐ ☐ Is float switch operational?

Align spray bars for reference and operate through a complete cycle.

☐ ☐ Does unit operate? If not:
☐ ☐ Is door locked?
☐ ☐ Is water off?
☐ ☐ Are controls set properly?
☐ ☐ If water goes into machine but it fails to operate, does unit have a preheat cycle?
☐ ☐ For units without a manual advance, is unit in the middle of a cycle?

At end of cycle:

☐ ☐ Does timer operate through entire cycle?
☐ ☐ Does heater operate?
☐ ☐ Does second cycle soap dispenser open?
☐ ☐ Do spray bars operate?
☐ ☐ Is dishwasher excessively noisy?
☐ ☐ Does water pump out?
☐ ☐ Are leaks apparent after removing the kick plate?

DISPOSAL

Yes No

☐ ☐ Any exposed wire connections?
☐ ☐ Is disposal grounded?
☐ ☐ Is condition of splash-guard acceptable?
☐ ☐ Are hammers missing, loose, or frozen?
☐ ☐ Any missing blades?
☐ ☐ Is there excessive rust on the impeller?
☐ ☐ Is casing corroded?
☐ ☐ Is dishwasher drain connection corroded?

Yes No

☐ ☐ Is sewer drain below disposal drain for proper drainage?

Flood sink and turn on disposal. If it does not operate:

☐ ☐ Is power to the unit available?
☐ ☐ Has reset button tripped?
☐ ☐ Is disposal jammed?
☐ ☐ Is there excessive vibration or noise?
☐ ☐ Are there leaks?

GAS RANGE

Yes No

☐ ☐ Is there a gas shut-off valve to range?
☐ ☐ Are gas branch line and connection to range constructed of recommended material?
☐ ☐ Are controls missing or broken?
☐ ☐ Any grates missing or broken?
☐ ☐ Is there a gas odor?

On conventional gas ranges, turn on each burner.

☐ ☐ Does each burner light? If not:
☐ ☐ Is gas shut off?
☐ ☐ Are pilots lit?
☐ ☐ Are burners slow to light?
☐ ☐ Does flame need adjustment?
☐ ☐ Does burner light completely?
☐ ☐ Does pilot need adjusting?

Note: *On electronic pilot ranges, turn each burner to "lite." There is no standing pilot, but all other checks are the same as with a conventional gas range.*

ELECTRIC RANGE

Yes No

☐ ☐ After lifting range cover, is condition of wires acceptable?
☐ ☐ Are electrical connections in a covered junction box?
☐ ☐ Are controls broken or missing?
☐ ☐ Are burner elements missing or damaged?

Yes No

Set control to low.

☐ ☐ Does element come on? If not:

☐ ☐ Is circuit breaker tripped?

☐ ☐ Is element plugged in?

☐ ☐ Does element glow?

☐ ☐ Is element controlled by a temperature control?

☐ ☐ Do signal lights operate?

Set control to medium.

☐ ☐ Do elements heat?

☐ ☐ Do elements have hot spots?

Set control to high.

☐ ☐ Do all coils glow?

☐ ☐ Does circuit breaker trip?

☐ ☐ On units equipped with a multiple-setting element, does the element operate at 4"?

☐ ☐ At 6"?

☐ ☐ At 8"?

☐ ☐ On ceramic cooktops, are there surface cracks?

Note: *Induction cooktops require special pans to operate elements.*

GAS OVEN

Yes No

☐ ☐ Is there a gas shut-off valve on the gas supply line to oven?

☐ ☐ Are the gas branch line and connection to oven constructed of recommended material?

☐ ☐ Is unit anchored in cabinet?

Identify any problems with door operation.

☐ ☐ Are hinges damaged?

☐ ☐ Are gaskets damaged or missing?

☐ ☐ Is door glass broken?

☐ ☐ Is door glass seal damaged?

☐ ☐ Are handles loose or missing?

☐ ☐ Are controls broken or missing?

☐ ☐ Are numbers worn off controls?

☐ ☐ Do oven lights operate?

☐ ☐ Is thermostat secured in oven?

☐ ☐ Does oven timer operate?

☐ ☐ Does minute timer operate?

☐ ☐ Is there a gas odor?

☐ ☐ Is finish damaged on continuous cleaning oven?

Yes No

☐ ☐ Set oven to bake at 350°F. Allow approximately 20 min.

Calibration check. Set oven to "bake" at 350°F. Allow 20 min. for thermostat to cycle three times.

☐ ☐ Does oven light? If not:

☐ ☐ Is gas shut off?

☐ ☐ Is pilot lit?

☐ ☐ Do flames need adjustment?

☐ ☐ Do burners light completely?

☐ ☐ Is calibration + or − 25°F?

☐ ☐ Does pilot need adjustment?

On electric pilot units there is no standing pilot, but all other checks are the same as with a conventional gas oven.

☐ ☐ On glow-coil units, do coils turn red?

Set control to broil.

☐ ☐ Do burners operate?

☐ ☐ If oven includes rotisserie, does it operate?

ELECTRIC OVEN

Yes No

☐ ☐ Is finish damaged on continuous cleaning oven?

☐ ☐ Is unit anchored in cabinet?

Check door operation.

☐ ☐ Are hinges damaged?

☐ ☐ Are gaskets damaged or missing?

☐ ☐ Is door glass broken?

☐ ☐ Is door glass seal damaged?

☐ ☐ Are handles loose or missing?

☐ ☐ Are controls broken or missing?

☐ ☐ Are the numbers worn off controls?

☐ ☐ Do oven lights operate?

☐ ☐ Is thermostat secured in oven?

☐ ☐ Is oven timer operating?

☐ ☐ Is minute timer operational?

SELF-CLEANING OVEN

Yes No

☐ ☐ Does door lock operate?

☐ ☐ Does window shield operate?

☐ ☐ Does the self-cleaning mode operate without setting the timer?

Yes No

☐ ☐ Operate at self-clean for 5 min. Does it operate?

On units without a selector switch, push timer in to manual mode.

☐ ☐ Does bake element operate? If not:

☐ ☐ Has circuit breaker tripped?

☐ ☐ Is element plugged in?

☐ ☐ If equipped with top and bottom oven, do both operate?

☐ ☐ Do elements have hot spots?

☐ ☐ Is calibration + or − 25°F?

Set selector control to broil.

☐ ☐ Do top elements glow?

☐ ☐ If oven includes rotisserie, does it operate?

CONVECTION OVEN

Yes No

☐ ☐ In addition to applicable checks listed above, does fan operate?

Note: *Report that self-cleaning oven was not checked through an entire cycle.*

MICROWAVE

Yes No

☐ ☐ Is cord damaged?

☐ ☐ Is microwave grounded?

☐ ☐ Is door glass broken?

☐ ☐ Are door hinges loose or broken?

☐ ☐ Is door latch loose or broken?

☐ ☐ Is door closing properly?

☐ ☐ Is cabinet damaged?

☐ ☐ Is there evidence of arcing?

☐ ☐ Is stirrer and/or cover damaged?

Place a microwave-safe container with one cup of water in the microwave. Set power to high and operate for 1 min.

☐ ☐ Does light operate?

☐ ☐ Does door interlock operate?

☐ ☐ Does water temperature reach a minimum of 120°F to 150°F?

Note: *State in the report that no radiation check was completed.*

KITCHEN EXHAUST

Using the ductless hood:

Yes No

☐ ☐ Is the grease filter missing or damaged?

☐ ☐ Is odor filter missing?

☐ ☐ Are electrical connections exposed?

☐ ☐ Do lights operate?

☐ ☐ Is fan operating on all settings?

☐ ☐ Does fan have excessive noise and/or vibration?

Using the ducted hood:

☐ ☐ Are vents in cabinet?

☐ ☐ Do vent pipes leak air in cabinet?

☐ ☐ Is vent into attic?

☐ ☐ Is grease filter missing or improperly installed?

☐ ☐ Is vent into crawlspace?

☐ ☐ Is excessive grease built up in well?

☐ ☐ Are there more duct elbows than allowed?

☐ ☐ Is fan operational?

☐ ☐ Does fan have excessive noise and/or vibration?

☐ ☐ Does unit draft?

☐ ☐ Is exhaust hood in place?

☐ ☐ Does motor overload trip when burners operate?

☐ ☐ Does exhaust vent contain water?

REFRIGERATOR

Yes No

☐ ☐ Are door hinges damaged?

☐ ☐ Is gasket damaged?

☐ ☐ Does door seal properly?

☐ ☐ Is plastic liner damaged?

☐ ☐ Is there interior or exterior water leakage?

☐ ☐ Is electrical cord damaged?

☐ ☐ Do interior lights operate?

☐ ☐ Are drawers covers and plastic rim pieces damaged?

☐ ☐ Is condenser coil clean with good air circulation?

☐ ☐ Is unit level?

☐ ☐ Is there compressor or fan noise?

☐ ☐ Is ice maker producing ice?

☐ ☐ Is refrigerator temperature 38°F?

☐ ☐ Is freezer temperature 0°F?

ICE MAKER

Yes No

- ☐ ☐ Are door hinges damaged?
- ☐ ☐ Is gasket damaged?
- ☐ ☐ Is plastic liner damaged?
- ☐ ☐ Are there interior or exterior water leaks?
- ☐ ☐ Is there ice?
- ☐ ☐ Is there excess corrosion?
- ☐ ☐ Does unit operate? If not:
- ☐ ☐ Is unit powered?
- ☐ ☐ Is water on to unit?
- ☐ ☐ Is there compressor noise?

TRASH COMPACTOR

Yes No

- ☐ ☐ Is unit properly anchored in cabinet?
- ☐ ☐ Is front panel damaged?
- ☐ ☐ Does door lock properly?
- ☐ ☐ Is key missing?
- ☐ ☐ Is bin damaged or missing?

Place a rolled-up newspaper upright in the bin and operate through an entire cycle.

- ☐ ☐ Does ram operate?
- ☐ ☐ Is there excessive noise and/or vibration?

WASHERS

Yes No

- ☐ ☐ Is automatic washer remaining in the house?
- ☐ ☐ Is washer equipped with lint filter?
- ☐ ☐ Any damage to tub?
- ☐ ☐ Is agitator damaged?
- ☐ ☐ Are door seals damaged or do they contain leaks?
- ☐ ☐ Is washer level?
- ☐ ☐ Any water damage on wall behind washer?
- ☐ ☐ Are hoses or valves leaking?
- ☐ ☐ Is washer grounded to cold water line?

Fill washer with water and operate through cycle.

- ☐ ☐ Does pump circulate water?
- ☐ ☐ Does pump remove water to drain?
- ☐ ☐ Is timer operational?
- ☐ ☐ Any excessive noise and/or vibration?

CLOTHES DRYER

Yes No

- ☐ ☐ Is clothes dryer remaining in the house?
- ☐ ☐ Is dryer operated with gas?
- ☐ ☐ Does dryer gas line contain a shut-off valve?
- ☐ ☐ Is proper material used for gas branch lines?
- ☐ ☐ Does automatic ignition operate properly?
- ☐ ☐ Is dryer operated with electricity?
- ☐ ☐ Does heat element operate?
- ☐ ☐ Does dryer have a lint trap?
- ☐ ☐ Is dryer vented to the exterior?
- ☐ ☐ Any excessive noise and/or vibration during operation?
- ☐ ☐ Does dryer operate with door open?

CENTRAL VACUUM SYSTEM

Yes No

- ☐ ☐ Is unit grounded?
- ☐ ☐ Is there damage to electrical cord?
- ☐ ☐ Is cabinet damaged?
- ☐ ☐ Are hinges broken?
- ☐ ☐ Is there evidence of rust inside tub?
- ☐ ☐ Does exhaust go outside or to garage?
- ☐ ☐ Is filter in place?
- ☐ ☐ Does central unit operate? If not:
- ☐ ☐ Do all outlets operate?

FOOD CENTER

Yes No

- ☐ ☐ Is shaft square?
- ☐ ☐ Does switch operate at all speeds?
- ☐ ☐ Is there excessive noise and/or vibration?

GARAGE DOOR OPENER

Yes No

- ☐ ☐ Any wood damage to panel(s) and/or frames?
- ☐ ☐ Does the door fit square in its frame?
- ☐ ☐ Any finger joints separating?
- ☐ ☐ Any loose or missing hardware?
- ☐ ☐ Is track damaged or loose?
- ☐ ☐ Are wheels loose or damaged?
- ☐ ☐ Any broken glass?
- ☐ ☐ Does door have excessive sag?

Before operating door opener, ensure that door is connected to cable. Operate opener.

- ☐ ☐ Does door open? If not:

Yes No

☐ ☐ Does another switch control opener?
☐ ☐ Is emergency release chain disengaged?
☐ ☐ Do wheels bind in track?
☐ ☐ Does door close properly?

Yes No

☐ ☐ Any adjustment required for opener?
☐ ☐ Does automatic reverse operate?

Note: State on inspection report that transmitters were not checked.

■ REPORTING GUIDELINES

Inspection reporting guidelines for appliances incorporating the above checklist:

Dishwasher. The inspector shall

* report as in need of repair any deficiencies in the door gasket, control knobs, and interior parts, including the dish tray, rollers, spray arms, and soap dispenser;

* report as in need of repair any interior signs of rust;

* report as in need of repair a door spring that does not operate properly;

* report as in need of repair deficiencies in the discharge hose or piping or the lack of back flow prevention;

* report as in need of repair units that are not securely mounted;

* report as in need of repair any water leaks;

* inspect the unit's operation in normal mode with the soap dispenser closed; and

* report as in need of repair spray arms that do not turn, soap dispensers that do not open or drying elements that do not operate.

Food waste disposer. The inspector shall

* report as in need of repair any deficiencies in the splash guard, grinding components, wiring and exterior;

* report as in need of repair a unit that is not securely mounted; and

* inspect the operation of the unit and report as in need of repair any unusual noise or vibration level and any signs of water leaks.

Range exhaust vent. The inspector shall

* report as in need of repair any deficiencies in the filter, vent pipe, light, and switches;

* inspect the operation of the blower and report as in need of repair any unusual sounds or vibration levels, or if the blower does not operate at all speeds;

* report as in need of repair a vent pipe that does not terminate outside the structure when the unit is not of recirculating type or configuration.

* report as in need of repair a vent pipe that is of inadequate material; and

* report as in need of repair the absence of a range exhaust vent.

■ REPORTING GUIDELINES *(Continued)*

Electric or gas ranges. The inspector shall

- report as in need of repair broken or missing knobs, elements, drip pans, or other parts; inadequate clearance from combustible material; or the absence of an anti-tip device;

- report as in need of repair signal lights and elements or burners that do not operate at low and high settings;

- report as in need of repair improper materials that are used for the gas branch line and the connection to the appliance; and

- report as in need of repair the absence of a gas shut-off valve, or a valve that is not properly located, is inaccessible, or leaks.

Electric or gas ovens. The inspector shall

- report as in need of repair any broken or missing knobs, handles, glass panels, door hinges, lights or light covers, or other parts, or inadequate clearance from combustible material;

- report as in need of repair deficiencies in the door gasket, tightness of closure, and operation of the latch;

- report as in need of repair an oven that is not securely mounted;

- report as in need of repair heating elements and thermostat sensing elements that are not properly supported;

- report as in need of repair deficiencies in the operation of the heating elements or the lighting, operation, and condition of the flame;

- report as in need of repair deficiencies in the operation of the clock and timer, thermostat, and door springs; and

- report as in need of repair any inaccuracy of the thermostat more than a 25°F range plus or minus of a 350°F setting, as measured by a thermometer.

Microwave oven. The inspector shall

- report as in need of repair any broken or missing knobs, handles, glass panels, or other parts, or a unit that is not securely mounted;

- report as in need of repair any deficiencies in the door and seal (the inspector is not required to test for radiation);

- report as in need of repair an oven that does not operate by heating a container of water or with other test equipment, as reasonably determined by the inspector; and

- report as in need of repair a light that does not operate.

■ REPORTING GUIDELINES *(Continued)*

Trash compactor. The inspector shall

- inspect the overall condition of the unit;

- report as in need of repair a unit that does not operate or operates with unusual noise or vibration levels; and

- report as in need of repair a unit that is not securely mounted in place.

Other built-in appliances. The inspector shall report as in need of repair any deficiencies in condition or operation of other built-in appliances not listed in this section.

Bathroom exhaust vents and electric heaters. The inspector shall operate the unit, and report as in need of repair unusual sounds, speed, and vibration levels or, when possible, vent pipes that do not terminate outside the structure.

Central vacuum system. The inspector shall

- inspect the condition of the main unit;

- report as in need of repair a unit that does not operate; and

- inspect the system from all accessible outlets throughout the house.

Doorbell and chimes. The inspector shall

- inspect the condition of the unit and report as in need of repair a unit that does not operate; and

- report as in need of repair any deficiencies in visible and accessible parts.

Attic power vents. The inspector shall

- report as in need of repair deficiencies in the operation and installation of the unit, including the wiring and mounting of the thermostat control, if so equipped and accessible; and

- report as in need of repair unusual sounds or speed and vibration levels.

Garage door opener. The inspector shall

- report as in need of repair deficiencies in the installation, condition, and operation of the garage door opener;

- operate the door both manually and by an installed automatic door control;

- report as in need of repair a door that does not automatically reverse during closing cycle, any installed electronic sensors that are not operable or not installed at the proper heights above the garage floor; and

- report as in need of repair door locks or side ropes that have not been removed or disabled.

■ REPORTING GUIDELINES *(Continued)*

Hydrotherapy or whirlpool equipment. The inspector shall

- report as in need of repair a unit that does not operate, leaks, or is inaccessible;

- report as in need of repair a unit that lacks a ground fault circuit interrupter or has an interrupter that does not operate;

- report as in need of repair switches that are not in a safe location or do not operate;

- report evidence of leaks under the tub if the access cover is available and accessible, reporting when the cover is absent or inaccessible (the inspector is not required to determine the adequacy of self-draining features of the circulation system); and

- report as in need of repair deficiencies in the ports, valves, grates, and covers.

Specific limitations for appliances. The inspector is not required to do the following:

- Operate or determine the condition of other auxiliary components of inspected items

- Inspect self-cleaning functions

11 Swimming Pools and Spas

Swimming pools, spas, hot tubs, and saunas are becoming more popular with residential homeowners. Swimming pools are constructed from concrete, fiberglass, and vinyl. A swimming pool system includes pumps, skimmers, filters, heaters, timers, cleaners, and numerous accessories. Spas and hot tubs are available in various sizes and shapes and are built above or below the ground. Hot tubs are wooden structures that are 4 feet (') deep and 5' to 12' in diameter. Saunas are wooden rooms that provide dry heat. Residential inspectors should have a thorough knowledge of plumbing and electrical systems to inspect swimming pools, spas, hot tubs, and saunas correctly.

■ SWIMMING POOLS

Swimming pools consist of a shell that holds water. They can be completely or partially in-ground, anchored to hillsides, or placed directly on the ground surface. Most permanent pools are in-ground, accessible from patio areas and adaptable to unified land schemes.

Permanent swimming pools are produced using various construction methods. The most common construction materials are air-sprayed concrete (referred to as *gunite*), poured concrete, fiberglass, and vinyl.

Construction

Concrete

Concrete is the most popular material used in the construction of in-ground and irregular swimming pools because of its workability, strength, stability, and flexibility of design. Concrete is reinforced with steel rebars to strengthen against failure due to soil expansion, contraction, and surface water pressure. The two concrete construction techniques used to produce swimming pools are air-sprayed (gunite) and poured concrete.

Most concrete swimming pools are air-sprayed using gunite. Gunite is a mixture of hydrated cement and sand applied over and under a grid of rebars placed directly against the soil. (See Figure 11.1.)

The dry gunite mixture is shot from a nozzle under high pressure to form a one-piece shell that is stronger than concrete alone. Gunite must be sprayed behind rebars and plumbing (main drain, inlet pipes, etc.) and against the soil so air pockets will not form. The shell must be the proper thickness, which is 4 inches (") to 6", to withstand soil and hydrostatic pressures.

The contractor should place covers over the main drain pipes and light openings to prevent their being filled with concrete. All openings must be checked and cleared as soon as the gunite crew is finished.

Gunite allows freedom of swimming pool size and shape. Steps and spas are formed at the same time the pool is excavated. The shell thickness and the number and size of rebars should be adjusted to meet structural requirements. If the swimming pool is built on filled ground, the gunite shell should be on concrete piers that rest on solid soil.

Gunite pools have several different interior finishes. Surfaces may be plastered in white or a variety of colors. Light colors provide a large solar heating benefit. The concrete surface can also be troweled smooth and painted. Ceramic tile is also a surface finish for gunite pools. Ceramic tile surfaces are attractive and easy to clean.

Pool builders install a band of ceramic tile along the water line both for the ease of removing minerals, oil, and dirt and for its attractiveness. Poured concrete pool construction has been almost totally replaced by gunite pool construction because of high labor costs, concrete curing time, and limitation of size and shape variations.

■ **FIGURE 11.1**

Gunite construction techniques produce swimming pools by spraying a mixture of hydrated cement and sand over rebars placed directly against the soils.

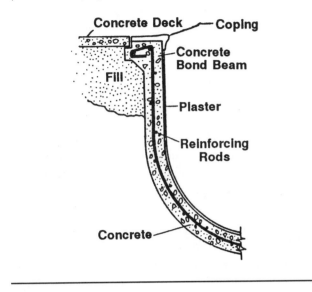

■ **FIGURE 11.2**

Fiberglass pools are placed in a bed of sand, and plumbing is installed. A concrete bond beam and deck are poured around the pool perimeter.

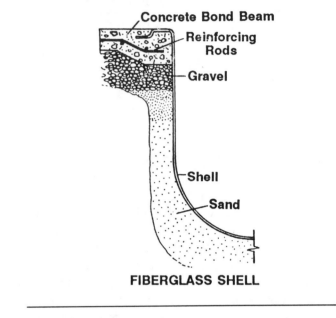

FIBERGLASS SHELL

Fiberglass

Fiberglass pools are limited in size owing to transportation limitations. The average fiberglass pool is 32′ long. Fiberglass pools are manufactured upside-down on a mold to produce a smooth inside surface. (Molds are limited to selected pool shapes and sizes.) A layer of gelcoat with the desired color is applied to the mold, followed by layers of resin-saturated fiberglass to produce proper thickness. Reinforcement is added as the fiberglass is laminated. The finished pool is lifted from the mold after resins have cured. Fiberglass shells are flexible and can absorb minor ground movement without structural damage.

Installation is a relatively easy process. After excavation, plumbing is installed and a bed of sand is contoured to fit the shell. A crane places the shell into the sand-filled excavation and plumbing is connected. Finally, the excavation is backfilled with sand at the same time water is added to the pool. A concrete bond beam and deck are poured around the pool perimeter. (See Figure 11.2.)

The major advantage of the fiberglass pool is low maintenance. The smooth fiberglass surface is easy to clean and prevents algae formation.

The color is manufactured into the material. If the surface is damaged, the alkaline content of the water is high, or the pool water is improperly maintained, it will

cause the pool surface to chalk and the finish to fade. At that point, it may become necessary to paint the fiberglass pool.

Resins used in the construction of fiberglass pools will harden and gain strength over time. Manufacturers of fiberglass pools offer warranties against structural failure. Kits are available for repairing fiberglass pool shells.

Vinyl

Vinyl has made swimming pools more affordable. Manufacturers can fabricate a vinyl liner to fit most pool shapes and/or sizes.

Vinyl pools must have a wall to support the weight of the water. These walls are plastic, metal, or wood and must conform to the vinyl liner configuration. Support walls carry a different warranty from that of the liner. Some manufacturers provide a 25-year (yr.) warranty. (See Figure 11.3.)

Molded plastic support walls are corrosion resistant and less expensive than metal or wood walls. Plastic panels are constructed of resin-impregnated fiberglass to form a strong, laminated wall with uniform thickness. Fiberglass panels require reinforcing steel in the wall to obtain the strength required to support the weight. Panels are also cast in a mold-resisting-polypropylene.

■ FIGURE 11.3

Vinyl-lined pools are placed over walls supported by braces. Walls and braces are made from plastic, metal, or wood.

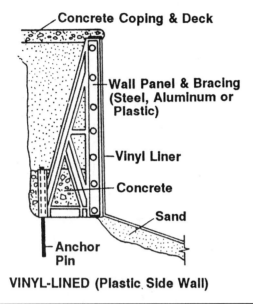

VINYL-LINED (Plastic Side Wall)

Fiberglass and polymer panels are structurally supported with struts when erected on-site. These struts can be metal or fiberglass.

Metal panels have proven to be a durable pool wall material. Galvanized steel, stainless steel and aluminum are used for support wall construction in vinyl-lined pools. Stainless steel is both strong and corrosion resistant but is the most expensive pool wall. Galvanized steel has strength and is protected from corrosion unless the surface is damaged. Aluminum is lightweight, corrosion resistant, and flexible.

Wood support walls should be pressure treated with a preservative. Wood wall panels are made from pressure-treated ½″ marine plywood. All of the wood that comes into contact with the ground and pool should be pressure treated, not just painted at the time of installation.

The pressure-treating process involves using approved chemicals that are forced into the wood fibers under a minimum of 100 pounds per square inch (psi). The chemicals are sealed into the wood and will not wash out. It is possible to purchase sidewall structures that are self-supporting, making them ideal for both in-ground and above-ground pools. Most above-ground and in-ground pools use either metal or fiberglass panels.

Vinyl liners are available in various colors and patterns. Common designs include imitation tile patterns and pebble designs in blue, black, white, and earthtones. Vinyl liners also can be purchased in solid colors for the pool bottom to absorb the sun's ultraviolet rays to reduce heating costs. Inhibitors have been developed to make vinyl liners more resistant to deterioration from sunlight, alkalinity, and pool chemicals. Most vinyl liners carry a 15-yr. warranty from the manufacturer.

Plumbing

Swimming pool construction must adhere to code requirements and safety precautions, and compliance with these may not be apparent on inspection of the pool. Groundwater can build up an extremely high pressure and raise a swimming pool out of the ground. Groundwater may be from underground springs or a high water table. To combat this problem, swimming pool contractors must install a hydrostatic valve in the main drain with a perforated drain pipe extending down into a gravel bed. Groundwater pressure causes the float in the hydrostatic valve to lift, allowing the groundwater to discharge to the pump and filter. When the groundwater pressure drops to a safe level, the float in the hydrostatic valve will reseat and will not allow pool water to leak. If there is a possibility of underground springs or a high water table or if underground water is suspected, it is a good idea to install a hydrostatic valve for concrete pools and fiberglass pool shells. An inspector cannot determine whether the swimming pool is equipped with a hydrostatic valve. To determine whether the swimming pool is level, the inspector should check the water level on the tile. Most contractors build swimming pools level within ¼″.

Swimming pools 1″ or more out of level indicate groundwater and/or expansive soil problems. Soils can expand as much as 50 percent or more and exert a force of 3 tons (t) to 16 t per square foot (sq. ft.), which is enough pressure to crack the sides of concrete pools and collapse walls of vinyl-lined and fiberglass pools. The sides, ends, and bottom of the pool should be inspected for cracks or other irregularities.

Plumbing installation for a swimming pool should be done by a licensed plumbing contractor who is familiar with swimming pool codes. Plumbing installation includes main drain lines, skimmer lines, return lines, and other lines that will not be accessible after the concrete is sprayed or poured. (See Figure 11.4.)

Plumbing must be pressurized to check for leaks before the concrete is installed. All plumbing should be checked for leaks when the pool and equipment have

■ **FIGURE 11.4**

Plumbing installation includes main drain lines, skimmer lines, return lines, and other lines not accessible after the swimming pool is constructed.

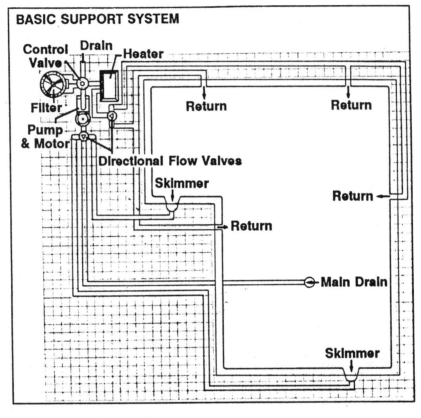

been connected. After the system has been operating regularly, the water circulation should be smooth. No air should be in the return line, evidenced by air bubbles at the pool returns. Air bubbles indicate a leak on the suction side of the pump. Another indication is when the pump has to be primed. Inspectors should not try to determine where a leak is located. Leaks on the pressure side of the pump appear as wet areas in the yard and/or loss of pool water.

Heaters are usually gas or electric. Gas heaters require that a gas service line be installed by a plumber, and gas lines must be pressurized and inspected.

Electrical System

Electrical work for a swimming pool should be completed by a licensed electrical contractor. The electrical system for a swimming pool must be protected by grounding (bonding) and/or a ground fault circuit interrupter (GFCI). The electrical contractor should install a number 8-gauge (ga.) bare copper wire to rebar used in concrete pools. The number 8-ga. bare copper wire is also connected to swimming pool lights, diving boards, slides, ladders, and the circulating pump case. The number 8-ga. bare copper wire is also called *bonding wire*. The pool and all equipment are bonded together to reduce the possibility of electrical shock. (See Figure 11.5.)

Pool lights, smaller pools, and spas are required to have a GFCI on all electrical circuits. The inspector should test the operation of all GFCIs.

Capacity

Pool capacity must be known to determine the correct size of mechanical equipment—e.g., pump filter and heater—and to maintain the chemical balance of pool water. The capacity of a vinyl-lined or fiberglass pool is usually furnished in the manufacturer's specifications. Concrete pools may not have identical

■ **FIGURE 11.5**

Electrical components of a swimming pool must be properly grounded.

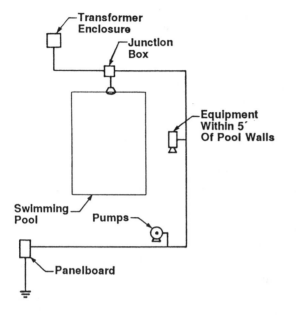

ft. by 7.5 provides the total gallonage of water in the pool. The average depth of a pool is determined by adding the depth at the shallow end to the depth at the deep end and dividing the sum by two.

For irregular pools, divide the pool into basic geometric shapes and find the number of gal. in each section. Add all totals to provide the total number of gal. in the pool.

For oval pools, multiply length × width × pi (3.14) × the average depth to provide pool capacity in cu. ft. For round pools, multiply the radius × pi (3.14) × the average depth to determine pool capacity in cu. ft.

Pumps

A swimming pool pump must have adequate power to cycle total water volume of a pool through the filter in a given number of hours. Turnover rate is the number of hours required to completely recycle the total water volume through the filter while filtering out dirt and debris. Turnover rates for residential pools range from 8 hours (hr.) to 12 hr. (See Figure 11.6.)

Pumps must be sized to overcome all resistance in the plumbing system. A spa built into a pool using the same pump must be sized correctly to maintain filtration requirements and operate the hydrojets in the spa. Some spas may require separate pumps independent of the pool pump.

capacity owing to variations in dimensions. Pool capacity is determined by multiplying the pool surface area by the average depth to determine the number of cubic feet (cu. ft.) of water in the pool. One cu. ft. of water equals 7.5 gallons (gal.). Multiplying the number of cu.

■ **FIGURE 11.6**

A swimming pool pump must have adequate power to cycle the total water volume of a pool through the filter in a given number of hours.

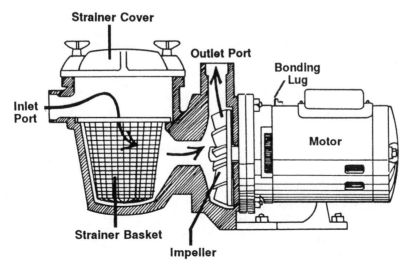

Flow rate is the number of gal. of water a pump cycles through the system per minute (min.). Flow rate is calculated by dividing pool capacity by turnover rate in hr. to obtain gal. per hr. This provides flow rate in gal. per min.

When the flow rate has been established, water resistance in the plumbing system is computed. System water resistance depends on the distance water must be pumped from the pool to the filter and the heater, the inside diameter of piping, and the number of fittings in the system.

Centrifugal pumps circulate water through the swimming pool system. Centrifugal pumps have a shaft-mounted impeller constructed of bronze, cast iron, or high-impact plastic driven by an electric motor. Proper pump size is chosen by the pool designer or pool contractor.

The centrifugal pump is used for swimming pools because it moves large volumes of water at low pressure. All pool pumps are self-priming. Once operating and when all air is removed from the system, the pump becomes a closed system. Most pools are designed with return lines below the pool's water level, which creates a closed system. Once a closed system is filled, water in the return lines causes a siphoning action that lifts water through the system. In a closed system, the height of the support system above the pool has little effect on resistance. Centrifugal pumps are water-cooled and must never operate dry. All swimming pool pumps must have a strainer basket on the suction side of the pump. The strainer basket traps leaves and debris that would clog or damage the pump's impeller.

Pool pump sizes are identified by horsepower (hp) and range from ½ hp to 3 hp. Large pumps are used to power hydrojets for spas.

To determine the electrical efficiency of a pump, divide the gal. of water by the pump rating in kilowatts (kw). If the pump is rated in hp, convert hp to kw by multiplying hp × 0.74. Kilowatts divided by the gal. pumped in 1 hr. yields the efficiency of the pump. The higher the number, the more efficient the pump.

Surface Skimmers

All swimming pools should be designed with one or more surface skimmers. Surface skimmers prevent oil, suntan lotion, floating algae, leaves, and debris from collecting and remaining on the surface of the pool and also play an important part in circulation. The main drain is located in the deepest part of the pool and will not pull these surface materials down. Skimmers are equipped with a strainer basket to trap leaves and large debris. (See Figure 11.7.)

Top-loading skimmers have an access cover that is flush with the pool deck. Top-loading skimmers are installed at the time the pool is constructed.

Front-loading skimmers are designed for above-ground pools and spas. The strainer basket is removed from the front through the skimmer opening to the pool. Skimmers are made of durable plastic and are installed as prefabricated units.

The surface skimmer is equipped with a weir. A weir is a gate that rises and falls with the water level so only a thin sheet of surface water is skimmed into the basket. Some surface skimmers have additional features, such as a low-water protector, an electrical pump control, and an automatic water level control. Surface skimmers may also use a cartridge filter, an automatic chlorinator, and a water flow adjuster between the skimmer and main drain for a more balanced system. Surface skimmers may have a connection for use when vacuuming the pool. If the pool is equipped with an overflow, the overflow pipe usually is located at the top of the skimmer.

The skimmer will be most effective if it is located on the downwind side of the pool. The wind pushes the surface debris to the skimmer.

■ **FIGURE 11.7**

Top-loading skimmers have an access cover, a floating weir, and a strainer basket.

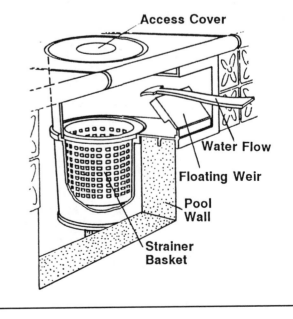

■ **FIGURE 11.8**

Three filters used with swimming pools and spas are high-rate sand, diatomaceous earth, and cartridge.

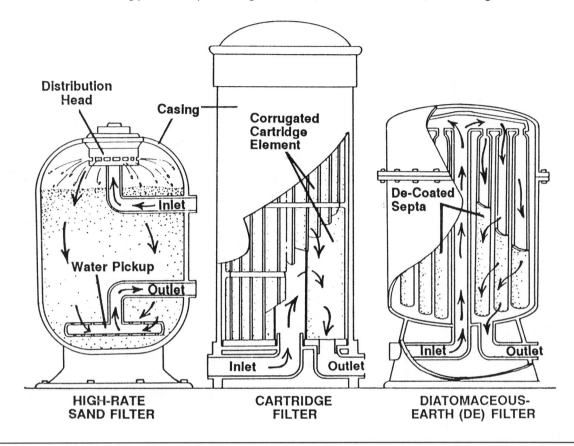

HIGH-RATE SAND FILTER   CARTRIDGE FILTER   DIATOMACEOUS-EARTH (DE) FILTER

Filtration Systems

A swimming pool filtration system is composed of the pump, surface skimmer, recirculating pipe and filter. Pumps and skimmers are manufactured from stainless steel, plastics, and bronze or materials that are nonferrous.

The filter system removes debris and solids from pool water. The filter system also dispenses chemicals throughout the pool water. A properly designed system should recycle all water in the pool through the filter in 8 to 12 hr. If proper circulation is not maintained, the pool water will become stagnant. Water seldom circulates through the filter system without pump operation.

If equipped with a heater, the filter also moves hot water evenly throughout the pool. The three pool filters are the high-rate sand filter, diatomaceous earth (DE) filter, and cartridge filter. (See Figure 11.8.)

If properly maintained, all three pool filters provide effective service. The filter case is manufactured from stainless steel, fiberglass, and/or high-impact plastic. A pool filter should last approximately ten years. Some communities specify the pool filter and equipment that must be installed. The pool filter size is measured in sq. ft. The DE filter size is determined by measuring the surface area of grids, which are called *septa*. The septa are clothlike membranes that are manufactured of a synthetic fabric that is not affected by pool chemicals. The grids or elements inside the filter are more effective than 1' of sand. The high-rate sand filter size is determined by measuring the surface area of the sand.

Small to medium-sized pools often have a cartridge filter installed in the skimmer. Cartridge filters are located below the skimmer basket and are plumbed to the main drain. Cartridge filters are commonly used with above-ground pools and vinyl-lined pools.

DE filters have a capacity of approximately 20 gal. of water per sq. ft. of filter area. High-rate sand filters are rated at approximately 20 gal. of water per min. per sq. ft. of filter area. Factors used to determine the filter size

■ **FIGURE 11.9**

The gas pool heater is the most economical.

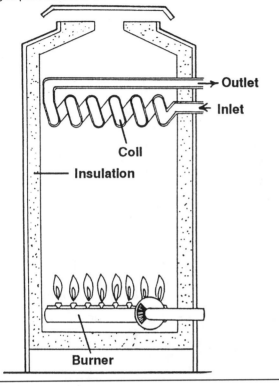

include the same elements used to determine the pump size: the pool capacity and turnover rate. The flow rate of the pump should match the filter size.

High-Rate Sand Filter

High-rate sand filters are manufactured of fiberglass, stainless steel, or high-impact plastic. High-rate sand filters are pressure vessels with a system of drains and water distribution that maintains a nonturbulent water flow through the filter. The filter consists of special grades of sands. Most filter manufacturers recommend sand of 0.45- to 0.55-millimeter (mm.) grain size or number 20 silica sand. Clean sand of this size removes particles as small as 15 microns from the water.

The filter is equipped with a pressure gauge to register operating pressures. Operating pressure ranges from 2 psi to 20 psi or higher, determined by variables such as distance between the pool and equipment, elevation of the pump, and size of the drain lines.

Manufacturers recommend backwashing the filter when the pressure increases by 50 percent over the operating pressure when the sand is clean. Backwashing the filter before it is required reduces filter efficiency. A

pool dealer provides an estimate of how often the filter requires backwashing.

The high-rate sand filter has a backwash valve connected to the plumbing between the pump discharge and filter. The backwash valve reverses the water flow, expels waste from the system, and cleans the sand. The pump motor must remain off when the backwash valve is moved.

High-rate sand filters require 50 to 250 gal. of water to backwash the filter. Water used during backwash is disposed of through a storm or sanitary sewer. However, with a sand filter, water may be drained into a dry well or a seepage pit. If the pool and filter are properly maintained, the sand lasts for several years.

DE Filter

Diatomaceous earth is a sedimentary rock composed of microscopic fossil skeletons of diatoms, small, freshwater marine plankton. DE rock is mined, crushed, washed, sized, and sold as a white powder. Filtering occurs through a thin layer of DE, which coats the septa. Grid material used for the septa supports the DE. The filter has no filtering ability without the DE coating and should not be operated without the coating. The pores in the septa become clogged and cannot be washed freely. This causes permanent damage, and the septa must be replaced.

The DE solution must be replaced after each backwashing. DE is mixed with water and poured into the skimmer with the pump operating to coat the septa. The required amount of DE is determined by the number of sq. ft. of filter area. Usually 1 pound (lb.) of DE is required for every 10 sq. ft. of filter area. DE is sold by volume, not weight. A 1-lb. container holds approximately ½ lb. of DE. The filter is cleaned by backwashing, with the backwash valve turned to reverse the flow of water in the tank and pump the waste from the system. The DE filter has a gauge on top of the filter tank to indicate pressure inside the tank. Waste material inside the tank increases pressure on the gauge.

It is necessary to know the operating pressure of the clean filter when the system is operating. It is impossible to predict the actual operating pressure because no two systems operate the same. Filter backwashing is normally required when the pressure increases 7 to 10 psi. Cleaning the filter when it is not necessary is a waste of time and money; however, when the filter is allowed to operate at excessive pressures (over 10 psi), it shortens the life of the pump and motor.

Waste from backwashing a DE filter is discharged to a storm or sanitary sewer. Waste from a DE filter should not be discharged to a dry well without a separation tank. A separation tank allows water to pass through a bag, which traps waste. After backwashing is complete, the bag is removed, emptied, washed and replaced in the separation tank. Clean water is discharged back to the pool. Without the use of a separation tank, DE will clog a dry well or drainfield.

Cartridge Filter

The cartridge filter is easy to clean, convenient and less complicated than the DE filter or high-rate sand filter. The life span of a cartridge is determined by pool use and environment.

The cartridge is suspended in a filter tank, and water is pumped through the cartridge. Dirt and debris in the water are trapped in the filter fabric, which does not consistently trap the smaller particles. Cartridge filters do not require backwashing and no filtering product is added after cleaning. The cartridge filter, however, requires approximately twice as many sq. ft. of cleaning surface as the DE filter.

The cartridge filter should have a pressure gauge at the top of the filter. The cartridge requires cleaning and/or changing when the gauge pressure increases approximately 8 psi over the normal operating pressure.

Heaters

Pool heaters are fueled by gas, oil, solar heat, and electricity. Where natural gas is available, the gas heater is the most economical. If natural gas is not available, the next economical energy choice would be propane gas or oil. (See Figure 11.9.)

A solar heating system also can heat pool water; however, it is not feasible in all parts of the United States. Solar covers can be used to raise water temperature and hold heat in the pool.

Several other heaters are used for heating pool water. Electric heaters have heating elements in the tank. Gas heaters use an open flame to heat water. Coil heaters have copper coils enclosed in a heat exchanger. The kind of energy used to heat pool water is a matter of preference.

To select the proper size of pool heater, it is important to consider the total pool surface area, spas, foundations, average air temperature of the coldest month the pool or spa will be used, and desired water temperature. Other factors that should be considered are wind patterns, pool location, and altitude.

The National Spa and Pool Institute recommends 78 degrees Fahrenheit (°F) as a comfortable temperature for pools. The American Red Cross and various health clubs recommend a temperature range between 78°F and 82°F. Temperature is a trade-off between comfort and cost. Fuel costs rise approximately 10 percent for each degree over 78°F.

To calculate the desired temperature rise from the proper-sized heater, subtract the average temperature for the coldest month the pool will be used from the desired pool temperature. The difference is the temperature rise that is required from the heater. Most pool heater manufacturers provide a chart that combines all of the information necessary to find the heater that will meet the requirements.

Gas heaters are rated in British thermal units (Btu). Electric heaters are sized in kw. A Btu is the amount of energy required to raise the temperature of 1 lb. of water 1°F. One kw. equals 3.412 Btu. To find the Btu rating of an electric heater, find the wattage on the nameplate/dataplate. Watts (w) × 3.412 equals the Btu rating.

The American Gas Association claims gas heaters are approximately 70 percent efficient and electric heaters are virtually 100 percent efficient in heat transfer. Electric heaters are less economical to operate than gas. Larger heaters require less time to reach and maintain desired temperatures.

Solar Heating

Solar energy can be used to heat swimming pools. The solar energy heating system normally is an open-loop system that pumps pool water through solar collectors on the roof. Water passes through solar collectors and is heated and carried back to the pool. The collectors act as the heat exchanger. A closed-loop solar heating system circulates antifreeze as a heat exchanger. (See Figure 11.10.)

The pool water is piped through the piping in the heat exchanger and is returned to the pool. In the open-loop system, collectors are usually made of plastic pipe. Several types of plastics are used. The drawback to the open-loop system is that if metal collectors are used, the collectors corrode and develop a scale buildup from improperly treated water or extremely hard water, causing serious damage to the system.

Swimming pool solar collectors lie flat on the roof and are usually made of black plastic with rubber man-

■ **FIGURE 11.10**

Typical solar system for a swimming pool.

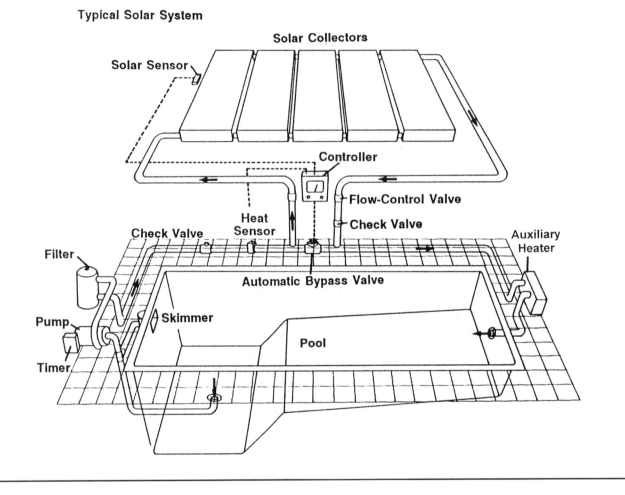

ifolds on top and bottom. It is important that the collectors be above the pool and have ⅛″ per ft. slope in the direction of flow. Collectors should have a flow rate of 2.0 to 2.5 gal. per min. per collector. At this flow rate, the temperature should rise 3°F to 7°F. Collectors located above the pool with an appropriate slope allow water to drain back into the pool when the system is off.

An automatic control has a sensor to compare the temperature at the top of the collectors with the temperature of a sensor in the pool pipe that carries the pool water. This second sensor is located in the bottom of the pipe and is sealed with silicone. The automatic control powers a diverter valve when the temperature differential is 5°F and de-energizes the valve at 2°F. The diverter valve is a three-way valve that routes pool water away from the bypass to the collectors. This non-positive-sealing valve is used to ensure collector drainage.

Because the diverter valve is not positive sealing, there must be manual valves in the piping system. Manual valves are required to isolate collectors and are usually ball type and located close to the diverter valve. Manual valves must be closed in the winter to prevent water from being forced through the collectors. If water gets into the collectors or collector pipes in the winter, they could freeze and split.

The automatic control system must be equipped with a vacuum breaker/vent valve. It should be located at the highest point in the piping system and positioned vertically. The vacuum breaker/vent valve allows air to vent during filling and air to enter during collector drainage.

Collectors

Swimming pool solar collectors are less expensive than domestic water heating collectors. They are con-

■ **FIGURE 11.11**

Automatically controlled pool timers maintain proper chemical balance and filtration for pool water.

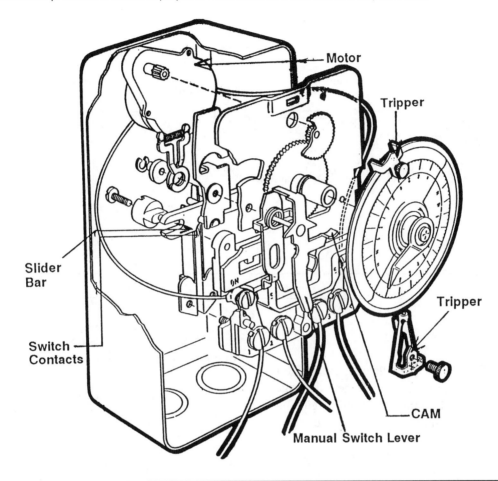

structed of black plastic that unrolls with a manifold at each end. The tubing that constitutes the piping system is usually polyvinyl chloride (PVC) pipe.

System Operation

An automatic controller monitors sensor temperature at the top of the collectors. It compares the collector temperature with the temperature of a similar sensor in the pool piping. If the collector sensor is warmer than the pool sensor, the controller opens a diverter valve, allowing the pool pump to move water through the collectors. If the collector sensor cools to pool sensor temperature, the controller breaks power to the valve. The valve shifts to allow pool water flow back through the pool piping as before.

Piping Slope

The collector piping must have a slight upward slope in the direction of water flow to allow water to return to the pool easily when the system is off.

Clocks and Timers

Automatically controlled timers maintain proper chemical balance and filtration for pool water. Timers operate equipment at preset times. (See Figure 11.11.)

The most common automatic control is a 24-hr. electric clock with adjustable contacts that operates the filtration system. A more sophisticated timer is programmable and operates the pool sweep, spa, heater and lights, as well as the filtration system. Timers can provide up to six program settings per day.

■ FIGURE 11.12

The deck should slope away from the pool to provide drainage, and the pool coping should be above deck level.

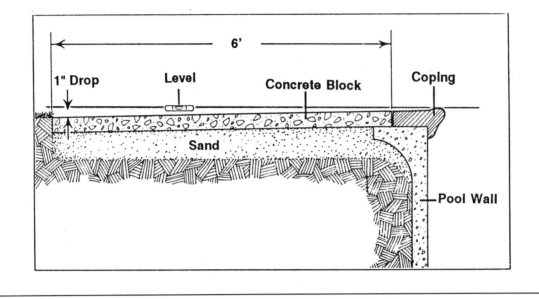

Automatic Cleaners

Two kinds of automatic pool cleaners are agitator and vacuum cleaners. Agitator pool cleaners dislodge debris from the sides and bottom of the pool by agitating the water. This allows water to circulate the debris and dirt to the skimmers and out the main drain. This system operates off the pool filter pump and does not use any additional energy. Vacuum pool cleaners roam the bottom of the pool and collect debris into a bag or are connected to the filtration system. Filtration systems have a pump to operate the vacuum independently of the pool filter pump. The pool sweep pump, however, should not operate unless the pool filter pump is operating.

Decking

The deck around the pool and any other paved surfaces are functional and versatile landscaping tools. Most pools are surrounded by a symmetrical or free-form deck. In addition to creating a pool frame, the deck provides a safe walkway around the pool. The pool deck should be designed to provide adequate space for pool furniture, slides, diving boards, and lounging.

When choosing decking material, the deck must be safe underfoot and not slippery when wet. The material should be heat reflective to create a cooler surface. The deck must slope away from the pool approximately 1″ in 6′. The slope prevents rainwater, water from a sprinkler or hose, and pool water splashed out on the deck from draining into the pool. (See Figure 11.12.) The deck surface should be easy to clean.

Poured concrete is the most common and versatile deck material. A properly reinforced concrete deck requires little maintenance and may be expected to last many years. Some fiberglass and vinyl-lined pools are designed with poured concrete decks as an integral part of the pool structure. The deck adds strength to pool walls.

The concrete surface may be finished in many different ways. Exposed aggregate is one of the most popular finishes for concrete decks. The pebble effect is attractive and provides a safe, nonslip, low-glare surface. Other surfacing materials are manufactured under different trade names. One of the most popular brands is Kool-crete. Kool-crete is available in several colors and is applied similarly to plaster over the finished concrete slab. It has a porous, nonslip surface that feels cooler than concrete and most other masonry materials.

Though concrete is the most common material used for pool decking, many other materials are used, such as brick, flagstone, tile, or wood. When these materials are used for decking, it is best if they are laid on a concrete slab. The concrete slab provides a solid, clean base and facilitates water drainage away from the pool.

Decking material is chosen to blend with or match other paved areas and resists acid, algae, bacteria, chemicals, fungi, and freezing. The inspector should observe

■ **FIGURE 11.13**

Swimming pool accessories include slides, ladders, and diving boards.

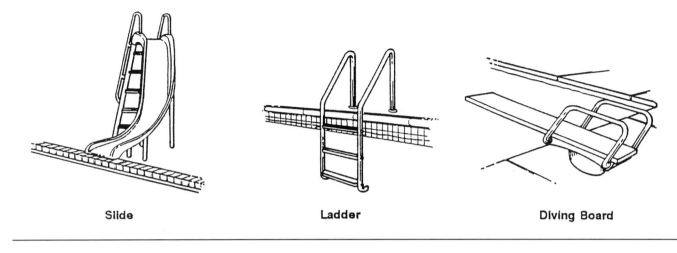

| Slide | Ladder | Diving Board |

the condition of the decking and check that the decking slopes away from the pool. If the pool has coping around it, the coping should be sealed to the deck.

Accessories

Swimming pool accessories include diving boards, slides, and ladders. (See Figure 11.13.) Accessories must be bonded to the pool steel with number 8 bare copper wire.

Diving Boards

Most city codes require that a pool have a 7½′ depth before a diving board is permitted. In addition, most local codes require minimum dimensions. Diving boards must be anchored to the deck.

Slides and Ladders

Pool slides must be anchored to the deck and should be located away from diving boards or other accessories. The water depth at the location of the slide must be 4′ for short slides and 6′ for long slides. Slides are manufactured from fiberglass with metal frames. Some slides have water jets to maintain wet and slippery surfaces. Safety requirements must be observed, which include the extension of the lip of the slide over the side of the pool. Water from these jets should run down the slide into the pool.

Gunite pools usually have built-in steps at the shallow end of the pool; however, many pool owners have ladders at the deep end. These ladders may be built into the side of the pool with grab rails on either side of the steps, or the ladders can be stainless steel, installed in the deck and extending into the pool.

Vinyl-lined pools and some fiberglass pools require ladders. Above-ground pools require a double access ladder to allow access to the pool as well as egress from it. If the pool is in-ground, the pool requires an inpool ladder. Ladders that come in contact with the water are usually stainless steel to prevent corrosion.

Pool Water Test Kit

Proper chemistry must be maintained to keep the pool water clean and disinfected. A pool water test kit is a necessary pool accessory. Pool water should be checked in hot summer months at least three to four times a week and at least once a week in colder weather. A water sample should be taken to a pool supplier to obtain a complete water analysis. The proper balance of acidity, alkalinity, and minerals in pool water must be maintained.

Fences

All swimming pools, spas, and hot tubs must be enclosed with a fence, building wall, or a wall that completely surrounds and obstructs access to the swimming pool.

The top of the obstruction, whether a fence or wall, must be a minimum of 48″ above grade measured on the side of the obstruction that faces away from the pool. The maximum clearance between grade and bottom of the fence or wall is 2″.

■ **FIGURE 11.14**

Freestanding spas, which are not connected to a pool, contain their own plumbing systems.

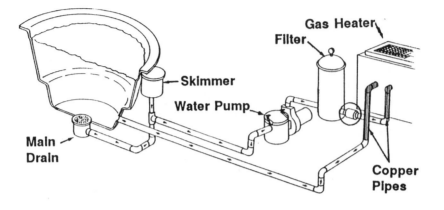

Where the fence has horizontal and vertical members, the horizontal members must be located on the pool side of the fence. The spacing between the vertical members should not exceed 4". When using a metal fence with vertical bars, the opening between the vertical bars must not allow passage of a 4"-diameter sphere.

All access gates must be self-closing and self-latching locking devices and should open out and away from the pool. The locking device must be located a minimum of 3" below the top of the gate, and there must be no opening within 18" of the locking device larger than ½".

Where a wall of a dwelling is part of the obstruction, the pool must be equipped with a power safety cover or all the doors with direct access to the pool must be equipped with self-closing and self-latching devices and alarms.

With above-ground pools, the ladder must be capable of being secured or removed to prevent access to the pool.

■ SPAS AND HOT TUBS

Spas and hot tubs are therapeutic and relaxing. Many physicians prescribe hydrotherapy for people with physical ailments.

Spa Construction

Concrete spas are available in various shapes and sizes. Plastered spas must have ceramic tile at water level to prevent mineral scale from forming on the plas-

tered surface. When the spa is an integral part of a pool, the same filtration and heating system can be used. Chemical water balance is maintained by using the valving and plumbing of the pool.

Economical spas are prefabricated from fiberglass in various sizes and shapes. These spas are freestanding and are not connected to a pool. (See Figure 11.14.)

Prefabricated spas are preplumbed and installed either above or below ground. The spa, whether gunite or prefabricated, holds 350 gal. to 1,000 gal. of water, with some exceptions. (See Figure 11.15.)

Larger spas require larger heaters. Maximum recommended temperature for water is 104°F. The best water temperature averages between 98°F and 100°F. Gas heaters are the most economical. Water should be frequently tested in a spa because chemicals dissipate faster in warm water.

Water action in a spa is created by a series of hydrojets or venturi jets. Venturi jets restrict water flow in a tube which raises water pressure at the nozzle. Airflow into the jets is regulated by air inlets that either are open pipes in the deck or have screw-on covers. (See Figure 11.16.)

Hydrojets have a booster that pumps air through the venturi. The pump must be protected from flooding by installing check valves or by installing the pump above the spa's water level.

Hot Tub Construction

Hot tubs are manufactured from cypress, cedar, oak, teakwood, or redwood. Redwood is the most desirable for hot tubs because of decay resistance. In addition,

■ FIGURE 11.15

Gunite and fiberglass spas are available in various sizes and shapes.

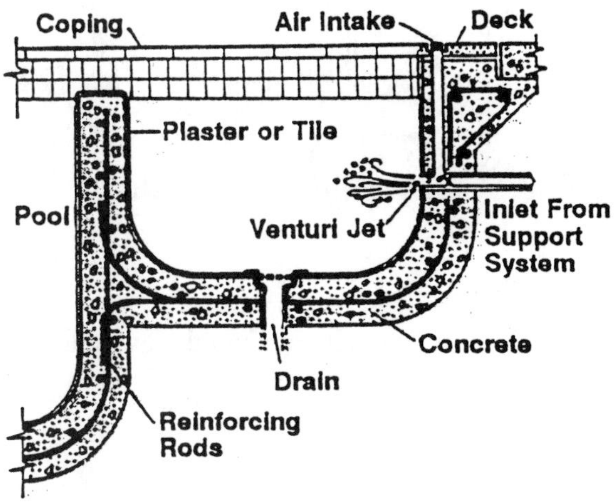

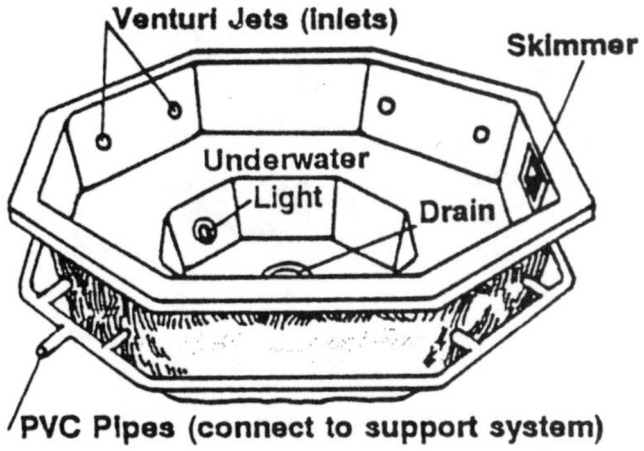

redwood will not splinter and is resistant to damage from chemicals and insects. Redwood and cedar are most suitable because they are fibrous and can absorb large amounts of water. The wood swells and seals itself to prevent leaks. Teakwood is the best choice because of its resistance to decay and its durability; however, the cost is prohibitive. Oak is hardwood, but requires high maintenance. Oak has layers of latewood (which makes up the grain) and heartwood that are susceptible to decay from the constant moisture.

The typical hot tub is 4' deep and ranges from 5' to 12' in diameter. A 4' deep and 10' diameter hot tub holds approximately 2,300 gal. of water and requires a foun-

■ FIGURE 11.16

Water action in a spa is created by a series of hydrojets or venturi jets.

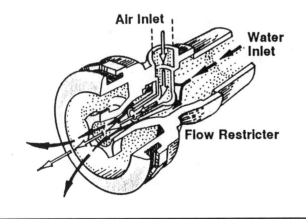

dation. Two factors critical in the installation of a hot tub are size and weight. For example, a hot tub holding approximately 2,300 gal. of water will weigh approximately 21,000 lb. when full of people and water. This hot tub requires a substantial foundation to hold the weight.

Before installing a hot tub, homeowners should check the local code requirements and obtain a building permit from the local authority.

A well-maintained hot tub should be drained and thoroughly cleaned approximately four times a year. The wood should not be allowed to dry out because it will not expand to reseal, causing the tub to leak and the wood to deteriorate more rapidly. A good hot tub, with proper maintenance, should last 10 to 15 yrs.

Hot tubs require a pump and motor, cartridge filter, and heater. (See Figure 11.17.) The motor can be 120V (volts) or 240V, and it requires a GFCI.

■ SAUNAS

Saunas originated in the Scandinavian countries, but have been popular in the United States for the past 25 to 30 yrs. Sauna manufacturers produce modular saunas as well as prefabricated saunas that may be assembled by the homeowner.

The sauna is an insulated wooden room heated 150°F to 200°F (sometimes higher) that provides a restorative environment for the body. The heat is very dry with usually less than 30 percent humidity, deep

■ **FIGURE 11.17**

Hot tubs require a pump and motor, cartridge filter, and heater.

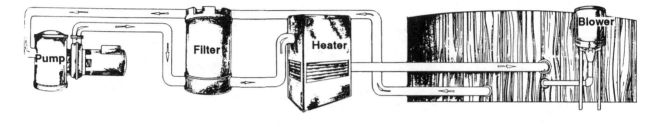

cleans the skin through induced perspiration, stimulates circulation, and reduces muscular tension. Robed only in a towel, users sit or lie on sauna benches for 10 to 20 min. If the user wants a burst of steam at intervals, water is thrown on the hot stones to produce steam and cause more perspiration to flow after. After the sauna, people normally take a cool shower, dive in the swimming pool, or flop in the snow. (See Figure 11.18.)

Saunas stimulate the cardiovascular system. A person who has a heart disease, has high blood pressure or diabetes, is taking antibiotics or other drugs, is pregnant, or is under the influence of alcohol, should not use the sauna without first checking with his or her physician. While a person uses the sauna, the pulse rate will increase and may cause dizziness or an upset stomach. If

this occurs, the person should leave the sauna immediately. Under no circumstances should a person stay in a sauna longer than 30 min.

Construction

Saunas may be freestanding or a separate room. A freestanding sauna must have a solid foundation. It will also be necessary to provide electricity, plumbing, and/ or gas. Saunas are built from redwood, cedar, spruce, Douglas fir, or cypress, and construction should be tongue and groove, double insulated, and sealed. The rooms are usually equipped with upper and lower benches, with the stove installed on a wall opposite the benches. The sauna should have adequate ventilation.

■ **FIGURE 11.18**

Saunas are rooms built from wood and are heated by a stove to temperatures that reach 150° F to 200° F.

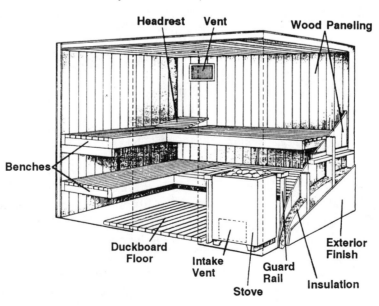

One vent will be behind the stove; the other vent will be on the opposite wall near the ceiling and will vent to the outside. Electrical work should be completed by a professional familiar with sauna codes, and the sauna drain should be properly plumbed. This is tied to the rebar in the footing in new south Florida construction.

The control panel, thermostat control, stove switch, timer, and light switch should be outside the room. Electrical wiring should withstand high temperatures and be moistureproof, and wires and controls should be in weathertight boxes. Doors must be double insulated and sealed. Sauna windows, regardless of size, should be double-pane, tempered glass.

Saunas must be properly vented to reduce high humidity, which causes mildew and wood rot. The residential inspector should check for mildew and wood rot around the exterior of a sauna.

Stoves

Electric stoves are wall mounted or freestanding. Heating elements are designed to heat a tray of stones, which may or may not come in direct contact with the element. Controls for the electric stove should be located outside the sauna. Room size dictates the size of the stove required to properly heat the sauna. Electric stoves are sized by kilovolt-amps (1KVA = 1,000 volt-amps). To find the proper size stove, the volume (vol.) of the room has to be known. This formula (volume = length × width × height) yields the vol. in cu. ft. Stove size should allow 1 KVA per 45 cu. ft. For example, a sauna measuring 6′ × 8′ × 7′ would have a volume of 336 cu. ft. Dividing 336 cu. ft. by 45 cu. ft. will show that a 7.5- or 8-KVA stove is needed for proper heating.

Gas stoves are thermostatically controlled and should be equipped with an automatic shut-off valve. The only difference between gas and electric stoves is the source of energy. It is important that the gas stove be properly sized for the room. It is again necessary to find the volume of the room. Gas heat is measured in Btus.

A sauna requires 1,000 Btus per 15 cu. ft. The 6′ × 8′ × 7′ room described above equals 336 cu. ft.; 336 divided by 15 equals 22.4. Therefore, it requires a 22,400 (22.4 × 1,000) Btu stove to properly heat the stones and room.

Clocks and Timers

The control panel should include a thermostat for temperature control and an on-off switch for the stove. All saunas should be equipped with an operational timer.

Accessories

Saunas should be equipped with a thermometer and hygrometer. The thermometer checks the interior temperature. The hygrometer measures humidity and should be installed on a wall away from the door, ventilator, and stove. Buckets and ladles used to throw water on stones should be made of wood, not metal.

Saunas need to be maintained after each use. They should be opened up to dry out. If there is covering or duck-board on the floor, it should be removed to allow the floor and covering to dry out. Depending on the amount of usage, the benches and headrests should be washed down with detergent to remove perspiration odors and stains.

■ REVIEW QUESTIONS*

1. What are the three types of pools?

   _____

   _____

   _____

2. When inspecting the swimming pool, the inspector must not attempt to leak test a pool on a residential inspection.

   A. True
   B. False

3. If the skimmer liner is cracked, it must be noted as a defect.

   A. True
   B. False

4. A swimming pool that has been winterized may be inspected.

   A. True
   B. False

5. The pool deck must always slope away from the pool.

   A. True
   B. False

6. When air bubbles are observed flowing through a swimming pool's returns, it indicates

   A. that the water level is too high in the pool.
   B. a leak on the suction side of the pump.
   C. that the pressure is too low on the filter gauge.

7. When the filter pump is not operating, the pool sweep pump and/or pool heater must operate.

   A. True
   B. False

8. All swimming pools and spas are required to be bonded and have GFCI-protected electrical equipment circuits.

   A. True
   B. False

9. Maximum water temperature for spa operation is 104°F.

   A. True
   B. False

10. All pool filters are required to have an operable pressure gauge.

    A. True
    B. False

11. A spa or hot tub can be prescribed by physicians for physical ailments.

    A. True
    B. False

12. Concrete spas are usually found as part of a swimming pool.

    A. True
    B. False

13. Prefabricated spas cannot be installed below ground.

    A. True
    B. False

14. A spa or hot tub must have a heater.

    A. True
    B. False

15. Water action in a spa or hot tub is created by a series of

    A. hydrojets.
    B. venturi jets.
    C. Both A and B
    D. Neither A nor B

16. Hot tubs always are manufactured from wood.

    A. True
    B. False

17. A hot tub does not need a foundation for support.

    A. True
    B. False

18. A hot tub should not be allowed to dry out.

    A. True
    B. False

19. A person with health problems should check with a physician before entering a sauna.

    A. True
    B. False

20. When a sauna is not vented properly, it can cause

    A. high humidity.
    B. mildew and wood rot.
    C. All of the above
    D. None of the above

■ INSPECTION CHECKLIST: SWIMMING POOLS AND SPAS

SWIMMING POOL

When inspecting a swimming pool, spa, hot tub, or sauna, the residential inspector should indicate that this is only a visual inspection. The inspector should not dismantle equipment or attempt to leak test a swimming pool or spa.

Yes No

☐ ☐ Can pool sides, bottom, main drain, inlet or return lines, light, or skimmers be observed?

☐ ☐ Are electrical or gas utilities operating properly?

☐ ☐ Has the pool been winterized or is water below the skimmer?

☐ ☐ Do weather conditions permit inspection?

☐ ☐ Does decking around the pool slope away from the pool? Check decking for cracks and/or scaling. If the pool has coping around the edges, the opening between the coping and deck should be sealed.

☐ ☐ Is the pool level? Observe the water level at the top of the pool. Measure from the top of the water to the coping or deck at different points around the pool.

☐ ☐ Are air bubbles present when the pump is operating? Air bubbles indicate a leak on the suction side of the pump. If the pump has to be primed, this indicates a leak on the suction side of the pump.

☐ ☐ Is the skimmer or skimmer liner cracked or broken? Skimmer covers should be in good working condition.

☐ ☐ Do the main drain cover, pool light, and built-in pool cleaner operate?

☐ ☐ Is pool light connected to a GFCI?

☐ ☐ Are the sides of the fiberglass pool bulging or distorted, implying either a leak or poor installation? Be extremely cautious if the fiberglass pool has been painted. Pay particular attention to patches or other repairs.

Yes No

☐ ☐ Is the surface of the vinyl-lined pool smooth? There should be no distortion or wrinkles in the liner. Wrinkles are an invitation to leaks. Pay particular attention to patches.

☐ ☐ Do the pump and filter equipment operate properly? Determine the filter system (i.e., high-rate sand, diatomaceous earth, or cartridge).

☐ ☐ Does the filter have a pressure gauge and, if so, is it operating?

☐ ☐ Does the timer operate properly? Unless the inspector is going to be around the pool for a long period of time, it is wise to disclaim checking the timer.

☐ ☐ Does the pool sweep operate properly? The filter pump must operate in order for the pool sweep pump to engage.

☐ ☐ Does the pool heater operate properly?

Note: *The filter pump must operate for the pool heater to operate.*

SPAS AND HOT TUBS

A freestanding spa or hot tub should have the same operating equipment as a swimming pool (i.e., pump, filter, and heater). In addition, the hot tub will have an air pump.

Yes No

☐ ☐ Are all 120V electrical circuits on a GFCI?

☐ ☐ Are all 240V circuits on separate circuits? All electrical work must be grounded.

☐ ☐ In a gunite spa, are the jets and blower operating properly? Note spa surface condition.

☐ ☐ In a fiberglass spa, are the pump, filter, heater,

Yes No

☐ ☐ In a hot tub, are the pump, filter, heater, jets, and blower operating properly?

☐ ☐ In a hot tub, is there evidence of wood rot and/or leaks? Observe the total tub perimeter.

☐ ☐ Are there leaks at the pump strainer or pump shaft?

☐ ☐ Does the pump vibrate or produce abnormal sounds?

☐ ☐ Is the filter equipped with a pressure gauge?

☐ ☐ Are there leaks around the filter or connections?

☐ ☐ Does the heater operate without leaks?

Note: *All equipment should operate for 10 to 20 min. to allow ample time for a proper inspection.*

SOLAR POOL HEATING

Yes No

☐ ☐ Are collectors facing south and not blocked from sunlight?

☐ ☐ Is collector tilt angle acceptable?

Yes No

☐ ☐ Can property damage result from installation?

☐ ☐ Have pipe hangers been used?

☐ ☐ Are manually operated isolation valves provided?

☐ ☐ Is controller bonded to the pool structure?

☐ ☐ Has the vacuum breaker/vent valve been properly installed?

☐ ☐ Are there leaks in piping and/or collectors?

☐ ☐ Are sensors installed properly?

SAUNAS

Yes No

☐ ☐ Is the sauna properly vented?

☐ ☐ Is the electrical wiring in weathertight enclosures?

☐ ☐ Is there evidence of mildew and wood rot?

☐ ☐ Are the controls for the stove located outside the sauna?

■ REPORTING GUIDELINES

Inspection reporting guidelines for swimming pools and spas incorporating the above checklist.

Swimming pools and equipment (spas and hot tubs). The inspector shall

- report the type of pool construction;
- report as in need of repair deficiencies in pool surfaces;
- report as in need of repair deficiencies in tiles, copings, and decks;
- report as in need of repair deficiencies in slides, steps, diving boards, and other equipment;
- report as in need of repair deficiencies in drains, skimmers, and valves;
- report as in need of repair pool lights that are missing, do not function, or lack ground fault circuit interrupter protection;
- report as in need of repair pump motors, controls, and sweeps that do not function or lack proper wiring and circuit protection;
- when inspecting a heater, report as in need of repair deficiencies that the standards of practice would require the inspector to report for a heating system;

■ REPORTING GUIDELINES *(Continued)*

- report as in need of repair gas heaters that use improper materials for the branch line and the connection to the appliance;

- report as in need of repair a gas unit that has no shut-off valve, an inaccessible valve, or a valve that leaks;

- report as in need of repair a pump motor, blower, or other electrical equipment, if visible, that lacks external grounding;

- report as in need of repair above-ground water leaks or deficiencies in the filter tank or pressure gauge; and

- report as in need of repair the absence of, or deficiencies in, fences, gates, or enclosures.

Specific limitations for swimming pools and equipment (spas and hot tubs). The inspector is not required to do the following:

- Dismantle or otherwise open any components or lines

- Uncover or excavate any lines or otherwise concealed components of the system or determine the presence of sub-surface leaks

- Fill the pool, spa or hot tub with water

- Determine the presence of subsurface water tables

- Inspect ancillary equipment such as computer controls, covers, chlorinators or other chemical dispensers, or water ionization devices or conditioners other than as required by this section

12

Termites and Other Wood-Destroying Insects

Many insects inhabit wooden structures when moisture conditions are excessive. Termites, particularly subterranean termites, dampwood termites, and Formosan termites, require moisture far beyond that normally found in residential structures. Beetles and carpenter ants also prefer moist wood structures.

■ TERMITES

Note: Some jurisdictions require separate licenses for termite inspections, and the inspector should check local codes.

Subterranean Termites

Termites cause tremendous wood damage. Termites break down dead wood and return it to the soil.

Lumber used in residential structures is susceptible to termites. The most common termites are the subterranean and drywood. Subterranean termites are active and found throughout the United States, although they are more predominant in the South and West. Subterranean termites live in colonies found in the soil. Each colony includes a king, a queen, workers, soldiers, and reproductives. (See Figure 12.1.)

The life cycle for subterranean and drywood termites is similar. Termites develop through three growth stages: egg, nymph, and adult.

Termite eggs are produced by a fertilized female, the queen. Termites hatching from eggs are nymphs and are white or cream colored, soft bodied, and blind. Nymphs have three pairs of legs, and though capable of moving, must first be cared for by adult termites. Later, nymphs feed on wood and care for themselves. In the

■ FIGURE 12.1

Subterranean termite colonies include winged reproductives, supplemental reproductives, workers, and soldier termites.

SUBTERRANEAN TERMITE COLONY

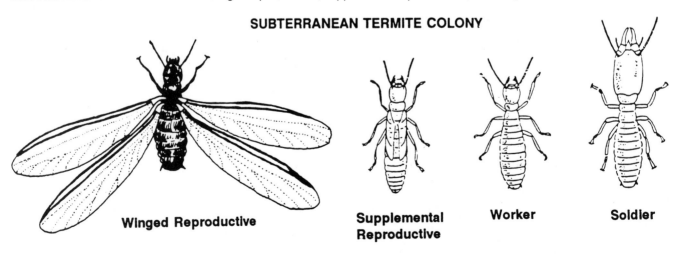

Winged Reproductive　　**Supplemental Reproductive**　　**Worker**　　**Soldier**

■ **FIGURE 12.2**

Termite life cycle tracks development from eggs to maturity.

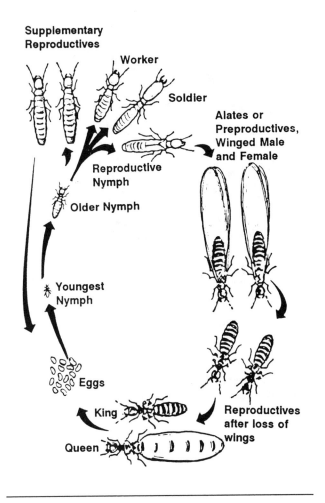

■ **FIGURE 12.3**

Subterranean termite shelter tubes located on a foundation wall are evidence of colony infestation.

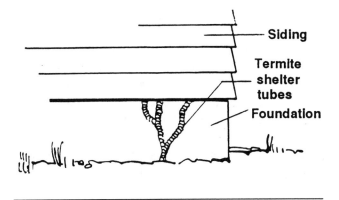

colony, some nymphs develop large heads, hard brown skin, and large jaws, or mandibles. These are the soldier termites. Other nymphs develop two pairs of wing pads on their backs and emerge as dark-colored, winged reproductives with fully developed eyes.

In very large colonies, some reproductives become mature males and females, but with arrested wing development. The supplemental reproductives may mate and never leave the colony. Reproductive needs of such colonies are often taken over entirely by supplemental reproductives. (See Figure 12.2.)

Worker termites are white and cannot live in sunlight. Termites require moisture, favorable temperatures, and a wood supply. Worker termites eat, digest, and share food with other members of the colony 24 hours a day. Because termites cannot live in sunlight or a

humid environment, workers dig tunnels to their food and water supply.

When wood is not immediately available, termites will construct shelter tubes leading from the soil to wood. These tubes serve as highways back to the colony and maintain the proper environment for termite survival. (See Figure 12.3.)

The tubes can go up walls, follow pipes, or stand free of support. Termites usually eat inside wood following the grain. Termite-damaged wood contains galleries, which are chamber-like voids in wood. Termite-damaged lumber may look sound on the outside but be hollow on the inside.

Residential inspectors should probe wood areas to detect termite damage. Check wood that is in direct contact with soil, such as exterior siding. Indicate damaged wood on the inspection report. With signs of active infestation, such as termite tunnels or active galleries, the inspector should suggest that a professional pest control company be consulted. The pest control applicator will apply chemical barriers around the house where termites are detected. Because termites cannot pass through these barriers and survive, termites in the residential structure will return to the soil and die. Those on the other side of the barrier cannot reach the home. When making an inspection under a house, use a respirator to protect against hazardous chemicals.

In areas of the country where termites are a major problem, builders often take preventive measures during construction. With slab-on-grade foundations, the ground is often treated before the slab is poured. Termite shields are often used in crawlspaces. These metal shields are placed over concrete piers, around pipes, and along perimeter walls. Termites can build their tunnels around metal, but shields make visual detection much easier.

Drywood Termites

Drywood termites are larger than subterranean termites. Drywood termite colonies appear in wood above ground. They have no connection with the ground and do not need the moisture provided by such a connection. These colonies are found in dead tree branches, dry tree stumps, and wood structures. Drywood termites can appear in all wood structures, from roof to subflooring. Infestation appears in and around a new colony and, if undisturbed, radiates outward. (See Figure 12.4.)

All nymphs in a drywood termite colony ultimately become either soldiers who protect the colony or swarmers (males and females, alates, kings, and queens) who leave the colony via a dispersal flight to pair off and start a new colony. A drywood termite colony never has the chance to accumulate large numbers of termites as does the subterranean termite colony because pairing occurs once every year. Because many new kings and queens are released, separate infestations in a single dwelling can be widespread and cause major damage to a wood structure.

Drywood termites do not build tubes. Drywood nymphs move to a new location only when wood is butted against infested wood. Drywood termites remove water from waste material and extrude pellet feces. When fecal pellets accumulate in the drywood termite channels and chambers, nymphs produce a kick hole to the outside and pellets are thrown out. The pellets on a flat surface reveal the presence of a drywood termite colony in the wood structure. The inspector should look for pellet piles when checking for drywood termites.

Drywood-termite-damaged wood contains chamber-like structures connected by galleries or tunnels that cut across the wood grain. Galleries have smooth surfaces and contain few or no fecal pellets.

Dampwood Termites

Dampwood termites are larger than subterranean or drywood termites. These termites are found in sound dead wood of standing trees, usually at their base, and in sound wood of fallen logs. Excessive moisture conditions caused by a leaky shower pan, poor drainage, a plumbing line leak, or poor ventilation can cause extensive damage to the timbers in the under areas of the

■ FIGURE 12.4

Drywood termite infestation causes structural damage in residential buildings.

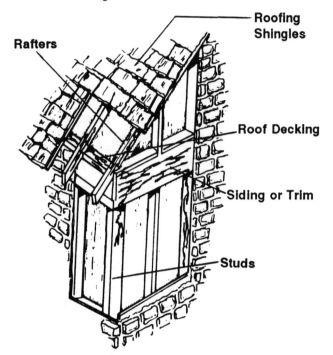

Rafters · Roofing Shingles · Roof Decking · Siding or Trim · Studs

Places where structural damage caused by drywood termites may be found.

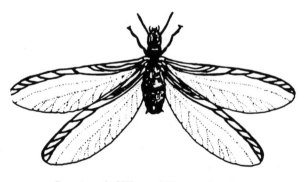

Drywood, Winged Reproductive

dwelling or if there is an excessive amount of moisture present. Dampwood termites produce pellets that look like drywood pellets, but larger. The pellets, usually found in the colony, tend to be caked together.

Swarms of dampwood termites have been recorded for almost every month of the year, but the peak of swarming season is late summer or early fall. A good-sized, healthy colony can have 4,000 termites.

Formosan Termites

Formosan termites are very active in Hawaii and were brought to the continental United States during and after World War II. Formosan termites are found in Texas, Louisiana, Florida, and South Carolina. These termites swarm from a well-developed colony. The winged reproductives swarm in the spring and fall in Hawaii. They swarm in the continental United States from March through July with peak swarming in June. Formosan termite soldiers are very aggressive.

The primary nest for Formosan termites is usually constructed below ground. Formosan termites are also capable of constructing aerial nests. An aerial colony is completely self-sustaining and has no connection to the ground. Sources of above-ground moisture are plentiful, even when no construction faults are evident. For example, Formosan termites have been observed drinking condensation that forms on cold water pipes and water that has gathered in rain gutters. Water gathering on flat roofs is an additional source. They have been recorded as remaining active for as long as eight months, living on the moisture from an auxiliary nest. Formosan termites have been known to penetrate mortar, asphalt, rubber, plastic, and creosote by secreting an acid substance from their frontal gland, and they also penetrate living trees and shrubs.

■ BEETLES

Powder-post beetles, furniture beetles, and old house borer beetles eat wood, but they cannot convert cellulose to nutrients. Beetles must obtain nourishment from starch and sugar stored in wood cells. Wood has no food value for beetles and is excreted as wood pellets, powder, or frass.

Woodboring beetles have four life stages: egg, larva, pupa, and adult. The life cycle of woodboring beetles varies. Some beetles complete a life cycle within a few months, while others live in wood for 20 to 30 years before emerging. Emergence holes of woodboring beetles are round, semicircular, or oval. Frass texture and location are used to identify beetles. (See Figure 12.5.)

Powder-post beetles are ⅛-inch (″) brown beetles. Larvae are small, whitish grubs that burrow through sound wood, packing the galleries with excrement. The life cycle of the powder-post beetle varies from three months to one year. Eggs are laid in wood pores, often before the wood is used for building material or fur-

niture. Powder-post beetles are often detected by finding galleries, exit openings, or fine powder sifting from the openings. Powder-post beetles attack only seasoned hardwoods. Emergence holes have ³⁄₃₂″ to ⅛″ diameters. Powder-post beetles can cause structural damage if infestation is not treated.

Furniture (or deathwatch) beetles are found in crawlspaces, studs, joists, and furniture. These beetles vary in size from ⅛″ to ⁵⁄₁₆″ in length and are black to reddish-brown. Furniture beetles attack both seasoned hardwoods and softwoods. Eggs are deposited in cracks in wood or near exit holes. Furniture beetles make emergence holes that vary in size from ¹⁄₃₂″ to ⅛″ in diameter. Furniture beetles develop in one to three years, depending on available food and moisture.

Old house borers attack suitable wood in new and old residential structures. Old house borers require seasoned softwood such as pine, spruce and fir, available in a wood surface without paint or other permanent finish.

Adult old house borers are ½″ to 1″ long. Old house borers excrete frass into wood tunnels. Extensive excavation along the grain results in a very thin shell of the original wood surface held in place by a few solid remnants of the wood interior. The emergence holes have slightly oval, ¼″ or less, diameters.

Old house borer infestation can continue for 3 to 12 years. Structural damage occurs in attics and other infrequently used areas. Infested wood is sometimes used in a new structure, and the emergence holes of adult borers may appear at the surface of hardwood, plaster, drywall, or paneling.

■ CARPENTER ANTS

Carpenter ants are wood-infesting insects found throughout the United States. They pose the biggest problems to control. They are not difficult to kill, as any one of a number of pesticides will easily cause their demise if the ants directly contact the wet material or the dust. But it is difficult to locate the nest or nests of carpenter ants, as they have the potential to travel long distances and hide in obscure places. Like carpenter bees, the carpenter ants do not feed on wood but merely excavate large, intricate galleries in it for the purpose of nesting and rearing their young. Initial evidence of infestation is often a small pile of sawdust debris that has sifted down from the gallery entrances, pushed out by the worker ants in an effort to keep living areas free of wood debris from their excavating activities.

■ **FIGURE 12.5**

Powder-post beetles, furniture beetles, and old house borer beetles exhibit unique wood-damaging characteristics.

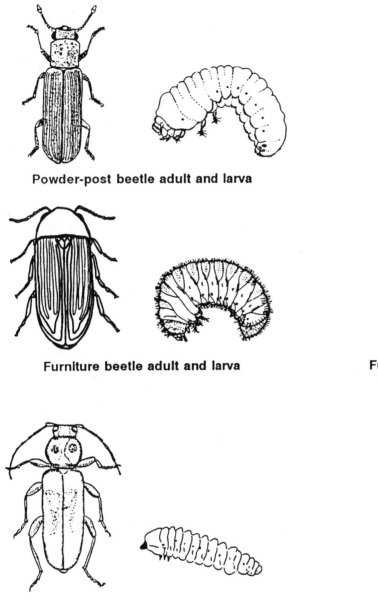

Powder-post beetle adult and larva

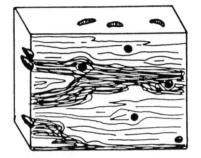

Powder-post beetle damage

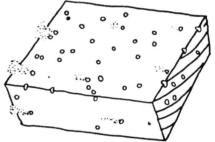

Furniture beetle exit holes and frass

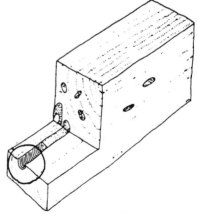

Old house borer emergence hole

Furniture beetle adult and larva

Old house borer adult and larva

Carpenter ants are social insects with one queen (rarely two) and a multitude of workers of various sizes, referred to as major, intermediate, and minor workers, depending on their size. In the mature colony division of labor is complete, with queens partaking solely in egg-laying and the various workers doing all the chores of egg and larval care and feeding, food gathering, nest construction and clearing, protection from enemies, etc. They cannot sting but have jaws strong enough to bite.

The life of a new carpenter ant colony begins as a mature colony produces eggs that develop into males and females with wings, referred to as *reproductives*. These new winged reproductives leave the nest for mating flights and disposal. Usually many carpenter ant colonies within a given area will swarm simultaneously, allowing for interbreeding among colonies and improvement of genetic traits within the species. Environmental factors such as temperature, moisture, light intensity, or the

■ **FIGURE 12.6**

Carpenter ants are among the largest ants found in the United States, ranging from ¼″ to ⅝″ long.

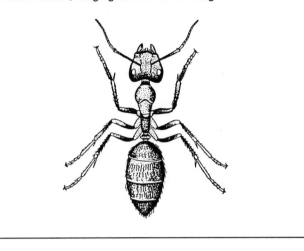

■ **FIGURE 12.7**

Carpenter ants and termites have distinct characteristics.

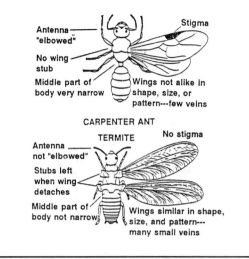

proper combination of several factors together trigger this emergence. Males and females frequently mate while in flight and the male dies shortly thereafter. The female needs to mate only once in her lifetime and stores the sperm in a spermatheca, withdrawing them one at a time for egg fertilization for her entire life. The female immediately searches for a suitable location for developing a new nest in which she seals herself. This may be a cavity in wood, under bark, etc. The female discards her wings and starts producing a new colony.

Carpenter ants are ¼″ to ⅝″ long and vary in color. Some carpenter ant species are glossy black, while others are red, red and black, or brown. (See Figure 12.6.)

Carpenter ants are predators of other insects, scavengers of organic debris, and decomposers of fallen trees. When endowed with wings during mating flights, carpenter ants closely resemble termites. (See Figure 12.7.) Characteristics used to separate these two groups of insects follow:

- Ants have a thin waist between thorax and abdomen, whereas termites have thorax and abdomen joined broadly and closely across adjacent surfaces.
- Ants have antennae that are elbowed at the middle. Termites have antennae with uniformly sized segments that resemble a string of beads.
- Termites or ants with wings have marked differences. Termites have four wings, all the same shape and size. Ants also have four wings, but the front wings are larger and have a different shape than the rear wings.

Carpenter ants are discovered by the

- presence of ant foragers inside the dwelling;
- presence of swarmers with wings, suddenly emerging on a spring day;
- rustling sounds within wood or hollow doors or walls, caused by ants engaged in colony activities; and
- appearance of small piles or layers of sawdust-like frass on floors, window ledges, or furniture.

Carpenter ants often nest in hollow spaces such as walls, hollow doors, and ceilings between multilevel dwellings. Other common infested locations include porch pillars, sills, joists, studs, and interior casings. Ants enter and exit through cracks around framing and vents. Carpenter ants prefer moist wood to chew and excavate. Carpenter ant galleries are identified by the following:

- No mud
- No fecal pellets
- Scraped, smooth interiors
- Loose-packed frass
- Large galleries at any angle respective to the wood grain

■ CARPENTER BEES

Carpenter bees are large bees capable of causing extensive damage to a wood structure. Carpenter bees are similar to bumblebees in size, but have a shiny, fat

■ **FIGURE 12.8**

Carpenter bees are ½″ to ¾″ long with a blue-black, green, or purple metallic sheen.

abdomen and are devoid of hair. Carpenter bees have quick, abrupt flying habits. (See Figure 12.8.)

Carpenter bees do not eat wood. Males and females team together to dig channels in wood to provide living quarters during winter. Carpenter bees provide a food supply for future larvae and then abandon them. Males and females emerge in the spring from their chambers to mate and begin new excavation. Carpenter bees frequently use old tunnels. A single carpenter bee has the ability to tunnel 12″ into wood in one season, and several pairs may work in the same wood structure.

Carpenter bees do not live in colonies. Several carpenter bees may inhabit the same wood structure, but each female carpenter bee has her own gallery.

Carpenter bees attack all wood, but they prefer softwoods that offer the least resistance to digging. Walls, fences, decking, poles, and planters are common targets for nests. In nature, the nesting places are logs, dead branches, trees, yucca flower stems, or softwood. The initial entry has a round hole on the side or bottom of wood and branches at a right angle inside. A cross section of galleries reveals holes with about ½″ to ¾″ diameters. An adult can excavate approximately 1″ in six days.

Female carpenter bees have a powerful stinger, but they are not aggressive and rarely sting. Male carpenter bees have no stinger. Carpenter bees return to larvae galleries in cold weather and hibernate until spring, when the cycle is repeated. After eggs are laid, carpenter bees live until midsummer and die.

Several species of carpenter bees are found commonly throughout the United States. Almost all areas have some type of carpenter bee, and backyard gardeners often become fond of them as they tunnel into wood with no particular structural importance.

Here is an address for an informational Internet site: www.pestworld.org

■ REVIEW QUESTIONS*

1. As long as no wood-to-soil contact exists, you may be relatively assured that termites cannot establish themselves.

   A. True
   B. False

2. Shelter tubes are an important means of termite entry from soil to sill.

   A. True
   B. False

3. The most common termites are

   A. subterranean and Formosan termites.
   B. dampwood and Formosan termites.
   C. subterranean and drywood termites.

4. Subterranean termites live in colonies in the soil.

   A. True
   B. False

5. Drywood termite colonies appear in wood below ground level.

   A. True
   B. False

6. Carpenter ants are ¼″ to ⅝″ long and vary in color.

   A. True
   B. False

Answers to all of the chapter review questions are located in Appendix C at the back of this book.

7. When endowed with wings during mating flights, carpenter ants closely resemble termites.

   A. True
   B. False

8. Powder-post beetles are often detected by locating exit openings or fine powder sifting from the openings.

   A. True
   B. False

9. Carpenter bees live in colonies.

   A. True
   B. False

10. What should a residential inspector do if he or she suspects termites?

    A. Do nothing
    B. Recommend inspection by qualified termite inspector
    C. Comment about termites

11. Usually all carpenter ant colonies in a given area swarm on the same day.

    A. True
    B. False

12. Most of the ants found in a carpenter ant colony do not have wings.

    A. True
    B. False

13. Carpenter ant colonies contain several distinct sizes of worker ants.

    A. True
    B. False

■ INSPECTION CHECKLIST: TERMITES AND OTHER WOOD-DESTROYING INSECTS

The inspection checklist is not included here for the following reasons:

To inspect for termite and wood-destroying insects requires special training and education. Most states require that the inspector be licensed through the Structural Pest Control Board. In states that require that real estate inspectors be registered or licensed, this registration or license does not cover termite and wood-destroying insect reports. Therefore, a checklist to perform this inspection is not included in the chapter. However, it is helpful to an inspector to be familiar with termites and wood-destroying insects.

13

Environmental Considerations

Environmental inspections are relatively new to the inspection field. Most environmental inspectors require special training and licensing by the Environmental Protection Agency (EPA). The residential inspector should not attempt to perform these inspections without proper training. There is no statute of limitations on environmental inspection, and it is called "from cradle to grave." This type of inspection carries great responsibility as well as liability. "Environmental" covers materials found to cause various diseases and allergies. Some of these materials are asbestos, radon, urea formaldehyde, and lead. Inspectors should check with the EPA Regional Offices in their areas to determine if they need special training and certification from the EPA to perform environmental inspections.

■ ASBESTOS

Airborne asbestos contamination in buildings is a significant environmental problem. Various diseases are connected with industrial exposure to airborne asbestos. Extensive use of asbestos products in buildings has raised concerns about exposure to asbestos. Surveys conducted by the EPA estimate that asbestos-containing materials (ACMs) are found in approximately 31,000 schools and more than 700,000 other public and commercial buildings in this country.

The presence of asbestos in a building does not indicate that the health of building occupants is necessarily endangered. As long as ACM remains in its original condition and is not disturbed, exposure is unlikely. When maintenance, repairs, or other activities disturb ACM or if it is damaged, asbestos fibers are released, creating potential hazards to building occupants. Although not required by federal law, prudent

building owners undergo steps to limit exposure to airborne asbestos. (See Figure 13.1.)

Physical Properties

The word *asbestos* is derived from a Greek word meaning indestructible. Asbestos has been widely used because it is inexpensive and virtually indestructible. It also possesses properties allowing applicability to a variety of physical forms and applications. Its primary desirable physical properties include chemical resistance (particularly to acids), bacterial resistance, incombustibility, thermal insulating ability, electrical insulating ability, mechanical strength, flexibility, and good friction and wear characteristics. Other important properties in industrial fabrication of composite materials containing asbestos include wet strength, ease of formation of slurries with water, and solid drying characteristics. Indirect applications include filtration and acoustical components made from ACM.

Asbestos is by definition a group of naturally occurring minerals. These minerals are hydrated silicates, crystalline in structure, and occur as parallel bundles of minute fibers. The physical disturbance of these bundles generally results in separation into smaller bundles or individual fibers, called *fibrils*. Perfect lengthwise cleavage is a characteristic of asbestos. A length-to-width ratio of at least 3:1 is one of the distinguishing characteristics of an asbestos material.

Asbestos minerals are divided into two major classes: the serpentine group and the amphibole group. The serpentine group is characterized by a lattice structure and contains chrysotile, which is white asbestos composed of fine silky fibers. The amphibole group comprises chained silicates (amosite, crocidolite, tremolite, anthophyllite, and actinolite).

■ **FIGURE 13.1**

Locations where asbestos may be found in a home.

Asbestos in the Home

Chrysotile and crocidolite are used in asbestos textiles and filtration products. Large amounts of chrysotile are used in asphalt flooring, vinyl floor tile, paving, and road surfaces. Chrysotile is also used in brake linings, clutch facings, gaskets, and reinforced plastics. Crocidolite is used in these products because it is resistant to acids and the effects of outdoor exposure.

Amosite is used primarily for high-temperature applications. It has effective acid and heat resistance, which allows acceptability as a product that requires less flexibility and workable characteristics compared with chrysotile. Anthophyllite, actinolite, and tremolite are used primarily in adhesives and cements. They are too brittle for textile products or fibrous reinforcement.

Major asbestos concentrations found in schools and other public and commercial buildings prior to the 1970s were located mainly in boiler rooms, steam tunnels, ceiling tile, floor tile, electric cable insulation and underground vaults for electric service transformers. In the 1970s, the EPA banned the spraying of commercial asbestos products and the use of premolded or wet applied thermal insulating products containing more than 1 percent of asbestos content. Mastic, popcorn ceilings, and composite products also were banned.

In January 1986, the EPA proposed an immediate ban on the manufacture, processing, and import of some asbestos-containing products and a 10-yr. phase-out of the surplus. Even with the ban and the fact that asbestos use has declined in recent years, asbestos is found in many homes, especially older ones. The dangerous situations occur when asbestos is exposed and friable.

Asbestos was little known until the 1800s. The industrial revolution, the change from a culture of organic substances such as bone, hide, and wood to a culture of large-scale extractions of metals and ores, provided the demand for asbestos. Asbestos use has remained relatively constant, and the material is still widely used. Asbestos is reported to be used in more than 3,600 products. Approximately 66 percent of all asbestos is used in cement products, flat sheets or siding tile, corrugated roofing sheets, rainwater pipes, gutters, and pressure pipes. These products contain 10 percent to 15 percent asbestos fibers, which function as fibrous reinforcement in the cement.

Some asbestos fibers have high tensile strength and thermal stability. Asbestos is a noncombustible noise absorber and thermal insulator. Asbestos is effective in condensate control and is resistant to corrosion and friction. Chrysotile accounts for approximately 93 percent of total consumption. The remaining 7 percent of asbestos used is in the amosite and crocidolite group. Crocidolite produced today is used in conjunction with chrysotile in the manufacture of asbestos cement pressure pipes. A small amount of amosite is frequently used in pressure-piping products as a filter aid. The typical asbestos mixture contains 60 percent chrysotile, 30 percent crocidolite and 10 percent amosite. In 1998, the use of asbestos in a variety of building products was banned or restricted.

Health Effects Associated with Asbestos Exposure

Asbestos has been used throughout the world since the early 1900s. Annual production increased from 400,000 tons (t) in the 1900s to 3.5 million t in the 1970s. Since that time, production has declined. The unique physical properties of asbestos and its virtual indestructibility are reasons it achieved widespread use. They are the same properties that make it hazardous to an individual's health. Asbestos is permanent once applied, installed, or used. When asbestos fibers become lodged in the lungs, they stay from cradle to grave.

Asbestos fibers have some unique health effects on people. Of all compounds capable of producing adverse effects on the human body, asbestos may have a longer latency period between exposure and subsequent appearance of disease than any other substance. For example, certain cancer types that develop from asbestos exposure may not appear until more than 40 years after exposure occurrence. Adverse health effects from asbestos exposure were first described in the early 1900s. Widespread concern about asbestos developed only recently as a result of extensive health problems developed among people heavily exposed during and immediately following World War II. In addition to several cancer types, asbestos may cause damage to the lungs not observed from exposure to other materials. Individuals vary considerably in their ability to withstand the disease. Some contract colds frequently, while others are almost immune to such infections.

Asbestos-Related Diseases

Asbestos has turned from a wonder fiber into a deadly problem. Airborne asbestos contamination in buildings is a significant environmental problem. Microscopic fibers are released into the air of a building and may be recirculated essentially forever. The tiny needle-like fibers pierce the lungs. Medical research indicates that the fibers cause many forms of cancer, and various other diseases have been linked with exposure to and extensive use of asbestos. Most people with asbestos-related diseases (asbestosis, lung cancer, and mesotheliomas) were exposed to high levels of asbestos while working in asbestos industries. Extrapolation of the relationship between exposure level and disease indicates that only a small proportion of people exposed to low levels will develop asbestos-related diseases. Smokers, children, and young adults are at greater risk.

Asbestos-related diseases are caused by inhalation or ingestion of asbestos fibers. That is, asbestos enters the body when a person breathes or swallows the fibers. The lungs are the primary site of adverse health effects. Common to all types of asbestos diseases is the long latency period, the length of time for the disease to develop after exposure.

Asbestos is a type of pneumoconiosis, a generic name for lung disease caused by inhalation of dust. Asbestosis causes disability and death. It is also a progressive lung disease, which means it progresses even after exposure is discontinued. The latency period for asbestosis is 5 to 10 yrs. with very heavy exposure; otherwise it may be 20 to 40 yrs.

Lung Cancer

Asbestos is a known human carcinogen. It is well documented that exposure to asbestos causes lung cancer. There is no known safe level of exposure to asbestos with regard to lung cancer. The lung cancer latency period caused by inhalation of asbestos is usually 15 yrs., with a peak of 30 to 35 yrs.

Mesothelioma

Mesothelioma is an unusual form of cancer rarely seen in the general population in the absence of asbestos exposure. The mesothelioma latency period is long, up to 40 yr. from the time of exposure to the onset of disease. It is an incurable form of cancer, usually fatal.

Smoking and Asbestos Exposure

Another important factor regarding asbestos and lung cancer is the synergistic, or multiplicative, effect of cigarette smoking. The risk of lung cancer among smokers who are not exposed to asbestos is approximately ten times that of a nonexposed nonsmoker. Nonsmoking asbestos workers have a risk of approximately five times that of nonexposed nonsmokers. However, the combined synergistic effect among those smokers who are also exposed to asbestos is not simply additive,

but multiplicative. Their risk of lung cancer is 50 to 55 times that of nonexposed nonsmokers. Also important to note is that if one stops smoking within 5 to 10 yr. after exposure, the risk of lung cancer may decrease close to that of a nonsmoker.

Other Cancers

In addition to lung disease and lung cancer, asbestos may be associated with increased incidence of gastrointestinal or digestive tract cancer such as cancer of the esophagus, stomach, or colon. This is presumably due to ingestion of asbestos fibers. With early detection of these cancer types, they may be curable. The EPA attributes as many as 12,000 cancer cases per year to asbestos materials.

Asbestos-Containing Materials

Asbestos may be found in cement products, fireproofing textiles, or thermal insulation. ACM in buildings is found in three forms: (1) sprayed or troweled on walls and ceilings (surfacing materials); (2) insulation around hot or cold pipes, ducts, boilers, and tanks (pipe and boiler insulation); and (3) a variety of other products such as ceiling and floor tiles, wall boards, and miscellaneous materials. ACM in the first two categories is of greater concern, especially if it is friable. Friable material may be crumbled, pulverized, or reduced to powder by hand pressure. Most ACM in the third category is nonfriable. Occupational Safety and Health Administration (OSHA) regulations specify work practices, and EPA rules govern the handling and disposal of asbestos. State regulations on these issues vary and may be more stringent than federal requirements.

Typical Locations for Asbestos

Asbestos may be found in various locations. Some of the areas include

- A/C and heat ductwork (exterior),
- boiler and boiler pipe insulation,
- ceiling tile,
- floor furnace vent pipes,
- floor tile,
- ironing board covers,
- mastic (glue),
- old linoleum
- ovens and dishwashers
- plaster on walls and ceilings,
- sheetrock and textures,

- stove top pads,
- toasters and clothes dryers,
- transite panels,
- transite siding and roofing,
- vibration dampers (A/C),
- water and steam line insulation, and
- water heater vent pipes.

Most of these materials do not represent a large threat in everyday life, owing to either their location or their particular class and use. For example, let's examine a transite water heater vent pipe. Transite is a dense, hard material, and the pipe generally is located from the ceiling through the attic to a roof vent, not within the living space. Its only function is to carry vent gas to the atmosphere above the house. Transite is a nonfriable substance that poses little threat as long as the vent pipe is intact and undisturbed. If the water heater is to be changed or moved, the homeowners should use a fully qualified contractor to handle ACM and remove the heater.

The vibration damper in the heating, ventilating, and air-conditioning (HVAC) system acts as an isolator and insulator between two pieces of equipment. It controls or eliminates the metal cabinet's rubbing or vibrating. This material is considered semifriable and causes a problem. The material sheds or releases fiber as air passes through and, with the normal amount of deterioration, is less than desirable. The amount of fiber released is small, but there is no known safe exposure to asbestos. This material is considered for abatement or removal.

■ RADON

Radon is a colorless, odorless gas that is difficult to detect without instruments. It is present almost everywhere. Radon is radioactive; therefore, it is hazardous. When radon decays, it emits radiation in the form of subatomic alpha particles. If alpha particles are inhaled, they directly affect cells and then dissipate.

Most radioactive materials are immobile solids, emitting their particles deep within the ground, and do no harm. However, gaseous radon finds its way to where people live. The combination of radioactivity and gaseous mobility and the formation of fine particles is more life threatening than radon's actual degree of radioactivity.

Formation

Radon is a natural link in the radioactive decay chain of elements, which begins with uranium. Uranium is scattered throughout the earth's crust. Wherever uranium is found, radon forms. Because radon is a gas and is mobile, it will not remain where found. At this time, nobody is certain where high concentrations of radon will occur. Rock formations such as the highly publicized Reading Prong (a corridor extending from Reading, Pennsylvania, into New Jersey, New York, and Connecticut) indicate areas of high radon concentrations. These areas have higher radon levels than other areas, although radon has been found throughout the United States in various levels.

The fact that a person lives in a neighborhood where high levels of radon have been found does not indicate that his or her house has a high level of radon. Some homes within high-concentration areas have been found to have low levels of radon. The only method to determine radon level in a residence is to test.

Testing

Whether radon gas is in a specific home is a function of both presence and air pressure. Testing for radon is not difficult; however, it is important that the detector be properly placed in the residence. Test kits are available from several sources, allowing the homeowner to test his or her own residence or have the test performed by a real estate inspector.

The exposure period ranges from one day to three months, depending on the type of detector used. There are different types of radon detectors:

Charcoal canisters.
1. Residence site preparation: operated normally for 24 hours prior to test.
2. Canister placement: one for every 400 sq. ft. placed at shoulder height away from air or water sources for 24 to 48 hours and then shipped to the laboratory.

Longer-term tests with electronic detection function such as an alpha-track. These take longer because the protocol takes into account climatic changes that affect air pressure in the house.

A third testing method involves a professional, but it is more expensive than the others. Normally, if excessive levels are detected using the first two methods, the third test is used to determine exactly where radon is entering the property. The professional called usually contracts his or her service to correct the problem.

Radon measurement expressed in picocuries (pCi, a unit of measure of radioactivity equalling one trillionth (10^{-12}) of one curie (Ci) where one ci = 3.7×10 disintegrations per second, is often expressed as a portion of a known volume of air—picocuries per liter of air, or pCi/L. The average home in the United States has approximately 1 pCi/L, to 2 pCi/L.

Outside air has approximately 0.1 pCi/L to 0.2 pCi/L. The EPA recommends that 4 pCi/L. be considered an action level.

People interpret this recommended level to mean that 4 pCi/L. is a safe level and anything higher is dangerous. This is not true. The figure of 4 was picked as a target because the EPA felt that reducing radon concentrations to this level, in most cases, is achievable. The risk escalates in proportion to the radon level and exposure time. In reality, any exposure reading of 4 pCi/L. or higher means the homeowner must act to reduce the radon level.

There are at least three ways of reducing radon levels in the home: (1) sealing holes and cracks gas may travel through, (2) ventilating the space to dilute radon with outside air, and (3) pressurization to keep radon out of the house. Each has advantages as well as limitations.

Sealing or plugging holes and cracks where radon may enter is the least expensive and probably the simplest. When sealing is used alone, only low to moderate reduction in radon levels is achieved. It is very difficult to locate all cracks and gaps when the house is settling and other stresses create more cracks as time passes. Old seals deteriorate and new cracks appear. (See Figure 13.2.)

Ventilation

Ventilate the lowest level of the house that is in direct contact with the primary source of radon (soil). If the house has a basement or crawlspace, this is the area to ventilate.

If the house sits on a concrete slab, the only ventilation choice is the living area. Open windows around all levels of the house. Radon is drawn into the house when air pressure in the basement or lowest level is less than air pressure in surrounding soil. It is imperative that any ventilation system does not reduce air pressure within the house and increase this pull. To guard against this, vents and windows must be opened equally on all sides of the house.

■ **FIGURE 13.2**

Sealing is a method used to reduce radon levels.

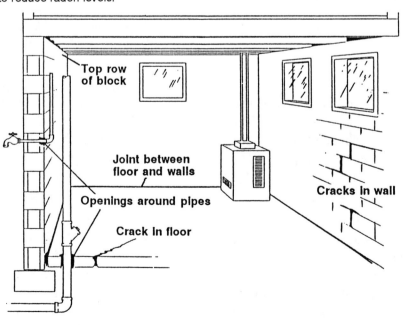

■ **FIGURE 13.3**

Natural ventilation is accomplished by opening basement windows or vents.

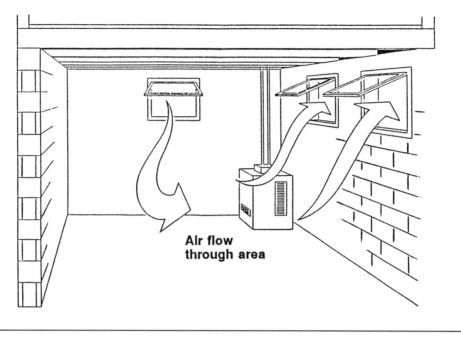

Air flow through area

Natural Ventilation

Natural ventilation replaces radon-laden indoor air with outdoor air. Some natural ventilation occurs in every house as air draws through cracks and openings because of temperature and pressure differences between indoor and outdoor air. In the average home, all interior air is replaced by outside air about once every hour. In technical terms, this is called 1.0 air changes per hour (ach). Newer homes, which are generally tight, may have air exchange rates as low as 0.1 ach, while older homes may have twice the average, or 2.0 ach. Use of natural ventilation in cold weather increases heating and cooling costs substantially. No installation costs are involved with this type of system unless a device is required to hold windows or vents open or to detect or prevent unauthorized entry through these openings. Tightly constructed homes with low air exchange rates are expected to benefit more from ventilation increases than homes with naturally high air exchange rates. (See Figure 13.3.)

Forced Ventilation

In forced ventilation, fans are used to replace radon-laden indoor air with outside air. The fans maintain the desired air exchange rate independent of weather conditions. When using forced ventilation, airflow between entry and exhaust points must be properly balanced. Otherwise, additional radon could be drawn in or moist air could be forced into walls and attics, causing structural damage.

The lowest level of the house should be ventilated. Closing off and not using a basement may be advisable. Ventilating all levels is recommended whenever outdoor weather conditions permit. Air should be blown into the house and allowed to exit, usually through windows or vents on adjacent or opposite sides. Exhaust fans should not be used because they pull air out of the house, which may decrease interior air pressure and cause more radon to be drawn inside. The air distribution and ventilation rate may be controlled by the size and location of fans, including the use of louvered air deflectors. The EPA's experience suggests that two or three fans be installed to dispense desired increased ventilation. (See Figure 13.4.)

Pressurization

Radon (a gas) will always move from high-pressure regions (ground) to low-pressure regions (house). The pressure differences are small. A furnace drawing in combustion air or a kitchen exhaust fan produces a significant difference in the rate radon enters the house. Pres-

■ **FIGURE 13.4**

A fan is installed to force outdoor air into the house to reduce radon levels.

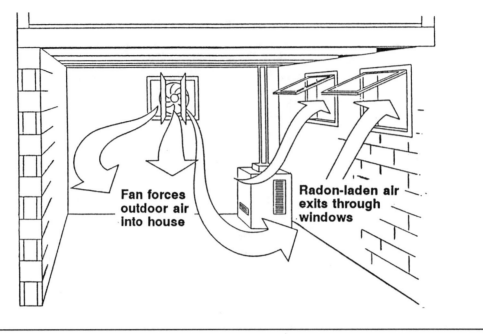

Fan forces outdoor air into house

Radon-laden air exits through windows

surizing the house or, more particularly, the basement is a strategy aimed at slowing or reversing this process.

One approach to pressurization is to eliminate articles that depressurize a house. For example, window fans should not be used as exhaust fans to ventilate the house. If outside air supplies wood stoves, fireplaces, furnaces, and gas dryers, their air consumption will not contribute to lowering air pressure in the house.

Other methods involve increasing air pressure, particularly in the basement or crawlspace. These approaches generally require test equipment unavailable to the average contractor or inspector. Ventilation, if feasible, is a simple approach.

■ UREA FORMALDEHYDE

In 1982, the United States Consumer Product Safety Commission voted to ban urea formaldehyde foam insulation (UFFI) as a hazardous consumer product. The agency determined that UFFI presents unreasonable injury risks to consumers. There is a risk of acute and chronic illness from the formaldehyde gas released from the foam insulation. In addition, it is not possible to predict prior to installation the amount of formaldehyde that will be released from the product. However, in many homes there is low-level off-gassing of formaldehyde

and the risk of injury to individuals living in these homes is reduced.

UFFI is manufactured at the job site by the installer. Urea-formaldehyde-based resin, a foaming agent, and compressed gas are fed into foaming equipment to form a product with the consistency of shaving cream. In retrofit applications, the foam is pumped through a hose and forced into the wall cavity, where it cures and becomes firm. During and after the installation process, formaldehyde gas may be released into the living quarters.

UFFI is not found in most American homes. Estimates place the number of UFFI-insulated homes at about 500,000, most of them insulated after the early 1970s. If you purchased your home prior to 1970 and have not added insulation, you probably do not have UFFI. If you own a newer home, check with the builder or contact the real estate agent and/or seller. Ask if foam insulation was installed in the walls of the house. If you had insulation added, check with the insulation installer or read the contract or bill of sale.

If your home has UFFI, some city, county, and state health departments conduct tests for a modest charge to report the amount of formaldehyde vapor present in the air. In the absence of these sources, you may consider contracting with a commercial laboratory to determine the formaldehyde concentration in the air. Locate *labo-*

ratories in the yellow pages for names of companies that perform this service. The formaldehyde level in a home is subject to variation because the release of formaldehyde from foam insulation is affected by temperature, humidity and other factors.

According to measurements in homes, UFFI continues to release formaldehyde gas for years. The levels are usually higher during the initial weeks following installation and gradually taper off. After the first year, levels generally decrease dramatically. However, higher temperatures and humidity may increase the formaldehyde off-gassing rate. In laboratory tests, formaldehyde off-gassing has continued for at least 16 months. Most homes emit the greatest amount of formaldehyde within the first year after installation.

Check your home or apartment for formaldehyde levels if the following circumstances occur for more than a few days and abate when you are away from home: symptoms of eye, nose, and throat irritation; coughing; shortness of breath; skin irritation; nausea; headaches; and dizziness. If you are not experiencing any acute health effects and the foam was installed more than a year ago, it is likely that the formaldehyde levels and health risks, including cancer, are greatly reduced. If you have experienced the symptoms previously described and your physician requires information for diagnosis, you may desire that a test be completed to determine formaldehyde gas concentration. You may also consider the test if you are concerned about the sale of your house with UFFI.

If the UFFI must be removed from the walls, interior and exterior wall panels or siding and foam insulation are removed. New insulation and wall panels or siding are installed. Wood surfaces that came in contact with the foam should be treated with a chemical neutralizing agent.

Formaldehyde has been in general use for more than 90 years and is a leading chemical in terms of quantity produced and variety of application. More than 50 plants belong to companies that are involved in direct production of formaldehyde, with a capacity exceeding 8.6 billion pounds per yr. When the multitude of end-use products are included, companies that manufacture formaldehyde products are responsible for the employment of more than 1.5 million people with an annual payroll exceeding $18 billion. These companies, producing thousands of industrial goods and consumer products, constitute roughly 8 percent of the gross national product (GNP) of this country alone.

Formaldehyde as a raw material is used in hundreds of everyday products such as hand lotion, shampoo, fin-

gernail polish, toothpaste, disinfectants, fumigants, and embalming fluids. It is also used to impart permanent press to natural and synthetic textiles and as a bonding agent in paper towels to make them absorbent. It is even present in paper used to wrap tobacco products, such as cigarette paper. The odor in new cars is from formaldehyde.

Formaldehyde also occurs naturally. As an example, trace amounts are generated in cooking and by burning wood, coal, gasoline, and diesel fuel. It is also released naturally by trees and plants (including vegetables such as carrots and cabbage) as a product of their life functions. Finally, formaldehyde is found in small quantities in the human body as a normal metabolite.

In short, formaldehyde is a part of our daily environment, whether it be in the exhaust fumes of transportation vehicles, in household and personal hygiene products, or in the extravagances in which we indulge, such as smoking. There are no federal regulations pertaining to the ambient air formaldehyde content in residences.

■ LEAD

Lead is a heavy, soft, malleable, ductal, plastic but inelastic, bluish-white metallic element. Found in combination with other materials, lead is used in pipe, cable sheaths, batteries, solder, and shields against radioactivity. Lead is also used in the construction of buildings, roofing, cornices, tank lines, electrical conduit, water pipes, and sewer pipes. In paint pigments, lead is used in yacht keels and in ornamental coatings.

In addition to serving many useful purposes, lead is one of the few naturally occurring substances that appears to have no use within the human body. High toxic effects can be detected at low measurable levels. Two-thirds of lead production goes into batteries that may be recycled; however, gasoline and paint, because they are not recyclable, cause widespread pollution. The areas of the body affected by lead exposure include red blood cells, the central and peripheral nervous systems, the kidneys, and the reproductive system.

Children and adults are affected differently in regard to lead exposure. Children are at greater risk of lead absorption and toxicity than adults. Symptoms of lead poisoning include fatigue, loss of appetite, irritability, sleep disturbance, behavioral change, developmental regression, clumsiness, vomiting, muscular irregularities, weakness, and abdominal pain. A child's developing nervous system is more susceptible to lead damage, and the number of exposure sources that affect children exceeds those affecting adults. Symptoms of lead poisoning are subtle and nonspecific, and a physical exam generally reveals little or nothing. The construction industry causes significant exposure when burning or sanding to remove old lead paint from surfaces or when cutting into bridges or lead-containing or painted metal structures.

Environmental exposures to lead may also contribute significantly to human exposure. Sources of environmental or public exposure to lead are dust, soil, water, and consumer products such as paints, ceramics, fishing weights, bullets, and solder.

Dust

Lead is commonly found in interior house dust, with the primary problem being lead-based paint. Houses with lead-based paint are more likely to have high levels of lead in dust than homes with no lead-based paint. Other sources of lead in dust include people and pets tracking in dust and dirt from outside the house. The level of lead in dust is thought to be the best indicator of potential lead problems in households. Possible places to find lead in household dust are on windowsills, in window wells, and on windows, floors, doors, door trim, and baseboards. Several reasons exist for the variety. First, lead-based paint was used on windows and doors, both wood and metal; on baseboards and trim; and also on the house exterior because of the paint's durability. Second, repeated opening and closing of windows and doors tends to damage paint, which may cause leaded dust if the paint contained lead. Other sources for lead dust contamination are if property is located near smelters, battery plants, or any industrial sources of airborne lead emissions. Quite often, this type of contamination is found in the attic.

Interior lead dust levels may be reduced by regularly cleaning floors, windowsills, and window wells. Wet mopping and wiping with a damp cloth on a regular basis may be effective in controlling accessible dust. Lead dust accumulation rates are more rapid if paint is in poor condition or if the home is under renovation. Ordinary vacuuming of lead dust is not recommended as a cleaning method.

Paint

Lead-based paint represents one of the highest potentials for lead exposure in humans, especially children. Homes built before 1965 are assumed to contain lead paint, and approximately 75 percent of homes built before 1978 contained some lead-based paint. Lead is now banned in consumer paints. Exposure to lead-based paint occurs from paint deterioration and the generation of lead dust that settles within and outside the home. Lead-based paint was designed to weather or chalk, resulting in a continuing source of lead-contaminated soil and dust. Lead is also encountered in sidewalk dust near homes with exterior lead-based paint. Exposure to lead-based paint also occurs occupationally. Lead-based paint abatement projects where paint is scraped or sanded may result in significant exposures to lead dust if not properly controlled. The construction industry has a potential for exposure because the ban on lead in paint does not extend to industrial applications. Homeowners may be exposed to lead through renovation projects, which also serve as a primary source of exposure for children.

Indoor household paint manufactured since 1978 should not contain lead in excess of 0.06 percent. For surfaces suspected of being covered with lead-based paint, sample chips of the paint should be sent to a laboratory for testing.

If paint is firmly attached to the surface with no blistering, peeling or flaking, it may be advantageous not to remove the paint. An alternative is to cover the existing paint with non-lead-based paint. If this option is chosen, special preparation of lead-based paint surfaces is required, which necessitates special equipment and trained personnel.

Testing for lead paint has a specific protocol and utilizes specialized equipment. A typical test for a 1200 sq. ft. home might include more that 200 readings and take 3 to 4 hours.

Soil

The soil surrounding a dwelling may be contaminated with lead from several different sources. The first source is the weathering and chalking of lead-based paint on the dwelling exterior. Many older homes used exterior lead-based paint, especially in colder climates such as the East and Midwest, because it was the most durable for these applications. The second source is airborne contamination from leaded gasoline. Although leaded gasoline has been phased out under an EPA ban, many millions of tons of lead entered the environment from this source until the late 1980s. For homes close to highways or major surface streets, considerable lead contamination of soil is possible. The third source is contamination from sources of airborne lead, such as lead smelters and battery manufacturing plants.

Lead in soil is a direct source of lead exposure to children playing in the yard, getting their hands dirty, and putting their fingers in their mouths. It is also a potential source of lead in interior house dust because soil is easily tracked into the house by humans and pets. Vegetables grown in lead-contaminated soil may take up lead and be ingested by the residents of the dwelling. If the area surrounding the dwelling is questionable, soil testing is highly desirable as part of an overall evaluation of lead in different media.

Sample Collection Techniques

Soil samples are generally collected using a soil recovery probe to collect core samples. A typical soil recovery probe consists of a 12-inch (″) stainless steel core sampler, replaceable 1″ diameter butyrate plastic inserts, a cross-bar attachment, and a hammer attached for use with hard or frozen soils. At each sampling location, a composite sample consisting of three to five soil cores mixed together should be extracted to achieve a representative sample of the area.

Lead is stable and persistent in soil. In most cases, it remains on or near the surface, which is especially true for metallic lead. Inorganic or metallic lead binds with the soil, which limits lead dispersion unless disturbed through erosion or mechanical factors. Various conditions, such as highly acidic soil or water, may cause formation of a lead solute that migrates farther into soils.

Water

Lead contamination of water is primarily due to corrosion of lead pipe, fixtures, and lead solder contained in water delivery systems. Ground water contamination by lead in soil is unlikely to occur in most instances. However, run-off of lead-contaminated soil may contaminate surface water. The EPA estimates that less than 1 percent of public water systems in the United States have incoming water containing lead levels greater than 5 ppb (parts per billion). Lead in drinking water, although rarely the sole cause of lead poisoning, can significantly increase a person's total lead exposure. Infants who drink baby formula and concentrated juices mixed with water have an increased exposure rate. The EPA estimates that drinking water accounts for up to 20 percent or more of a person's total exposure to lead.

How Lead Enters Our Water

Lead is unusual among drinking water contaminants because it seldom occurs naturally in water supplies like rivers and lakes. Lead enters drinking water primarily as a result of corrosion or the wearing away of materials containing lead in the water distribution system and household plumbing. These materials include lead-based solder used to join copper pipe, brass, and chrome-plated brass faucets and, in some cases, pipes made of lead that connect the house to the water main. In 1986, Congress banned the use of lead solder containing greater than 0.2 percent lead and restricted the lead content of faucets, pipes, and other plumbing materials to 8 percent.

When water stands in lead pipes or plumbing systems containing lead for several hours, the lead in the pipes or solder may dissolve into the drinking water. The first water drawn from the faucet in the morning or late in the afternoon after water has not been used for several hours may contain a higher level of lead. The lead level may be lowered by flushing the water lines before using the water. Cold water should be used for cooking and drinking because hot water dissolves more lead more quickly than cold water.

Sampling Technique for Drinking Water

Because the most likely sources of lead in drinking water are internal to the dwelling, lead tends to build up in water stagnant in pipes overnight. Therefore, as stated above, the highest levels of lead in tap water are usually encountered in the first water from the tap in the morning. The sampling strategy outlined below is designed to differentiate between different sources of lead in tap water.

- First Sampling: Take 250 cubic centimeters (cc.— about ½ pint) of water from the cold water kitchen tap after no water usage for at least 8 hours—morning first draw.
- Second Sampling: Take 750 cc. (about 1½ pints) immediately after the first sample without wasting any water in between.
- Third Sampling: Take 250 cc. after the water turns cold or any other indication that the water is representative of the service line.
- Fourth Sampling: Take 250 cc. after the water has run for three additional minutes after the third sample or

after the water has otherwise been determined to be representative of water in the main.

These samples should be sent to the laboratory for analysis of lead content. Laboratory results are usually reported in units of parts lead per billion parts water (ppb). The EPA has recently (May 1991) established a new National Primary Drinking Water Regulation for lead with an action level of 15 ppb for water in dwellings (20 ppb for 250-cc. samples). The test results should be interpreted in terms of these levels.

The inspector should check with his or her local EPA office to determine whether any special certification or licensing is required before attempting any type of environmental inspection or test. Many environmental courses held at colleges and universities are open to inspectors wanting to gain more knowledge. Remember, on all environmental inspections, no statute of limitations exists. The term used is *from the cradle to the grave*. Before performing these types of inspections, the inspector should be certain he or she is qualified.

■ REVIEW QUESTIONS*

1. Real estate inspectors should not inspect for asbestos unless they are trained and certified by the EPA.

   A. True
   B. False

2. The major concentrations of asbestos are found in buildings built prior to the 1970s.

   A. True
   B. False

3. The formaldehyde off-gassing rate will not increase with high temperatures and humidity.

   A. True
   B. False

4. If the UFFI must be removed from the walls, it is not necessary to install new wall panels or siding.

   A. True
   B. False

5. The EPA attributes up to how many cancer cases per year to asbestos materials?

   A. 2,000
   B. 12,000
   C. 20,000

6. Formaldehyde is used as a raw material in products such as

   A. hand lotion.
   B. shampoo.
   C. fumigants.
   D. All of the above
   E. None of the above

7. Radon may be found throughout the United States.

   A. True
   B. False

8. Exhaust fans may be used for removing radon from the house.

   A. True
   B. False

9. Testing for radon may be accomplished by what type of detectors?

   A. Alpha-track
   B. Charcoal canister
   C. Either A or B
   D. Neither A nor B

10. Radon measurement is expressed in picocuries.

    A. True
    B. False

11. Which process is used to reduce radon levels in the home?

    A. Sealing
    B. Ventilating
    C. Pressurization
    D. All of the above

12. 4 pCi/L. is a safe radon level.

    A. True
    B. False

---

* Answers to all of the chapter review questions are located in Appendix C at the back of this book.

■ INSPECTION CHECKLIST: ENVIRONMENTAL CONSIDERATIONS

ASBESTOS

Yes No

☐ ☐ Does the home have insulated heating ducts or hot water pipes? Look for batting, tape, chalk-like plaster or corrugated cardboard wrapping around pipes and ducts.

☐ ☐ Was the home built before 1985? These houses could have asbestos.

☐ ☐ Does the house have asbestos siding, shingles that are deteriorating?

☐ ☐ Does the house have vinyl floor tiles or linoleum? These floor coverings could contain asbestos. The mastic that holds the floor covering to the floor could also contain asbestos.

☐ ☐ Does the house have plaster sprayed on or troweled on interior ceilings and walls?

☐ ☐ Does the house have blown-in insulation in the attic and walls?

☐ ☐ Does the house have mastic, putty, caulking, cement?

If any of the questions were answered "yes," the inspector should recommend that the house be tested for possible contamination.

RADON

Yes No

☐ ☐ Has the house been tested for radon?

☐ ☐ Are there any exposed cracks in the slab?

☐ ☐ Is the crawl space exposed to gravel or soil?

☐ ☐ Is the crawl space used as the return air for heating and cooling?

☐ ☐ Is the floor of the crawl space covered with plastic and sealed around plumbing risers and ducts?

☐ ☐ Is there a sump in the crawl space that is not sealed?

☐ ☐ Are there any open heating and cooling ducts?

☐ ☐ Is the crawl space damp?

☐ ☐ Is the crawlspace ventilated properly?

☐ ☐ Do the basement floors and/or walls have cracks or unsealed openings?

☐ ☐ Is the basement damp or are there signs of recent water damage?

Yes No

☐ ☐ Does the basement have standard water drains?

☐ ☐ Does the basement have any areas of exposed soil?

UFFI (UREA FORMALDEHYDE)

Yes No

☐ ☐ Does the house have UFFI insulation that is at least 10 years old?

Note: *Formaldehyde is not likely to be a problem.*

☐ ☐ Is the house less than five years old? *Note:* House should be tested.

☐ ☐ Does the house have UFFI insulation in the walls?

Note: *Check behind electrical outlets and check for plugged holes uniformly spaced on exterior of house.*

☐ ☐ Has the house been renovated within the past 24 months?

Note: *New carpet, vinyl, furniture and cabinets can release formaldehyde fumes.*

☐ ☐ Is the house a manufactured or mobile house?

☐ ☐ If any of the questions were answered "yes," the house should be tested.

LEAD PAINT

Yes No

☐ ☐ Was the house built before 1978?

☐ ☐ If the house was built before 1978, is the interior or exterior paint peeling or cracking?

☐ ☐ If paint is peeling or cracking, is it cracking in a pattern of uniform squares?

LEAD IN WATER

Yes No

☐ ☐ Was the house built before 1930? The water lines and connectors may contain lead.

☐ ☐ Was the house built after 1930? The water lines are copper joined with lead solder.

☐ ☐ Does the house have dull gray soft metal water lines? Water lines are probably lead.

Yes No

☐ ☐ Is there rust-colored water, stained dishes? Corrosion is occurring, and if lead is present it will leach into the water supply.

☐ ☐ Is the plumbing copper? Pipes may be joined with lead solder.

☐ ☐ Are the plumbing fittings brass? Brass fixtures may leach lead into water.

Yes No

☐ ☐ Does the house have a submersible well pump?

☐ ☐ Is the house located in an industrial area?

☐ ☐ Has the house been remodeled or renovated?

If any of the questions were answered with "yes," the presence of lead is possible. The soil, water, paint, and dust should be tested for lead contamination.

Appendix A

The American Society of Home Inspectors, Inc.

■ STANDARDS OF PRACTICE AND CODE OF ETHICS

1. Introduction

1.1 The American Society of Home Inspectors, Inc. (ASHI) is a not-for-profit professional society established in 1976 whose volunteer membership consists of private, fee-paid home inspectors. ASHI's objectives include promotion of excellence within the profession and continual improvement of its member's inspection services to the public.

1.2 These Standards of Practice:
   A. provide inspection guidelines.
   B. make public the services provided by private fee-paid inspectors.
   C. define certain terms relating to these inspections.

2. Purpose And Scope

2.1 Inspections performed to these guidelines are intended to provide the client with a better understanding of the property conditions, as observed at the time of the inspection.

2.2 Inspectors shall:
   A. observe readily accessible installed systems and components listed in these Standards.
   B. submit a written report to the client which shall:
      1. describe those components specified to be described in sections 4-12 of these Standards.

   2. state which systems and components designated for inspection in these Standards have been inspected.
   3. state any systems and components so inspected which were found to be in need of immediate major repair.

2.3 These Standards are not intended to limit inspectors from:
   A. reporting observations and conditions in addition to those required in Section 2.2.
   B. excluding systems and components from the inspection if requested by the client.

3. General Limitations and Exclusions

3.1 General limitations:
   A. inspections done in accordance with these Standards are visual and are not technically exhaustive.
   B. these Standards are applicable to buildings with four or less dwelling units and their garages or carports.

3.2 General exclusions:
   A. Inspectors are NOT required to report on:
      1. life expectancy of any component or system.
      2. the causes of the need for a major repair.
      3. the methods, materials and costs of corrections.
      4. the suitability of the property for any specialized use.
      5. compliance or non-compliance with applicable regulatory requirements.

6. the market value of the property or its marketability.
7. the advisability or inadvisability of purchase of the property.
8. any component or system which was not observed.
9. the presence or absence of pests such as wood damaging organisms, rodents, or insects.
10. cosmetic items, underground items, or items not permanently installed.

B. Inspectors are NOT required to:
1. offer or perform any act or service contrary to law.
2. offer warranties or guarantees of any kind.
3. offer or perform engineering, architectural, plumbing, or any other job function requiring an occupational license in the jurisdiction where the inspection is taking place, unless the inspector holds a valid occupational license in which case he/she may inform the client that he/she is so licensed, and is therefore qualified to go beyond the ASHI Standards of Practice, and for an additional fee, perform additional inspections beyond those within the scope of the basic ASHI inspection.
4. calculate the strength, adequacy, or efficiency of any system or component.
5. enter any area or perform any procedure which may damage the property or its components or be dangerous to the inspector or other persons.
6. operate any system or component which is shut down or otherwise inoperable.
7. operate any system or component which does not respond to normal operating controls.
8. disturb insulation, move personal items, furniture, equipment, plant life, soil, snow, ice, or debris which obstructs access or visibility.
9. determine the presence or absence of any suspected hazardous substance including but not limited to toxins, carcinogens, noise, contaminants in soil, water, and air.
10. determine the effectiveness of any system installed to control or remove suspected hazardous substances.
11. predict future conditions, including but not limited to failure of components.
12. project operating cost of components.
13. evaluate acoustical characteristics of any system or component.

3.3 Limitations and exclusions specific to individual systems are listed in following sections.

4. System: Structural Components

4.1 The inspector shall observe:
A. structural components including:
1. foundations
2. floors
3. walls
4. columns
5. ceilings
6. roofs

4.2 The inspector shall:
A. describe the type of:
1. foundation
2. floor structure
3. wall structure
4. columns
5. ceiling structure
6. roof structure
B. probe structural components where deterioration is suspected. However, probing is NOT required when probing would damage any finished surface.
C. enter underfloor crawl spaces and attic spaces except when access is obstructed, when entry could damage the property, or when dangerous or adverse situations are suspected.
D. report the methods used to observe underfloor crawl spaces and attics.
E. report signs of water penetration into the building or signs of abnormal or harmful condensation on building components.

5. System: Exterior

5.1 The inspector shall observe:
A. wall cladding, flashings and trim.

B. entryway doors and representative number of windows.

C. garage door operators.

D. decks, balconies, stoops, steps, areaway, and porches including railings.

E. eaves, soffits and fascias.

F. vegetation, grading, drainage, driveways, patios, walkways and retaining walls with respect to their effect on the condition of the building.

5.2 The inspector shall:

A. describe wall cladding materials.

B. operate all entryway doors and representative number of windows including garage doors, manually or by using permanently installed controls of any garage door operator.

C. report whether or not any garage door operator will automatically reverse or stop when meeting reasonable resistance during closing.

5.3 The inspector is NOT required to observe:

A. storm windows, storm doors, screening, shutters, awnings and similar seasonal accessories.

B. fences.

C. safety glazing.

D. garage door operator remote control transmitters.

E. geological conditions.

F. soil conditions.

G. recreational facilities.

H. outbuildings other than garages and carports.

6. System: Roofing

6.1 The inspector shall observe:

A. roof coverings.

B. roof drainage systems.

C. flashings.

D. skylights, chimneys and roof penetrations.

E. signs of leaks or abnormal condensation on building components.

6.2 The inspector shall:

A. describe the type of roof covering materials.

B. report the methods used to observe the roofing.

6.3 The inspector is NOT required to:

A. walk on the roofing.

B. observe attached accessories including but not limited to solar systems, antennae, and lightning arrestors.

7. System: Plumbing

7.1 The inspector shall observe:

A. interior water supply and distribution system including:

1. piping materials, including supports and insulation.

2. fixtures and faucets.

3. functional flow.

4. leaks.

5. cross connections.

B. interior drain, waste and vent system including:

1. traps; drain, waste, and vent piping; piping supports and pipe insulation.

2. leaks.

3. functional drainage.

C. hot water systems including:

1. water heating equipment.

2. normal operating controls.

3. automatic safety controls.

4. chimneys, flues, and vents.

D. fuel storage and distribution systems including:

1. interior fuel storage equipment, supply piping, venting, and supports.

2. leaks.

E. sump pumps.

7.2 The inspector shall:

A. describe:

1. water supply and distribution piping materials.

2. drain, waste, and vent piping materials.

3. water heater equipment.

B. operate all plumbing fixtures, including their faucets, and all exterior faucets attached to the house.

7.3 The inspector is NOT required to:
A. state the effectiveness of anti-siphon devices.
B. determine whether water supply and waste disposal systems are public or private.
C. operate automatic safety controls.
D. operate any valve except water closet flush valves, fixture faucets and hose faucets.
E. observe:
1. water conditioning systems.
2. fire and lawn sprinkler systems.
3. on-site water supply quantity and quality.
4. on-site waste disposal systems.
5. foundation irrigation systems.
6. spas, except as to functional flow and functional drainage.

8. System: Electrical

8.1 The inspector shall observe:
A. service entrance conductors.
B. service equipment, grounding equipment, main over current device, main and distribution panels.
C. amperage and voltage ratings of the service.
D. branch circuit conductors, their over current devices, and the compatibility of their ampacities and voltages.
E. the operation of a representative number of installed lighting fixtures, switches and receptacles located inside the house, garage, and on its exterior walls.
F. the polarity and grounding of all receptacles within six feet of interior plumbing fixtures, and all receptacles in the garage or carport, and on the exterior of inspected structures.
G the operation of Ground Fault Circuit Interrupters.

8.2 The inspector shall:
A. describe:
1. service amperage and voltage.
2. service entry conductor materials.
3. service type as being overhead or underground.
4. location of main and distribution panels.
B. report any observed aluminum branch circuit wiring.

8.3 The inspector is NOT required to:
A. insert any tool, probe or testing device inside the panels.
B. test or operate any over current device except Ground Fault Circuit Interrupters.
C. dismantle any electrical device or control other than to remove the covers of the main and auxiliary distribution panel.
D. observe:
1. low voltage systems.
2. smoke detectors.
3. telephone, security, cable TV, intercoms, or other ancillary wiring that is not a part of the primary electrical distribution systems.

9. System: Heating

9.1 The inspector shall observe:
A. Permanently installed heating systems including:
1. heating equipment.
2. normal operating controls.
3. automatic safety controls.
4. chimneys, flues, and vents.
5. solid fuel heating devices.
6. heat distribution systems including fans, pumps, ducts, and piping, with supports, dampers, insulation, air filters, registers, radiators, fan-coil units, convectors.
7. the presence of an installed heat source in each room.

9.2 The inspector shall:
A. describe:
1. energy source.
2. heating equipment and distribution type.
B. operate the systems using normal operating controls.
C. open readily openable access panels provided by the manufacturer or installer for routine homeowner maintenance.

9.3 The inspector is NOT required to:
A. operate heating systems when weather conditions or other circumstances may cause equipment damage.
B. operate automatic safety controls.
C. ignite or extinguish solid fuel fires.
D. observe:

1. the interior of flues.
2. fireplace insert flue connectors.
3. humidifiers.
4. electronic air filters.
5. the uniformity or adequacy of heat supply to the various rooms.

10. System: Central Air Conditioning

10.1 The inspector shall observe:
  A. central air conditioning including:
    1. cooling and air handling equipment.
    2. normal operating controls.
  B. distribution systems including:
    1. fans, pumps, ducts, and piping, with supports, dampers, insulation, air filters, registers and fan-coil units.
    2. the presence of an installed cooling source in each room.

10.2 The inspector shall:
  A. describe:
    1. energy sources.
    2. cooling equipment type.
  B. operate the systems using normal operating controls.
  C. open readily openable access panels provided by the manufacturer or installer for routine homeowner maintenance.

10.3 The inspector is NOT required to:
  A. operate cooling systems when weather conditions or other circumstances may cause equipment damage.
  B. observe non-central air conditioners.
  C. observe the uniformity or adequacy of cool-air supply to the various rooms.

11. System: Interiors

11.1 The inspector shall observe:
  A. walls, ceilings, and floors.
  B. steps, stairways, balconies, and railings.

  C. counters and a representative number of cabinets.
  D. a representative number of doors and windows.
  E. separation walls, ceilings, and doors between a dwelling unit and an attached garage or another dwelling unit.
  F. sumps.

11.2 The inspector shall:
  A. operate a representative number of primary windows and interior doors.
  B. report signs of water penetration into the building or signs of abnormal or harmful condensation on building components.

11.3 The inspector is NOT required to observe:
  A. paint, wallpaper, and other finish treatments on the interior walls, ceilings, and floors.
  B. carpeting.
  C. draperies, blinds, or other window treatments.
  D. household appliances.
  E. recreational facilities or another dwellingunit.

12. System: Insulation & Ventilation

12.1 The inspector shall observe:
  A. insulation and vapor retarders in unfinished spaces.
  B. ventilation of attics and foundation areas.
  C. kitchen, bathroom, and laundry venting systems.

12.2 The inspector shall describe:
  A. insulation and vapor retarders in unfinished spaces.
  B. absence of same in unfinished space at conditioned surfaces.

12.3 The inspector is NOT required to report on:
  A. concealed insulation and vapor retarders.
  B. venting equipment which is integral with household appliances.

■ GLOSSARY OF TERMS

Automatic Safety Controls: Devices designed and installed to protect systems and components from excessively high or low pressures and temperatures, excessive electrical current, loss of water, loss of ignition, fuel leaks, fire, freezing, or other unsafe conditions.

Central Air Conditioning: A system which uses ducts to distribute cooled and/or dehumidified air to more than one room or uses pipes to distribute chilled water to heat exchangers in more than one room, and which is not plugged into an electrical convenience outlet.

Component: A readily accessible and observable aspect of a system, such as a floor, or wall, but not individual pieces such as boards or nails where many similar pieces make up the component.

Cross Connection: Any physical connection or arrangement between potable water and any source of contamination.

Dangerous or Adverse Situations: Situations which pose a threat of injury to the inspector, and those situations which require use of special use of special protective clothing or safety equipment.

Describe: Report in writing a system or component by its type, or other observed characteristics, to distinguish it from other components used for the same purpose.

Dismantle: To take apart or remove any component, device or piece of equipment that is bolted, screwed, or fastened by other means and that would not be dismantled by a homeowner in the course of normal household maintenance.

Engineering: Analysis or design work requiring extensive preparation and experience in the use of mathematics, chemistry, physics, and the engineering sciences.

Enter: To go into an area to observe all visible components.

Functional Drainage: A drain is functional when it empties in a reasonable amount of time and does not overflow when another fixture is drained simultaneously.

Functional Flow: A reasonable flow at the highest fixture in a dwelling when another fixture is operated simultaneously.

Household Appliances: Kitchen and laundry appliances, room air conditioners, and similar appliances.

Inspector: Any person who examines any component of a building, through visual means and through normal user controls, without the use of mathematical sciences.

Installed: Attached or connected such that the installed item requires tools for removal.

Normal Operating Controls: Homeowner operated devices such as a thermostat, wall switch, or safety switch.

Observe: The act of making a visual examination.

On-site Water Supply Quality: Water quality is based on the bacterial, chemical, mineral, and solids content of the water.

On-site Water Supply Quantity: Water quantity is the rate of flow of water.

Operate: To cause systems or equipment to function.

Primary Windows and Doors: Windows and/or exterior doors which are designed to remain in the respective openings year round and not left open for the entire summer.

Readily Operable Access Panel: A panel provided for homeowner inspection and maintenance which has removable or operable fasteners or latch devices in order to be lifted off, swung open, or otherwise removed by one person, and its edges and fasteners are not painted in place. Limited to those panels within normal reach or from a 4-foot step-ladder, and which are not blocked by stored items, furniture, or building components.

Recreational Facilities: Spas, saunas, steam baths, swimming pools, tennis courts, playground equipment, and other exercise, entertainment, or athletic facilities.

Representative Number: For multiple identical components such as windows and electric outlets one such component on each side of the building.

Roof Drainage Systems: Gutters, downspouts, leaders, splash blocks, and similar components used to carry water off a roof and away from a building.

Safety Glazing: Tempered Glass, laminated glass, or rigid plastic.

Shut Down: A piece of equipment or a system is shut down when it cannot be operated by the device or control which a home owner should normally use to operate it. If its safety switch or circuit breaker is in the "off" position, or its fuse is missing or blown, the inspector is not required to reestablish the circuit for the purpose of operating the equipment or system.

Solid Fuel Heating Device: Any wood, coal, or other similar organic fuel burning device, including but not limited to fireplaces whether masonry or factory-built, fireplace inserts and stoves, wood stoves (room heaters), central furnaces, and combinations of these devices.

Structural Component: A component which supports non-variable forces or weighs (dead loads) and variable forces or weights (live loads).

System: A combination of interacting or interdependent components, assembled to carry out one or more functions.

Technically Exhaustive: An inspection is technically exhaustive when it involves the extensive use of measurements, instruments, testing, calculations, and other means to develop scientific or engineering findings, conclusions, and recommendations.

Underfloor Crawl Space: The area within the confines of the foundation and between the ground and the underside of the lowest floor structural component.

■ CODE OF ETHICS OF THE AMERICAN SOCIETY OF HOME INSPECTORS, INC.

Honesty, justice, and courtesy form a moral philosophy which, associated with mutual interest among people, constitutes the foundation of ethics. The members should recognize such a standard, not in passive observance, but in a set of dynamic principles guiding their conduct. It is their duty to practice the profession according to this code of ethics.

As the keystone of professional conduct is integrity, the members will discharge their duties with fidelity to the public, their clients, and with fairness and impartiality to all. They should uphold the honor and dignity of their profession and avoid association with any enterprise of questionable character, or apparent conflict of interest.

1. The member will express an opinion only when it is based on practical experience and honest conviction.
2. The member will always act in good faith toward each client.
3. The member will not disclose any information concerning the results of the inspection without the approval of the clients or their representatives.
4. The member will not accept compensation, financial or otherwise, from more than one interested party for the same service without the consent of all interested parties.
5. The member will not accept nor offer commissions or allowances, directly or indirectly, from other parties dealing with their client in connection with work for which the member is responsible.
6. The member will promptly disclose to his or her client any interest in a business which may affect the client. The member will not allow an interest in any business to affect the quality of the results of their inspection work which they may be called upon to perform. The inspection work may not be used as a vehicle by the inspector to deliberately obtain work in another field.
7. An inspector shall make every effort to uphold, maintain, and improve the professional integrity, reputation, and practice of the home inspection profession. S/He will report all such relevant information, including violations of this Code by other members, to the Association for possible remedial action.

Appendix B

The National Association of Home Inspectors, Inc.

■ STANDARDS OF PRACTICE AND CODE OF ETHICS

1. Purpose, Scope and General Statements

1.1 The Standards of Practice (Standards) provide the minimum standards of performance for a written residential home inspection performed by a member of the National Association of Home Inspectors, Inc. (NAHI).

1.2 The Standards define and clarify the purpose, conditions, limitations, exclusions, and certain terms relating to an inspection.

1.3 The Standards identify those items, components, and systems included in the scope of an inspection.

1.4 The Standards apply only to the inspection of buildings with one (1) to four (4) dwelling units.

1.5 The Standards apply to a visual inspection of the readily accessible areas of the included items, components, and systems to determine if, at the time of the inspection, they are performing their intended function without regard to life expectancy.

1.6 The purpose of the inspection is to identify visible defects and/or conditions that, in the judgement of the Inspector, adversely affect the function and/or integrity of the items, components, and systems inspected with the health and safety of the dwelling occupant(s) in mind.

1.7 Inspections performed under the Standards are basically visual and rely upon the opinion, judgement, and experience of the Inspector, and are not intended to be technically exhaustive.

1.8 Inspections shall be performed in a time period sufficient to allow compliance with the provisions of the Standards.

1.9 Inspections performed under the Standards shall not be construed as a compliance inspection of any code or governmental regulation. In the event a law, statute, or ordinance prohibits a procedure recommended in the Standards, the Inspector is relieved of the obligation to adhere to the prohibited part of the Standards.

1.10 Inspections performed under the Standards are not an expressed or implied warranty or a guarantee of the adequacy, performance, or useful life of any item, component, or system in, on, or about the inspected property.

1.11 Detached building(s) and detached garage(s) located on the property will be inspected under these Standards only if specifically listed in the inspection report.

1.12 The National Association of Home Inspectors recommends that its members perform inspections in accordance with these Standards, the Code of Ethics, and applicable law(s). The Standards are not intended to limit members from performing additional inspection services.

2. General Limitations and Exclusions

2.1 Inspections performed under the Standards exclude any item(s) concealed or not readily accessible to the Inspector. The Inspector is not required to move furniture, personal, or stored items; lift floor coverings; move attached wall, ceiling coverings, or panels; or perform any test(s) or procedures(s) which could damage or destroy the item(s) being evaluated.

2.2 Excluded are the following: appliances, recreational facilities, alarms, intercoms, speaker systems, radio controlled operators, and security devices.

2.3 The determination of the presence of or damage caused by termites or any other wood-damaging insects or organism is excluded.

2.4 The Inspector is not responsible for the determination of air quality, presence of airborne substances and conditions, or odors that may be harmful or unpleasant to certain individuals or animals.

2.5 Use of special instruments or testing devices, such as amp meters, pressure gauges, moisture meters, gas detectors and similar equipment is not required.

2.6 The inspection is not required to include information from any source concerning previous property, geological, environmental or hazardous waste conditions, or manufacturer recalls or information contained in Consumer Protection Bulletin. The inspection is not required to include information from any source concerning past or present violations of codes, ordinances, or regulations.

2.7 The inspection and report are opinions only, based upon visual observation of existing conditions of the inspected property at the time of the inspection. THE REPORT IS NOT INTENDED TO BE, OR TO BE CONSTRUED AS, A GUARANTEE, WARRANTY, OR ANY FORM OF INSURANCE. The Inspector will not be responsible for any repairs or replacements with regard to the property or the contents thereof.

2.8 The Inspector is not required to determine property boundary lines or encroachments.

3. Site

3.1 Components for Inspection.
- 3.1.1 Building perimeter, land grade, and water drainage directly adjacent to the foundation.
- 3.1.2 Trees and vegetation that adversely affect the structure.
- 3.1.3 Walks, grade steps, driveways, patios, and retaining walls contiguous with the structure.

3.2 Procedures for Inspection.
The Inspector will:
- 3.2.1 Describe material and inspect the condition of the driveways, walkways, grade steps, patios, and other items contiguous with the inspected structure.
- 3.2.2 Observe the drainage, grading, and vegetation for conditions that adversely affect the structure.

3.3 Limitations.
The Inspector is **not** required to:
- 3.3.1 Inspect fences or privacy walls.
- 3.3.2 Evaluate the condition of trees, shrubs, and/or other vegetation.
- 3.3.3 Evaluate or determine soil or geological conditions, site engineering, or property boundaries.

4. Foundations

4.1 Components for Inspection.
- 4.1.1 Foundation walls, first-floor systems, other support and substructure components, stairs.
- 4.1.2 Ventilation (when applicable).
- 4.1.3 Grade slab and/or floor slab.

4.2 Procedures for Inspection.
The Inspector will:
- 4.2.1 Identify the type of structure and material comprising the structure and other items inspected.
- 4.2.2 Observe the condition and serviceability of visible, exposed areas of foundation walls, grade slab, bearing walls, posts, piers, beams, joists, trusses, subfloors, chimney foundations, stairs, and other similar structural components.

4.2.3 Inspect foundations for indications of flooding, moisture, or water penetration.

4.2.4 Observe subfloor crawl space ventilation and vapor barriers.

4.2.5 Operate the sump pump when present.

4.2.6 Inspect the visible and accessible wooden members.

4.2.7 Observe the visible condition of floor slab when present.

4.3 Limitations.
The Inspector is **not** required to:

4.3.1 Enter subfloor crawl spaces with headroom of less than 3 feet, obstructions, or other detrimental conditions.

4.3.2 Move stored items or debris or perform excavation to gain access.

4.3.3 Enter areas which may contain material hazardous to the health and safety of the Inspector.

4.3.4 Operate sump pumps equipped with internal/water dependent switches.

5. Exterior

5.1 Components for Inspection.

5.1.1 Visible structural components.

5.1.2 Wall covering, trim, and protective coating.

5.1.3 Windows and doors.

5.1.4 Attached porches, decks, steps, balconies, handrails and guardrails, and carports.

5.1.5 Visible exterior portions of chimneys.

5.2 Procedures for Inspection.
The Inspector will:

5.2.1 Identify the type and material comprising the exterior components inspected.

5.2.2 Observe the condition of the components from the ground level.

5.2.3 Observe the condition of a representative number of visible windows and doors.

5.2.4 Inspect accessible porches, decks, steps, balconies, and carports.

5.3 Limitations.
The Inspector is **not** required to:

5.3.1 Inspect buildings, decks, patios, and other structures detached from the house.

5.3.2 Evaluate function of shutters, awnings, storm doors, storm windows and similar accessories.

5.3.3 Inspect or test the operation of security locks, devices, or systems.

5.3.4 Evaluate the presence, extent, and type of insulation and vapor barriers in the exterior walls.

5.3.5 Examine the interior of the chimney flues or determine the presence or absence of flu liners.

5.3.6 Inspect for safety glass or the integrity of thermal window seals.

6. Roof Coverings, Flashings, Gutters, and Downspouts

6.1 Components for Inspection.

6.1.1 Roof covering material.

6.1.2 Rain gutter and downspout system.

6.1.3 Visible portions of roof flashings.

6.1.4 Roof ventilation.

6.1.5 Roof soffits and fascias.

6.1.6 Roof skylights and other roof accessories.

6.2 Procedures for Inspection.
The Inspector will:

6.2.1 Describe type of roofing and gutters.

6.2.2 Observe the condition of visible roof material, rain gutter and downspout systems, visible portions of roof flashings, roof soffits and fascias, roof vents, skylights and other roof accessories visible from the exterior.

6.2.3 If possible, inspect the roof surface and components from arms-length distance or with binoculars from the ground.

6.2.4 Inspect flat roofs where internal accessibility is readily and safely available.

6.3 Limitations.
The Inspector is **not** required to:

6.3.1 Walk on or access a roof where it could damage the roof or roofing material or be unsafe for the Inspector.

6.3.2 Remove snow, ice, debris or other conditions that prohibit the observation of the roof surfaces.

6.3.3 Inspect internal gutter and downspout systems and related underground drainage piping.

6.3.4 Inspect antennas, lightning arresters, or similar attachments.

7. Roof Structure, Attic and Insulation

7.1 Components for Inspection.
   7.1.1 Roof framing, sheathing and decking.
   7.1.2 Attic insulation and ventilation.

7.2 Procedures for Inspection.
   The Inspector will:
   7.2.1 Describe material comprising the roof structure in the visible attic area.
   7.2.2 Observe the condition of the visible roof structure and attic components where readily and safely accessible.
   7.2.3 Investigate evidence of the presence of water penetration.
   7.2.4 Determine the presence of attic insulation and its approximate thickness.

7.3 Limitations.
   The Inspector is **not** required to:
   7.3.1 Enter attic spaces not readily accessible, if headroom is less than 3 feet, or if inspection could damage ceilings or insulation.
   7.3.2 Break or otherwise damage the surface finish or weather seal on or around access panels and covers.
   7.3.3 Operate powered roof ventilators.

8. Attached Garage(s)/Carport(s)

8.1 Components for Inspection.
   8.1.1 Exterior and interior walls and ceilings, floors, windows, doors, roof, and foundation.
   8.1.2 Electrical system and components.
   8.1.3 Plumbing system and components.
   8.1.4 Heating systems or units.

8.2 Procedures for Inspection.
   The Inspector will:

8.2.1 Identify type and material of door(s), exterior walls, roof (if applicable), and other items to be inspected.

8.2.2 Observe the condition and function of listed components; electric, plumbing, heating and similar systems.

8.2.3 Check the condition and operation of accessible garage door(s).

8.3 Limitations.
   The Inspector is **not** required to:
   8.3.1 Inspect or operate equipment housed in the garage area except as otherwise addressed in the Standards.
   8.3.2 Operate the auto reverse function of a vehicle door if the condition or type indicates possible damage could occur from such operation.

9. Electrical

9.1 Components for Inspection.
   9.1.1 Entrance of the primary service from masthead to main panel.
   9.1.2 Main and sub-panels including feeders.
   9.1.3 Branch circuits, connected devices, and lighting fixtures.

9.2 Procedures for Inspection.
   The Inspector will:
   9.2.1 Identify type and location of primary service (overhead or underground), voltage, amperage, and over-current protection devices (fuses or breakers).
   9.2.2 Determine the existence of connected service grounding cable(s) and observe their condition.
   9.2.3 Inspect the main and branch circuits for over-current protection and condition.
   9.2.4 Determine presence of aluminum branch circuit wiring at the main and sub-panels.
   9.2.5 Test and/or verify operation of a representative number of accessible switches, receptacles and light fixtures.
   9.2.6 Test and/or verify grounding and polarity of a representative number of receptacles in proximity to plumbing fixtures or on the exterior.
   9.2.7 Verify operation of ground fault circuit interrupters (GFCI), if present.

9.2.8 Observe the general condition of exposed wiring.

9.3 Limitations.
The Inspector is **not** required to:
9.3.1 Insert any tool, probe or testing device into the main or sub-panels.
9.3.2 Activate electrical systems or branch circuits which are not energized.
9.3.3 Operate overload protection devices.
9.3.4 Inspect ancillary systems, including but not limited to: burglar alarms, home protection systems, low voltage relays, smoke/heat detectors, antennas, electrical de-icing tapes, sprinkler wiring, swimming pool wiring, or any systems controlled by timers.
9.3.5 Move any objects, furniture, or appliances to gain access to any electrical component.
9.3.6 Test every switch, receptacle, and fixture.
9.3.7 Remove switch and outlet cover plates.
9.3.8 Inspect electrical equipment not readily accessible or dismantle any electrical device or control.
9.3.9 Verify continuity of connected service ground(s).

10. Plumbing

10.1 Components for Inspection.
    10.1.1 Visible water supply lines.
    10.1.2 Visible waste/soil and vent lines.
    10.1.3 Fixtures and faucets.
    10.1.4 Dome'stic hot water system and fuel source.

10.2 Procedures for Inspection.
    The Inspector will:
    10.2.1 Identify material of the main line and water supply lines.
    10.2.2 Verify the presence of a main water supply valve.
    10.2.3 Identify type of sanitary waste piping.
    10.2.4 Identify type and capacity of domestic water heating unit(s).
    10.2.5 Inspect the condition of accessible and visible water and waste lines.

10.2.6 Inspect and operate fixtures and faucets.
10.2.7 Inspect and operate the domestic hot water system.
10.2.8 Inspect and operate drain pumps and waste ejector pumps when possible.
10.2.9 Test the water supply for functional flow.
10.2.10 Test waste lines from sinks, tubs and showers for functional drainage.

10.3 Limitations.
The Inspector is **not** required to:
10.3.1 Operate any main, branch or fixture valve, except faucets, or determine water temperature.
10.3.2 Inspect any system that is shutdown or secured.
10.3.3 Inspect any plumbing components not readily accessible.
10.3.4 Inspect any exterior plumbing components or interior or exterior drain systems.
10.3.5 Inspect interior fire sprinkler systems.
10.3.6 Evaluate the potability of any water supply.
10.3.7 Inspect water conditioning equipment, including softener and filter systems.
10.3.8 Operate freestanding or built-in appliances.
10.3.9 Inspect private water supply systems.
10.3.10 Test shower pans, tub and shower surrounds, or enclosures for leakage.
10.3.11 Inspect gas supply system for materials or leakage.
10.3.12 Evaluate the condition and operation of water wells and related pressure tanks and pumps; the quality or quantity of water from on-site water supplies; or the condition and operation of on-site sewage disposal systems such as cesspools, septic tanks, drain fields, related underground piping, conduit, cisterns, and equipment.
10.3.13 Inspect and operate fixtures and faucets if the flow end of the faucet is connected to an appliance.

11. Central Heating

11.1 Components for Inspection.
 11.1.1 Fuel source.
 11.1.2 Heating equipment.
 11.1.3 Heating distribution.
 11.1.4 Operating controls.
 11.1.5 Flue pipes, chimneys and venting
 11.1.6 Auxiliary heating units.

11.2 Procedures for Inspection.
 The Inspector will:
 11.2.1 Identify the type of fuel, heating equipment, and heating distribution system.
 11.2.2 Operate the system using normal control devices to determine function.
 11.2.3 Open access panels or covers provided by the manufacturer or installer, if readily detachable.
 11.2.4 Observe the condition of normally operated controls and components of the systems.
 11.2.5 Observe visible flue pipes, dampers and related components for safe operation.
 11.2.6 Observe the condition of a representative number of heat sources in each area of the house.
 11.2.7 Inspect the installation and operation of fixed supplementary heat units.

11.3 Limitations.
 The Inspector is **not** required to:
 11.3.1 Activate or operate heating or other systems that have been shut-down.
 11.3.2 Activate or operate heating systems that do not respond to normal controls.
 11.3.3 Inspect equipment or remove covers or panels that are not readily accessible.
 11.3.4 Dismantle any equipment, controls, or gauges.
 11.3.5 Inspect the interior of chimney flues.
 11.3.6 Inspect heating system accessories, such as humidifiers, air purifiers, motorized dampers, heat reclaimers, etc.
 11.3.7 Inspect solar heating systems.
 11.3.8 Activate heating, heat pump systems, or other systems when ambient temperatures or other circumstances are not conducive to safe operation or may damage the equipment.
 11.3.9 Evaluate the type of material contained in insulation and/or wrapping of pipes, ducts, jackets and boilers.
 11.3.10 Operate digital-type thermostats or controls.
 11.3.11 Evaluate the capacity, adequacy, or efficiency of a heating or cooling system.
 11.3.12 Test or operate fireplaces, stoves, space heaters, or solar heating devices.
 11.3.13 Determine clearance to combustibles.

12. Central Air Conditioning

12.1 Components for Inspection.
 12.1.1 Cooling equipment.
 12.1.2 Cooling distribution.
 12.1.3 Operating controls.

12.2 Procedures for Inspection.
 The Inspector will:
 12.2.1 Identify the type of central air conditioning system and energy sources.
 12.2.2 Operate the system using normal control devices.
 12.2.3 Open access panels or covers provided by the manufacturer or installer, if readily accessible.
 12.2.4 Observe the condition of controls and operative components of the complete system, conditions permitting.
 12.2.5 Observe the condition of a representative number of the central air cooling outlets in each habitable area of the house.

12.3 Limitations.
 The Inspector is **not** required to:
 12.3.1 Activate or operate cooling or other systems that have been shut down.

12.3.2 Inspect gas-fired refrigeration systems, evaporative coolers, or wall or window-mounted air conditioning units.

12.3.3 Check the pressure of the system coolant or determine the presence of leakage.

12.3.4 Evaluate the capacity, efficiency, or adequacy of the system.

12.3.5 Operate equipment or systems if exterior temperature is below 60° Fahrenheit or when other circumstances are not conducive to safe operation or may damage the equipment.

12.3.6 Remove covers or panels that are not readily accessible.

12.3.7 Dismantle any equipment, controls, or gauges.

12.3.8 Check the electrical current drawn by the unit.

12.3.9 Operate digital-type thermostats or controls.

13. Interior

13.1 Components for Inspection.
13.1.1 Walls, ceilings, floors, windows, and doors.
13.1.2 Steps, stairways, balconies, railings.
13.1.3 Fireplaces.
13.1.4 Electric outlets and fixtures.
13.1.5 Plumbing fixtures and components.
13.1.6 Heating and cooling distribution.

13.2 Procedures for Inspection.
The Inspector will:
13.2.1 Observe the visible condition of the surfaces of walls, ceilings, and floors relative to structural integrity and evidence of water penetration.

13.2.2 Verify the presence of steps, stairways, balconies, handrails and guardrails and observe their condition.

13.2.3 Describe type, material, condition and operation of a representative number of windows, doors and their hardware.

13.2.4 Inspect the exterior condition of the kitchen cabinets and countertops.

13.2.5 Observe the condition of fireplaces, dampers, fire boxes and hearths readily visible.

13.2.6 Locate and observe a representative number of electrical outlets/fixtures and wiring in each room as described in Section 9.

13.2.7 Comment on presence or absence of smoke detectors.

13.2.8 Observe condition and operation of plumbing fixtures and components in each room as described in Section 10.

13.2.9 Observe a representative number of heat and/or air conditioning sources and returns, if applicable, in each room as described in Sections 11&12.

13.3 Limitations.
*The Inspector is **not** required to:*
13.3.1 Ignite fires in a fireplace or stove to determine the adequacy of draft, perform a chimney smoke test, or inspect any solid fuel device in use.

13.3.2 Evaluate the installation or adequacy of inserts, wood burning stoves, or other modifications in a fireplace, stove, or chimney.

13.3.3 Determine clearance to combustibles in concealed areas.

13.3.4 Determine cosmetic condition of ceilings, walls, floor coverings, and components.

GLOSSARY OF TERMS

Activate: To turn on, supply power, or enable systems, equipment, or devices to become active by normal control means. Examples include turning on the gas or water supply valves to the fixtures and appliances and activating electrical breakers or fuses.

Adversely Affect: Constitute, or potentially constitute, a negative or destructive impact.

Appliance: A household device operated by use of electricity or gas. Not included in this definition are components covered under central heating, central cooling, or plumbing.

Evaluate: To ascertain, judge, or form an opinion about an item or condition.

Foundation: The base upon which the structure or a wall rests; usually masonry, concrete, or stone, and generally partially underground.

Function: The action for which an item, component or system is specially fitted or used or for which an item, component or system exists; to be in action or perform a task.

Functional: Performing, or able to perform, a function.

Functional Drainage: A drain is functional when it empties in a reasonable amount of time and is not subject to overflow when one of its *supply* faucets is left on.

Functional Flow: Sufficient water flow to provide uninterrupted supply to the highest, unrestricted tap (faucet farthest from the source) when a single intermediate, unrestricted tap is operated simultaneously with uninterrupted flow.

Habitable: In a condition suitable for human habitation.

Habitable Spaces: Rooms or spaces used for sitting, sleeping, bathing, toilets, eating or cooking. Not considered habitable spaces by these Standards are closets, halls, storage spaces and utility areas.

Heat Source: A heat source may be a radiator, convector unit, radiant panel, heat pipe, ductwork, grille, register, or other device(s) from which heat is intended to be emitted.

Inspected Property: The readily accessible areas of the buildings, site, items, components, and systems included in the inspection.

Intended Function: Performing or able to perform the usual function for which an item is designed, or fitted; and be in a condition (state of repair) appropriate to this function, its age and location. [See Function]

Observe: To see through visual directed attention.

Operate: To cause equipment or systems that have been activated to perform their intended function(s), such as turning on a water faucet or turning up the thermostat on an activated heating system.

Readily Accessible: An item or component is readily accessible if, in the judgement of the inspector, it is capable of being safely observed without movement of obstacles, detachment or disengagement of connecting or securing devices, or other unsafe or difficult procedures to gain access.

Representative Number: A sufficient number to serve as a typical or characteristic example of the item(s) inspected.

Shut-down: A system or equipment is considered to be shut-down when its normal control device(s) will not cause it to become activated or operational. The Inspector is not required to activate or operate safety devices (fuses, breakers, etc.) in the "off" position. It is not the responsibility of the Inspector to put these controls in the "on" mode, nor to ensure that the equipment or systems to be tested are operable at the time of the inspection.

Slab on Grade: Structures that have no crawl space and are in direct contact with the soil. Slabs may or may not have supporting piers or pads.

Technically exhaustive: An inspection is technically exhaustive when it involves the use of measurements, instruments, testing calculations and other means to develop scientific or engineering findings, conclusions, and recommendations.

Verify: To confirm or substantiate.

CODE OF ETHICS

To maintain the integrity and high standards of skill and practice in the home inspection profession, the following rules of conduct and ethics shall be binding upon the use of the Standards of Practice (Standards) of the National Association of Home Inspectors, Inc. (NAHI):

1. The Inspector will act as a disinterested third party and will discharge his duties with integrity and fidelity to the public, with fairness and impartiality to all parties.

2. The Inspector shall uphold the honor and dignity of this profession and avoid association with any enterprise of questionable character or apparent conflict of interest.

3. The Inspector will express an opinion only when it is based on practical experience and honest conviction.

4. The Inspector will always act in good faith toward the client.

5. The Inspector will not disclose any information concerning the results of the inspection without the approval of the client for whom the inspection was performed.

6. The Inspector will not accept compensation, financial or otherwise, from more than one interested party for the same service on the same property without the consent of all interested parties.

7. The Inspector will not accept nor offer commissions or allowances, directly or indirectly, from other parties dealing with the client in connection with work for which the Inspector is responsible.

8. The Inspector will promptly disclose to the client any interest in any other business which may affect the client, the quality or the result of the inspection. The Inspector will not knowingly use the inspection process to obtain work in another field.

9. The Inspector shall make every effort to uphold, maintain and improve the professional practice, integrity and reputation of NAHI. He will report all violations of this Code by other members, and any other relevant information, to NAHI for possible remedial action.

10. An appraisal or opinion of the market value of the inspected property will not be expressed by the Inspector within the context of the inspection.

11. Use of the NAHI logo and name is limited to those persons holding the designation of Member. Provisional and Affiliate Members may use specifically designated logos in advertising.

Appendix C

Chapter Review Answers

CHAPTER 1

No Review Questions

CHAPTER 2

No Review Questions

CHAPTER 3

1. A
2. B
3. A
4. D
5. A
6. A
7. D
8. A
9. B
10. B
11. D
12. A
13. A
14. B
15. D
16. sump
17. sump
18. B
19. B
20. D
21. A
22. A

CHAPTER 4

1. D
2. A
3. A

Construction
1. A
2. C
3. A
4. A
5. ridgeboard
6. D
7. A
8. lower chord
   web members
   upper chord
   gusset plate
9. B
10. masonry
    metal
11. A
12. D
13. A
14. A
15. A
16. B
17. B
18. A
19. C
20. C
21. A
22. A
23. A
24. B
25. B
26. A

EIFS
1. D
2. C
3. A
4. A
5. A

CHAPTER 5

1. B
2. C
3. A
4. C
5. B
6. D
7. A
8. A
9. B
10. A
11. D
12. A
13. A
14. A
15. B
16. A
17. C
18. D
19. D

CHAPTER 6

1. septic, aseptic, mechanical
2. aseptic
3. B
4. A
5. C
6. anode rod
7. B
8. A
9. D
10. A
11. A
12. A
13. D
14. B
15. A
16. A
17. A
18. C
19. B
20. A
21. B
22. D
23. A
24. C
25. A
26. B
27. A

28. A
29. A
30. A
31. D
32. D

CHAPTER 7

1. A
2. A
3. D
4. A
5. B
6. A
7. B
8. fuses
   circuit breaker
9. driven rod
   copper water line
10. black, red, blue
11. white
12. A
13. A
14. A
15. D
16. A
17. C
18. B
19. D
20. B

CHAPTER 8

1. incomplete
2. blocked vent
   too long run
   too many elbows
   vent pipe too small
   downdraft
3. limit
4. yellow
5. convection
6. induced power vent
7. derates
8. spillage
9. amprobe
10. A
11. B
12. dismantle the furnace and visually inspect
    heat exchanger
13. carbon monoxide
14. A

15. opens
16. humidistat
17. convection
    conduction
    radiation
18. A
19. B
20. D
21. A
22. A
23. D

CHAPTER 9

1. 60
2. vapor
3. A
4. A
5. reversing
6. 80
7. balance point
8. B
9. A
10. B
11. cycle off due to high head pressure
12. hot
13. evaporator coil
14. defrost control and/or reversing valve
15. A
16. A
17. A
18. E
19. A
20. C
21. B
22. A

CHAPTER 10

1. A
2. A
3. continuous feed
   batch feed
4. C
5. A
6. A
7. open
8. low
   medium
   high

9. A
10. A
11. 350, 3
12. B
13. A
14. B
15. B
16. corrosion
17. A
18. 4
19. steam, odors, and grease vapors
20. A
21. A
22. cycle selection
    water temperature
23. protect the shaft seal
24. A
25. D
26. D
27. A
28. A

CHAPTER 11

1. gunite, fiberglass, vinyl lined
2. A
3. A
4. B
5. A
6. B
7. B
8. A
9. A
10. A
11. A
12. A
13. B
14. A
15. C
16. A
17. B
18. A
19. A
20. C

CHAPTER 12

1. B
2. A
3. C
4. A
5. B
6. A
7. A
8. A
9. B
10. B
11. A
12. A
13. A

CHAPTER 13

1. A
2. A
3. B
4. B
5. B
6. D
7. A
8. B
9. C
10. A
11. D
12. B

Glossary

A

abatement asbestos control beyond a special operations and maintenance program.

absolute humidity amount of moisture in the air, indicated in grains per cu. ft.

absolute pressure gauge pressure plus atmospheric pressure (14.7 lb. per sq. in.).

absolute temperature temperature measured from zero.

absorb/adsorb to take in and make a part of, as would a sponge.

absorber dark surface that absorbs solar radiation and converts it to heat; a component of a solar collector.

accessible (as applied to wiring methods) capable of being removed or exposed without damaging the building structure or finish or not permanently closed in by the structure or finish of the building.

acid demand acid required to lower the pH and alkalinity of pool water to the proper level.

acoustical tile special tile made of wood, mineral, cork, metal, or fiber that is installed on ceilings and/or walls to control sound.

acrylonitrile-butadiene-styrene (ABS) pipe used for drains, waste, and venting.

activated carbon specially processed carbon used to clean air.

activated charcoal highly absorbent charcoal that is free of contamination.

active system solar heating system using mechanical means of heat collection, storage, and distribution.

admixture material other than water, aggregate, or hydraulic cement added to concrete before or during mixing to modify the concrete's properties.

AGA American Gas Association.

aggregate crushed stone, crushed slag, or water-worn gravel used for surfacing a built-up roof, or any such granular mineral material (e.g., sand) used with hydraulic cement to form concrete or mortar.

aggregate, lightweight aggregate with a dry, loose weight of 70 lb. per cu. ft. or less.

air chambers pressure-absorbing devices that eliminate water hammering. Air chambers should be installed as close as possible to valves or faucets and at the end of long runs of pipe.

air circulation refers to air velocity, air volume, and airflow patterns.

air cleaner device used for removal of airborne impurities.

air diffuser air distribution outlet designed to direct airflow into desired patterns.

air ducts pipes that carry warm and cold air to rooms and return back to the heating or cooling system.

air gap (drainage system) unobstructed vertical distance through the free atmosphere between the outlet of a water pipe and the flood level rim of the receptacle into which it discharges.

air gap (water distribution system) unobstructed vertical distance through the free atmosphere between the lowest opening from any pipe or faucet supplying water to a tank, a plumbing fixture, or another device and the flood level rim of the receptacle.

air-heating collector solar collector, such as a thermosiphoning air panel (TAP) or window box collector, designed to absorb solar energy, convert it to heat and transfer the heat, to air flowing from the house, through the collector, and back to the house.

air lock bubble of air that restricts the flow of water in a pipe.

air return air that returns from conditioned or refrigerated space to the source.

air-saturated mixture of dry air and saturated water vapor, all at the same dry bulb temperature.

air velocity rate of flow of air, measured in ft. per min.

471

air volume change volume of fresh air equal to the volume of the space; a ventilation standard measured in the number of changes of air per hr.

algae marine plant life that grows in the presence of sunlight and carbon dioxide.

algaecide/algicide chemical that kills algae.

algae discoloration type of roof discoloration caused by fungus growth.

algaestat chemical that inhibits algae growth.

alluvium material such as sand, silt, or clay deposited on land by streams.

alpha particle energized particle made up of two protons and two neutrons that is ejected from a radioactive atom.

ambient encompassing atmosphere or environment.

ambient temperature temperature of fluid, usually air, that surrounds an object on all sides.

ammeter electric meter used to measure current, calibrated in amperes.

amp measurement of electrical current in a circuit at any given time.

ampacity current-carrying capacity of electric conductors expressed in amperes.

amperage unit of electric current equivalent to 6.28 quintillion electrons passing a given point in 1 sec.

ampere flow of electricity through electrical wire.

amprobe tester that is designed to determine running currents, overloads, and balanced circuits.

anchorage (1) device used to anchor tendons to a concrete member in post-tensioning; (2) device used to anchor tendons during the curing of concrete in pretensioning.

annual fuel utilization efficiency (AFUE) rating that measures the average annual seasonal efficiency of a boiler or furnace by measuring the heat produced from a given amount of fuel.

anticipating control one that is artificially forced to cut in or out before it originally would, thus starting cooling before needed or stopping heating before the control point is reached. It reduces the temperature fluctuation or override.

appliance utilization equipment, generally other than industrial, normally built in standardized sizes or types; installed or connected as a unit to perform one or more functions, such as dishwasher, electric range, air-conditioning, etc.

approved acceptable to the authority having jurisdiction.

apron paved area, such as a garage entrance, on the junction of the driveway to the street.

architectural shingles see **laminated shingles.**

area divider raised, double wood member attached to a properly flashed wood base plate that is anchored to the roof deck. It is used to relieve the stresses of thermal expansion and contraction in a roof system where no expansion joints have been provided.

area wall metal or concrete wall that forms open area.

areaway open space that allows light and air to a window.

ARI Air Conditioning and Refrigeration Institute.

armored cable two or more insulated wires wrapped in a metal sheathing.

asbestos group of naturally occurring, silicate minerals that separate into fibers.

ash dump trap door that allows ashes to drop to a pit below for removal.

asphalt dark brown to black cementitious material in which the predominating constituents are bitumens, which occur in nature or are obtained in petroleum processing.

asphalt felt asphalt-saturated felt or an asphalt-coated felt.

asphalt plastic cement asphalt-based cement used to bond roofing materials, also known as *mastic* or *flashing cement.*

atmospheric pressure pressure that gases in air exert on the earth, measured in lb. per sq. in.

atom smallest particle of an element that can exist alone or in combination.

atrium space intended for occupancy within a building extending vertically through three or more floor levels of the building and enclosed at the top.

B

backfill earth that is placed around piping, foundations, walls, etc.; Also refers to the material frequently used to fill the void between a swimming pool wall and sides of the excavation.

backflow flow of water or other liquids, mixtures, or substances into the distribution pipes of potable water supply from any source or sources other than the intended source.

backflow preventer device that prevents the reverse flow of water, due to atmospheric or higher pressure, by means of a positive check valve.

background radiation average radiation from all sources found in the surroundings.

back nailing practice of nailing the back portion of a roofing ply.

back siphonage flowing back of used, contaminated, or polluted water from a plumbing fixture or vessel into a potable water supply due to a negative pressure in the pipe.

back surfacing fine mineral matter applied to the back side of shingles to prevent them from sticking.

backwashing cleaning the pool filter by reversing the flow of water.

bacteria microscopic organisms not conducive to a healthy pool.

balance point where the heat pump capacity exactly matches the heating loss.

balancing damper baffle or plate used to control the volume of flowing air in a confined area.

balcony a railed platform projecting from the face of a building above ground level with an entrance from the building interior.

ballast transformer that steps up the voltage in a fluorescent light.

balloon frame a framing system in which studs and corner posts extend from the sill to the plate and upper story floor joists are carried on ledgers or girts let into the studs.

balusters vertical rods or spindles supporting a rail.

balustrade row of balusters topped by a rail, edging a balcony or a staircase.

barge board fascia or board at gable just under edge of the roof.

bark outer layer of trunk and limbs that provides protective covering for the tree.

barometer instrument for measuring atmospheric pressure. It can be calibrated in lb. per sq. in. or inches of mercury in a column.

baseboard board along floor attached to wall and partitions in a building to hide gaps and imperfections.

base flashing portion of the flashing attached to or resting on the deck to direct the flow of water onto the roof covering.

base flood elevation the elevation in relation to mean-sea-level (National Geodetic Vertical Datum) having a 1 percent chance of being equaled or exceeded in any given year.

basement any building story having a floor below grade.

basement floor slab 4″ to 5″ thick concrete that forms basement floor.

base ply first ply when it is a separate ply and not part of the shingle system.

base sheet saturated or coated felt placed as the first ply in some multiple built-up roof membranes.

batt insulation in blanket form, rather than loose filling.

batten small, thin strips covering joints between wider boards on exterior building surfaces.

beam principal horizontal wood, steel, or concrete members of a building.

bearing capacity ability of ground material to safely support a load.

bearing pressure force exerted from the foundation to the ground.

bearing wall wall that supports a floor or roof of a building.

bedrock solid rock that underlies soil and other unconsolidated material exposed at the surface.

berm a low dike-like earthen structure used to control surface drainage, mark property boundaries.

beta particle energetic electron ejected from an atom during radioactive decay.

beveled siding clapboard with a thick butt and a thin upper edge lapped to shed water.

bibcock or **bib** water faucet connected to a hose. Also referred to as a *sill cock* or *hose bib.*

bimetal two dissimilar metals that heat and cool at different rates to open or close a circuit automatically. This method is most commonly used in circuit breakers, thermostats, and pilots on some types of furnaces.

bimetal strip temperature-regulating or temperature-indicating device that operates on the principle that two dissimilar metals with unequal expansion rates, welded together, will bend when temperature changes.

bitumen generic term for an amorphous, semisolid mixture of complex hydrocarbons derived from any organic source. Asphalt and coal tar are the two bitumens used in the roofing industry.

bleeding (1) process of drawing air from a water pipe; (2) seeping of resin or gum from lumber.

blisters an enclosed pocket of air mixed with water or solvent vapor, trapped between impermeable layers of felt, or between the felt and substrate.

blind nailing practice of blind nailing (in addition to hot mopping) all the plies of a substrate to prevent slippage.

blower fan used to force air under pressure.

BOD biochemical oxygen demand

body feed air fed into a diatomaceous earth filter during the filtering cycle.

boiler at high pressure (steam), furnishing pressure at 15 psi or more; at low pressure (hot water), furnishing steam at a pressure less than 15 psi or hot water at not more than 30 psi.

boiling temperature temperature at which a fluid changes from a liquid to a gas.

bond adhesive and cohesive forces holding two roofing components in intimate contact.

bonded tendon prestressing tendon bonded to concrete either directly or through grouting.

bonding permanent joining of metallic parts to form an electrically conductive path to ensure electrical continuity and capacity to safely conduct any current likely to be imposed.

bonding jumper reliable conductor to ensure the required electrical conductivity between metal parts required to be electrically connected.

bottom land normal flood plain of a stream subject to flooding.

boulder rock fragment larger than 2′ in diameter.

box metal or plastic enclosure within which electrical connections are made; used for splitting circuits and connecting switches, receptacles, or fixtures; also referred to as a *J-box* or *junction box*.

brace wood, steel, or other material used to stiffen a structure.

braced framing construction technique using posts and cross-bracing for greater rigidity.

branch any part of the piping system other than the main, riser, or stack; or a drain pipe that collects waste from two or more fixtures for conveyance to a drain.

branch circuit circuit conductors between the final overcurrent device protecting the circuit and outlets.

branch circuit (appliance) branch circuit supplying energy to one or more outlets to which appliances are connected. Such circuits have no permanently connected lighting fixtures not part of an appliance.

branch circuit (general purpose) branch circuit that supplies many outlets for lighting and appliances.

branch vent vent connecting one or more individual vents with a vent stack.

brands airborne burning embers released from a fire.

brazing method of joining metals with nonferrous filler using heat between 800° F and the melting point of the base metals.

brick veneer structure that consists of an outer brick wall and an inner wood frame wall.

brick veneer brick used for outer surface of a framed wall.

bridging metal or wood placed diagonally between joists to prevent joists from twisting.

British thermal unit (Btu) heat energy required to raise the temperature of 1 lb. of water 1°F.

bronchi air passages to and of the lungs.

brooming embedding a ply of roofing material by using a broom to smooth out the ply and ensure contact with the adhesive under the ply.

Btu see **British thermal unit.**

Btuh Btus per hour.

building structure that stands alone or separated from adjoining structures by fire walls with all openings protected by approved fire doors.

building drain lowest drainage piping system to receive discharge from soil and waste from drainage pipes inside walls of the building; discharges to the sewer.

building line line established by law beyond which the building shall not extend.

building paper paper placed outside sheathing to prevent water and air from leaking in; also used as a tarred felt under shingles or siding to keep out moisture or wind.

built-up roof flat or low-sloped roof consisting of multiple layers of asphalt and ply sheets.

bundle package of shingles. There are three, four, or five bundles in 1 square (100 sq. ft.).

burner domestic heating boilers are generally low pressure with maximum working pressure of 15 psi for steam and 30 psi for hot water.

bus bar main power terminal to which circuits are attached through either fuses or circuit breakers. One bus bar serves the hot side; the other serves the neutral side.

butt edge bottom edge of the shingle.

butt joint joining point of molding or wood.

B-X cable trade name for a flexible electrical cable with a rubber coating, and armored with a flexible steel outer covering.

C

cable two or more insulated conductors wrapped in a metal or plastic cover.

calcium hypochlorite chemical compound of calcium and chlorine used to disinfect water.

Calendar (cylinder) a machine with rollers between which paper, cloth, plastic, etc., is run in order to give it a smooth or glossy finish. To process paper, cloth, plastic, etc., in a calendar.

calibrate to fix, check, or correct graduations of a measuring instrument, such as a pressure gauge.

calibration the relationship of the dial setting and the cut-in temperature of the thermostat.

cambium layer of actively growing cells beneath the bark in woody parts of trees.

cantilever projecting joist or beam, without support at one end, that is used to support an extension of a structure.

cant strip beveled strip of wood or wood fiber that fits into the angle formed by the intersection of a horizontal surface and a vertical surface. The 45° slope of the exposed surface of the cant strip provides a gradual angular transition from the horizontal surface to the vertical surface.

cap flashing that portion of the flashing attached to a vertical surface to prevent water from migrating behind the base flashing.

capacitor condenser-type electrical storage device used for starting and/or running circuits on many electric motors.

capillarity action by which the surface of a liquid, where it is in contact with a solid, is elevated or depressed, depending on the relative attraction of the molecules of the liquid for each other and for those of the solid.

capillary attraction upward movement of a liquid through a cellular structure of fibrous strands or other solids.

capillary tube type of refrigerant control, usually consisting of several feet of tubing having a small inside diameter and coiled near the evaporator coil.

cap sheet granule-surfaced coated sheet used as the top ply of a built-up roof membrane or flashing.

carriage structural member that supports steps or treads of stairs.

cartridge filter filter using a cartridge element that can be cleaned or replaced.

casing window and door framing.

caulking to fill a joint with mastic or asphalt cement to prevent leaks.

cementitious friable materials that are densely packed into a nonfriable material.

centigrade scale temperature scale used in the metric system. The freezing point of water is 0°C and the boiling point is 100°C.

central heating system boiler or furnace flue connected and installed as an integral part of the structure and designed to supply heat adequately for the entire structure.

cfm cubic feet per minute.

chain number of atoms or chemical groups united like links in a chain.

chair rail wooden molding placed on a wall around a room at chair-back level.

chalk line line made on the roof by snapping a taut string or cord dusted with chalk.

charge amount of refrigerant in a system.

chase groove in masonry wall or through a floor to accommodate ducts and pipes.

check valve a valve or other device that allows fluids to flow in only one direction.

chemical piping piping that conveys concentrated chemical solutions from a feeding apparatus to the circulation piping.

chimney vertical masonry shaft of reinforced concrete or other approved noncombustible heat-resisting material enclosing one or more flues. The chimney removes the products of combustion from solid, liquid, or gaseous fuel.

chimney breast inside face or front of fireplace chimney.

chimney cap protects chimney brick from weather. The chimney cap is generally made from concrete.

chimney connector pipe or breaching that connects a heating unit (such as a fuel-burning appliance) to the chimney.

chimney effect tendency of air or gas in a duct or another passage to rise when heated, due to its lower density caused by a difference in temperature. Typically, the air is replaced by cooler, denser air flowing in through lower level openings.

chimney flashing sheetmetal flashing that provides a tight joint between chimney and roof.

chlorinated polyvinyl chloride (CPVC) plastic pipe used with hot or cold water.

chlorophyll essential chemical for process of photosynthesis whereby carbon dioxide and water convert to sugars and oxygen to provide nutrition and energy to plants.

choke tube throttling device used to maintain correct pressure between the high and low side in the refrigerating mechanism; sometimes referred to as *capillary tube.*

circuit path of electrical flow from a power source through a fixture and return to ground or neutral. Also refers to the tubing, piping, or electrical wire that permits a flow from an energy source back to the energy source.

circuit breaker device that interrupts electrical flow automatically in case of an overload in the circuit. The circuit breaker can be reset by either a switch or push-button.

circuit vent branch vent that serves two or more traps and extends from the last fixture connection of a horizontal branch to the vent stack.

circulation piping system piping between the pool structure and mechanical equipment, which includes suction piping, face piping, and return piping.

cistern tank used to catch and store rain water.

Class A highest fire resistance rating for roofing as per ASTM-E-108. It indicates that roofing is able to withstand severe exposure to fire originating from sources outside the building.

Class B fire resistance rating that indicates roofing material is able to withstand moderate exposure to fire originating from sources outside the building.

Class C fire resistance rating that indicates roofing material is able to withstand light exposure to fire originating from sources outside the building.

clay fine-textured soil that usually forms hard clods when dry and is sticky when wet. Moist clay soil that is squeezed between thumb and forefinger forms a long, flexible ribbon. Fine clays high in colloids lack plasticity at all moisture levels.

clay loam soil that breaks into clods that are hard when dry. Moist clay loam soil that is squeezed between thumb and forefinger forms a thin ribbon that breaks readily, barely sustaining its own weight. The moist soil is plastic and forms a cast that can bear much handling. When kneaded in the hand, it will work into a heavy compact mass. Clay loam is defined as moderately fine soil.

cleanout door door to ash pit at the bottom of a chimney.

clearance distance separating the appliance, chimney connector, plenum, and flue from the nearest surface of combustible material.

clerestory window or strip of windows, generally between two levels of roof, that allows light to enter the interior of a building.

closed cut valley method of valley treatment in which shingles from one side of the valley extend across the valley, while shingles from the other side are trimmed 2" from the valley center line. The valley flashing is not exposed.

CO/ALR receptacles and switches rated 20 amps or less and directly connected to aluminum conductors. Must be marked CO/ALR.

coal tar bitumen dark brown to black, semisolid hydrocarbon formed as a residue from the partial evaporation or distillation of coal tar. It is used as the waterproofing agent in dead-level or low-slope built-up roofs. It is different from coal tar pitch because it has a lower front end volatility.

coarse-grained soils soils that consist of individual particles that are seen by the naked eye, such as sand and gravel. Compacted coarse-grained soils are dense with few voids.

coated base sheet felt that has been impregnated and saturated with asphalt and then coated on both sides with harder, more viscous asphalt to increase its impermeability to moisture. A parting agent is incorporated to prevent the material from sticking in the roll.

coating a layer of viscous asphalt applied to the base material in which granules or other surfacing materials are embedded.

coefficient of performance (COP) ratio of work or energy applied compared with energy used.

coil any heating or cooling element made of pipe or tubing connected in series.

coil blower consists of a metal cabinet, a filter, a blower, an air-conditioning coil, and electric controls. Blower coils are used for air-conditioning only, even though electric heat is available.

cold process roofing continuous, semiflexible roof membrane, consisting of plies of felts, mats, or fabrics that are laminated on a roof with alternate layers of cold-applied roof cement and surfaced with a cold-applied coating.

collar preformed flange placed over a vent pipe to seal the roof around the vent pipe opening; also called a *vent sleeve.*

collar beam tie that prevents the roof from spreading; connects similar rafters on opposite sides of the roof.

collection act of trapping solar radiation and converting it to heat.

column vertical steel or wood structural member that provides support for framing. Also, a slender, upright structure, generally consisting of a cylindrical shaft, a base, and a capital; a supporting or an ornamental member in a building.

combination valve multiport valve intended to perform more than one function.

combined chlorine chlorine that is combined with other chemicals and used to disinfect pool water.

combustion rapid oxidation accompanied by heat and light; a process of burning.

composite concrete flexural members members of precast and cast-in-place concrete elements or both, constructed in separate placements, but so interconnected that all elements respond to loads as a unit.

compressibility, soil reduction of voids under a load.

compressible excessive decrease in volume of soft soil and underload.

compression the force being applied to the wood grain. Example with a waterbed in the center span of a floor joist, the top edge is in compression and the bottom edge is in tension.

compression valve valve used in water supply lines inside the residential structure because it is reliable and easy to repair.

compressor pump of a refrigerating mechanism that draws a vacuum or low pressure on the cooling side of the refrigerant cycle and compresses the gas into the high-pressure or condensing side of the cycle.

concealed rendered inaccessible by the structure or finish of the building. Wires in concealed raceways are considered concealed, even though they may become accessible by withdrawing them.

concealed nail method application of rolled roofing in which all nails are driven into the underlying course of roofing and covered by a cemented, overlapping course. Nails are not exposed to the weather.

concrete mixture of hydraulic cement, fine aggregate, coarse aggregate, and water, with or without an admixture.

condensate water extracted from air by the evaporator coil during the cooling cycle. Also refers to the pump device used to remove moisture that collects under the coils.

condensation liquid or droplets that form when a gas or vapor is cooled below its dew point. Occurs when warm, moisture-laden air comes in contact with a cold surface.

condenser part of the refrigeration mechanism that receives hot, high-pressure refrigerant gas from the compressor and cools gaseous refrigerant until it returns to the liquid state.

condenser comb comb device made of metal or plastic that is used to straighten the metal cooling fins on the condensers and/or the evaporator coils.

condensing unit that part of the refrigerating mechanism that pumps vaporized refrigerant from the evaporator, compresses it, liquefies it in the condenser, and returns the liquid refrigerant to the refrigerant control.

conduction passage of heat energy through a material by molecular excitation.

conductor wire or some other material that will carry electric energy.

conduction (thermal) process of heat transfer through a material medium in which the kinetic energy is transmitted by the particles of the material from particle to particle without the displacement of particles.

conductor, bare conductor with no covering or electrical insulation.

conductor (thermal) material that readily transmits heat by means of conduction.

conduit tubing through which wires are run. It can be metal or plastic and rigid or flexible.

connector, pressure (solderless) device that establishes a connection between two or more conductors or between one or more conductors and a terminal by mechanical pressure and without the use of solder.

consistency, soil feel of the soil and ease with which a lump is crushed by the fingers.

containment work area isolated from the rest of the building to prevent escape of asbestos fibers.

contaminant substance (dirt, moisture, etc.) foreign to a refrigerant or refrigerant oil in a system.

continuity tester device used to determine whether the circuit is complete.

continuous load load where the maximum current is expected to continue for 3 hr. or more.

control automatic or manual device used to stop, start, and/or regulate flow of gas, liquid, and/or electricity.

control, combustion safety primary safety control that responds to flame properties, sensing the presence of flames and causing the fuel to shut off in the event of flame failure.

control, high-low limit automatic control that responds to liquid level changes and pressure or temperature changes and limits the operation of the appliance to be controlled.

control, primary safety automatic safety control to prevent abnormal discharge of fuel at the burner in case of ignition failure or flame failure.

convection heat transfer in air, water, or another fluid by currents resulting from the medium's falling when cooler and heavier and rising when warmer and lighter.

convection heat transfer of heat by means of movement or flow of a fluid or gas.

convector radiator that supplies a maximum amount of heat by convection, using many closely spaced metal fins fitted onto pipes that carry hot water or steam, thereby heating the circulating air.

conversion boiler or furnace originally designed for solid fuel but converted to use liquid or gaseous fuel.

cooling season portion of the year when outdoor heat makes indoor cooling desirable.

coping covering piece placed on top of a masonry wall that is exposed to the weather. It is usually sloped to shed water.

copper-clad aluminum conductors conductors drawn from a copper-clad aluminum rod with the copper metallurgically bonded to an aluminum core.

corbel horizontal projection from a wall that forms a ledge or supports a structure above the ledge (similar to a bracket).

corner bead wood or metal strip protecting the outside corners of plastered walls.

corner bracing diagonal strips used to keep framing square and plumb.

corner post vertical member at the corner of framing to receive inner and outer covering material.

cornice decorative element made of molded members usually placed at or near the top of an exterior or interior wall.

corrosion the gradual deterioration or wearing away of metal through rusting or by the action of chemicals.

count total number of particles released within the time period the measurement took place; e.g., counts/minute.

counterflashing formed metal or elastomeric sheeting secured on or into a wall, a curb, a pipe, a rooftop unit, or another surface to cover and protect the upper edge of a base flashing and its associated fasteners.

course row of shingles or roll roofing running the length of a roof. Also refers to a horizontal row of cinder blocks, bricks, or masonry material.

coverage surface area (in square feet) to be continuously coated by a specific roofing material, with allowance made for a specific lap.

crack separation or fracture occurring in a roof membrane or roof deck, generally caused by thermally induced stress or substrate movement.

crawlspace area beneath some types of homes that is constructed so that the floor is raised slightly above the ground, leaving a space between the two through which one can crawl to access utilities.

creep permanent deformation of a roofing material or roof system caused by the movement of the roof membrane that results from continuous thermal stress or loading.

cricket peaked saddle construction at the back of a chimney to prevent accumulation of snow and ice and to deflect water around the chimney.

cripple wall a framed stud wall extending from the top of the foundation to the underside of floor framing for the lowest occupied floor level.

cross connection physical connection between two separate piping systems, one of which contains potable water and the other containing water of unknown or questionable safety or steam, gas, or chemicals, whereby there may be a flow from one system to the other; the direction of flow depends on the pressure differential between the two systems. See **backflow** and **back siphonage.**

crown sighting the top edge of the board, the crown is the high point or arched top up.

curing hardening of concrete over a period of time.

cutback any bituminous roofing material that has been solvent thinned. Cutbacks are used in cold process roofing adhesives, flashing cements, and roof coatings.

cut-in temperature or pressure valve that closes a control circuit.

cut-in point the temperature at which the thermostat calls for system operation.

cutoff any device for cutting off the flow of a fluid, a gas, or a connection.

cutout open portions of a strip shingle between the tabs.

cut-out temperature or pressure valve that breaks or opens a control circuit.

cut-out point the temperature at which the thermostat stops calling for heating or cooling.

cyanuric acid used in pool water to prevent chlorine loss.

cycle series of events that repeat the same events in the same order.

cycle rate the number of times per hour that the heating or cooling equipment is cycled on at half-load conditions.

cycling loss heat lost from a furnace while warming up or cooling down.

D

damp-proofing coating on foundation wall to provide water barrier.

daughter atomic species; immediate product of radioactive decay of a given element.

dead front without live parts exposed to a person on the operating side of the equipment.

dead-level term used to describe an absolutely horizontal roof; zero slope.

dead-level asphalt roof asphalt that has a softening point of 140°F (60°C) and that conforms to the requirements of ASTM D312, type 1.

dead load vertical load due to the weight of all permanent structural and nonstructural building components, such as walls, floors, roofs, and fixed service equipment.

decay spontaneous decrease in the number of radioactive atoms in radioactive material.

deck surface installed over the supporting framing members, to which the roofing is applied.

deflection the amount a board will bend when under load.

dehumidifier device used to remove moisture from air in enclosed areas.

dehumidify to remove water vapor from the atmosphere.

delaminate to separate into layers (to separate from the substrate).

delamination separation of the plies in a roof membrane system or separation of laminated layers of insulation.

demand factor ratio of the maximum demand of a system or part of a system to the total connected load of a system or the part of the system under consideration.

deodorizer device that absorbs various odors by the principle of absorption. Activated charcoal is a common substance used for this device.

depressurization phenomenon that occurs when the air pressure outside a building is higher than that inside.

design head total head requirements of the circulation system at the design rate of flow.

device unit of an electrical system that is intended to carry, but not utilize, electric energy.

dew point temperature at which vapor (at 100 percent humidity) begins to condense and deposit as a liquid.

diatomaceous earth (DE) type of filter aid.

diatomaceous earth filter pool filter designed to use diatomaceous earth as the filtering medium.

differential (as applied to refrigeration and heating) the difference between cut-in and cut-out temperature or pressure control.

diffuser grill over an air supply duct having movable or stationary vanes to distribute the supply air to a specific area or in a specific direction.

diffuse radiation solar energy that scatters as it passes through atmospheric molecules, water vapor, dust, and other particles or translucent glazing.

dimensional lumber when dimensional lumber is used in framing floors, ceilings, and roofs, the crowns of the boards should be installed up. This way, the board's natural camber helps the structural integrity and reduces low spots. When the walls are built, the crowns should all be installed in the same direction.

dimmer switch that allows control of a light's intensity.

direct gain system passive solar heating system in which sunlight penetrates and warms the house interior directly.

direct radiation radiation that comes directly from the sun, without being reflected or diffused.

disinfectant chemical used to destroy bacteria and germs.

disposal field area containing a series of one or more trenches lined with coarse aggregate and conveying the effluent from the septic tank through vitrified clay pipe or perforated, nonmetallic pipe, laid in such a manner that the flow will be distributed with reasonable uniformity into natural soil.

distribution act of moving heat energy from the point of collection or storage to the point of use.

dormer framed window unit projecting through the sloping plane of a roof, often containing a window or ventilating louver.

dose quantity of radiation absorbed.

double coverage application of asphalt roofing such that the lapped portion is at least 2″ wider than the exposed portion, resulting in two layers of roofing material over the deck.

double glazing insulating window pane made of an air space sealed between two thicknesses of glass.

downspout pipe for draining water from roof gutters; also called a *leader.*

downwarping tendency of the outside perimeter of the foundation to settle.

draft usually refers to the pressure difference that causes a current of air or gases to flow through a flue, chimney, heater, or space.

draft gauge instrument used to measure air movement.

draft hood device placed in and made part of the vent connector (chimney connector or smoke pipe) from the appliance or in the appliance itself that is designed to (1) ensure the ready escape of the products of combustion in the event of no draft, backdraft, or stoppage beyond the draft hood; (2) neutralize the effect of stack action of the chimney flue on appliance operation.

draft indicator instrument used to indicate or measure chimney draft or combustion gas movement. Draft is measured in units of 0.1″ of water column.

draft regulator device that functions to maintain a desired draft in oil-fired appliances by automatically reducing the chimney draft to the desired value. It is also called a *barometric damper* and is referred to as an *air balance,* an *air stat,* or a *flue velocity control.*

drain any pipe or device that carries waste water or waterborne waste in a building drainage system.

drainage proper removal of excess water from the foundation.

drainage, waste and vent piping (DWV) used for drainage and venting systems.

drier device used to remove moisture from a refrigeration system.

drip edge noncorrosive, nonstaining material used along the eaves and rakes to allow water run-off to drip clear of underlying construction.

drip pan pan-shaped panel or trough used to collect condensate from the evaporator coil.

droop an indoor temperature control condition where the room remains below the thermostat setting. This control occurs in mild cooling conditions and is caused by the cooling anticipator resistor, which provides a false heat source for the thermostat to maintain relative humidity control.

drum humidifier humidifier that utilizes a drum covered with a porous foam medium that revolves through a water reservoir. Air passing over the wet medium is moisturized.

dry bulb temperature air temperature as indicated by an ordinary thermometer.

drying edge effect removal of moisture from the soil along the perimeter of the foundation.

dry rot brown rot fungi that conduct water.

dry wall wall surface of plaster board.

duct pipe or conduit through which air is delivered.

duplex receptacle device that includes two-plug outlets.

E

EAC electronic air cleaner.

earth tube tube buried in the earth, with one or both ends connected to the house. Air drawn through the tube to the house is cooled by the enveloping earth. In an open-loop tube, one end is open to the outside air. In a closed-loop tube, both ends are connected to the house and house air is continuously circulated through the tube.

eave lower edge of a sloping roof projecting beyond the wall.

eaves flashing additional layer of roofing material applied at the eaves to help prevent damage from water backup.

edging strips boards nailed along eaves and rakes after cutting back existing wood shingles to provide secure edges for reroofing with asphalt shingles.

effective temperature overall effect of air temperature, humidity, and air movement on a human.

efflorescence white powder that forms on the surface of bricks.

effluent treated sewage from a treatment plant or septic tank.

elbow any fitting that produces a bend in the pipes it connects.

electrolysis decomposition into ions of a chemical compound in solution by the action of an electric current passing through the solution.

electronic leak detector electronic instrument that measures electronic flow across an air gap. Changes in electronic flow indicate the presence of refrigerant gas molecules.

electrons negatively charged particles that orbit the nucleus of an atom.

electrostatic precipitator air cleaner that removes primarily dust particles from the air by electrically charging them so that they will be attracted to and collected on a plate of the opposite charge.

embedment (1) the process of pressing a felt, an aggregate fabric, a mat, or a panel uniformly and completely into hot bitumen or adhesive; (2) the process of placing a material into another material so that it becomes an integral part of the whole material.

enclosed surrounded by a case, a housing, a fence, or walls that prevent people from accidentally contacting energized parts.

enclosure case or housing of an apparatus or the fence or walls surrounding an installation to prevent personnel from accidentally contacting energized parts or to protect the equipment from physical damage.

entrance canopy roof extending over entrance door.

Environmental Protection Agency (EPA) agency of the U.S. government tasked with the responsibility for regulating, advising on, and assisting in resolving environmental issues.

equilibrium moisture (1) the moisture content of a material stabilized at a given temperature and relative humidity, expressed as a percentage of moisture by weight; (2) the typical moisture content of a material in any given geographic area.

evaporation physical process of changing a liquid to a vapor through the addition of heat energy.

evaporative cooler system in which the absorption of latent heat by evaporation of water cools the air it contacts.

evaporator coil device made of a coil of tubing that functions as a refrigerant evaporator.

excess fines excess silt and clay in soil.

excess lime excess carbonates in soil that restrict the growth of some plants.

expansion joint structural separation between two building elements designed to minimize the effect of the stresses and movements of a building's components and to prevent these stresses from splitting or ridging the roof membrane.

exposed capable of being inadvertently touched or approached nearer than a safe distance by a person. The term is applied to parts not suitably guarded, isolated, or insulated.

exposure that portion of the roofing exposed to the weather after installation.

exposure (human) presence of people in an area where levels of an airborne contaminant are elevated; technical definition: the total amount of airborne contaminant inhaled by a person, typically approximated by the product of concentration and duration.

exposure (material) amount or fraction of material visible.

exposure 1 grade plywood type of plywood approved by the American Plywood Association for exterior use.

F

face piping piping with all valves and fittings used to connect the filter system as a unit.

fascia wood or other trim covering the ends of the rafters.

fast intake rapid movement of water into soil.

feathering strips tapered wood filler strips placed along the butts of old wood shingles to create a level surface when reroofing over existing wood shingle roof; also called *horsefeathers*.

feeder all circuit conductors between the service equipment or the source of a separately derived system and the final branch circuit overcurrent device.

felt fibrous material saturated with asphalt and used as an underlayment or a sheathing paper.

fertility, soil quality that enables soil to provide plant nutrients, in adequate amounts and in proper balance.

fiberglass mat asphalt roofing base material manufactured from glass fibers.

fibrous spongy, fluffy, and composed of long strands of fibers.

fill-type insulation loose insulating material applied by hand or mechanically blown into wall spaces.

filter device for removing small particles from water or air moving through a system.

filter aid or **medium** nonpermanent, fine-grain material—e.g., diatomaceous earth and alum—used in a filter to trap particles suspended in pool water.

filter cycle operation of filter between backwashes.

filter rate average rate of water flow per square foot of filter area.

filter rock specially graded rock and gravel used to support filter sand.

filter sand permanent, special-graded filter medium.

filter septum part of the filter element in a diatomite-type filter on which a cake of diatomite or another nonpermanent filter aid may be deposited.

filter waste discharge piping piping that conducts wastewater from a filter to a drainage system.

fine-grained soils soils consisting of microscopic particles, such as silts and clays.

finish flooring tongued and grooved hardwood strips, or plywood.

finish grade line top of ground at the foundation.

firestop blocking placed in any vertical channel in a building, such as between studs in an exterior wall or interior partition; its purpose is to slow down progress of a fire by blocking off the flue-like effect of such a channel.

firewall a wall between sections of a building; the wall is constructed of relatively fireproof material.

fixture light or another electrical device that is permanently attached and is connected permanently to the property's wiring.

fixture drain drain from the trap of a fixture to the junction of that drain with any other drain pipe.

fixture unit quantity expressing the load-producing effects on the plumbing system, which is based on an arbitrary scale.

fla full-load amperes.

flashing pieces of metal or roll roofing used to prevent seepage of water into a building around any intersection or projection in a roof, such as vent pipes, chimneys, adjoining walls, dormers, and valleys. On flat built-up roofs, it seals the edges of a membrane at walls, expansion joints, drains, gravel stops, and other areas where the membrane is interrupted or terminated. Base flashing covers the edges of the membrane. Cap flashing or counterflashing shields the upper edges of the base flashing. Galvanized metal flashing should be a minimum 26 ga.

flashing cement see **asphalt plastic cement.**

flashing content trowelable mixture of cutback bitumen and mineral stabilizers, including asbestos or other inorganic fibers.

flashings metal used around angles or junctions on exterior walls, chimneys, or roofs to prevent leaks.

floating slab concrete-reinforced slab poured inside foundation walls or footings and separated by an expansion joint. This process of pouring the slab separately allows the slab to rise or fall without causing cracks at the edges of the footing.

flood coat top layer of bitumen in which the aggregate is embedded on an aggregate-surfaced built-up roof.

flood level rim top edge of a receptacle from which water overflows.

flood plain nearly level alluvial plain that borders a stream and is subject to flooding unless protected artificially.

flooring paper felt paper laid on rough floor to stop air infiltration and noise.

flue liner fireclay tile not less than ⅝" thick that provides a smooth flow and protection from leakage.

flushometer valve device that discharges a predetermined quantity of water to fixtures for flushing purposes and is closed by direct water pressures.

flush valve device located at the bottom of the tank for flushing water closets and similar fixtures.

foam plastic insulation a plastic that is intentionally expanded by the use of a foaming agent to produce a reduced-density plastic containing voids consisting of open or closed cells distributed throughout the plastic for thermal insulation or acoustical purposes.

footing portion of the foundation (a concrete base) that transfers the structural load to the ground.

footing drain tile perforated drain pipe or pipe with cracks at joints to allow underground water to drain away from the basement.

foundation masonry and concrete foundation walls, usually below ground level, that support house structure.

four-way switch switch that is used to control a light from three or more locations.

fpm feet per minute.

framing joists, studs, rafters, and beams of a residential structure.

free tab shingles shingles that do not contain factory-applied strips or spots of self-sealing adhesive.

freezing point temperature at which liquid will solidify on removal of heat. The freezing temperature of water is 32°F.

french drains underground perforated pipe that removes subsurface water from the property.

Freon trade name for family of synthetic chemical refrigerants. It is a colorless gas.

fresh water water having a specific conductivity less than a solution containing 6,000 parts per million of sodium chloride.

friable capable of being crumbled, pulverized, or reduced to powder by hand pressure.

frieze board a horizontal trim piece immediately below the cornice soffit.

fuel oil liquid mixture derived from petroleum that does not emit a flammable vapor below 125° F.

fullway valve gate valve designed to permit straight, full, and free flow or no flow.

fungi, decay fungi that are major destroyers of the strength of wood, such as white rot and brown rot.

fungi, stain fungi that feed on wood at a slow rate, causing discoloration but little damage.

fungus plant that does not contain chlorophyll.

fuse device that stops the electrical flow in case there is a circuit overload for any reason. Fuses cannot be reset; they must be replaced.

furring framework used over masonry where a finished wall is applied.

G

gable upper portion of a sidewall that comes to a triangular point at the ridge of a sloping roof.

gable roof type of roof containing sloping planes of the same pitch on each side of the ridge with a gable at each end.

galleries chamber-like voids in wood caused by termites or other wood-destroying insects.

galvanized metallic zinc coating.

gambrel roof type of roof containing two sloping planes of different pitch on each side of the ridge with a gable at each end. The lower plane has a steeper slope than the upper.

gamma rays short-wave electromagnetic radiation; a high-energy photon emitted spontaneously by a radioactive substance.

gas valve device used for controlling the flow of gas.

gas vapor phase or state of a substance.

general purpose circuit circuit that serves a number of light and/ or receptacle outlets.

girder main structural member carrying the weight of a floor or partition. Often used to support floor joists in a pier-and-beam foundation. Piers support the girder and transfer the load to the ground.

glass fiber felt felt sheet in which glass fibers are bonded into the felt sheet with resin. They are suitable for impregnation and coating. They are used in the manufacture and coating of bituminous waterproofing materials, roof membrane, and shingles.

glass fiber mat thin mat composed of glass fibers with or without a binder.

glazing (1) fitting glass into window frames and doors; (2) glass plastic or other transparent or translucent material designed to transmit light.

glue lams pre-engineered, built-up 2x4s or 2x6s laminated flat on top of each other; used for beams and excessive spans for floor joists or headers.

gph gallons per hour.

gpm gallons per minute.

grade surface of the ground surrounding the home. Below grade means the part of the house (i.e., basement) that is lower than the surface level of the ground.

grade beam a beam placed at or near ground level, usually performing the function of a foundation.

grade line see **finish grade line.**

granules ceramic-coated, colored, crushed rock that is applied to the exposed surface of asphalt roofing products.

gravel course, granular aggregate, containing pieces approximately ½″ to ⅝″ in size and suitable for use in aggregate surfacing, in built-up roofs, and as fill under slab to allow drainage and guard against a damp floor. A pebble is an individual piece.

gravel stop flanged device, frequently metallic, designed to provide a continuous finished edge for roofing materials and to prevent loose aggregate from washing off the roof.

grease trap see **interceptor.**

greenhouse effect phenomenon in which heat is trapped in a glazed enclosure due to glazing's ability to admit short-wave solar radiation while retarding the reradiation of long-wave heat energy.

green lumber unseasoned lumber that has not properly dried and tends to warp and/or bleed resin.

ground fault in an electrical circuit allowing electricity to flow into the metal parts of the structure; also known as a *short circuit.*

ground electricity electricity always seeks the shortest path to earth. Neutral wires carry electricity to the ground in all circuits. An electrical panel must have a ground connected to either the copper cold water line or a rod driven into the ground.

ground fault circuit interrupter (GFCI) safety device that senses any shock hazard and interrupts the flow of electricity in the circuit.

ground wire electrical wire that will safely conduct electricity from the structure into the ground.

gusset bracket or brace used to strengthen a structure.

gutter trough that channels water from the eaves to the downspouts.

gypsum board gypsum wallboard, gypsum sheathing, gypsum base for gypsum veneer plaster, exterior board, or water-resistant gypsum backing board.

H

habitable space a space in a structure for living, sleeping, cooking, or eating. Bathrooms, toilet rooms, closets, halls, storage or utility spaces, and similar areas are not considered habitable spaces.

half-life unit of measure for decay of a radioactive substance. If the half-life of a substance is two years, then half of its radiation will disappear after two years; then half of the remainder after another two years, and so on.

hardness quantity of dissolved minerals—e.g., calcium and magnesium—in the water.

header structural member carrying a wall load above the opening for windows and doors.

headlap shortest distance from the butt edge of an overlapping shingle to the upper edge of a shingle in the second course below; the triple coverage portion of the top lap of strip shingles.

heat warming of a building, an apartment, or a room by a stove, a furnace, or electricity.

heat, latent term used to describe the heat energy required to change the form of a substance without changing its temperature.

heat, sensible term used in heating and cooling to indicate any portion of heat that changes only the temperature of the substance involved.

heat, total sum of latent and sensible heat.

heat anticipator (sometimes called a *preheat resistor*) a bias heater that shuts off the thermostat before the room reaches the thermostat setting; the heat anticipator minimizes overshoot.

heat exchanger device used to transfer heat from a warm or hot surface to a cold or cooler surface.

heating control controls temperature of a heat transfer unit that releases heat.

heating plant the furnace, boiler, or other heating devices used to generate steam, hot water, or hot air, which is then circulated through a distribution system. It uses coal, gas, oil, wood, or electricity as its source of heat.

heating season portion of the year when outdoor cold makes indoor heating necessary.

heel end of rafter that rests on wall plate.

hermetic system refrigeration system that has a compressor driven by a motor contained in a compressor dome or housing.

hex shingles shingles that have the appearance of a hexagon after installation.

high-efficiency term applied to heating and air-conditioning units that supply more heating or cooling for each energy dollar invested.

high-pressure cut-out electrical control switch operated automatically by the high-side pressure. It opens the electrical circuit if the head pressure is too high or the condensing pressure is reached.

high-rate sand filter sand filter designed for flow rates in excess of 5 gallons per minute (gpm) per sq. ft.

high side parts of a refrigerating system that are subjected to undercondensing or high-side pressure.

hip inclined external angle formed by the intersection of two sloping roof planes; runs from the ridge to the eaves.

hip roof type of roof containing sloping angles of the same pitch on each of four sides; contains no gables.

hip shingles shingles used to cover the inclined external angle formed by the intersection of two sloping roof planes.

holiday area where a liquid-applied material is missing.

homogeneous (material) similar in appearance and texture.

homogeneous (worksite) contains only one type of asbestos-containing material and uses only one type of abatement method.

horsefeathers see **feathering strips.**

hot stuff or hot roofer's term for hot bitumen.

hot water potable water heated to at least 120°F and used for cooking, cleaning, washing dishes, and bathing.

hot wire conductor that carries electricity to a light and/or receptacle.

humidifier device used to add and control the humidity in a confined space.

humidistat humidity-sensing control that cycles the humidifier on and off.

humidity moisture, dampness. Relative humidity is the ratio of the quantity of vapor present in the air to the greatest amount possible at a given temperature.

HVAC heating, ventilation and air-conditioning.

hybrid system solar heating system that combines passive techniques with active devices such as fans or blowers to assist in the collection, storage, or distribution of heat.

hydration chemical reaction between water and cement in a concrete mix.

I

ice dam condition formed at the lower roof edge by the thawing and refreezing of melted snow on the overhang. It can force water up and under shingles, causing leaks.

ignition transformer transformer designed to provide high-voltage current; used in some heating systems to ignite fuel.

incline or **slope** slope of a roof expressed either as a percentage or as the number of vertical units of rise per horizontal units of run.

indirect gain system solar heating system in which sunlight directly warns an absorber located between glazing and living space; heat is then distributed from the absorber to the living space naturally or by fans.

infiltration downward entry of water into immediate soil surface or other material, as contrasted with percolation, water movement through soil layers or material. Also refers to heat leakage by convection currents through cracks around windows and doors.

inlet fittings fittings or fixtures through which circulated water reenters the pool.

insolation incident solar radiation; total amount of direct, diffused, and reflected solar radiation striking a given surface.

insulated glazing two or more layers of glazing material mounted in a single frame and separated by insulating air spaces.

insulating board or **fiber board** low-density board made of wood, sugar cane, or similar materials, usually formed by a felting process, dried and pressed to a specified thickness.

insulation nonconductive covering that protects wires and other electricity carriers. Generally refers to material high in resistance to heat transmission placed in walls, ceilings, or floors of a structure.

interceptor device designed and installed to separate and retain deleterious, hazardous, or undesirable matter from normal wastes and permit normal sewage or liquid wastes to discharge into the drainage system by gravity.

interlocking shingles individual shingles that mechanically fasten to each other to provide wind resistance.

ionizing radiation radiation capable of exerting enough energy to knock electrons loose from around an atom; includes such particles as alpha and beta rays, neutrons, and x-rays. This is the most damaging type of radiation to human health.

isolation pads small rubber pads that are placed under the corners of a furnace to prevent any vibration from being transmitted to the floor or the surface the unit sits on.

J

joist structural members or beams that hold the floor or ceiling; floor and framing lumber, laid on end , to which flooring and lath are attached.

K

kilowatt (kw) unit of electrical power equal to 1,000 watts (w). A kilowatt hour is the standard measure of electrical consumption.

kip a unit of force equal to 1,000 pounds.

L

laminated shingles strip shingles containing more than one layer of tabs to create extra thickness; also called *three-dimensional shingles* or *architectural shingles*.

lap to cover the surface of one shingle or roll with another.

lap cement asphalt-based cement used to adhere overlapping plies of roll roofing.

latewood slow growth period of a tree responsible for creating annular rings.

lath mesh made from sheet metal or gypsum board onto which plaster is applied.

leaching bed tiles in trenches carrying treated wastes from septic systems.

leader a pipe-like length of metal which carries rainwater from the gutter to the ground or other place of disposal; sometimes called a downspout or rain leader; exterior drainage pipe to convey storm water from roof or gutter drains to building storm drain, combined building sewer, or other means of disposal. Also see *downspout*.

leak detector instrument such as a halide torch, an electronic sniffer, or soap solution used to detect leaks.

lean-to small building whose rafters pitch, or lean, against another building or against a wall.

ledger wood that is attached to a beam to support joists.

leveling legs small bolts that are screwed into the bottoms of the corners of a furnace or another appliance. Threaded feet can be adjusted to raise and lower the corners so the appliance sits level.

limit control used to open or close electrical circuits as temperature and/or pressure limits are reached.

lintel horizontal structural member that spans a door, a window, or another opening to carry the weight of walls above.

liquid indicator located in the liquid line, provides a glass window that allows the liquid flow to be observed.

liquid limit moisture content at which soil passes from a plastic to a liquid state.

liquid line carries liquid refrigerant from the condenser or liquid receiver to the refrigerant control mechanism.

live load load superimposed by the use and occupancy of a building, not including the wind load, earthquake load, or dead load.

load amount of work imposed on a refrigerating system or the required rate of heat removal.

load-bearing wall strong wall that is capable of supporting weight.

loam mixture of rich soil composed of clay, sand, silt, and organic matter.

loop vent same as a circuit vent except that it loops back and connects with the stack vent instead of the vent stack.

louvers series of slanted slats spaced at intervals to admit a free flow of air.

low-side pressure pressure in cooling side of the refrigerating cycle.

low-side pressure control used to keep low-side evaporating pressure from dropping below a given pressure.

low-slope application method of installing asphalt shingles on roof slopes between 2" and 4" per ft.

lra locked rotor amps.

M

magnetic south south as indicated by a compass; magnetic south's relationship to true south varies with geographic location.

main outlet outlet at the deep portion of the pool through which the main flow of water leaves the pool when drained or circulated.

main sewer see **public sewer.**

main vent principal venting system artery; where vent branches may be connected.

manometer instrument, usually a U-shaped tube, used for measuring the pressure of gases or vapors.

mansard roof type of roof containing two sloping planes of different pitch on each of four sides; contains no gables. The lower plane has a much steeper pitch than the upper, often approaching vertical.

manual or **mechanical differential** the difference (in degrees F) between cut-in and cut-out temperature with no electrical load connected to the thermostat.

masonry stone, brick, concrete, hollow tile, or building units or materials, bonded together with mortar to form a wall, pier, or similar mass.

masonry primer asphalt-based primer used to prepare masonry surfaces for bonding with other asphalt products.

Mastic see **asphalt plastic cement. melting point** temperature at which a substance will melt at atmospheric pressure.

membrane flexible or semiflexible roof covering or waterproofing layer whose primary function is the exclusion of water.

mesh square or circular opening of a sieve.

metal flashing see **flashing.**

Metallic coating see **galvanized**.

micron one millionth of a meter.

milli combining form denoting one thousandth; for example, 1 millivolt equals one thousandth of a volt.

MG/L milligrams per liter.

mineral fiber felt felt with mineral wool as its principal component.

mineral granules or stabilizers finely ground limestone, slate, traprock or other inert materials, naturally or synthetically colored, added to asphalt coatings, such as roofing shingles, surface cap sheets and granule-surfaced sheets, for durability and increased resistance to fire and weathering.

mineral-surfaced roofing asphalt shingles and roll roofing that are covered with granules.

miter joining of two pieces of material (wood, metal) at an angle that bisects the junction.

mitigation to fix; to reduce the severity of.

modulus of elasticity refers to a board's ability to regain its original form once a load has been applied. The modulus of elasticity is used in determining suitable spans for various woods.

moisture barrier treated paper or metal that prevents water from passing into floors and walls.

molding strip of decorative material with a planed or curved narrow surface prepared for ornamental application; also used to hide wall imperfections.

molecule smallest particle of a substance that still maintains the chemical properties of the parent substance.

monitor in the case of a computer, the screen; in the case of the count/measurement process, the act of measuring.

monolithic concrete poured (solid) concrete.

monolithic slab concrete foundation wall and floor slab poured as one piece.

mopping application of hot bitumen to the substrate or to the felts of a built-up roof membrane with a mop or mechanical applicator.

mopping, solid continuous mopping of a surface, leaving no unmopped areas.

mopping, spot mopping pattern in which hot bitumen is applied in roughly circular areas, leaving a grid of unmopped, perpendicular bands on the roof.

mopping, sprinkle random mopping pattern wherein heated bitumen beads are strewn onto the substrate with a brush or mop.

mopping, strip mopping pattern in which hot bitumen is applied in parallel bands.

mortar material composed of cement, aggregate, and water used for bonding masonry units.

motor control device to start and/or stop a motor under certain temperature or pressure conditions.

mud-jacking foundation repair process whereby a cement grout is pumped beneath a slab to produce a lifting force that floats the slab to a desired position. The cement grout is pumped through small holes drilled through the concrete.

mullion framing of slender material that divides the panes of glass in windows.

multichannel analyzer (MCA) electronic device for measuring and recording the radiation spectrum emitted during radioactive decay. Not unlike an electronic calculator, it has the ability to perform simultaneous add or subtract functions on all channels.

N

nailing (1) In the exposed nail method, nail heads are exposed to the weather. (2) In the concealed nail method, nail heads are concealed from the weather.

National Electrical Code (NEC) set of rules drafted by the National Fire Protection Association governing safe wiring methods. Local codes can be different and take precedence over NEC requirements.

negative pressure occurs when the air pressure in the home is less than the air pressure outside the home (vacuum).

neon tester device with a small neon bulb and two leads that proves a circuit is carrying current.

neoprene synthetic rubber (polychloroprene) used in liquid-applied and sheet-applied elastomeric roof membranes or flashings.

nesting method of reroofing with new asphalt shingles over old shingles in which the top edge of the new shingle is butted against the bottom edge of the existing shingle tab.

neutral conductor that completes the circuit. It always has white insulation on the wire.

neutron uncharged particle present in all known atomic nuclei (except hydrogen).

newel post that terminates the railing.

no-cutout shingles shingles consisting of a single, solid tab with no cutouts.

nominal lumber size the commercial size designation of width and depth in standard sawn lumber and glued laminated lumber grades; somewhat larger than the standard net size of dressed lumber.

normal slope application method of installing asphalt shingles on roof slopes between 4" and 21" per ft.

nosing rounded and projecting edge of stair treads or edge of a landing.

O

off cycle part of the refrigeration cycle; when the system is not operating.

offset ledge occurring at a change in the thickness or width of a wall.

oil burner device for burning oil in heating appliances such as furnaces, boilers, water heaters, and ranges. A burner of this type can be a pressure-atomizing gun type, a horizontal or vertical rotatory type, or a mechanical or natural draft-vaporizing type.

on center spacing for joists, studs, and rafters in construction from the center of one member to the center of the next member.

one ton of cooling removal of heat from a conditioned space at the rate of 12,000 Btus per hour.

open circuit interrupted electrical circuit that stops the flow of electricity.

open metal trusses pre-engineered metal welded sections utilizing triangulation construction.

open valley method of valley construction in which shingles on both sides of the valley are trimmed along a chalk line snapped on each side of the valley. Shingles do not extend across the valley, and the valley flashing is exposed.

open webbing floor trusses pre-engineered wood in typical 2x4 wood triangulation construction.

operating differential the difference (in degrees F) in cut-in and cut-out temperature when the thermostat is actually operating equipment. Operating differential is less than mechanical differential.

organic felt asphalt roofing base material manufactured from cellulose fibers.

organic matter plant and animal residue in various stages of decomposition in soil.

orientation alignment of a building along a given axis to face a specific direction, such as along an east/west axis to face south.

orifice accurate size opening for controlling fluid flow.

OSSF on-site sewage facility.

outside air external air; ambient air; atmosphere exterior to a refrigerated or conditioned space.

overcurrent any current in excess of the rated current of equipment or the ampacity of a conductor. It may result from overload, short circuit, or ground fault.

overhang upper part of a building (such as a roof) extending beyond the lower part.

overload condition that exists when a circuit is carrying more amperage than the circuit was designed to carry. Overloading causes heat, which causes the wire to get hot and the fuses to blow or the circuit breakers to trip because they are designed to sense heat.

overload protector temperature-operated, pressure-operated, or current-operated device that will stop operation of the unit without damaging it if a dangerous condition should arise.

oversize selecting equipment for a living space that has more Btus and/or tonnage than is necessary to heat or cool the space.

P

pallets wooden platforms used for storing and shipping bundles of shingles.

parent material unconsolidated organic and mineral material in which soil forms.

parging rough coat of mortar applied over a masonry wall as protection or finish.

Particleboard a generic term for a panel primarilly composed of cellulosic materials (usually wood), generally in the form of discrete pieces or particles, as distinguished from fibers. The cellulosic material is combined with synthetic resin or other suitable bonding system by a process in which the interparticle board is created by the bonding system under heat and pressure.

passive system a solar system using natural means to heat collection, storage and distribution.

peak levels levels of airborne contaminant that are much higher than average and occur for short periods of time in response to sudden releases of the contaminant.

ped individual natural soil aggregate, such as a granule, prism, or block.

pentachlorophenol (penta) wood preservative that is highly toxic to both fungi and insects, insoluble in water, and permanent.

percolation ability of soil to absorb water.

perimeter beam edge around the foundation that adds stiffness and stability to the slab.

permeability quality of soil that enables water to move downward through the profile. Permeability is measured as the number of inches per hour that water moves downward through saturated soil.

permeable having pores through which gases may pass.

personal computer analyzer (PCA) printed circuit addition to a personal computer that transforms it into a multichannel analyzer.

pH measure of acidity or alkalinity of water. For example, a pH of 7 is neutral; above 7 is alkaline; and below 7 is acidic.

phase, soil subdivision of a soil series based on features that affect its use and management; for example, slope and thickness.

phloem conductive tissue that moves sugars produced by the tree's foliage down the tree into the roots for use or storage.

pH value numerical designation of acidity and alkalinity in soil. See **reaction, soil.**

picocurie (pCi) unit of measure of radioactivity; one trillionth (10^{-12}) of 1 curie (Ci), where Ci = 3.7×10^{10} disintegrations per sec.; often expressed as a portion of a known volume of air—pCi/L.

pier a platform structure supported by pilings, extending from land into water.

piers members that transfer the building load to the ground.

pilaster projection of the foundation wall used to support a floor girder or to stiffen the wall.

piling structural members driven into the ground and used to support vertical loads.

pitch degree of roof incline expressed as the ratio of the rise, in feet, to the span, in feet.

plasticity index (PI) range of moisture content in which the soil remains plastic. The PI rating is the shrink-swell potential.

plastic limit moisture content at which soil changes from semisolid to plastic.

plates horizontal wood members that provide bearing and anchorage for walls, floor, ceiling, and roof framing.

plenum chamber air compartment to which one or more distributed air ducts are connected.

plumbing system includes (1) aseptic, an adequate potable water supply system; (2) septic, a safe and adequate drainage system; and (3) mechanical, ample fixtures and equipment.

ply layer of felt in a built-up roof membrane system. A four-ply membrane system has four plies of felt—i.e., four layers of felt.

plywood a wood structural panel comprised of plies of wood veneer arranged in cross-aligned layers. The plies are bonded with an adhesive that cures on application of heat and pressure.

pneumatic devices that use compressed air, as in pressure tanks boosted by pumps.

pointing treatment of joints in masonry by filling with mortar to protect against weather or to improve appearances.

polarized outlets outlets that are designed with the neutral slot larger than the hot side. An appliance with a polarized plug can be plugged into only an outlet with the proper polarity.

polyvinyl chloride (PVC) plastic pipe used with cold water. PVC piping becomes soft when exposed to heat or hot water.

pond water accumulation on roof surface that is incompletely drained.

poorly graded coarse-grained soil or soil material consisting mainly of similar size particles. Because of little difference in particle size, density is increased only slightly by compaction.

portable pool prefabricated swimming pool constructed on-site, which may be disassembled and reerected at a new location. It is generally installed on the ground surface without excavation.

positive drainage drainage condition in which consideration has been made for all loading deflections of the deck and additional roof slope has been provided to ensure complete drainage of the roof area within 24 hours of precipitation.

post-tension reinforcement method of prestressing in which tendons are tensioned after concrete has hardened.

potable water water with no impurities present in amounts sufficient to cause disease or harmful physiological effects and conforming in its bacteriological and chemical quality to the requirements of the Public Health Service drinking water standard or meeting the regulations of the public health authority having jurisdiction.

ppb parts per billion.

ppm parts per million.

precast concrete plain or reinforced concrete element cast in other than its final position in the structure. Can be erected in sections; more common with commercial or pier construction.

precoat initial coating of diatomaceous earth medium on the filter septa at the start of a cycle.

prefabrication components, such as walls, trusses, or doors, constructed before delivery to the building site.

pressure drop pressure difference between the high side and the low side in a refrigerator mechanism.

pressure regulator, evaporator automatic pressure-regulating valve, mounted in the suction line between the evaporator outlet and the compressor inlet to maintain a predetermined pressure and temperature in the evaporator.

pressure suction pressure in the low-pressure side of a refrigerating system.

prestressed concrete reinforced concrete in which internal stresses have been introduced to reduce potential tensile stresses in concrete resulting from loads.

pretensioning method of prestressing in which tendons are tensioned before concrete is poured.

prevalent levels levels of airborne contaminant occurring under normal conditions.

primary air air mixed with gas prior to exiting the burner port.

primary control directly controls operation of a heating system.

profile, soil vertical section of soil extending through all horizons into the parent material. Sequence of natural layers in the soil from the surface to the parent material, which has not been changed by leaching or by plant roots.

programmable sensor a sensor with the capability to assign setpoints to selectable periods of time.

protector, circuit electrical device that will open an electrical circuit if excessive electrical conditions occur.

psi pounds per square inch.

psig pounds per square inch gauge; the means used to measure pressures higher than those that are expressed in inches of water column.

psychrometric chart chart that shows relationships between the temperature, pressure, and moisture content of the air.

P-trap trap with a vertical inlet and a horizontal outlet.

public sewer common sewer directly controlled by public authority.

pump, automatic oil device that automatically pumps oil from the supply tank and delivers it in specific quantities to an oil-burning appliance. It is designed to stop pumping automatically in the event of damage to the oil supply line.

pumping down using a compressor or pump to reduce pressure in a container or system.

purlin timber laid horizontally to support common rafters of a roof.

purging releasing compressed gas to the atmosphere through some part or parts for the purpose of removing contaminants from that part or parts.

Q

quick-setting cement asphalt base cement used to adhere tabs of strip shingles to the course below; also used to adhere roll roofing laps applied by the concealed nail method.

R

rabbet groove cut in a board to receive another board.

racking roofing application method in which shingle courses are applied vertically up the roof, rather than across and up. Racking is not a recommended procedure.

radiant heat infrared energy that is emitted from the outer surfaces of a solid fuel-burning fireplace.

radiant heating method of heating a building by means of electric coils, hot water, or steam pipes installed in the floor, walls, or ceilings.

radiation movement of energy through space by electromagnetic waves; e.g., the transfer of heat by heat rays.

radon naturally occurring, colorless, odorless, radioactive, inert gaseous element formed by the radioactive decay of radium atoms; symbolized by Rn^{222}; half-life 3.82 days.; one of the decay products of radium—polonium and bismuth. Each is an ultrafine radioactive particle that further decays until a stable, nonradioactive lead atom is formed, stopping the chain.

rafter supporting framing member immediately beneath the deck or furring strip, sloping from the ridge to the wall plate.

raintight constructed or protected so that exposure to a hard rain will not result in the entrance of water under specified test conditions.

rake inclined edge of a sloped roof over a wall.

random-tab shingles shingles on which tabs vary in size and exposure.

range pressure and/or temperature settings of control that change within limits.

rapid sand filter filter designed to be used with sand as the filter medium. The flow rate will not exceed 5 gpm per sq. ft.

reaction, soil measure of acidity or alkalinity of soil, expressed in pH values. Soil with pH of 7.0 is described as neutral. The degree of acidity or alkalinity is expressed as follows:

extremely acid	pH below 4.5
very strong acid	4.5 to 5.0
strong acid	5.1 to 5.5
medium acid	5.6 to 6.0
slightly acid	6.1 to 6.5
neutral	6.6 to 7.3
mildly alkaline	7.4 to 7.8
moderately alkaline	7.9 to 8.4
strong alkaline	8.5 to 9.0
very strong alkaline	9.1 and higher

rebar term used for reinforced steel; a deformed steel put in concrete to improve its tension quality.

receptacle outlet that provides power to lamps and other electrical appliances; also called a *duplex receptacle.*

receptor plumbing fixture that receives the discharge from indirect waste piping.

refrigerant substance circulated under pressure within a cooling system that produces the refrigerating effect.

refrigerant control device that meters refrigerant and maintains a pressure difference between the high-pressure and low-pressure sides of a mechanical refrigerating system while the unit is operating.

region of interest (ROI) portion of the spectrum from which radiation counts are taken. It is set to include the various radon progeny and exclude other elements in the decay process.

register grille covered opening in a floor or wall where hot or cold is introduced into a room.

reinforced concrete concrete containing reinforcement (metal bars or wire mesh) prestressed or nonprestressed, and designed on the assumption that the two materials act together in resisting forces.

reinforcing bar (rebar) steel bar used to reinforce concrete slabs, foundations, footings, piers, etc. The size of reinforcing bar is indicated by a number that represents ⅛″ diameter.

relative humidity percentage of water vapor contained in a given amount of air at a specific temperature compared with the amount it contains when 100 percent saturated. For example, if the weight of the moist air is 1 lb. and if the air could hold 2 lb. of water vapor at a given temperature, the relative humidity is 50 percent.

release tape plastic or paper strip that is applied to the back of self-sealing shingles. This strip prevents the shingles from sticking together in the bundles and need not be removed for application.

relief valve safety device designed to open at a preset pressure before a dangerous pressure is reached.

relief vent auxiliary vent that permits additional circulation of air in or between drainage and vent systems.

reroofing practice of applying new roofing materials over existing roofing materials.

resolve to distinguish different objects with a microscope.

retrofit addition of a solar heating system to an existing house.

return air air delivered to the furnace to be treated.

return air grille metal louvered grille over an opening to the return air plenum through which air enters the system for treating.

return piping circulation piping that extends from the outlet side of the filter to the pool.

ridge uppermost, horizontal, external angle formed by the intersection of two sloping roof planes.

ridge board board at the top intersection that aligns and receives the top ends of the rafters.

ridge pole longitudinal plank to which the ridge rafters of the roof are attached.

ridge shingles shingles used to cover the horizontal, external angle formed by the intersection of two sloping roof planes.

rise vertical distance from the eave line to the ridge.

riser vertical board closing the spaces between the treads of a stairway.

risk the likelihood of developing a disease as a result of exposure to a contaminant.

roll roofing asphalt roofing products manufactured in roll form.

roof covering material placed on a roof.

roofer trade name for the worker who applies roofing materials.

roofing wood, asphalt, tile, slate or metal that forms protection against the weather.

roofing tape asphalt-saturated tape used with asphalt cement for flashing and patching asphalt roofing.

roof insulation rockwool or fiberglass in blanket form placed between roof rafters or ceiling joists.

roof rafters structural members that rest on the plate and support the roof.

roof sheathing boards that provide the base for the finished roof.

roof system system of interacting roof components (not including the roof deck) designed to weatherproof and normally to insulate a building's top surface.

room heater self-contained, freestanding heating appliance intended for installation to heat space and not designed for duct connections; space heater.

rpm revolutions per minute.

run horizontal distance from the eaves to a point directly under the ridge; one-half the span.

run-off precipitation discharged into stream channels. Water that flows off the land surface without sinking into the soil is surface run-off. Water that enters the soil before reaching surface streams is groundwater run-off or seepage flow from ground water.

run time equipment operating time.

S

safety control device that stops the refrigerating unit if unsafe pressures and/or temperatures are reached.

saline water water having a specific conductivity in excess of a solution containing 6,000 parts per million of sodium chloride.

sand soil consisting of separate, individual rock or mineral fragments from 0.05 mm. to 2.0 mm. in diameter. Most sand grains consist of quartz. As a soil textural class, soil is 85 percent or more sand and not more than 10 percent clay.

sandstone sedimentary rock containing predominantly sand-size particles.

sandy loam soil that contains sand, silt, and clay. Individual sand grains are seen and felt readily. If squeezed when dry, sandy loam forms a cast that readily falls apart, but if squeezed when moist, a cast forms that bears careful handling without breaking. Sandy loam is moderately coarse soil.

sash frame for holding the glass pane or panes of a window or door.

saturant asphalt used to impregnate an organic felt base material.

saturated felt asphalt-impregnated felt used as an underlayment between the deck and the roofing material.

saturation condition existing when a substance contains a maximum amount of another substance for that temperature and pressure.

scale hard mineral deposits normally found on heater coils and pool walls.

schrader valve spring-loaded valve that permits fluid or air to flow in one direction when the center pin is depressed and in the other direction when a pressure difference exists.

screeded slab wooden floor built on a concrete slab.

scuttle hole small opening to the attic, roof, or crawlspace.

sealant mixture of polymers, fillers, and pigments used to fill and seal joints where moderate movement is expected. It cures to a resilient solid.

season energy efficiency ratio (SEER) ratio of total cooling output (Btuh) to power input (watts) for the season.

secondary air air that enters the flame from the area around the burner.

seepage movement of water through soil.

selective surface special coating with high solar absorbing and low thermal emitting properties; used on the surface of an absorber element to increase collector efficiency.

self-sealing shingles shingles containing factory-applied strips or spots of self-sealing adhesive.

self-sealing strip or **spot** factory-applied adhesive that bonds single courses together when exposed to the heat of the sun after application.

selvage that portion of roll roofing overlapped by the succeeding course to obtain double coverage.

sensible heat heat energy that changes the temperature of a substance without changing its state.

sensor a device that measures and communicates temperature of the conditioned space in which it is located to a system controller.

separation tank device used to clarify filter rinse water or wastewater.

septic system comprises all piping, appurtenances, and treatment facilities used for the collection and disposal of sewage, except plumbing inside and in connection with buildings served, and the building drain.

septic tank watertight receptacle that receives discharge of a building's sanitary drain system or part thereof and that is designed and constructed so as to separate solid from liquid, digest organic matter through a period of detention, and allow the liquids to discharge into the soil outside the tank through a system of open-joint or perforated piping or through a seepage pit.

sequence control group of devices that act in series or in a time order.

service conductors and equipment for delivering electrical power from the supply system to the wiring system of the property.

service cable service conductors constructed in the form of a cable.

service conductors supply conductors that extend from the street main or from transformers to the service equipment of the premises supplied.

service drop overhead service conductors from the last pole or another aerial support to and including the splices connecting to the service entrance conductors at the building.

service panel main fuse box or circuit breaker box for the property; also called the *electrical panel*.

service valve device attached to the system that provides openings for gauges and/or charging lines.

set point the temperature at which the thermostat indicator is set.

sewage ejector ejector used with sanitary systems below the city sewage system or when the drainfield is higher than the septic tank.

sewer tile glazed waterproof clay pipe with bell joints.

sewer trap a device in a sewer system that prevents sewer gas from entering a branch pipe leading to a structure.

shading slight differences in shingle color that may occur as a result of normal manufacturing operations.

shake wooden shingle, usually edge grained.

shale sedimentary rock formed by hardening of a clay deposit.

shear wall a wall designed to resist lateral forces parallel to the plane of a wall.

sheathing first layer of outer wall covering nailed to the studs. In roofing, the exterior grade boards used as a deck material.

sheathing board insulation board secured to the outside of a frame wall.

shed roof roof containing only one sloping plane; has no hips, ridges, valleys, or gables.

shield in the case of radon counting, used to preclude background radiation from adding to the canister level being counted.

shim thin, tapered wood or metal used for leveling or tightening a stair or other building elements.

shingle (1) a small unit of prepared roofing material designed to be installed with similar units in overlapping rows on inclines normally exceeding 25 percent; (2) to cover with shingles; (3) to apply any sheet material in overlapping rows like shingles.

shingling (1) procedure of laying parallel felt so that one longitudinal edge of each felt overlaps, and the other longitudinal edge underlaps, an adjacent felt. Normally, felts are shingled on a slope so that the water flows over, rather than against, each lap; (2) application of shingles to a sloped roof.

short circuit occurs when a hot and a neutral wire contact each other, causing the fuses to blow or the circuit breaker to trip.

short cycling continual starting and stopping of a system over a shorter than normal time period.

shrink-swell shrinking of soil when dry and swelling when wet. Shrinking and swelling cause major damage to roads, foundations, and other structures.

siding finished covering of outside wall of a frame building.

sieve apparatus with apertures for separating sizes of material.

sight glass glass tube or glass window that shows the water, oil, or refrigerant in a heating and/or cooling system.

sill plate board secured to the top of a foundation wall on which the framing rests.

silt soil consisting of separate, individual mineral particles that range in diameter from the upper limits of clay to the lower limits of fine sand. As a soil textural class, soil is 80 percent or more silt and less than 12 percent clay.

silt loam silt loam soil has a moderate amount of fine grades of sand and a small amount of clay with more than half of the particles being the size of silt. When dry, it may appear cloddy, but lumps are broken readily, and when pulverized, it feels soft and floury. Whether wet or dry, it forms casts that are handled freely without breaking. Silt loam is defined as medium soil.

single coverage asphalt roofing that provides one layer of roofing material over the deck.

skim filter surface skimmer combined with a vacuum filter.

skimmer weir part of a skimmer that adjusts to water level changes, ensuring continuous water flow to the skimmer.

skylight glass opening in roof.

sleeper timber laid on the ground to receive joists; or strips of wood laid over a concrete floor to which the finished wood floor is nailed and/or glued.

sling psychrometer measures humidity with wet and dry bulb thermometers. It is moved rapidly through the air when measuring humidity.

slope inclination of land surface from the horizontal. Slope percentage is the vertical distance divided by the horizontal distance, multiplied by 100. A 20 percent slope is a drop of 20' in 100' of horizontal distance.

smoke detector device installed in the plenum chamber or in the main supply air duct of an air-conditioning system to shut off the blower automatically and close a fire damper in the presence of smoke.

smoke test test made to determine the completeness of combustion.

smooth surface roof built-up roof membrane surfaced with a layer of hot-mopped asphalt, cold-applied asphalt-clay emulsion, cold-applied asphalt cutback, or sometimes unmopped, inorganic felt.

soffit exposed underside of the roof projection or eaves, frequently with an opening for attic ventilation.

soft rot decay fungi that attack wood from the surface inward and cause cavities to form.

soil surface layer of earth that supports plant life.

soil gases gases that fill the pores between soil particles. They move through or leave the soil and rock, depending on the pressure.

soil pipe pipe that directs house sewage to receiving sewer, building drain, or building sewer.

soil separates mineral particles less than 2 mm. in diameter. Names and sizes of separates recognized in the United States, in mm., are as follows:

very coarse	2.0 to 1.0
sand	1.0 to 0.5
coarse sand	0.5 to 0.25
medium sand	0.25 to 0.10
fine sand	0.10 to 0.05
very fine sand	0.05 to 0.002
silt	less than 0.002
clay	

soil stack vertical piping that terminates in a roof vent and carries off the vapors of a plumbing system.

soil survey inventory and evaluation of soils used to determine the suitabilities and limitations of land use.

soil texture relative amounts of sand, silt, and clay in a soil.

solar chimney ventilating device using solar energy to create a chimney effect, drawing warm air out of the house and inducing a flow of cool air into the house.

solderless connectors screw-on or crimp-type devices that join two or more wires by means of mechanical pressure and without the use of solder; also called *scotch locks, wire nuts,* and *nuggets.*

solenoid valve electromagnet with a moving core that serves as a valve or operates a valve.

source known amount of radioactive substance used in calibrating counting equipment.

span distance between supports of a beam, girder, arch, or truss. In roofing, the horizontal distance from eaves to eaves.

span ratings maximum center-to-center spacing for supports over which plywood panels should be placed in construction applications.

specialty eaves flashing membrane self-adhering, waterproofing, shingle underlayment designed to protect against water infiltration due to ice damage or wind-driven rain.

split separation in roofing material resulting from movement of the substrate.

split system air-conditioning installation that places the condensation unit outside or far from the evaporator.

spray humidifier humidifier that utilizes a water valve and nozzle that sprays water onto a porous foam medium. The air passing over the wet medium is moisturized.

spread footing rectangular base placed beneath the foundation to distribute the building load over a greater area.

square unit of roof measurement covering 100 sq. ft. of roof area.

square-tab shingles shingles on which tabs are all the same size and exposure.

stack vent vertical outlet in a built-up roof system designed to relieve any pressure exerted by moisture vapor between the roof membrane and the vapor retarder or deck.

stair rail bar used for a handhold for stairs.

stair riser see **riser. stair stringer** sloping board that supports the ends of steps.

stair tread horizontal strip where the foot is placed to walk up and down stairs.

starter strip asphalt roofing, applied at the eaves, that provides protection by filling in the spaces under the cutouts and joints of the first course of shingles.

static pressure resistance or friction loss of a duct system or a piece of equipment, such as a filter or an evaporator, to airflow.

steep slope application method of installing asphalt shingles on roof slopes greater than 21″ per ft.

step flashing flashing application method used where a vertical surface meets a sloping roof plane.

step footing footing with steps to follow the contour of the slope and grade of the land.

storage mass medium that absorbs solar heat and holds it until required to heat the house.

storm sewer used for conveying rainwater, surface water, condensate, cooling water, or similar liquid waste.

storm sewer tile underground pipe that receives water from downspouts and carries it to the sewer.

stratification tendency of warm air to rise and collect in layers near ceilings and upper stories of buildings and cooler air to collect near floors and lower stories.

stress intensity of force per unit area.

strip shingles asphalt shingles that are approximately three times as long as they are wide.

stud vertical wood members of house framing.

subatomic particles parts of an atom—electrons, protons, and neutrons.

subflooring boards or sheet material laid over joists or plywood, over which a finished floor is laid.

suction line tube or pipe that is used to carry refrigerant gas from the evaporator to the condenser.

suction piping portion of circulation piping located between the pool and structure and the inlet side of the pump, usually including the main outlet piping, skimmer piping, and surge tank piping.

sump hole in the basement floor designed to collect water, from which the water either drains or is removed via a sump pump.

superheat temperature of vapor above the boiling temperature of its liquid at that pressure.

supply air treated air that is carried from the furnace to the living space for the purpose of conditioning that space.

surface skimmer device located in the pool wall that skims the pool surface by drawing pool water through a self-adjusting weir.

swale wide, shallow depression that channels surface water off of property; e.g., for storm water drainage.

swamp cooler see **evaporative cooler.**

sweating (1) condensation of moisture from air on a cold surface; (2) method of joining two pieces of copper together with heat from a torch and a thin layer of solder.

swimming pool constructed or prefabricated pool used for swimming or bathing; 18″ or more in depth.

T

tab exposed portion of strip shingles defined by cutouts.

talc see **back surfacing.**

tank separate tank connected directly or by pipe to an oil-burning appliance.

tar brown or black bituminous material, liquid or semisolid in consistency, in which the predominating constituents are bitumens obtained as condensates in the processing of coal, petroleum, oil shale, wood, or other organic materials.

tarred felt felt that has been saturated with refined coal tar.

tectum a rooflike structure or covering.

telegraphing shingle distortion that may arise when a new roof is applied over an uneven surface.

temperature degree of hotness or coldness as measured by a thermometer, usually in degrees Fahrenheit.

temperature and pressure (T-P) relief valve safety valve installed on a hot water storage tank to limit temperature and pressure of water.

tendon steel element such as wire, bar, rod, or strand, or a bundle of such elements, used to impart prestress to concrete.

tensile strength the force pulling at the grain.

termite shield metal baffle to prevent termites from entering framing.

terrace relatively level step constructed in the face of a graded slope surface for drainage and maintenance purposes.

Terra-cotta clayware used in facing of buildings, flue liners for chimneys, etc.

terrazzo highly polished flooring made of cement and marble chips.

test cut sample of the roof membrane, usually 4″ in size, that is cut from a roof membrane to: (1) determine the weight of the average interply bitumen poundages; (2) diagnose the condition of the existing membrane—e.g., to detect leaks or blisters. The National Roofing Contractors Association (NRCA) recommends that the test cut procedure *not* be used as a means of determining the quality of a roof system.

thermal protector (as applied to motors) protective device for assembly as an integral part of a motor or motor compressor; when properly applied, protects the motor against dangerous overheating due to overload and failure to start.

thermal storage wall wall constructed of heavy masonry materials or an array of containers holding water or phase change materials positioned behind glazing and designed to absorb and store solar heat.

thermocouple device that generates electricity using the principle of two dissimilar metals that are welded together; when the junction is heated, a voltage measured in millivolts is developed across the open ends.

thermopane window double pane that is hermetically sealed with vacuum between the two pieces of glass.

thermosiphoning natural air circulation of liquid in an enclosed space by convective currents.

thermosiphoning air panel (TAP) air heating collector attached to the exterior of a south-facing house wall.

thermostat temperature-sensitive electrical circuit control that is responsive to air temperature.

thimble term applied to a metal or terra-cotta lining for a chimney or furnace pipe.

three-dimensional shingles see **laminated shingles.**

through-wall flashing water-resistant membrane or material assembly, extending through a wall and its cavities, positioned to direct any water entering the top of the wall to the exterior.

tie timber, rod, or chain holding two or more structural members together. A loop of reinforcing bar or wire enclosing longitudinal reinforcement.

tile field drain tile laid to distribute septic tank effluent over a pre-planned area or to provide subsoil drainage in wet areas.

toenail to drive nails at an angle into corners or joints.

top lap portion of the roofing covered by the succeeding course after installation.

topsoil upper part of soil that is the most favorable material for plant growth. Topsoil is rich in organic matter and used to top dress lawns and flower beds.

transfer act of transferring stress in prestressing tendons from jacks or pretensioning bed to concrete member.

transom sash over a doorway.

transpiration removal of soil moisture by vegetation.

trap fitting that provides a liquid seal to prevent emission of sewer gases without affecting the flow of sewage or wastewater.

travelers two of the three conductors that run between switches in a three-way installation.

tread see **stair tread.**

trombe wall thermal storage wall consisting of a masonry wall positioned behind glazing.

truss a rigid, open web structural member designed and engineered to carry roof or floor loads.

truss combination of structural members arranged and fastened together so external loads applied at the joints will result in only direct stress in members.

turnover rate hours required for the circulation system to filter and recirculate a volume of water equal to pool volume.

Twisting (or warping) viewing from the end of the board irregularities in various directions

two piece thermostat system consisting of a sensor mounted in the controlled space communicating to a controller that establishes the systems' operation.

U

UL approved approved by Underwriters Laboratories.

underlayment asphalt-saturated felt used beneath roofing to provide additional protection for the deck.

underpinning formerly a term of significance denoting that portion of a foundation above lot grade when it was constructed of a material different than that of the lower part, such as required on all mobile or manufactured homes; skirting material placed around the outside perimeter of a pier-and-beam structure.

undersize selecting equipment for a living area that has inadequate tonnage and/or Btus to heat or cool that space.

Underwriters Laboratories (UL) independent testing agency that examines and tests electrical components for possible safety hazards. It also classifies roof assemblies for their fire characteristics and wind-uplift resistance for insurance companies in the United States.

unit vent fixtures installed back to back in separate rooms.

unsanitary contrary to sanitary principles, injurious to health.

V

vacuum reduction in pressure below atmospheric pressure.

vacuum breaker device to prevent backflow (back siphonage) by means of an opening through which air may be drawn to relieve negative pressure (vacuum).

vacuum fitting piping from the suction side of a pump connected to a vacuum fitting located below the water level.

vacuum pump special high-efficiency compressor used for creating high vacuums for testing or drying purposes.

valley internal angle formed by the intersection of two sloping roof planes.

valve device used for controlling fluid flow. Also used for regulating draft, located on the exhaust side of the combustion chamber, which is usually located in a chimney connector.

valve, expansion type of refrigerant control that maintains a pressure difference between the high-side and the low-side pressures in a refrigerating mechanism; often referred to as an *automatic expansion valve* or *AEV.*

vapor word usually used to denote vaporized refrigerant rather than the word *gas.*

vapor barrier nonporous sheet or coating that prevents water vapor from saturating insulation.

vapor charged lines and component parts of a system that are charged at a factory.

vapor lock condition where liquid is trapped in a line because of a bend or improper installation, which prevents the vapor from flowing.

vapor retarder any material used to prevent the passage of water vapor through a wall or roof.

vault arched ceiling.

veneer a layer of material applied to another surface for ornamental or protective purposes.; out-facing of brick, stone, or other material placed on a wall for protection or decoration.

vent any outlet for air that protrudes through the roof deck, such as a pipe or stack; any device installed on the roof, gable, or soffit for the purpose of ventilating the underside of the roof deck.

ventilation natural or mechanical means of supplying or removing air to or from a space.

vent pipe see **vent system.**

vent sleeve see **collar.**

vent stack vertical vent pipe installed to provide air circulation to and from the drainage system and extending through one or more stories.

vent system (as applied to plumbing) pipe or pipes installed to provide an airflow to or from a drainage system or to provide air circulation within such a system to protect trap seals from siphonage and back pressure. Also refers to a gas vent or chimney and vent connector; if used, assembled to form a continuous, unobstructed passageway from the gas appliance to the outside atmosphere for the purpose of removing vent gases.

verge edge of tiles, slate, or shingles, projecting over the gable of roof.

vermiculite aggregate used in lightweight concrete, formed by the heating and consequent expansion of a micaceous mineral.

venturi throat that forces an air/gas mixture to accelerate and then quickly decelerate.

vestibule small hall at entrance of a building.

volt (V) measure of electrical potential. Volts x amps = watts.

voltage control to provide some electrical circuits with uniform or constant voltage.

voltmeter device that measures voltage in a circuit and may perform other electrical tests.

W

wainscoting lower facing of interior wall when different from remainder of wall facing.

wall member, usually vertical, used to enclose or separate spaces.

wall, bearing wall supporting vertical load.

wall, cavity wall built of masonry units, plain concrete, or a combination of materials arranged to provide an air space within the wall.

wall, cover inner surface of wall, of plaster on lath, gypsum board, or plywood.

wall, curtain nonbearing wall between columns or piers and not supported by girders or beams.

wall, exterior wall, bearing or nonbearing, that is used as an enclosing wall for a building, other than a party wall or fire wall.

wall, foundation wall below first floor extending below adjacent ground level and serving as support for a wall, a pier column, or another structural part of a building.

wall, nonbearing wall that supports no vertical load.

wall, panel nonbearing wall in framed construction, built between columns or piers and supported at each story.

wall, parapet part of wall above the roof line.

wall, party fire wall on an interior lot line, used or adapted for joint service between two buildings.

wall, retaining wall designed to prevent lateral displacement of soil or other materials.

wall framing vertical studs and horizontal members, soleplates, top plates, and window and door headers of exterior and interior walls that support ceilings, upper floors, and the roof.

wall insulation blanket of wool or reflective foil placed inside walls.

water hammer loud thump of water in pipe when valve/faucet is suddenly closed.

waterproofing treatment of a surface or structure to prevent the damage of water passage under hydrostatic pressure.

water service pipe pipe from the water main or other sources of potable water to the water distribution system of the building served.

water supply system consists of the water service pipe, water-distributing pipes, necessary connecting pipes, fittings, control valves, and all appurtenances in or adjacent to the building or premises.

water table projecting ledge or molding that throws off rainwater.

watertight constructed so moisture will not enter the enclosure under specified test conditions.

water vapor water in the form of a gas.

watt (w) measure of the power an electrical lamp or appliance consumes.

weather stripping metal, wood, plastic, or other material installed at doors or windows to retard air passage, water, moisture, or dust around the openings.

weep holes openings that allow entrapped water to escape and provide ventilation in the space between the brick and frame wall, or in a pipe for drainage.

wet bulb temperature lowest temperature that will register on a thermometer having its bulb enclosed in a wet wick over which air is circulating.

wet vent vent that receives discharge other than waste from water closets.

wind chill factor still air temperature that would have the same chilling effect on human skin as the combination of the recorded wind speed and air temperature.

windload forces superimposed on a building or structure by movement of an air mass at a specified velocity.

window box collector small air heating collector placed in a window on the south side of a house.

wire mesh welded wire fabric used to reinforce concrete.

withe (1) partition between two chimney flues in the same stack; (2) inner and outer walls of a cavity wall.

wolmanized wood chemically pressure-treated lumber that resists wood rot and termite damage.

wood rot damage caused by fungi that feed on wood.

working level (wl) unit of measure of the exposure rate to radon and radon progeny; defined as the quantity that will result in a specified potential alpha energy. It is expressed in working level months (wlm); e.g., 1 wl for 1 working mo. (173 hr.) is 1 wlm. Originally developed to measure cumulative exposure of uranium miners, it is today used as a measurement of all human exposure.

woven valley method of valley construction in which shingles from both sides of the valley extend across the valley and are woven together by overlapping alternate courses as they are applied. The valley flashing is not exposed.

X

xylem layer in trees that moves water and nutrients up from the roots to the foliage.

Y

yoke vent pipe connecting upward from a soil or waste stack to a vent stack for the purpose of preventing pressure changes in the stacks.

Z

zoned system heating and air-conditioning system capable of maintaining varying conditions for various rooms or zones.

*I*ndex